THE
CHARITY SCHOOL MOVEMENT

LC
4096
G7
J6
1964

THE
CHARITY SCHOOL
MOVEMENT

A Study of
Eighteenth Century Puritanism
in Action

M. G. JONES

LIBRARY

MAY 26 1964

FAIRFIELD U.

ARCHON BOOKS
1964

First published by
Cambridge University Press
in 1938

✓ This edition published by
Archon Books, The Shoe String Press Inc.
Hamden, Connecticut

First edition   1938
New impression   1964

Printed in Great Britain

CONTENTS

63028

PART TWO

Appendices

I. ENGLAND

II. SCOTLAND

III. IRELAND

IV. WALES

WALES, *cont.*

ILLUSTRATIONS

PREFACE

This book is an attempt to present a study of eighteenth-century elementary education, not as the history of educational ideas, nor as the history of administration, in which two garbs the history of education usually appears, but as the study of a neglected aspect of social history. Its main interest lies in the different reactions of philanthropic men and women in England, Scotland, Ireland and Wales to the movement for establishing schools on a religious basis for the children of the poor.

In expressing my thanks to those who have helped me in collecting materials for this book I must mention first my gratitude to the Secretaries of the Society for Promoting Christian Knowledge in London and the Society for Propagating Christian Knowledge in Edinburgh who gave me access to the Societies' papers when they were not, as they are to-day, open to public inspection. The first part of this book is based primarily on the wealth of material which languishes almost unknown in the archives of the London Society. Its minute books, letter books, miscellaneous papers and, above all, the invaluable abstracts of correspondence cannot safely be neglected by students of eighteenth-century religious and social history in the four countries of the British Isles, for the charity school movement in its different forms owes its inception to the London Society. In its archives may be found the carefully considered plans of the members of the Society for the education of the poor and of the organization which it established to this end. Of even greater importance are the letters which poured into the Society's offices from correspondents in England, Scotland, Ireland and Wales, informing it of the local conditions which permitted or frustrated the realisation of the Society's ideals.

The records of the Scottish S.P.C.K. (now kept at H.M. Register House, Edinburgh) are equally valuable for an appreciation of religious, social and economic problems in the Highlands and Islands of Scotland. They provide an even more detailed and complete picture of local conditions than that which is given by the London S.P.C.K. The minute books of the Society and of its executive body, the Committee of Directors, are throughout the century remarkably full of detail. Unlike the London Society which, after the first quarter of the eighteenth century was diverted from the education of the children of the poor to mission work overseas and the publication of religious works at home, the Scottish S.P.C.K. maintained continuously its interest in the schools which it set up. Its minute books, its miscellaneous papers, including the returns of parish ministers to specific enquiries and its correspondence with the "innovators" in agriculture and industry in the Highlands, provide the material for a detailed study of the prevailing religious and social conditions in the north of Scotland.

To the Bishops of Durham, Ely, Lincoln, Llandaff, Norwich, Peterborough, St Davids and Worcester I owe much gratitude for their permission to use the materials in the diocesan archives. The *Speculum Diœceseos Lincolniensis*, edited by the Rev. R. E. G. Cole, Archbishop Herring's *Visitation Returns*, edited by Canon Ollard and the late Rev. P. C. Walker, and the Wake MSS. at Christ Church, Oxford, which contain many references to schools for the children of the poor in the first half of the eighteenth century, suggested to me the possibility of finding similar stores of information in the returns to other episcopal visitation inquiries in the later half of the century. Unfortunately none of the above registries appear to possess returns comparable in detailed information with those inaugurated by Archbishops Wake and Herring. Here and there as in the returns to the visitation articles of the Bishop of Ely in 1787, or in miscellaneous papers like those in the diocesan registry at Worcester, there is evidence of considerable activity in the education of the children of the poor, and it is difficult to believe that among the mass of unknown and unclassified materials in the diocesan registries there is not further information of the interest of the church in education.

From the librarians of the British Museum, the National Libraries of Scotland, Ireland and Wales, the University Libraries of Cambridge, London, Edinburgh, Aberystwith, Bangor and Cardiff, the Bodleian and Christ Church, Oxford, Marsh's Library and the Library of Trinity College, Dublin, and the Public Libraries at Cardiff, Bristol, Gloucester, Dumfries, Newcastle-on-Tyne, Brentford, the Friends' Library, Bishopsgate, London, the Libraries of the Congregational and Baptist Unions, I have received unfailing courtesy and help. To them and to the Headmasters and Headmistresses who have given me access to their school-records I wish to express my appreciation and my thanks.

Among those who have taken a kindly interest in the book or have put me in touch with sources of information unknown to me I am especially grateful to the late Principal J. H. Davies of Aberystwyth, who placed his library at my disposal, to the late Dr Thomas Shankland of Bangor, whose study of the S.P.C.K. in Wales was the pioneer work in the subject, and to the friend who called my attention to the invaluable and hitherto unknown reports of the schools of the Welsh Trust for 1675 and 1678. The Reports, printed in full in the *Bulletin* of the Board of Celtic Studies, vol. ix, Part i, November 1937, establish the claim of Wales to be the pioneer of charity school instruction and make clear the active participation in it of the clergy and churchwardens of the Established Church. I am greatly indebted to Dr Thomas Richards and Mr R. T. Jenkins of Bangor for their advice and criticism, and to the Rev. Arvon Davies, Miss D. M. Griffith and to Mr T. J. Owen for information. Professor Timothy Corcoran, of University College, Dublin, and the late Mr Robert Dunlop, one-time lecturer in Irish History at Manchester University, made suggestions which I have incorporated in Chapter VII. Dr John Mason of Queensferry, Edinburgh, generously lent me his MS. material on the schools of the Forfeited Estates in the Highlands, and Professor J. W. Adamson gave me much valuable advice many years ago when I began to write this book and later, when it was completed.

I want also to thank those of my pupils who have, from time to time, sent me information, or have copied materials for me. To Mrs J. H. Clapham, who has given unremitting care to the making of the index, and to my other friends Dr M. D. George, Miss H. M. Cam, Miss I. F. Grant, Dr H. M. Wodehouse, and in particular Professor Eileen Power, whose help has throughout been generously given, I find it difficult to express my gratitude.

M. G. J.

GIRTON COLLEGE CAMBRIDGE

September 1937

PART I

CHAPTER I

INTRODUCTION

"Charity is doing good to the souls and bodies of men."
ROBERT NELSON

I

"THE AGE OF BENEVOLENCE"

The eighteenth century in English history has been endowed with a
number of epithets, which enshrine its leading characteristics. In philosophy it is the age of reason, in politics the age of Whig ascendancy, in
economic history the age of the industrial revolution; it is sometimes
forgotten that it was, *par excellence*, the age of benevolence. In its
sustained humanitarianism and generous philanthropy it supports with
extraordinary and unswerving consistency the title bestowed upon its
closing years by Hannah More.[1] The range of its philanthropy was
remarkable. The call of the mission field at home and abroad, the
distress of religious refugees, the misery of negro slaves, foundling
children and climbing boys, the brutalities of the criminal law, the
hardships of the very poor, the aged and infirm, the struggle of the
"second poor" to keep their heads above water, the suffering of the
sick and diseased and those in prison, never failed to stir the consciences
and untie the purse-strings of the pious and philanthropic men and
women of eighteenth-century England. The charity school was their
favourite form of benevolence. It is the most striking of the many social
experiments of the age. To it was applied the new method of associated
philanthropy and the new device of joint-stock finance. Thousands of
schools were set up and hundreds of thousands of children, for whom no
other means of education existed, were instructed by its means during
the eighteenth century. The common tendency to date the provision
of elementary education from 1870, or from the foundation of the

[1] More, Hannah, *On the Religion of the Fashionable World, Collected Works*,
vol. II, p. 302.

National and the British and Foreign School Societies in the early years of the nineteenth century, or from the establishment of Sunday schools at the end of the eighteenth century, has obscured the efforts of educational enthusiasts throughout the eighteenth century to provide a means of free education for the lower orders in the four countries of the British Isles. Yet it is difficult to find any interest more continuous and sustained, and, at the same time, more representative of the age than the schools which were established for the children of the poor.

For the eighteenth century was marked by a very real sense of pity and responsibility for the children whose physical and spiritual interests were lamentably neglected, coupled with a determination to reform them by application of what Defoe aptly called "the great law of subordination".[1] The political and religious unrest of the seventeenth century contributed in no small degree to the desire of the upper and middle classes to establish social discipline among the poor, who in contemporary opinion were peculiarly susceptible to the poison of rebellion and infidelity. An organisation which would provide for them religious and social discipline would solve two acute problems of Church and State, the growth of irreligion and of pauperism. Instruction in Bible and catechism during the formative years of childhood, before the infant population was ready for apprenticeship or service, would build up a God-fearing population and, at the same time, would inoculate the children against the habits of sloth, debauchery and beggary, which characterised the lower orders of society.

It would be a misreading of the age of benevolence to see in the prominence enjoyed by the principle of subordination a harsh and unsympathetic attitude of the superior to the lower classes. Far from it. The eighteenth century was an age of well-defined social distinctions, and it used a language in accordance with its social structure. Expressions of patronage on the one hand and of subserviency on the other, so unpleasing to an age indifferent to etiquette, were then common form and were recognised as such. That the well-being of the State and the happiness of individuals were bound up with the injunction that men should do their duty in the station of life to which they were called, was a well-entrenched belief, peculiarly apposite to the poor, but it was not, on that account, lacking in sympathy or social compunction. The charity schools came into being chiefly, although by no means ex-

[1] Defoe, D., *Everybody's Business is Nobody's Business*, 1725.

clusively, as a comparison of the movement in the four countries of the British Isles demonstrates, to *condition* the children for their primary duty in life as hewers of wood and drawers of water.

In this conception of education, as indeed in the whole social philosophy of the age, John Locke's psychology played a part of the first importance. It came to the aid of the "great society" in much the same way as the psychology of the behaviourist school to-day supports the political and social theory of states engaged in building a new order, upon the foundation of children conditioned for the part they are to perform. Locke's essay *Concerning Human Understanding* provided a psychology, and his *Thoughts Concerning Education* a method of education which exercised a profound influence upon his own and subsequent ages. His theory of the *tabula rasa* was a powerful stimulus to philanthropists and reformers. From Locke they learned that education is a discipline of mind and body, dependent upon the formation of good habits. By him they were told that "as children will not have time and strength to learn all things, most pains should be taken about that which is most necessary, and that principally looked after which will be of most and frequentest use to them in the world".[1] By habitual response to carefully selected stimuli the evil hereditary and environmental influences which surrounded the poor from birth would be modified, and, though they remained hewers of wood and drawers of water, they would be conditioned to perform these duties as good Christians and faithful servants.

In the provision and management of schools for the poor the clergy of the Established Church played a leading part. The schools were, in essence, catechetical schools established to give instruction in reading the Bible and catechism and, sometimes, in writing and casting accounts. They were of prime utility to urban and country clergy, from whom they received, in general, steady encouragement. But of equal importance in the history of the schools was the active and unfailing interest of laymen in the new work. The eighteenth century, it has been said, witnessed a steady laicisation of religion, which is the key-note of its ecclesiastical development.[2] In nothing is this more clearly shown than in the lay control and lay support of schools primarily engaged in giving children specific religious and moral teaching. It is significant,

[1] Locke, J., *Some Thoughts Concerning Education*, 1693, Section 94.
[2] Sykes, N., *Church and State in England in the Eighteenth Century*, p. 379.

too, that the lay organisation and support of work which had been regarded as essentially clerical was not confined to men. As subscribers to societies and as managers, trustees and teachers of schools, women of all classes strengthened and supported the lay element.

But whether lay or clerical, men or women, the champions of schools for the poor, throughout the eighteenth century, were drawn predominantly from the "middling class", and the schools were financed by the modest benefactions of "middling-class" philanthropists. The single benevolence of the great and wealthy did not disappear. Here and there noble lords and ladies, royal princes and high ecclesiastics, founded schools or supplied funds for their upkeep, but the movement for their establishment and the funds for their maintenance depended, in the main, upon the conjoint philanthropy of an unnumbered company of men and women, who, throughout the four countries of the British Isles, were profoundly influenced by an ethic at once puritan and middle class in character.

The ambiguities arising from the use of the word puritanism tend to obscure its character in the eighteenth century. If puritanism be regarded as an exposition of theological dogma, the eighteenth century was little interested in it, but if it be regarded, as Troeltsch has suggested that it may legitimately be considered, as the expression of an austere and devout religious temper, apart from any particular dogmatic implications, then it dominated the social life of the age to an extent not commonly recognised.[1] Conduct, not dogma, stamped the puritan of the eighteenth century. Men of such a temper were to be found, throughout the British Isles, in the Church and in the Sects. Whether they found their standards in the scriptures, as expounded by the Anglican Church, or regarded the Bible as the sole and self-interpreting exponent of doctrine and duty, they endeavoured to live their lives in punctilious conformity with Christian teaching. They were united, not by a specific form of church constitution, but by a pietism, or precisianism, which aimed at promoting by an austere personal discipline the glory of God and the inner sanctification of the individual.

Historians, in recent years, have suggested a connection between puritan ethics and the development of a bourgeois capitalist civilisation. That capitalism was a driving force in economic life long before the

[1] Troeltsch, E., *Die Soziallehren der christlichen Kirchen und Gruppen*, 1912, *passim*.

religious changes of the sixteenth and seventeenth centuries, does not upset the contention that puritanism contributed to its development. The relationship may easily be exaggerated, but it cannot be denied that an ethic which not only permitted the pursuit of wealth, but encouraged it as a religious duty, was an immeasurably important factor in the change from the medieval to the modern economic system. It provided religious sanctions for the acquisition of wealth which the middle classes, the backbone of puritanism, made peculiarly their own.

The consecration of self and of work to the glory of God, which provided the puritan with a unity of purpose and habits of conduct, was not confined to his economic activities. It was carried over to a marked degree into his social relationships. It taught him that wealth, which with the steady increase of trade flowed so easily into his pockets, was a trust, whose expenditure was governed by the same rule as its acquisition—the glory of God—and since God could best be glorified by making man fit to glorify Him, the puritan was irresistibly drawn towards the service of man, who through misery, or ignorance, or debauchery, deprived God of the glory which was His due. To men of such a mould charity was obligatory. In a world of indifferents they were the active conscientious Christians. They differed from their contemporaries in the intensity of their convictions, in the austerity of their conduct, and in the compassionate paternal discipline which they lavished on the poor and unfortunate. And, since they were drawn in the main from the "middling classes" comfortably endowed with this world's goods, they found an outlet for their spiritual activities in philanthropy, giving ordered charity to the poor as compensation for their own abundance. It is impossible to read the voluminous writings of such men and women in the eighteenth century without experiencing a conviction of their sincerity and humanity. They saw life steadily, but they did not see it whole. Like Cobbett and Engels in the first half of the nineteenth century, they were profoundly distressed by the misery they saw around them, but, whereas Cobbett, bringing down his "mutton fist" on the fundholders, whom he regarded as primarily responsible for the wretchedness of the poor, and Engels, remorselessly uncovering the greedy capitalist behind the appalling conditions of his creation, are clear that there is something rotten in the constitution of the social order and demand material reforms, the eighteenth-century puritans accepted the inequalities of wealth and poverty as the will of

God. They showed no disposition to "pry into the state of society". They found the only remedy for the squalor, ignorance and vice which they deplored in the more faithful application of Christian charity by the rich, and uncomplaining acquiescence by the poor. Not permanent material reforms in this world, but the promise of spiritual rewards in the world to come, was their panacea for present ills. It was beyond the range of their mentality to conceive that the poor were poor because Society was an ill-regulated machine, or that the body politic was, as a whole, responsible for the disease which attacked it. Enough for them that the poor were there; the poor on unimpeachable authority would always be there; and puritan asceticism, which impelled man to work for the glory of God, not in the cloister but in the world outside, busied itself with schemes of ordered and systematic charity on their behalf. This is the key to the vast and organised philanthropy of the age.

Robert Nelson, at the beginning of the century, is representative of eighteenth-century puritanism at its best. A Jacobite, a High Churchman, a non-juror, his life conformed throughout to puritan standards. To the social problems of his day he brought the same high conscientiousness, the same independence of mind which marked his religious and political opinions. Counting among his friends the rich and powerful, this sturdy puritan of the "middling classes" did not lack the courage to appeal to persons of quality and estate to amend their ways, and to remain for twenty years of his life a member of the unpopular non-juring communion. Kettlewell, Hickes, Dodwell, Leslie and Francis Lee were in no small degree responsible for his voluminous writings and widely read devotional works.

When the non-juring clergy were precluded from pastoral service and were handicapped by poverty, the devout and well-to-do layman made himself responsible for attending to the spiritual welfare of his generation. The religious societies won his support because "their pious and devout practices prepared the minds of the laity for that discipline which is wanted in the Church". To his passion for godly discipline may be attributed his membership and support of the societies for the reformation of manners. But the charity schools which he set up, and the movement which he fostered for their extension, are the most striking testimony to his puritan spirit. The superiority of prevention to cure as a means of social reform attracted him and his contemporaries. Solomon's wisdom, "Train up a child in the way he should go: and when he is old, he will not depart from it", supplied a guiding principle; to form the child instead of reforming the man was a sound commonsense proposition which appealed to the puritan mind.[1] To it Nelson bent his efforts from 1699 to his death in 1715. He corresponded with fellow enthusiasts for charity school instruction in York, Beverley, Oxford, Cirencester, Leicester, Tring and Bray; he was a manager of St Andrew's parish charity school, Holborn; he was responsible for the schools attached to St George's Chapel, Windsor; he drafted the printed forms used in the establishment of the schools; he compiled a catechism for the children, drawn from *The Whole Duty of Man*; he busied himself in finding teachers for St Anne's school, Soho, and for the charity schools at Bath, and to his organising powers fell the duty of arranging the anniversary meetings of the London charity schools. His puritan spirit abhorred so strongly the dramatic performance of *Timon of Athens* played by the boys of Clerkenwell charity school, that he requested the Bishop of London to withdraw the schoolmaster's licence. It would not be easy to find a more complete example to fit the contemporary definition of a puritan or precisian as one who is "more devout and withal more conscientious and exemplary than is ordinary; though in the way of the church of England"[2] than Robert Nelson. "You must endeavour", he wrote in a characteristic letter to a young kinsman, "that the great end to which you were sent into the world, which was not to sport away your time in pleasure, nor only to get a fair estate, but to fit and prepare yourself for a happy eternity in the enjoyment of God by a constant and universal obedience to all His holy laws, be prosecuted steadily and vigorously by all those ways and means which God has established for the working out of your salvation.... The virtue and holiness I mean are to a large extent to comprehend your duty to God, your neighbour, and yourself, and is what the Apostles call living righteously, soberly, and godly in this present world.... God has given us the Holy Word to instruct us in the particulars of our duty. He has encouraged our addresses to Him by promising to hear our prayers.... He has instituted the Holy Sacrament to be a continual memorial of the Sacrifice of Christ's death.... You

---

[1] The marginal note to Proverbs xxii, 6 in the Authorised Version gives *catechise* as an alternative to *train*.

[2] *The Life of Mr Thomas Firmin, by one of his most intimate acquaintances*, 1698, p. 6.

must accustom yourself to meditate upon such divine subjects as occur in the course of your reading, that you may stir up all the faculties of your soul to a vigorous prosecution of them. I desire you to live by rule and method and divide the day into such proportions that a proper time may be assigned for all your actions, that the hours of your devotion, of your business, and your diversions may all be stated." The intimate relationship between religion and charity, which St James in his Epistle declared to be the essence of religion, was the guiding principle of this most typical of puritans. "I must particularly recommend to you the practice of charity, by which I mean doing good to the souls and bodies of men.... Comfort your friends that mourn and are afflicted with seasonable discourses of piety, and reprove, prudently and quietly, all your companions where you find they transgress God's laws. But never unnecessarily vex or grieve any man's mind, for thereby you hurt his soul. As to their bodies you must, according to your abilities, relieve their wants, and supply their necessities, and in order for this purpose...dedicate and lay apart a proportion of your gains, or your income when it is certain, for alms-deeds which will make the work easy and delightful, and you, moreover, ready to embrace any opportunity that offers for doing good, because you are beforehand provided with the means."[1]

At the close of the century Hannah More showed the same characteristics. In the years which separated the Evangelical from the High Churchman the Methodist revival swept like a flood across England, modifying so profoundly its social and religious life that it is, at times, difficult to believe that a bare sixty years separate the England of Fielding from the England of Jane Austen; but the change in the religious and moral conduct of the people was not reflected in the lives of the godly men and women who devoted themselves to the glory of God. The precisian of the Evangelical movement at the end of the century is a replica of the precisian of "classical puritanism" in its early years. It is true that Christ the Law-giver in the writings of the one is replaced by Christ the Saviour in the writings of the other, but in the practice of piety which they proclaimed in their writings, and lived in

[1] Secretan, C. F., *Memoirs of the Life and Times of the Pious Robert Nelson*, 1860, pp. 188 *et seq. passim*: see also S.P.C.K. Letter Books and Abstracts of Correspondence; Minute Books of the Blue Coat School, Bath; Nelson, R., *An Address to Persons of Quality and Estate*, 1715.

their lives, there is no difference. Hannah More, poet and playwright, the friend of Dr Johnson and Horace Walpole and David Garrick, and, like Nelson, a welcome visitor in the houses of the great, shared his sense of social responsibility and his belief in godly discipline. Her *Thoughts on the Manners of the Great*, her *Estimate of the Religion of the Fashionable World*, appeals to the upper classes to regulate their lives in conformity with the teaching of Christ, were the counterparts of Nelson's *Appeal to Persons of Quality and Estate*. To teach the great that philanthropy without godly discipline on the part of the philanthropist was a mockery, she wrote her courageous remonstrances. To convince the well-to-do farming and trading community that prosperity required unceasing moral vigilance, she addressed to them her *Stories for Persons in the Middle Ranks*; to show the poor that poverty was God's discipline and man's opportunity, she worked among them, and in her leisure poured forth a reckless profusion of tracts for their edification. Passionately anxious to form the poor to habits of piety and virtue, she, too, saw in the children the easiest and most certain means of moral regeneration.

Between Robert Nelson and Hannah More stretched a long line of pious men and women, whose differences in religious doctrine, social conditions and personal character serve but to throw into more marked relief their fundamental similarity of outlook and behaviour. England, Scotland, Ireland and Wales alike produced them. The steady unswerving practice of piety and charity remained their dominant characteristics. And behind this small army of precisians, trained by never-relaxing discipline for godly service, moved a vast assembly of camp followers, who compressed the religion of duty and discipline "into the slender compass of a little pecuniary relief".[1] When poverty indecently thrust itself beneath their noses, they suffered from a temporary stirring of conscience, and uneasily opened their purses; when a preacher of eloquence portrayed the separation of the sheep from the goats on the day of judgment, contributions found their way into the collection box in the hope that "Satan be non-suited at a small expense".[2] More distressing to precisians than the irregular drip of conscience money was the craze for philanthropy, which, at intervals, through the

[1] More, Hannah, *op. cit.*
[2] Mandeville, B., *The Fable of the Bees*, Part II; *Essay on Charity and Charity Schools*, 1723, p. 247.

century, seized upon the fashionable world, in whose easy benevolence Hannah More found not Christianity but a substitute for Christianity. The Robert Nelsons and Hannah Mores, "concentrating the powers and affections of the soul into one steady point",[1] spent themselves in service; the charitable mob paid its guinea and crowded to the annual charity sermons to hear its generosity extolled and its investment for the next world approved.

The dedication of time and money to charity was but a part of the puritan conception of philanthropy. Giving alms, as the stout puritan Defoe had asserted, was no charity. True religion did not command, nor did it desire promiscuous almsgiving. Generous impulses, stirred by the sight of poverty or distress, called for restraint, and puritan ethics demanded that the almsgiver should both rationalise his almsgiving and require social interest on his investment. Charity must promote the glory of God by promoting the usefulness of man. It is in this combination of methodical and utilitarian qualities that the charity of the eighteenth century is sharply distinguished from its predecessors, and in none of the many charitable undertakings, which the century initiated and developed, is this combination more conspicuous than in the movement for erecting charity schools for the education of the poor. Methodical organisation distinguished the movement from its inception. When the State, after a brief period of activity during the Commonwealth, relapsed into a quiescence, which left no hope of action on its part, voluntary societies came into being. They occupied an intermediary position between private-venture education on the one hand, and state-controlled education on the other. In England, Scotland, Ireland and Wales, societies were formed to promote the work, conditions of membership were drawn up, executive committees appointed, local correspondents enrolled, qualifications for teachers laid down, individual investigation of candidates for admission to the schools undertaken and rules and regulations for the conduct of the scholars, their dress, their instruction, and their text-books meticulously described.

The success of the voluntary societies was closely bound up with what contemporaries termed the joint-stock method of finance. In industry and commerce joint-stock companies, during the seventeenth century, had tapped new sources of capital, hidden hitherto in the

[1] More, Hannah, *op. cit.*

stockings of maiden ladies and country clergy. Nonconformists had built their meeting houses and paid their ministers by a joint-stock method of subscription. Education could show an even earlier application of the method, in the grammar schools set up and financed by medieval gilds and by private persons in Elizabethan times.[1] When, therefore, eighteenth-century reformers for the education of the poor required funds to finance their work the joint-stock method supplied them with a means. Schools did not cease to be endowed by those who could afford to endow them, and elementary schools accumulated considerable property by endowment throughout the century, but the joint-stock subscription method drew supplies for education, not only from the well-to-do but from the vast army of the "middling classes", the main support of the schools, whose guinea subscriptions hurt them no more, as an enthusiast for this form of charity pointed out, "than the paying of a little tradesman's bill".[2] The new method aroused extraordinary interest and response. "By contributions and a joint-stock", said the Bishop of St David's, recommending the device in a charity school sermon, "the bottom of charity is enlarged."[3]

Methodical association of the charitable in joint-stock societies for promoting the education of the poor explains in great part the public support of the charity school movement. There remains one other factor to be considered. An analysis of the sermons preached and pamphlets written on behalf of the schools reveals the strong and deep-seated utilitarianism which characterised the eighteenth century. Rational methods for the collection and dispersion of charity demanded rational objects on which to expend it. The education of the poor did not in itself provide such an object. There was no conception of popular education as the foundation of a common citizenship and little belief in it as a panacea for the ills which flesh is heir to. Instead, the conviction that the education of the poor was economically unsound and socially destructive was well entrenched. To meet opposition the utilitarian value of the schools was kept well before the public in sermons which

[1] Leach, A. F., Articles on Schools in *Encyclopaedia Britannica*, 11th ed. 1911; *The Journal of Education*, June–July 1908; *The National Observer*, Sept.–Oct. 1896; *The Dictionary of English Church History*.
[2] Blake, W., *The Ladies' Charity School House Roll, Highgate* [n.d.].
[3] *Sermon preached by the Bishop of St David's on behalf of the Charity Schools in and about London and Westminster*, May 3, 1739.

appealed for their support. In some the ignorance and infidelity of the poor in city slum or remote village held a prominent place, and men and women were urged with fervour and compassion to save the souls of the children for the glory of God. In others, the value of instruction as social discipline held first place. Sloth and debauchery, the twin sources of social evil, would, it was asserted, disappear if the children of the poor were trained to habits of order and decency in the schools. Other preachers moved their hearers by expatiating on the value of the schools to the Protestant faith and the Hanoverian Succession. Children armed with the Bible, *The Whole Duty of Man*, and the Anglican or Westminster catechism, would form, in Dr White Kennett's words, "little garrisons against Popery",[1] and the Mother of Superstition, who fed her children on ignorance, would be powerless against an instructed proletariat. That these propagandist motives for the support of the schools were closely inter-connected, often appearing together, is plain from an analysis of the sermons preached on their behalf in England, Scotland, Ireland and Wales. They appealed to all whose minds were formed in the puritan mould, but the relative strength of the different motives varied with different individuals and was profoundly affected by the different national problems of the four countries of the British Isles. When piety, politics and discipline made a united appeal, as in England in the early years of the century, or when one of them was strong enough to attract widespread support, as in Wales in the middle years, the movement made rapid headway. It slackened speed whenever religious, social or political changes diminished, in popular estimation, the utilitarian value of the schools, but by the end of the century, in spite of the failure to establish a national system of popular education, it had prepared the ground for the advent of the State in this work of "national concern".[2]

[1] Kennett, White, Archdeacon of Huntingdon, *The Charity Schools for Poor Children recommended in a Sermon*, May 16, 1706.

[2] See *Directions given by Edmund, Lord Bishop of London, to the Masters and Mistresses of the Charity Schools within the Bills of Mortality and Diocese of London assembled for that purpose in the Chapter House of St Paul's*, Nov. 14, 1724.

II

NUMBERS AND DISTRIBUTION OF
THE CHARITY SCHOOLS

The provision of education for the children of the poor by the liberality
of the rich was not a new phenomenon in the eighteenth century. Over
500 endowed grammar schools were returned by the Commissioners
of Inquiry Concerning Charities in the nineteenth century as existing
in England and Wales at the end of the seventeenth century.[1] The
children for whom they were intended were not drawn exclusively from
a particular class, nor confined to a particular neighbourhood. Rich
men's sons and poor men's sons were eligible, though the frequent
mention of the poor suggests a desire to keep the door open for their
reception, rather than an expectation that they would prove the majority
of the scholars.[2] Archbishop Cranmer's oft-quoted words, when one
of the Commissioners, appointed in 1540 to elect the scholars of the new
grammar school at Canterbury, urged the admission of the sons of
gentlemen only, represents, in general, the ideals of the founders of the
grammar schools. "If the gentleman's son be apt to learning let him
be admitted; if not apt let the poor man's child being apt enter his
room."[3]

The organised attempt to establish a system of popular education in
the eighteenth century had its roots in the seventeenth century when,
under the pressure of new intellectual and social forces, endowed
English, or elementary, schools, in which religion and the three R's
were taught, appeared in increasing numbers. Sometimes these schools
were attached to the grammar schools, and served as preparatory
departments to them:[4] more often they owed their existence to the

---

[1] *Reports of the Royal Commission to Inquire Concerning Charities for the Education
of the Poor.* (Lord Brougham's Commission.) 44 vols. Published at intervals from
1819 to 1837, with Analytical Digest in 2 vols. 1842. The total here given is approximate only, since among the schools returned by the Commissioners as endowed
schools before 1700 some are of unknown date; others were elementary schools at
the date of the inquiry; others were never in fact anything but elementary schools;
they "taught grammar only if the children remained long enough at school".

[2] *Report of the Schools Inquiry Commission*, 1868, vol. I, p. 122.

[3] Strype, J., *Memorials of Thomas Cranmer*, ed. 1694, Book I, chap. xxii, p. 88.

[4] See St Olave's School, Southwark, in Foster Watson's *English Grammar
Schools*, 1908, p. 150.

desire of their founders to provide non-classical instruction for the children of parents who were not able or who did not wish "to keep their children at grammar". No less than 460 such schools were returned in the reports of the Commissioners of Inquiry Concerning Charities as existing in England and Wales at the end of the seventeenth century, for pedagogy, most neglected of the arts, had shared in the astonishing intellectual activity of the "century of genius".[1] It became fashionable. Men distinguished in religion, administration and letters did not disdain to apply the "new philosophy" to education. A spate of pedagogical writings and of legislation bore witness to the enthusiasm for educational reform. The lively interest of the Long Parliament, and of the Protector, was responsible for the part played by the State from 1640 to 1660. It was with "learned and wise" members of Parliament that the celebrated Bohemian bishop, Comenius, planned to discuss his scheme for a Seminary of Christian Pansophia;[2] Milton, pleading for the distribution of culture "to all extream parts which now be too much neglected", revealed in his *Ready and Easy Way to Establish a Free Commonwealth* that a design to make the whole nation "more industrious, more vigorous at home, more potent, more honourable abroad" was under consideration by the Long Parliament;[3] the House of Commons, in the resolutions of 1641, declared its intention of vindicating itself from "the imputations laid upon it, of discouraging learning", by authorising the application of Church revenues "to the advancement of piety and learning",[4] and Cromwell, occupied with affairs of State, did not consider it waste of time to plan a new university in the North and a "Forraigne Correspondency" with learned men in Europe at one end of the scale, and a scheme of industrial instruction for the children of the Irish poor at the other.[5]

The three Education Acts of 1649 illustrate the pre-occupation of the Commonwealth State with education. Under the "Act for the Better Propagation of the Gospel in Wales" over sixty free schools were set

[1] These figures must be received with reserve. Pre-seventeenth century charities applied to education were seldom founded for the purpose.

[2] Comenius, J. A., *Opera Didactica Omnia* [etc.], 1657, Part II, Introduction.

[3] Milton, J., *Prose Works*, vol. III, p. 427.

[4] *Journals of the House of Commons*, June 18 and July 9, 1641.

[5] Letters Patent, Durham University, May 15, 1657, from the Allen Tracts and Reprints, *Collectanea Dunelmensis*; Commonwealth Records, Ireland, A 27, 28, folio 156.

up and financed in the Principality, with funds secured by the dis-establishment and partial disendowment of the Church in Wales.[1] By Chapter 31 of the same year the firstfruits and tenths, which since the reign of Henry VIII had accrued to the Crown, were used to augment the salaries, stipends, allowances and provisions of preaching ministers and schoolmasters. The allocation of this money to education "preceded by 184 years the first grant made by the English Parliament under the modern education system".[2] Chapter 45, the third of these remarkable measures, recognised the responsibility of the State and of the community to the natives of the New England Colonies, and set up a machinery for this purpose which was the prototype of voluntary efforts when the State withdrew its encouragement. By it a society of sixteen persons was appointed to propagate religion and education, and the collection of voluntary contributions was authorised throughout the parishes of England and Wales to finance the work.[3]

Nor was the enthusiasm for education confined to organising and financing a State system of schools. Influenced by Comenius's ardent advocacy of a new curriculum and new methods of instruction, a group of distinguished Englishmen, among them Milton, Drury and William Petty, denounced the monopoly of the classics in education, and demanded a place for the mathematical, natural and political sciences.[4] With the exception, however, of a reformed curriculum, including science, mathematics, history, geography and modern languages, introduced into some of the Dissenting academies in the later seventeenth and eighteenth centuries, pedagogic practice remained unaffected by pedagogic theory.[5] Long after Milton's day "pure trifling at Grammar

[1] Scobell, Hen., *Acts of Parliament Under the Commonwealth*. Feb. 22, 1649: "Act for the Better Propagation and Preaching of the Gospel in Wales and redress of some grievances."

[2] De Montmorency, J. G., *State Intervention in English Education*, 1902, p. 100.

[3] Scobell, Hen., *op. cit.* chap. 45, 1650.

[4] Milton, J., *Of Education*, 1644; Drury, J., *The Reformed School*[n.d.]; Petty, W., *The Advice of Mr S. Hartlib for the Advancement of some particular Parts of Learning*, 1648.

[5] See Parker, I., *Dissenting Academies in England and Wales. Their Rise, Progress and their Place among the Educational Systems of the Country*, 1914; McLachlan, H., *English Education Under the Test Acts*, 1931; Roberts, H. P., "Non-Conformist Academies in Wales, 1662–1862", in *The Transactions of the Honourable Society of Cymmrodorion*, 1928–9.

and Sophistry" remained the main business of study in grammar schools and universities. One reform of immeasurable importance was, however, achieved. The vernacular language slowly established itself as the proper medium of instruction. Latin, hitherto the only key to culture, began to share its function with English, when school text-books in English replaced school text-books in Latin.

The association of the vernacular with the new learning of the mathematical and natural sciences permitted "a diffusion of knowledge among ordinary people". The popularisation of science, the arrival of the daily press and the literary journals, the growth of libraries and the extension of the printing press, hitherto confined to London and the towns, afford some measure of the intellectual activity of the age. Literature began to adapt itself after the Revolution to a new public. "A learned body or clerisy as such gradually disappeared and literature in general began to be addressed to the common miscellaneous public."[1]

The increase of endowed English or elementary schools in the second half of the seventeenth century was closely associated with the victory of the vernacular tongue, and the spread of new intellectual interests. Wills and deeds of gift, endowing them, are to be found expressly forbidding the teaching of Latin. They emphasised the importance of reading and writing in English, and, here and there, they made provision for the teaching of mathematics. But the extension of instruction in the second half of the seventeenth century from endowed grammar school to endowed English school left the bulk of the people still without the means of education. Those among the lower orders who could afford to educate their children sent them to the pay schools, which steadily grew in number throughout the century; those who could not afford the small fees demanded were unable to share in the advancement of learning. The desire that they should participate was a contributory factor to the movement for charity school education in the eighteenth century with which it is seldom credited.

The eighteenth century, which witnessed the establishment of but 128 grammar schools in England and Wales, between 1700 and 1799,[2]

---

[1] Coleridge, S. T., *Literary Remains*, vol. I, pp. 230 *et seq.*

[2] These figures must be received with reserve, for the official estimates of the number of grammar schools do not agree. The Report drawn up by Horace Mann for the British Government in 1854 returned them at 128; the Schools Inquiry Commission in 1868 at 124.

was a period of remarkable activity in elementary education in all four countries of the British Isles. Thousands of schools were endowed and innumerable bursaries for schooling were bestowed, by charitable men and women, for the education of the children of the poor. Equally remarkable was the establishment of schools for elementary instruction maintained, not by endowments, but by subscriptions, and as the contributions were made at the pleasure of the donors the voluntary or subscription school made its appearance side by side with the endowed school.

It has been customary to separate these two groups of elementary schools into categories called respectively the endowed non-classical and the charity or subscription schools. The terminology is unfortunate. It has accentuated their differences rather than their similarities. In the eyes of the law, schools founded by endowment were subject to a control from which the voluntary schools were exempt, but in all other respects, in their purpose, personnel and practice, the majority of the endowed and subscription elementary schools of the eighteenth century were alike. Both types were charity schools, both aimed at the moral improvement of the poor through instruction, both based the education they offered on religious knowledge, both, when they could afford it, gave gratuitous instruction, clothing and apprentice fees to their pupils, and for both the Society for Promoting Christian Knowledge in England and Wales and the Incorporated Societies in Scotland and Ireland, which co-ordinated the individual efforts of the charitable into the charity school movement, used the term "charity school". Their supporters were indifferent to the manner in which funds were raised. Endowments and subscriptions were equally welcome to them. Their interest lay not in the means employed, but in the provision of instruction for the children of the poorer classes.

Investigation of the early accounts of the schools, published by the societies which organised them, confirms the use of the term "charity school" as an omnibus term covering "all schools of a like nature".[1] Endowed schools, established long before the societies began their work,[2] old endowments for education recovered by the Commission

---

[1] *Account of the Charity Schools*, 1704, p. 13.

[2] *Account of the Charity Schools*, 1707. "Little Houghton, Northamptonshire, £12 per ann. left by a private person in 1667 for teaching the poor children of this place."

of Charitable Uses,[1] recent endowments attached by munificent benefactors to particular schools,[2] or left unattached as bursaries for the
schooling of a specified number of children,[3] free schools on which
charity schools "were now engrafting"[4] and even "old decayed grammar
schools"[5] were returned by them, with the new subscription schools, as
charity schools. The subscription method offered a novel and unlimited
means for the education of poor children. It was a new and popular
method of raising funds, but it did not replace the older method of
endowment. Subscription schools were not encouraged, the S.P.C.K.
informed its correspondents, "where the want is supplied by an endowed school".[6] They were supplementary. Schools founded by
"noble lords" and "gracious ladies", by "pious gentlemen" and
"private gentlewomen", appear in the reports side by side with
schools financed by the modest subscriptions of "middling-class" philanthropists. Frequently, too, schools which began life as voluntary, or
subscription schools, changed their status during the century, when, by
the accumulation of gifts and donations, they became endowed schools.[7]
An age which lacked precise terminology and classification called
them indifferently English, or elementary, or free, or non-classical,

[1] *Account of the Charity Schools*, 1712. "Artleborough, A rent charge of £6 a
year left about 28 years ago for teaching poor boys lately recovered by a Commission of Charitable Uses."

[2] *Account of the Charity Schools*, 1714. "Badminton, Gloucestershire, A school
built by a Lady of Quality and endowed by her."

[3] *Account of the Charity Schools*, 1724. "Dean, Bedfordshire, Between £20 and
£30 settled by a private person for teaching."

[4] S.P.C.K. Abs. of Correspondence, Letter from the Rev. John Strype, Sept. 2,
1709.

[5] *Account of the Charity Schools*, 1712. "Soham, Suffolk, A Grammar
School converted by the feoffees to a Charity School for about a hundred
children."

[6] S.P.C.K. Abs. of Correspondence, March 2, 1716–17.

[7] The *Account of the Charity Schools*, 1714, states explicitly that the overplus of
subscriptions and gifts should be used to purchase lands and build school-houses.
See also *Account* of 1707 for Spofforth, Yorkshire: "Within twelve miles are six
catechetical schools which are already, or will be, endowed within the space of a
year." See also the *Report of the Charity Commissioners on the Blue Coat School,
Southmolton, Devon*, vol. III, 1830. The school was established by subscription in
1711; in or about the year 1730 the sum of £156 was laid out in purchasing, in the
name of the Mayor and Burgesses of Southmolton, the reversion in fee of an estate
in the parish of Warkleigh.

or catechetical, or charity schools, but the movement for their establishment was a single movement.[1]

Comparison of the children attending the endowed and subscription schools, and the arrangements made for their instruction and apprenticeship, offers corroboratory evidence. It has sometimes been assumed that the endowed and subscription schools of the eighteenth century differed in the class of children whom they instructed; the one providing education for the children of the "second", or respectable, poor of the parish, who kept off the rates and, since the passing of the Poor Law Act of 1601, regarded the innumerable charitable endowments for education as their perquisites;[2] the other drawing its pupils from the pauper families of the slums, who were dependent upon the rates for their support. It is possible to find confirmation of this view in the records of particular schools whose managers "enquired narrowly" into the incomes of the parents; some admitted only the children of house-keepers, others only those of paupers and indigent parents, but comparison of the subscription schools returned by the Societies in the eighteenth century and of the eighteenth-century endowed schools returned by the Commissioners of Inquiry Concerning Charities in the early years of the nineteenth century does not, in general, support this distinction. The pupils of both types of school were, alike, drawn from all the ranks of the labouring poor. Contemporaries did not discriminate between them. "Patriots and philanthropists of earlier days", said Archdeacon White Kennett, addressing the London charity schools at their anniversary service in 1706, "founded grammar schools...that a number of poorer children might have learning gratis." But their intention had proved unsatisfactory. The grammar schools reached but a fraction of the poor; they provided no instruction for girls, and their curriculum of Greek and Latin was "too high for the meaner sort of boys born for the spade, and the plough, and the lower trades". "Worthy persons", who desired to assist in education, were encouraged by the preacher to *endow* or *subscribe* to *English* schools, in which these

---

[1] See the *Report of the Royal Commission on the Poor Laws [etc.]*, 1909, p. 455, for the definition of a charity.

[2] See Tudor, O. D., *The Law of Charities and Mortmain*, 4th ed. 1906, p. 105.

children could learn "the plaine accomplishments which best become the generality of the people".[1]

The vast corpus of wills and deeds of gift entombed within the forty-four volumes of the reports of the Commissioners of Inquiry Concerning Charities in the early nineteenth century provide an elaborate proof of the response of eighteenth-century philanthropists to this and kindred appeals. "For the children of the labouring poor", "for children of the poor labourers of the parish", "for the sons of the poor and also of farmers and others", "for the children of such day labourers and other inhabitants least able to pay for the instruction of their children", "for children whose parents have nothing but their labour", appear again and again in the reports. Sailors, soldiers, servants, artificers, mechanics, labourers and petty tradesmen were the lower orders whose children, Mrs Trimmer reported in 1792, filled the endowed and subscription charity schools.[2]

The children who attended them received instruction and clothing which marked them off from the children of the grammar schools on the one hand and of the private-venture school on the other. Here and there Latin formed part of the curriculum, but the emphasis in endowed and subscription charity school was laid throughout upon a "Christian and Useful education". To this end "the Knowledge and Practice of Religion" formed the backbone of the instruction offered, and, except in rare instances, the curriculum was confined to the three R's, and "when practicable" to handicrafts that "the children may be inured to labour".

As the century grew older, and the movement spread into Scotland, Ireland and Wales, modifications of the character of the schools became noticeable. The "christian and useful" elements in the curriculum received different emphasis at different times and in different places, the

---

[1] Kennett, White, *op. cit.* See also the sermon preached on behalf of the Charity Schools in and about London and Westminster by the Rev. G. Ridley on May 5, 1757. He answers his question "Who are the children of the poor?" by reminding his hearers of 5 Eliz. c. 4: "The Statute provides that no Merchant trafficing beyond the sea, Mercer, Draper, Goldsmith, Ironmonger, Imbroiderer or Clothier shall take for his apprentice any but his own sons or the sons of Freeholders of 40s. a year if they live in Market Towns not corporate. Now in these and other agreeable and advantageous walks of life which may have grown up in the State since Queen Elizabeth's time we shall meet with few or none of these children. The schools are for the children of the poor engaged in low and laborious occupations."
[2] Trimmer, S., *The Œconomy of Charity*, 1801, vol. I, pp. 81–91.

provisions of clothing and apprenticeship associated with both endowed and subscription charity schools frequently failed, and the success or failure of an individual school was reflected in the changing social status of its pupils. But while these, and other modifications, permitted variation within the charity school movement, the schools, as a whole, conformed to type. They provided a particular kind of education for a particular class of children, financed in great part by a particular method, and, by so doing, they established the idea of elementary education not, as in earlier ages, as a stage preliminary to the grammar schools, by which "boys of parts" might climb to the universities, but as a system complete in itself.

From 1699, when the Society for Promoting Christian Knowledge co-ordinated the movement, until the appearance of Sunday schools, in the last quarter of the eighteenth century, the endowed and subscription charity schools were the chief, and, in many places, the only means of education for the children of the poor. For them thousands of schools were set up and financed in the British Isles.[1] When the remarkable enthusiasm evinced in England in the reigns of Anne and George I slackened at the end of the third decade of the century, Wales became the scene of extraordinary enthusiasm for adult and infant education, resulting in the instruction of over 158,000 children between 1737 and 1761. In Ireland the success of philanthropists in establishing 170 schools on "the English pattern" in the early years of the century was increased in 1733 by the grant of a charter from the Crown to the Incorporated Society, which built and financed over fifty endowed boarding schools in the course of the next half century. Scotland, whose proud boast was the existence of a school in every parish, did not remain unaffected by the popular interest in the instruction of the poor, when it discovered that there were parishes which had no parish schools, and parishes, so vast in extent, that the legal school served but a fraction of the children. Two charters to incorporate a Society for the provision of charity schools in the Highlands and Islands and other remote parts were sought and obtained in 1709 and 1730, and its activity added over 500 schools to those provided by the neighbouring countries of the British Isles.[2]

[1] It is remarkable that the charity school movement began and flourished when England was engaged in a long and expensive war.

[2] See Appendices IV, 3; III, 1, 2; II, 1.

While it is possible to estimate with some degree of accuracy the extent of the charity school movement in Scotland, Ireland and Wales, it is not possible to offer even an approximate estimate of the number of schools set up in England in the course of the century, or of the numbers of children attending them, for the main sources of information do not provide the data required. The London S.P.C.K. had no coercive powers. It encouraged the trustees and managers of old and new schools to join it and to adapt them to the new scheme of instruction, but it could not oblige them to do so. Unlike the Incorporated Societies in Scotland and Ireland it did not manage, or finance, the schools associated with it, and had little control over them. It was dependent upon the grace of its local correspondents for the returns which it published, and, as minute and letter books show, neither polite request nor vigorously worded demands could ensure a regular return of the schools and pupils.[1] From the end of the first quarter of the century, when the zeal of the Society was gradually transferred from the charity school movement to missionary work over-seas and the establishment of a great publishing business at home, little effort was made to secure up-to-date returns. Lists of schools and of the numbers of scholars replaced the full and detailed accounts of the early years. From 1725 abbreviated tables of schools, county by county, took their place.[2] In 1736 they too disappeared. The London schools were reported in some detail to the end of the century, and show a slow increase in numbers and endowments, but the totals, only, of the country schools were returned. Unhappily their value is negligible. They became common form. The same number of schools and children were returned unchanged year after year, 1329 schools and 23,421 scholars in 1723, and precisely the same number in 1799. Figures such as these establish the continuity of the movement in England, but are valueless in estimating its development.

Returns from the S.P.C.K. do not, however, exhaust the evidence of a widespread and continuous charity school movement in the eighteenth century. The schools which did not stay the course must not be forgotten. References to schools born one year "to decline" the next are strewn throughout the correspondence of the Society. Others whose demise was unpitied and unsung have left no record at all.

---

[1] Sometimes whole counties failed to make returns. Herefordshire and Monmouthshire schools were frequently omitted in the reports. S.P.C.K. Minutes, June 18, 1723.   [2] See Appendix I, 4.

Further, the reports of the S.P.C.K. omit all reference to the establishment of Nonconformist and Methodist charity schools. As an Anglican Society, established to organise the instruction of the poor in the tenets of the Anglican faith, the S.P.C.K. gave no place to them in its reports, and as neither Dissenters nor Methodists established a central body for the organisation and co-ordination of their schools, their numbers are unknown. The histories of local Nonconformist and Methodist churches, of Quakers, Jews and Huguenots, show that schools, supported by their members, in which children learned to read the Bible and sometimes to write and cast accounts, were not uncommon. The existence of over thirty endowed elementary schools founded by Nonconformists, revealed in the Charity Commissioners' reports, is proof of non-Anglican interest in the education of the poor.[1] It is not too great an assumption to make that many of the non-Anglican churches established subscription charity schools, whose existence was unrecorded, for the children of the poor of their communions.

The two main sources of information in the early nineteenth century are also unsatisfactory. The figures of endowed and subscription schools returned by the Select Committee appointed in 1816 to Inquire into the Education of the Lower Orders were only roughly approximate; those of the Commission to Inquire Concerning Charities in England and Wales, which published its invaluable reports from 1819 to 1837, were incomplete. Analysis of the Commissioners' returns shows that over eleven hundred endowed elementary schools were set up in the eighteenth century, and that in addition over a thousand unattached charities were left for elementary education in the same period.[2] As the Commissioners were however precluded by their terms of reference from enquiring into the state of those schools which at the time of their investigation were financed wholly or in the main by subscription, the voluntary schools were ignored. Their numbers were unrecorded in the voluminous survey.

The incomplete character of the returns of the S.P.C.K. and the Charity Commissioners rob them of value in estimating the extent of the English charity school movement. Nor would a sum in simple addition assist in arriving at an approximate estimate, for investigation of the two main sources of information makes clear that the returns overlap. Some of the schools listed by the S.P.C.K. can be identified with

[1] See Appendix I, 3.   [2] See Appendix I, 1, 2.

schools returned by the Commissioners a hundred years later. There are others, and they form the majority, whose identification is impossible. The data for comparison are either inadequate or lacking altogether.

Nevertheless it is possible to establish a steadily maintained interest in the education of the poor throughout the eighteenth century. The extraordinary enthusiasm evinced in the first quarter of the century did not come to an end when religious, political and economic opposition combined to try and destroy it in the second quarter of the century. Not only did Scotland, Ireland and Wales take up the theme, but the schools in England weathered the storm, and added to their number. The nation, wrote Hanway in 1766, "abounds" in charity schools.[1] Local histories, S.P.C.K. records, the answers to episcopal visitation articles of enquiry, the returns to Parliament of ministers and church-wardens of the parishes in England and Wales, made under the Act of 1786,[2] and the steady stream of gifts and donations endowing new and re-endowing already established schools and bursaries returned by the Charity Commissioners, bear witness to the immense number of charities earmarked for the education of the poor in the second half of the eighteenth century. Nor should the importance of the comparison made in 1776 by Adam Smith, a balanced and informed observer, between the English charity schools and the Scottish parish schools be forgotten. They were not, he admitted, as universal as the Scots schools, but that the comparison should have been made at all is confirmation of the numerical strength and wide extent of the charity schools in the third quarter of the century.[3] It is, too, sometimes forgotten that the advent of the Sunday school in the last twenty years of the eighteenth century was but a continuation of the earlier attempts to provide education for the children of the poor. The combined influence of the religious revivals and of the industrial revolution modified the original idea of day-school instruction and forced Sunday charity schools, organised by the same means and financed by the same methods as the older charity schools, into prominence. In 1787 it was estimated that there were a quarter of a million children in the Sunday charity schools.[4]

[1] Hanway, J., *An Earnest Appeal for Mercy to the Children of the Poor*, 1766.
[2] 26 Geo. III, c. 58.
[3] Smith, Adam, *An Inquiry into the Nature and Causes of the Wealth of Nations*, 1776, Book V, chap. 1, Art. 2.
[4] Statistics of the pupils in attendance at the eighteenth-century charity schools

But perhaps the most impressive evidence of a continuous movement for elementary education in the eighteenth century is to be found in the rapid development of the voluntary movement for the establishment of schools for the children of the poor under the National and the British and Foreign School Societies in the early nineteenth century, which can be explained only by the existence of a large number of voluntary schools enjoying well-established support. How many schools returned by the two nineteenth-century societies as "National" and "British" schools were already in existence when the Societies began their work cannot be ascertained, but there are enough scattered references to show that the normal development of the eighteenth-century subscription charity school was to become a nineteenth-century "National" or "British" school. According to Lord Brougham's estimates there were, in 1818, about 18,500 day schools in England and Wales at which 644,000 children received instruction. Of these, above 4100 were endowed schools, containing 165,432 pupils. The remainder of the schools, 14,300 in number, were unendowed. They were maintained by school fees, or by voluntary contributions. Their pupils reached a total of 478,000. Among them were 310,000 paying pupils, and no less than 168,000 children whose schooling was financed by charity. To these should be added some part of the 5100 Sunday schools and their 452,000 pupils, returned in 1818, but as the number of children who attended both day and Sunday schools is unknown, to add them together would make the total unduly big.[1] While Lord Brougham's figures cannot be accepted as accurate, they afford a measure of the strength of the voluntary school movement in the early years of the nineteenth century before the National and the British and Foreign School Societies had made any considerable headway. Lamentably inadequate as the schools were when the rise in population threw out of gear old standards and old methods, they establish a movement for popular instruction in the eighteenth century of no inconsiderable extent.

are seldom reliable. The notoriously irregular attendance of the children and the carelessness of the teachers in making returns rob them of value. The totals returned appear as a rule to be unduly large. Most probably they refer to the number of children whose names were on the school lists, not to those in attendance.

[1] See Brougham's speeches in the House of Commons, June 28, 1820 and in the House of Lords, May 21, 1835. Hansard, *Parliamentary Debates*, 3rd Series, vol. II, cols. 49–89 and vol. XXVII, cols. 1293–1333.

CHAPTER II

ENGLAND

ORGANISED CHARITY

"For as much as the pious Instruction and Education of Children is the Surest Way of Preserving and Propagating the Knowledge and Practice of True Religion, it hath been very acceptable for Us to hear that for the attaining these Good Ends many Charity Schools are now created throughout this Kingdom by the Liberal Contributions of our Good Subjects; We do therefore earnestly recommend it to you, by all Proper Ways to encourage and promote so excellent a Work, and to Countenance and Assist the Persons principally concerned in it as they shall always be sure of our Protection and Favour."

> Letter of Her Majesty Queen Anne to the
> Archbishops of Canterbury and York,
>
> August 20, 1711.

I

PAUPERISM AND POPERY

Two factors in particular were responsible for organised efforts in the early eighteenth century to provide education for the children of the poor. Of these pauperism was the more fundamental. It was, throughout the century, the leading domestic problem. The breakdown of the Tudor poor law, after forty years of competent administration under the early Stuart kings, forced the problem of the poor into prominence in the last half of the seventeenth century, and kept it there throughout the eighteenth century. The accuracy of Gregory King's astonishing statement that more than half of the population in the year 1688 was a charge upon the community may be called in question, but, read in conjunction with the writings of contemporary publicists, it establishes the existence of an immensely large class of dependent and semi-dependent poor.[1]

[1] King, Gregory, *Natural and Political Observations and Conclusions upon the State and Condition of England*, 1696, ed. by G. Chambers, 1804.

The existence of this class was not in itself a distressing phenomenon to the reformers of the seventeenth and eighteenth centuries. It was accepted without more than occasional comment. Poverty was the source of wealth, for it provided the reservoir of cheap labour which was deemed an essential requisite in a country whose economics were those of mercantilism. But the state of the poor at the end of the seventeenth century called for reform on two sides. In the first place the poor had become too heavy a charge upon the national income, and, secondly, their moral delinquencies, attributed in part to the "monstrous increase in Deism, Profaneness and Vice",[1] threatened the stability of society.

In this double charge against the poor the children played a part which did not fail to evoke compassion. The lot of the parents, as Richard Baxter pitifully remarked, would have been easier if they had but contained themselves from marriage,[2] for the swollen ranks of the poor were steadily recruited by long families of children. Locke, writing a few years after King, stressed the part which the children played in forming the national deficit. A labouring man and wife when in health might, he held, be able to maintain themselves and two children without recourse to the rates, but the families of the labouring poor were normally in excess of this number, and their children were an ordinary burden to the parish. At twelve years of age, or thereabouts, they were apprenticed, or put out to service, and the responsibility of the parish for them ended. But from babyhood to apprenticeship they were usually maintained in idleness.[3]

That was one side of the picture. On the other was the appalling condition in which the majority of these children lived. London and the towns, "where the children swarmed like locusts in the streets",[4] called early upon the attention of reformers and philanthropists. The City was "congested with children", some of whom—the orphans, whose parents had left them penniless, and the foundlings and bastards —were the especial concern of the poor law officials. Desertion was

---

[1] *First Circular Letter from the Honourable Society for Promoting Christian Knowledge to their Clergy Correspondents in the several Counties of England and Wales,* 1699.

[2] Baxter, R., *The Poor Husbandman's Advocate to Rich Racking Landlords,* ed. by F. J. Powicke, 1926.

[3] Locke, J., *Report to the Board of Trade,* 1697.

[4] For a vivid and detailed account of the condition of the London poor see M. D. George's *London Life in the Eighteenth Century,* 1925.

common. Children "laid in the streets" obtained a settlement in the parish in which they were born, and, as it was a main object of parish policy to prevent such children from becoming a charge upon the rates, the proportion of those that lived to grow up was small. As babes they were handed over to the parish nurses, who, as a parliamentary report of 1716 stated, were "void of commiseration and religion".[1] Those that were permitted to live by their "barbarous foster mothers" were sold, for apprenticeship in such cases was but a euphemism, so young that "'tis little better than murdering them."[2]

Children who lived with their parents in the slums and alleys of London and Westminster were little better off. The filthy single rooms and cellars in which parents and children were "heaped up",[3] afforded opportunity for neither cleanliness nor decency. It was noticed by Josiah Child that the children of the poor were more unhealthy, and "more than ordinarily subject to many loathsome diseases".[4] Gin drinking, which spread with alarming rapidity in the second quarter of the eighteenth century, took its toll of the children. Men, women and children, reported His Majesty's Justices of the Peace at Hick's Hall in 1736, shamefully and constantly indulged themselves in the practice.[5]

The moral state of the children was no less disquieting. The labyrinthine courts and alleys in which the poor lived were not only the most dirty and dilapidated but, as a recent writer has pointed out, were also the most dangerous districts ,where anarchy, drunkenness and thieving were rife.[6] In this "vast wood and forest" where, wrote Henry Fielding, the London magistrate, in 1751, "the thief may harbour with as great security as wild beasts do in the deserts of Arabia and Africa",[7] children were brought up to trades of begging and stealing. Here, from babyhood, they contracted the evil habits which prepared them for "the hangman's harvest".[8] From these lanes, and alleys, courts and by-

[1] *Journals of the House of Commons*, March 8, 1715–16.
[2] *The Ladies' Memorial Praying for a Charter for the Foundling Hospital*, 1739.
[3] Strype, J., 1735 ed. of Stow's *Survey of London*, Book II, p. 711.
[4] Child, Sir J., *A New Discourse on Trade*, 1670, p. 81.
[5] *Report of H.M. Justices of the Peace at Hick's Hall*, January Sessions, 1735–6, pp. 16, 17. Printed in an Appendix to *Distilled Spirituous Liquors, the Bane of the Nation*, 1736.
[6] George, M. D., *op. cit.* chap. II, *passim*.
[7] Fielding, H., *Inquiry into the Causes of the late Increase of Robbers*, 1751, p. 76.
[8] Bellers, J., *Proposals for Raising a Colledge of Industry*, 1695, p. 11.

places they were drawn to form the infant army, ten thousand strong, of blackguard boys, the wicked, idle, pilfering vagrants, thieves, robbers, gamblers, pickpockets, blasphemers and caterpillars of Defoe's full-flavoured denunciation.[1]

Two methods for their rescue and reform were presented to the public at the end of the seventeenth century. In their search for a panacea men of the eminence of Hale, Child, Locke and Bellers, influenced by the success of their contemporaries abroad in solving a similar problem, urged the establishment of workhouses and working schools, which would act as a deterrent of pauperism, and, by making the poor self-supporting, would accustom them from babyhood to "a civil and industrious course of life". "The subtle Dutch", according to Josiah Child, had solved the problem of the sustentation of their poor by settling them on work in houses established for the purpose.[2] Locke's weighty report to the Board of Trade in 1697 proclaimed his belief in the same means. It is significant that the most effective method he could devise was the establishment of working schools in every parish, which all children, above three and under fourteen years of age, should be obliged to attend. Under such control their moral, religious and physical well-being would be cared for, the first by the discipline of manual work on week-days, the second by "constant attendance" at church on Sundays, and the last by a plentiful supply of bread instead of the scanty ration allowed to them by their parents.

London reformers, who favoured the workhouse and working school, had an example before them in Thomas Firmin's "spinning school in the nature of a workshop", where children who "never bring anything to their parents, nor earn one penny to their keep and the good of the Nation" were taught to spin, and earned a few pence, weekly, by their efforts.[3] The failure of Firmin's scheme did not prevent the development of his idea. In the London workhouse, opened in 1698, the children were set to spin wool, knit stockings and make new their linen clothes and shoes, and, when they left the house at the age of twelve or fourteen years, they were apprenticed or put out to service.

Over against this group of reformers, who found in the discipline of

---

[1] Defoe, D., *Everybody's Business is Nobody's Business*, 1725.

[2] Child, Sir J., *op. cit.*

[3] Firmin, T., *Some Proposals for the Employment of the Poor for the Prevention of Idleness*, 1678.

labour the cure for existing ills, were a body of men and women who approached the problem from the standpoint of religion. They found their panacea in the discipline of catechetical instruction for the infant poor, before they were ready for apprenticeship and service. They attributed the social evils of the day in part to the inadequacy of the Tudor poor law, which had failed to recognise that "instruction was as primary a need as maintenance" for the children of the poor,[1] but chiefly to the indifference of the clergy to their duties, and in particular to the duty of catechising the children of the parish. They were perturbed to find tens of thousands of children in London and the towns and country-side without the means of religious and social discipline, children to whom neither church nor school offered, as they did to the children of the superior classes, a means of religious salvation and moral improvement. For the weekly catechising of the children in church, during the evening service, as enjoined by prayer book and canons, had fallen, by the end of the seventeenth century, into general disuse. On parents and priests rested the dual obligation of sending youth to church and of catechising them when there. The detailed returns to the visitation enquiries of Bishops Wake and Gibson of Lincoln, in the first quarter of the eighteenth century, show that the practice was fairly general in Lent, but was neglected during the rest of the year, and this was so, it should be remembered, in a diocese whose bishops were conspicuous, not only for their piety and learning, but for their persistent and searching efforts at reform, lasting for eighteen years. It is the recurring theme of contemporaries, both laymen and clerics, that the "decay of catechising" was the explanation of "the barbarous ignorance observable among the common people, especially those of the poorer sort",[2] but it is apparent that factors other than its neglect contributed to its decay. The earnest priests "unexceptionable in their

[1] *Sermon preached by the Bishop of Bristol at the Anniversary Meeting of the Gentlemen concerned in Promoting Charity Schools lately erected in the Cities of London and Westminster,* May 9, 1745. "...In the new legal provision for the poor in Queen Elizabeth's reign poor children had a part. But maintenance alone was not sufficient for children because their case always requires more than maintenance. Maintenance for the adult poor may be enough. Maintenance and Education are necessary for children of the poor, and Education is essential for children whose parents are able to maintain but utterly neglect their children...."

[2] *First Circular Letter, ut supra.*

lives and labours"[1] (and, contrary to the general belief, there were many of them) who did not leave their duty undone were faced by a technical difficulty which goes some way to explain the neglect. Prayer book and canons enjoined the instruction and examination of the children of the parish on Sundays after the second lesson at evening prayer, but, unless the children could read or their parents co-operated in giving instruction between whiles, the weekly catechetical exercises were, as every teacher knows, condemned to failure, for one Sunday's lesson was forgotten before the next came round. The labouring poor had neither schooling enough, nor books, nor leisure to instruct their children during the week. Hence on Sundays, though "sometimes great numbers of the middling sort came",[2] there were parishes in which few or none of the very poor attended the weekly instruction and examination.

And as the poor would not go to church, so they could not go to school. Shenstone's *Schoolmistress* has established the belief that "every village mark'd with little spire" had, in the eighteenth century, at least its dame school, where the village children learnt the A.B.C. and the horn-book. But it is easy throughout the century, and especially in its early years, to find country town and village without any school of any kind, and, where there were schools, the very poor could not afford the dues charged in the free schools, nor the weekly pence demanded by the village dame and parish clerk, whose schools formed the common schools of the people. For schooling not only involved positive expenditure, it entailed also a negative loss of earnings; the child of school age contributed his pence to the weekly budget, or, at least, relieved his parents of his keep by begging for his food. Because of this the children of the poor were "abandoned to the wildness of their own nature, like brutes of the earth without any knowledge of God or Christ".[3] And pity, which has not always a smiling face, moved God-fearing men to take up the burden of their instruction.

Faced by two possible ways of disciplining the infant poor, the response of the English public was, for the first quarter of the eighteenth

[1] S.P.C.K. Abs. of Correspondence, Letter from Dr Knight, Broughton, Oxon, June 1, 1700.

[2] S.P.C.K. Abs. of Correspondence, Letter from Dr Hutchinson, Bury St Edmunds, Oct. 9, 1700.

[3] Watts, Isaac, *An Essay Towards the Encouragement of Charity Schools, particularly those that are supported by Protestant Dissenters* [*etc.*], 1728, p. 12.

4

century, overwhelmingly in favour of catechetical instruction. The idea
appealed in the first place because it was but a variant of an old practice.
Provision for the poor scholar had commonly been made in the old
grammar and English schools, and innumerable charities existed for his
education, clothing and apprenticeship. Schools for catechetical instruction, which would be free, in the strict sense of the word, i.e. would
involve neither parents nor parish officers in entrance fees or fire and
candle dues, and would, if funds permitted, provide the children with
clothing, was but the extension of a method already in existence. The
workhouse, on the contrary, was a new device, not indigenous, but
foreign in origin, and English public opinion, always slow in accepting
new ideas from foreign sources, paid but half-hearted attention to its
advocates.

Again, the charity school was a cheap method of effecting reform.
Any unoccupied house or room could be utilised as a school. The
wooden benches, slates and pencils, and the few books, which formed
the school's equipment, could be purchased at a trifling expenditure. A
neat and even smart uniform for the girls cost but sixteen shillings, for
the boys even less,[1] and one teacher, passing rich on twenty pounds a
year, could, it was believed, discipline, with ease, the minds and bodies
of pupils of all ages and at all stages. A workhouse, set up on the
Continental plan, involved considerable expenditure of money. New
buildings were essential to house the workers, stock for their labours
and implements wherewith to fashion it cost money; above all, wages
for officials, both numerous and competent enough to organise, control
and instruct the mixed company of men, women and children whom
the house was designed to shelter and discipline, could not but present
a heavy bill.

But it was to the more favourable economic conditions which prevailed in England during the reigns of Anne and George I that the
charity school owed its financial support. Trade was rapidly and
population but slowly increasing; labour was in demand for spinning
and carding in the clothing counties; corn was cheap, and, in some parts
of England, wages were rising. Workhouses, it was urged, were unnecessary. Their advocates were mercilessly attacked by Daniel Defoe,
who ridiculed the idea of building expensive houses throughout the
country in order to provide the poor with work which was crying out

[1] See Appendix I, 7.

to be done. In his famous tract, *Giving Alms no Charity*, he denounced
the folly of diverting industry from its natural channels, and attacked
the bill, sponsored by Sir Humphrey Mackworth, to set up workhouses
in every parish. Luxury, sloth and idleness, Defoe declared, in true
puritan fashion, to be the national causes of poverty and unemploy-
ment. "The general taint of slothfulness demanded not workhouses but
moral and religious regulation." The charity schools, whose purpose
was to build up moral and religious habits of the infant poor, won his
whole-hearted approval. This was the right way to begin reform. The
orderly and disciplined charity children afforded in his eyes a delightful
and pleasing spectacle. "The institution of Charity Schools is laudable,
the end most agreeable to all that is just and good."[1] Defoe's point of
view won general support. Mackworth's bill was turned down, and the
charity schools, which undertook to provide the discipline necessary to
reform the poor, increased in numbers and public esteem.

The second factor responsible for the "enthusiastic support" of the
charity schools, rather than of the workhouse, in the early years of the
eighteenth century, is to be found in the religious policy of the day.
Rome and its machinations constituted a danger to the Protestant
Succession, which Anglicans and Nonconformists could not fail to
recognise, hence catechetical schools, which would breed up sturdy
Protestants to bulwark the faith against the assaults of Rome, met with
immediate support. To Anglican and Dissenter alike Rome was the
parent of ignorance and sedition. Separated by a deep cleavage in
doctrine and politics they were one in their desire to curb its power.
Children who had learned the Anglican catechism, the psalms and
prayers, declared the Archdeacon of Huntingdon, in a peroration to a
charity school sermon in 1706, "would never stoop to beads and Latin
charms, nor bow their necks to the dark slavery of Rome".[2] To prevent
the spread of a religion, "absurd in itself and oppressive to the liberty
and the souls of men",[3] Anglican and Dissenter made common cause
to rescue the children of the poor from "the Great Devourer" by
establishing charity schools on their behalf.

---

[1] Defoe, D., *Charity still a Virtue, or an Impartial Account of the Trial and
Conviction of the Rev. W. Hendley for Preaching a Charity Sermon at Chiselhurst*,
1719.   [2] Kennett, White, *op. cit.*

[3] Milner, J., *Sermon preached for the benefit of the Charity School in Gravel Lane,
Southwark*, 1743.

II

THE SOCIETY FOR PROMOTING
CHRISTIAN KNOWLEDGE

Public interest in the schools, aroused by the social and religious benefits their establishment promised, was mobilised and co-ordinated by the new Society for Promoting Christian Knowledge, one of the several associations of the early eighteenth century for the reform of the lower classes. The religious societies set up in William and Mary's reign had taught that the care of the poor was a Christian duty. Perturbed as they were by the atheism and indifference of the fashionable and intellectual world, the devout men, "young in years and of the middling classes", who formed groups for prayer and the exchange of spiritual experiences, were profoundly disturbed by the ignorance and indifference of the poor. Practising the injunction to care for the widows and the fatherless they succeeded in arousing among clergy and laymen a sense of responsibility to the sick and distressed, and to the children, whose parents could not afford to send them to school.[1]

A different method of approach was made by the societies for the reformation of manners. Not the "persuasive of Christianity", but the rigours of the criminal law was their cure for the vice, indolence and intemperance of the poor. It was to supplement the loose and ineffective administration of the law that the societies for the reformation of manners came into being, and a certain measure of success may be attributed to them.[2] It did not, however, escape the sharp eyes of

[1] Woodward, J., *Account of the Rise and Progress of the Religious Societies in the City of London*, 1697.
[2] *Accounts of the Societies for the Reformation of Manners in London and Westminster and other parts of the Kingdom*, 1699, forty-four Reports, 1694–1738. See also Dr Josiah Woodward on the relation of the Societies for the Reformation of Manners to the S.P.C.K. "I cannot but take notice with great thankfulness to God of a very honourable and beneficial society—erected about two years ago in this City—by which the Propagation of Christian Knowledge at home and abroad is vigorously endeavoured, which seems to fill up all that could be thought deficient in the Methods that were before set on foot in order to the general Amendment of the lives and manners of men. For whilst the Societies for Reformation pluck up the Weeds and prepare the ground this 'sows the good Seed'." *Account of the Rise and Progress of the Religious Societies in the City of London*, 1701. Third ed. 1701.

Daniel Defoe that the main result of their activities was but to drive beneath the surface some of the outward manifestations of profaneness and debauchery, and it was the failure to do more than this which switched reforming interest from adults to children.[1]

Upon the ground so prepared came the news of Hermann Francke's work at Halle, which exercised a remarkable influence upon the charity school movement in England, Wales and Ireland.[2] The children of the poor, "who lived their lives like cattle without any knowledge of God and spiritual things", were provided by Francke and his pietist friends with "food for the soul as well as the body" in the poor school and orphanage erected for them. Pietism, originally a movement of asceticism within the Lutheran Church, endeavoured to correct the emphasis laid by Luther upon the doctrine of justification by faith by a mystical and emotional absorption in good works. By a life devoted to the rescue of neglected and godless children God's will would be done and the glory of God supremely vindicated by the establishment in each child's heart of the *unio mystica* with the Deity. Hence it followed, in the rules laid down by Francke in his *Short and Simple Instruction*, that the first essential was to place in the hands of a child the means by which, with God's grace, he could prepare his soul for salvation. To this end a rigidly ascetic method of instruction was evolved. In a school day of seven hours more than half was devoted to the religious discipline of Bible reading, catechism, prayers, public worship and pious exercises. Part of the remainder of the time was given to the godly discipline of labour.[3]

[1] Defoe, D., *The Poor Man's Plea*, pp. 10, 28.

[2] See also *Welch Piety*, 1752–3; and *Pietas Concagiensis, or the History of the Green Coat Hospital, Cork*, 1721.

[3] Francke, A. H., *A Short and Simple Instruction how poor children are to be guided to True Piety and Christian Wisdom, formerly drawn up for Christian Teachers and now by desire printed*, 1707. See also his *Pietas Halliensis, or a Public Demonstration of the Footsteps of a Divine Being yet in the World, or an Historical Narrative of the Orphan House and Other Charitable Institutions at Glaucha, near Halle in Saxony*; and his *Historische Nachricht*, 1709. For Francke's life and work see Richter, K., *A. H. Francke, Schriften über Erziehung und Unterricht*, Leipsic, 1872; *Zum Gedächtnis August Hermann Francke, zu seinem zweihundertjährigen Todestage am 8. Juni, 1927*, Hgg. von Friedrich Mahling, Carl Mirbt und August Nebe, Halle (Saale), 1927; Weber, M., *The Protestant Ethic and the Spirit of Capitalism*, trans. by T. Parsons, with a foreword by R. H. Tawney, 1930. I am indebted to Dr Lore Leibenam, of the Deutsch-Englischer Kulturaustausch, Halle, for information

With the mystical and emotional elements of pietism English puritans had little in common, but there is no great difference between the *Praxis Pietatis* of German pietist and English puritan. When the founders of the Society for Promoting Christian Knowledge, profoundly concerned by the lamentable condition of the infant poor in the Metropolis, conceived the idea of welding together the separate and occasional charity of the benevolent into an organised movement for the education of the poor, it was religious discipline on the German pattern which they commended as a cure. "Whereas", they stated in the form of subscription to the charity schools, "it is evident to common observation that the growth of Vice and Debauchery is greatly owing to the gross ignorance of the principles of the Christian Religion, especially among the poorer sort. And also whereas Christian Vertue can grow from no other root than Christian Principles, we, whose names are underwritten, being touched with zeal for the honour of God, the salvation of the souls of our poor brethren, and the Promoting of Christian Knowledge among the poor...do hereby promise to pay yearly during pleasure...towards the setting up of a school within this parish for the teaching poor children...to read and write and repeat the Church Catechism."[1] The same note was struck in the first circular letter of the Society to the clergy in England and Wales, inviting them to become corresponding members and to forward its aims.

The five persons of "Honour and Quality" who founded the Society for Promoting Christian Knowledge in 1699 were men conspicuous for their piety and public spirit. Four of the five were laymen, the fifth, who planned the constitution of the Society, and whose name is an honoured one in the annals of the Anglican Church, was a parish priest. Dr Thomas Bray's *General Plan of the Constitution of a Protestant Congregation or Society for Propagating Christian Knowledge* consisted of two parts, one a scheme for carrying the Gospel to the Plantations abroad, the other for the establishment of catechetical schools at home. Together the proposed scheme formed in his mind a Congregation *pro Propaganda*

relating to the close personal relation of leaders of the charity school movement in England, Francis Lee, Henry Hoare and Dr Slare with Francke and the pietists in Germany; see also Lee, Francis, *History of Montanism*, with preface by Dr George Hicks, 1709, stating that Lee "put Mr Hoare and Mr Nelson upon founding of Charity schools upon the same plan as that of Halle in Germany".

[1] S.P.C.K. Minutes, March 16, 1698–9.

Fide.[1] In 1701, by Royal Charter, the Society for Propagating the Gospel in Foreign Parts (the S.P.G.) was carved out of the original Society, and its activities were confined by its letters of incorporation to missionary work in the English Plantations in America. The Society for Promoting Christian Knowledge (the S.P.C.K.) retained its character as a voluntary society, and was, as such, subject to no defined limitations. It was free, if it so desired, to concentrate its efforts upon the education of the children of the poor, the establishment of parochial libraries, the provision of religious literature for adults, or upon mission work over-seas.[2]

Little is known of the personal lives of the small group of philanthropists who founded the S.P.C.K. Ralph Thoresby, in his *Diary*, has left a picture of Thomas Bray, in his old age, teaching, with prodigious pains, the children in the charity school of his parish, St Botolph's, Aldgate.[3] Colonel Colchester, his friend and colleague, had, some time before the formation of the Society, set up a charity school on his estate at Westbury-on-Severn, where the village children were set to work upon writing, the primer, the Testament, and the horn-book.[4] Mr Justice Hook, the third of the original members, comes to life in the minutes of the S.P.C.K. as a good friend of the children and a man of robust faith in education. Of Lord Guilford, son of Charles II's Lord Keeper North, Swift and Burnet present contrary portraits. The Dean condemned him as "a mighty silly fellow"; in the Bishop's opinion he "did not want sense or application to business".[5] Sir Humphrey Mackworth, M.P. for Cardiganshire, the last of this band of enthusiasts, was a leading *entrepreneur* of the day, deputy-governor of the Mine Adventurers of England, who combined his interest in education for children with company promotion of a questionable character.[6]

[1] The Original Draft of Dr Bray's scheme is in the library of Sion House.
[2] For the work of the S.P.C.K. see Allen, W. O. B. and McClure, E., *Two Hundred Years, 1698–1898, The History of the Society for Promoting Christian Knowledge*, 1898.
[3] Thoresby, R., *Diary*, vol. II, May 26, 1703. See also *Public Spirit illustrated in the Life and Designs of Dr Bray*, 1746.
[4] The Colchester Papers, May 18, 1699.
[5] For the life of John Hook, judge and serjeant-at-law, see Woolrych, H. W., *Lives of Eminent Serjeants-at-Law*, 1869.
[6] Cokayne, G. E., *The Complete Peerage*, ed. by H. A. Doubleday, D. Warrand, and Lord Howard de Walden, 1926, vol. VI, p. 212.

The interest and unremitting care of these men and their associates during the early years of the Society is profusely illustrated in its minute and letter books. Frequent meetings were called to consider the methods of raising funds and the management of the schools. Justice Hook set out to collect subscriptions, Lord Guilford was sent to arouse the interest of the Archbishop of Canterbury, emissaries from Hermann Francke of Halle, laden with advice, were welcomed and consulted, and one and all worked at high pressure answering letters and enquiries from laymen and clerics requesting information, or financial help or books, or for assistance in finding that rarest of all rare birds, the competent teacher.

The appeal of the founders, who represented the church, the aristocracy, the country gentry, the law and big business, to remedy evils "which cry aloud to Heaven" by creating charity schools for the instruction of poor children in reading the Bible and the catechism met with immediate and general support. They were joined by men as conspicuous for their piety as for their charity. The names of Archbishops Tenison and Sharp, the Bishops of Gloucester, London, Chichester, Salisbury, Bath and Wells, Worcester, Bangor, Chester, Sodor and Man, Gideon Harvey, William Whiston, Ralph Thoresby, White Kennett, William Wake, Josiah Woodward, Humphrey Wanley, Samuel Wesley, Robert Nelson, John Philipps, Edmund Gibson and John Chamberlayne appeared early in the lists of the subscribing members of the Society. They were representative of the different schools of thought within the Church, the latitudinarian, non-juring and High Church parties. Subscriptions, ranging from £1 to £10, received in the first twelve months, gave the directing committee of the Society £450 wherewith to advertise its aims and functions. Chamberlayne undertook the duties of secretary, and circular letters were sent to the clergy in London and the country, urging them to join in the good work, and to set up schools in their parishes. Scotsmen and Irishmen, fired by the success of the English experiment, asked for and received guidance and advice in organising similar movements in their countries. Sir John Philipps carried the work into Wales and schools were opened in the Isle of Man and in the Scilly Isles. Nor did the confines of the British Isles limit the Society's influence. "The Protestant Countries of Europe" asked that *Accounts of the Charity Schools* might be sent to them. As a result schools were set up on the English model in Sweden,

Denmark, Holland, Switzerland, in several parts of Germany, "and in the great towns in the Dominions of the Czar of Muscovy".[1]

Early in 1699 the Society made a tentative beginning of its work as publisher and distributor of books by printing and publishing Keith's *Narrative and Catechism*. In an age when books were scarce and dear it supplied its members with devotional literature and sent them, at cost price, Bibles, testaments, prayer books and primers for the use of the children and the teachers in the schools.

Unlike the Incorporated Societies set up in Scotland and Ireland the London S.P.C.K. did not manage and only rarely financed the schools. Local control was the basis of its scheme. Its policy was to excite the interest and support of the parish clergy and laymen in the work. It advertised and encouraged the new method of subscription, because it allowed men of moderate means to contribute to the schools, but it did not thereby exclude from its membership the managers and trustees of schools supported wholly, or in the main, by endowment. Its aim was to make religious instruction the backbone of education in all sorts and conditions of schools. It served both as an appointments bureau for teachers and as an insurance society for courageous parishes which responded to its appeal. As a central directing body it helped London and country schools to hold their own against apathy and obstruction. The value of its work may be measured by the decline of the charity school movement in England when the Society's interests were diverted from the schools to the foreign mission field and to the development of a great publishing connection.

III

LOCAL MANAGEMENT

The organisation of the charity schools financed by endowment does not call for special comment. Like other charitable endowments they were governed by the terms of the trusts which established them. As educational charities they were legally under the supervision of the Crown; in practice their funds and their administration were vested in trustees, usually members of families resident in the neighbourhood, who, subject always to observance of the trusts governing them,

[1] *Account of the Charity Schools*, 1711.

exercised independent and irresponsible control. Sometimes a body of trustees was specially created for the administration of the school; sometimes the trust was vested in a body already existing, such as the mayor and burgesses of the town; sometimes the heirs of the founders, or the proprietors of lands paying rent-charges to the schools, formed the school governors. In their hands, as a rule, rested the right of appointment of the schoolmaster and mistress and the selection of the children, normally those resident in the parish, for instruction. Financially independent, and enjoying powers of administration, the trustees of the endowed charity schools were less amenable to the guidance and patronage of the S.P.C.K. than were the managers of the subscription schools, whose method of finance and organisation was the Society's peculiar contribution to the cause of popular education. But the greater financial independence of the endowed schools did not prevent them from asking the Society's help when they wanted books and teachers, or from seeking advice when, as frequently happened through ignorance of or indifference to the law, their endowments were "very much abused".[1]

In the subscription charity schools the laborious task of raising funds to finance the schools and of providing them with managers fell upon the subscribers, and local piety was equal to the task.[2] The methods adopted varied little from place to place. Usually, as the first annual *Account of the Schools* reported, the idea of opening a school for poor children living in the parish was suggested either by the minister of the parish to some of his parishioners, or by two or three parishioners to the minister, and such others as they thought would join them. When four or five supporters were secured they advertised "the Necessity and Usefulness of the Design", and "commonly met with so good Success"[3] that they were able to set up a school in seven or eight months' time.

[1] S.P.C.K. Abs. of Correspondence, Letter from the Rev. R. Lloyd, Yarpol, Herefordshire, March 28, 1713.

[2] The local character of the schools was defined in an early letter from the S.P.C.K. to Edmund Gibson, Bishop of Lincoln, Jan. 18, 1718. The Grey Coat School, he was informed, was always reckoned as a charity school; the workhouse in Bishopsgate was not so reckoned "because it is as it were a *general* charity for all the Foundlings and destitute children of the City". The Foundling Hospital, in Gray's Inn Fields, was another general charity, and, as such, is not included in the history of the charity school movement.

[3] *Account of the Charity Schools*, 1704.

With few exceptions the schools, though in the parish, were not controlled by the vestry. They were managed by the voluntary subscribers living in the parish and were financed by local collections and subscriptions. Schools, whose control was in the hands of the bishop of the diocese, or the guardians of the poor, or the lord of the manor, are to be found,[1] but in general the local subscribers at their general meetings were the ultimate authority, and "what shall be agreed upon at such meetings by the majority of the subscribers there present shall be observed".[2] An attempt, in the second decade of the century, to treat the London charity schools as parish schools, met with sustained and successful opposition from the general committee of trustees, a body organised to preserve to the subscribers the control of the London schools.[3]

The charity school movement not only introduced new methods of organisation and finance into education, it provided also an opportunity, of which they were not slow to avail themselves, to the "middling classes" to interest themselves in work of social reform. While persons of wealth and quality continued to endow schools and act as patrons, the lists of benefactors to both endowed and subscription schools, and the innumerable small bequests recorded by the Charity Commissioners for schooling, show that the supporters of the education of the poor in the eighteenth century were drawn, in an overwhelming majority, from middle-class people, living in the neighbourhood of the schools. Their success in establishing thousands of schools for the lower orders, for whom, in his opinion, education, other than that derived from compulsory attendance at morning and evening service in Church on Sundays, was neither necessary nor desirable, called forth the envenomed and biased attack of the schools' most bitter critic, Bernard Mandeville. In his famous essay *On Charity and Charity Schools* he ascribed the "enthusiastick passion" of small tradesmen and shopkeepers for the schools to the opportunity they afforded the ambitious middle-class hypocrite of social advancement. Such inconsiderable persons counted for nothing in the vestry. The charity schools gave them an opportunity for asserting themselves. "If you should ask these worthy rulers why they take upon themselves so much trouble to

---

[1] E.g. Blewbury; Hull; Chippenham; see *Account of the Charity Schools*, 1714.
[2] *Account of the Charity Schools*, 1704.
[3] *Vide* chap. IV.

the detriment of their own affairs and loss of time, either singly or the whole body of them, they would all unanimously answer that it is the regard they have for religion and the church, and the pleasure they take in contributing to the good and eternal welfare of so many poor innocents, that in all probability would run into perdition in these wicked times of scoffers and free thinkers. They have no thought of interest; even those who deal in and provide these children with what they want, have not the least design of getting by what they sell for their use, and, though in everything else their avarice and greediness after lucre be glaringly conspicuous, in this affair they are wholly divested from selfishness and have no worldly ends." The motive "carefully conceal'd", but revealed by Mandeville in his rôle of an eighteenth-century Freud, was "the satisfaction which delights mean people in governing others". "It is chiefly this which supports the tedious slavery of schoolmasters. If there be the least satisfaction in governing the children it must be ravishing to govern the schoolmaster himself. What fine things are said and perhaps wrote to a governor when a schoolmaster is to be chosen! How the praises tickle!"[1]

The full and detailed minutes of the charity school set up in St Margaret's parish, Westminster, later known as the Grey Coat Hospital, furnish an exceptional opportunity of inspecting the foundation of one of the earliest of the London charity schools, and, at the same time, provide an excellent commentary upon Mandeville's relentless criticism. The six inhabitants of the parish, who collaborated in setting up the school, were Westminster tradesmen; one a cheesemonger, another a draper, a third a bookseller, while the remaining three were general dealers in soap, and candles, brooms and leather goods. These men contributed "freely and liberally" towards the charges of the school; they induced other substantial persons to join them, and called a meeting of subscribers to consult upon a scheme for the charity. "Several of the inhabitants of Westminster", runs the first entry in the school's minute book, "having taken into their serious consideration the great misery that the poor children of the parish do generally suffer, by reason of their Idle and Licentious Education; their Nurses, or those that provide for them, generally suffering, if not encouraging, them to wander about and begg, by which Means the Evil Customs and Habits they contract thereby become, for the most part, the Curse and Trouble

[1] Mandeville, B., *Essay on Charity and Charity Schools*, 1723, *passim*.

of all places where they live, and often, by their Wicked Actions, are brought to Shameful and Untimely Death; to prevent the like miseries for the future, in the said Parish, as much as in them lay, the persons hereafter named in particular did think it proper and convenient to erect a free school in the said Parish, where 40 of the greatest objects of charity they could find should, from time to time, be educated in sober and virtuous principles, and instructed in the Christian Religion. And for their Incouragement in their Learning they did propose that the said 40 children should be clothed, as hereafter directed, and when fit to go out Apprentices should be carefully placed out to Honest Masters, who should take care as well of their good Principles as instruct them how to get an honest livelyhood, by their labours and industry in the World."

A house was taken in the Broad Walk, and fitted up as a school at a cost of £1. 2s. 9d. A choice was made of a schoolmaster and eleven "desirable objects" were chosen as the first pupils of the school. For the master's guidance a scheme of management was drawn up which bears lasting witness to the disinterested philanthropy of the founders of the Grey Coat Hospital. "The principall designe of this Schoole" was declared to be the education of poor children in the principles of piety and virtue; the master was bidden "to study to endeavour to win the love and affection of the children, thereby to invite and encourage them, rather than by correction to force them to learne". "Reason as well as experience", these wise and generous-minded shopkeepers remarked, "having plainly shewn that too great severity does rather dull than sharpen the wits and memory." Such education was the cause why "so many children rejoice at all opportunity to neglect their Learning, which they find to them a grief and vexation when they come to years of Discretion".

The responsibility of the managers of the new school did not end with the appointment of the schoolmaster and the drafting of rules for his guidance. The trustees of St Margaret's were unsparing of their time and care. They met every week to supervise the charity they had set up. They ordered the new grey coats for the children, and were present when the tailor tried them on. They supplied the mothers with grey yarn to make stockings for the children and prevailed upon their own wives and daughters to make the caps and stitch the bands which constituted the boys' uniforms. Convinced believers in the value of inspection, they evolved schemes for testing the children's progress in learning, at first making themselves each responsible for the examination of five of the children, and later arranging on every quarter day a general examination by the whole body of governors, putting on a file specimens of the children's writing "to judge, from time to time, of their progress in learning".

Nor were these Westminster tradesmen careless of the temptations to which they were exposed as patrons and governors of the school. They did their best, in an age when there was no professional body of teachers, to find suitable men and women for the school; they dealt fairly with the children, who presented themselves for admittance, choosing them at first by an elaborate device of lot, and later by taking it in turns to nominate pupils. Finally, they protected their good name from the charge of diverting public money to their own advantage, "as if we were persons who undertook the Trust for lucre and self-interest", by a self-denying ordinance, undertaking that "No trustee of the school shall furnish or provide the same with any sort of provisions or necessaries of what-so-ever, and that this Order shall be sett up in Capital Letters in a Frame over the Trustees' Chamber door".[1]

Three primary duties of organisation rested upon the shoulders of the governors of the charity schools. In the first place successful school management involved the drawing up of a scheme of instruction for boys and girls from about the age of seven to twelve or fourteen years; supervision of their work and behaviour; provision of clothing and, occasionally, of maintenance grants; inspection of the teaching and conduct of the masters and mistresses, and never-ceasing endeavour, both by personal appeal and by the circulation of written rules and regulations, to induce the parents to co-operate in the education of their children. The rigidity and simplicity of the elementary curriculum, and of the methods followed by eighteenth-century pedagogues, involved the governors in little organisation, once the school was started, for each day's work repeated that of its predecessor. Inspection of children and teachers varied with the interest and responsibility of the managers. Minute books of London and urban schools bear witness to their constant and careful supervision. At their monthly meetings they

[1] Minute Book, No. I, 1698, St Margaret's Charity School, Westminster, *passim*. See also Day, E. S., *An Old Westminster Endowment*, 1902.

read the reports of the masters and mistresses on the behaviour of the children, "in their manners, wearing of their cloaths, and absence from school", and, like the governors of the Grey Coat school, they are to be found hearing the children read and say their catechism, examining their writing, encouraging them and their parents with gifts of money, food and clothing, reproving the children and dismissing them from the schools for misconduct.

A burden of special responsibility rested upon the shoulders of trustees and managers of schools which lodged and maintained the children. Never numerous in England, they appeared slowly and irregularly in London and the towns, when school funds permitted the experiment to be made. Disillusionment with day-school instruction was, in general, the cause of their establishment. The supporters of the early schools in the metropolis and elsewhere went out of their way to rescue the poorest and most vicious of the children and turned away those "who were not real objects of charity".[1] It was from the slums of Westminster, Rogue's Alley, Pickpocket Alley, Thieving Lane and Bandyleg Walk, purlieus of ill-repute, that the pupils of the charity school in St Margaret's parish were drawn. School managers elsewhere chose their pupils deliberately from "the worst boys in the parish", or from children of "known evil habits and customs", or from among those who were "the curse and trouble of all places where they live".[2] They drew their pupils from the most evil and beggarly homes, with the result that the discipline of school was undone directly school hours were over. Some device appeared necessary to keep the children from the contaminating influence of parents and relatives, and of ensuring more regular attendance. The transformation of the Grey Coat day school into the Grey Coat Hospital, of the Ladies' charity school in St Sepulchre's parish into a boarding school, of the girls' charity school in the parish of St George's in the East into Raine's Hospital, were explained by their supporters on these grounds.[3] Outside London similar conditions produced a similar remedy. "The only cure", wrote the vicar of Old Swinford, struggling to keep the children away from

[1] *The Schools Inquiry (Taunton) Commission*, 1868, 21 vols., vol. xv, *Report on Coulson's Hospital, Bristol.*
[2] S.P.C.K. Minutes, *passim.*
[3] See Day, E. S., *op. cit.*; *The History and Plan of the Ladies' Charity School of St Sepulchre's, London*, 1805; Hadden, R. H., *An East End Chronicle* [n.d.].

work, bad for their health and morals, at the coal pits, "is a Hospital." Liverpool, faced by the same problem, turned the Blue Coat day school into Blundell's Hospital.[1] The heavy expenses involved explain why the hospitals were not common in England, just as their lack of adequate and effective inspection and control explain their unsavoury reputation.

No general charge of cruelty and neglect was brought against the hospitals in England like that directed against the Irish charter schools by John Howard and Sir Jeremiah Fitzpatrick. Reports of ill-treatment but rarely found their way into school minute books, but there were not lacking observers who were conscious that all was not well with the hospital schools. From responsibility for the misery which the Squeers and Mrs Manns of the eighteenth century inflicted upon their unhappy victims it is impossible to absolve the managers and trustees. Ceaseless and untiring supervision was demanded. It does not appear that the hospitals received it.

After-school care, the second self-imposed duty of the school's governors, was an even more laborious burden than school management, for it involved co-operation with the parents and with the potential employers of the children's labour. By the Poor Law Act of 1601 parish officers were empowered to put out the parish children, i.e. the orphans and bastards and the children whose parents were in receipt or threatened to be in receipt of parish relief, until the boys were twenty-four years and the girls twenty-one years of age, or were freed from their apprenticeship by marriage.[2] One of the objects of the compulsory apprenticeship of pauper children was to relieve the parish of their maintenance and support by binding them to masters who, in return for apprenticeship fees, gave them board and lodging. The small fees paid by the poor-law officers for putting out the pauper children condemned them to the lowest of unskilled labour, and, as a recent study of the pauper children of the metropolis has shown, committed them all too frequently to the keeping of brutal and incompassionate employers.[3] "The master may be a tyger of cruelty," declared a writer on the maintenance of the poor in 1738, "he may beat, abuse, strip

[1] S.P.C.K. Abs. of Correspondence, Letters from Mr Halifax of Old Swinford, March 28, 1719 and B. Blundell, Liverpool, May 6, 1735.
[2] 43 Eliz. c. 2.
[3] For the condition of the pauper children in the metropolis see the admirable chapter by M. D. George, op. cit.

naked, starve or do what he will to the poor innocent lad; few people take much notice and the officers who put him out least of anybody."[1]

The after-care duties of the charity school managers were designed to save the charity children from such a fate. The instruction they received in the schools was intended as a preliminary to apprenticeship and service. Its aim was to make good and honest apprentices and servants out of the children of the poor, and, as school managers were aware that the lessons of the schoolroom would soon be forgotten if the children were employed by the type of men and women upon whom parish officers unloaded their unwanted goods, they extended their care of the children to after-school years and endeavoured to put them out to families who in Isaac Watts's words "had a due Character for Sobriety and Diligence".[2]

According to Bernard Mandeville the schools failed in their after-school care. Decent and respectable people, he alleged, were shy of employing the charity children either as apprentices or as servants. "Few men of substance will have anything to do with these children; they are afraid of a hundred inconveniences from the necessitous parents, so they are bound, at least most commonly, either to sots and neglectful masters, or else such as are very needy and don't care what become of their prentices, after they have received the money." He completed his indictment of the managers by asserting that the governors of the charity schools "don't deliberate so much what is best but what tradesmen they can get that will take the boys with such a sum".[3]

School minute books and reports again permit considerable modification of Mandeville's sweeping statement. In spite of their unfavourable environment and undesirable parents the children of the slums responded in a remarkable fashion to the new instruction. They were, reported an observer in 1728, "as much distinguished from what they

---

[1] *Enquiry into the Causes of the Increase of the Poor*, 1738, p. 12.

[2] Watts, Isaac, *op. cit.* p. 9. See also the *Circular Letter of the S.P.C.K. to its Clergy Correspondents*, 1714: "The Trustees shall see that the Masters to whom the children are apprenticed are persons of a sober and religious life and conversation, who will cultivate and improve their christian disposition. Hear them read the Bible and some other good books; make them repeat what they have learn'd at school, see they are constant in their morning and evening devotions and not only carry them to Church to be catechised there...but sometimes send or go with them to their Minister to be catechised and instructed by him in private."

[3] Mandeville, B., *op. cit.*

were before as is a tamed from a wild beast",[1] and the proof of their reformed character is established by the requests to the school for servants and apprentices, not only from "the lesser tradesmen" and artisans, but also from "respectable tradesmen" and professional men.[2] Managers who, taking their duties seriously, used their influence to find good homes and suitable work for the children were, contrary to Mandeville's opinion, not few and far between. Those whose schools were in good repute could afford to be particular. They "inquired narrowly" into the would-be master's character. When they were satisfied, it was a common custom for the children to go "on trial" to see if they and their masters approved of one another, and, well aware that there were employers who grabbed the fees and turned away the apprentices before the requisite twelve months had expired, so that "the money given with the lad is all lost and the youth perhaps quite ruined", some of the school managers wisely refused to pay more than half of the fees when the children were bound, and handed over the remainder only if at the end of the year the apprentice was still living with his master.[3]

[1] *A Memorial Concerning...an Orphanotrophy or Hospital for the Reception of Poor Cast-off Children or Foundlings, in order to the Saving of the Lives of many poor Innocents yearly, and to the rendering of all useful to the Public, instead of hurtful Members thereof; as those who survive by being brought to begging generally prove. By a Rector of one of the Parish Churches without the City Walls*, 1728 (?).

[2] "No sooner", wrote Hendley in his widely read *Defence of Charity Schools*, "is a child of any of these charity schools fit to be put out an Apprentice but there shall be two or three masters perhaps of different trades and Handicrafts immediately soliciting the Trustees to have him and will sooner take him with £4 or £5 than a youth who had no other education than what he has had in his father's homestall, with Ten or Twenty. And I have often myself heard them give the reason for it viz that they are instantly useful to them and prove the soberest, faithfullest and best of servants." See also Archbishop Secker's similar testimony in his *Collected Works*, vol. v, pp. 105–37, 3rd ed., Dublin, 1758.

[3] Minutes of the Grey Coat Hospital, Aug. 27, 1700; St Martin's in the Fields Charity School for Girls, April 4, 1705; Feb. 7, 1706. It was, reported Henry Newman, Secretary to the S.P.C.K. from 1708 to 1743, a general rule among the trustees of the London and Westminster charity schools to decline to allow boys to take service as errand-boys unless security was given by the master that after three or four years' service he would bind the lads to some trade or handicraft and "even this they declined doing except they were well satisfied with the character of the master as well as the security given". Letter, March 29, 1733. In this way it was hoped to prevent blind alley occupations.

After-school care did not cease when the children began their service or apprenticeship. Their careers were followed up. Cases of alleged ill-treatment were examined by the trustees, and causes of difference between employers and apprentices were brought before them, when both sides were heard and judgment given. To keep in touch with the children after they had left school some of the governors ordered them to attend the school's anniversary services in the parish church, and rewarded each youth and maid who came with money and gingerbread. Others held special services for their late pupils and "dined" them afterwards. "If it appears that the children have behaved well," said the kindly Dr Isaac Watts, in an address to the supporters of Dissenters' charity schools, "give them some token of your favour, ten or twenty or thirty shillings the first year or two after they are gone from school. This will greatly encourage them to pursue the practice of piety and virtue."[1]

It is not possible to arrive at even an approximate estimate of the number of children put out to service and apprenticeship from the English charity schools. Many of the schools could not afford apprentice fees, others, while recording the names of the masters to whom children were apprenticed, omit to tell how many children were sent out. The *Accounts* of the London charity schools published annually by the S.P.C.K. from 1704 recorded the number of children placed by the schools in and about London and Westminster, but careless returns to the Society rob these figures of exactitude. The list of 1733 (the first in which these details were returned) states that out of 20,000 children instructed in the metropolitan schools since the beginning of the century, 7139 boys had been put out apprentice, and 3366 to service; while of the girls 1383 had been apprenticed and 3873 put to service, making a total of 15,761 children placed by the London schools in thirty-five years. The payment of apprentice fees, ranging from 30s. to £5, was a heavy strain upon the financial resources of the schools, and explains the limitation of this side of their activities. Service, which did not, as a rule, demand payment of a premium, was the favoured method of putting to work, and was the predominating method of the girls' schools. Most commonly the girls were settled in domestic service, or were apprenticed to sempstresses or mantua-makers; many of the boys were placed with the Thames watermen and fishermen, but the jobs obtained by the children were not confined to domestic service, or to

[1] Watts, Isaac, *op. cit.* p. 9.

the notoriously hard and dangerous river labour. In school minutes and reports are recorded the names of boys and girls apprenticed to butchers, and bakers, and candlestick-makers; to weavers, shoe-makers, cheesemongers, barbers, joiners, tailors, carpenters, glovers, bricklayers, saddlers, coopers, and dyers. Clear-starchers, fan-makers, bookbinders, booksellers, wig-makers, linendrapers, and makers of musical instruments all drew apprentices and servants from the schools.

More exhausting to patience and forbearance than school management or after-care were the incessant difficulties arising from finance. The subscription schools, in the years before endowments began to accumulate, were entirely dependent upon the gifts and subscriptions of local supporters, who, because they paid the piper, insisted on their right to criticise the tune. Their contributions fluctuated with their approval or disapproval of the way in which the school was conducted and its funds administered. "Aspersions on the way the money goes", and accusations that the trustees lined their own pockets by supplying the schools with low-class goods at high-class prices, though doubtless of value in establishing standards of rectitude among managers and trustees, did not make their self-imposed duty of collecting and administering school funds the easier. "Everyone who gave us 2d.", asserted the members of the Amicable Society, in the parish of St Mary's Rotherhithe, when refusing to set up a charity school, "would think he had the right to make what reflections he thought proper."[1] Complaints that the teachers were tinged with disloyalty to the House of Hanover, or that the result of education had been to make the charity children impertinent to their betters, or that the schools had not brought about the moral reformation in the parish which had been promised, resulted in a drop in the subscriptions and in the collections taken at the church door on Sundays.

Criticisms of the manner in which the schools were run it was possible to meet; more difficult to cope with was the falling off in subscriptions when the novelty of the schools began to wane or the original supporters disappeared. Charity schools in Mandeville's opinion "were in fashion like hoop'd up petticoats, by caprice, and no more reason can be given for the one than for the other".[2] Few if any of the parish charity schools, drawing their revenues from the middle

[1] Minutes of the Amicable Society, Rotherhithe, 1739.
[2] Mandeville, B., *op. cit.*

classes of the neighbourhood, were subject to the wholesale withdrawal of support from which the Ladies' charity school at Highgate suffered, when the score of noble dames who founded it tired of their pet charity. Neither cajolery nor invective moved the unstable wills and hearts of these "choicest flowers of nature" to pay their arrears of subscriptions for the support of the "40 poor fatherless boys, decently cloathed in blue lined with yellow, and constantly fed all alike with good wholesome diet" whom they had undertaken to educate and put out to trades.[1] Enthusiasm was not always easy to maintain; death removed supporters; interest easily switched from one new concern to another and managers were left to run the schools, as best they could, on the uncertain and fluctuating income which handicaps all voluntary effort.[2]

A financial problem of a different character became prominent as the movement grew in popularity and extent. Endowments left to the schools by men and women, many of whom had subscribed in their

[1] Blake, W., *The Ladies' Charity School House Roll, Highgate* (n.d.). In the copy of this book in the British Museum the names of the following ladies are written: the Marchioness of Winchester, the Countesses of Bedford, Salisbury, Denbigh, Essex, Radner (*sic*) Northumberland, Viscountess Ranelagh, the Ladies Clinton, Falconbridge, Tweedale, Wharton, Hollis, Capell, Falkland, Pemberton, and "four beloved ladies of this mighty city", Mrs Love, Madam Pilkington, Lady Player and Lady Clayton, the wives of "great merchants of eminent quality and degree." See also Ralph Thoresby's *Diary, 1677–1724*, vol. I, p. 161, ed. J. Hunter, 1830.

[2] See *An Appeal for the Charity Schools at Deptford*: "The Charity Schools at Deptford, which are maintained by subscriptions, consist of 25 Boys and 25 Girls. But were intended to consist of 50 Boys and 50 Girls each had the Constitutions extended so far. They are all cloathed and taught to read and write and so far as is necessary for their circumstances to cast accounts. The Parishioners are upon all occasions of Charity generally very bountiful and have been so in this. But by the death of a principal subscriber just at our first setting out; by the removal of several inhabitants and by the discharge of several hands formerly employed in H.M. Shipping and Dockyards the number of our Poor is so increased and the income of many Tradesmen so diminished that though the necessities of the people call for an enlargement of these schools yet the undertakers have found it very difficult to support them in the first condition. Upon these accounts upon the example of other Poor Parishes adjoining to the Cities of London and Westminster the schools of Deptford beg the assistance of their wealthier neighbours hoping at least to find an equal regard with others because the parents of these children are employed and have their whole dependence upon the Service of H.M. and the Govt."
Presumably the appeal was successful, as the Deptford schools retained their position in the list of the London and Westminster schools.

lifetime to their upkeep, frequently went astray. A form of bequest, drawn up by the S.P.C.K. "so as to prevent any scruple about paying it", was not always used, and urgent letters to the Society show that trustees experienced much difficulty in securing legacies left to the schools. Benefactions they complained were "swallowed up without attaining the end proposed". Real property too went astray for want of proper legal precautions. To country clergy, eager to secure endowments for the schools, the Society's legal advisers sent help, explaining the intricacies of the Act 9 Geo. II, c. 36, and informing their correspondents of the course to be followed in conveyancing land to particular schools. Not once, but several times, were bills introduced into Parliament for "the more easie recoverie of small gifts and legacies". "The conceal'd or misapplied legacies", wrote Henry Newman, Secretary to the S.P.C.K., as early as 1711, "have induced me to believe that many more might be detected if the Archbishop of Canterbury would authorise some person to inspect the register of wills in Doctors' Commons. If only one will in 50 would yield any advantage it would abundantly answer the pains of our Inquisition. They are mostly gifts in Reversion that are subject to this fate."[1]

The trouble persisted throughout the charity school movement and was responsible in great measure for its limited success. The disappearance and mismanagement of endowments left for the education of the poor was attested by the *Reports of the Select Committee appointed to Inquire into the Education of the Lower Orders 1816 to 1818* and by the *Reports of the Royal Commission appointed to Inquire Concerning Charities 1819 to 1837*. Even in the schools enjoying a permanent income and a legal constitution the administration was signally defective. The trust deeds of the schools endowed the schools' governors with almost complete irresponsibility and at the same time restricted them from introducing reforms or modifying the original constitutions. Occasionally the Court of Chancery, which exercised original and inherent jurisdiction over charities anterior to and irrespective of the

---

[1] S.P.C.K. Minutes, June 21, 1711; *Circular Letter of the S.P.C.K. to its Clergy Correspondents*, 1709; Abs. of Correspondence, Letters from Rev. T. Tanner, Norwich, Oct. 21, 1709; E. Edwards, Embleton, Northumberland, March 17, 1710–11; R. Lloyd, Yarpol, March 28, 1713; E. Warren, Suffolk, April 28, 1713; E. Kelsall, Boston, Lincolnshire, Dec. 20, 1714; Dr Colbatch, Orwell, Cambridgeshire, March 30, 1742.

Elizabethan Statute of Uses, established an ambulatory tribunal under the statute as a means of enquiry into the affairs of particular schools whose property had gone astray.[1] After the middle of the century this cumbrous and not always effective method was replaced by the method of Information by the Attorney-General, but the voluntary charities had not even this modicum of protection and control. Lacking a legal constitution, their management had no continuity and their funds no permanence. The rough and ready device of inscribing on a tablet in the parish church particulars of the parish charities was the common method of protection against misappropriation. Opportunity was not lacking for dishonest trustees to help themselves and their friends to school property, or to line their own pockets by supplying their own goods at their own prices to the schools. It is however permissible to attribute the fate of a number of endowments intended for the education of the poor to the ephemeral character of many of the charity schools set up by one generation to be forgotten by the next, and to the difficulty which school managers and trustees experienced of establishing a legal right to legacies and endowments.[2] Indifference and ignorant mismanagement rather than deliberate chicanery characterised the abuse of the charities for the education of the poor.

Local information of parish charities was not seldom forthcoming in the returns made by the clergy and churchwardens to the episcopal visitation enquiries, but almost complete ignorance of the value and extent of the vast number of charities earmarked for education in

[1] 43 Eliz. c. 4.

[2] See Nicholas Carlisle on the "Lost Charities" in his *Historical Account of the Origin of the Commission appointed to Inquire Concerning Charities in England and Wales*, 1828. The Statute of Mortmain, 9 Geo. II, c. 36, laid down "that no lands or tenements or money to be laid out thereon shall be given for or charged with any charitable uses whatsoever unless by Deed indented, executed in the presence of two witnesses 12 Calendar months before the death of the donor and enrolled in the Court of Chancery within 6 months after its execution (except Stocks in the Public Funds which may be transferred within 6 months previous to the donor's death) and unless such gifts shall be made to take place immediately and be without power of revocation...and that all other gifts shall be void". The statute was enacted, says Mr Carlisle, "in the apprehension, grounded on experience, that persons on their death beds might make large and improvident dispositions even for good purpose to defeat the political ends of the Legislature. And it will be seen in the reports how largely the benevolent intentions of well disposed persons have been frustrated by its operation."

the country existed until the Act of 1786 authorised the return to Parliament by the clergy, churchwardens and overseers of all the parish charities in England and Wales.[1] Meagre as were the details presented to Parliament in 1788, it was clear that many donations had been lost and that others were in danger of being lost by neglect and maladministration. Charity estates all over the country, declared Lord Eldon in the early years of the nineteenth century, were dealt with in a manner "most grossly improvident",[2] and, as the reports of the Commissioners bear witness, flagrant cases of indifference and mis-direction were found among those relating to the education of the poor.[3] At the beginning of the nineteenth century the abuse of charities had become a matter of public concern.

IV

THE SCHOOLS OF LONDON
AND WESTMINSTER

Local interest in the charity schools spread with extraordinary celerity in the metropolis after the foundation of the S.P.C.K. "Conspicuous as ever for the Holy Zeal of Charity which everywhere appears in the Great City"—London adopted the Society and the schools with enthusiasm. Parish vied with parish in setting up schools. In May 1699 the Society's agents reported the first of the voluntary efforts in St George's, Southwark, where the minister and others had subscribed sixteen pounds per annum towards a school in the parish. A week later the parish officers of St Andrew's, Holborn, joined with subscribers in setting up a school. In June, schools in Poplar and Whitechapel and St Martin's in the Fields were opened. In July, St Giles's, Cripplegate, and Hungerford Market followed suit. In October, schools were being founded in St Paul's, Shadwell; St Leonard's, Shoreditch; St Clement Danes, and St James's, Westminster; in November, in Greenwich and

---

[1] 26 Geo. III, c. 58.

[2] Lord Eldon, c. 13, Ves. 580, quoted in Brougham, H., in *A Letter to Sir Samuel Romilly M.P. upon the Abuse of Charities*, 1818.

[3] See *Reports of the Commission to Inquire Concerning Charities for the Education of the Poor*, 1819–37, under the parishes of Stow-in-the-Wold, Naunton in the Cotswolds, Bourton in the Water (Glos.), Stoke Gabriel (Devon.)

St Anne's, Westminster. By the end of the year schools were "perfected" in St John's, Wapping; St Paul's, Shadwell; St Margaret's, Westminster; St Botolph's, Aldgate and St Botolph's, Bishopsgate.[1] Five years later, in 1704, when the Society published its first report, thirty-two of the parishes of the cities and liberties of London and Westminster had established charity schools. In twelve of these parishes two or more schools were opened; in all there was a total of fifty-four schools, and in these schools over two thousand children were taught reading, some writing and arithmetic, and all were given instruction in their duties to God and man through catechetical instruction. In 1729, a quarter of a century later, there were 132 schools and 5225 pupils.

The ease with which subscriptions were collected and donations secured is further proof of London's interest in this particular charity, an interest consistently retained throughout the century. The Society's report of 1704 shows that the fifty-four charity schools were in receipt of annual subscriptions amounting to £2164. St Andrew's, Holborn, which counted the generous and pious Robert Nelson among its subscribers, headed the list with £194 per annum; St Mary's, Whitechapel, had received gifts amounting to the large total of £1090. The poorer schools made up their financial deficiencies by ingenious devices; the parish of St Paul's, Shadwell, farmed its street lamps; two of the trustees of St Katharine's near the Tower were land-tax collectors, who gave their poundage to the school; the ladies of St Sepulchre's, Southwark, undertook to clothe and educate fifty-one poor girls; clergy who could not raise funds for a school taught children gratis; the master of Cripplegate free school offered to teach forty poor boys for nothing. Religious Societies assisted the parishes with donations and supplied teachers to the schools from their members.[2] The Society of St Ethelburga, in St Ethelburga's parish, set up a school at its own expense.[3] The societies for the reformation of manners made special collections for these "excellent nurseries of piety", magistrates handed over the fines for profaneness and debauchery to school trustees,[4] and perambu-

---

[1] S.P.C.K. Minutes, under dates.

[2] *A Memorial giving some account of the meetings of the Jacobites and Papists in and near London*, 1716.

[3] *Bicentenary Magazine of the Central Foundation Girls' School, London*, 1926.

[4] *Account of the Charity Schools*, 1706.

lations of the parish were held for the special purpose of soliciting subscriptions. When the movement got under way the city wards offered a new and larger unit than the parish for the establishment of schools, and for the union of one or more parish schools into ward schools. The little school in St Alfage parish, struggling to instruct fifty boys on subscriptions and collections whose total did not reach £20 a year, was, before 1712, merged in the ward school of Cripplegate-within-the-Walls. The Bridge and Candlewick ward schools for boys and girls replaced the parish schools of St Michael, Crooked Lane, and St Magnus the Martyr.[1] By the end of the first quarter of the eighteenth century support of the charity schools was the favourite form of practical piety in London, and it is clear that the schools were objects of pride to its citizens. On Sunday evenings, after service, supporters of the schools and parents of the children crowded to the parish churches to hear the public catechism of the children;[2] anniversary services, which commemorated the founding of a school, were regarded as red-letter events in the parish. Special sermons, advertised in the newspapers, attracted crowded congregations, and swelled the schools' funds; over £100 on these occasions was collected at the church doors. Rich and poor, masters and servants, flocked to the church to see "children well-matched, march two and two, in good order, all whole and tight in the same clothes", into pews reserved for them.[3] Famous preachers, especially those in lawn sleeves, were in great demand. A text on charity introduced the congregation to a dissertation on charity in general, and ended by an account of the particular charity in its new clothes and shining faces sitting in the front pews. The congregation was reminded that this collection of "virtue rendered visible" was manufactured by their generosity out of ignorance, poverty and debauchery, and their attention was called to the little brands saved from the burning, and transformed by the charity schools into sturdy Protestants and useful members of society.[4] Hymns, written especially

[1] *Accounts of the Charity Schools*, 1712, 1733.

[2] Kennett, White, *A True report of the Charity Schools*, 1706. See also "Account of the Times and Places of the public examination of several Charity Schools in and about London", printed as a supplement to the annual *Account*, 1712.

[3] Mandeville, B., *op. cit.*

[4] *Sermon preached by Canon Gastrell of Christchurch* at the *Annual Meeting of the Charity Schools [etc.]*, June 5, 1707.

for the occasion in praise of benefactors and sung by the children, were a special feature of the services.

Belief in the efficacy of the new catechetical instruction was enthusiastically held. In the opinion of the Prebendary of Durham in 1718 the schools were of greater consequence to religion than any other design which had been put on foot since the Reformation. His successor eight years later attributed the prosperity of the country to their existence. They had "contributed to hinder a sinful nation from filling up the measure of its iniquities". The virtue and knowledge generated by the schools, declared the Archdeacon of Cardigan, "will produce plentiful harvest in the next age".[1]

These "popular orations," as Bernard Mandeville called them, were not confined to the clergy. Richard Steele, in *The Spectator*, roundly stated that the charity schools were "the greatest instances of public spirit the age had produced", and urged that no good work was more worthy of a generous mind. "Would you do a handsome thing without return? Do it for an infant that is not sensible to the obligation. Would you do it for the public good? Do it for one who would be an honest artificer. Would you do it for the sake of Heaven? Do it for one who shall be instrumental in the worship of Him for Whose sake you gave it." A year later Addison's enthusiasm in *The Guardian* was even greater. "I have always looked upon the institution of Charity Schools, which of late has so universally prevailed throughout the whole nation, as the glory of the age we live in."[2]

In 1704 a joint procession and service for 2000 children, selected from the charity schools in London and Westminster, was held in St Andrew's Church, Holborn, and drew forth a eulogy from John Strype. "It was a wondrous surprising as well as pleasing sight", he wrote, "that happened on June 8, 1704, when all the boys and girls maintained at the schools in their habits walked two and two with their masters and mistresses, some from Westminster and some through London, with many parish ministers going before them and all meeting at St Andrew's Church where a seasonable sermon was preached by Dr Willis upon Genesis 8. 19: 'I know Him that He will command

[1] *Sermons preached at the Annual Meetings of...the Charity Schools* [*etc.*], June 5, 1718; June 2, 1726; May 3, 1750.

[2] *The Spectator*, No. 294, Feb. 6, 1712; *The Guardian*, No. 105, July 11, 1713.

His children etc.'"[1] So excellent a method of advertisement was not allowed to lapse. A group of charity school enthusiasts, with Robert Nelson at their head, formed a Society of Patrons of the Anniversary of Charity Schools to organise an annual gathering of all the London charity schoolchildren. Notices in the papers informed the public where they could see, and members of the Society where they could join, the procession, and Londoners flocked in their thousands to the services, so that no church was big enough to hold them.[2] Attempts to obtain permission to use the new and unfinished church of St Paul's was frowned upon by Sir Christopher Wren, and it was not until 1782 that the anniversary services were held in the cathedral. To accommodate the huge gatherings, estimated at 12,000 persons, wooden galleries were erected at considerable expense to hold "the little Eleemosynaries". There was no difficulty in raising the necessary funds for these occasions. The handsome collections taken at St Paul's; the contributions made by the City Companies, and a grant of £500 in 1785 from the City Council, testified that London's pride in its pious charity had in no way abated in the course of the century.[3] William Blake's picture of the children in his poem *Holy Thursday* expresses the pride and compassion aroused on these occasions:

T'was on a Holy Thursday, their innocent faces clean,
The children walking two and two, in red and blue and green,
Grey-headed beadles walk'd before, with wands as white as snow,
Till into the high dome of Paul's they like Thames' waters flow.

O what a multitude they seem'd, these flowers of London town!
Seated in companies they sit with radiance all their own.
The hum of multitudes was there, but multitudes of lambs,
Thousands of little boys and girls raising their innocent hands.

[1] Strype, J., 1720 ed. of Stow's *Survey of London*, Book V, p. 43.
[2] See S.P.C.K. Letters, Letter of Henry Newman, Secretary of the S.P.C.K., to the Countess of Hartford (*sic*), April 28, 1731, telling her of the Anniversary Meeting of the Charity Children the next day at 11 a.m. "If your Ladyship should be inclin'd to honour the audience with your company I am persuaded you will with pleasure see 3 or 400 charity children at their devotions with the same readiness as the Guards perform their exercise, and I am sure Lord Beauchamp and Lady Betty will thank your ladyship for the pleasure of accompanying you to such a sight as the Nation and perhaps all Europe cannot parallel."
[3] Guildhall MSS. London Journals, July 23, 1783–69, fol. 24.

Now like a mighty wind they raise to heaven the voice of song,
Or like harmonious thunderings the seats of Heaven among.
Beneath them sit the aged men, wise guardians of the poor;
Then cherish pity, lest you drive an angel from your door.[1]

The display of virtue rendered visible was not confined to the anniversary gatherings. On great national occasions, such as the celebrations of the Peace of Utrecht, stands were erected in the Strand where the children occupied a conspicuous position, not only that they might see the great but that the great might see them, a spectacle which gave much satisfaction to the spectators. A hundred years later, at the end of another great war, the charity children were exhibited to the distinguished peacemakers, the King of Prussia and Marshal Blücher and the Tzar Alexander, who was moved to tears "by the singing of the Old Hundredth Psalm by the children in full chorus".[2]

The London charity schools as a whole escaped the difficulties which handicapped the charity school movement elsewhere. The never-failing pride of the City in the schools, the willing compliance of leading ecclesiastics to preach the popular anniversary sermons which untied the purse-strings of the rich, the plentiful supply of "qualified" and experienced teachers, and the easy absorption of boys and girls by the London labour market, put the London schools in a class apart from the schools elsewhere. More important still, the incomes of the schools, obtained partly by subscriptions and partly by collections, though fluctuating, seldom dropped to a point too low to support them. The large well-to-do middle-class population made it easy to secure new subscribers when the old ones dropped off, and a steady flow of gifts and donations placed the London schools in the assured position of schools financed in whole or in part by endowments at the beginning of the nineteenth century. In 1799 their number, in and about London and Westminster, reached 179 and the children taught in them 7108.[3]

[1] Blake, W., *Songs of Innocence, circa* 1784.
[2] Allen, W. O. B. and McClure, E., *op. cit.* p. 149.
[3] *Account of the Charity Schools,* 1799.

V

THE COUNTRY SCHOOLS

The "Holy Zeal" which manifested itself in London did not manifest itself with equal fervour in the urban and country districts outside the Metropolis. Associated charity depended for its success on organisation as well as enthusiasm, and an age which could call upon neither the penny post nor the daily press did not find the organisation of the pious in small towns and remote villages an easy task. To it the S.P.C.K. devoted its energies, when, eight months after its formation, the rapid progress of the London schools allowed it to turn its attention elsewhere. A circular letter addressed by the Society to the clergy of the several counties of England and Wales in 1699 informed them of the success of the London experiment and urged them to use their "utmost endeavours to prevail with all pious and well behaved Christians in ye several parts of the nation to joyn their hearts and purses in advancing to perfection so excellent and glorious a work".[1]

The response was neither uniform nor general. The English country clergy in the eighteenth century have been the butt of contemporaries and of posterity. Eachard's and Hildrop's pictures of a contemptible ministry were popularised by Fielding's Supple and Thwackum, and by the licentious clergy of the eighteenth-century stage. The existence of indifferent and dissolute parish priests is too well attested to be denied. It is, however, sometimes forgotten that eighteenth-century literature produced also the Vicar of Wakefield, Dr Harrison, Dr Bartlett and Parson Adams. The correspondence of the S.P.C.K. and the little used returns to the questionnaires sent out by the diocesans and archdeacons to the parish clergy show men of earnest character and a high sense of duty at work unostentatiously in their remote and unknown country livings. While eighteenth-century literature presents two sharply contrasted types of country parson, eighteenth-century records equally refuse to establish a typical figure. But while this is so, the majority of Anglican clergy shared in common a characteristic fear of enthusiasm and a consequent "absence of zeal and of the fire of love" for which puritan excesses in the seventeenth century were in part responsible, and which in its turn was to promote the reaction of the Methodist and

[1] Quoted by Allen, W. O. B. and McClure, E., *op. cit.* p. 43.

Evangelical revivals. This attitude was well defined in the early years of the century. The clergy societies which the S.P.C.K. envisaged throughout the length and breadth of the country, creating new life and vigour, suggested to many Anglican priests an unpleasing blend of the religious societies and of the societies for the reformation of manners; the first offended them because they smelled of the Presbyterian classes, "encouraging fanaticism, contrary to 25 Henry VIII, cap. 19",[1] the second because they involved co-operation with Dissent. These two objections imposed a barrier to the ideals of the new education society behind which apathy and indifference could sit at ease. The law was invoked to show that such societies were contrary both to civil and ecclesiastical law, plurality of livings to demonstrate the impossibility of undertaking new obligations in parishes set far apart, and the poverty of the people provided religious indifference with an economic weapon. If schools were set up children could not be spared from work to attend them. Letters received from the Society's correspondents demonstrate the opposition which faced the supporters of the schools. Clerics were not wanting who regarded the Society's proposals as an infringement of parochial independence. "They would not submit to be directed by men whose names they were not to know"; others were alive to the censure implicit in the new scheme, "for if the clergy should now associate for these purposes, it would be a reflection on them, as if they had hitherto neglected their duties". Huntingdon clergy were "cold", Gloucestershire clergy "lacked warmth", Surrey clergy were "very averse". In the towns the same antagonism showed itself. Attempts to form a clergy society in Bristol were ineffectual; in Carlisle the Archdeacon objected to societies of any kind "declaring that so far as his influence could prevail he would keep all people from joining them"; in Plymouth the Society's correspondents tried in vain "to attempt societies of the Clergy".[2]

Progress was, however, assured when the higher clergy began to

[1] S.P.C.K. Abs. of Correspondence, Letter from the Rev. Leevis, Acrise, Kent, Feb. 28, 1699–1700.
[2] S.P.C.K. Abs. of Correspondence, Letters from Dr W. Bernard, Malden, Surrey, April 19, 1700; Mr Tatem, Sutton-on-the-Hill, Derbyshire, June 12, 1700; Mr Mapletoft, Huntingdon, Oct. 12, 1700; Mr Defray, Old Romney, Kent, Dec. 6, 1700; Mr Bedford, Bristol, April 10, 1700; Mr Gilpin, Scaleby, Cumberland, April 23, 1700; Mr John Gilbert, Plymouth, April 23, 1700.

bless the scheme and encouraged clergy and laity to support it. The pious and learned Symon Patrick, Bishop of Ely, encouraged the efforts of town and gown in Cambridge. The warm approval of Gilbert Burnet, Bishop of Salisbury, promoted the setting up of many schools in Wiltshire and Berkshire. In the Isle of Man Bishop Wilson, with the assistance of Lady Elizabeth Hastings, opened thirteen schools, and filled them with pupils, by imposing a fine of one shilling upon parents who neglected to send their children.[1] Most outstanding of the efforts of these years were those of the two early eighteenth-century Bishops of Lincoln. In Epworth town, in the Isle of Axholm, its parson Samuel Wesley, "labouring ten years to carry on the business of reformation" among his indifferent and profligate parishioners, had, as early as 1700, acquainted his diocesan with the method of the new Society, and had secured his approval and permission to form a clergy society and also a society of laymen "to get a charity school erected among us as a mighty advantage, for the people are so extream ignorant that not one in twenty can say the Lord's Prayer right, nor one in thirty the Beliefs". With the aid of such schools he envisaged not only the present generation but two generations "secured for piety and virtue".[2] Wesley's reforming work in his own parish was developed on a larger scale by his able and distinguished diocesans William Wake and Edmund Gibson. In 1706 Wake held his primary visitation, addressing, in preparation for it, a letter of advertisement to the clergy of the diocese. It was short and to the point. The answers to the questions, "How often and at what time do you catechise in your Church?" "Is there any Public or charity school endowed or otherwise maintained in your parish?" asked by him, shed considerable light upon the provisions for religious and secular education in the great diocese. They showed that catechising, commanded as a duty on Sunday and Holy days throughout the year, had been relegated to Lent; that in many cases the poor did not send their children to be catechised, and that there were parishes which had no school of any kind. The second and third visitations in 1709 and 1712 showed a marked increase in the number of schools and

[1] See Crutwell, C., *Life of Bishop Thomas Wilson*, 2 vols. 1781; *21st Report of the National Society*, 1832.

[2] S.P.C.K. Abs. of Correspondence, Letters from Mr Samuel Wesley, Epworth, June 16, 1701. See also S.P.C.K. Papers, An Account of the Religious Society begun in Epworth in the Isle of Axholm, Feb. 1, 1701–2.

in the number of children attending them.[1] In 1714 the S.P.C.K. called the attention of its members to the example set by the Lincoln diocese, which had established over 200 charity schools. When Wake was translated to Canterbury, in January 1715–16, Gibson carried on his work in the diocese of Lincoln, where his vigour in setting up charity schools gave a foretaste of his determination years later, as Metropolitan, to control them. "Spilsby, Brickat, Algarkirk, Friestone, Donnington, Fishtoft, Frampton, Leak, Quadring, Swineshead, Skirbeck, Wigtoft, and Wyberton have no schools", he wrote impatiently to one of his clergy, who had asked what philanthropic parishioners could do to further the good work. He bade him "to take five or more parishes and set up schools in them", and lest parson and patrons should imagine that their responsibility came to an end when the schools were set up, he commanded them to overlook the ordering of the charity, and "to see that it is applied to the end for which it was given".[2] Before the end of his episcopate in 1723 the schools in the Lincoln diocese numbered 268.

The attitude of the diocesans affected the progress of the movement, but in the country, as in London, the onus of making the new scheme a success fell upon the parishes, and, to an extent unparalleled in the towns, the country schools were dependent upon the interest and enthusiasm of the parish clergy. They initiated the movement, and managed and inspected the schools which were set up. Letters from north, south, east and west poured into the Society's offices in London, telling of the progress made, or the disappointments suffered by the clergy promoters. To the demand for advice and requests for sympathy, unfailing supplies were given by the standing committee of the S.P.C.K., which read the voluminous correspondence at its meetings, and instructed its secretary to reply. It is true that the letters were received from but a small proportion of the clergy in England and Wales, but there is more than enough evidence to dissipate the belief that the country clergy in the first half of the eighteenth century were as a whole lax and indifferent to their duties. Among those who threw themselves with enthusiasm into the work of catechetical instruction were men of outstanding character and ability. Letters from Samuel Wesley at

[1] See *Speculum Diœceseos Lincolniensis sub Episcopis Gul. Wake et Edm. Gibson*, Part I, 1705–23. The Lincoln Record Society, 1913.

[2] S.P.C.K. Abs. of Correspondence, Letter from Edmund Gibson, Feb. 10, 1714–15.

Epworth, Thomas Tanner at Thorpe Bishop's, John Strype at Low Layton, Erasmus Saunders at Blockley, and Laurence Echard at Louth, reveal a strong sense of responsibility to the poor, and an eagerness to participate in a scheme for their improvement, which was shared by innumerable parish priests whose names were, and are, unknown to contemporaries and to posterity. Letters, nominating the country clergy for membership of the Society, present pictures of the eighteenth-century parson very different from those usually portrayed.

The poverty of the majority of the clergy and the common eighteenth-century policy of using plurality of livings as the only cure did not make clergy societies easy to initiate or charity schools easy to set up,[1] yet many of the clergy, whose parishes were too poor to finance a charity school, opened them at their own expense; others paid for the schooling of a specified number of parish children at the village school, or supplied them with books: those who could not afford to pay a teacher, mindful of the 78th canon of 1604, took over the duties of schoolmaster,[2] or prevailed upon the parish clerk to teach the children of the poor gratis. In villages and market towns where there was not "a competent number of children for a school", or where parents could not spare the children in the day-time from work, they made arrange-

[1] Out of a total number of 10,000 benefices in the early years of the eighteenth century 4000 benefices, with revenues not exceeding £50 a year, were discharged from the payment of fifteenths and tenths. See Ecton, J., *Liber Valorum et Decimarum*, 1711, and *A State of the Proceedings of the Corporation of the Governors of Queen Anne for the Augmentation of the Maintenance of the Poor Clergy*, 1721, which show that the revenues of 5597 benefices were less than £50 p.a. 2122 of these were in receipt of less than £30 p.a.; 1200 of less than £20 p.a. A hundred years later the *Diocesan Returns Respecting Non-Residence* in 1810 reported that the revenues of 3397 livings were under £150 a year. Non-residence, due in part to lack of parsonage houses, or suitable lodging, was common. The salaries of the unbeneficed clergy were on an even lower level. The cheapest curates, wrote Archbishop Tenison to Queen Anne, were sometimes allowed but £5-£6 for the service of the Church. For a recent authoritative account of the English clergy in the eighteenth century see Dr Norman Sykes, *Church and State in England in the Eighteenth Century*, 1935.

[2] "In what parish or chapel soever there is a curate which is master of arts, or batchelor of arts, or is otherwise well able to teach youth, and will willingly do so, for the better increase of his living and training up of children in principles of true religion, we will and ordain that a license to teach the youth of the parish where he serveth be granted to none by the ordinary of that place but only to the said curate." Canon 78, 1604. From Cardwell, E., *Synodalia*, vol. I, 1842.

ments with "proper persons" to teach the children at odd times, remunerating them by payments by results, 2s. 6d. for each child who could name the letters of the alphabet, 5s. when he could read and say the church catechism, 15s. when he could write and cast accounts. They preached sermons on behalf of the schools, or gave their Easter dues, or permitted the offertory to be applied for school purposes, and, when the people were so poor that they could not send the children to school, they raised funds for their clothing, and even paid the parents a few pence a week as a maintenance grant if they would allow the children to attend school.[1] To some of the clergy the idea of instructing the children in the catechism came as a surprising innovation. "I ask the children questions", wrote the vicar of Ugborough in Devon. "This is a novelty, for very few clergymen in these parts do more than make the children barely repeat the words of the catechism. . . .I am heartily sorry I did not follow the method sooner." From Stratford in Suffolk came the request for books. "I have encouraged reading by a new method, that of giving books to the masters of each of my charity schools to sell to the parents who have a child in the school." From Box in Wiltshire, where the vicar, an enthusiastic musician, had fired children and adults with a love of music, came letters telling the Society that the children "whose singing far surpasses expectation" could now master thirty psalms and hymns.[2]

The primary problem of finance was met at first, in the country as in London, by the subscription method. All sorts and conditions of people, gentle and simple, from the first lady in the land at Windsor to the pit-boys in the Northumberland collieries, made contributions to the upkeep of the schools. But the sparse and poor country population, the absence of the trading and manufacturing middle class, whose contributions were the backbone of the London schools, and the open hostility of the big and important farming middle class to the education of the poor, flung many of the country schools upon the generosity of the local nobility and gentry, some of whom undertook during their lifetime to educate and clothe some or all the poor children of the village, or made arrangements to endow the schools after their death. Many of the schools, returned in the early reports of the S.P.C.K., as

[1] *Accounts of the Charity Schools, passim.*
[2] S.P.C.K. Abs. of Correspondence, Letters from Mr Cranch, Oct. 15, 1751; Mr White, July 30, 1747; Mr Millard, May 30, 1718.

for example those at Badminton, Chipping Camden, Chippenham, Poole, Cranbourne, Woburn, owed their inauguration to the beneficence of "Persons of Honour and Quality". They put up school-houses and endowed them for the education of all, or for a specified number of the children of the parish, or they left part of the expenses of running the school to be met by the contributions of the minister and the inhabitants. But the numbers of the charitable were too few to ensure the success of the movement in the English country-side. Associated philanthropy, on the lines laid down by London, presented problems of organisation and finance which were difficult if not impossible to meet. "Only one person beside myself", wrote the vicar of Monmouth despairingly, "appeared at the annual meeting." The death or disapprobation of even one or two subscribers was sufficient to bring the experiment to a close. It is clear from the constant references of the clergy correspondents to "the decline of the schools" that the "inconstancy of subscribers" was a prime cause of failure. Enthusiasm was not easy to evoke, and the unwillingness of the inhabitants "to part with so much money as they at first in a general heat subscribed", made sustained effort impossible. Any excuse was good enough to withdraw subscriptions. "The inferior sort" refused their support because the schools did not, as they expected, "ease them of the Poor's levye"; "the superior sort" because the schools unfitted the children for their function as labourers and servants.

The poverty and apathy of the parents provided a difficulty which was again more acute than in London, where the advantages which accrued to the children from instruction in the three R's gave them a market value, albeit a low one. The farmers, the chief employers of country labour, on the contrary, denounced the folly of instructing country lads and lasses in the "theoretic parts" of reading and writing, and parents, who could in good times send the children out to find work, and in bad times to beg, placed between the Scylla of priestly displeasure and the Charybdis of the farmers' resentment, preferred to keep their children away from school. Finally, when difficulties of finance and parental indifference were overcome and the children were collected for instruction, it proved impossible to attract as teachers to the village schools the type of men and women whose methods were in no small degree responsible for the sustained success of the London schools. "The country clergy", wrote the vicar of Hullavington, Wiltshire, "cannot bring the schools to the perfection they desire them."[1] These were persistent difficulties which did not grow easier as the century grew older.

VI

THE URBAN SCHOOLS

In the cities and large towns the movement fared better than in the country-side. In them, gallant efforts were made to emulate London's example. The numbers of ignorant and neglected children in the provincial towns forced themselves upon public notice, and laymen and ecclesiastics responded to the call of the Society to set up schools in their behalf. Bristol counted at the end of the first decade of the century six schools to its credit, two of which, a hospital and a day school, were endowed by Edward Colston, "eminent for his great charity".[2] Newcastle-on-Tyne in 1712 furnished a remarkable record. £20 a year was settled for ever by a gentleman for the education and elevating of forty-four poor children of St John's parish. The master, beside his salary, had a house "settled for the use of the school for ever" by the corporation. Forty shillings per annum were set aside for books. A legacy of £100 was left to the school; the subscriptions amounted in 1712 to £37. 5s. 2d. and the collections taken in church to £18. 2s. 7d. In the parishes of St Nicholas and St John were two more schools, one for forty boys the other for twenty girls, "for whose maintenance another Gentleman has settled £60 per annum for ever". In the parish of St Andrew the instruction of thirty boys was paid for by money left to pious uses. Eighty-seven girls and three boys were taught to spin at the expense of the Corporation and a considerable number at the charge of private persons. In the parish of All Hallows seventy-two children were taught and clothed. Every subscriber to this charity might clothe

[1] S.P.C.K. Abs. of Correspondence, Letter from Mr Pye, Monmouth, May 11, 1717; Letter from the Rev. Amb. Pimlowe, Rector of Great Dunham near Swaffham, Norfolk, April 29, 1740; Letter from Mr Wright, Oakham, Rutland, March 27, 1714; Letter from Mr Fox, Potterne, Wiltshire, Aug. 9, 1712; Letter from Mr Jackson, Hullavington, Wiltshire, Jan. 23, 1717–18.

[2] See Garrard, T., *Edward Colston the Philanthropist, His Life and Times*, 1852. Colston's bequests to charity schools included, in addition to the boys' hospital and the charity school in Temple Street, gifts and donations to the schools in the parishes of St Philip, St Thomas, St Michael, St Augustine and Redcliffe, Bristol, the charity school at Mortlake and to eighteen charity schools in Lancashire.

a boy or girl as he pleased. Finally, a private gentleman paid for the teaching of four children "so as to make up the number of 300 children in all these schools".[1]

In the industrial towns and in the mining districts it was less easy to get the children to school, since their labour was, except in times of slump, in demand for carding, spinning and spooling or for work as pit-boys, underground. "Our misfortune", wrote the vicar of Bradford, Wiltshire, in 1717 to the Society, "is that there is too much business here, so that some can spare but little time for learning." A scheme was evolved by the vicar, in co-operation with the children's employers, who promised to pay a schoolmaster a crown a year for each child, if he would undertake to teach them for two hours a day, during the breakfast and dinner breaks at 9 and 3 o'clock. At Whickham, in the North Durham coal-field, even this miserable compromise proved unworkable. The heavy labour, reported the rector to the Society in 1721, usually brought men to their graves in the middle of their age and their widows depended on the full-time work of the children, who worked from the age of six in the pits underground. "If attendance at school be rigorously demanded", he lamented, "the poor families would starve. All that can be done is to prevail with those that live near the school to come part of the day when they have left their work."[2]

The two University towns applied themselves with vigour to the setting up of schools. At Cambridge the professor of mathematics, William Whiston, as early as 1702, stirred the University and the Town so effectively that provision was made for the instruction of 300 boys and girls in "the knowledge and practice of the Christian Religion and other things suitable to their condition", forty-two of whom were clothed by the master of St John's College.[3] Oxford, under the equally effective leadership of John Watts of St John's College, subscribed generously to the new schools, one of which was managed by the vice-chancellor and proctors and several heads of houses, and two others by the mayor and aldermen and a committee of elected subscribers. Here, as in London, elaborately organised anniversary services on St Luke's day were held which advertised the schools to town and

---

[1] *Accounts of the Charity Schools*, 1712 and 1714.

[2] S.P.C.K. Abs. of Correspondence, Letter from Mr Rogers, vicar of Bradford, Wiltshire, July 8, 1717, and Mr Tomlinson, vicar of Whickham, Feb. 20, 1721.

[3] *A short Account of the Rise, Progress and Present State of the Charity Schools in Cambridge*, 1763. See also Whiston, W., *Memoirs written by himself*, 1753, *passim*.

gown. The trustees and the children met at Carfax Church, where the children "performed an exercise" which consisted of the repetition of the catechism, the account of St Luke's festival from Mr Nelson, a speech by the senior boy, a hymn, and an account of the schools. The professor of Arabic "performed the examining part", the chaplain of Christ Church preached the sermon, and two dons in their formalities stood at the church door with plates for the collection. The commemoration, which aroused keen interest in the University, ended with a procession of children and trustees to the Angel Inn, where they dined in company.

At Bath and Tunbridge Wells the two well-run schools attracted widespread interest. They drew their support, not from the middle classes, as at Bristol and Newcastle, nor from the professional classes as at Cambridge and Oxford, but from the aristocracy who thronged to the waters in the season. The school at the Wells, reported the *Account* of 1712, was maintained by the contributions of the nobility and gentry. The "performances" of the children in the charity schools at Bath became a recognised entertainment for the fashionable world, and added a new attraction to the famous spa. To create a Roman holiday for Lady Lyttleton and Lady Bulkeley, the mistress of the girls' school made the children "perform to admiration". Even the babies who could not read were able "to answer their part out of the catechism book broke into short questions". The Duke of St Albans, unwilling to miss a new entertainment, prevailed upon the schoolmaster to arrange a public examination of his boys, which His Grace and his friends very much applauded. The Duchess, being indisposed, and unable to be present, desired that there might be yet another entertainment arranged on purpose for her. This time even greater success was scored by a combined examination of the boys and girls. Her Grace, with three or four ladies and as many gentlemen in attendance, were so pleased with the performance that they stayed above three hours, and when they went away they gave five guineas to the children, and half a guinea each to the master and mistress.[1]

Before the end of the first quarter of the century charity schools had been set up in every English county. In the first *Account of the Schools*

[1] S.P.C.K. Abs. of Correspondence, Letters from R. Watts, St John's College, Oxford. April 16, Oct. 19, 1709. See also *An Account of the Charity Schools in Oxford*, 1715; S.P.C.K. Abs. of Correspondence, Letters from J. Leeson, Bath, March 24, 1712; Jan. 22 and March 10, 1712–13.

published in 1704 fifty schools and "about five thousand" pupils were returned by the Society. Twenty-five years later the number of schools had swollen to 1419 and the number of children to 22,303. Of these 5225 were pupils of the 132 schools in London and Westminster, the bulk of the remainder were pupils in the urban schools. The village schools, in comparison, were small in number and in size, but the cities and chief towns and many of the market towns had, in the same quarter of a century, set up schools for the education of the poor. Blue coat schools, grey coat schools, green coat schools, red, green and blue maids' schools were a characteristic feature of urban society. In their distinctive dress, wearing "badges of their benefactors' bounty", they were a perpetual reminder to the townsfolk of their benevolence. As in London, so in the provinces, some of the schools became the recipients of considerable benefactions, which, in the course of the century, changed their legal and financial status from that of voluntary to that of endowed schools. They weathered the storms of opposition and the cold winds of neglect, and handed on to a later age endowments which have been used to provide secondary education for the children of the poor.

Charity school badge. Designed for the boys of the Grey Coat Hospital, Westminster, attending Neale's Mathematical School in Hatton Garden.

CHAPTER III

ENGLAND

CHARITY AND DISCIPLINE

"Children are made tractable and submissive by being early accustomed
to Awe and Punishment and Dutiful Subjection. From such timely
Discipline the Publick may expect Honest and Industrious Servants."

An Account of the Charity Schools lately erected, 1708.

I

"THE LITERARY CURRICULUM"

Of the two possible methods for disciplining the children of the poor
in the eighteenth century that of religious instruction was adopted by
the endowed and subscription schools associated with the Society for
Promoting Christian Knowledge when it began its work of reform.
Godly discipline supplied both the principles and the methods of
instruction. School text-books, directions drawn up for the teachers,
the prayers and hymns written for the children, and the sermons
preached on their behalf, make clear that the conception of a liberal
education found little place in the minds of the men and women who
were responsible for the charity school movement. They envisaged, in
accordance with the social philosophy of the age, a stratified society,
based upon a rigid class system. This did not mean that the occasional
"bright lad of parts" lacked encouragement to proceed to the grammar
school or university. Social and religious discipline bulk so large in the
ideals and methods of the charity schools that the occasional attempts
of enlightened supporters to provide an educational ladder for the
children is forgotten. The efforts of the enlightened Mr Justice Hook,
one of the five founders of the S.P.C.K., in 1700, and of William Stubbs,
Archdeacon of St Albans, in 1709, to send the brightest of the London
children to a grammar school and from there to the university or to
some place of technical instruction, failed not because of the Society's
lack of interest but from lack of funds.[1] Resolutions of the S.P.C.K.

[1] S.P.C.K. Wanley MSS. vol. I, Scheme of Serjeant Hook for a *General School*;
S.P.C.K. Minutes, Oct. 27, 1709.

and of benefactors to and managers of the schools in England, Scotland, Ireland and Wales, directing that special care should be given to and higher education provided for "lads of bright genius and constant application", who "excelled in the pregnancy of their parts", illustrate the efforts made to provide opportunities of more advanced instruction for the children of the poor. Knowledge, said Dr Joseph Butler, Bishop of Bristol, in a sermon preached before the Society on behalf of the charity children, had increased since the common use of the art of printing and literature had become general. "If this be a blessing we ought to let the poor in their degree share it with us."[1] But these voices crying in the wilderness did not affect the common opinion that if the labouring poor were to be educated at all their own happiness and the good of the nation required a particular type of education designed for a particular end. The children were to be rescued from idleness and vagrancy, washed and combed, and instructed in their duties by the catechism, that they might become good men and women and useful servants. The schools did not exist to develop their intellectual powers, nor to steer them towards equality of opportunity. Such conceptions were outside their range. Good to the souls and bodies of the children of the labouring poor could best be achieved by transforming them into pious and respectful members of the community, rendering unto Caesar the things which were Caesar's and to God the things which were God's. "Principles, not opinions, are what I labour to give them",[2] said Hannah More at the end of the century, and, during the hundred years which preceded her labours in the Mendips Anglican and Nonconformist divines, with wearisome reiteration, appealed to the public to provide the children of the poor with an education proper to their rank in life, one which would, in Isaac Watts's words, "teach the duties of humility and submission to superiors", and of "diligence and industry in their business".[3] "Such little portions of Holy Scripture as recommend industry, gratitude, submission and the like vertues" were recommended as their daily fare.[4] "There must", de-

---

[1] *Sermon preached by the Bishop of Bristol at the Anniversary Meeting of the Charity schools in and about London and Westminster*, May 9, 1745.

[2] *The Journal of Martha More*, ed. A. Roberts, 1857, p. 9, Letter of Hannah More to Mr Bowdler.   [3] Watts, Isaac, *op. cit.* p. vi.

[4] *Sermon preached for the Benefit of the Charity School in Gravel Lane, Southwark, by the Rev. S. Chandler*, Jan. 17, 1727-8.

clared the Bishop of Norwich in a charity school sermon, "be drudges of labour (hewers of wood and drawers of water the Scriptures call them) as well as Counsellors to direct, and Rulers to preside.... To which of these classes we belong, especially the more inferior ones, our birth determines.... These poor children are born to be daily labourers, for the most part to earn their bread by the sweat of their brows. It is evident then that if such children are, by charity, brought up in a manner that is only proper to qualify them for a rank to which they ought not to aspire, such a child would be injurious to the Community."[1]

The sober school uniform worn by the boys and girls in most of the urban schools was designed to drive home the lessons of poverty, humility and submission. "The clothes which are bestowed upon them once in a year or two", said Dr Isaac Watts, "are of the coarsest kind, and of the plainest form, and thus they are sufficiently distinguished from children of the better rank, and they ought to be so distinguished." "There is no ground for charity children to grow vain and proud of their rayment when it is but a sort of livery."[2] "No gaiety of colour," said the Bishop of Oxford, supporting Dr Watts, "no trifling orna- ments, nor any distinction between them and other children which they can possibly be tempted to take pleasure in. It is good that they should bear the yoke in their youth."[3] Most of the children, the preacher of the anniversary sermon informed his hearers in 1706, were "modestly but neatly apparelled or at least wear some becoming badge of their benefactors' bounty".[4]

Social discipline was supported by the school prayers and hymns. "Make me dutiful and obedient to my benefactors, and charitable to my enemies. Make me temperate and chaste, meek and patient, true in all my dealings and content and industrious in my station", was the opening prayer of the girls' charity school in Sheffield.[5] Hymns ex-

[1] *Sermon preached by the Bishop of Norwich at the Anniversary Meeting of the Charity Schools in and about London and Westminster*, May 1, 1755.

[2] Watts, Isaac, *op. cit.*, p. 43.

[3] *Sermon preached by the Bishop of Oxford at the Anniversary Meeting of the Charity Schools in and about London and Westminster*, 1743.

[4] *Sermon preached by the Dean of Ely at the Anniversary Meeting of the Charity Schools in and about London and Westminster*, 1708.

[5] *The Poor Girls' Primer*: for use in the Sheffield Girls' Charity School, 1789. Quoted by Birchenough, C., *History of Elementary Education in England and Wales*, 1920, p. 190.

pressing gratitude to their patrons formed part of the anniversary services. They were learnt in the schoolroom and sung by the children in church.

> Obscured by mean and humble birth
> In ignorance we lay.
> Till Christian Bounty called us forth
> And led us unto day.
>
> Oh, look for ever kindly down
> On those that help the poor
> Oh, let success their labours crown
> And Plenty keep their store.[1]

To the course of study prescribed for the children in the charity schools eighteenth-century educationalists gave the grandiloquent title of "The Literary Curriculum". It fell into three main sections. First and foremost, occupying the greater part of a six-hour school-day, and demanding the chief efforts of the teachers, was religious instruction. "To the End that the chief Design of this School, which is for the Education of Poor Children in the Knowledge and Practice of the Christian Religion, as Professed and Taught in the Church of England, may be the better promoted, the Master shall make it his chief Business to instruct the Children in the *Principles* thereof, as they are laid down in the Church Catechism, which he shall first teach them to *pronounce* distinctly, and plainly, and then, in order to practise shall explain it to the meanest Capacity, by some good Exposition approved by the Minister."[2] These instructions, drawn up by the London schools for their teachers, were followed throughout the country. For more explicit directions the managers and teachers were referred by the S.P.C.K. to *The Christian Schoolmaster*, a hand-book written at its request by the Rev. Dr James Talbot, vicar of Spofforth, which formed the teacher's manual of instruction in endowed and subscription charity schools throughout the eighteenth century.[3] The Doctor, to whom Locke's *Thoughts Concerning Education* was clearly not unknown, informed his readers that the minds of the children were like blank

---

[1] *Hymn Sheet*, printed for the Anniversary Service of the Charity School in St Mary's Parish Church, Rotherhithe, 1792.

[2] *Account of the Charity Schools*, 1704.

[3] Talbot, Dr James, *The Christian Schoolmaster*, 1707; see also the *Report of the National School Society*, 1837.

paper or smooth wax, on which it was their duty to imprint "the fundamental duties of our Holy Religion", without a moment's delay. No time should be lost by the master to instil these principles into the youngest of his scholars. "It will be advisable that those who cannot read should immediately, upon their first admission to the school, be taught to say the Creed and the Lord's Prayer, with the explanatory answer belonging to each, by frequent repetition from the mouth of the master." In the same way the younger scholars were to learn a short prayer to be said every morning and evening, and a grace to be said before and after meat. This much, in Doctor Talbot's opinion, was sufficient for children of tender age and understanding. When the children could read the prayers were to be "enlarged, in proportion to their capacity", and they were set to learn the whole of the catechism by heart in order that they should be able to give an audible and ready account of it in church.

When religious principles were thus inculcated the teacher was bidden by *The Christian Schoolmaster* to show the moral application of every article in the Creed, and of every commandment in the Decalogue. All proper methods were to be taken to discourage and correct the beginnings of vice, and particularly of cursing and swearing, taking God's name in vain, and the profanation of the Lord's day. Idleness, of all vices the most odious and contemptible, was to be nipped in the bud by severe punishments, for industry, next to the immediate service of God, was the principal end of all education. The teacher's exhortations were reinforced by rules of conduct learnt by heart from text-books written especially for the children. At the end of the century Mrs Trimmer's famous *Teacher's Assistant* with its emphasis on direct moral instruction illustrates its importance in the charity school curriculum.[1]

---

[1] See *The Poor Girl's Primer*, used in the Sheffield Girls' Charity School, 1789.

Lesson V

Learn to spin Wool and Linen.
Learn to sew Shifts and Shirts and Caps.
Learn to knit Hose.
Learn to bake and brew and wash.
Learn to clean Rooms and Pots and Pans.

Lesson VI

Do no wrong.
It is a sin to steal a Pin.

The duties "especially requisite" for children bred in the charity schools followed. Among them that of subjection held first place; gratitude, a duty of utmost importance, could best be paid by morning and evening prayer for the reward of benefactors in this world and the next. Meekness, which occupied the third place in the table of duties, was incumbent on those who were poor and low. "Children fed by charity ought in a more special manner to be clothed with humility."

The Society's regulations for the instruction of children in the three R's lacked the definition which marked its scheme of religious and moral instruction. Teachers were referred by it to *The Christian Schoolmaster* for the methods used with success in the London schools. Reading

> Swear not at all, nor make a Bawl.
> Use no bad Words.
> Live in Peace with all as much as you can.

Quoted by Birchenough, C., *op. cit.* pp. 190–1. See also Mrs Trimmer, *The Teacher's Assistant*, vol. I, Lecture VIII, on "Moral Duties":

Instructor. There is one kind of dishonesty which is often practised without thought by workmen, and that is wasting the time for which they are paid and the materials belonging to the Trade or Manufacture they work at. Of the same nature with this is the crime of many household servants who take every opportunity of being idle and who make no scruple of wasting provisions or giving them away without leave; nay too often they go farther and pilfer tea and sugar, and other things which they suppose will not be missed, but they should remember that nothing is hid from the eye of God and that the Day of Judgment will come when they will be called to account for all their bad actions.

Questions. Is it honest for workmen to waste and destroy the materials and implements which they make use of?
A. No.
Q. Who do these things belong to?
A. Their master.
Q. Whose eyes see you when your master is not by?
A. God's.
Q. Who do victuals and drink properly belong to in a family?
A. The Master or Mistress.
Q. Is not robbing them of these things the same as taking their money?
A. Yes.
Q. Who sees people when they are pilfering tea and sugar and such things?
A. God.
Q. Does God approve of such actions?
A. No.
Q. What will God do to thieves of all kinds?
A. Punish them.

lessons began with the letters of the alphabet, and went on, by the alphabetic-spelling method, to "the true spelling of words and the use of stops". The reading-book for these infant scholars, whose ages ranged upwards of six years, was the Anglican catechism. Such portions as had not already been learnt by heart were chosen, so that "by frequent repetition of words, while they are thus practising to read them, they may become familiar both to their eye and memory". From the catechism the children were transferred to the Book of Common Prayer, in which they learnt to read the daily offices of the Liturgy, the Common Prayer for Morning and Evening, the Collects, and the Athanasian and Nicene Creeds. These were followed by the Psalms of David in the Prayer Book version. Select psalms, such as the first, eighth, fifteenth and twenty-third, were learnt by heart. When this was accomplished the children passed on to the New Testament, beginning with the sermon on the mount in St Matthew's Gospel, and the miracles and parables. "The remarkable stories in the Historical Books of the New Testament" were reserved for Sundays or Holy days. The Old Testament was regarded as the crown of biblical instruction. It was not approached until the earlier stages of reading had been mastered. Parts of the Prophets and Ecclesiastes were learnt by heart, and finally "some plain useful treatise such as '*The Whole Duty of Man*'", with its "powerful arguments and easy familiar style", was presented to the charity children when the school years came to an end.[1]

Week-day instruction in the Bible and catechism did not complete the moral and religious training provided for the children. On Sundays

---

[1] *The Whole Duty of Man.* This famous book was first published in 1658. It was entitled *The Practice of Christian Graces or the Whole Duty of Man, laid down in a plain way for the use of the meanest reader; divided into XVII Chapters, one thereof being read every Lord's Day, the whole may be read over thrice in the year. Necessary for all Families.* It sprang immediately into great popularity, and was the most widely read of devotional works until the second half of the eighteenth century. Over twenty English editions were issued within a hundred years of its first publication and translations of it appeared in Welsh, French, German and other languages. It was a text-book for schoolchildren on the one hand, and for candidates for ordination on the other. Its extraordinary popularity was due to its straightforward style, and simple directions for the practice of Christian duties. Its authorship is still a matter of dispute. See Introduction to a recent edition in the *Ancient and Modern Library of Theological Literature* [n.d.].

and Holy days the teachers accompanied them to church, and sat with them in the pews reserved for them, and schools which possessed a competent schoolmaster and enthusiastic managers arranged for quarterly public examinations of the children in their schoolrooms on Sunday evenings, when patrons and subscribers crowded to hear the children perform and took part in their examination. "You may see them on a Sunday evening at their quarterly exercises of Letters and Religion in a most edifying manner," reported Dr White Kennett, "some of them are spelling the hardest words, with more exactness than many adult persons can do, who yet think themselves masters of the English tongue. Some are reading with such an emphasis and clear pronunciation as may instruct, if not shame, those Men and Women who come to hear them. Others are making speeches, holding Dialogues, or by turns rehearsing some chosen part of Scripture, or likewise reciting some particular clauses in the Acts of Parliament restraining Vice and Immorality. And all with such an air of Christian Breeding that I perceive gives a wonderful satisfaction to those friends and neighbours who so well spend the evening of a Christian Sabbath."[1]

The art of writing was approached when, and only when, the children could read "competently well". They were permitted, when they could write without a copy, to transcribe some useful sentences of Scripture, or, on red-letter days, a fable of Aesop's, and the method of self-correction was introduced by bidding the children compare their transcripts with the original, and correct their mistakes before showing up the work to the master. Arithmetic, the advanced course of the charity school boys' education, one to which few were qualified to enter, since it was not open until reading and writing were "perfected", was confined to the first four rules, whose use "in the ordinary management of accounts" was recognised.

Singing, as a school subject, forced its way, for a brief period, into some of the schools. Here, again, London led the way. The children, taught to sing in the parish charity schools, were encouraged by the parson to play a part in the church services on the Sabbath. Enthusiastic support for the new practice was received by the Society from all parts of the country. Letters from country clergy begged it to find them masters who could teach singing in the London method, and reported the "uncommon delight" of children and adults in learning

[1] Kennett, White, *True Report of the Charity Schools*, 1706, p. 34.

church music. But the new subject met with opposition in high quarters. There were complaints that so much "fine singing" undermined social discipline, for the children who "sang singly" acquired a pride in themselves. The Society, always sensitive to public opinion, urged the abolition of the solo, and approved of singing only in "full chorus". This fine distinction was ignored by the Bishop of London, Edmund Gibson, in his address to the teachers of the London charity schools in 1724. Fine singing, like fine writing and fine needlework, had no place, in his opinion, in schools designed to make good Christians and good servants. Such accomplishments tended to grow by degrees "unto a more polite kind of education", and must be stopped in time. Here and there courageous or indifferent school managers ignored the bishop's instructions, but the enthusiasm of children and teachers was nipped in the bud by his action. Singing did not become a recognised subject of the elementary school curriculum.[1]

The literary curriculum of the charity schools did not rule out vocational instruction. In the girls' educational programme it was the predominant element. Reading and repeating the catechism played as important a part in the instruction of charity school girls as in that of the boys, but writing was seldom taught, and arithmetic was even more rare. Plain needlework, knitting, sometimes spinning, and, when possible, housewifery took their place, that the girls might be prepared specifically for one type of work, never adequately supplied, that of domestic service. It was less easy "to inure the boys to labour" by vocational instruction. The most favoured method in an age of rapidly developing trade and commerce was to prepare them for sea-service. The Legislature had made an attempt to provide a means of supply by authorising any two or more justices of the peace and mayors of towns to bind and put out any one over ten years of age chargeable to the parish, as apprentice to any master of an English ship,[2] and in the first half of the eighteenth century a considerable pamphlet literature came to its aid, urging the setting up of schools near ports, harbours and

[1] S.P.C.K. Abs. of Correspondence, Letters from the incumbents of Box, Pottern, Yeovil, Prestbury; Minutes, Nov. 4, 1708; *Directions given by Edmund, Lord Bishop of London, to the Masters and Mistresses of the Charity Schools within the Bills of Mortality and Diocese of London assembled for that purpose in the Chapter House of St Paul's*, Nov. 14, 1724.
[2] 2 Anne, c. 6.

7

creeks where youths might be instructed in all those parts of mathematics which prepared them to become seamen. This, it was held, was the only way to secure "enough sailors for the Royal Navy, for merchantmen, for the recovery of the fishing trade and for improvement of them all".[1]

An early response to the demand for ship's boys was made by a group of London charity school managers. Specially intelligent lads in the schools of Farringdon Ward Within, St Dunstan's in the West, St Andrew's, Holborn, and other adjacent schools, were, by arrangement with the trustees, sent on three days of the week to Neale's Mathematical School in Hatton Garden, where they received vocational instruction in the art of navigation.[2] Parents whose children were privileged to attend this central school gave a bond of £10 as security that the boys should go to sea, when the course was completed. Neale's trustees undertook to find them masters, and joined with the managers of the charity schools to fit the boys with clothing and instruments proper to their calling. Dover, Brighton, Exeter, Combemartin, Bridgewater and other towns on, or near, the coast followed London's example, and included mathematics and navigation in the curriculum of their boys' charity schools.

It is, however, clear that except for a few "children of parts" the literary curriculum of the charity schools was restricted to the Bible and catechism. With occasional help from Aesop's *Fables* and *The Whole Duty of Man* they provided the religious, moral and intellectual pabulum for the children. The restriction was deliberately imposed, for the only alternative literature for children in the early years of the century was the chap-book and ballad.[3] The pious men and women who managed the charity schools did not regard the chap-book with the equanimity of Mr Bickerstaff in *The Tatler*, or Mr Burchill in *The Vicar of Wakefield*. In their opinion the corruption of youth was "not a little owing" to the loose and immoral character of books such as

[1] Brokesby, Francis, *Of Education*, 1701, pp. 47–51.

[2] The school was endowed by Joseph Neale in 1705 to provide instruction for lads attending these specified charity schools in the Art of Navigation, to fit them for Sea Service, either on Men-of-War or Merchantmen. It was opened in 1715.

[3] Locke, J., in *Some Thoughts Concerning Education*, found a difficulty in naming easy pleasant books suited to a child's capacity. He suggests two, *Reynard the Fox* and Aesop's *Fables*, "the only book almost that I know fit for children". Quick's ed. 1902, pp. 133, 164.

Laugh and be Fat, "a collection of the most indecent stories", or *The Irish Rogues and Rapparees*, which "in the coarsest language" celebrated the deeds of highwaymen. The moral sense of the children was, they held, depraved by books which were gross and indelicate, and their sense of right and wrong confused by "posing the actions of lawless felons as objects of interest and attention".[1]

Nor were the ballads which competed with the chap-book as the favourite literature of the lower orders regarded by them as suitable for the children. "The profane and loose poems set to music" were, like the chap-books, agents of corruption. In the absence of suitable books for children in the early eighteenth century the Bible became and remained the school reading-book.

After the middle of the century there was less excuse for the restriction of charity school instruction to Bible and catechism. The publication in 1744 of Newberry's *Pretty little Pocket Book*, "designed to make Tommy a good boy and Polly a good girl", created a new branch of literature.[2] *The Liliputian Magazine*, *The Governess, or the Little Female Academy*, *Mother Goose's Melodies* and the *Tale of Goody-Two-Shoes* followed one another in quick succession. In the last quarter of the century children's books reached a high level of literary excellence, and, in such tales as Mrs Trimmer's *Story of the Robins* and Hannah More's *Sacred Dramas for Children*, reached an even higher level of moral excellence. But nowhere is there evidence that the charity schools provided books such as these for their pupils.[3]

Their lack would have been of less consequence had the methods of instruction been less rigid. The Old and New Testaments abound in stories expressed in language vivid enough to grip a child's imagination, and simple enough for his understanding. But to make the Bible into a reading primer defeated the end of charity school instruction. Correct pronunciation, rather than clear understanding, became the test of biblical knowledge. Mrs Trimmer's damaging criticism of charity school instruction at the end of the century, when a variety of school-books were available and school methods had improved, sums up the case against the literary curriculum of the schools. "The children", she wrote in 1792, "are first taught to read in a spelling book, the lessons

---

[1] S.P.C.K. Abs. of Correspondence, July 31, 1729.
[2] See Darton, F. J. H., *Cambridge History of English Literature*, vol. XII, p. 377.
[3] See Appendix I, 6.

of which chiefly consist of sentences collected from the Scriptures, most of them in figurative language; as soon as they can read and spell a little, they are put into the New Testament, and go through that in the same manner, without regard to anything further than improvement in the art of reading. They learn, by stated regular tasks, the columns of spelling in the spelling books; and in some schools they are taught English Grammar, writing and arithmetic. Once or twice a week the scholars are catechised, that is, they stand up in classes and answer in rotation the questions in the Church Catechism, and explanations of it. They learn, perhaps, besides, chapters, prayers etc. by heart, and are sometimes taught psalmody. They go to Church twice every Sunday, and, where there is a weekly duty performed, they also attend on Wednesdays, Fridays and Holidays. When the scholars leave school to go out into the world as servants or apprentices, a Bible, Common Prayer Book, and *Whole Duty of Man* are given to them, and it is supposed, from the years they have been at school, that they must necessarily be furnished with a competent share of Christian knowledge to enable them to read with advantage and improvement as long as they live."[1] Formerly, she added, in 1802, it was the custom everywhere for young children to commit whole chapters to memory: "This is now we believe laid aside excepting in Charity Schools."[2]

[1] Trimmer, Sarah, *Reflections on the Education of Children in Charity Schools*, 1792, pp. 18, 19.

Mrs Trimmer's method of teaching to read, as set forth in her *Charity-School Spelling Book*, was not free from the faults she deplored. Part II introduced the children to disyllabic words and led them by way of moral lessons, some disguised as fables, to the Old Testament, whose topography provided unlimited exercise in the pronunciation of proper names, as, for example:

"And they went from Mithcah, and pitched in Hashmonah.

And they departed from Hashmonah, and encamped at Moseroth.

And they departed from Moseroth, and pitched in Benejaakan."

This was followed by the difficult words of the Gospels, definitions of biblical terms, the catechism and prayers.

[2] *Idem*, 1806 ed.

II

LABOUR

Restricted as was the literary curriculum to instruction in the three R's, religion and morals the charity schools were subjected to vehement and destructive criticism throughout the eighteenth century. The attack upon them was launched simultaneously from two sides. Strongest and most sustained was that of the vast army of persons who were opposed to any form of education for the poor. It drew its strength from the prevailing mercantilist policy of the century, which demanded as an essential of economic nationalism an adequate supply of cheap labour. The stress laid upon the importance of a favourable balance of foreign trade in theories of mercantilism relegated to a less prominent position the importance of labour, cheap enough to allow English goods to compete with those of the foreigner in the markets of the world, but in the fierce and prolonged struggle for national predominance the labouring classes in England played a part of primary importance. All available capital was required to push English trade abroad. Economies were possible only in labour at home. The passive acceptance of low wages and detestable conditions of life may be regarded as the contribution paid by the labouring classes to the development of economic nationalism.

That the price paid was a heavy one did not penetrate the consciousness of the English public in the eighteenth century. The function of the poor was to provide manual labour; it was their duty, just as it was the duty of the middle classes to develop trade by their wits. From such premises it followed that any scheme of social improvement which would unfit the poor for their work as hewers of wood and drawers of water was, to the great bulk of middle class opinion, ruled out.

Opposition to the charity school movement illustrates the prevailing opinion. The children were drawn in the main from the ranks of the labouring poor, many of them were the offspring of parents in receipt of poor relief. They were the reservoir from which future labour supplies could be drawn. Schools for their instruction, it was vehemently urged, upset the economic order of things, since they unfitted the children for their function in society. Criticism of the schools on these lines appeared early in the history of the charity school movement. It reached its apotheosis in 1723, when Bernard Mandeville, in his *Essay on Charity and Charity Schools*, vehemently asserted that poverty was the only means of ensuring an adequate supply of labour for the hard and dirty work of the world. Like Arthur Young, half a century later, he held that the lower ranks must be kept poor, or they would never be industrious, for no one would undertake the unpleasant duties of life unless compelled to do so by necessity. The attempt to divert the labour of children of the poor by education from the hard and dirty labour which was their lot and portion drew forth his fiercest attack. "The more a shepherd and ploughman know of the world the less fitted he'll be to go through the fatigue and hardship of it with cheerfulness and equanimity." Compulsory attendance of the poor at church on Sundays would provide them with all the education they required, and would leave them free for work on week-days. School learning was not work. It encouraged idleness since, while "thinking with their books", the children's bodies contracted habits of idleness. "To divert children from useful labour until they are 14 or 15 years old is a wrong way to qualify them for it when they are grown up."[1]

Much of the violence of Mandeville's essay was due to his antagonism to the High Church party, who were the warm supporters of the schools, but there was more than enough agreement with his economics to set and keep the tide of public opinion running strongly against the schools. His argument was repeated again and again in the history of the schools, and may be found even more vigorously expressed at the beginning of the nineteenth century.

The second attack upon the schools was made on a narrower front. So marked was the improvement of the children in the charity schools that they threatened not only the economic, but also the social order, for the charity children, whose education was superior to that of the common schools, supported by the influence of their patrons and by the apprenticeship funds at the disposal of school managers, entered into unfair competition with their betters. They crowded out the children of tradesmen in the already over-stocked manual trades, and, because they could read and write and cast accounts, they forced their way into the business of shopkeepers and retailers of commodities, and even pushed aside the children of a superior class from domestic service.

[1] Mandeville, B., *Essay on Charity and Charity Schools, passim.*

Such criticism had its root in the distinction which existed between the poor who were relieved by the rates and the poor who, while they were *in* the parish, were not *on* the parish, but managed to maintain themselves without recourse to rate aid. The duty of training the children of the poor for a life of toil by putting them out to apprenticeship or service had rested, since the passing of the Poor Law Act of 1601, on the shoulders of the parish officials, who defrayed the expense from the rates. The "second poor", as a later age designated them, found their relief not in aid from the rates, but from charity. "The new fangled charity schools", it was alleged, in an attempt to "breed up beggars to what are called scholars", diverted charity from the children of lesser tradesmen, decayed merchants, helpless widows and poor housekeepers who were "scarce able out of their little substance to teach their children to write and cast accounts, and to put them out apprentice to those of their own degree". "What benefit can accrue to the public", demanded "Cato" in *The British Journal*, "by taking the dregs of the people out of the kennels and driving their betters into them?"[1]

Opposition to the schools on these lines appeared early in the history of the charity school movement. It was accompanied by strictures on the conduct of the children educated in the schools, who were "inclined to put too great a value upon themselves", and "held themselves above being bound to any servile employment".[2] Instead of the humility and submission with which the school discipline should have imbued them, it was evident that the charity children suffered from a mild epidemic of swelled head. In a world of ignoramuses they could read and cast accounts; among a shabby and poverty-stricken community they were decently and even smartly clothed. On Sundays and anniversaries, when they marched in ordered ranks through the streets or sat in pews reserved for them in church, they found themselves the cynosure of all eyes. Little wonder if like Marjorie Fleming they were "all primmed up with majestick pride".

Scarcely had the S.P.C.K. been formed before it was requested to consider setting the children of the charity schools to work, that they might be "inured to labour", and, as the attack on the schools developed, the schools' supporters, perturbed by the general criticism,

---

[1] "Cato" [John Trenchard], in *The British Journal*, June 15, 1723.
[2] S.P.C.K. Abs. of Correspondence, June 6, 1706; Oct. 16, 1725.

began with one accord to make excuse. The utmost care, they assured the public, was taken to breed up the children to the meanest services. Prelates seized the opportunity offered to them in charity school sermons to deplore the undue elevation of mind of the charity children, and urged that unnecessary subjects such as writing and accounts should henceforth be omitted from the curriculum. When the Foundling Hospital was opened in 1739 the trustees were careful to state that the children would not be educated in such a manner as to put them on a level with the children of parents who had the humanity and virtue to preserve them, and the industry to support them.[1] Even Dr Isaac Watts, whose views on education were more liberal than those of his contemporaries, was apologetic in his support of the education given in the schools. "There are none of these poor who are, or ought to be, bred up to such an accomplished skill in Writing and Accompts as to be qualified for superior posts; except here and there a single Lad whose bright Genius and constant Application and Industry have outrun all his Fellows."[2]

Disillusionment with literary instruction for the labouring poor as a satisfactory method of reformation gripped its supporters only less completely than disapprobation gripped its opponents. The reformed manners and morals so confidently promised by the Society in the early years still tarried, and public opinion turned once again to the alternative method proposed by social reformers at the end of the seventeenth century. After the passing of the General Act of 1723, workhouses appeared rapidly, and working schools, on Locke's model, sometimes financed by charity, followed in the wake of the workhouse. Enthusiastic reports of the miraculous improvement effected in the moral character of the workers, and of the decrease in the rates, spread far and wide. The children of St Albans's workhouse, who were employed in making horsewhips and in spinning, helped by their emulation and industry "to banish idleness and begging from this and neighbouring parishes".[3] Workhouses and working schools which combined catechetical instruction with the godly discipline of labour answered, as their enthusiastic advocate, Matthew Marryott, averred, "all the ends of

[1] *Regulations of the Foundling Hospital*, 1749.
[2] Watts, Isaac, *op. cit.* pp. 37 *et seq.*
[3] Marryott, M. [*Account of the Workhouses in Great Britain* [etc.], 1725, pp. vi] and 119.

charity to the poor in regard to their souls and their bodies". Spinning linen and woollen thread, making lace, knitting stockings, throwing silk, and picking oakum were the common employments of the children. Spinning conferred remarkable benefits upon them. By an unprecedented transference of skill it qualified the children for all sorts and conditions of labour, such as wool-drawing, pin-making, letter-founding, weaving, printing, shoe-making and painting. In the juvenile industrial world it played the part usually attributed to the classics in the world of learning.

In the famous spinning school at Findon in Northamptonshire discipline was maintained by a life of strenuous toil. The girls were set to work, taught, lodged and wholly maintained by their labour. The working school at Artleborough, Northamptonshire, which shared with Findon in the same county a reputation as the model working school of the day, attracted widespread attention. It owed its fame to the energy of the remarkable Mrs Harris, its first mistress, who, in the early years of the century, at the request of several poor people in the neighbourhood, had taught the children for a penny a week. Reading and knitting were the subjects of instruction, and, when her pupils had mastered these, she looked round for a new world to conquer and found it in the spinning-wheel. The parents, when approached, agreed that the schoolmistress should receive the profits of the children's labour for two months to repay her for her trouble, after which time "to encourage the children's industry she contented herself by taking $2d.$ a week from those that Spin, $1\frac{1}{2}d.$ a week from those that Knit and $1d.$ a week from those that learned only to read", and allowed them to keep their earnings, "some $2d.$ others $3d.$ and others about $5d.$ a day". The enthusiasm of the parents for this new and eminently satisfactory method of education was not less than that of the school managers, for a method which enabled children, some of whom were as young as four years of age, to be self-supporting, provided, in their opinion, the most favourable means of moral discipline, and promised a reform in the manners of the infant population of the town. Accordingly, to enable the very poor to take full advantage of these opportunities, "two public spirited persons paid all the pence, three half pence, and two pence for 63 children that they might gain the more for their own and their parents' support". Forty fee-paying pupils of "creditable and substantial parents" brought the number of scholars to above a hundred. In the summer months school work began at five or six in the morning, and continued until eight or nine at night; in the winter the hours were from six or seven a.m. to seven or eight p.m. "There was allowed", says the report commendingly, "only a short intermission for dinner." During the fifteen hours' day the mistress was on constant duty in a school-house constructed so that she might see two floors at the same time, and direct and order all the children at pleasure. And her duties did not end here. She bought the yarn and the jersey for knitting and spinning, and handed them over to the Northampton and Wellingborough dealers, one of whom was not above attempting to deduct a penny in the shilling for his private gain. He met his match in the schoolmistress, who discontinued dealing with him.

The intellectual and spiritual development of the children was not neglected by this busy and efficient woman. God and mammon were served at the same time, "the children learning the catechism and prayer book and collects for the day with other good lessons in such a way that they were no hindrance to their manual work". After harvest time the untiring schoolmistress took the whole school into the bean-fields, where they gathered enough stubble to serve as firing through the winter, and on Sundays she listened to the "Heavenly music of the children", who sang "handsomely cloathed, the greatest part of their own getting" in the gallery of the parish church, erected specially for them by public subscription. The townspeople could well afford the gift of a gallery to church and school, since the profits of the school was a benefit estimated at a figure between £500 and £600 per annum to the town.[1]

It is not astonishing that Mrs Harris's experiment at Artleborough attracted widespread attention. Here was a happy combination of moral discipline, school work, religious training and profitable labour. Here were no difficulties arising out of mitching and loitering and non-attendance, since parents co-operated with teachers in keeping the children's noses to the grindstone. The schoolmistress was overwhelmed by requests for advice. Managers and trustees asked that their teachers might be allowed to spend two or three weeks at Artleborough "to pursue her method", before taking up their duties. References to her success are scattered through the minutes and correspondence of the

---

[1] Rawlinson MSS., Papers of Henry Newman; S.P.C.K. Letter Book, Dec. 15, 1722; *Account of the Workhouses* [etc.], pp. 155 *et seq.*

S.P.C.K.;[1] the *Account of the Workhouses*, published in 1725, gives a glowing account of the experiment. The Dublin Incorporated Society saw in Mrs Harris's plan the ideal method for Ireland, and Wales and Scotland learnt with interest not unmixed with envy of a school which was not only untroubled by financial difficulties, but actually paid its way. Political arithmeticians worked out the sums which would accrue to the national income if the restless energy of the children were harnessed in this way to industry. Visions of gold and silver mines appearing in every county of England, if the literary schools were turned into working schools, gripped the public imagination, and it is not surprising to find that "a prejudice, a kind of fashion, had set in against the schools" with their literary curriculum, or that the whole nation was "running so strongly" in favour of the new method that subscribers threatened to withdraw their subscriptions unless the curriculum of the schools was drastically altered, and labour given its rightful place.[2]

In this modification of the original idea of catechetical instruction for the poor the S.P.C.K. played a leading part. It could not ignore the fact that the schools were dependent for their existence on public support. The public paid the piper and could therefore call the tune. Aware that the introduction of labour into the curriculum would serve not one but several ends, it came into line with the popular demand. By making the schools self-supporting the charity school movement, which, from its inception, had been severely limited by the capricious

---

[1] S.P.C.K. Letter Book. Letter of Henry Newman, Dec. 15, 1722. "It is", wrote the Secretary approvingly, "worth while for any gentlemen minded to set up a working school to go thither to see how eagerly the children press to go to school by 5 o'clock in the summer mornings, and grudge every hour they spend out of it; they make Reading and Writing their diversion, and the gain they make by their labour makes 'em impatient to return to it again, and all this conducted by one old woman, who could scarce write her name when she first opened her school." One enthusiastic supporter sent a pasteboard model of the school to the Society.

[2] *Account of the Workhouses* [etc.], pp. 89, 162. "Suppose", wrote the S.P.C.K. to its correspondents, "England and Wales to contain Ten Thousand Parishes and that but Ten persons in every Parish, one with another, were by some method employed, who were perfectly idle before, then the whole number of Persons so set to work would be One Hundred Thousand, and if they would work but 300 days in the year and, one with another, earned but a Half-penny a day the produce of their labour at the year's end would amount to £62,500." *S.P.C.K. Circular Letter*, 1736.

assistance of its supporters, would be able to stand on its own feet. Further, by allowing the children to retain the wages they earned, the co-operation of parents would be secured, and the irregular attendance of the children, which handicapped all attempts at providing education for the poor until the era of compulsory attendance, would disappear. The Society, alive to these economic considerations, had called the attention of managers and subscribers, as early as 1704, to the results achieved by the Grey Coat Hospital in St Margaret's parish, Westminster, where school trustees and parish officers had combined to provide religious instruction, clothing, maintenance and labour for the children taken in on the parish account, and had defrayed part of the heavy expenses of a combined working and boarding school by the earnings of its pupils.[1] When opposition began to manifest itself to the schools the Society urged its correspondents to modify the literary instruction by "introducing all proper measures to inure the children to labour and industry", lest "the advantages they received from a pious education should incline them to put too great a value upon themselves". In 1719 they again earnestly exhorted and entreated their correspondents to get any kind of labour added to the curriculum, such as husbandry in any of its branches, spinning, knitting or other useful employment which will "effectually obviate an objection to the charity schools that they tend to take the poor children from off these servile offices which are necessary in all communities and for which the wise Governor of the World had by his Providence designed them".[2] Reviewing, in a letter to a correspondent in December 1722, the history of the charity school movement, the Society's secretary, Henry Newman, made the significant statement that the time for change had come. The original idea of rescuing the poor from the grossest ignorance of their duty to God and man had in his opinion "been wonderfully helped". Over thirty thousand children were now taught reading and the catechism, but "twenty four years of experience had shewn that a working school is in all respects preferable to one without labour and more in keeping with the present trend of public opinion".[3]

In 1724 the Society invited Matthew Marryott to discuss with it the pros and cons of workhouse instruction and a year later, impressed by

---

[1] *Account of the Charity Schools*, 1704.
[2] *S.P.C.K. Circular Letters*, 1712 and 1719.
[3] S.P.C.K. Letter Book, Dec. 15, 1722.

the advantage which the residential workhouse possessed over the day charity school in its power to enforce discipline, published the *Account of the Workhouses*, enthusiastically recommending these new brooms to public favour. The replies of the Society to the stream of letters from its correspondents, asking for advice upon the most suitable employments to be introduced into the older charity schools, or extolling the superiority of the new method to the old, show that a desire to inculcate the godly discipline of labour and to increase the school funds at one and the same time was an attractive one. The girls' charity school in St James's parish, Westminster, was turned into a working school, devoted to the maintenance and instruction of forty poor girls. The charity schools at Stroud and Stockport were united to the workhouses, a modification of their original character which was claimed as economically advantageous to the children who lived with their parents, and morally advantageous to the orphans in the workhouses.[1]

Seldom in the voluminous correspondence of the S.P.C.K. was objection taken to the new scheme, and its danger to the children exposed. It is therefore of peculiar interest to note that although the influence of the S.P.C.K., the financial interests of the schools trustees, the warm approval of the parents, and a solid weight of public opinion demanded that the charity children should contribute towards the expenses of their education and the increase of the national income, the attempt to screw out of their labour a contribution commensurate with the expense and effort entailed was a failure. The Grey Coat Hospital, Westminster, the first of the schools to introduce spinning-wheels and spinning mistresses to train the children in manual labour, abandoned the practice in 1734, on the ground that the money earned by them was so little, and the hindrance to education so great, that it was wise to relinquish the attempt, and the thirty spinning-wheels were sold for £1.[2] Indeed, five essentials seldom to be found in isolation, never in combination, were required for the success of school labour; raw materials, cheap enough to minimise the wastage of experimental and unskilled labour; work which could be adapted to the strength and capacity of the learners, "all weak, some sickly, all young"; a market for the defective work which the children commonly turned out; regular attendance of the children at school; and, last, trustees with

[1] *Account of the Workhouses*, etc., pp. 59, 102, 135.
[2] Minutes of the Grey Coat Hospital, vol. III, 1734.

sufficient leisure to supervise and teachers competent to teach, not only the catechism and the three R's, but the technical employments followed by the children. Essentials such as these involved the charity schools, just able to pay their way in clothing, instructing and apprenticing the children, in an expenditure too heavy for their resources, too burdensome for their organisation, too distasteful to a profession which can wield a pen with greater ease than a tool. Further, any Tom, Dick or Harry could play the manager of a catechetical school, but trustees with a requisite technical knowledge could not, as Dean Tucker of Gloucester remarked in one of the few public statements which poured cold water on the scheme, be made in an instant.[1] Only in the girls' schools, where learning was combined with domestic labour, was the method successful. The demand for trained and respectful servants is never met by the supply. The difficulty of finding competent domestic service, which harasses the housewife to-day, was shared by her sister in the eighteenth century, and schools which, like the working schools at Kendal, used the older girls to do the housework and prepare the meals, or like Mrs Cappe's school at York, gave the girls training in the elements of housecraft and in religious and moral instruction, were able to keep their heads above water.[2] Elsewhere the new method proved unsatisfactory. In the hands of an exceptional teacher like Mrs Harris at Artleborough or in a neighbourhood "so happy as to fall into a proper method of employing poor children"[3] financial success and moral improvements were, the S.P.C.K. informed its correspondents, assured, but behind the personal and administrative difficulties lay the hard economic fact that it was not easy to find work suited to children so young and inexperienced, and that, as Cary had found by experience in the Bristol workhouse, it was even more difficult to secure a satisfactory sale of the goods turned out.[4] "From all of which", said Dean Tucker in the sermon referred to, "it clearly appears that the setting up of working schools or the introducing of labour into our present charity schools is not so easy as many people have thought." Indeed,

[1] *Sermon preached at the Anniversary Meeting of the Charity Schools*, May 7, 1766; see also the admirable address of the Bishop of Bristol on a similar occasion in 1745.
[2] Cappe, C., *Account of Two Charity Schools for the Education of Girls in York*, 1800.
[3] *Account of the Charity Schools*, 1735.
[4] Cary, J., *An account of the proceedings of the Corporation of Bristol*, 1700.

the difficulties were so great that although spinning, stocking, and lace schools were to be found at all times in districts suitable for their industry, the catechetical schools finding the strain too great for their organisation did not, with few exceptions, persist in the new method. The struggle between the discipline of labour and literature for the control of the charity school curriculum ended in the defeat of labour. If success had crowned the efforts of the working charity schools the history of elementary education in the British Isles would have followed a different course. The discipline of labour would have reinforced and probably would have replaced the discipline of literature in the schools. As it was the victory of the three R's established the traditional curriculum of the elementary school, but it did so at the cost of alienating public opinion. The enthusiasm which supported the charity school movement in the early years of the century was never regained.

In the country districts the attack upon the schools was more successful. The farming middle class consistently opposed all forms of instruction for the children of the poor, whose *raison d'être*, they held, was to supply casual labour when required. It was less easy to prove that the village charity schools and endowments for schooling did not divert infant labour from husbandry, than it was to illustrate the economic folly of introducing labour into the urban schools. Faced with a threatened collapse of the charity school movement in the country, ecclesiastics, who as a body had supported the proposal for the introduction of labour in the urban schools, took up cudgels on behalf of the rural schools. Preacher after preacher protested that the country schools exercised no detrimental effect upon the supply of labour. They pointed out that the number of rural schools was too small, "considering the extent through which they are dispersed", to produce such a result, or that the Registers of Births and Burials showed "well before the creation of charity schools, as since, that our villages produce more hands than they can supply with work". They asserted that a reserve of children to meet the occasional labour shortage on the farms was unnecessary, since "the poor of Ireland and of the more populous countries of Great Britain who travel all over the Kingdom for harvest work" met in great measure such requirements. "Does the plough stand still nowhere but where there is a school of charity?" pertinently asked Isaac Watts. The select preacher at the anniversary meeting in 1757 carried the war into the enemies' camp by attributing any failure of hands in agriculture to the action of the landlords in throwing their estates into large farms, with the result that "the same quantity of land now supports, but one Family, which formerly maintained two or three or perhaps half a dozen". The remedy for such a state of affairs he held was in the hands of the landlords.[1] But in spite of pulpit oratory subscriptions fell off. Numbers of schools "declined", and many came to an abrupt end. Had not a considerable number of the country schools been endowed specifically in the first half of the century for teaching religion and the three R's, it is probable that the movement in rural England would have collapsed. As it was, belief in the spade and the plough, as superior instruments of godly discipline, successfully restrained the movement in the English country-side.

III

THE TEACHERS

The lack of competent masters and mistresses, upon whom rested the immediate responsibility of disciplining the infant mind and character, handicapped charity school education, as it handicapped all educational efforts in the eighteenth century. It is curious that an age marked by the advance of human intelligence in science, law and philosophy saw no corresponding movement in education. South and Butler in the first half of the century, Gibbon and Adam Smith at the end, united in deploring the intellectual stagnation of the Universities. The quality of the material which the Universities sent out as teachers reacted directly upon the grammar schools, which, with a handful of exceptions, declined in numbers and prestige, and indirectly upon the innumerable private-venture schools, which honeycombed London and the towns. As for the parish clerk and village dame, their scholastic qualifications were as a rule negligible, often beneath contempt.

One of the outstanding contributions of the charity school movement to education was the introduction of a new type of teacher into elementary instruction. The London charity schools demanded both full-time attendance and moral and intellectual qualifications from the men and women they appointed. Until the advent of the charity schools,

---

[1] *Sermons preached at the Anniversary meetings of the Charity Schools in and about London in* 1731, 1738, 1743, 1755, 1757; Watts, Isaac, *op. cit.* p. 22.

teachers of the poor lacked any kind of professional status. Instruction in the elements was not a whole-time job, nor did it require specific qualifications. Sometimes the work of teaching school was used as a means of providing old age pensions to the aged and decayed, or was "the refuse of other callings", the discarded servants or ruined tradesmen of Macaulay's rhetorical denunciation, "who would not be able to write a common letter, who do not know whether the earth is a square or a cube, and cannot tell whether Jerusalem is in Asia or Africa: whom no gentleman would trust with the key of his cellar and no tradesmen send on a message".[1]

More often the work was regarded as a by-industry to be carried on in conjunction with another job. Howitt's description of his teacher William Woodcock, who boasted that he nourished both minds and bodies of his pupils in his dual capacity as schoolmaster and baker, portrays him coming into the schoolroom out of the bakehouse, with his shirt sleeves rolled up to his shoulders. He "would hear our lessons; and then, having set us our copies, he strutted humming away again to set his bread".[2] Reuben Dixon, whom Crabbe commemorated in *The Borough*, was both shoe-maker and master of a common school.[3] The office of parish clerk was frequently united with that of village teacher. Even in the grammar schools the incumbent of the parish, or his curate, were to be found officiating as schoolmaster.

The masters of the London charity schools were, on the contrary, appointed as full-time teachers. They were expected to give all their time and energy to their school work. Instructions drawn up by the S.P.C.K. and the trustees of the London schools ordered them to be in attendance at school during the hours appointed for teaching, viz. from 7 to 11 in the morning, and from 1 to 5 in the evening, during the summer half of the year, and from 8 to 12 in the morning, and 1 to 4 in the evening, in the winter half, "so that they might improve the children in good learning" and prevent "the Disorders that frequently happen for want of the master's presence and care".[4]

Further, the new type of teacher was expected to produce evidence

---

[1] Macaulay, T. B., Speech in the House of Commons, April 19, 1847. Hansard, *Parliamentary Debates*, 3rd Series, vol. XCI, cols. 1016–7.

[2] Howitt, W., *The Boy's Country Book*, 5th ed. 1863, chap. xv.

[3] Crabbe, W., *The Borough*, Letter XXIV.

[4] *Account of the Charity Schools*, 1704.

of his moral and intellectual fitness for teaching the children entrusted to him. "Skill in the learned languages, poetry and oratory"[1] was not required by the charity school managers. They laid stress instead upon good character and religious knowledge. A contrast was thus presented to the common schoolmaster, whose indifferent moral and intellectual qualifications were seldom called in question by the humble parents who "heave our coals and clean our cause-ways".[2] Early in the century the qualifications required from the teachers in the new schools were drafted by the S.P.C.K. It was expected that the master should be:

1. A member of the Church of England, of a sober life and conversation, and not under the age of twenty-five years.
2. One that frequents Holy Communion.
3. One that hath a Good Government of himself and his Passions.
4. One of a meek Temper and humble behaviour.
5. One of a good Genius for teaching.
6. One who understands well the Grounds and Principles of the Christian Religion, and is able to give a good Account thereof to the Minister of the Parish or Ordinary on Examination.
7. One that can write a good Hand, and who understands the Grounds of Arithmetic.
8. One who keeps good order in his family.
9. One who is approved by the Minister of the Parish (being a subscriber) before he be presented to be Licensed by the Ordinary.[3]

To these requirements *The Christian Schoolmaster* added "virtues peculiarly suitable to the office", such as patience and humility, sagacity and judgment, justice and equity, meekness and forbearance, candour and sweetness of disposition. The fortunate possessor of these virtues, the author agreed with the Society, did not need learning. "These institutions are not for masters of schools preparing scholars for the Universities or the professions, but for teaching children of a lower class and consequently of lower talents."[4]

From the women teachers the same religious and practical qualifications were demanded. Few of them were required to teach writing;

[1] Talbot, Dr James, *op. cit.*
[2] Crabbe, W., *op. cit.*
[3] *Account of the Charity Schools*, 1704.
[4] Talbot, Dr James, *op. cit.*

fewer still arithmetic. Knitting and "plane needlework" were expected in their stead.[1]

During the early years of the charity school movement the S.P.C.K. was overwhelmed by requests from managers and trustees to find teachers for the schools, and the Society endeavoured to secure the services of men and women who, in its opinion, were qualified to take up the work. It acted as an employment agency bringing together teachers who were seeking posts, and trustees who were seeking teachers. The letter books and minutes of the Society testify to the elaborate care taken by it to fit the right man and woman to the right place. Only those candidates who were personally known to members of the Society were recommended by it.[2] The religious societies which, from the time of their establishment in William and Mary's reign, had attracted large numbers of pious young men of the "middling classes", provided reservoirs from which the schools drew many of their male teachers. Some of the applicants were parish priests, but managers and Society had little liking for men who wished to fill two posts at the same

[1] See Minutes of the Charity School for Girls in the Parish of St Martin in the Fields, Jan. 1, 1700. Qualifications for the Mistress of the School:
1. That she shall be a member of the Church of England and of a sober life and conversation.
2. One that has frequented the Communion once a month (at least) for some years.
3. One that keeps good orders in her family (if she have one).
4. One that hath a command of her passions.
5. One that is of an ingenious mind, willing to learn and apt to teach.
6. That she be solidly grounded in the true Principles and Practice of Christianity so as to give a good account thereof to the Minister of the Parish upon examination.
7. One that is sufficiently grounded in the English Tongue so as to be able to teach her scholars to read, and also one who understands knitting, writing, plane work so as to be able to instruct her scholars in the same, in order to fit them either for Service or Apprenticeship.

[2] "Mr Bickerton a clergyman was this day with us", wrote Henry Newman to the Rev. Ed. Gregory at Wotton-under-Edge, Gloucestershire, "to recommend William Harrison of Droitwich for your school. We told him the Society would not recommend any person whom they had not personal knowledge of and good Testimonials as to his past life, but that if he thought it would be worth while to come to Town to be discussed with about his qualifications, the Society might be able in a little time to have it in their power to recommend him if he answered the character given him." S.P.C.K. Letters, Feb. 11, 1720–1.

time. They preferred the services of those who would devote their whole time and energy to the new work, and since the applicants were many and the posts few, the London school trustees had little difficulty in finding the men and women they required. There were so many applicants that the Society dissuaded young men in the provinces from coming to London in search of teaching posts. "Many country Candidates", wrote the secretary in 1715, "are still unprovided for."[1]

In an age when the English country clergy were passing rich on £40 a year the salaries paid by the London charity schools to their teachers were by no means unattractive. The average salary for a master in a London school at the beginning of the century was £30 a year, with coals, and, sometimes, a house rent free. For a woman £24 per annum was the maximum; usually her pay was less. In the second half of the century it is possible to find some of the London schoolmasters in receipt of incomes from £50 to £65 a year. Sometimes husband and wife, since marriage did not debar a woman from teaching, were appointed, respectively, master and mistress of the boys' and girls' schools in the parish, and enjoyed a joint salary.[2]

It was not, however, easy to find suitable candidates for the provincial schools. Letters from trustees in Bristol, Exeter, Southampton, Bath and elsewhere testify to the difficulty of schools outside London in securing the services of satisfactory persons. The local material did not satisfy them. They wanted men and women from the metropolis, trained in the new methods, but their resources did not enable them to offer salaries commensurate with those offered in London. In the villages the difficulty of staffing was acute. "The men of known and approved piety",[3] whom Samuel Wesley demanded for the success of the charity school movement, were not easy to find. Country managers reminded the London Society that there were compensating advantages which accrued from living outside London. "£20 a year in the Country where living is so cheap that one can board for £10 to £12 per annum is as good as £30 a year in Town", they asserted.[4] But the bait seldom proved attractive. "Masters don't care to go into the country", said

---

[1] S.P.C.K. Letters, Oct. 18, 1715.

[2] S.P.C.K. Letters, May 26, 1713.

[3] Wesley, Samuel, An Account of the Religious Society begun in Epworth in the Isle of Axholm, Lincolnshire, Feb. 1, 1701–2, sent by him to the S.P.C.K.

[4] S.P.C.K. Abs. of Correspondence, Aug. 19, 1719.

Henry Newman bluntly in a letter to a correspondent, "but upon consideration of having so much as they have here."[1] The qualified and experienced masters, whom country parsons and trustees requested the Society to find for them, were unwilling to abandon a permanent well-paid post in London for one of uncertain tenure and lower salary in the country.[2] The endowed and subscription schools of rural England were therefore, for the most part, forced to fall back upon existing material. The parish clerk, the village dame, the religious poor woman, the private-venture schoolmaster were retained by the patrons of the new schools, with instructions to teach the catechism, reading, and, sometimes, writing to all the children of the parish, free, gratis or for nothing, or to teach a specified number without charge, and, to eke out their salaries, they were, here and there, allowed to take pay scholars. The difficulty of raising funds sufficient to run and equip schools on the London model explains why the movement made relatively little headway, after the early years, in the country-side. The English charity school movement, unlike that of Wales, Ireland and the Highlands, was emphatically urban in character.

More than once in its early years the S.P.C.K., impressed by the need of trained teachers, approached the idea of a seminary for their professional training, and it was not until it became clear that the expense involved was beyond its means that it abandoned the idea.[3] When a training college proved impossible, belief in professional training remained. The pupil-teacher method of recruiting was introduced; promising elder lads taught the children under the master's superintendence, and, if they showed genius for teaching, they were apprenticed so that they "might gain the art of teaching school on the old master's methods".[4] Newly elected teachers were bidden by the Society with commendable wisdom to take into consideration the different capacities, temper and inclination of the children, and to

[1] S.P.C.K. Letter Book, May 26, 1713.
[2] S.P.C.K. Abs. of Correspondence, Jan. 20, 1718–19. See also the *Account of the Charity Schools*, 1714, for a list of nineteen "eminent London Teachers" sent by the S.P.C.K. from London to the country. "They are ready to inform any persons that shall apply to them in the methods used in the London Schools."
[3] S.P.C.K. Minutes, Oct. 7, 14, 21, 1703; Sept. 14, 1736; Abs. of Correspondence, Oct. 25, Nov. 18, 1708; see also *Sermon preached by Dr Waterland before the Society*, June 6, 1723, and Nelson, R., *Address to persons of Quality and Estate*, 1715.
[4] Minutes, St Martin's in the Fields Charity School for Girls, Nov. 15, 1715.

consult with the experienced masters of the "perfected schools" for
the better understanding of their duties, before they began their new
work, and school managers were urged to make it possible for novices
to have liberty, on certain days of the week, to go and hear their elders
teach, and to take part in teaching under their supervision.[1] Minute
books of the schools and the Society tell of the efforts of teachers and
trustees to carry out the recommendations of the Society, and to create
a professional spirit. Country schools sent their masters and mistresses
to London to be instructed in the "London method", and "eminent
London teachers" voluntarily exiled themselves in the country to teach
their method in urban and village schools.[2]

The men and women who earned their livelihood as school teachers
have suffered hardly at the hands of contemporaries and of posterity.
Literature seldom finds them attractive, history as a rule ignores them.
The charity school teachers, humblest of their kind, were as a rule too
insignificant for praise or blame. Once or twice during the century
they were dragged from the obscurity of their classrooms and pilloried
in public. Mandeville depicts them as the most despicable of their kind,
"starving wretches of both sexes that, from a natural antipathy to
working, . . . think themselves qualified to become masters and mistresses
of charity schools". His portrait has stereotyped the popular conception
of the charity school teacher, but, like the eighteenth-century parson,
the eighteenth-century teacher refuses to conform to type. It is impossible to deny that the masters and mistresses were, as a body,
ill-equipped for their work, or that they conducted themselves and their
schools satisfactorily only when they were subject to constant supervision
and inspection. Among them were ignorant, lazy, dishonest and incompassionate men and women. They are to be found neglecting their
duties, manipulating school funds, and behaving with gross and
abominable cruelty to the children committed to their charge. The
boarding schools and hospitals, which in England were, fortunately,
but a small proportion of the total number of charity schools,[3] readily
lent themselves to such masters and mistresses, who, secure in their
fastnesses from interference in the intervals between the visits of

---

[1] *Account of the Charity Schools*, 1704.
[2] *Account of the Charity Schools*, 1714.
[3] See Appendix I, 3; see also the evidence of Mr Fearon before the Schools
Inquiry Commission, 1868, vol. VII, pp. 867–8.

governors and managers, were able to exploit the children for their own ends, and lined their pockets with money saved from the children's rations. School records reveal the disquieting fact that, when the care of trustees and managers was relaxed, masters and mistresses showed themselves to their unhappy pupils in unsuspected colours. Girls, as well as boys, were so cruelly flogged at the Grey Coat Hospital that the matron was arrested, and was allowed out on bail with difficulty. In the same school the boys deliberately smashed the windows to ensure an enquiry from the governors, and, on another occasion, the girls, for the same end, set fire to the wood-work. When the governors made enquiry into the "rebellion" they were answered that the children were so "utterly wretched" from constant flogging and semi-starvation, that they could endure it no longer.[1]

Similar conditions existed in the girls' charity school at York, at the end of the century. The children, thirty in number, were boarded by a master and mistress who consistently underfed and ill-treated them. They were, reported Mrs Cappe in 1795, generally diseased in body and mind; their appearance was sickly and dejected, their ignorance extreme.[2] It is unlikely that the incidents of recorded neglect comprise a fraction of the cases in which the teachers ill-treated their pupils. There are too many allusions to men and women who ruled like the petty tyrants of Mandeville's diatribe, too many rumours of the unmerciful practices which Isaac Watts and Samuel Chandler deplored, to permit the recorded cases to be treated as exceptional. Blake's *Holy Thursday* in his *Songs of Experience* is a reminder that sometimes "the human heart is forged iron":

Is this a holy thing to see	Is that trembling cry a song?
In a rich and fruitful land,	Can it be a song of joy?
Babes reduc'd to misery,	And so many children poor?
Fed with cold and usurous hand?	It is a land of poverty!

And their sun does never shine,
And their fields are bleak and bare,
And their ways are fill'd with thorns:
It is eternal winter there.[3]

---

[1] Minutes, Grey Coat Hospital, Feb. 19, March 11, 1788; June 30, 1789; Jan. 30, 1796.

[2] Cappe, C., *op. cit.*   [3] Blake, W., *Songs of Experience, circa* 1794.

But, while it is not difficult to find instances of brutal treatment and harsh discipline in the records of charity boarding schools, it does not appear that the teachers in the day schools were remarkable for similar behaviour. Indeed there is reason for believing that, while to spare the rod and spoil the child was a principle acceptable alike to eighteenth-century pedagogue and parent in all classes of society, excessive punishments were less general in the charity schools than in the public schools, or in the common schools of the people. Busby's "awful reign" at Westminster passed into a proverb; the floggings administered by Butler at Shrewsbury, Keate at Eton, and Parr at Norwich acquired public fame. Blows, kicks and cuffs, the use of the cane, the strap, and the bastinado were of daily occurrence in the common schools. Samuel Bamford showed neither surprise nor indignation at the brutal chastisement he received at the first school he attended. Lovett's story of the schoolmaster who hung up one of his scholars by his two thumbs because he played truant does not suggest that such punishment was uncommon.[1]

Two factors contributed to protect the charity children of the day schools from the unbridled passions of teachers such as these. The schools were, in the first place, publicly managed and publicly financed. They drew the bulk of their endowments and subscriptions, and recruited their managers and trustees, from persons who lived in the neighbourhood of the schools, and were jealous of the privilege which accrued to them of nominating pupils to the schools. They acted as patrons to the children. They were interested in their conduct and their appearance, and they took up cudgels on their behalf when parents or children complained. Explanations were demanded, and when they were not satisfactory, subscriptions were withdrawn. In the early years of the movement the aid of the Society was sought in making investigation into cases of misconduct. When the school managers did their duty the charity children suffered less than their contemporaries from brutality disguised as discipline.[2]

---

[1] Bamford, S., *Early Days*, 1849; *Life and Struggles of William Lovett*, 1876. See also Barnard, H., *English Pedagogy*, vol. II, p. 336, for a curious and horrifying medley of punishments used in English and Continental schools throughout the ages.

[2] See Minutes, St Martin's in the Fields Charity School for Girls, March 6, 1706; S.P.C.K. Minutes, Nov. 25, 1703.

In the second place the parents were, as a rule, drawn from a class which, though many of them were eager for their children to have the advantages of education, could not but regard the time spent by them in school as an economic disadvantage. They were not concerned, as were parents who paid fees for schooling, to keep their children's noses to the grindstone. Mitching, truancy and elopement occur with monotonous regularity in the minutes and reports of the schools. As compulsion could not be used to oblige parents to send their children to school, nor fines be imposed for neglect to do so, parents and children had the whip-hand of masters and mistresses. Boys and girls absented themselves from school when their parents wanted their services at home or in the streets. Parents, mothers in particular, faced masters, mistresses and managers with effrontery when their children were punished for absence from school, or for misbehaviour when there. Nothing is more surprising and entertaining than the behaviour of parents and children, which school reports and minute-books reveal. Instead of a uniformly down-trodden and inarticulate labouring class, gratefully and humbly accepting the favours bestowed upon them, there appear children with more than their fair share of original sin, and parents whose powers of vituperation were immeasurably superior to those of teachers or trustees. They are to be found bullying the teachers before the children in the classroom, disturbing them "in a clamorous manner", using abusive language, withdrawing their offspring when they objected to the punishments inflicted upon them, while the children, instead of showing distaste for their charity uniforms and badges, could with difficulty be parted from them until "the law was put on them". At Bath the "barbarian mothers", objecting, as mothers not infrequently do in all classes and in all ages, to the encroachment of school work and school exercises on their children's time, marched in a body to the school and so hectored the unfortunate schoolmistress that "the discipline of her school was seriously hindered".[1]

But it is possible to credit the charity school teachers with more positive praise. They carried on their work, in many cases, faithfully and efficiently against the most serious of educational handicaps, those of a narrowly limited period of schooling, and irregular attendance. A school course for four years was outlined by the S.P.C.K. and *The*

[1] S.P.C.K. Abs. of Correspondence, Aug. 17, 1715.

Christian Schoolmaster, and was, in general, adopted by the London schools. The success of the London method was due in no small degree to the length of the school course. Some of the big urban schools followed suit, but in the small towns and villages, as the bitter complaints of the clergy correspondents and the reports of the Charity Commissioners bear witness, the length of time allowed by parents and poor-law officers was normally two years or less. When it is remembered that the children came to school at all ages, from six years of age onwards, and with "varying degrees of scholarship", some able to read, others ignorant of their letters, the difficulties of the single-handed teacher become apparent. Even more serious was the irregular attendance of the children. Teachers in the country schools found their schools "almost void of children" in the summer months, and especially in harvest time. In the towns the teachers fought a losing battle against the indifference of the parents and the temptations of the streets. Only in the hospital schools where the children, of use in running the establishment, were retained until their early teens, and where irregular attendance did not obtain, were conditions favourable to the pedagogue.

That charity school instruction, handicapped by the limitations of a rigid curriculum, an inadequate period of schooling and irregular attendance of the children, attained any measure of success may be attributed to the number of men and women, entombed in school records and the minute-books of the S.P.C.K., who were lacking neither in intellectual qualifications nor in a sense of responsibility to the children. Sims of Cripplegate, whom Henry Newman affectionately calls "the Father of the Charity Schoolmasters", is easily discernible in the Society's minutes as an educational enthusiast. Better qualified than most of the charity schoolmasters, for he appears to have been the author of *Nolumus lilium defamari*—a vindication of the common grammar—published in 1709, he reported to the Society in 1700 that he had discovered a secret by which he could teach the alphabet in a day's time and that he had taken forty poor boys into the school. The secret, which was not divulged, was presumably a success. The Society's agents reported favourably upon the school and so great was Sims's reputation that managers of country schools sent him young men to train and instruct before taking up their new posts, and eagerly appointed those who had served as ushers under him. Dixon of St Andrew's, Holborn, the most revered of charity schoolmasters, was, like Sims, a man of considerable attainments. His *English Instructor*, whose lessons were "formed on the plan of the Church Catechism inculcating on tender minds their duty to God, their neighbours and themselves", went through twenty-one editions before his death in 1761. At the Grey Coat Hospital the library of the master, William Dear, bears lasting witness to his intellectual interests, just as the school records disclose him as a man little fitted for the dual task of teacher and master of the Hospital.

Among the mistresses in the schools were women of attainments and character. The first mistress of the girls' school in St Martin's parish possessed unusual qualifications and personality. "Being examined for the office", the school minutes record, "she says she is a single woman aged about 40; of the Church of England, had in her apprenticeship taken the Sacrament once a month, since that once a week; has read besides the Bible, Bishop Taylor's, Dr Scots', Dr Horneck's and Dr Sherlock's Books; has for these 20 years past brought up several children and has made it her chief business to instruct them in religion, so that all but one being brought to the minister received the Communion at 15 years of age; writes a very good hand and understands knitting and plane work." The two other applicants on the short list had read but two devotional works apiece and frequented the Communion but three times a year. Mrs Mary Harbin was appointed mistress at a salary of £24 a year "with the conveniency of a lodging". Every third Thursday in the month she laid before the trustees a report of the behaviour of the girls, "in their manners, wearing of their clothes and absence from school". Examination of her pupils showed that the mistress had been very industrious in her teaching and that most of the children were much improved since their first coming to school. For sixteen years Mrs Harbin was "an indefatigable mistress to the school, admirably qualified and, in every way, capacitated for her sex's instruction", and the sorrow of the managers when they reluctantly dismissed her in 1716, because she was a non-juror, disaffected to "the present happy Establishment" and could not find it in her conscience to teach her girls to pray for King George in the school prayers, is not obscured by the formal minutes which record her examination and dismissal.[1]

[1] Minutes of St Martin's in the Fields Charity School for Girl's, Nov. 25, 29, 1716.

The efficient organisation and the remarkable results achieved at Bath, Artleborough, Blewbury and Findon, the four model schools of the provinces, were the work of the teachers appointed to the posts. Although public opinion to-day would condemn their methods as warmly as public opinion then commended them, changed conceptions of education cannot obscure the reforming zeal of the teachers or their devotion to duty. No pains were spared by Robert Nelson and Edward Jennings, to whose enthusiasm the Bath schools owed their origin, to find the right man for the post. "The Society is very much concerned", wrote Henry Newman in 1710, "that a master has not yet been provided. We have seen several but we doubted of their being acceptable, because one wanted age and a good presence, another was married and expected £40 a year; a third was in orders and therefore not so likely to attend to the duty of the school; a fourth wanted experience in London methods."[1] But in June 1711 the trustees of St Andrew's school, Holborn, gave leave to their much valued master, Henry Dixon, to go to Bath for a year, "till the school is formed, upon conditions that he shall return at the end of the twelve month". "The great rejoicings" which greeted the appointment were maintained when the schoolmaster began his work. By March 1712–13 he had effected a remarkable change in the town. "The whole body of people is wonderfully mended", and convincing proof of the widespread esteem and affection felt for the man and his work was witnessed in church on Sundays "when some of the best people in the Town sent their children to sit among the charity children". At the end of the twelve months, when the schoolmaster desired to return to London, the Bath trustees were unwilling to let him go. "I can assure you", wrote Robert Nelson, supporting them in a letter to Dixon, "that all your friends in town were much concerned when they heard you had thoughts of quitting Bath; they take your success in that place to be an indication of the call of Providence to reside there, and can you be insensible of God's great goodness which vouchsafes to make you so great an instrument of His service?"[2] Dixon, thus reproved, remained at his post and continued the work of reformation in Bath, "where he prevailed over the children in the tenderest and most affectionate manner". "He hath done so

[1] S.P.C.K. Letters, Letter of Henry Newman to Robert Nelson, June 16, 1711.
[2] Secretan, C. F., *Memoirs of the Life and Times of the Pious Robert Nelson*, 1840, p. 127.

much good in a short time", wrote a correspondent to Henry Newman in 1712, "as many men would be glad to be able to say they have done in the whole of their lives." And the good so done was not quickly forgotten; "worthy and considerable men bred up by him took pride in visiting him in his old age, bringing with them their children and grandchildren whom he with pleasure beheld".[1]

Under Dixon and his indefatigable colleague in the girls' school, Bath became a recognised training centre for young teachers of the neighbourhood and a centre of educational activity. "Any master or mistress", reported the Society, "may be very well informed of the London methods by going to Bath and conversing with the master and mistress aforesaid and seeing their way of managing the schools." And, not content with occasional visits and conversation, the schoolmaster gathered together the teachers of the neighbourhood in one of the earliest educational societies, "that they might consult the best methods of teaching their children".[2]

That these are not isolated instances of men and women possessing by no means contemptible intellectual and personal qualities is shown by the correspondence of the S.P.C.K. "Men who valued themselves or their parts" were not uncommon. Unfortunately they did not always combine the moral and practical qualifications required, so that "men of inferior parts", who had disciplinary powers, and little else to recommend them, were preferred to them.

[1] *The Parent's and Schoolmaster's Spiritual Assistant, for grounding their children and those under their care in Sound Christian Principles according to the Church of England agreeable to the late Mr Henry Dixon's instructions in the Charity School at Bath* [etc.], 1761, Preface.

[2] *Account of the Charity Schools*, 1712; S.P.C.K. Abs. of Correspondence, May 5, 1716.

CHAPTER IV

ENGLAND

CHARITY AND POLITICS

"High Church and Ormonde!"

I

THE TORY OFFENSIVE

It was the unhappy fate of the English charity schools to act as pawns in the game of party politics played between High and Low Churchmen in the first quarter of the eighteenth century. When the earliest of the London schools were set up fear of Rome was acute and became more so when the Jesuits were granted permission by James II, in 1685, to build a chapel in the Savoy. Their superior, Andrew Poulton, at once opened a charity grammar school for the education of poor children who numbered, it was alleged, over 400, more than half of whom were the children of Protestant parents.[1] This alarming success created so much concern among Anglicans and Dissenters that Dr Symon Patrick, then dean of Peterborough, and Dr Tenison, then rector of St Martin's in the Fields, using charitable funds at their disposal, set up two Anglican charity schools as counter-attractions, one in the parish of St Margaret and the other in the parish of St James, Westminster. It was these two institutions that later generations declared to be "the original root" of the English charity schools. "The Jesuits", said Patrick in his autobiography, "set up a school to teach youths for nothing, which we thought would drive many into their snare, and therefore we agreed to do the same." Almost simultaneously Protestant Dissenters, sharing the same fear of the Jesuit seminary, opened a school for the children of watermen and fishermen in Gravel Lane, Southwark, which they, in their turn, claimed to be the parent charity school of the

---

[1] Patrick, Symon, Bishop of Ely, *Autobiography*, 1839, pp. 127 *et seq.*; Clarke, J. S., *Life of James II, Collected out of Memoirs out of his own hand*, 1816, vol. II, pp. 79–80.

Metropolis.[1] The separate attempts of Anglicans and Dissenters to meet the Jesuit peril in 1685 did not prevent their combination to maintain the Hanoverian Succession against the common foe. Although membership of the Society for Promoting Christian Knowledge was confined to members of the Anglican Church, Dissenters gladly supported their fellow Protestants in the struggle with "The Mother of Superstition and Sedition". Unable to finance an adequate number of schools in connection with their churches, they welcomed the parish charity schools as the first line of defence against the spread of a religion "absurd in itself and oppressive to the liberty of the souls of men";[2] they sent their children to the schools in spite of the fact that they were there "educated in a church way", and so liberal were their contributions that they sometimes exceeded those of the schools' Anglican supporters.[3]

Unhappily the approximation of Church and Dissent, which William III and his bench of bishops desired, was opposed by the High Church party, whose policy of exclusiveness in Church and State steadily gained ground when Anne became Queen. To establish its position no means were too insignificant. It captured the Religious Societies and made a determined bid to capture the schools. The bitter struggle for their possession may be regarded as a minor engagement in the long drawn out battle between the High Church party, recruited mainly from the lower clergy, who were strongly antipathetic to their Hanoverian and latitudinarian superiors and who counted among their ranks many who were ardently legitimist on the one side, and on the other side, "those they call low-churchmen", whose devotion to the Protestant Succession, and to the House of Hanover as its symbol, involved them in a policy of toleration towards Dissent and of sustained opposition to Tories and Jacobites. After the extraordinary outburst of popular enthusiasm for the High Church party expressed during Dr Sacheverell's trial in 1710, and the Tory triumph at the polls in the same year, the High Anglican campaign began in earnest with an attack

[1] Chandler, S., *Sermon preached for the benefit of the Charity School in Gravel Lane, Southwark*, Jan. 2, 1727–8, p. 40.

[2] Milner, J., *Sermon preached for the benefit of the Charity School in Gravel Lane, Southwark*, 1743.

[3] Wake MSS. Arch. W. Epist. 15, Universities, Charities and Religious Societies, 1715–18. Memorial Representing the Origin and Design of the Charity Schools, the First Method of Supporting them [etc.].

upon the Dissenting supporters of the charity schools, when "preachers distinguished for their discretion, temper and moderation in the early days of the movement were replaced by men who very indiscreetly fell a-railing at the Dissenters and did very unseasonably publish how much the charity would tend to put an end to their schism".[1] Recrimination from the pulpit, which did much to cool Dissenting enthusiasm for the schools, was followed by the High Tory crusade of 1711, and the passing of the Act against Occasional Conformity, and culminated in 1714 in the Schism Act, which attempted to debar Dissenters from having schools even for the education of their own children. This harsh and unconscionable Act, which shows the danger with which religious liberty was threatened in Anne's reign, "did so utterly alienate them that there is not now a dissenter within my knowledge", wrote an indignant Low Churchman, "who has not withdrawn his subscription to the schools or can be induced to renew it".[2]

The policy of High Anglican exclusiveness was not confined to the elimination of Nonconformist support to the schools. When they had succeeded in depriving the little garrisons of their Dissenting allies High Churchmen estranged from them their Low Church supporters by the selection of masters and mistresses who did not attempt to conceal their Jacobite sympathies, and of preachers who used the charity school sermon to express High Anglican politics. Low Churchmen, in their turn, began to withdraw their subscriptions, and bitter religious feelings and party rancour replaced the amiable agreement of the schools' early years. "Scarce anywhere", says Ralph Thoresby in his *Diary* for 1710, "without unhappy disputes, even among the nearest relations, about the wretched distinctions between anglicans and low churchmen."[3] It appeared inevitable to the Low Church supporters of the schools, to whom High Anglican and Jacobite were synonymous terms, that the charity schools, set up to maintain the Hanoverian Settlement, would, if nothing were done to prevent them, fall entirely into the hands of disaffected persons, who enjoyed an unrivalled opportunity for poisoning the children with seditious principles. The year 1715 crowned their suspicions with certainty. At the Brentford election in May "children with the badge of common charity

---

[1] Memorial, *op. cit.*
[2] Memorial, *op. cit.*
[3] Thoresby, Ralph, *Diary, 1677–1724*, vol. II, p. 69, ed. J. Hunter, 1830.

on their backs" joined in the riots and tumults in the streets,[1] and during the months of the Rebellion, charity school boys, conspicuous in their characteristic uniforms, formed part of the High Church mob in the streets. They wore the Pretender's favours in their caps and shouted vigorously for "High Church and Ormonde". The teachers, too, brought the schools into disrepute, as Henry Newman, secretary to the S.P.C.K., unwillingly admitted in a letter to the Bishop of Lincoln.[2] Rumours that a non-juring catechism containing principles for Popery and against the Government was used in London and country schools created great alarm.[3] The little garrisons, founded by sanguine Whigs to withstand Rome and rebellion, appeared in danger of betrayal from within.

The defeat of the rebels at Preston in 1715 called a temporary halt to High Anglican pretensions. In the same year William Wake, one of the ablest of Hanoverian bishops, was translated from Lincoln to Canterbury, in which post his hearty concurrence with the Whig Government was confidently expected. It appeared to Low Churchmen that the moment had arrived for a strong counter-attack upon the High Tory entrenchments in the London charity schools.

No estimate is less easy to make than one of the strength of Jacobitism during the first half of the eighteenth century. Those who openly championed the Pretender's cause were few in number, but behind them was an army of sympathisers whose numbers were unknown. Their activities were secret and unostentatious but, as the Wake manuscripts and the letters and minutes of the S.P.C.K. testify, many of them found shelter and opportunity in the religious societies and in the charity schools of the metropolis. It has been stated more than once that the charges of Jacobitism brought against the trustees and teachers of the charity schools were without foundation and that the assertions of press and publicists were merely political weapons in the party struggles of the age. But, while it is true that Whigs and Low Churchmen often violently exaggerated the importance of facts and opinions which told against the Jacobites, there is considerable evidence that

[1] See *The Flying Post*, April 26, 1715; S.P.C.K. Minutes, April 28, 1715.
[2] S.P.C.K. Abs. of Correspondence, Letter from Henry Newman to Edmund Gibson, May 31, 1716.
[3] S.P.C.K. Abs. of Correspondence, Dec. 24, 1718, referring to letter of an earlier date: also Letter Book, Jan. 27, 1718–19.

Jacobitism had entrenched itself in many of the London charity schools, where its presence was a source of anxiety, not only to the Whig Government, but to level-headed ecclesiastics, such as Wake and Gibson, and to the executive committee of the S.P.C.K.

The change in the character of the religious societies, which supplied the schools with not a few of their trustees and teachers, was brought to Wake's notice soon after his translation to Canterbury in a memorial signed by Dr Thomas Bray, the founder of the S.P.C.K. The pious, useful and modest character of the religious societies in King William's day had degenerated, the memorial stated, since the trial of Dr Sacheverell; they had become bodies disaffected to Church and State, "little better than seminaries to prepare our youth for Jacobite conventicles". The society in Whitechapel was "notorious for disaffection", the society in the parish of St Lawrence Poultney "drink to the Pretender", in the Vintry Ward's society there was "much downright Jacobitism", and the society of charity schoolmasters, which held its meeting in the Ward, was of the same stamp. The Government, a later petition urged, "should have a narrow eye upon them, virulent malice appearing to be in the young men's breasts against the King".[1] It would be easy to write down these and similar reports as the extravagant expression of Whigs and Low Churchmen obsessed by the Roman peril, did not the Archbishop's strong condemnation of the religious and political activities of the societies "running into the corruption of Popery", and "disputing and determining the rights of Princes", confirm the allegations of sedition and disaffection brought against them. "It were better", wrote Wake, "that the Religious Societies should be wholly dissolved than such Libertys be taken and such Practices be allowed of....I can never account either Such Persons good Christians, or their meetings, for such purposes as these, to have anything to entitle them to the character of Religious Societies."[2]

[1] Wake MSS. Arch. W. Epist. 15. A Memorial giving some account of the Jacobites and Papists in and near London, under the heads of (1) Religious Societies, (2) Jacobite Conventicles, (3) Popish Seminaries: A second Report upon the same, August 24, 1716.

[2] S.P.C.K. Abs. of Correspondence, Letter from the Archbishop of Canterbury to be communicated to the visiting Stewards of the Religious Societies in and about London, April 3, 1718. This letter repeats one written for the same purpose in 1716, which I cannot find: it is referred to in the *Circular Letter of the S.P.C.K. to its Correspondents* in 1716.

II

THE WHIG ATTACK

The Whig attack on the schools began with the struggle over the Close Vestries Bill in 1716. The need for reforming the close or select vestries of the metropolis had occupied the attention of the legislature since the last decade of the seventeenth century. The evil consequences to the parish of a semi-permanent oligarchy answerable to no superior, usurping to itself the sole power and disposal of public moneys and stock, cried out for remedy, and, since in 1716 the select vestries of the metropolis were regarded as the strongholds of the Tory, Church and Jacobite party, the Whig Government prepared to cleanse an Augean stable, and remove a strongly entrenched foe at one and the same time, by opening the vestry and transferring the powers, formerly wielded by the oligarchy, to a lay body elected by the substantial householders of the parish. The proposed reform "sought virtually to disestablish the clergyman from his immemorial participation in local government, to place in a completely subordinate position the Churchwardens who were the most ancient officers of the parish",[1] and to transfer to an elected body the right of appointing the masters and mistresses of the charity schools in the parish and of the selection of the pupils to be admitted. The bill, by attempting too much, accomplished nothing. At once the cry was raised that the Church was in danger and Anglicans, high and low, closed their ranks to oppose lay control of the schools. The general body of London charity school trustees, composed of managers drawn from the schools, in London and Westminster, took vigorous action. The schools, they asserted in a petition to the House of Lords, though *in* the parish were not maintained *by* the parish; they were supported by the voluntary subscriptions of men and women who, thereby, secured the right of appointing the teachers and nominating the children who were to be admitted. To hand these powers over to an elective body would check the flow of subscriptions and would "tend to discourage, if not totally to dissolve, the said schools".[2]

[1] Webb, S. and B., *English Local Government from the Revolution to the Municipal Corporations Act. The Parish and the County*, 1906, p. 255.
[2] Petition of Trustees of Charity Schools in London and Westminster, House of Lords Archives, June 5, 1716.

The bill succeeded in passing the Commons, in spite of the efforts of the S.P.C.K. to bestir members to vote against it;[1] in the Lords the Archbishop, showing not for the first time or last time his independence of Whig policy when he considered that the Church was in danger, made a set speech against it and as "not a peer", says the Nonconformist historian, Edmund Calamy, had "the courage to speak for it afterwards, it was thrown out by a considerable majority".[2] The stables remained uncleansed; the High Tory party still controlled the vestries, and trustees and managers were left in possession of the schools.

A triumph such as this was not without its dangers. The Archbishop in a letter to Edward Jennings, chairman of the committee of the trustees of the London schools, warned him that the failure of the Government to establish control of the schools placed the burden of cleansing them from suspicion of sedition and disaffection upon the trustees. "I can now with satisfaction acquaint you that I presented your Petition on the behalf of all our Charity Schools yesterday to the House, and that the effect was as happy as could have been wished. For the bill was rejected, and therefore the danger which threatened these pious nurseries for the present is no more. But indeed I can't tell you how soon it may return if some effectual care be not taken by you to purge them from all such masters and mistresses as instill any factious or seditious principles into their children, and rigorously to animadvert upon all, whether Children or Teachers, who either appear or suffer them to appear at any times further to affront the Government, and bear a part in those Tumults and Riots which are so great a scandal as well as a prejudice to the good order and peace of the Realm."[3] The Archbishop requested the trustees to enquire diligently into the grounds of the complaints against the schools, and followed up his appeal to them by a letter to the S.P.C.K. asking it to restrict its membership to persons who were well affected to the King and his Government, and to refuse to assist the country schools unless the masters and mistresses

[1] S.P.C.K. Minutes, May 10, 1716: Letter Book, May 16, 1716, Letter to Sir Richard Marsham, M.P.

[2] Calamy, E., *Historical Account of my own Life*, 1829, vol. II, pp. 352–3; see also the *House of Lords Journal*, May 25, 26 and June 1 and 5, 1716, vol. XX, pp. 365, 366, 368, 372, and Oldmixon, J., *History of England*, 1735, vol. II, p. 633.

[3] S.P.C.K. Abs. of Correspondence, Letter of the Archbishop of Canterbury to Edward Jennings and the Worthily Respected Governors and Directors of the Charity Schools in and about London and Westminster, June 6, 1716.

were equally well affected.[1] The Society, the loyalty of some of whose members was not beyond question, was profoundly disturbed. It deplored the behaviour of masters and scholars who "at this critical junction so freely Pray, Drink and Swear for a Popish Pretender"; it instructed its secretary to send out *questionnaires* to its country correspondents, whose replies suggest that disaffection was not considerable in the country districts, and it made a standing order that no person be admitted as a resident or corresponding member "unless the Society is satisfied of his having taken the oath that he is well affected to his Majesty King George and his Government". But the tempered exhortations of the Archbishop and the co-operation of the Society produced little effect.[2] When the trustees, forming the committee of the London charity schools, met to consider the Archbishop's injunctions much talk resulted in little wool. They examined and found guilty of disaffection and sedition the masters of the charity schools in St Anne's, Aldersgate, St Anne's, Westminster, and of Castle Baynard Ward, and recommended their dismissal to the managers. They rejected with indignation a charge brought against the Society of Schoolmasters as "Forg'd, False, Scandalous and malicious" and voted *nemine contradicente* that the schoolmasters in general were very well affected to King George and his Government, and they crowned their report by recommending that a handful of small boys should be whipped for wearing bows in their caps, or for begging money for bonfires, or for crying "High Church and Ormonde", or, because, after the manner of small boys, they had used "provoaking language".[3]

It would, however, be unwise to assume that this poor haul of victims was an adequate representation of the fish in the sea of disaffection. The general committee of trustees numbered among its

---

[1] S.P.C.K. Abs. of Correspondence, Aug. 21, 1716.

[2] S.P.C.K. Abs. of Correspondence, Aug. 21, 1716; Wake MSS. *loc. cit.* Extracts from several Letters showing the good affection to the present Government of the Persons employed in the Charity Schools; S.P.C.K. Minutes, Aug. 30, 1716.

[3] Wake MSS. Arch. W. Epist. 27. General Meeting of the Trustees of the Charity Schools in and about London and Westminster; the case of Thomas Wild, Master of the Charity School in Castle Baynard Ward, Nov. 2, 1716; punishments for the children engaged in the tumults; resolution of the trustees of the several charity schools [etc.]. See also S.P.C.K. Letters. Letter from Henry Newman to the Bishop of London, July 10, 1724; *The Evening Post*, Oct. 6–9, 1716; *The British Gazetteer*, Oct. 13, 1716.

members men who were clearly not unsympathetic to High Church tenets and whose loyalty to the Crown was not above suspicion. But, though it might, and indeed did, with the Archbishop's warning in mind, recommend the managers of the schools to deal faithfully with the disaffected teachers and children in their midst, it had no power to enforce its recommendation. Each school was a law to itself; no licence was required to teach the three R's, and school managers could choose whom they would without fear of interference from bishop and ordinary. The S.P.C.K., which had played a leading part in the establishment of the schools, could advise and persuade; it, too, had no power to enforce a policy on unwilling trustees, some of whom were members of its own body. It is therefore not surprising to find that the number of disaffected teachers was not identical with the several masters examined and reproved by the general committee. Within school minute-books are hidden the names of men and women dismissed for disaffection to the Crown and Government; the correspondence of the S.P.C.K. and paragraphs in the daily and weekly papers bring charges against others whose fate is unknown, and, if some of the charges lacked convincing references to chapter and verse, there are enough to support the contention that "charity school teachers were mischievous in dispersing their poison". In June and again in October the general committee of trustees recommended the dismissal of the master of Castle Baynard Ward school as one unfit to teach in any charity school, but in November the master, whose disaffection was notorious, was still in office, and, though the committee reported the matter to the Society, and the Society to the Archbishop, the school managers showed no disposition to remove him.[1]

Roused by the ineffectiveness of Archbishop and Society in controlling the trustees and teachers a drastic change in the government and administration of the schools was demanded by a body of Low

---

[1] "I send herewith a copy of the Minutes of the General Meeting of Trustees in Oct. 1716", wrote Henry Newman to the Bishop of London, Dr Edmund Gibson, in 1724, "by which your Lordship will see with what spirit they proceeded to censure some masters after they had acquitted all the masters in general at the beginning of their meeting, and Mr Parker of St Katherine's, and Mr Brewster of St Anne's, Blackfriars, are looked upon to this day by some people with an evil eye for the information they honestly gave on that occasion. And Mr Wild, one of the Masters, dismissed from his school, had his salary paid after his dismissal, and is now restored again." S.P.C.K. Letters, 1724.

Churchmen, whose memorial is a valuable commentary on the early history of the charity school movement. Recalling the happy beginnings, when Churchmen and Nonconformists had combined to set up and support the schools, they demanded that their present management by Jacobites and other disaffected persons should end, either by suppression of the schools, or by their complete reorganisation. The first of these two courses was in their opinion impolitic, since to turn thousands of helpless children into the streets would bring odium upon His Majesty's happy government, and an increase of popularity to the disaffected party. They proposed therefore, as the basis of reform, that the Crown should grant a charter incorporating persons whom His Majesty should think fit to be trustees and managers of the schools. To this body corporate, under the presidency of the Archbishop, should be entrusted the appointment and dismissal of teachers, the inspection of schools, the power to withhold permission to preach charity sermons, "poisoning the people with the utmost prejudices to their superiors in both Church and State", from all those who were not approved by His Grace as president; the supervision of all charity school funds, so as to secure benefactions from unreasonable defalcation and embezzlement, and finally, the right to levy a tax of twopence a cauldron on coals imported to London as a means of making up deficiencies from subscriptions and benefactions. If these reforms were introduced the petitioners confidently believed that many of the old subscribers, both Anglicans and Dissenters, who had withdrawn their interest because of the late disorders would renew their subscriptions.[1] But once again the Archbishop, who clearly disliked any scheme of reform which admitted even the thin edge of the wedge of State interference in the schools, disappointed his party. The plan of incorporation failed to secure his support. He contented himself by demanding from the chairman of the committee of trustees a promise that henceforward all persons exercising control over the schools should testify their fidelity and loyalty by making the following declaration: "I am fully satisfied of the just right of His Majesty King George to the Crown of these Realms and I will undertake by the Grace of God to behave myself, as it becomes a subject well affected to His said Majesty and His Government."

[1] Wake MSS. Arch. W. Epist. 15. Memorial Representing the Origin and Design of the Charity Schools [etc.].

Archbishop Wake failed to win his point. The committee of trustees replied that they thoroughly approved the proposal but were doubtful whether, at such a moment, it was prudent to propose it "lest it might be rejected", and the Archbishop wisely did not put the matter to the test. Instead he requested the S.P.C.K.[1] to consider the matter and to come to some resolution upon it. The Society printed the declaration in the *Annual Account of the Charity Schools* for the year 1718, and urged its residential and corresponding members to insist on its observance, but again in spite of the efforts of Primate and Society the conduct of the disaffected teachers continued to raise "jealousies among charitable benefactors". Teachers, it is true, were removed for disaffection, but, as the Society's correspondents lamented, there was little difference between those turned out and those put in their places.

Never were Jacobite hopes higher than in the summer of 1718. Two restless and discontented European powers were not unwilling to use the Jacobite cause as a pawn in their ambitious schemes. Elizabeth Farnese and Cardinal Alberoni promised Spanish help; Charles XII of Sweden, it was believed, would himself lead the Jacobite rising in England. Byng's victory over the Spanish fleet at Cape Passaro and Stanhope's diplomatic triumph in forming the Quadruple Alliance of England, France, Austria and Holland relieved the Government momentarily of anxiety from these two quarters. But the tension in England was nevertheless acute. Uncertainty is an unrivalled breeder of fear, and no one was in a position to estimate the Jacobite strength or to deny the possibility of Jacobite success. Atterbury, Bishop of Rochester, the recognised leader of the High Church party and the idol of the majority of the clergy, was strongly suspected by the Government of Jacobite intrigues, though it was not until later years that contemporary suspicions of his treasonable practices were proved to be well founded. "Certain relief is near at hand",[2] he wrote to Mar at the end of 1717, and as the tension increased, Whigs and Low Churchmen, searching for treason in all sorts and conditions of unlikely places, were not above manufacturing it when supplies were inadequate. While the kings and queens were too well watched to steal a move, the unhappy pawns were again dragged into action, this time by a frivolous case built up against the schools in general and that of St Anne's,

[1] S.P.C.K. Minutes, June 5, 1718; S.P.C.K. Abs. of Correspondence, May 22 and June 2, 1718.   [2] Doran, J., *London in Jacobite Times*, 1877, p. 299.

Aldersgate, in particular. Its managers had requested the rector of Chislehurst to allow them to send a detachment of the parish charity children, and a lecturer to preach on behalf of the school, to his church. This not unusual practice for raising funds would probably have passed unnoticed if St Anne's school had not already enjoyed unpleasing notoriety by the disaffection of its master, and if Atterbury had not been the rector of Chislehurst's diocesan. The combination of these two facts transformed the school's request and the rector's permission into a Jacobite plot. When the little contingent arrived at Chislehurst they were hauled before the High Sheriff of the county and two Whig justices, who, after demanding by what right they went strolling and begging through the country without a licence, detained one of the trustees in prison. At the end of the morning service in Chislehurst church, when the school's trustees carried round the patens for the collection, the two justices rose from their seats and forbade it. The congregation, whose sympathies were unmistakable, refused to obey; they too rose from their seats and flung their contributions into the plates, whereupon the justices, after an unseemly struggle, in which they tore the patens from the hands of the trustees and ordered the congregation, guilty of rioting, to disperse. The affair did not end there. The rector, the lecturer and the trustees were taken into custody and were bound over to appear at quarter sessions, but so great was the sympathy for the defendants that it was found impossible to bring in a true bill against them and the charge was left over until the next assizes. As it was obvious that no case of treason could lie against them, they were charged with unlawfully strolling up and down the country, and with conspiracy to extort unlawful charity to the sum of £3 in a parish of which they were not members. It was left to the counsel for the prosecution to reveal the true significance of the charge, in a speech which portrayed the disastrous effect upon the Hanoverian Settlement of this nefarious and illegal scheme of raising money which, if allowed to persist, would enable charity schools to "make head way against the Government". He begged the jury to bear in mind that though but £3 had been collected in the little parish of Chislehurst, if the ten thousand parishes of England made similar contributions, enough money would be raised to "bear the Chevalier's charges into Italy, and help him to consummate the marriage with the Princess Sobieski, upon whom he might get new Pretenders, to the great disquiet of the

Protestant interest". The case, said the judge, Sir Lyttleton Powys, had raised a question which was now answered; the defendants' plea that they had been given permission by bishop and incumbent to stroll about the country and collect money was disallowed; the Statutes 4 and 5 Anne, Chapter 14, were quoted against them; the collections had been made without lawful authority and heavy fines would in future be imposed upon those who should presume to offend in like manner. Although the court, by concentrating on this aspect of the case, disguised its real significance, there were few who failed to realise that if the Whig lawyers and justices had their way "they would suppress all the charity schools throughout England".[1]

Five years later the attack upon them was renewed with extreme vehemence by "Cato" in *The Independent Whig*, and by Bernard Mandeville in his famous essay *On Charity and Charity Schools*. Complaints of disaffection had not ceased in 1718, but the Chislehurst affair was a warning which the general committee of trustees could not ignore. They showed a greater willingness to co-operate with Primate and Society in removing "causes of jealousie", and even claimed that they were indispensable in securing the good behaviour of the teachers. In spite however of their greater circumspection, their Jacobite sympathies made the schools objects of suspicion, particularly at those times when Jacobite intrigues were rife. The immediate cause of the new outburst was the discovery of yet another Jacobite plot in 1722, in which Atterbury was clearly involved. The bursting in 1720 of the South Sea Bubble, bringing grave discredit on the Government, synchronised with the birth of a son to the Pretender and inflamed Jacobite hopes. During the summer of 1723 public excitement threatened a repetition of the Sacheverell disturbances. In the London churches prayers were offered for Atterbury; verses comparing him with Archbishop Laud, "Whose Christian courage nothing fears but God", were written in his honour, and pictures of him in prison, holding Laud's portrait in his hands, found eager buyers in the crowds

---

[1] Wake MSS. Arch. W. Epist. 27. Report, not dated, of the Chislehurst affair. See also Howell, T. B., *State Trials* [etc.], vol. xv, cols. 1407–22, and for a report of the trial, *The Weekly Journal*, Dec. 6, 1718. The best account of this remarkable affair is given by Daniel Defoe in his tract, *Charity still a Christian Virtue*, or *The Impartial Account of the Trial and Conviction of the Rev. Mr Hendley for Preaching at Chislehurst* [n.d.].

who thronged to see him pass from the Tower to his trial in West-minster. When the trial was over and the High Anglican party were discredited by their leader's treasonable intrigues, Mandeville and "Cato" focused attention upon the contribution of the charity schools to the prevalent disaffection. Before 1723 the struggle for the control of the schools between High and Low Churchmen had been waged in semi-obscurity. Now, the envenomed pens of the most widely read publicists of the time dragged the schools into the full light of day and prepared the way for a bitter controversy in press and pamphlet throughout the summer months of 1723. "Cato" in *The British Journal* played his heavy artillery directly upon the High Church party, whose "newfangled charity" he denounced as a threat to public security by debauching the principles of the common people. "They are taught, as soon as they can speak, to babble out 'High Church and Ormonde', they are bred up traytors before they know what Treason signifies." No longer, he asserted, was there a dread of popery, for a corrupt section of the clergy had successfully used the schools to undermine the fear of Rome and to threaten the Revolution and the Establishment. The managers were denounced as "staunch Jacobites or furious High Churchmen", often of debauched lives and principles, and they em-ployed as teachers men who manufactured the ringleaders of the city mobs, and bred up the children to fight the Pretender's battles.[1]

Opprobrium so unmeasured defeated its own ends. Low Churchmen who had helped to found the schools, High Churchmen who had captured them, trustees who managed them, and subscribers who financed them, shared the common indignation provoked by "Cato's" attack. While they girt up their loins to defend the schools the Grand Jury of Middlesex presented authors, publishers and printers of *The British Journal* for libel, "as blasphemously reflecting upon God and Religion in general, scurrilously exposing and traducing the great Duty of Christian Charity to the Scandal and Offence of all pious and well dispos'd Christians, but more particularly villifying and traducing the

---

[1] *The British Journal*, June 15, 1723. Under the pseudonym of "Cato", John Trenchard, sometimes alone and sometimes in collaboration with his amanuensis Thomas Gordon, published *The Independent Whig* and wrote in *The London Journal* and *The British Journal*. The two men were bitter and consistent opponents of the High Church Party; see *The Fable of the Bees, or Private Vices, Public Benefits*, by Bernard Mandeville, ed. F. B. Kaye, 2 vols., Oxford 1924.

members of the Church of England for their excellent piety in contributing to erect and maintain Charity Schools for the Instruction and Education of Poor Children, a Design so good and so much tending to the Honour of God and the Service and Glory of our Country, so universally applauded and practised by almost the whole Body of Dissenters themselves as the most laudable institution of the best of Charity, which this Libeller has endeavoured maliciously to insinuate and represent as impious seminaries, set up to threaten the Publick, introduce Popery, to carry on the Pretender's interest by these poor innocent children bred up in no other Principles but the plain doctrines of Christianity, which all the Kingdom knows. We therefore present the same as a most insolent, malicious, scandalous Libel to receive such condign Punishment as in Justice it deserves."[1]

The London press drove home the attack of the Grand Jury. *The British Gazetteer*, indignantly repudiating "Cato's" statements, asked him to prove his assertions. "We have had", it stated, "the opportunity of being acquainted with the Directors of more than one [of the schools] and know several honest and worthy persons who would abhor the thought of supporting anything that had the least tendency towards either disloyalty or faction." *The Saturday Post* reported in full, and with warm approval, the Grand Jury's presentment. *Appleby's Weekly* applauded it, and hoped that some public course would be taken to punish the offenders. *The London Journal* on July 21st deplored the attempt "to discourage one of the noblest instances of charity" because of the behaviour of "silly masters and mistresses seven years ago", and the following week entered the lists again by challenging "Cato" to produce a single disaffected master or mistress. "If any one master be suffered by the Trustees to continue in any School against whom Proof can be brought that he is disaffected to the Government, or that he does not as faithfully teach the children obedience and loyalty to the King...then I will gratify Catiline with a licence to pull down the Schools and hang up the Masters." "Philo-Britannicus" on July 27th defended the schools as "one of the greatest instruments of Religion and Virtue, one of the purest Bulwarks against Popery, one of the best Recommendations of the people to Divine Favour". "Cato's" attack on clergy and schools, he pointed out, was inspired by hostility to

[1] *The Report on the Presentment of the Grand Jury of the Co. of Middlesex* on July 3, 1723, is printed in full in *The Saturday Post* for July 20, 1723.

religion. Christianity was attacked under the guise of defending Protestantism. *The Saturday Post* on the same day devoted more than half its columns to an able leading article in defence of charity schools, finding in them the surest bulwark against Rome, and the only means of securing equality of opportunity for the poor, and attributed the onslaught upon them to "free thinkers, fanatics and atheists", who were "inspired by their conviction that charity schools strengthen the Church of England".[1]

Greater and more sustained opprobrium overwhelmed Bernard Mandeville and his contribution. *The Fable of the Bees*, by which poem he is most widely known, had created little stir when it was first published in 1714. Its second edition in 1723 became the book of the day, and remained a favourite object of vituperation from the pulpit for over a hundred years. Its sudden fame, as Mandeville lugubriously admitted, was due, not to the intrinsic merits of the poem, but to the fact that it was bound up in the same cover as his essay *On Charity and Charity Schools*, whose attack on the most popular form of philanthropy brought press and pulpit, trustees and teachers and the vast army of subscribers into the lists against him. The essay emphasised the social and economic rather than the political dangers of popular education, but in it Mandeville held up the schools' supporters to ridicule and contempt. *The Bees* had made an attack on virtue and religion for the intelligentsia, "who can think abstractedly"; the essay was a brutally plain statement which did not require learning to be understood. Under the sting of his whip the *Vulgus*, whom he despised, counter-attacked in their turn and Mandeville found himself confronted by two popular forces working in unison, the popular enthusiasm for the Church and the popular enthusiasm for philanthropy. Nothing is more remarkable in the vehement controversy of 1723 than the easy victory of the schools and their supporters against their redoubtable antagonists. By the end of July "Cato" had ignominiously retired from the editorship of *The Independent Whig*, and in August Mandeville, whose book, like "Cato's" journal, had been presented by the Middlesex Grand Jury as a common nuisance, was driven into a public vindication of his works in *The London Journal*, in which he protested that he had been misrepresented. The attack on the schools had failed.[2]

[1] *The British Gazetteer*, June 22 and 29, 1723; *The Saturday Post*, July 27, 1723; *Appleby's Weekly*, July 20, 1723; *The London Journal*, July 20, 1723.
[2] See *The British Journal*, Aug. 3, 1723 and *The London Journal*, Aug. 10, 1723.

There is however seldom smoke without fire; popular indignation roused by the unmerciful attack on their clerical supporters obscured the fact that the schools had been, for over a decade, an object of suspicion to the Low Church party and to the Whig Government. That they were instruments of religion and virtue was not contested; that the religion and virtue inculcated was of the desirable Hanoverian brand was less clear, nor was it unlikely, after the recent spectacular vindication of the schools, that disaffection which, as their supporters now admitted, had tarnished the loyalty of the schools would not be again a matter of concern to the Government and the Establishment.[1]

The opportunity was not given to disaffection to dig itself in. While the Government was preparing to take action against Atterbury, Edmund Gibson, staunchest of Hanoverian bishops, was translated from Lincoln to London. The man and the moment had arrived to root out sedition from the schools for ever. The menace of Popery could in Dr Gibson's opinion be met and overcome only by the united action of Protestants great and small, old and young, against the common foe. This time there were to be no half measures, no circuitous approach through disaffected school trustees. As one of the earliest members of the S.P.C.K. he shared the views of his friend Dr White Kennett and his master Archbishop Tenison in the function of the charity schools as "little Anglican garrisons against Popery".[2] As rector of Lambeth and as canon of Chichester he possessed first-hand knowledge of the value of the schools to the Church and their need of control. In his Lincoln diocese he followed in Archbishop Wake's footsteps, devoting time and energy to the movement for their establishment. The two hundred schools which Wake returned to the Society in 1714 steadily increased in number during Gibson's episcopate. The sermon preached by him at the anniversary meeting of the London charity schools, in 1716, on *The peculiar Excellence and Reward of Supporting Schools of Charity*, left no doubt in the minds of his hearers that the function of the schools was to instruct the children "not to speak evil of persons, but to

[1] S.P.C.K. Letters, Letter of Henry Newman to the Bishop of London, Jan. 27, 1718–19.

[2] Kennett, White, *Sermon preached at the Anniversary Meeting of the Charity Schools in and about the Cities of London and Westminster*, May 16, 1706.

reverence authority, and pay all duty honour and obedience to the powers that are".[1]

The Bishop's new office placed him not only in control of the most important see in the kingdom, but, as the relations between Archbishop Wake and the Government became colder and more estranged, made him also an "active partner in the firm of Townshend and Walpole".[2] The partnership which, in Gibson's words, was based on "the clear Church Whig bottom" of "the Protestant succession, the Church Establishment and the Toleration"[3] lasted until "the Imperious Hildebrand the Second" in 1736 refused to sacrifice his church to his party.[4]

In 1723 the Government and its ecclesiastical adviser were of one mind in their determination to secure the pious nurseries as "a bulwark and defence of our Reformation". To Lord Townshend, Secretary of State, Dr Gibson proposed in his office as Bishop of London "to take some notice of the Charity Schools in the city and diocese and the masters and mistresses of them, that they might at least be sensible that they were under inspection, and be more cautious in giving offence to the Government". He would, he said, summon them to the Chapter House of St Paul's and would there deliver to them a "well considered charge". Townshend approved the proposal as one which tended extremely to the good of the Church and the service of His Majesty's Government, and the Bishop called together all the masters and mistresses of the London charity schools which were in his diocese, and harangued them on their duties to the Church and the Government. The usefulness of the schools in promoting religion and virtue was, he pointed out, so manifest that it must be the wish of all serious and good men to see them flourish and increase. If therefore abuses or corruption of any kind could be found among them, the course that prudence and piety directed was to reform the abuse, but not to destroy the institution. The rapid multiplication of the schools in all parts of the kingdom had made them a "National Concern", hence "it behoves them that while they are promoting the ends of religion they give no

[1] Gibson, E., *Sermon preached at the Anniversary Meeting of the Charity Schools in and about the Cities of London and Westminster*, May 24, 1716.

[2] Sykes, N., *Edmund Gibson, Bishop of London, 1667–1748. A Study in the Politics and Religion of the Eighteenth Century*, 1926, p. 83.

[3] Gibson MSS. IV, 32, quoted in Sykes, *op. cit.* p. 408.

[4] Bishop Gibson Pamphlets, XV, 16, Sion College Library.

jealousy of any kind to the Civil Government". In particular the schools in the two Cities of London and Westminster, from which the rest took their rise, and which were more immediately under the Eye of the Government than schools in other parts, should be a pattern to the rest. And yet complaints had reached him of "Inconveniences and Abuses" in both city and country schools. He had called together the teachers to consider these objections and to remove them by drafting rules for their future conduct which could leave no reasonable ground for complaint.

The first part of Bishop Gibson's discourse dealt faithfully with the dangerous tendency to introduce social experiments which would set the children above the mean and more laborious status and offices of life. More serious—"a heavy objection indeed and a point that the Government was nearly concerned to look after"—was the charge of disaffection levelled against the schools. "I hope and believe that there is not at present the like ground to complain of Disaffection in our Charity Schools as there was some years ago. While the Protestant Succession remained doubtful and no stone was left unturned to defeat it, some Persons, who had their views a different way though otherwise Virtuous and Good Men, endeavoured to get the Management of the Charity Schools into their own Hands and to make them instrumental in nourishing and spreading an Aversion to the Protestant Succession." The misconduct of teachers and children was then notorious; but much of that leaven had now, in the Bishop's opinion, worked out. "For some years past the Behaviour of the Children had been in the main inoffensive and the teachers have studied to give proofs of their sincere affection to the Government." As long as they continued in this way the Government would protect them, but unless it could be assured that a succession of disaffected persons was not "perpetually nursing in our schools" it would not long tolerate such places of education. This judicious criticism, assuring his hearers that bygones would be bygones, enlisted them on the side of authority. It was followed by the Bishop's proposals for a future regulation of the schools which would purge them from all suspicion of disaffection to the Government. To this end the children were to pray constantly in morning and evening prayers for the king and royal family by name, adding these or like words: "We beseech Thee also to pour down thy Blessings in a plenteous manner upon our Gracious Sovereign King George and upon all the Royal Family. Grant that he may enjoy a long and happy Reign over us and that there may never be wanting one descended from him to sit upon his Throne and to preserve the True Religion in these Nations."

All marks of disrespect to the king and royal family were to be discouraged, whether they appeared by words or songs or pictures, and punishments for such offences were to be given "in such a public manner as may both justify the schools from the Imputation of Disloyalty and make the Offender an Example to the rest". No opportunity was to be lost of possessing the minds of the children with a "just and favourable impression of the King, his Family and Administration, or of giving them a just impression of the Terrors of a Popish Reign and of the persecution and cruelties which Protestants are to expect under a Popish Prince". Finally, oblivious of the contradiction his recommendations involved, the Bishop counselled the teachers to inculcate in the children "the Sinfulness of disturbing the Government, and the folly as well as the Sinfulness of meddling with matters which do not belong to them and which are so far above them", and he warned the teachers that their conduct would not in future lack supervision. "I shall think it my duty to make enquiry from time to time into the conduct and behaviour of the several masters and mistresses."[1]

Dr Gibson's charge, intended for the schools in his own diocese, was spread far and wide by the agency of the S.P.C.K. Every school connected with the Society received a copy, and with it a letter, desiring the cultivation of a proper spirit of loyalty. Where Wake had failed Gibson succeeded. Writing four years later Dr Isaac Watts, a vigorous critic of the disaffected Anglican schools, accepted the Bishop's statement that much of the "Leaven of Disaffection", formerly in the schools, had "worked out".[2] For the remaining three-quarters of the century the Society, in its published reports, directed the trustees to give instruction to the children in their duty to the Hanoverian king, and, from time to time, ecclesiastics in charity sermons reminded the schools that they were still the bulwark and defence of the Reformation, but the need of such instruction and commendation lapsed when Jacobitism ceased to menace the Protestant Succession. The schools which had

---

[1] *Directions given by Edmund, Lord Bishop of London, to the Masters and Mistresses of the Charity Schools, within the Bills of Mortality and Diocese of London, assembled for that purpose in the Chapter House of St Paul's*, Nov. 14, 1724. Reported in full in *The Daily Courant* for Monday, Nov. 16, 1724.

[2] Watts, Isaac, *op. cit.* p. 45.

10

strayed were, by the combined efforts of the Bishop and the Society, brought safely back to the Hanoverian fold, and were not allowed to wander again.

> "Well fed, well taught, array'd in godly zeal,
>   To serve our Holy Church and Commonweal"[1]

was henceforth the children's duty. They learnt their lesson well. Not even the Rebellion of 1745 produced more than a ripple of excitement among pupils and teachers.

III

THE NONCONFORMIST REACTION

While Jacobitism left little mark on the internal history of the schools after the Bishop of London's effective purging, the struggle to control them permanently affected the English charity school movement. Its influence was clearly shown in the gradual withdrawal of the S.P.C.K. from the part which it had hitherto played in the movement. Already perturbed by the social and economic criticism of its work, and anxious to avoid political complications within its own body, which included members of both High and Low Church parties, it turned, with a growing enthusiasm, to missionary work abroad, and to its publishing work at home, neither of which involved politics. Even more noticeable was the estrangement of Low Church supporters of the schools after the temporary success of Jacobite intrigues, and of High Church supporters when Jacobite hopes collapsed, which deprived the movement of two main sources of supply. Last and most important in its permanent effect was the split which it established between Church and Dissent in the business of elementary education, which has not since been healed. Many Dissenters, who had given generous support to the Anglican schools, withdrew both pupils and subscriptions and, when they could afford to do so, opened schools attached to their own Churches.[2]

---

[1] *Charity in Perfection this side Heaven, or the Great Happiness and Advantage of Erecting Charity Schools.* A Poem, by J. B., under-master of the Charity School at St Alban's, Holborn, 1716. In Sion College Library, 45. A. 6, No. 4.

[2] S.P.C.K. Abs. of Correspondence, Nov. 14, 1716; Jan. 21, 1716–7; *Letter Book,* xx, July 28, 1730.

The bitter attack upon the Dissenters in Anne's reign made a breach in the friendly co-operation of Church and Dissent in the education of the children of the poor which had characterised the last years of the seventeenth century. So great was "the enmity in the charity schools towards Dissenters" that the distinguished Nonconformist Matthew Henry, minister of Mare Street Meeting House, Hackney, urged his fellow Nonconformists to follow the example of the Established Church and set up charity schools of their own, in which charity and moderation would be taught to all and evil overcome by good. His death in 1714, synchronising with the passing of the Schism Act, which forbade any person to keep a public or private school unless he were a member of the Church of England, wrecked his scheme of organised effort.[1]

The Dissenters' charity schools expressed the determination of ardent and devoted Nonconformists to provide instruction for the children of the poor of their communions in schools maintained and controlled by them. The few records which remain show that their supporters were affected by the same passions for godly piety and godly discipline which moved the supporters of the Anglican charity schools. Fear of Rome and distrust of High Anglican pretensions were even more acute. The school in Gravel Lane, Southwark, was the answer of the Nonconformists to the Roman peril in the last years of the reign of James II. The school in Shakespeare Walk, Ratcliffe Highway, originally in the parish of St Paul's, Shadwell, was set up by voluntary subscribers in 1712, "out of compassion, and benevolence and from a zeal for the maintenance of religious liberty". The school at Horsely Down, Southwark, was the symbol of the united protest of Baptists, Independents and Presbyterians against the exclusiveness of High Church policy at the end of Anne's reign, "when Churchmen refused to Dissenters the right of openly teaching their own children how to worship God".[2]

[1] Henry, Rev. Matthew, *Reasons for Promoting the Interest of Charity Schools* [n.d.].
[2] See *Sermons preached by the Rev. Samuel Chandler for the benefit of the Charity School in Gravel Lane, Southwark, Jan. 1728, and by the Rev. Peter Robinson for the benefit of the Protestant Dissenting Charity School at Horsely Down, March 3, 1779;* see also Bourne, M. A., in *The Educational Record,* Feb. 1902, and Ivimey, J., *History of the English Baptists,* 1824, vol. III, p. 116.

After the repeal of the Schism Act in 1718 the pillars of Nonconformity, Isaac Watts, Samuel Chandler and Philip Doddridge, again encouraged the establishment of Nonconformist charity schools in which children would be in no danger of learning to hate the present Government or "to rail at the Protestant Succession, which is the Glory of Great Britain the Defence of the Reformed Religion and the securest guard of the Liberties of Europe".[1] The number of Dissenters' charity schools set up as a result of these and similar appeals is not known. Thirty-eight non-Anglican endowed schools were returned by the Commissioners of Inquiry Concerning Charities in the early part of the nineteenth century.[2] To this small total, schools which were not financed by endowments must be added. As Dissenters were for the most part "poor folk", and the subscription school was the school of the philanthropic poor man, it may safely be asserted that the subscription school was the type commonly favoured by the Dissenting Churches, few of which could afford to provide clothing, as did the Anglican schools, for their scholars.[3] Unfortunately no collective returns similar to those of the Anglican societies testify to their number and extent. The schools whose existence is recorded in sermons preached on their behalf, or in the local histories of parishes in London, Bristol, Downend, St Albans, Mangotsfield, Northampton, Ribchester, Calne, Pulton and Daventry, represent a remembered few out of a greater number whose names are forgotten.

Lack of associated effort and the apathy which characterised the Nonconformist Churches in the first half of the eighteenth century prevented the rapid advance of Nonconformist charity schools which might have been expected when the danger which had threatened Nonconformity in Anne's reign was removed, but the exaggerated autonomy which regulated the life of the older Dissenting congregations in the eighteenth century precluded any form of associated effort, other than for prayer and the exchange of religious experiences. To some of them association was regarded as fatal to civil and religious liberty. Nor except for the Society of London Ministers of the Three Denominations, whose interests were mainly political, was there organised co-operation between the sects. Hence the famous school at Horsely Down, Southwark, the combined effort of the three leading

[1] Watts, Isaac, op. cit. p. 44. [2] See Appendix I, sect. 3.
[3] Watts, Isaac, op. cit. p. 41.

Nonconformist denominations, stands as a rare eighteenth-century example of Nonconformist association for elementary education.[1]

A more serious handicap to the development of Nonconformist charity schools for the children of the poor was the concentration of Dissenting interest upon the provision of higher education. The heavy financial obligations of members of the Nonconformist churches made some at least among them unwilling to shoulder further responsibilities. For, in addition to the upkeep of their fabrics, and the maintenance of their ministers, they were obliged, since penal legislation and university statutes had closed the doors of the universities to conscientious Dissenters, to provide other means for the training of young men for their ministries.[2] The Dissenting academies, in which candidates for the ministry and, as time went on, an increasing number of lay pupils, received an education not only in the established classical curriculum of grammar school and university, but also in modern studies, were the characteristic contribution of Nonconformity to education in the eighteenth century.[3] It absorbed "great contributions" in money and in personal effort. Instruction in the elements to the children of the poor appeared, in comparison, unimportant. There were Nonconformists, as Isaac Watts lamented, who saw no reason why the poor should not send their children to the Anglican schools in the parish which offered not only education but clothing and apprenticeship fees as well. The difference, they held, was "not so great or so formidable, but that the poor should be willing to accept of such an Education for their Children, since they were not able to bring them up without the Charity of others",[4] and it became increasingly difficult, as the religious animosities of the early years of the century evaporated, to arouse the rank and

---

[1] Ivimey, J., *op. cit.* vol. IV, p. 39; vol. III, p. 116.

[2] "At Oxford members were required on admission to subscribe to the Thirty-Nine Articles and to take the oath of Supremacy. On taking a degree this had to be repeated, with the addition of subscription to the three Articles of the Thirty-Sixth Canon. At Cambridge admissions were free but in order to proceed to the degrees of B.A., B.C.L., or B.M. a declaration was required in the form 'I, A.B., do declare that I am a bonâ fide member of the Church of England'. While for all other degrees it was necessary to subscribe to the three Articles of the Thirty Sixth Canon." Bellot, H. H., *University College, London, 1826–1926*, p. 5.

[3] See Parker, I., *Dissenting Academies in England*, 1914; McLachlan, H., *English Education under the Test Acts, 1662–1820*, 1931.

[4] Watts, Isaac, *op. cit.* p. 42.

file of the Dissenters to the defence of religious liberty by the provision of schools for the children of their poor. Strong centres of Nonconformity, such as Bristol and Northampton, where the Dissenting congregations were large and the Churches prosperous, managed to maintain their schools, but it may be doubted whether the number of Dissenting charity schools was considerable throughout the greater part of the eighteenth century.[1] When Methodism regenerated the older Nonconforming Churches and revived the interest in education, schools, financed in whole or in part by charity, were set up by them. Their number and their strength were not realised until their supporters succeeded in forcing the withdrawal of Lord Brougham's bill in 1820 for the provision of a system of rate-aided schools, controlled by the clergy of the Established Church, and in riveting the system of voluntaryism upon elementary education. It is not possible to estimate the number of these schools in the later years of the eighteenth century, but that they were both numerous and widespread appears incontestable.

[1] At Bristol "The Presbyterians raised a fund of £4,000 by voluntary subscriptions for erecting a charity school for Cloathing, Dieting, and Apprenticing the children". This was the Stokes Croft School. *See* S.P.C.K. Abs. of Correspondence, June 27, 1721.

CHAPTER V

ENGLAND

CHARITY AND THE RELIGIOUS REVIVALS

"It is the discipline of the heart more than the instruction of the head for which Sunday Schools are chiefly valuable."
Letter of the Bishop of Chester, Dr Beilby Porteus, to the Clergy of the Diocese, 1785.

I

METHODISM

In the early years of the eighteenth century the charity school movement under the guidance of the Society for Promoting Christian Knowledge held out promise of establishing elementary education as "a national concern",[1] but the twofold attack upon the schools by critics of their curricula and religious partisans, and the withdrawal of active interest in the movement by the Society slowed down the pace of the early years. Before it could recover from this set-back two of the most powerful forces of the eighteenth century, in unison, dealt a heavy blow at the attempts to establish an adequate number of day schools for the children of the poor, by deflecting public interest from the schools.

It is remarkable that the influential and highly organised Methodist Societies made, during the eighteenth century, little direct contribution to the movement for popular instruction. Throughout the first thirty years of the century a handful of earnest and conscientious laymen and clerics had slowly, and with difficulty, built up a tradition of popular instruction. In establishing that tradition an Anglican Society had played a conspicuous part, but Methodism made no organised attempt

---

[1] Gibson, E., *Directions given by Edmund, Lord Bishop of London, to the Masters and Mistresses of Charity Schools, within the Bills of Mortality and Diocese of London, assembled for that purpose in the Chapter House of St Paul's*, Nov. 14, 1724.

to carry on the old tradition, and played but a secondary part in initiating the new tradition of Sunday school instruction.

Yet no two men in the England of their age were more alive than were John Wesley and George Whitefield to the neglected condition of the children of the poor. In the early years of their long ministries they shared the interest and enthusiasm of their pious contemporaries for the education of poor children. At Epworth and Wroot in the Isle of Axholm, John Wesley witnessed one of the early efforts of a parish minister to set up charity schools for the catechetical instruction of the children.[1] Whitefield was an early member of the S.P.C.K., and Thomas Broughton, from 1743 to 1777 secretary to the Society, was the mutual friend of both men. The Holy Club at Oxford evinced the same interest in practical piety that its prototypes, the old religious societies of William and Mary's reign, had done. Its members cared for the sick and prisoners and for the children of the poor, some of them going into the villages and "calling the children together and teaching them their prayers and their catechism".[2] Wesley, his friend Gambold relates, opened a school in Oxford where the children were taught to say the catechism and to knit and spin; he paid the schoolmistress and clothed some of the children,[3] and, on his journey from the Moravian settlement at Herrnhut, in 1723, he made a detour to visit Hermann Francke's son at Halle. He recorded in his *Journal* the impression left upon his mind by the famous orphanage and school, in whose likeness he planned the Orphan House at Newcastle.[4] Whitefield, in 1736, took charge of the two or three small charity schools in Oxford maintained by the Methodists, and when his fame as a preacher spread abroad was "constantly applied to", by churchwardens and school managers of charity schools in London and elsewhere, to preach for the benefit of the children. "The Blue coat boys and girls", his *Journal* relates, "looked upon me as their great benefactor", for he had the power, even greater than that with which Mandeville had endowed the wearers of lawn sleeves, to loosen the purse-strings of his hearers. "People gave so

[1] S.P.C.K. Papers, An Account of the Religious Society begun in Epworth in the Isle of Axholm, Feb. 1, 1701-2; see also *Speculum Diœceseos Lincolniensis sub Episcopis Gul. Wake et Edm. Gibson*, Part I, pp. 157, 175.

[2] Wedgwood, J., *John Wesley and the Evangelical Reaction of the Eighteenth Century*, 1870, p. 56.

[3] Tyerman, L., *The Oxford Methodists*, 1873, pp. 158-9.

[4] Wesley, J., *Journals*, ed. N. Curnoch, 1909-13, vol. II, pp. 50-52.

liberally to the charity schools", he reported in 1737, "that this season nearly £1000 was collected at the several churches, besides many more contributions and subscriptions sent in."[1]

Their interest did not end here. Both men were concerned in the effort to set up an Orphan House in Georgia, where they had found, on their missionary journeys, many children in miserable circumstances, without education, "hurt by bad examples, and hard services". "I thought", said Whitefield, "that I could not better show my regard to God and my country than by getting a house and land for these children, where they might learn to labour, read and write, and, at the same time be brought up in the nurture and admonition of the Lord."[2] At Kingswood the two friends co-operated in setting up a charity school for the children of the colliers, "a race of wild fierce savages", whose name was a terror to the inhabitants of Bristol, since "they feared not God neither regarded man".[3] Here the children were taught to read, write and cast accounts, and "more especially by God's assistance to know God and Jesus Christ whom he hath sent".[4] But the personal interest of the founders of Methodism during their early years in the education of the poor was not transformed by them into an organised effort to provide schools for the children. Nowhere in their diaries and correspondence is there evidence of the conviction with which the S.P.C.K. inaugurated its work "that the Glory of God and the good of mankind could not be more universally and effectually secured than by an organised attempt to erect schools for the children of the poor". The idea of a national system of schools, on a parochial basis, apparently engaged the minds of Wesley and Whitefield as little as the crying need for improvement in the condition of the inferior clergy.[5]

The explanation of this lack of organised effort on the part of a society which, in great part, owed its amazing influence to its masterly and efficient organisation, is not to be found in indifference to the

[1] Whitefield, G., *Journal*, ed. W. Wale, 1905, pp. 67, 80, 81.
[2] Tyerman, L., *Life of the Rev. George Whitefield*, 1890, vol. 1, p. 348.
[3] Wedgwood, J., *op. cit.* p. 180.
[4] Wesley, J., *Journals*, Nov. 27, 1739; see also Whitefield, G., *Journal*, under date March 29, 1739. The charity school set up at Kingswood for the colliers and other inhabitants of the village should not be confused with Kingswood School, with which Wesley's name is intimately connected. It was opened in 1748 and provided education of a secondary character, at a charge of £14 p.a.
[5] Southey, R., *Life of John Wesley*, 1820, p. 176.

spiritual and moral welfare of the children. Their condition continually called forth expressions of distress from philanthropic members of the Society, and it is inconceivable that men bent, as were Wesley and Whitefield, and their vast band of followers, on the saving of souls could have been careless of the children. Lack of funds, in its turn, cannot be urged as an explanation. It is true that in the eighteenth century Methodism drew the bulk of its followers from the poorer classes, some of whom could with difficulty contribute the weekly penny to the Class, but, almost from the beginning, and increasingly so in the course of the century, it made an appeal to the middle and professional, and to the upper classes, who could well have contributed to any organised effort. In Wales Griffith Jones, a personal friend of Whitefield, whose work was well known both to him and Wesley, had established a system of "locomotive schools" throughout the length and breadth of the country, "without any settled fund visible",[1] and what Griffith Jones could do in "poor Wales" the two great Methodists could have done in England.

Nor was other-worldliness an explanation. The deep and intense spiritual awareness of the Methodists did not detract from their interest in temporal matters. They were bidden by their founder to improve the present hour. "Above all things", was Wesley's urgent plea, "do not make the care of future things a pretence for neglecting present duty."[2] The old puritan ideal of diligence in daily work and austerity in personal conduct, which they made their own, demanded concentration on the things of this world, and the steadily improving economic and social status of this new body of puritans was proof that they were not without temporal rewards.

The lack of organised effort in the establishment of schools for the children of the poor was due in the main to the concentration of reforming zeal upon the adult, in the belief that it was the quicker and more certain method of national regeneration. This is clearly stated by the Countess of Huntingdon, whose two charity schools at Ashley and Markfield were discontinued after 1742. "Many things agreeing", she wrote in a letter to Wesley, "have determined me to lay aside the school at Markfield, and for that end I have discharged the school-masters. It is but too plain the time has not yet come. . . . I believe longer experience,

[1] Whitefield, G., *Journal*, March 9, 1739.
[2] Wesley, J., *Collected Works*, ed. 1872, vol. v, p. 390.

with much better observation will prove this an undeniable truth, that a school will never answer the end of bringing forth any of the Gospel fruits of holiness till the parents are first made Christians. The parents must lay up for the children, not the children for the parents."[1]

It is significant, as testifying to Wesley's support of this opinion, that the Orphan House at Newcastle housed no orphan children. The forty poor children and their teachers for whom the trust deeds of the establishment provided "never had an existence save in the intentions of Wesley". "There is a clause", replied the trustees to a demand for information from the Charitable Trusts Commission in 1855, "referring to the education of forty poor children, but this does not appear, so far as any certain information can be obtained, ever to have been carried into effect during Mr Wesley's lifetime."[2] The House, fitted up with pulpit and forms and classrooms, and used as a preaching house, demonstrates the switching of interest from the infant to the adult poor. Not until the Methodist organisation for the salvation and reform of the adult was complete did Methodism turn with enthusiasm to the cause of popular education.

The concentration of interest on the adult did not, however, mean that the spiritual and moral regeneration of the children was neglected. Far from it. If it is not possible to point to any considerable number of charity day schools set up by the Methodists in the second half of the eighteenth century, nor to claim for them a vigorous initiation of the Sunday school movement, it is not difficult to attest their concern for the religious instruction of the children. Parents who joined the Society were expected "to lay up for their children". It was their duty to see that the lessons in the Methodist hand-book, *The Instruction for Children*, were learned by the children, just as it was the duty of the preachers, in their visits to the homes or in the class, to test the children's work. Where there were as many as ten children in a class the preachers were bidden twice at least, every week, to meet them. "Do this", they

---

[1] *The Life and Times of Selina, Countess of Huntingdon*, 1840, vol. I, p. 51.
[2] Stamp, W. W., *The Orphan House of Wesley*, 1863, pp. 16, 228. This statement is not strictly true. A letter of Wesley to Atmore in the *Wesleyan Methodist Magazine*, 1848, states that a Sunday school of 800 children was held in the Orphan House in 1799.

were urged, "not in a dull, dry, formal manner, but in earnest with your might."[1] Upon parents and preachers rested the duty of teaching the children to read the Bible and other religious literature. Such a method of "direct, immediate and palpable utility", as Southey called it, goes a long way to explain the remarkable growth of a reading public at the end of the century, to which contemporaries bear witness.[2]

A second factor, explaining the lack of organised educational effort, is to be found in the characteristic Methodist attitude towards philanthropy. On no aspect of social life was John Wesley's teaching more powerful and explicit than upon the duty of regarding the possession of this world's goods as a trust held from God. "The Christian was instructed that he was entitled to supply his own reasonable wants together with those of his family," says a recent writer on the movement, "but beyond this he had no further defensible claim to use property for his own desires."[3] The remainder, in accordance with Wesley's teaching, was to be delivered to God, through the poor. Their wants were to be supplied out of that part of God's substance which he had placed in their hands for this purpose. Again and again in his writings and addresses does he stress the moral function of property. Not a tenth, nor a half, nor three-quarters, but all surplus wealth

---

[1] Minutes of the Methodist Conference first held in London by the late John Wesley in 1744, Aug. 12, 1766.

[2] To the growth of a reading public at the end of the eighteenth century James Lackington, bookseller and publisher, bears remarkable testimony: "I cannot help observing that the sale of books has increased prodigiously within the last twenty years. According to the best estimation I have been able to make I suppose that more than four times the number of books are now sold than were sold twenty years since. The poorer sort of farmers and even the poor country people in general who before that period spent their winter evenings in relating stories of witches, hobgoblins, etc., now shorten the nights by hearing their sons and daughters read tales, romances etc., and on entering their houses you may see Tom Jones, Roderick Random, and other entertaining books stuck upon their bacon-racks etc., and if John goes to town with a load of hay he is charged to be sure not to forget to bring home Peregrine Pickle's adventures and when Dolly is sent to market to sell her eggs she is commissioned to purchase the history of Pamela Andrews. In short all ranks and degrees now read." From *Memoirs of the First Forty Years of the Life of James Lackington*, 1791, p. 350.

[3] Warner, W. J., *The Wesleyan Movement and the Industrial Revolution*, 1930, p. 208.

remaining after the necessities of life had been provided for were to be given to those in need of it. "Those who fail to do so", said Wesley in one of the most powerful of his addresses, "are not only robbing God, continually embezzling and wasting their Lord's goods, and by that very means corrupting their own souls, but also robbing the poor, the hungry, and the naked, wronging the widows and the fatherless, and making themselves accountable for all the want, affliction and distress which they may, but do not remove."[1]

This characteristic emphasis upon the social duty of charity among Christians was united with an equally characteristic emphasis on the methods to be employed. Highly organised and efficient control was necessary if the Gospel was to be carried, without delay, to those that sat in darkness and in the shadow of death, but philanthropy did not require organised control and direction; it was a personal matter, dependent on the spirit of the giver. Men "hungering and thirsting to do good" should be left to fix their own measures and methods. It was expressly directed that whatever was done should be done "in as secret and unostentatious manner as is possible".[2] A disposition rather than an organisation for philanthropy was thus established, which explains, in great part, the generous support of members of the Methodist Connection for the amelioration of human distress, whether that of poverty, or sickness, or imprisonment, or slavery; it explains, too, the lack of organised effort in tackling any of the leading social problems of the age.

The combination of these two characteristics makes it impossible to arrive at any numerical estimate of the schools supported by the Methodists for the education of poor children. The charity day and Sunday schools, established by them, were financed by local contributions and controlled by the local societies. Their numbers were not returned to a central organisation. They received no advertisement. Here and there in the journals and correspondence of leaders of Methodism, in local histories of Methodist societies, and in the reports of the Charity Commissioners are references to the setting up of day schools for the children of the poor. London, Bristol, Bradford, Halifax, Ironbridge, Leytonstone supply details of schools which, it is probable, could have been paralleled in other cities and towns in

[1] Wesley, J., *Collected Works*, vol. v, p. 375.
[2] *Ibid.*, p. 330.

the second half of the century.[1] Wesley's *Journal* bears witness to his interest in and encouragement of Sunday schools. That the interest of his followers did not flag after his death is attested by Jonathan Crowther's undisputed claim, in the early nineteenth century, that the Methodists had done "more that all the other denominations of Christians in establishing, supporting, teaching, and encouraging Sunday schools".[2] Nevertheless, when allowance is made for schools whose work was without record, it cannot be denied that the direct contribution of Methodism to the cause of popular education in the eighteenth century was a curiously negative one. It provided no leaders, it established no organisation, it was content to limit the instruction of the children in home, and class, and school to the Bible and catechism. Moreover, it diverted public attention from the need of daily instruction in the three R's for the children of the poor during the middle years of the century, when the tradition of such instruction was in need of restatement, and it supported, at the end of the century, the miserable compromise of the Sunday school.

II

THE SUNDAY SCHOOLS

The relation of the Methodist movement to popular education in the eighteenth century was not confined to the creation of a reading public and the establishment of a few day charity schools. The new evangel, accompanied by a deepened sense of the spiritual needs and claims of the individual, broke the lethargy of the Anglican and Nonconformist Churches. It inspired the Anglican Church to take a lead in the provision of catechetical schools for the children of the poor, when the social and economic conditions at the end of the century called for fresh effort. The enthusiasm of two devoted Anglicans, Robert Raikes

---

[1] See *Methodism Vindicated. A reply to Clapham by a Member of the Church of England*, 1795, p. 55: "Respecting the education of their children", wrote this appreciative Anglican contemporary, "it is notorious that not any body of Christians has made greater exertion towards the attainment of so valuable an end than the Methodists, witness their noble seminary at Kingswood, their numerous Charity Schools in London and elsewhere, exclusive of frequent instruction which they received from the Preachers who meet them in a body once a week."

[2] Crowther, J., *The Methodist Manual*, 1810, p. 214.

and Sarah Trimmer, for Sunday school instruction, revived the tradition of popular education associated with the Church during the earlier years of the century. The idea found particular favour with the Church of England, but no small part of the success which the new method achieved was due to the co-operation of Methodists and Dissenters. To Wesley, who was over eighty years of age when Raikes began his work, the Sunday school was "one of the noblest institutions which has been seen in Europe for some centuries".[1] Not once but several times did he preach on behalf of the Sunday schools and their pupils.

It is possible to find Sunday schools scattered throughout England and Wales before Raikes began his work in Gloucester, in the spring of 1782, just as it is possible to find day charity schools before the foundation of the S.P.C.K. Joseph Alleine at Taunton, Madam Boevey at Flaxley Abbey, Theophilus Lindsay at Catterick, Hannah Ball at High Wycombe, Thomas Stock at Brecon, are among the early founders of Sunday schools for the children of the poor. Raikes, by his personal efforts and through the instrumentality of his paper *The Gloucester Journal*, which from its beginnings was conspicuous for its philanthropic spirit, and later by his articles and letters in *The Gentleman's Magazine*, transformed a local and particular device for the instruction of the children of the poor into a system of schools, so numerous and so popular that they explain the tendency of early nineteenth-century publicists to think of the education of the poor in terms of Sunday school instruction.[2]

The Sunday school movement, one of the several expressions of the philanthropic spirit which characterised the later years of the eighteenth century, was a revival and a continuation of the earlier day charity school movement. It supplemented the inadequate number of schools for the children of the poor set up in the early half of the century. It was a voluntary movement, financed, as was the earlier movement, by the subscriptions and donations of the middle classes. It was a rescue

[1] *Wesleyan Methodist Magazine*, 1845, p. 118, Letter of Wesley to Charles Atmore.

[2] See Malthus, T. R.: "It is surely a great national disgrace that the education of the lowest classes in England should be left entirely to a few Sunday Schools", *Essay on the Principle of Population as it affects the future improvement of Society*, 1798, Book IV, chap. 9; see also the remark of Sir James Kay-Shuttleworth that "the Sunday School was the root from which sprang our system of day-schools", Smith, F., *Life of Kay-Shuttleworth*, 1923, p. 6.

movement, designed to save the souls of the children of the very poor. Like its forbear it was concerned, primarily, with the towns; its methods of instruction followed closely on the lines laid down by the charity schools; its curriculum, like theirs, was based upon the bed-rock of Bible and catechism. The difference between the two types of charity school lay not in the impulse which prompted them, nor in the methods which established them, but in the limitation of the instruction given in the Sunday Schools to one day in the week.

The choice of the Sabbath as the day of instruction was dictated by the course of events known as the Industrial Revolution, to whose influence the distress of the working classes at the end of the century is commonly ascribed. A quantitative study of the relation of wages to prices, or of pauperism to enclosure, and a recognition of the part played by the continuous wars of the later eighteenth century in the creation of distress make clear that it alone was not responsible for the suffering usually ascribed to it. Nevertheless this ill-termed movement of long drawn out and gradual change, affecting the lot of the farmer as profoundly as it did that of the industrial worker, was responsible, in great measure, for the detestable conditions of life and labour from which children and adults suffered in rural and industrial England at the end of the century. As far as the infant population was concerned, no revolutionary change was introduced by it into their employment. Child labour, an established practice when Defoe wrote in the early years of the century, had continued in spite of the efforts of educational reformers to keep the children at their books until they were old enough for apprenticeship. Throughout the eighteenth century children from six to twelve years of age were to be found working in the fields and the mines and in domestic industry; indeed one of the constant complaints brought against the charity schools was that they diverted cheap and unskilled workers from the labour market. But while child labour was no new thing, the increase in the number of children who lived to grow up, and of those engaged in industry, presented a new phenomenon at the end of the century.

The rise in population and the massing of the people in towns, two of the characteristic features of the revolution, were not undiluted evils, but they brought with them attendant ills, physical and spiritual, not least of which was the palpable failure of the existing schools to provide education for the children of the new urban proletariat. Modern authorities show that the reduction in the death rate rather than the rise in the birth rate was the main explanation of the unprecedented rise in population from 1780, and ascribe it primarily to the revolution in hygiene and medical skill, which characterised the later eighteenth century. But whatever the cause, the increase could not be gainsaid. In no sphere of life was it more spectacular than among the infant poor in the towns. "Few parish children", said Hanway, writing in the sixties, "live to be apprenticed",[1] but from the eighties onwards death could no longer be relied upon to remove with celerity the unwanted infants. The number for whom no educational facilities existed, and the absorption in manufacturing areas of both "workhouse brats" and "free children", who lived at home with their parents in industrial work during a twelve-hour day, presented a problem far more difficult to meet than that which had presented itself in the early years of the century. Then, "the dirty infantry of the streets, degenerating into beasts, without any knowledge of God and Christ", had aroused the pity and distress of pious men and women. A hundred years later men and women of the same complexion suffered the same distress of mind when they found "multitudes of children", after work hours on week-days, and from noon till night on Sundays, prowling "in the shapes of wolves and tygers" through the streets, and treating with indifference the command to keep holy the Sabbath Day.[2]

The new puritans of the Methodist and Evangelical revivals were stirred in their consciences as their predecessors had been. That poverty was intense and ruthless did not leave them undisturbed. They worked for its alleviation, by establishing soup kitchens and clothing clubs and friendly societies, but it was the evil tendencies that came from idle and dissipated habits which acted as a trumpet call to action. To sloth and debauchery preachers and publicists who, at the end of the century were still unable to discriminate between symptoms and causes, attributed "the anti-social" and "atheistical" conduct of the lower orders, who filled the prisons, "gave mournful and horrible employment to the hangman", and "shocked the neighbouring nations by their habits".[3]

[1] Hanway, J., *An Earnest Appeal for Mercy to the Children of the Poor*, 1766.
[2] *The Universal Magazine*, Letter from Robert Raikes, June 5, 1784.
[3] *Sunday Schools Recommended. A sermon preached by George Horne, D.D., Dean of Canterbury and President of Magdalen College, Oxford*, 1785.

11

To curb the "iniquity of the age" social reformers at the end of the century founded new societies for the reformation of manners, and set to work to reclaim a godless and thriftless adult population by a campaign against "the low and debased pleasures of the poor", but the main efforts of social and religious reform were concentrated, once again, upon the children, who "in temper and disposition and manners can scarce be said to differ from the brute creation".[1] Money was collected, offers of voluntary help poured in, and schools for the instruction of the poor were established with extraordinary rapidity, but, because poverty was acute and industry was in the saddle riding mankind, the reformers of the late eighteenth century were obliged to adapt themselves to the limits of which it approved. The machines could not spare the children on week-days, but on Sundays the children took their revenge, disturbing the Sabbath peace of respectable citizens in the towns and of farmers in the country-side. An organisation which would sweep the children off the lanes and streets into school was welcomed by the rural and urban middle-class adults with enthusiasm.

Again, as at the beginning of the century, all sorts and conditions of persons seized upon the new plan with passionate zeal. In dogma, Methodists, Evangelicals and Dissenters lacked agreement, but in their desire to rescue the children of the poor from the evils which they united in abhorring, they were of one mind. They showed the same compassion for the wretched offspring of the streets, and the same spendthrift expenditure of time and energy, and, mingled with these familiar characteristics was the not less familiar desire to instil social discipline, "so that men may learn to submit cheerfully to their stations". "The aim of the Sunday School", said its sponsor Robert Raikes, "is the reformation of Society...one only practicable by establishing notions of duty and discipline at an early stage."[2]

The Sunday school was peculiarly well suited to this end; without upsetting the economic order of things it allowed a combination of the discipline of labour on week-days with the discipline of religion on the Sabbath. It satisfied the demands of Godly piety and of Godly discipline. "The points aimed at", the early supporters of the school assured the public, "are to furnish opportunities of instruction for the

---

[1] *The Universal Magazine.* Letter from Robert Raikes, June 5, 1784.
[2] *The Gentleman's Magazine*, vol. LIX, 1784, Letter from Robert Raikes, Nov. 25, 1783.

poorer parts of the parish without interfering with any industry on the week-day, and to inure children to early habits of going to Church and of spending the leisure hours of Sunday decently and virtuously. The children should be taught to read, and be instructed in the plain duties of the Christian Religion with a particular view to their future character as labourers and servants."[1]

The setting up of the new schools recalls again the inception of the charity school movement. At Gloucester Robert Raikes and his co-adjutor Thomas Stock, curate of St John the Baptist, visited the parents and urged them to send their children to school, and brought persuasion to bear upon the children, who, as earners of their daily bread, were less amenable to parental control than were "unemployed children". "I go round to the Houses of the Poor," wrote Raikes, to a correspondent, "enquire how the children behave, make the wicked and disobedient kneel down and beg pardon of their parents, point out to them how greatly it is within their own power to improve their situation and increase their Happiness and Comforts, by such Behaviour. The deserving I reward with books, and some articles of clothes, as a pair of shoes etc." The response, after some early rebuffs from "the mockers and scoffers", was remarkable. The children presented themselves in crowds on Sunday mornings at the schools. They came "with great regularity". Cold, dark, rainy mornings did not deter them. They clamoured to be heard the chapters and hymns they had learnt by heart, an honour allowed to none who could not produce clean hands and face. "What is yet more extraordinary", wrote Raikes, in 1784, "is that within this month, the little raggamuffins have in great numbers taken it into their heads to frequent the early morning prayers which are held every morning at the Cathedral at 7 o'clock. I believe there were 50 this morning. They assemble at the house of one of the mistresses, and walk before her to the Church, two and two, in as much order as a company of soldiers. I am generally at Church, and after service they all come round to me, and make their bow, and, if any animosities have arisen, to make complaints."[2]

---

[1] *Sermon preached in the Church of St Nicholas, Rochester, on the Occasion of the Introduction of Sunday Schools, June 24, 1785, to which is added an Appendix containing various arguments on the Utility and Importance of the Institution* [etc.].

[2] Raikes, R., MS. Letter to the Rev. A. Price of Northleach, Dec. 13, 1785, in Ely Diocesan Registry; see also *The Gentleman's Magazine*, 1784, vol. LIX.

From all parts of the country came similar stories. Funds were raised by the methods of subscription and donation and by collections in the churches on Sundays. The number of schools and of children attending them varied from place to place. In Wales and the industrial districts of the north of England, the children came *en masse*. The manufacturing towns of Yorkshire, Bradford and Leeds, in particular, were prominent in erecting Sunday schools. "At Bingley", reported John Wesley in 1784, "the school contains 250 children, taught every Sunday by several masters, and superintended by the curate; so many children in one parish are restrained from open sin, and taught a little good manners at least, as well as to read the Bible. I find these schools springing up wherever I go."[1] At York, the enthusiastic children assembled at the schools every Sunday morning at 8 o'clock, and after two hours schooling were taken in regular order to church by their teachers. At 2 p.m. they met again in the schoolroom and were again led to church, after which they continued at school until 7 o'clock, when the daylight would permit, and in winter until 6 o'clock. The clergy and merchants of Bristol entered upon the new plan with spirit. Canterbury was aroused to establish schools for the children engaged during the week in spinning wool and winding silk. Birmingham, under the leadership of the celebrated Dr Joseph Priestley, minister of the New Meeting, took up the good work with enthusiasm.[2]

Reports of the remarkable reformation effected in the manners and morals of the children and adults followed close upon the heels of the schools' inauguration. "Quietness, decency and order replaced noise, prophaneness and vice" in Manchester; the colliers of the Forest of Dean, "a most savage race", and their children were civilised by the schools. The country round Painswick, Gloucestershire, changed its character after the Sunday schools were introduced in 1784 by a wealthy cloth manufacturer of the neighbourhood. Formerly the children had been "the nuisance of the place". They were ignorant, profane, clamorous, filthy, impatient of restraint. On Sundays the farmers and their families dared not leave their orchards unguarded when they attended service at Painswick Church. Either they or their servants were under the necessity of staying at home to protect their property. Within two years a "remarkable reformation" had taken place. To

[1] Wesley, J., *Journals*, July 18, 1784.
[2] *The Origin of Sunday Schools*, 1841.

advertise it to the neighbourhood and to the country at large Raikes, who had helped to promote the Painswick schools, selected the local feast day (the first Sunday after the nineteenth of September) when, according to immemorial custom ,"drunkenness and every species of clamour, riot and disorder filled the town", as a suitable occasion for an anniversary service on behalf of the schools. The magistrates and gentry and farmers, the husbandmen, craftsmen and "the usual crowd that attended the feast", came to survey "the truly affecting sight" of so many young people, lately more neglected than cattle in the fields, now cleanly, quiet, observant of order, submissive, courteous in behaviour. The church was filled, the galleries and aisles thronged like a play-house, while the ale-houses were empty. The collection taken at the door reached the unexpected total of £57, and the schools flourished.[1]

Pressure to induce the children to attend the Sunday schools was throughout vigorously and effectively applied. Employers in town and country who subscribed to the schools, or paid the teachers, or built schools for the children they employed, combined with the clergy and their lay helpers to drive the children into the schools, but their action does not explain the enthusiasm of children and parents for learning. The whining schoolboy, whose irregular attendance was the bane of the schoolmaster's life until the advent of compulsion, seemed for a short period in the history of education to have disappeared. The novelty of the schools offers an explanation of this change; prizes of books and clothing offers another; the "sympathy of numbers" a third and the kindly welcome and personal interest of superintendent and teachers yet another, but powerful as were these attractions the desire of the poor for instruction at the end of the eighteenth century was the prime cause of the interest aroused in parents and children. The steady growth of radical thought, the extraordinary development of scientific, mathematical and economic knowledge, which marked the later eighteenth century, and the Methodist revival, which, it is sometimes forgotten, was profoundly important as an intellectual force, contributed to make parents and children desirous of education. The limitation of the early charity school movement was due in no small degree to the indifference, and, at times, the hostility of the poor to instruction. The Sunday school movement owed its astonishing success to the desire of the poor for learning, combined with the creation of a means which

[1] *The Gentleman's Magazine*, vol. LVII, p. 73.

enabled them to obtain it without the diminution of the earnings, "all little enough", which they received in a six-day working week.

But whatever the prime cause of the enthusiasm, and it varied from group to group, the interest of the children was real enough to support the heavy burden of the new plan of education. Into one day was stuffed an amazing amount of instruction. Throughout the Sabbath, in church and school, learning and discipline marched side by side. Methods were improved when Mrs Trimmer broke through the practice of a century and wrote books for the use of the children in the schools, but normally, as in the charity schools, both "infant" and "advanced" scholars used the Bible, the common prayer book, the catechism and one or more commentaries as the text-books of instruction. "I examine the most forward of the children", wrote the rector of the united parishes of St Alphege and St Mary, Northgate, Canterbury, "and explain the Catechism, and the use of the Prayer Book. I exercise them in repeating after me the Lord's Prayer and the Creeds, and all the responses. We have gone through, likewise, *Fox*, on *Public Worship* and his *Introduction* etc. and also *Crossman's Introduction* etc., the *Church Catechism broke into short questions* and *Mann's Catechism*. The books in common use are *The Child's First Book*, *Fisher or Dixon's Spelling Book*, the Catechisms before mentioned, particularly Mann's; the *Divine Songs* of the pious and excellent Dr Isaac Watts, and every child is furnished with a Common Prayer Book and Testament to carry to Church."[1] This was strong meat for babes. Appetites which were not destroyed by so heavy a diet of pious pabulum were healthy if under-nourished.

The zeal of the children was matched by that of the clergy and their army of lay helpers. Explanatory Bible instruction was the order of the day, and it could not be left to the private-venture teacher, from whom the Sunday schools recruited the bulk of their masters and mistresses. "Four decent well-disposed women who kept school for teaching to read" worked under the personal supervision of Raikes and Stock in Gloucester. Such teachers were easy enough to find and were glad to undertake the new work for 1s. or 1s. 6d. a Sunday. They could be entrusted with instruction in letters and reading, but they were seldom capable of giving the explanatory religious teaching which the new plan demanded. In the towns, and especially in the villages, Sunday

[1] *Sermon preached by the Dean of Canterbury, ut supra.*

school promoters lamented that the common school teachers were "totally unqualified". On the clergy and the respectable laymen of the parish fell the duties of superintendence and exposition. They read Raikes's accounts of the schools at Gloucester and Painswick, and followed his lead, visiting the poor families in the parish, consulting with the parents, collecting money to pay the teachers, and superintending the schools. "I am at Chapel", wrote the rector of the united parishes of St Alphege and St Mary, Northgate, Canterbury, "when school begins. I superintend all myself. I stay till 11, and then we all go to Church together. I take 30–40 of the most advanced children, hear them read the psalms, the Collects, the Epistle, the Gospel and the lesson of the day. I explain things to them. At 1.30 we meet at school again and at 2.30 we return to Church; after Church we all return to School."[1] "That clergyman is peculiarly fortunate", wrote the hard-worked vicar of Boughton Blean, Kent, "who has respectable laymen in his parish, willing to assist him with his purse and sharing the duties of superintendence with him."[2]

The redoubtable Mrs Sarah Trimmer, Raikes's female counterpart in these early years of the Sunday school movement, established schools at Brentford, which became famous, and secured the patronage of King George and Queen Charlotte for a school at Windsor. She appealed in her widely read book *The Œconomy of Charity* to young ladies of the upper classes to grace the schools with their presence, and exercise a civilising influence upon the children. Ignorance, she assured them, need not deter them from offering their services as teachers, for it was not intended that the children of the poor should be instructed in the branches of a liberal education, but merely in English to enable them to read the Gospels. The "disgusting circumstances", which accompanied all such collections of dirty ragged children, would do them no harm, for dirt, although unpleasant, was not contagious; no apprehension of danger, she urged, should restrain Christians from engaging in a work to which Providence so evidently called them.[3]

Few aspects of the Sunday school movement are more remarkable than the *naïveté* of the clergy who set up schools in their parishes. That they should contrast the evil habits of the ragged and disorderly

---

[1] *Sunday Schools Recommended, ut supra, Appendix I.*
[2] *Sunday Schools Recommended, ut supra, Appendix II.*
[3] Trimmer, Sarah, *The Œconomy of Charity*, 1787, vol. I, pp. 71, 72.

children transformed by the schools into clean, decent and orderly members of society was but a natural and justifiable conceit, but seldom, if ever, does their responsibility for the godless and undisciplined children appear to strike them. They state with pride that children who had never been inside a church since they were baptized now attend "with regularity and circumspection". And yet the canons enjoining the catechising of the children in church on Sundays still held place and bishops harangued their clergy, urging them to catechise the children, in precisely the same manner as Ken and his contemporaries had done in the early years of the century. To many of the clergy catechetical instruction in school on Sundays appeared as a new and welcome idea. Their pleased surprise is a significant commentary on the apathy of the Church before the revival.

In broad outline the Sunday school movement was a replica of the early charity school movement. The similarity extended to the establishment of a central organisation when, in 1785, the Sunday School Society set to work to systematise and co-ordinate the schools. Unlike the S.P.C.K. the new Society was undenominational in character. Jonas Hanway and the Dissenter, William Fox, an intimate friend of Robert Raikes, were its founders; Henry Thornton, the London banker and a leading member of the famous Clapham Sect, was its first president. Its aim was to give financial assistance to laymen and clerics who were anxious to set up Sunday schools until the schools could stand on their own feet. In the *Plan of a Society* the "most liberal and catholic principles were adopted", in the hope that "persons of *all* denominations of the protestant faith will be induced to unite".[1] Cordial and zealous support was received from the public. Within six months over £1000 were received in subscriptions and five new schools were opened in London. The Bishops of Llandaff and Salisbury warmly approved of the Society. The Dean of Lincoln recommended it in his charge to the clergy of the Archdeaconry of Nottingham; and Dr Priestley in Birmingham welcomed the idea "with all the energy and zeal which characterised his powerful mind". Under the enthusiastic patronage of Church and Dissent the schools spread with amazing rapidity. Undenominational Sunday schools were set up at Colchester, while those at Stockport afforded a remarkable illustration of united effort. In the

[1] First Circular Letter of the Sunday School Society, 1784, printed in *The Origin of Sunday Schools*, 1841.

new and elaborate school buildings the children were gathered for morning school: from there they were taken by their teachers to church or chapel, and met again at the school when the services were over. Above 1800 children were in attendance at the largest of the Stockport schools.[1] In 1787 Raikes claimed that a quarter of a million children attended tbe schools.[2] The number cannot be substantiated, but the rapid progress of the movement was attested by the reports of the Sunday School Society. 201 affiliated schools with 10,232 children were returned by it in 1787 and 1086 schools with 69,000 pupils in 1797.[3]

Unhappily the cordial co-operation of Church and Dissent, which marked the early years of the Sunday school movement, as it had marked those of the early charity school movement, did not survive the advent of revolutionary and atheistical thought from France. Political unrest, when the century was drawing to a close, checked the undenominational trend of the early Sunday schools. Methodist and Dissenter were suspected by the Anglicans of disseminating the Jacobinical principles of sedition and atheism in the schools. To protect the Church from this alleged anti-social and anti-religious danger, the leaders of the Anglican Church charged the parochial clergy to withdraw from association with Dissent, and establish Sunday schools under their own control. "Schools of Jacobinical religion and Jacobinical politics abound in this country in the shape of charity schools and Sunday schools", asserted the Bishop of Rochester in his charge to the clergy of his diocese in 1800. In them the minds of "the very lowest orders" were taught to despise religion and the laws of all subordination. The proper antidote for the poison of the Jacobin schools, he declared, was the establishment of schools for the same class of children under the management of the parochial clergy. Sunday schools must be established under clerical inspection and control.

Pronouncements such as these had an immediate effect. Jacobinism split the Sunday school movement just as Jacobitism had split the early charity school movement. History repeated itself, but with a difference. As at the beginning of the century Dissent withdrew from association with the Church, so this time the Church withdrew from association with

---

[1] Wild, W. I., *History of the Stockport Sunday School*, 1891.

[2] Gregory, A., *Robert Raikes, Journalist and Philantropist. A History of the Origin of Sunday Schools*, 1877, p. 92.

[3] *Plan of a Society...for the Support of Sunday Schools*, 1787 and 1797.

Dissent. "A vigilant eye"[1] was kept upon the teachers in the Church schools. Nothing was left to their discretion. The fear of infidelity roused to action those who were indifferent to ignorance and vice, and renewed efforts were put forth by the Anglican clergy and their lay helpers to set up schools under their own control, and free from the horrors of French importations. Undenominationalism had been tried and failed.

Like the Methodist class the Sunday school in its turn diverted public interest from the earlier tradition of day school instruction. It established instead the conviction, from which supporters of full-time education in the nineteenth century found it difficult to dislodge public opinion, that Sunday was the proper and most suitable time for the children of the poor to receive instruction. But if there is little to be said for the eighteenth-century Sunday schools as educational institutions, their importance as a means of social betterment can with difficulty be over-estimated. Their universality was perhaps their most remarkable feature. They were national institutions, in a sense in which the day charity schools, restricted in numbers, and able to instruct but a selected number of pupils, had never been. The new schools forced the idea of education, free and universal, into prominence, and kept it there. Moreover, they conveyed the simple and humane teaching of Christ to hundreds of thousands of children and adults, for whom no other means of religious and moral instruction existed, at a time when the stress of war and the new industrialism threatened to dehumanise the lower ranks of society. "The fierce antagonism of misconceived class interests"[2] was in some degree transcended by the shared enthusiasm of children, teachers, and employers for the Sunday school.

III

SCHOOLS OF INDUSTRY

Not all the children who attended the Sunday schools were at work during the week. Raikes in his *Journal* stated that his attention was diverted from the state of the prisoners in Gloucester gaol to the state of the ragamuffins playing on *week-days* in the streets. On Sundays

---

[1] *Charge of the Bishop of Rochester to the Clergy of the Diocese,* 1800.
[2] Unwin, G., *Samuel Oldknow and the Arkwrights. The Industrial Revolution at Stockport and Marple,* Manchester, 1924, p. 41.

their ranks were enlarged, and the disorder increased, by the children released from employment, "cursing and swearing in a manner so horrid as to suggest to any serious mind an idea of hell".[1] The unemployed children created a problem in themselves. Congregated in districts where manufactures were absent, or not highly developed, they lacked even the modicum of discipline which children, engaged in field or workshop, received. Idle and untrained, their plight appeared to social reformers at the end of the eighteenth century to demand a more sustained and intensive training than the Sunday schools were capable of giving. Hence towards the end of the century the industrial school appeared again in full sail.

Had Pitt's poor law scheme of 1795 been approved, parish schools of industry for the compulsory attendance of children whose parents were on the rates would have made unnecessary schools established by charity. But vested interests were too powerful to allow Pitt's bill to become law and the demand for juvenile labour was too strong to permit an enthusiastic welcome for a movement which would divert it from the mines and manufactures which clamoured for it, and it was left to voluntary effort to set up schools where children could be "inured to labour". This time attempts were not made to graft labour on to the charity school curriculum. That struggle had been waged and lost. The new schools were working schools, and, except for a short period devoted to learning to read, the school hours were engaged in industrial work. Learning was relegated to the Sunday schools attended by the children on the Sabbath.

But once again the attempt to set up working schools was a failure. It was not easy to arouse interest in industrial schooling when children could be subjected to the discipline of labour in workshops without the expenditure of charity or rate aid. It was useless for Mrs Trimmer, to whose enthusiasm the movement at the end of the century owed much of its vitality, to proclaim the advantage of the working school to the workshop. The workshop had come to stay and as industry expanded the working school gave way before it.

Mrs Trimmer's belief in the moral value of industrial schools ran parallel to her passionate conviction that the religious well-being of the country was bound up with the Sunday school. The discipline of

---

[1] Raikes, R., Letter to Colonel Townley, Nov. 25, 1783; quoted in Gregory, A., *op. cit.* p. 57.

religion combined with the discipline of labour was, in her opinion, the only cure for the evils of the age, but, while her belief in the moral value of labour was second to none, her indignation was aroused by the type of discipline to which the factories subjected their infant workers. Close daily contact with adults whose conduct and language was deplorable was subversive of child morality. The value of industrial training disappeared when children heard and were unchecked in the use of profane language, and the indifference of employers to the physical care of the children they employed moved her to indignant protest. "I cannot think of the children who work in the manufactures without the utmost commiseration", she wrote. It was impossible to view with equanimity countenances "pale and sodden" in which "the roses of health should bloom", or to see limbs, which should be straight, robust and active, stunted in their growth and distorted by sitting in one continued posture. Nor did the industrial training they received compensate for the bad moral and physical conditions in which the children worked. In the shops which she knew, the children were kept at work "in one particular branch of the manufactory for which their size will disqualify them after a few years, when they are turned into the world unacquainted with any useful art to gain a livelihood". It would be an act of charity, she pleaded, to deflect children's labour from the factories into the industrial schools, in which the health and morals of the children were cared for by the teachers and "labour was mixt with learning".[1]

Schools at Lewisham, Bamborough Castle, Epping, Old Brentford, Chester, Oakham, Boldre, Kendal, Weston (Somerset), St Albans, Lincoln, Harding-Fordbury, Norwich, and Edgware Road, London, were singled out by the later eighteenth-century reformers as worthy of praise and imitation.[2] In some the children spun flax and wool, in others they put heads on pins, or "closed" boots and shoes. They knitted stockings and made shirts, and everywhere the girls learnt sewing and, in some of the schools, cooking and housewifery. Schools which could afford to do so paid the children wages of 1s. to 1s. 6d., or even 2s. 6d. a week. The hopes of enthusiasts rose high. They made the same elaborate calculations that the political arithmeticians had

[1] Trimmer, Sarah, The Œconomy of Charity, vol. 1, pp. 190–200.
[2] See Reports of the Society for the Betterment of the Poor, 1797–1800; see also The Œconomy of Charity, vol. 1, pp. 193–296.

made at the end of the seventeenth century of the advantage to the
nation of the children's labour. The work of 100,000 persons re-
munerated at only one halfpenny a day would, they estimated, in a year
of 300 days produce a total of £625,000. They pleaded for a national
system of industrial schools and called public attention to the improvement in manners and morals enjoyed by places in which the schools
were set up.

At Bamborough Castle and Lewisham the schools, like those of
Artleborough and Findon seventy years before, were temporarily successful, for their organisation was in the hands of enthusiasts who could
make bread out of stones and the desert to blossom as the rose. At
Brentford, Mrs Trimmer's own particular care, there was no manufactory of any kind and the children, ragged, dirty and disorderly, were
always in the streets. A school for girls was first opened where spinning,
learnt on a wheel given by a benevolent lady, knitting, and plain
needlework were taught. At the end of two years it was closed as an
economic failure. A school for boys, opened later, gave twenty
children instruction in carding and spinning coarse wool. Twice a
week, for two hours in the evenings, a master attended to teach them
to read and write. The school lasted for two years and then, to the
distress of Mrs Trimmer, came to an abrupt end.[1] Schools which set
out to give girls domestic training were at the end of the century, as at
all times, more successful.[2] But the schools of industry were, except in
districts suited to their existence, economic failures. Spinning, the
normal occupation of the schools, was, in the opinion of many well-
informed men, as detrimental to the health and well-being of the
children as the work in shops and factories which Mrs Trimmer
deplored. The economic value of spinning schools, according to Sir
Thomas Eden, was, as a rule, negligible. "The experience of eight
years", he wrote in 1797, "has proved that although schools of industry
may flourish for a while under the active zeal of the first promoters, yet,
when after a few years' trial they are left to the superintendence of less
interested administrators, they dwindle into the ordinary state of the

---

[1] Trimmer, Sarah, *The Œconomy of Charity*, vol. I, pp. 296–310. See also *Some
Account of the Life and Writings of Mrs Trimmer*, 1786.
[2] See Cappe, Catherine, *Account of Two Charity Schools for the Education of Girls
…in York interspersed with Reflections on Charity Schools and Friendly Societies in
General*, 1800.

parish poor house."[1] In 1803 the Parliamentary Returns made under Mr Rose's Act, and covering the greater part of England and Wales, show that the number of children between five and fourteen years of age receiving parish relief was 188,794. Of these but 20,336 had received, or were receiving, instruction in schools of industry.[2]

No study of elementary education in the late eighteenth century would be complete without an account of the work of the "great man" of the Evangelical party, Hannah More. It combined the two objects upon which eighteenth-century reformers had laid stress, instruction in religion and in labour for the children of the poor. Martha More's *Journal*, and Hannah More's *Letters and Tracts* present a picture of village life in Somerset at the end of the century which, if it is typical of the rest of England, does not warrant a belief in the social and religious progress of the century. There are the same ignorant and poverty-stricken labouring people, the same despotic farming middle class, the same indifferent and indolent clergy, which the early years of the century revealed. In the Mendip villages, to which her attention was called by Wilberforce in 1787, Hannah More found the people almost pagan, savage and depraved, brutal in nature and ferocious in their manners. Thirteen adjacent villages were without resident clergy of any kind. Every house in Cheddar presented a scene of the "greatest ignorance and vice". The inhabitants of Shipham and Rowberrow, the two distressed mining villages at the top of the Mendips, equalled Cheddar in depravity and ferocity. No constable would venture there to execute his office. Blagdon's reputation had won for it the title of "Botany Bay" or "Little Hell". Allowing for the common tendency of reformers to paint the background to their work in dark colours, the conditions of the labouring classes in the Mendip villages, revealed by the More sisters, remains one of almost unrelieved gloom. In the summer of 1789, incited by Wilberforce, who offered to find the funds required for this "work of practical piety", and with the example of Robert Raikes and Sarah Trimmer before them, they hired a house, appointed "the excellent Mrs Baber" as schoolmistress, and opened school at Cheddar. When these preliminary steps had been taken they courageously faced the combined opposition of the local clergy, who

[1] Eden, Sir T., *The State of the Poor*, 1797, vol. II, pp. 400–1.
[2] 43 Geo. III, c. 144; *Parliamentary Returns*, 1803.

could explain the disinterested action of two middle-aged ladies only in terms of French radicalism or Methodistical enthusiasm, of intolerant farmers, who held religion to be a "very dangerous thing", calculated to "ruin agriculture", and of the labouring poor, who suspected their efforts to get hold of the children as a preliminary step to carrying them off and selling them as slaves.

More than a dozen schools were, in the next ten years, set up and controlled by the two sisters.[1] They combined the character of Sunday schools, in which reading and religious knowledge were taught, industrial schools in which children, who were not employed in labour, were given daily instruction in "such coarse works as may fit them for servants", and evening schools where adults were taught to read. Their object, tersely stated by Hannah More, was "to train up the lower classes to habits of industry and virtue". For this reason writing, an unnecessary accomplishment, was forbidden.

No more convincing evidence exists of the social isolation and neglect suffered by some, at least, of the labouring classes at the end of the eighteenth century, than the response of children and adults to the efforts of the educational enthusiasts of the age. When the piety and sincerity of Hannah and Martha More disarmed the minds of the labouring poor in the Mendip villages of fear and antagonism, they crowded to the schools, as the children in the towns did to the Sunday schools, because in them they found social interests and religious consolation hitherto denied to them. The competitions and prizes for good behaviour, the school feasts, the meetings of the Friendly Society, organised by the sisters, made village life one of active co-operation. The response of the villagers shown in the efforts to change their habits of life so as to win approval from their mentors, affords a measure both of their needs and of the efforts of the sisters to satisfy them. It is easy to criticise the Trimmers, Raikes and Mores, and their fellows throughout the eighteenth century. Hannah and Martha More in particular lend themselves to adverse judgments from an age which has little sympathy with their religious point of view, and detests their social philosophy. They were too condescending, too self-righteous,

[1] At Belmont, Blagdon, Axbridge, Barnwell, Cheddar, Congresbury, Cowslip Green, Barley Wood, Flax Bourton, Nailsea, Rowberrow, Shipham, Weston, Wedmore, Winscombe, Yatton. See Thompson, H., *The Life of Hannah More*, 1838, p. 95.

too austere; worse, they turned a blind eye on the causes of the
evils they deplored, attributing the ignorance and depravity of a class
not to detestable social and economic inequalities, but to infidelity and
lack of religious knowledge. This much may, however, be claimed
for the precisians of the eighteenth century, that, as a body, they
possessed and cultivated a sense of responsibility to the poor and
ignorant, and spent themselves in service. Among them Hannah More,
courageous, compassionate and unselfseeking, holds no inconspicuous
place.[1]

At the end of the eighteenth century there were in England three
types of charity schools for the children of the poor. They were alike
in that they were schools which provided education for a class and that
their primary end was to condition the children for their work in life.
They formed in the minds of contemporaries a tight little self-contained
educational system for the lower orders. But the arrival of Sunday
schools and schools of industry, characterised respectively by a severely
limited period of instruction, and a severely limited curriculum, thrust
the older charity schools, both those which were endowed and those
which were dependent upon subscriptions, into a new position. No
longer were they the only schools which provided free instruction for
the children of the very poor. Below them, as educational institutions,
stood the Sunday school and the industrial school, and as the end of the
century approached it became clear that the older charity schools had
established for themselves a new status. Their pupils were not now the
scum of the parish, for the poor who could afford to send their children
to a day school, in which no remuneration was offered for labour, and
no training was given to fit them for manual work, were the superior
poor; the education their children received was a superior education,
which fitted them for work of a superior character. While the children
of the Sunday schools were supplying the demand for labour in the
mines and workshops, artisans and tradesmen were demanding boys
who could read and write and cast accounts. For not the least remark-

---

[1] For the work of the More sisters see *The Mendip Annals, the Journal of Martha
More*, ed., with additional matter, by Arthur Roberts, 1859; *The Letters of Hannah
More*, ed. by Brimley Johnson, 1925; *Memoirs of the Life and Correspondence of
Hannah More*, by W. Roberts, 1835, and the *Works of Hannah More* in eleven
volumes, 1854.

able feature of the industrial revolution was the increase of retail trade. Neither Sunday school scholars, nor, as Sir Thomas Bernard discovered at the Foundling Hospital, the children trained to labour, nor, it would appear, a large enough number of children educated in the pay schools, were competent for work of this kind, but the charity school boy, with his "literary education", was in request for this work of considerable importance.[1]

This hierarchy of schools for the lower orders suggested to educationalists at the end of the century the advisability of grading the children attending them, according to their social condition and intellectual qualities. "There are", said Mrs Trimmer, in an essay curiously reminiscent of the detestable Mandeville's, "degrees of poverty as well as of opulence. If it is improper to educate the children of the higher orders promiscuously, it surely must be equally so to place all the children of the poor upon the same footing, without any regard to the different circumstances of their parents, and of their own genius and capacity." The new Sunday charity schools provided a remedy for this promiscuity. They were admirably designed to sift the children of the poor. Their work was probationary. In them could be tried out the capacities of the children. From them "dull and bad children", suited for employment in manufactures, and in the inferior offices of common servants, could be drafted to the industrial schools, where they would receive suitable training. The endowed and subscription day charity schools on the other hand could then be reserved for the children of "the first degree among the Lower Orders". The comprehensive education which they offered would qualify children of parts and respectability for work as teachers in the different types of charity schools, or for apprenticeship to superior trades, or for domestic service in respectable families.[2]

The existence of a hierarchy of schools providing instruction for all classes of the poor at the end of the century may be regarded as evidence of the alleged improvement in the condition of the labouring classes

[1] Bernard, Sir T., *Account of the Foundling Hospital*, 2nd ed. 1799, pp. 66–7; *Report of the Society for Bettering the Condition of the Poor*, 1799, p. 277.

[2] Trimmer, Sarah, *Reflections upon the Education of Children in Charity Schools*, 1792, *passim*. See also the opinion of the Rev. J. S. Howson, a witness before the Commission on...Popular Education in England, 1861, on the "working upward" class tendency of the endowed elementary schools, vol. XXI, Part IV.

12

during the eighteenth century, but it cannot be ignored that, narrow as was the conception of the early charity schools, they offered a more liberal curriculum and a more generous plan of instruction than the Sunday schools which industrialism and evangelicalism established as the schools for the poor at the end of the century.

PART II

CHAPTER VI

SCOTLAND

CHARITY AND "CIVILITIE"

"There was perhaps never any change of national manners so quick, so great, and so general, as that which has operated in the *Highlands*, by the last conquest, and the subsequent laws. We came thither too late to see what we expected, a people of peculiar appearance, and a system of anti-quated life. The clans retain little now of their original character; their ferocity of temper is softened, their military ardour is extinguished, their dignity of independence is depressed, their contempt of govern-ment subdued, and their reverence for their chiefs abated. Of what they had before the late conquest of their country, there remain only their language and their poverty. Their language is attacked on every side. Schools are erected in which *English* only is taught, and there were lately some who thought it reasonable to refuse them a version of the holy scriptures, that they might have no monument of their mother-tongue."

DR JOHNSON, Journey to the Western Islands of Scotland, 1773.

I

"THE REMOTE PARTS"

Scotland alone of the four countries of the British Isles could lay claim at the beginning of the eighteenth century to a national system of education. On paper the claim appeared a sound one. John Knox's *First Book of Discipline* had commanded all parents, irrespective of social position, to see to the training of their children in learning and virtue, and had planned a hierarchy of schools for their instruction, of which the parish schools were the foundation. "A certain time must be appointed to reading and to learning the Catechism, a certain time given to Grammar and the Latin tongue, a certain time to Arts, Philosophy and to the other tongues, and a certain time to that study in which they intend chiefly to travail for the profit of the Common-wealth."[1]

[1] Knox, J., *First Book of Discipline*, 1560, ed. C. Lemox, 1905, p. 384.

To translate this comprehensive scheme of compulsory education
into practice greater unity of purpose and more generous funds were
required than Scotland in the sixteenth century could supply. Church
and State approached the problem of education from different stand-
points. The Reformed Kirk claimed the tithes and the whole patrimony
of the old Church for the use of the ministry, the schools and the poor.
The Estates, while readily giving parliamentary sanction to the new
faith, objected to "these devout imaginations". They refused sanction
to the *First Book of Discipline*, and the Scots lords with characteristic
pertinacity claimed their share of the plunder. The artichoke of church
patrimony disappeared leaf by leaf until nothing but a remnant was left
to finance a national scheme of education. Nevertheless the Church
of Scotland, handicapped by inadequate funds, harassed by religious
dissensions and faced by the extreme poverty of the lower ranks of
the people, displayed a belief in the value of popular education which
was a constant challenge to the Government. It struggled faithfully,
as the records of the General Assembly bear witness, to provide the
people with instruction. When the Presbyterian Church was revived
in 1638 there was renewed activity in setting up schools. The
Estates re-affirming in 1646 the Act of 1633 made the establishment
of a school in every parish a legal duty of the heritor and, by the
famous Act of 1696, not only laid upon them the obligation of setting
up a school and paying the schoolmaster's salary, but appointed commissioners to ensure its execution.[1] In spite, however, of the new
machinery for default, progress was slow and uncertain. Kirk Sessions
records show that for a hundred years after the passing of the Act there
were parishes in which it was ignored, and at the end of the century
there were Lowland parishes in which no parish school had ever been
set up.[2]

It was, however, when the Highland Line was crossed that the
discrepancy between paper schemes and actual conditions was conspicuous. Secure in their "remote corners", in the huge Highland and
Island parishes, the heritors ignored their duty and left the peasantry
without provision for instruction. The proprietors, the well-to-do

[1] Acts of the Parliament of Scotland, 1633, c. 5, vol. v, p. 21; 1646, c. 45, vol. vi,
p. 216; 1696, c. 26, vol. x, p. 63.
[2] Sinclair, Sir J., *The Statistical Account of Scotland*, 21 vols. 1790–95, vol. ii,
p. 69; vol. iii, pp. 140, 420; vol. ix, p. 387.

tacksmen and tenant farmers, solved the problem of their children's education by employing private tutors at home or by sending their sons abroad, or as weekly boarders to the nearest burgh or private school, but for the poorer classes of the community there was no such solution. Their children were "void of religion and education";[1] for them the legal means had failed and it was left to voluntary effort to do in the eighteenth century what the law had failed to accomplish.

It is conceivable that the *praefervidum ingenium Scotorum* of the Lowlanders would, in itself, have provided a sufficient incentive for the organisation of popular education in the Highlands, without the formation of a Society to this end. For the material and spiritual conditions of its people which were, in Southern opinion, lamentable, offered a constant challenge to the Lowland Scot. It is, however, as easy to exaggerate the conditions which called for reform as it is to exaggerate the value of the reforms introduced. An age which finds beauty in Highland scenery and charm in Highland simplicity, and is not blind to the high moral quality of Highland loyalty, finds it difficult to appreciate the attitude of mind of early eighteenth-century reformers of Highland life. General Stuart of Garth in 1822 roundly declared that the libels made upon his countrymen were without foundation, and recent studies of the social history of the Highland people go some way to support his contention.[2]

On the other hand it is undeniable that Lowlander and Englishman, enjoying the benefits and possessing the standards of what Adam Smith termed a commercial civilisation, had no difficulty in finding much to criticise and condemn in the social and economic life of the Highlands. They set off with a hearty dislike of the "rude geography" of the Highland region. Its scenery was to them without charm. "The stupendous vulgarity and horrid gloom" of the mountains oppressed them.[3] In these they saw, not beauty, but barriers to the penetration of "civilitie". Rapid rivers destitute of bridges, and liable to sudden floods, made easy intercourse with the civilised South an impossibility.

[1] *Sermon preached before the Society for Propagating Christian Knowledge in Scotland*, 1735.

[2] Stuart, D., *Sketches of the Character, Manners, and Present State of the Highlands of Scotland*, 1822, *passim*; see also Grant, I. F., *The Story of an Old Highland Farm, 1769–82*, 1924; Cunningham, A., *The Loyal Clans*, 1933.

[3] *Letters from a Gentleman in the North of Scotland to a Friend in London* [written about 1726], 2 vols. 1754, vol. II, p. 10.

Progress, even on horseback, was a slow and painful business. Carts and carriages were almost unknown. The courses, for there were few roads, and they in bad repair, lay over rock and river-beds, and wide stretches of bog, which no stranger dared to cross until a native, born and bred upon them, "shook the ground with his feet" to test its safety. Twenty-four times in one hour did an intrepid school inspector, who was at pains to count his trials, cross the same river in the neighbouring parishes of Lord Reay's country at the end of the century.[1] A "barbarous climate" added yet another physical barrier to the missionaries of Southern civilisation.

More disturbing to them than geography and climate were the miserable and squalid conditions in which the poorer classes lived. One after another, travellers from the South, be they Government officials, or curious foreigners, or members of the Jesuit mission, or correspondents of the Society for the Propagation of Christian Knowledge, expressed their concern for a people lacking in the most elementary comforts and barely able at times to support life. For this state of things clan relationships, the characteristic feature of Scottish agrarian life, were in the main responsible. They had, as Marshall put it, "riveted" a system of small holdings upon the people. In order that the proprietors and tacksmen or "gentlemen middlemen" might provide themselves with the warriors they required, the land was burdened with "a load of tenantry", which it could not support.[2] A farm of thirty acres, reported Walker in 1802, would have ten sub-tenants, their families and the tacksmen's servants upon it; in all about seventy-one persons. Such a number of people living by agriculture upon so small a property was not to be found elsewhere. The land was held on a short lease from the proprietor, or more commonly, from a tacksman who, to support his dignity, secured from his sub-tenants, farmers, cotters and crofters, rent in excess of that which he paid and services which, according to Walker's estimate, formed more than one-third of the sub-tenants' whole labour.[3] Indifferent farmers—for their interests

[1] *Abstract of the Proceedings of the Society in Scotland for Propagating Christian Knowledge*, 1800, p. 179.

[2] Marshall, W., *General View of the Agriculture of the Central Highlands of Scotland*, 1794, pp. 25, 33.

[3] Walker, J., *An Economical History of the Hebrides and Highlands of Scotland*, 1802, vol. I, pp. 52–5, 180, 240.

lay not in improved agrarian economy, but in the numbers of their tenants—the tacksmen were responsible for much of the poverty and misery which perturbed the Southern visitors, and, by their lack of interest in the instruction of their tenants, for much of the apathy of the peasantry towards education. The harsh climate and barren soil contributed to make the sub-tenants' life a hard one. His methods were primitive and ineffective. Land in such high altitudes was not put under the plough until February or March; sowing was correspondingly delayed and autumn rains accompanied the gathering of the late harvest. His implements were, in their turn, equally unsatisfactory. The Aberdeenshire plough was "beyond description bad".[1] In Skye and other parts of the Highlands the *cas chrom*, or foot-plough, was commonly used. Harrows, sometimes fastened to the tails of the horses, were, declared Lord Kames, "more fit to raise laughter than to raise soil".[2] Corn was thrashed with the flail and winnowed by being flung into the air.

Partly as a result of these conditions, food supplies were short and uncertain. The scanty crop of oats, bear, rye, or mixed grain, which in many parts represented Highland agriculture, amazed the traveller from the lands where wheat was the staff of life. In summer, reported the Jesuit missionaries to the General of the Order in Rome, the people fed mainly on milk; in winter on animal food.[3] In spring-time, when food was scarce and supplies of oats or meat were lacking, the condition of men and beasts was often pitiable, and when famine seized upon the country, as it did during the "Seven Ill Years" from 1696 to 1703, and at other times which have escaped the notice of historians, families were found dead in the ditches and behind the hedges. Generalisations are as dangerous in Scottish as in Irish history, but it appears undeniable that a large proportion of the Highland people lived on the verge of starvation. The farms were so small and so poor as to give scanty subsistence even in good years. Burt, one of General Wade's officers engaged in building the new military roads of 1726, comparing the physique of the labouring classes with those in England and the Low-

---

[1] Anderson, J., *General view of the Agriculture of Aberdeen*, 1794, p. 77.

[2] Kames, Lord, *The Gentleman Farmer*, 1776, p. 46.

[3] Stonyhurst MSS., Report of the Scottish Mission of the Society of Jesus for the year 1702, given in Forbes Leith, *Memoirs of the Scottish Catholics during the Sixteenth and Seventeenth Centuries*, vol. II, pp. 293 *et seq.*

lands, found them decidedly smaller in stature. "Nor is it likely", he remarked, "that they should be rendered larger than other people seeing that they were half starved in the wombs, and never afterwards well fed."[1]

The housing conditions of the sub-tenants and cottagers were equally deplorable. "Hovels so little that a man must almost creep on hands and knees to get into them" were shared in winter-time with the cows and young store cattle. They lacked comfort and cleanliness. Brooding in the smoke over the fire was Burt's description of their inmates' existence when the barbarous winter climate kept even Highlanders indoors.

The conditions which travellers from the South described with a pity not unmixed with contempt were not peculiar to the Highlands. Wales and Ireland, Westphalia, or Picardy, can provide parallel descriptions of a "dwarf peasantry" scratching a bare subsistence from the soil, while want and squalor equal, if not superior, to that which travellers deplored in the Highlands could have been found in the slums of English and Lowland towns. In the towns such conditions could be ignored; in the Highlands they captured the attention of those who found their way across the mountains, and in the breasts of philanthropists they created an itch for reform. Idle people, improperly provided for, were a nuisance to their Lowland neighbours, whose cattle they drove in order to support themselves; they were also a political danger, since "broken men" gladly took service under any fighting leader. No less offensive to puritan morals was the "lazy and mean and contented manner of living" which Southern reformers found so deplorable and so difficult to understand.[2] The Highlanders often lacked bread but they did not lack "superiority to want".[3] In their search for an explanation of so curious a phenomenon the reformers of the Highlands ascribed it, not without justice, to an organisation of society which, finding its most honoured occupation in arms, ran directly counter to the belief that labour was the will of God and its performance the test of grace. Pasture farming and the cattle trade, the

---

[1] *Letters from a Gentleman*, vol. I, pp. 85, 120; see also the Report of the Scottish Mission, in Forbes Leith, *op. cit.*

[2] Laing MSS., Edinburgh University Library, Div. II, No. 623.

[3] Simond, L., *Journal of a Tour and Residence in Great Britain, 1810–11–15*, p. 398.

two occupations of any importance in the Highlands, were in the eyes of their critics detrimental alike to moral and economic improvement. "Looking after cows", as the S.P.C.K. remarked contemptuously, did not constitute work.[1] And this was never more so than in the summer months from May to August when men, women and children migrated in a body with their cattle and household goods from the winter houses along the sea coast or in the glens to the shealings or summer dairies in the upland pastures, where they spent their time "stretched in crowds, basking themselves in the sun, or else in the whiskey house, and left the black cattle, the staple of these countries, to look after themselves".[2]

No less deplorable was the indifference to industry and trade. The backward country, its critics averred, offered employment in husbandry, fishing, manufactures, handicrafts, and navigation. Supplied with an abundance of fish, with enough wool for a stocking trade and quantities of seaweed for the manufacture of glass, with a soil admirably suited for the raising of flax and potatoes, the people preferred to live without labour, "sauntering through life".[3] That the Highlands were incapable of development on the lines laid down by "a commercial age" is doubtful, but in the eighteenth century the gospel of work broke against the indifference of its people to comfort and ambition. The proud indolence which the French traveller Simond found so attractive aroused Protestant reformers to redoubled efforts to inculcate industrious habits among adults and children. Unlike the Frenchman they did not hold that Highland poverty "need not be pitied, much less despised".[4]

Equally perturbing to the puritan reformers of the Highlands was the blend of superstition and imagination which found expression in a wealth of fairy lore and pagan rites. Popery, the Presbyterian divines alleged, had "pandered to paganism" in an endeavour to re-establish its former position in the Highlands.[5] By diluting the faith it had left

[1] *State of the Society in Scotland*, 1729, p. 38.

[2] Laing MSS. *loc. cit.*

[3] *Account of the Rise, Constitution, and Management of the Society in Scotland*, 1714, p. 5; see also *The Highlands of Scotland in 1750*, from MS. 104 in the King's Library, B.M., ed., with introduction, by Andrew Lang, 1898. This is probably the letter of one Mr Bruce, a government official employed in surveying the forfeited and other estates in the Highlands after the Forty-Five.

[4] Simond, L., *op. cit.* p. 398.

[5] *State of the Society in Scotland*, 1748, p. 53.

the unhappy Highlanders without true religion. The new presbyters, un-like the old priests, set out with passionate determination to rescue them from the thraldom of fairies and ghosties, water-kelpies and brownies, whose capricious and sometimes diabolical behaviour contributed a vivid and dramatic quality to a bucolic existence. Incantations to the elements, offerings to beasts of prey, ceremonial feasts and curious rituals at different seasons of the year, aroused not the sympathy, but the profound distress of men whose highly intellectualised form of religion had been swept bare of childish things. The Highlanders, they held, "had not tasted the Heavenly Gift", and, constrained to save a people who had no desire to save themselves, "ministers were ordained and teachers set apart to visit the dark places and point the way to Salvation through the remission of Sins".[1]

The twin devils of sloth and superstition were in themselves suffi-cient to spur to action men whose minds were formed in the puritan mould, but, strengthening their determination to introduce Southern "civilitie" to a barbarous people, was the conviction which they shared with the Government that only by control of the Highlands could the Hanoverian Crown and the Protestant Succession be made secure. Law in the Highlands was the will of the chiefs; loyalty, to an unknown number of Highlanders, meant obedience to the House of Stuart. Highland law and Highland loyalty could therefore, when occasion arose, open a back-door into England for England's enemies. The annual sermons, preached on behalf of the Scottish S.P.C.K. in Edinburgh and in London, and the petitions presented to the Government during the first half of the century, expressed the fear and horror of Lowlanders and Englishmen for the fierce and warlike Highlanders, "averse from labour and inured to rapine", who "scorned the arts of peace" and were "ready for every bold and desperate action". Accustomed to no subjection except "a slavish dependence upon their chieftains" they accepted "pernicious Notions of Government, artfully instilled into their minds". "Theft and robbery with them is esteemed only a Hunting, not a Crime, Revenge and Murder is counted only a Gallan-trie."[2] A long series of Statutes and Orders-in-Council, supplemented by the building of the forts in the Great Glen, later known as Fort William and Fort Augustus, the road-making of General Wade, and

[1] *Sermon preached before the Society in Scotland*, 1741.
[2] *Memorial Concerning the Disorders in the Highlands*, 1703.

the periodic attempts to establish a permanent armed force, beginning in the seventeenth century and culminating in the Black Watch, were the legal and military means used by the Government to restrain the power of the Highland chiefs and to exercise political control in the North.

No less urgently did the power of the priests call for delimitation, for the Jacobite movement in politics coincided with the counter-reformation movement of the Church of Rome in Scotland.[1] While the Reformed Church had neglected the Highlands, "the restless emissaries" of the Catholic Church, who "compass land and sea to gain one proselyte", had made a sustained and courageous attempt to recover the North for Rome.[1] Their advance during the seventeenth century was considerable. Franciscans and Lazarites from Ireland strengthened the efforts of the Jesuits and secular clergy already in the North. They carried the Faith to "the Outer Isles", Uist, Canna, Eigg, and Skye, of "the barbarous Hebrides", and to the mainland country round and about Moidart, Arisaig, Knoydart and Glengarry, and set up schools in Glengarry and Barra, where the chief himself instructed the people "in the fear of God and the purity of the true faith", and "kept them firm against the assaults of heresy".[2]

Still more significant of the growing activity of Rome was the appointment in 1694 of Bishop Nicholson as Vicar Apostolic and Bishop Peristatum of Scotland—the first Roman Catholic bishop to be appointed since the Reformation. Fresh activity on the part of the Roman Church followed the appointment of this active and zealous prelate. In his *Statuta Missionis* he laid down the rules and regulations under which the work of the Church was henceforth to be carried on, dividing up the country into district missions, exhorting the priests to lead edifying and Christian lives and bidding them threaten with public penance and deprivation of the sacraments parents who permitted their children to be brought up in heresy. In 1700 there were reported to be in Skye no less than six priests and only five ministers. In South Uist, Canna, Knoydart, Moidart, Glengarry and neighbouring

[1] For a recent study of the Roman Church in Scotland see Maclean, D., *The Counter-Reformation in Scotland, 1560–1930*, 1930.
[2] Extract from a report of Thomas Nicholson, vicar-apostolic of Scotland, to the Congregation of Propaganda, 1700. Printed in Bellesheim, A., *History of the Catholic Church of Scotland*, trans. by Hunter Blair, 1883, vol. IV, Appendix VIII.

parishes, nearly all the inhabitants were Papists. During his itinerary through the Highlands in the summer of 1700, Nicholson claimed to have confirmed over 3000 persons. Five years later, to assist Nicholson in his labours, James Gordon was appointed coadjutor-bishop and Vicar Apostolic by Pope Clement XI. In 1707, Gordon reported to the Congregation of Propaganda that in his Highland itinerary of that year he had confirmed 2740 persons. Figures such as these, as a recent analysis has shown, cannot be sustained; they serve, however, to make clear that "a serious landslide to Rome" had taken place in and about the Great Glen of Inverness.[1]

Even more significant of the Roman revival was the establishment in 1712 at Scallin in the Braes of Glenlivet of a seminary for the sons of the local gentry who desired to enter the Church of Rome, and could not afford to go abroad for their instruction. No better choice for such a college could have been made. Surrounded by mountains which cut it off from interference with the world outside, it controlled the seven parishes within its frontiers, and succeeded, in half a century, in changing a population mainly Protestant into a population almost wholly Catholic.[2]

The activity of the Roman Church was in striking contrast to the passivity of the Church of Scotland. Disturbed by feuds within its own body, at open enmity with the Protestant Episcopal Church, and lacking the funds requisite for organising the Church in the Highlands as it had been established in the Lowlands, it made little headway in a country which, its preachers lamented, were "without true Religion". Of the "thousand parishes of Scotland" less than two hundred were to be found in the North.[3] Their vast size, "as large as Lowland Counties or German Kingdoms", particularly those of the Western Highlands and Islands, and the scattered population, in farms and townships set far apart, demanded not one parish minister, as appointed by law, but a body of clergy wearing seven-leagued boots. Some of the parishes extended for sixty miles in length by twenty in breadth, and mountain ranges, "whose heads touch heaven", and "arms of the sea", running

---

[1] Maclean, D., *op. cit.* p. 196.

[2] See Blundell, Dom Odo, *The Catholic Highlands of Scotland*, 1907, pp. 24 *et seq.*; *Ancient Catholic Houses of Scotland*, 1909, pp. 186 *et seq.*; Hunter, H., *Brief History of the Society for Propagating Christian Knowledge in Scotland*, 1796.

[3] Chambers, R., *History of the Rebellion of 1745-6*, 1827.

inland for miles, made others impassable. "Those who are strangers", said the Society in Scotland for Propagating Christian Knowledge, in an attempt to make its English supporters appreciate the size of the Leviathan parishes, and the difficulty of travelling in the North, "look upon the Highlands of Scotland as only a few Mountains and Glens of a small extent, but such would be informed that from the Mull of Kintyre to Farohead in Strathnaver they would be in a straight Line, from South to North, upward of two hundred miles, without counting the Turns, Peninsulas, and Arms of the Sea which come up into the Land, from Faroe Head to John o' Groat's House, it will be more than sixty miles, and this beside the vast number of Inhabited Islands which lye on this Coast, some whereof are large and populous." [1]

The lack of an adequate body of clergy was reflected in the scarcity of parish churches, and the distance of the church from the scattered homesteads was often so great that few persons could enjoy the ordinary means of instruction. Often the congregation attended services in the fields, and when the winter weather made this impossible they were, for several months in the year, deprived of the opportunity of assembling together for religious worship.

Alarmed by the activity of the Church of Rome, the Estates and the Church of Scotland early in the eighteenth century took action to meet the danger. In 1700 Parliament re-enacted the old laws, which had fallen into desuetude, against Jesuits and "trafficking papists", whose malice and subtlety were believed to be at the bottom of intrigues at home and abroad, and ordained that whosoever should disarm and seize them should, if they were convicted, receive 500 merks for his reward.[2] Honoured in the breach rather than in the observance, Parliament's attempt to restrict Roman propaganda produced little effect. The Assembly, wiser in its generation, adopted a constructive scheme whereby new presbyteries were established in the Highlands; Lorne in 1704, Tain in 1706, Dornoch in 1707, Caithness in 1709, Skye in 1712 and Dingwall in 1716. From 1724, when the Royal Bounty helped to replenish an exhausted exchequer, it appointed and sent out additional ministers, itinerant preachers and catechists to the remote parts. Had funds permitted, the division of the huge parishes and the setting up of new churches and schools would have set up an effective

---

[1] *State of the Society in Scotland*, 1729, p. 36.
[2] Act of the Parliament of Scotland, 1700, c. 3, vol. x, pp. 215–9.

barrier to the Roman advance. But the Church had not the means
or the energy for large-scale reform. Education, one of the subordinate crafts of Plato's *Statesman* for the creation of right opinion
and the elimination of wrong, came to the aid of arms and the law by
organising instruction on a voluntary basis in the "Principles of our
Happy Religion and Constitution", which, it was confidently believed,
would transform a disloyal and rebellious people into a peaceful and
loyal one.

II

THE FIRST PATENT OF THE SOCIETY IN SCOTLAND FOR PROPAGATING CHRISTIAN KNOWLEDGE, 1709

North of the Tweed, the charity school movement developed an
independent organisation for its threefold task. A praying society
formed in Edinburgh in 1698 was, according to the historian Wodrow,
the origin of the Scottish S.P.C.K.[1] Its members, among whom were
"several gentlemen of weight and distinction", corresponded with the
societies for the reformation of manners in England and learned from
the "outed" episcopalian minister, James Kirkwood, corresponding
member in Scotland of the English S.P.C.K., and from London
members of the Society, of the growing belief of English reformers in
the education of the children of the poor as the panacea for social,
religious and political ills. Kirkwood, who had been chaplain to Breadalbane, was alive to the neglected condition of the Highlands. He
prevailed on Sir Francis Grant, afterwards Lord Cullen, Robert Baillie
and George Meldrum, "men of knowledge, solid piety and estates",
to form a voluntary society to set up schools and libraries in the Highlands.[2] They collected money and sent a schoolmaster to open school
in the parish of Abertarf "in the heart of the popish country". Eighteen
months later, the school was closed, because the schoolmaster met with
"repeated discouragements from the inhabitants".[3] But his discourage-

---

[1] Wodrow, R., *Correspondence*, vol. III, p. 193.

[2] The Kirkwood MSS., Church of Scotland Library, Edinburgh, L.S. 16. 1. 3.
I am indebted to the Rev. Donald Maclean for calling my attention to these MSS.

[3] *Account of the Constitution and Management of the Society in Scotland*, 1714, p. 8.

ment was not shared by the Edinburgh gentlemen. "Finding it impossible in their private capacity to carry on so great and public a work", they drew up, in 1703, a memorial describing the disorders in the Highlands and Islands, and urged that vacant stipends in the Church, mortifications, private subscriptions, and a general collection throughout the country, should be authorised to raise funds for "charity schools, where religion and virtue might be taught to old and young".[1] The attempt to secure parliamentary support failed, but in the following year, the Church of Scotland, always sympathetic to the efforts of the Society, gave the support which the Estates withheld. The Assembly ordered its committee of education to explore the needs of the Highlands for instruction, and to find out what encouragement might be expected from the different districts, if it were possible to establish schools in them. When the returns were received the Assembly circularised the Presbyteries and persons of influence in the kingdom, requesting their assistance for a Society to Propagate Christian Knowledge in the Highlands and Islands and remote corners of Scotland.[2]

In 1708 the abortive French invasion in support of the Old Pretender stirred even the indifferent to action. Ready and generous response from nobles and commons, clerics and laymen, and from the Church of Scotland and the Estates, made it possible for the Edinburgh gentlemen in 1709 to apply to the Crown for letters of incorporation. Out of the large body of subscribers the Lords President and other Lords of Council and Session were empowered, by the first patent of 1709, to nominate the first eighty-two members of the new society, all of whom were, as the patent laid down, members of the Protestant communion, and, from this body, a president, a secretary, and a committee of fifteen directors were appointed as the executive of the new organisation.[3]

The task which faced the Edinburgh Society was immeasurably more difficult than that which had confronted the London S.P.C.K. Unlike the English Society, which left the control of the schools in the hands of locally elected trustees and managers, the Society in Scotland acted, from the beginning, as a central organising and controlling body

---

[1] *Memorial Concerning the Disorders in the Highlands*, 1703.
[2] Acts of the General Assembly of the Church of Scotland, Act 5, Sess. 5, 1707.
[3] See *An Account of the Society in Scotland*, 1774, Appendix I.

13

for all the schools set up under its auspices. It received and disbursed the funds for propagating education in the Highlands; it decided where the schools should be set up, and how long they should remain in their stations; it drew up the curriculum, appointed, paid, and dismissed the teachers; received the reports from its local committees, and at intervals sent out inspectors to report upon the schools. By its patent of incorporation it was declared capable of purchasing and enjoying lands, tenements, rents, tacks, liberties, privileges and jurisdictions in fee and perpetuity not exceeding the yearly value of two thousand pounds sterling. Restrained by its patent from encroaching upon its capital, the Society set up and maintained the schools out of income; its stock remained inviolate. Not until increase of funds permitted were new schools established. Losses arising from insufficient knowledge or errors of judgment were promptly cut, and, since the working expenses of the Society were confined to an honorarium of £25 each paid to its treasurer, bookseller, and clerk, the income was devoted to the setting up of schools, and only when the state of the finances allowed, to the propagation of the gospel among the American Indians, and to the publication of the Gaelic Bible at home. The Society's funds, controlled from headquarters, were not subject to the defalcations from which so many of the English schools suffered at the hands of dishonest or incompetent local trustees and managers, nor did the Society in Scotland forget, as the Incorporated Society in Ireland forgot, that the first essential of sound finance is to cut the coat according to the cloth. Its excellent business management was recognised by contemporaries and by posterity. Annual sermons were preached on its behalf in the High Church in Edinburgh, and both Anglicans and Nonconformists joined the Corresponding Society in London and contributed to its funds. The General Assembly of the Church of Scotland made collections for it throughout the parishes of Scotland; part of the Royal Bounty of £1000 paid annually by the Crown to the Assembly for the reformation of the Highlands and Islands, and other places where Popery and ignorance abound, was used to augment the salaries of the schoolmasters. Philanthropists, local magistrates and parish clergy in England and the Lowlands, impressed by the aims and methods of the Society, endowed it with funds for general purposes, or left benefactions to particular schools.[1] It remained for all these contributions a poor Society, whose

[1] See Hunter, H., *op. cit.*

work was narrowly circumscribed by inadequate funds. Until the last decade of the century its income was less than £2000 a year.[1]

A slow but steady increase in the number of schools was maintained throughout the century. Starting off with five schools in 1711, the year of the Fifteen found the number increased to twenty-five. The Rebellion supplied a fresh stimulus to both Government and Society to provide the Highlanders with education. An Act for the more effectual securing the peace of the Highlands in Scotland, passed in the first year of George I's reign, empowered Commissioners, appointed by the Crown, to make a full report of the educational requirements of the Highlands.[2] The report, when presented in the following year, stated that 151 schools, exclusive of those already established, were necessary, and urged the granting of competent salaries of £20 per annum to the schoolmasters appointed. By Acts of Parliament in 1718 and 1719 the forfeited estates of the rebels were vested in the Crown for public use and a sum of £20,000 was earmarked for the erection and maintenance of schools in the Highlands of Scotland.[3] But in spite of the efforts of the General Assembly and of the Society,[4] not a penny of the £20,000 was ever received by the Society for its educational work.

While the State delayed, the Society acted. By the middle of the century 150 schools were in existence, and a new scheme to provide industrial instruction had been put forward. Eight years later the schools under the first patent numbered 176. In the third quarter of the century a halt was called by the withdrawal of contributions from the Royal Bounty, paid since 1729 to schoolmasters, who acted as catechists. As a result the Society was obliged to reduce its expenditure. Schools whose pupils numbered less than thirty-five pupils were, "except those in parishes where papists reside", closed. In 1760 the total had dropped to 146. Within a few years, gifts and subscriptions allowed new schools to be opened, and the Society recovered from this set-back.

In the last quarter of the eighteenth century a new and unexpected

---

[1] *Abstract of the Proceedings of the Society in Scotland for Propagating Christian Knowledge*, 1792. The Society announced an accession to its funds in 1791 of £10,000 "from a most generous but unknown benefactor", and of £20,000 from the late Lord Van Vryhouven of Holland. Other large legacies were left to it in the last decade of the century.   [2] 1 Geo. I, c. 54.   [3] 4 Geo. I, c. 8; 6 Geo. I, c. 11.
[4] MSS. Church of Scotland Library, Edinburgh, Portfolio 42.

source of supply added twenty-four schools to those controlled by the Society under its first patent. The growing interest of the Government in education as a means of pacification and "civilitie" had been reflected in its educational policy after the Forty-Five. Acts disarming the Highlands, abolishing heritable jurisdictions, tenure of ward holding and Highland dress, passed immediately after the Rebellion, were, a few years later, followed by remedial legislation of far-reaching importance in religion, industry and education.[1] The rents and produce of the estates forfeited by the rebels to the Crown were applied to "civilising and improving the Highlands of Scotland". The management of the estates was entrusted by the Crown to Commissioners, funds were set apart and "Publick Schools" were erected on the said estates, or in other parts of the Highlands and Islands of Scotland, for instructing young persons "in reading and writing the English language and in the several branches of agriculture and manufacture". The schools which, as a rule, were set up in places where no school was accessible, "or where there was but one charity school which can benefit only a few neighbouring farms",[2] made no inconsiderable contribution to the loyalty, virtue and "civilitie" of the North. But in spite of their good record they were forgotten when the Crown, in 1784, was empowered to restore the forfeited and annexed estates to the former proprietors or to their heirs.[3] Financial provision had been made for all other officials employed by the Commissioners since the annexation of the estates, but, from lack of proper representation, the claims of the men and women teachers in these State-controlled schools to compensation was ignored. The Society, alive to the value of the work of the dispossessed teachers, and indignant at their neglect by the Government, took up cudgels on their behalf. It volunteered to take them into its service, and to pay the salaries formerly allowed to them by the Commissioners of the annexed estates, on condition that the Commissioners paid to the Society a lump sum of £2500. While the Board deliberated, the Society, "sensible that the school-masters might starve before the money was obtained", paid them from its own funds, and when the Barons of Exchequer in Scotland handed over the sum required in 1785, added sixteen schools to its establishment under the first patent, and

[1] 20 Geo. II, cc. 43, 50, 51; 25 Geo. II, c. 41..
[2] H.M. General Register House, Forfeited Estates Papers, Portfolio 6.
[3] 24 Geo. III, c. 57.

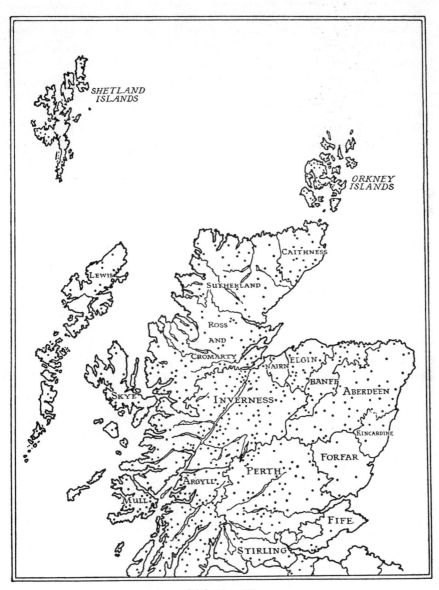

SCOTLAND

Map showing the distribution of the Schools of the Scottish S.P.C.K.

eight under the second patent.[1] In 1809, a hundred years after the Crown had granted a charter of incorporation to the Society, there were, in Scotland, 189 schools under the first patent, in which about 13,000 children received instruction.[2]

The minute books of the general committee of the Society, and of the smaller executive body of directors, bear witness to the sustained and consistent interest of the members in the schools they established. Unlike the London Society, whose enthusiasm was diverted from the founding of schools by the rival claims of missionary work abroad and the production of devotional literature at home, the Scottish S.P.C.K., while sharing these interests, was not diverted from its original purpose. The limited funds at its disposal were, in its opinion, laid out to better advantage in work at home than abroad. "Ten schools in the Highlands", it declared, "may be maintained for the expense of one missionary among the Indians and more certain and essential service done by them."[3] The minute books at the end of the century show no slackening of interest in the work of education.

The increase in number of the schools, while testifying to the sustained interest of the Society, was to a great extent neutralised by the

[1] The Schools on the Annexed Estates, as returned in the Appendix to the *Abstract of the Proceedings of the Society*, 1786:

Estate	Schools	Estate	Schools
Perth	Strelitz	Lochiel	Kinlocharkaig
	Craigneich		Strathlochie
	Glenartney		Mamore
Arnprior	Strathyre	Clunie	Clunie
Lochgary	Lochgary	Cromarty	Coigach
			South Uist
Strowan	Kinlochrannoch		
	Finnart		
	Glenorchty		
	Camagran and Carrie		

Also Spinning Schools at:

Crief	Boglot, near Callander
Muthil	Kinlochrannoch
Auchterarder	Clunie
Callander	Dunblane.

[2] See *Abstract of the Scheme of the Society's Establishments for the year 1809*, p. 47. See also Map, p. 181, and Appendix II, 1.

[3] Appendix to *Abstract of the Proceedings of the Society*, 1784, p. 45.

growth of population in the Highlands and Islands. In the second half of the century, in spite of emigration and the clearances for sheep walks, the population rapidly increased. That of the Hebrides was almost doubled. The schools kept pace with the advance, but failed relatively to improve their position. In 1728, 1758 and 1808 the numbers of children returned as attending the schools were respectively 2757, 6409 and 13,000.[1]

Two characteristics of the charity school movement in the Highlands call for particular attention. The schools were not, as the Society was careful to inform its supporters, rivals to the legal schools. It did not propose to relieve indifferent or hostile heritors from their legal obligations to support the parish schools. It refused consistently to send a schoolmaster to parishes which had not a parish school. The apathy and indifference of many of the heritors to their obligations was a serious handicap to the Society's work. Dr Hyndman, reporting as late as 1761 to the General Assembly of the Church of Scotland on the state of the Highlands, deplored the loss suffered by great parts of the country, "which, having no parish schools, could receive no aid from this excellent institution". Nor again would the Society undertake to set up a school unless the heritors, or a sufficient number of the inhabitants, would promise to provide the schoolmaster with a dwelling-house and schoolroom, grass for his cow and turfs for his fire. The charity schools were "supplementary" or "assistant" schools to the parish school, and they were deliberately set up at stations in the vast parishes remote from the legal school "lest one should hinder the success of the other".[2] Further, the Society's schools were not permanent institutions. The "impropriety" of fixed schools in the Highlands was a tenet of the Society's organisation. The thinly spread population, and the difficulties inherent in Highland geography, made the fixed school everywhere "ridiculous in the extreme", and on the north-west mainland and islands, where, reported Walker, there was scarce anything that could be called a village except Oban, Fort William and Stornoway, a useless extravagance.[3] Such schools afforded instruction only to children in their immediate neighbourhood, and allowed others, who lived at a distance and were "equally the sub-tenants of the

[1] Hyndman, J., Report to the General Assembly of the Church of Scotland, 1761.
[2] S.P.C.K. Minutes, March 18, 1731.   [3] Walker, J., *op. cit.* vol. I, p. 53.

same proprietor and consequently entitled to this favour, to grow up in savage ignorance".[1] Hence to allow Mahomet to go to the mountain the Society evolved the idea of ambulatory schools, later used with remarkable success in Wales. In the more populated parishes the schools were fixed for two or three years at one station, and were then removed to another; in districts where the children were few and the homesteads scattered the itinerant schoolmaster gave what instruction he could for a few months and went his way.[2]

It appears, however, from a comparison of the annual reports of the Society in the last quarter of the century that the itinerant character of the schools was not uniformly maintained. Some of the schools remained in the same station year after year. Occasionally, as for example in the eighties when "the rage of the Highland proprietor for sheep farming" caused depopulation in the converted areas, the argument in favour of circulating schools was refurbished, and the schools were removed by the Society from stations formerly full of adults and children, but "now occupied only by a shepherd and his dog", to other stations where there was still work for them to do.[3] By the beginning of the nineteenth century many of the schools had ceased to circulate. It is significant that the Gaelic Society, suggesting to its supporters in 1811 the advisability of ambulatory schools in the Highlands, referred them to the Welsh circulating schools as examples of the method to be followed.[4]

The local management of the schools, set up by the conjunct action of Society, heritors, and inhabitants, was in the hands of ad hoc committees. In each Presbytery the Society nominated the members,

---

[1] Forfeited Estates Papers, Portfolio 11, Memorial respecting the Obligations and Discharge required by the Barons of Exchequer upon their paying £2500 to the Society for Propagating Christian Knowledge [etc.].

[2] Endowed schools set up in places selected by their founders were exempt from the rule. Rainings's school at Inverness differed from the usual Society school in that it was fixed at Inverness. Wodrow states that "this noble foundation of a thousand pounds sterling" was "mortified" to the Assembly of the Church of Scotland which put it in the hands of the S.P.C.K. The Society set up the school in Inverness, finding it inconvenient to have scattered schools in the Highlands because "the boys were never masters of English which renders them useless afterwards". *Analecta*, vol. III, p. 357.

[3] Forfeited Estates Papers, Portfolio 11.

[4] *First Report of the Society for the Support of Gaelic Schools*, 1812, p. 15.

instructed them to meet four times in the year under the presidency of the moderator, to consider "the circumstances of the country", and to advise the Society where the schools should be placed and when salaries should be augmented or reduced. In co-operation with the minister and Kirk Session, sometimes with the baillie or other civil magistrate, they descended upon the school once each quarter and subjected the master and his pupils to a severe examination, testing his skill as a teacher of writing, arithmetic and church music, and their proficiency in the three R's and their knowledge of the principles of the reformed religion. They inspected the attendance lists, listened to the master's grievances, and constrained the parents, Protestants and Catholics, to send their children to school, and the inhabitants, great and small, to make contributions in money or in kind.[1] The reports of the committees, together with a "presbyterial certificate" testifying to the master's faithfulness and diligence, were transmitted annually to the Society, which paid no salary until the schoolmaster's work and conduct had been reported as satisfactory.[2]

So careful and thorough a method of inspection was not always consistently maintained. Local committees were not seldom rapped over the knuckles by the Society for neglect of their duties, and in particular for failing to report those heritors who did not honour their obligations. Nevertheless, compared with the indifference and incompetence of many of the local bodies of trustees in England as revealed by the Charity Commission reports, and the gross negligence of the local committees of the Incorporated Society in Ireland, the local educational authorities in the Highlands, like the central body at Edinburgh, were models of efficiency and responsibility.

III

THE HIGHLAND SCHOOLMASTER

Success in a threefold attack upon "barbaritie, jacobitism and poperie" required an army of well-equipped teachers. No pains were spared by the S.P.C.K. to find the right men to garrison the little stations in the

[1] S.P.C.K. Minutes, March 18, 1731.
[2] See the *Statutes and Rules of the Society in Scotland*, 1732, pp. 36–7. In 1790 the Presbytery of Dunkeld had twenty-seven schools under its inspection.

distant and popish parts of the country. The Scots Society did not demand from its teachers the qualifications, which, by the Act of 1696, were demanded from the parish schoolmasters, who, often the product of burgh school and university, taught not only the recognised subjects of the elementary curriculum, but, at times, prepared boys for the junior classes in the universities. These men prided themselves upon their knowledge of Greek and Latin, and on their proficiency in theology, philosophy, and literature and were regarded as the secular counterpart of the minister. Sometimes they were his equal in social position and intellectual power. To their co-operation is attributable the keen interest of the Lowland Scot in education. When the S.P.C.K. aspired to give the Highlands and Islands the religious and educational advantages which had been denied them by politics and geography, it was content to accept lower intellectual qualifications from its candidates. Its teachers fell into two categories, the "fixed teachers" who were engaged to teach the pupils for two years or more to read English, to write, and to cast accounts, and the "petty itinerants" who needed only the art of reading as their qualification for appointment. Latin, the hall-mark of scholarship, was ruled out. It was not required for charity school teachers, who were expressly forbidden to teach it to their pupils.[1]

Religious, political and moral qualifications, on the other hand, bulked large in the Society's requirements. No candidate was considered who was not well affected to the Government and whose manner of life was not approved by the Presbytery within whose bounds he resided. Personal attestation of his piety, loyalty, prudence and gravity was demanded by the Society, which ordered the candidates, when distance did not involve delay and too heavy an expense, to present themselves in Edinburgh for examination.[2] Possibly little difficulty in finding teachers would have presented itself, since pedagogy in Scotland conferred social distinction, and an opportunity for instructing others seldom fails to attract a Scotsman, but by a well-planned scheme of bursaries for Gaelic-speaking pupil-teachers the Society recruited from within its own body most of the teachers it required. "Lads o' pairts", ambitious to become teachers, were never lacking. Those among them who were "deficient in cultivation" were

[1] *Rules, Directions and Orders of the Society concerning the Schools*, 1729, p. 43.
[2] S.P.C.K. Minutes, Nov. 1, 1711; March 6, 1712.

put by the Edinburgh committee under a well-qualified master for improvement at the Society's expense.[1]

The minute-books and reports of the Society support the contention of its historians that the men selected for the lonely and onerous duty of schoolmaster were "of respectable talents, and attention to duty", loyal to the House of Hanover and to the reformed religion. Among them were men of intellectual distinction. The bard, Alexander Macdonald, who left his school and his church to become Poet Laureate to Prince Charles Edward in 1745, was a good classical scholar; Dugall Buchanan and Ewen MacLachlan were distinguished poet-teachers; and John Macdonald of the charity school at Bunloit, near Glen Urquhart, was recognised throughout Scotland as a theologian of repute.[2] It is not impossible to find among them men whose loyalty to the House of Stuart was greater than to a Society dedicated to the service of the House of Hanover, and who, when testing time arrived, left their schools to aid the Stuarts. Nor is it impossible to find others who were of indifferent moral character, careless of their duties, and

[1] S.P.C.K. Minutes, Nov. 3, 1720; June 6, 1723. Article 16 of the Statutes and Rules of the Society, 1732, reads as follows: "The Society being desirous to encourage some of their poor Scholars who may be found to be of more than ordinary Capacity for Learning, that these may be a Seminary out of which Schoolmasters may be had for teaching Schools, and that they may in the meantime be assisting to their own Masters who have numerous Schools in teaching the other Scholars, and that the Choice and Maintenance and Premium of such Bursars may be duly regulated, the Society appoints... that none shall have Claim to the weekly Maintenance and Premium allowed to the Society's Bursars or poor scholars, but such as shall be recommended and certified for that Effect, not only by the schoolmaster who at the Time teaches him, but also by the Minister of the Parish within which the School is settled, and the Visitors of the School appointed by the Presbytery...." The parents of the scholars were then required to promise that the lad should, when capable, serve as schoolmaster in any place of the Highlands and Islands. The Society, after receiving the certificate and obligation, duly signed, granted to the poor scholar twelve Pennies *Scots* every day "providing they attend their School the whole Week", and promised also a suit of clothes and a pair of shoes at the end of two full years attendance, and, if the poor scholars "incline to continue a third Year to be further perfected in order to be put in a Capacity to teach a School, they were to get Eighteen Pennies *Scots* each Day... or else they shall be boarded and maintained the said third Year at Rainings' School in Inverness...".

[2] Maclean, Magnus, *Historical Development of the Different Systems of Education in the Highlands*, p. 169. Publications of the Gaelic Society of Glasgow, 1895–1906; Mackay, W., *Education in the Highlands in the Olden Times*, 1921, Inverness, *passim*.

harsh in their behaviour to their pupils. But, as the Society claimed and as the reports of the parish ministers in 1755, and those of the *Statistical Account*, testify, they were "a body of laborious and meritorious men deserving well of their country".[1] Supervised, as a rule, with meticulous care by Presbytery and Kirk Session, there was not much opportunity for indifference or neglect of duty, and it must be remembered that salaries were not paid by the central office unless satisfactory reports had been received from the visiting Commissioners.

The regulations drawn up for the guidance of these Highland teachers closely resembled those which the London S.P.C.K. devised for its teachers in the Anglican charity schools. Curricula and methods were similarly rigid and restricted. Religious instruction was the backbone of the curriculum. It alone was capable of making men fit members of society. The masters were bidden to train up their scholars in the knowledge and principles of the reformed religion, by frequent repetition and exposition of the shorter catechism. Every morning and afternoon they were to lead the children in prayer. They were to encourage them to pray in private, and to beg a blessing before, and to give thanks after meat. Except during the three weeks' "vaik" in summer, the schoolmaster was to instruct his pupils daily in the true spelling of English words, the distinction of syllables, and the points and stops. Some portion of the Holy Scriptures was to be read every day in English, and when the children could read "competently well", instruction in writing and arithmetic was to follow. On Sundays the schoolmaster escorted his pupils to church and was responsible for their good behaviour there, and on Monday mornings the attentiveness of the scholars to the minister's lengthy and doctrinal discourse was tested by an examination of its content.

So far the duties of the Highland schoolmaster corresponded with those of his English counterpart, but, unlike the English teachers, his work did not cease when his day pupils were dismissed. Men who combined the offices of teacher and catechist called together the children for Sunday school in the church, where they read the scriptures and were publicly catechised by him. Night schools for servants and adults, who could not leave their work in the day-time, were within his province, and on

[1] *Report of the Secretary to the Corresponding Board of the Society in Scotland,* 1803, p. 56.

Saturday afternoons, when his pupils enjoyed holiday, he was bidden to visit the old and the sick who could not come to church.

Upon the tact and prudence of the schoolmaster depended the attendance of his pupils at school. The authority of Kirk Session and Presbytery could be brandished only at intervals. When the backs of the school visitors were turned, the schoolmaster could rely only upon his personal influence to persuade parents, indifferent to their children's schooling, or in need of their help in the fields or on the hill-sides, to spare them for their lessons, or to induce those who came to remain. In an age which believed that to spare the rod was to spoil the child, the Scots Society was surprisingly humane and in advance of its age. Brutal behaviour by the masters was kept in check, as far as it was possible to do so, by meticulous regulations prescribing the type of punishments permitted by the Society. Blows on the head, with the fists, or kicks on the body, were forbidden; when chastisement was deserved it was to be inflicted on the hand or breeches with a tawse. Most difficult of the schoolmasters' task in "papistical parts" was to induce Roman Catholic parents to send their children to school. It is a lasting monument to the Society that the intolerance and persecution which stained the records of both Roman and Presbyterian Churches in the Highlands were, by its express orders, eliminated from the organisation of the schools. It forbade the teachers in its employ to apply compulsion of any kind to the children of Papists. Further, it ordered them to use gentle means of persuasion only, and bade them take "double care of such children when they came".[1] Unfortunately it does not follow that the Society's instructions were uniformly carried out, or interpreted in a spirit of toleration. Threats and caresses and promises of material advantage, reported the Jesuit Mission to Propaganda, were the means used by the implacable Presbyterian clergy and teachers to fill the schools, and it is unlikely, when religious bitterness was acute, that parents or children escaped moral or physical pressure from minister and schoolmaster. On the other hand, the growing numbers of Catholic children who, with the approval of their priests, attended the schools to be "instructed in literature" at the end of the century suggests that the Society's denunciation of religious intolerance was more than a pious expression.[2]

[1] S.P.C.K. Minutes, Nov. 1, 1711; June 4, 1724; Aug. 3, 1732; Jan. 6, 1715; Jan. 7, 1731; *Statutes and Rules* [etc.], Art. 14.
[2] Report of Dr John Kemp, printed in Hunter, H., *op. cit.*

The financial remuneration for work which was both onerous and responsible did not err, even according to eighteenth-century standards, on the side of extravagance. While the salaries of the parish school-masters, by the act of 1696, were not to be less than 100 merks Scots (£5. 11s. 1⅓d.) or more than 200 merks Scots (£11. 2s. 2⅔d.), the fixed teachers in the Society's schools were paid, by a resolution of the Society in 1711, a minimum salary of 100 merks and the itinerant, or petty, teacher a maximum of 100 merks but it is possible to find amounts both more and less which were received by the Society's teachers. The schoolmaster at Badavochill received £22 a year, his fellow at Hoy but £2, and the salaries of individuals varied according to the funds at the Society's disposal in a manner most disconcerting to the recipient. The poet-schoolmaster, Alexander Macdonald, was paid £16 per annum in 1729, £18 in 1732, £15 in 1738 and £12 in 1744.[1]

The small salaries paid by the Society are a measure both of its limited resources and of contemporary estimates of the teaching profession. They did not, as the Society recognised, form a living wage. Unlike the parish schoolmaster, who was permitted by law to charge such fees as he could collect, and whose perquisites were often a considerable source of income, the charity schoolmaster was expressly forbidden, in the early years of the movement, to demand anything from his scholars, who were to be taught gratis. Only from "gentlemen or others in plentiful circumstances, who thought fit to send their children to the schools, and freely offer to pay for their education",[2] were the masters permitted to accept fees. The absence of a middle class, the poverty of the people and their indifference to education, made this permission of small pecuniary value. Many of the parents in the early years of the Society "cared so little for education that they had to be courted to send their children to school".

It was not the intention of the Society that its teachers should be entirely dependent upon the salaries paid to them. Before a school was set up it insisted that a house and a kail-yard should be provided by the heritors, or other influential persons, and that the inhabitants of the stations should provide the schoolmaster with turfs and grass.[3] No other single factor was as responsible as this regulation for the limited

[1] Mackay, W., *op. cit.* p. 36.
[2] *Rules, Directions and Orders of the Society concerning the Schools*, 1729, No. 9.
[3] *Statutes and Rules of the Society*, 1732, p. 38.

scope of the Society's work in the Highlands. Constantly, as the reports reveal, local lairds and substantial tenants failed to honour their promises. Among the heritors were men who, to the end of the century, put up strong opposition to the instruction of the vulgar, and the unfortunate teacher, when he arrived at his new station in distant glen or remote island, found neither schoolhouse, nor dwelling, nor kail-yard, nor grass, and out of his inadequate salary was obliged to provide himself and his family with these necessaries. Lack of local support was responsible for the Society's resolution of 1765 demanding from heritors and parents a formal obligation both of financial help and of assistance in kind, *before* the schoolmaster arrived.

Unorthodox methods of increasing the inadequate salaries were not infrequently used by the ill-paid teachers. Some received land instead of grass, or rented farms in the neighbourhood, and when seasonal work demanded their attention on the land, they put in deputies to do their school duties and scandalously absented themselves from school.[1] Towards the end of the century neither salary nor contributions provided the teachers with enough to live upon. Prices rose steadily through the eighties and nineties, and although wages rose too, the lag between them made the teachers' remuneration a beggarly pittance. While the livings of the greater part of the clergy had been considerably increased, reported the ministers again and again in the *Statistical Account*, no addition had been made to the salaries of the parish and Society schoolmasters. "Common tradesmen and day labourers earn a great deal more than the generality of schoolmasters can possibly do."[2] In the Society's schools the average salary was £12 a year, while the average wage of a casual labourer, the Society stated in 1799, was 1s. 2d. a day. The Society's secretary, on a tour of inspection in the Highlands in 1790, reported that the situation of many of the teachers was abject in the extreme, for there were not lacking proprietors who in these years of general poverty and distress tried to starve out the schoolmaster. They refused to contribute payments in kind for his upkeep, and threw the whole weight of his accommodation and supplies upon the shoulders of the people, who, in their turn, with equal injustice,

[1] S.P.C.K. Misc. Papers, 252; Remonstrance of the S.P.C.K. to the Synod of Ross for permitting the schoolmaster of Stennes to absent himself from school.

[2] Sinclair, Sir J., *op. cit.* vol. XI, p. 161.

attacked the schoolmasters as "engines of oppression".[1] The appeals of the Society for funds to meet the situation were only in part successful. In 1800 it was decided to reduce the number of schools from 208 to 198 so as to augment the salaries of the teachers who remained, but when this was done the average salary in 1803 was under £13 a year, a beggarly pittance which failed to attract the type of man desired. It is not surprising to find the Society in the first quarter of the nineteenth century perturbed by the inefficiency of its teachers, some of whom, it declared, were comparatively illiterate, and by the indifference of others "to the great and leading object of these institutions".

IV

ENGLISH OR ERSE?

Such were the duties and remuneration prescribed by the Society for the teachers in its employ. Armed with its rules and regulations they were sent out to do battle for the Hanoverian Settlement, and the Presbyterian Church, against the combined forces of "disloyalty, ignorance and irreligion". The most remote and backward parts of the Highlands were deliberately chosen as stations for the new schools. St Kilda, whose inhabitants were "not far reformed from Heathendom" and "had scarce ever heard the Gospel before the schoolmaster came among them",[2] was the scene of the first venture in 1709. Abertarf, where not many years before the fierce and inhospitable inhabitants had boycotted the Protestant schoolmaster, was chosen with equal deliberation as the scene of the second venture. Neither the Society nor its teachers lacked courage. Forty years later the inhabitants of Abertarf and Glengarry were still a thorn in the flesh of southern officials. They were reported as drunken, quarrelsome, churlish and inhospitable, "the very dregs of mankind" and "the plague of their neighbours".[3] When due allowance is made for official Whig distaste for rebel Jacobites after the Forty-Five, there yet remains a picture of a people whose hostility cannot have made the life of the charity schoolmaster an easy one.

[1] *Abstract of the Proceedings of the Society*, 1792.
[2] *Account of the Rise Constitution and Management of the Society in Scotland*, 1714, p. 18.
[3] Lang, A. (ed.), *The Highlands of Scotland [etc.]*, p. 108.

Undeterred by the hostility of the clansmen the teachers marched onward to the Highlands of Aberdeenshire and set up two more schools in and about the Braes of Mar and the heads of the rivers Don and Dee. In the same year a fourth school, whose charges were defrayed by the Countess of Sutherland, was established in the bounds of the Presbytery of Sutherland, a fifth in the parishes of Duirness and Farr, then in the Presbytery of Caithness; a sixth in the Presbytery of Skye; a seventh at Blair Atholl "in the Duke of Atholl's Highlands as suggested by his Grace"; an eighth in the parish of Glenelg; a ninth in the small Isles and Continent of Orkney; a tenth in North Zetland. Before the middle of the century schools had been set up in twenty-four Presbyteries of the North and in some of the remote corners of the Lowland Presbyteries.[1]

While the Presbyteries on whose shoulders rested the local responsibility of the schools were not uniformly encouraging in the early years, the heads of clans, especially, reported the Society, the Popish ones, were either hostile or indifferent. A new attempt to set up a school at Abertarf met with failure. The proprietor could not be prevailed upon to build the school-house, nor the Popish parents to send their children. The schools at Erlisbog and Glenelg, in the Presbytery of Skye, met with so much discouragement that they came to an end in 1713. At Aberlour in 1714 the priests, whose "insolence" the schoolmaster lamented, set up a rival school. Letters from the Society's teachers at Lairg in Sutherland deplored the "disesteem of education" among the people. The laird of Houston Sharp refused the Society's commission to set up a school.[2] In the Lovat country Lord Lovat, who, reported the Commissioners in 1750, had done more to revive the clannish spirit which had declined since the Revolution than any man in the whole country, consistently discouraged the establishment of the schools. "He declared himself an enemy to all who educated their children at them."[3]

The opposition of the Roman priests and missionaries was a less serious deterrent to the success of the charity schools than the indifference and occasional hostility of the chiefs. The persistence of the

[1] MSS. Church of Scotland Library, Edinburgh, Portfolio 42.
[2] S.P.C.K. Minutes, June 3 and 6, 1714; March 12, June 4, 1713; August 12, 1714; June 3, 1714; Jan. 6, 1714; July 13, 1713.
[3] Lang, A. (ed.), *The Highlands of Scotland* [etc.], pp. 188–9.

14

Roman faith in the Highlands, and the increase in the number of their communicants, which the Presbyterian preachers consistently asserted, and which Webster's census of 1755 and Walker's report ten years later confirmed, was a never-ceasing anxiety to the Protestant interest. To check its progress the catechetical teachers of the Royal Bounty and the masters of the charity schools put up a sturdy defence. Highland Protestantism owes no small debt to them. But, compared with the vigorous and sustained educational policy of the Roman Church in Ireland, the Catholic Church in the Highlands lacked force. The priests did not view with indifference the schools set up by the S.P.C.K., and were alive to the danger of this new Presbyterian weapon. Bishop Nicholson's report to Propaganda, telling of the contributions made by the public to the Society in the hope that the schools would put an end to Popery in the Kingdom, revealed his acute anxiety. But Rome, while recognising *"una certa campagnia a titolo di propagare la fede Christiana tra i Barbari, ma diretta in fatto alle perversione dei Cattolici, che si contengono costante in tutto quei paesi..."* [1] did not attempt to meet the danger, as the Roman Church did in Ireland, by encouraging a rival system of schools. Its only weapon, one not always used, as the reports of the S.P.C.K. testify, was the threat of public penance and the deprivation of the sacraments to parents who permitted their children to attend the schools. [2] But rarely did the local committee of the Society report the existence of Popish schools. The Protestant schoolmaster, as the only educational agency in many parts of the Highlands, could and did attract the children of Roman Catholic parents to the schools.

For opposition from Catholic gentry and Roman clergy the Society was prepared. It was a condition of the struggle for "true religion" which in time, by "God's good grace", would be broken down. Far more difficult to overcome was an obstacle of the Society's own making, its opposition to the Gaelic tongue. Sharing the conviction of English-speaking people that the English tongue was the heaven-sent medium of religion and civilisation, the Society early in its existence

[1] Archiv. Propag. Acta, fol. 175, 9 April 1726, quoted in Bellesheim, A., *op. cit.* vol. IX, p. 169. See also *Instructions for Mr John Tyrie, Roman Catholic Missionary to the Highlands, 1731, revealed in a letter to the Duke of Newcastle,* London, 1747.
[2] S.P.C.K. Minutes, August 12, 1714.

decided that the extirpation of Erse, "the rude speech of a barbarous people and one of the chief causes of the continuance of barbaritie and incivilitie among the inhabitants of the Highlands and Islands,"[1] was the first step to reform. Schoolmasters were reminded that one of the chief designs of the schools was to teach the poor to read English. They were forbidden to teach the children to read or speak Irish "except when turning it into English", and were instructed to appoint censors from among the older pupils whose duty it was to "delate transgressors" of the rule. For over half a century the Highland schoolmaster laboured at the Herculean task of instructing an illiterate peasantry to read the Bible and the shorter catechism in a foreign tongue.

This was the primary difficulty which handicapped the Society's efforts in the first half of the century. The eager desire for education which impressed contemporaries in Ireland and in Wales was absent in the Highlands. Only occasionally did the inhabitants send in petitions asking for a school to be set up. While Irish reports tells of parents on their knees begging the Incorporated Society to take their children into the schools, and *Welch Piety* describes the crowding of men, women and children into barn or church to be taught by the schoolmasters, the sheep in the Highlands were not eager to be fed with English foods. Instead, there are frequent lamentations of "the inveterate prejudices of the Highlanders to education", of the "rooted aversion of the people to the schools", and bitter complaints that the inhabitants in the neighbourhood of the schools were unwilling to contribute to the schoolmasters' keep appear in the minutes and reports of the Society. It was not until 1766 that the committee of directors recommended that the regulations prohibiting the teaching of Erse should be rescinded and that the schoolmaster should be instructed to teach the children both English and Erse "in those places where Erse is generally spoke".[2]

[1] Act of the Privy Council for Erecting Parish Schools, Dec. 10, 1616; see also S.P.C.K. Minutes, March 6, June 6, 1766.

[2] "The division of language among the different districts of the eastern parts of the North of Scotland", reported the Society's School Inspector in 1800, is "a striking phenomenon, which has never yet been sufficiently accounted for. In *Lord Reay's country* Gaelic is the only language spoken by the common people. In six parishes of the ten which constitute the Presbytery and shire of Caithness *English* is the general language. In the other four Gaelic is the dialect of the common people; as it is in all the parishes of the counties of *Sutherland* and *Ross*, and also

The change of policy in 1766 was not due to a change of attitude towards the superior qualities of the English tongue as the instrument of religion and civilisation, but was a belated recognition of the fact that children who were taught to read aloud the Scriptures in English did not understand what they read. For years at a time the teacher, in accordance with the Society's regulations, instructed his pupils in the spelling of words, the distinction of syllables, with the points and stops, which is necessary to right reading, "until many of them could read fluently yet, through intire ignorance of the English language, hardly understood a word of what they read".[1]

For a method so inept the schoolmaster was not to blame. Teachers and school visitors who, in the course of half a century, had questioned its wisdom and efficacy, had no means of teaching the reading of the scriptures except through the English language. For neither the Bible, nor the catechism, nor devotional literature with the exception of the psalms, was available in Gaelic. Copies of Bishop Bedell's Irish Bible were scarce and the Irish dialect so different from the Gaelic that the inhabitants "could not fully understand it".[2] To read the Scriptures the children were perforce obliged to learn English. In 1739 the first attempt was made to help the schools by the publication of a Gaelic and English vocabulary, but it was not until 1758 that *The Mothers' Catechism*, in Gaelic, prepared by one of the Society's schoolmasters, and not until 1767 that a translation of the New Testament, made by James Stewart of Killen, was ready for the press. The Society, before 1766, was alive to the need of a Gaelic version of the Scriptures, but the charge of maintaining a steadily growing number of schools absorbed its revenues. In 1767 it met the heavy expense involved in printing 10,000 copies of the New Testament in the express hope that "the children will make more progress in the Knowledge of the English

of *Cromarty*, with the exception of three parishes, viz. *Cromarty itself, Rosemarkie* and *Avoch*, in which English alone is spoken. Immediately after crossing the Murray Firth *Gaelic*, excepting in *Fort George* and *Inverness* among strangers and people of better fashion, who speak English, the *Gaelic* resumes its influence, and continues along the coast to *Nairn*, where it ceases. It prevails through the whole of *Inverness-shire*, the high districts of *Aberdeen* in the line of Braemar, and through the Highlands of *Perthshire* to *Dunkeld*, where it gives place to English alone and unmixed." Appendix to the *Report of the Society*, 1800, p. 15.

[1] *Proceedings of the S.P.C.K.*, 1780, p. 78.
[2] *Sermon preached before the Society in Scotland*, 1765.

language by thus learning to translate from the Gaelic into English than they have done hitherto".[1]

The translation of the New Testament was followed years later by the printing of a Gaelic version of the Pentateuch which "was read with avidity by the people, exciting in them a thirst for knowledge and a desire to learn the English language which they never before discovered".[2] In 1782 the Society and the General Assembly of the Church of Scotland made a conjoint appeal throughout the parishes of Scotland for funds to raise the £1300 required to print a Gaelic version of the whole Bible, but the poverty of the country was so great in this year of scarcity, that many parishes could afford no contribution. Twenty-five years elapsed before a complete edition of the Gaelic Bible appeared, and, by a curious irony, when the means were forthcoming for instruction in Gaelic a pronounced distaste for it was shown. "A general prejudice", lamented the Society, which a hundred years before had prohibited its use, "existed against the use of Gaelic as a school language." Conscious at the beginning of the nineteenth century of the advantage of understanding the English tongue, Highland parents were resolved to have their children "taught English chiefly if they attend school at all".[3]

---

[1] *Sermon preached before the Society*, 1765. So momentous a change of policy was not made with precipitation. The opposition of some of the members of the Society to the translation of the Scriptures into Gaelic called forth "a generous indignation" from Dr Samuel Johnson. "Sir," he wrote to William Drummond, Bookseller to the S.P.C.K. in Edinburgh, "I did not expect to hear that it could be in an assembly convened for the propagation of Christian Knowledge a question whether any nation uninstructed in religion should receive instruction; or whether that instruction should be imparted to them by a translation of the holy books into their own language. To omit for a year or for a day, the most efficacious method of advancing Christianity in compliance with any purposes that terminate on the side of the grave, is a crime." Boswell, *Life of Johnson*, Globe ed., pp. 181–2.

[2] *Abstract of the Proceedings and Correspondence of the S.P.C.K.*, 1784, p. 35.

[3] *Report of the Sub-Committee of the Society on the Visitation of the Schools*, 1825, p. 26.

V

THE SECOND PATENT, 1738

During the first half of the eighteenth century instruction of the peasantry in the reformed religion and the English tongue formed the chief design of the schools, but belief in the efficacy of the shorter catechism and a foreign language as instruments of civilisation were shaken by the continuous political unrest and by the rising of the clans against the Government. The schools had not checked the rebellion of 1715. Indeed, as the Presbyterian preachers admitted, it was from the remote mountains where the schools had been set up that the Highlanders, "like a dark torrent through a peaceful land, spread fear and death on every side".[1] Seeking for a cause of the continuance of "incivilitie" in spite of the increasing number of schools, puritan reformers and government officials found it in the "incurable sloth and idleness" of the Highland people. When therefore a proposal was made to supplement the education given in the schools under the first patent by instruction in husbandry and industry, it met with ready response.

Two factors in particular contributed to the setting up of schools for technical instruction. In the thirties, when the Society applied to the Crown for extended powers, enthusiasm for working schools was at its height in England and Ireland. The Society in Scotland, always in close touch, through its correspondents, with the S.P.C.K. in England, and aware of the progress of the new Incorporated Society in Ireland, was moved to follow its neighbours' examples in the new method of instructing the poor. Schools which would teach young people to labour "when their minds are young and their tempers like willow" suggested a means of reforming the Highlands and other remote parts which had not yet been used. It appealed alike to laymen and cleric. Sermons and reports expressed approval of a method which combined instruction in religion and industry for the lower ranks of mankind. "The discipline of labour", said the preacher, "will teach them most rationally to serve God."[2]

[1] *Sermon preached before the Society in Scotland*, 1750.
[2] *Sermon preached before the Correspondent Board in London of the Society in Scotland*, 1787.

The second factor was the growing interest of landed proprietors and the monied middle classes in land reform after the Union in 1707. Beginning before the eighteenth century, "the improving movement" in Scottish agriculture produced, in the course of the century, an agricultural revolution. Lands lying runrig were enclosed, chiefly for the purpose of planting and grazing, but here and there, as the century grew older, for agriculture also. The market for black Highland cattle in England, opened by the Union, offered limitless opportunities, if the difficulty of supplying winter feeding could be met. Hence the growing interest in the provision of artificial grasses and root crops for cattle. The individual efforts of men like Sir Robert Gordon of Gordonstone and Sir Alexander Grant of Monymusk, in the early years of the eighteenth century, were strengthened in the twenties by the association of proprietors in the Honourable the Society of Improvers in the Knowledge of Agriculture in Scotland. Two similar Societies, one of Buchan farmers, and another of agriculturists in Ormiston, were local organisations at work for the same end in the thirties. The Edinburgh Society for Encouraging Arts, Sciences and Agriculture was founded in 1735. Enthusiasm was widespread; even the Highlands and remote corners did not remain unaffected by it.[1]

Closely associated with the improving movement in agriculture was the attempt to increase the raising of flax and the manufacture of linen. From the seventeenth century the industry, which was to become, in the eighteenth century, the leading industry of Scotland, had received attention from the State. Acts of Parliament had been passed to encourage it by enforcing standards of quality, but without marked effect. The quality of the cloth was unsatisfactory and the trade suffered in consequence. The Union, by establishing free trade between the two kingdoms, struck a blow at the hitherto protected woollen industry in Scotland, but, by removing at the same time duties on the export of Scottish linen into England and the Colonies, gave great, though not immediate, encouragement to the industry. Built upon the bedrock of custom, for flax was grown throughout the Lowlands and was considered especially well suited to the small-holdings of the Highlands, the manufacture of linen promised golden returns. Custom,

[1] See *An Essay on Ways and Means for Inclosing and Planting in...Scotland*, 1729; *Select Transactions of the Society of Improvers in Scotland*, ed. by R. Maxwell, 1743, XLIII–XLVII.

too, was able to produce "a tolerable store of spinners and weavers who may easily be improved into good artists", for the flax was spun, bleached and woven in hall and cottage. "Every woman", wrote Miss Muir of Caldwell, recalling her memories of the twenties and thirties, "made her web of wove linen, and bleached it herself".[1] It needed but the support of the State to make the manufacture of linen cloth the backbone of Scottish industry, and in 1727, by the Act for Encouraging and Promoting Fisheries and other Manufactures and Improvements in Scotland, the Board of Trustees for Manufactures was set up.[2]

Grants made under the Act of Union to improve Scottish industry, and further sums, which accrued from the malt tax when its annual yield was in excess of £20,000, had accumulated during the twenty years which had elapsed since 1707. An income of £4000 was at the disposal of the new Board of Manufactures. Part of the income was applied to the linen manufacture. Premiums for the growing of lint and hemp seed were offered, and prizes were presented to housewives making linen cloth. A sum of £150 was, under the Board's scheme, put aside for the establishment of spinning schools, four of which, at a cost of £10 a school, were to be set up in the Highlands, where indolence and poverty reigned supreme, and spinning was "least understood".[3]

It was at this stage that enthusiasm for improving land and linen joined forces with enthusiasm for improving the manners and customs of the Highland people. As early as 1726 the Convention of Royal Burghs, which from the Union to the establishment of the Board of Trustees had taken trade and industry under its wing, had played with the idea of introducing spinning into the charity schools and any other schools where there were upwards of thirty pupils, "for the encouragement of younge children between the age of 8 and 14 to dress and spin flax and hemp and coarse wool".[4] The S.P.C.K., in no way averse from the idea, but precluded by its patent from using funds for technical instruction, prepared itself for an extension of its powers. In 1738 it made representations to the Crown, and received from it a second patent enabling it to raise funds and to set up Schools in suitable places

---

[1] *The Caldwell Papers*, 1854, vol. II, pp. 260 *et seq.*
[2] 13 Geo. I, c. 3.
[3] Warden, A. J., *The Linen Trade, Ancient and Modern*, 1867, p. 447.
[4] *Records of Convention of Royal Burghs*, vol. V, p. 427; quoted in Dean, I. F. M., *Scottish Spinning Schools*, 1930, p. 59.

for "the breeding up of young people to handy labour, trades and manufactures", which experience had shown would be of great benefit, not only to themselves, "but likewise to the nation in general and better answer to the inclination of the contributors for promoting piety and virtue".[1]

Anxious to use its new powers to the best advantage, the Society invited the public, through the Edinburgh papers, to send funds and suggestions. Land and linen at once clamoured for assistance, and by 1742 sufficient money had dribbled in to allow the Society to make a tentative experiment in the new method of education. A successful appeal for a schoolmaster to teach agriculture in the parish of Muthil in Perthshire, marked the inauguration of the second patent. The proprietor undertook to provide the schoolmaster appointed by the Society "with a house, and a little farm, gratis, where he may breed the boys at school to all the parts of husbandry". The Society's schoolmaster in a neighbouring parish "thoroughly acquainted with all the parts of farmery, having been for some years at that trade in England", was appointed to the new school stationed at Auchtermuthil in which labour was to be joined to learning. But in spite of a promising beginning, the experiment was a failure. There were difficulties with the tack, and these did not disappear when the school was removed to Callendar. The farm, situated on a "barren muir", was too remote to attract pupils and required considerable expenditure of money for initial improvements; finally, the schoolmaster appeared incapable of coping with his job. In the opinion of the minister of the parish, he was incompetent both as a farmer and as a domine. The experiment came to an abrupt end in 1744.[2]

The Rebellion of 1745 called a temporary halt to schemes of technical instruction, and it was not until fear and confusion had abated that the civilisation of the Highlands began in earnest. Upon the estates forfeited to the Crown the Crown's Commissioners set up fifteen schools, whose curriculum combined religious, literary and technical instruction.

[1] For recent studies of eighteenth-century education in Scotland see Dean, I. F. M., *Scottish Spinning Schools*, 1930, and Mason, John, *History of Scottish Experiments in Rural Education*, 1935. I am indebted to Dr Mason for calling my attention to the schools set up on the forfeited estates and for the use of his manuscript materials relating to the schools of the S.P.C.K.

[2] S.P.C.K. Minutes, April 1, 1742; Jan. 6, March 17, 1743; March 23, 1744.

They were expressly designed to promote "the Protestant Religion, Good Government, Industry and Manufactures and the Principles of Duty and Loyalty to His Majesty, His Heirs and Successors and to no other use or purpose whatsoever". Eight spinning schools for girls were also established by the commissioners on the estates.[1]

The Government's activity did not diminish that of the Society. On the contrary, the failure of the Rebellion afforded it an opportunity of asserting that the schools had played their part in its collapse, since the "common people" had not risen in 1745 as they had done in 1715. It claimed that as "the prime movers" of the Rebellion came from those corners which were least affected by the charity schools, the need of an increased number of schools was clearly shown. "Knowledge, Industry and Labour" could not, it asserted, fail to exercise the desired influence.[2] Hence, six years after the Rebellion it made its second experiment under its new patent, this time in co-operation with a local association of gentlemen and farmers under the leadership of Robert Scott of Duninald, who presented a scheme for the instruction of boys in the principles of Christianity, good morals, the history of Great Britain, the art of husbandry, agriculture, gardening, geometry and land measuring. A schoolmaster was engaged in 1752, at a salary of £12 a year, to carry out the modest requirements of the promoters at Craig in Montrose. Four years later, as the Society was unable to extract from Scott or his friends any report of progress in the school, or of the work of the schoolmaster, it withdrew its support.[3]

Co-operation with the linen industry met with a greater measure of success. Half-way through the century the influential Board of Fisheries and Manufactures began to establish little colonies in the Highlands "to wean the inhabitants of these countries from their evil habits of idleness and disaffection to the Government". Conspicuous among the enterprising local heritors who gave encouragement to the work was Lord Deskford, a trustee of the Linen Board and later, as the Earl of Findlater, a famous "improver" in Banffshire. At Portsoy in 1751, where an embryo factory village had been set up, the Society, at Lord Deskford's request, agreed to support a schoolmaster, if his loyalty to

[1] 25 Geo. II, c. 46.
[2] *State of the Society in Scotland*, 1748, p. 54.
[3] S.P.C.K. Minutes, March 19, 1752; Minutes of the Committee of Directors, Jan. 25, 1756.

the Government was assured, to instruct the children in the mornings in religion and the three R's, and to supervise their work at the spinning school, or at the loom, or the stocking-frame, or in assisting the fisher-men and gardeners of the little colony, in the afternoons, according to their ages or capacities.[1] A similar plan was followed at Logierait, where a school was set up at the request of a company of Perth linen manufacturers in the same year.[2]

Some measure of the restricted scope of technical instruction open to the Society under its second patent is provided by its minute books for the year 1755. While funds available for the schools under the first patent amounted in this year to the interest on the capital of over £18,000, expenditure under the second patent was limited to the interest on the paltry sum of £336. 14s. 5d. Funds permitting a more sustained effort were necessary if the Society was to play its part in the economic reconstruction of the Highlands. Answers to a *questionnaire* addressed to the parish ministers in twenty of the Highland Presby-teries provided the Society with much needed information on the educational requirements of the Highlands, and incited it to co-operate in the ambitious schemes for setting up manufacturing villages at Lochcarron and Glenmoriston.[3]

The famous experiment at Lochcarron was a combined effort of the proprietor, the Board of Manufacturers and the Society for Propagating Christian Knowledge. A hundred acres of land, "very capable of improvement", were rented from the laird by the Board, twelve of which were devoted to the building of a manufacturing village as near as possible to the kirk. A dwelling-house and a storeroom of stone and slate were set up in a central position for the chief undertaker appointed by the Board, and on the outskirts of the village were the huts of clay and wattle made for the expert craftsmen from the South. Two primary factors were required for the success of the experiment at Lochcarron as elsewhere. The first was to attract skilled craftsmen of unquestioned loyalty to the Government from the South, and to keep them contented with their lot in their new environment. To this

[1] S.P.C.K. Minutes of the Committee of Directors, Dec. 8, 1750.

[2] S.P.C.K. Minutes, Jan. 5, 1751; Minutes of the Committee of Directors, Dec. 8, 1750; *State of the Society*, 1752, p. 45.

[3] S.P.C.K. Papers. Returns by Parish Ministers to the Society in Scotland for Promoting Christian Knowledge, 1755.

end the laird of Lochcarron undertook to protect them in their new homes, amidst unfriendly and sometimes hostile inhabitants; to provide them with summer grass and winter fodder at the current prices, and to make himself responsible for any cattle, horses, or sheep stolen from them by the natives. The undertaker, on his part, assisted the new-comers to grow lint and raise flax, paid them their wages, and supervised their work and their accommodation.

The second condition, compared with which the first was a simple matter, was to attract the children of the natives to the new factories. For assistance on this side of the experiment the proprietor, on the advice of the Board, appealed to the Society. The inhabitants, he declared, were "alert to the need of a schoolmaster to teach their children in writing and arithmetic", and, as they were well disposed to the manufacturers, he proposed that the children should be instructed also in the craftsmen's arts.

After mature consideration the Society made its first big contribution to technical instruction in the Highlands. It not only appointed a schoolmaster under the first patent at a salary of £15, but supplemented him with a ploughman at the same salary, a shoe-maker, cartwright and blacksmith, each at a salary of £10 a year, and a spinning mistress, who was paid 1s. a quarter for each child instructed by her. To encourage parents too far distant, or too poor, to spare their children for instruction, it authorised each of its male teachers at Lochcarron to take five apprentices, and undertook to pay £5 a year for the lodging and maintenance of each one. But neither skilled instructors nor maintenance allowances succeeded in breaking through the stubborn conservatism of the Highland people. While the school proper was crowded with children, who came to learn the three R's, the craftsmen instructors waited in vain for pupils to present themselves. The blacksmith and cartwright, reported the undertaker to the Society in 1756, had each one apprentice awaiting indenture, the shoe-maker "had not got offered any apprentice", and the ploughman, whose advanced methods in preparing the ground for oats, barley and potatoes were watched with open and interested curiosity by the natives, had only "one offer of an apprentice". The spinning mistress was slightly less unpopular. She could boast of three pupils. When, in 1760, the five years allotted to the experiment came to an end, the Society decided to bring it to a close, and the unfortunate craftsmen, drawn from the South to introduce industrial arts into the Highlands, made their ways home again.[1]

The Glenmoriston experiment began with the same eager anticipations, and met with the same disappointment. The site was recommended to the Linen Board by the principal undertaker for the linen industry in the district as a suitable "concentrical spot" for an industrial colony, for it lay within twenty Scots miles west of Inverness in the bosom of an inland glen far removed from the main highway. The Board of Trustees again appealed to the Society to co-operate in setting up a school. Their appeal describing the ignorance and irreligion which prevailed among the natives in the glen cannot have failed to awaken memories of the Society's earlier efforts in the Presbytery of Abertarf, when its first schoolmaster, half a century before, had retired in discomfort before the fierce and inhospitable Macdonalds. In 1755, the "great ignorance and irreligion" of the inhabitants was still the most striking characteristic. "They know no more", reported the undertakers of the Linen Board to the Society, "than by hearsay that there is a God, and were they to be asked for anything further they would be found to be as ignorant as the wild Americans. Any of them that profess religion are gross papists, and it can hardly be otherways, as they are deprived of the means of knowledge and education, having no schools among them, no minister to instruct them, nor publick worship, and being thus neglected the Popish priests who are indefatigable in making Proselytes, corrupt the minds and morals of the people and instill into them Rebellious principles, destructive to the principles of our happy Constitution and Revolution." To a man they had taken part in the Rebellions of 1715 and 1745.[2]

The undertakers' claim that the appointment of a schoolmaster, a shoe-maker, a tailor, a cartwright, a smith and a farmer would remedy the existing state of depravity and afford an effectual means of civilising the people, impressed the Society, but an expenditure on the scale suggested was beyond its purse. It appointed a schoolmaster, and gave a grant of £10 per annum towards the salary of a mechanic, whom it

[1] S.P.C.K. Minutes of the Committee of Directors, Feb. 6, March 5, 1755; March 3, 1756; Oct. 10, 1759; see also Minutes of the Board of Manufactures, July 18, Aug. 2, 1754, quoted by Dr John Mason, *op. cit.* pp. 12 *et seq.*

[2] S.P.C.K. Minutes, June 5, 1755; Minutes of the Committee of Directors, March 20, 1755.

authorised to take five apprentices, making an allowance for their board and maintenance as it had done at Lochcarron. At the end of five years this experiment, too, was written down as a failure. Two apprentices only during the period had been indentured; both had run away to enlist; and in 1762 the Society withdrew its encouragement.

These two expensive failures would have restrained the Society from further experiments in technical instruction, had not a legacy of £2000 obliged it again to consult the public as to the best means of using public money. The new bequest was earmarked for the second patent, and the capital sum was to be spent, and not put into stock. Once again, through the Edinburgh newspapers, the Society appealed for suggestions, and, after one or two tentative experiments, decided to apply part of the legacy to binding out promising male pupils in its schools to trades and agriculture in the Highlands, and to farmers and artisans in the Lowlands, on the understanding that the boys should return to the Highlands, bringing their improved technique with them, when their apprenticeship was ended. Thirty-five lads from the Highlands and Islands had been appointed to farmers, weavers, flax-dressers, carpenters, wheelwrights, blacksmiths, and other craftsmen by the year 1769, and some of them, the Society's *Accounts* report, returned when their apprenticeship was at an end to the Highlands,[1] but the sparse references to this side of the Society's work in its later records suggests that its success was strictly limited. Twelve hundred pounds of the legacy were devoted to the instruction of girls, who had learnt to read in the Society's schools, in spinning, and the manufacture of stockings. Twenty spinning mistresses were to be appointed under the scheme, each with a salary of £15 for every hundred girls taught, and the greater part of the sum was to be expended on wheels and reels for the pupils when they had learnt to spin and to knit. To meet the difficulty of attendance the spinning mistresses, like the teachers under the first patent, were to be itinerant, teaching the craft at such stations, and for such a length of time as the Society should decide.[2]

The dislike of Highland women to instruction in handicrafts may be measured by the Society's reports of 1774, which showed that there were but twelve spinning mistresses in its employ, and not one of them

---

[1] *State of the Society in Scotland*, 1769, pp. 14, 15; see also Mason, John, *op. cit.* pp. 32 *et seq.*

[2] S.P.C.K. Minutes, March 3, 1763; *State of the Society*, 1769, p. 13.

had sufficient pupils to earn the maximum salary of £15. It was not until 1783 that there were upwards of twenty spinning schools in the Highlands. In 1787, when the Society took over the schools on the restored estates, the number was increased to thirty-six. Ten years later, helped by two big legacies, a total of ninety-four schools was reached "at which it is computed, for the returns from these schools are neither so regular nor so exact as from those on the first (patent), are educated about 2350 young people, chiefly females".[1]

It is impossible to contend that the schools set up under the second patent had not, as the Society admitted, "generally miscarried".[2] Land reform tarried in the remote and backward parts. Improvements on the estates of the Duke of Gordon and Lord Findlater excited the admiration of Andrew Wight when on his tour of inspection for the Commissioners of the forfeited estates in 1773, and in the less barren islands of Colonsay and Islay the improvers made some advance, but in general Highland agriculture was unaffected by the improving movement of the eighteenth century, and as the barren country-side offered little hope of farming for profit, the incentive for an agricultural revolution was lacking. "The husbandmen of Scotland", said Wight in 1778, "go languidly on in the old beaten track."[3]

Industrial results were only less unsatisfactory; yet if the attempts of the Society in Scotland to provide instruction for the youth of the Highlands in handicrafts be compared with those which prevailed in the English charity schools, some measure of success might reasonably have been expected, for local proprietors and undertakers were eager to make the experiment a success, and willingly employed specialist teachers who possessed the requisite technical knowledge of the several handicrafts to be taught. But against these two advantages the scales were heavily weighted by the difficulty of growing flax in the Highlands on a large scale, and of transporting the cloth from the remote places to market. Above and beyond these two difficulties was the deep-rooted objection of the Highlanders to handicraft occupation. Although the schools were set up in the midst of the native population and premiums and apprentice fees were offered to attract children whose homes were distant from the schools, parents could not be

---

[1] *Abstract of the Proceedings of the Society in Scotland* [etc.], 1797.
[2] Hunter, H., *op. cit.* 1795, p. 68.
[3] Wight, W., *Present State of Husbandry in Scotland*, 1778, vol. I, p. 185.

induced to allow their children to abandon their customary mode of livelihood for that which was new and strange. Handicrafts were sedentary occupations carried on inside a house and, as such, were unfitted for the male Highlander who, in the picturesque phrase of Mrs Grant of Laggan, "never sits at ease at a loom; it is like putting a deer in the plough".[1] Such handicrafts as were practised were regarded as women's work. The spinning schools, the residue of the conjoint efforts of Society, trustees and proprietors to establish working schools in the Highlands, owed their relative success to the fact that they drew their pupils from the female section of the community. The gifts of wheels and reels to girls who attended the schools extended the craft among the women folk, many of whom, reported the Society's inspector in 1802, formerly employed in the labour of the fields "most unsuitable to their sex, are now occupied in spinning, sewing and knitting stockings and the like appropriate employments", which enabled them to gain a "considerable subsistence for themselves".[2]

VI

THE END OF THE CENTURY

There are few instances in history of a transformation so rapid and complete as that which changed the interests and character of the Highland people in the course of half a century. Before the end of the eighteenth century they had ceased to be a political danger to the Protestant Succession and to the English Government. The penalising acts after the Forty-Five had drawn the teeth of opposition to the Crown. Still more effective in the pacification of the Highlands was the "Healing Act" of 1752.[3] By the restoration of the forfeited estates in 1784 the policy, begun thirty years before, was completed and, as the country settled down under the new conditions, the North followed the example of the South, and transferred its allegiance from the House of

---

[1] Mrs Grant of Laggan, *Letters from the Mountains between 1773 and 1807*, vol. I, p. 103.

[2] *Report of the Secretary of the Society in Scotland*, 1803, p. 55; *Account of the Funds, Expenditure and General Management of the Affairs of the Society*, 1796, p. 53. See also Sir John Sinclair, on the influence of the dame schools at the end of the century upon the home industries of knitting and spinning, in *The Statistical Account*, vol. I, pp. 244, 580.   [3] 25 Geo. II, c. 41; 24 Geo. III, c. 57.

Stuart to the House of Hanover. Liberal legislation may claim a share in the changed political atmosphere which marked the end of the century.

More remarkable even than the political differences was the change which had taken place in the social life of the Highland people. If they had not beaten their swords into ploughshares they had, in the words of a contemporary, "melted down into the votaries of peace".[1]

The transformation of the Lowlands in the eighteenth century has usually been attributed to the threefold influence of a dominating Church, an unusually efficient system of parish schools, and a widespread industrial organisation, but in the Highlands the parishes were too vast, the ministers too few, and the population too dispersed to allow the Church to control the life of the people as it did in the South, or to permit preaching and disputation to play the prominent part which is ascribed to them in the moral and intellectual development of the Lowlands. Nor did industrialism irrigate the North with the commercial civilisation which had helped to metamorphose the South.

It is to the influence of education, coupled with the new economic conditions of the second half of the century, that the changes in the Highlands, which astonished contemporaries, must in the main be attributed; and of the different agencies which were responsible for the instruction of the Highland people in southern "civilitie" the charity school played a leading rôle. It would be an untrue representation of the facts to confine the influence of education to the efforts of the S.P.C.K. Its work was too circumscribed by lack of funds to claim for it more than a share in the transformation. The work of the ministers and catechists, the teachers in the parish schools, the Royal Bounty schools, the schools on the forfeited estates and the dame schools, which at the end of the century were to be found here and there in village and clachan, is too well recognised to be forgotten. Cattle drovers returning from their journeys across the Border, traders who brought new standards of material comfort with their wares, inquisitive travellers encouraged by legends of the fine military roads to visit the Highlands, soldiers recruited for service in the Highland regiments on the Continent, coming home on leave, have received recognition as missionaries of southern civilisation. One and all contributed to break down the isolation and ignorance of the Highland people. It is nevertheless to

[1] *Sermon preached before the Society in Scotland,* 1759.

the charity schoolmaster, whose work has not received due recognition, that the greater share of the responsibility belongs. With the Bible in one hand and the three R's in the other he penetrated to the most remote and backward parts, teaching and preaching as he went, and, as in Wales, he left behind him men and women who could read the Bible and could, moreover, teach others to read it too. But for the exertions of the S.P.C.K. and its teachers, the Highlands, declared the Gaelic Society in its *First Report* of 1811, "would, in great measure, have been destitute of the means of education".[1]

The effect of the schools on the religious, political and economic history of the Highlands is not easy to estimate. It may fairly be claimed for them that they made a contribution to the spirit of religious toleration, for in an age and in a country of bitter religious animosities the Society set its face against persecution and proselytism. It would be unwise to suggest that individual teachers did not use both means to fill their schools, but it is significant of the Society's reputation that its inspector, travelling in the Highlands at the end of the century, told of the help and co-operation of the Roman priests, and of the welcome given to him in Roman parts of the country by proprietors "whose religious opinions prevented them not from promising countenance and support".[2]

[1] *First Report of the Society for the Support of Gaelic Schools in the Highlands and Islands of Scotland*, 1812, p. 11.

[2] *Report of Dr Kemp, Secretary to the Society, upon his Tour of Inspection of the Schools, in the Highlands and Islands*, 1791, p. 61. The Secretary's itineraries in 1787, 1790 and 1791 illustrate the "remote character" of the schools, upon which the Society's Reports lay stress, and the difficulty of transit, since the inspection could be made only in the summer months. The following is an abstract:

1787. Set out from Perth to Crieff and Killin, thence by the coast of Lorn to the Isle of Mull, and a variety of islands in its neighbourhood. Returned to the mainland and travelled by Appin and Fort William, through Lochaber to Fort Augustus; from thence by the north side of Lochness into Ross and Cromarty shires and through the counties of Sutherland and Caithness; returned by Inverness, Fort George, Strathspey, and Badenoch.

1790. Visited schools in the Highlands of Perthshire, Strathtay, Breadalbane, Glenlyon, Rannoch and Atholl. Hence to the head of the Spey in the Parish of Laggan; followed the course of the river and visited schools in the parishes of Kingussie, Duthill, Rothiemurchus, Alvie, Abernethy, and Cromdale; the schools in the parishes near to Inverness and Inverness Town. Thence by a very indirect course, "following the direction of the schools wherever they led him", he covered

In the political history of the North it is more difficult to establish the importance of the schools. It was asserted by the Society that "the lower kind of people" did not respond to the appeal of the Stuarts in 1745 as they had done in 1715. It is not easy to produce proof of this alleged difference, but it is at least possible that "the spreading of the English tongue", "the Knowledge of the Principles of Christianity", and "instruction in Loyalty to the King and Subjection to the Government" played the part ascribed to them by the Society in the failure of the Forty-Five.[1]

More considerable and more certain is the influence which the charity school movement exercised upon the social and economic condition of the Highland people, for it shares the responsibility, with the changing economic conditions of the second half of the century, in inciting adventurous spirits to leave the country. Although the depopulation of the Highlands culminated in the clearances for sheep farming of the later eighteenth and of the nineteenth century, a slow and steady trickle of Highlanders into the Lowlands persisted throughout the century, and, beginning with Oglethorp's colonising efforts in Georgia in the first quarter of the century, the stream of Highlanders who left the country to find homes across the seas seldom dried up.

A persistent cause of the emigration was the inability of the country to support a population too large for its primitive agriculture. By substituting an economic for a military organisation of society the Rebellion of 1745 accelerated the exodus. A rise in rents was the logical result of the disappearance of military service, and the resumption of leaseholding by the proprietors was, to improving landlords, the first essential. Small holdings were thrown by them into larger units, and were leased to farmers from the South, who brought improved agricultural methods with them, or the holdings were, with increasing speed in the later years of the century, put down under grass for sheep. From Argyle and Inverness-shire emigration began on a considerable

the Highlands of Nairn, Murray, Banff and Aberdeen, and returned by Strathdon, Cromar, Braemar, Glenshee and Forfar.

1791. Set out from Perth and Strathearn, proceeded through the parishes of Callendar, Aberfoil, Buchanan, Luss, Arrochar, and Lochgoilhead to Inverary. Visited the parishes west of the town, rode by the western coast of Kintyre to Campbelltown; sailed to the Island of Arran; returned to Kintyre; crossed Lochfine into Cowal, and travelling by the east coast of Kintyre came back to Inverary.

[1] S.P.C.K. Minutes. June 4, 1747.

scale in the sixties. The seventies witnessed a remarkable exodus of families from Skye, Islay, Orkney, the Hebrides and from the northern mainland. The great emigrations of 1786 and 1788 were accelerated by the famines of 1782 and 1783, which are still remembered in local tradition. In the last decade of the century most parts of the Highlands were in process of depopulation and many great tracts of country, once inhabited by men, were now occupied by sheep.[1] As the changes slowly and irregularly made themselves felt emigration abroad or chronic under-employment at home was the alternative which faced the Highland people.

A spectacular increase of population in parts of the Highlands coincided with the rise in rents. It is doubtful whether the Highlands under reformed agrarian conditions could have supported the population in the first half of the century without recourse to the aids of war and cattle-raiding; it seems clear that no improvements in agriculture could have coped with the increasing numbers in the second half of the century, when a large population lived permanently on the verge of subsistence. Faced by a slow declension in the means of livelihood, Highlanders of courage and initiative left the country in a steady stream with their wives and children, leaving behind them the more dependent members of the community, who, from lack of courage, or untoward circumstances, or passionate love of country, did not join the immigrant train.

In stirring the vigorous to action, and providing the consolation of religion for those that remained behind, the charity schools played a part of considerable importance. Unlike the English Society, whose efforts were, in the main, directed towards the establishment of social discipline by means of religious instruction, the Scots Society was concerned chiefly with the desire to convey the blessings of southern civilisation to the people of the Highlands and Islands. To this end it taught them to read and speak English, and, in so doing, it provided the means whereby adventurous spirits prepared themselves to leave the country, and push their fortunes abroad. The minutes and reports of the S.P.C.K. show that some part at least of the eager desire of the

[1] Forfeited Estates Papers, Portfolio 11; see also Adam, M. I., "The Causes of the Highland Emigrations, 1783–1803", and "Eighteenth Century Landlords and the Poverty Problem", in *The Scottish Historical Review*, vols. XVIII and XIX, 1921–2.

peasantry to read and speak the English tongue in the second half of the century, when the Society no longer insisted upon its inclusion in the curriculum, was due to their recognition of the fact that English was an invaluable equipment for immigrants to English-speaking lands.[1] Towards the end of the century the Society reported a growing opposition to the schools from proprietors and farmers. While emigration was normally welcomed by heritors and sheep-owning tacksmen, there were among them those who, fearing a lack of cheap labour, refused to contribute to the schools on the ground that "education encouraged the common people to leave the spade and the plough and push their fortunes abroad".[2] To the sturdy men and women determined to "get education" the opposition of unsympathetic heritors to the schools acted as an incentive to emigration. Emigrants from Moidart, Arisaig, Knoydart and North and South Morer explicitly asserted that this was a reason for leaving their homes.[3] Nor was the growing interest of the people in education confined to potential emigrants. Less adventurous spirits, who were too poor to comply with the Society's condition that the schoolmaster should be supplied with a house and a schoolroom, set to work to supplement the legal and charity schools by their own efforts. From the neighbouring charity schools they selected lads "qualified to become teachers of others", and offering them board and lodging in lieu of pay, sent them round the villages in rotation to teach the children for a few months at a time.[4]

It is by this action of the Highland people that the work of the charity schools in the Highlands should be judged. When the century opened the conditions of Highland life were favourable neither to physical nor to intellectual development. Possessing, by virtue of clanship, freer social intercourse with their superiors than was customary among the English or Lowland peasantry, their extreme poverty and devotion to their chiefs robbed them of the advantages which should have accrued from greater social independence. The second half of the century, which witnessed the breakdown and gradual disappearance of the old organisation of society, deprived them of their customary social relations without providing any form of compensation. Coinciding as

[1] Appendix to *Report of the Society*, 1825, p. 26.
[2] Appendix to *Report of the Society*, 1800, p. 22.
[3] *Abstract of the Proceedings of the Society*, 1792, pp. 46–7.
[4] *Report of the Secretary to the Society*, 1789, p. 67.

this did with economic changes which were unfavourable to their interests, their position, at the end of the eighteenth century, was less satisfactory than in its early years. From the chief turned landlord they received little material help or advice for improving their position. Indeed, by the introduction of the potato and by their opposition to emigration, the Highland landlords, in the second half of the eighteenth century, encouraged rather than discouraged the maintenance of a large supply of under-employed labour. "Theirs was the detested maxim", said Burt, in terse criticism of Highland chiefs at the beginning of the century, "that to render the people poor would double the tie of their allegiance", and the same criticism is made by the S.P.C.K. at the end of the century, when it pertinently remarked that the outcry against the charity schools was due to the desire of some of the gentry "to keep the people at home in ignorance and subjection".[1]

The English tongue and the Gaelic Bible suggested two ways of escape from conditions which were fast becoming intolerable. Far from undermining the characteristic independence of the Highlanders the charity schools provided them with the only means of translating it into effective action. To men of vigour and courage the English language offered a new world across the seas; to those who remained behind the schools made possible independent access to the consolations of the Bible.

In the nineteenth century Scotland enjoyed a well-deserved reputation as a literate and instructed nation. The charity schoolmaster and his Highland pupils merit no small share of the general approbation.

[1] See *Abstract of the Proceedings of the Society*, 1792, p. 44: "There are proprietors who even in the present time are not ashamed to avow it as their principle that knowledge of all kinds except in the occupations of common life, is not only useless, but pernicious to the vulgar: that it renders them dissatisfied with their condition and ambitious of altering it for the better either at home or abroad."

CHAPTER VII

IRELAND

CHARITY AND PROSELYTISM

"Who will say that the extreme poverty of the parents was not intended to open an effectual door to the preservation and conversion of these children?" *Sermon preached by John Thomas, D.D., Canon of St Paul's Cathedral, on behalf of the English Protestant Working Schools in Ireland*, April 2, 1747.

I

THE PROTESTANT ASCENDANCY

The peculiar political and religious conditions prevailing in Ireland in the eighteenth century were responsible for the tragic failure of the Irish charity school movement. A sense of pity and a passion for reform no less sincere than those which had driven men to action in England and the Highlands were conspicuous in the early years of the movement, for a people whose poverty, ignorance and squalor were more intense, in the opinion of contemporaries, than those which obtained elsewhere in Europe, called loudly for help. It was the unhappy fate of Ireland that succour was bestowed in a form which did little to improve material conditions, and much to exacerbate religious and political differences.

The charity school movement in Ireland was predominantly rural in character. It was concerned in the main with the lower tenantry and in particular with the cottier class, which formed the bulk of the peasantry.[1]

---

[1] "One of the most curious and unfortunate blunders which have been made about the Irish cottier", wrote Professor Cairnes in his *Fragments on Ireland*, published in *Political Essays*, 1873, "is that which confounds him with the peasant proprietor, under the general description of a representative of the *petite culture*. In fact, the two forms of tenure are, in that which constitutes their most important attribute—the nature of the cultivator's interest in the soil which he tills—diametrically opposed: and the practical results stand as strongly in contrast as the conditions. It would be difficult, perhaps, to conceive two modes of existence more utterly opposed than the thriftless, squalid, and half-starved life of the peasant of

Their wretched condition was the salient feature of Irish social history in the eighteenth and nineteenth centuries. The poor, menial and un-propertied condition of this class was not the creation of the eighteenth century. Irish agrarian history has established its existence from early times. It was "the constant element" in Irish society, for "the tempest which devastated the castle swept over the cabin".[1] Wars and confiscations which sent landowners to "Hell or Connaught" left the cottiers undisturbed. They remained as hewers of wood and drawers of water to their new masters, their conditions little affected by the change. At the end of the seventeenth century their numbers were estimated by Sir William Petty at 600,000 out of a total population of 1,200,000. In the eighteenth century their ranks were steadily recruited from above.[2]

The well-known descriptions of Petty and Stevens show that the husbandry of this large class was as backward and their conditions of life as squalid as those of the Highland people.[3] There was the same primitive agriculture, the same mean housing, the same subsistence level of existence, but the Irish peasantry suffered from additional disadvantages, material and spiritual, which helped to make them the most "beggarly, wretched and destitute" of Christian and civilised peoples.[4]

The new land system, by which lands which had escheated to the Crown after the rebellions of the seventeenth century passed in fee

Munster and Connaught, and that of the frugal, thriving, and energetic races that have, over a great part of Continental Europe—in Norway, in Belgium, in Switzerland, in Lombardy—and under the most various external conditions turned swamp and deserts into gardens...Between the métayer and the cottier there is the broad distinction that while the rent of the former is a fixed proportion of the produce, determined by custom, that of the cottier is whatever competition may make it—the competition, we repeat, of impoverished men bidding under the pressure of prospective exile or beggary...Cotterism (omitting the condition of personal freedom and regarding it simply in its economic aspect), was thus, in fact, serfdom reduced to a money standard and modified by competition," pp. 159–66.

[1] Sigerson, Dr G., *History of Irish Land Tenures*, 1871, p. 36.

[2] Petty, Sir W., *Political Anatomy of Ireland*, 1672, p. 9. For criticism of his figures see O'Brien, G., *The Economic History of Ireland in the Eighteenth Century*, 1918, chap. 1.

[3] Petty, Sir W., *op. cit.*; *Journal of John Stevens, 1689–1691*, ed. by R. H. Murray, Oxford, 1912.

[4] Berkeley, Bishop, *The Querist, 1735-6-7*, in Frazer, A. C., *Life and Works of Bishop Berkeley*, 4 vols., 1901.

simple to Protestant landowners, made a notable contribution to the existing distress. Rack-renting became the characteristic feature of estates held by the absentee landlord and resident proprietor. The agents of landlords living in England and the middlemen, to whom proprietors leased their lands on long lease, were alike in their indifference to the cultivation of a soil which, unlike that of the Highlands, was rich and fertile, and to the need of the lower tenantry for some form of tenant right for their protection. Holding their small farms on short leases, normally for one year, and lacking security of tenure in a country where competition for land as the main and, in many parts, the only source of livelihood was acute, the "little farmers" could escape eviction only by paying rent in excess of that which their holdings could afford. As a result their rents were invariably in arrears and improvements not only lacking but actually suppressed by them. More often than not eviction followed and the small tenants swelled the already overcrowded ranks of the cottier class.

Designed deliberately to check Irish landowning, the penal laws of the eighteenth century, prohibiting Roman Catholics from obtaining lands from Protestant owners by gift, sale and inheritance, or from holding a lease of more than one life, made their contribution to the depression of the agricultural classes.[1] The Catholic gentry excluded by these measures from "durable and profitable tenure", turned their efforts to grazing, for pasture farming required little capital and less labour. This "policy of self defence" brought in quick returns and was "suited to men confined to a fugitive property"[2]. It was equally advantageous to Protestant landowners not so confined, but to the tillage farmers and labourers turned off the land it spelt disaster. The victory of pasture over agriculture in the first half of the century was primarily responsible, according to contemporary opinion, for the misery and idleness of the people and for the dispersion of the "schuloag race", "communities of industrious housekeepers, called yeomanry in England", who were the backbone of the Irish tenantry.[3] Unable to retain their farms when their leases expired, they, too, swelled the cottier class from above. Indifference on the part of landowners and middle-

---

[1] Irish Statutes, 2 Anne, c. 6; 8 Anne, c. 3.
[2] Taaffe, Viscount, *Observations on Affairs of Ireland from the Settlement in 1691 to the Present Time*, Dublin, 1766, p. 12.
[3] Taaffe, Viscount, *op. cit.* pp. 12, 13.

men, and the levelling down of the schuloags, deprived the main industry of the country of guidance and leadership. "The lower tenantry", said Arthur Young in the last quarter of the century, "labour under a total want of countenance and support."[1]

To the distress arising from the land system and the decay of agriculture the Established Church made its contribution. Tithes, justifiable when the tithe-payers were members of a church supported by them, were an intolerable burden to a people who, by a large majority, were not members of its communion, and were, perforce, obliged to contribute to the support of the Roman clergy who ministered to them, maintaining thus "a double set of clergy".[2] The immunity of pasture land from tithe aggravated the grievance of the tithe-payers. While the large graziers, who could best afford to contribute to the revenues of the Anglican Church, were exempt from its incidence, the method of its collection added to the distress of the small tillage farmer, on whom the chief burden fell. Seldom were the tithes collected by the clergy in person. Sometimes they were farmed out to tithe-farmers, "the middlemen of the clergy",[3] who fleeced both the parson and the peasantry. More commonly they were collected for the clergy by proctors, who enjoyed in contemporary Irish literature an unsavoury reputation. They were, in Froude's words, "perhaps of all the carrion birds who were preying on the carcase of the Irish peasant the vilest and most accursed".[4]

The hand of God contributed to the misery inflicted by man. Famine, always a lurking danger in Ireland, was general in the first half of the century. Swift, Sheridan, Berkeley, Boulter and Dobbs are among those who tell of the appalling distress after the years of famine from 1726 to 1729, when thousands quitted their homes to get bread elsewhere.[5] "They are every day dying and rotting by cold and famine,

---

[1] Young, A., *Tour in Ireland...made in the years 1776, 1777, 1778*, ed. C. Maxwell, 1925, Part II, p. 198.

[2] Wakefield, E., *An Account of Ireland, Statistical and Political*, 2 vols., 1812, vol. II, p. 809. [3] O'Brien, G., *op. cit.* p. 144.

[4] Froude, J. A., *The English in Ireland*, 1881, vol. II, p. 493.

[5] Swift, J., *Short View of the State of Ireland*, 1727; *Modest Proposals for Preventing the Poor of Ireland from being a Burden to their Parents and Country*, 1729; Sheridan, T., *The Intelligencer*, No. 6, 1728; Frazer, A. C., *Life and Works of Bishop Berkeley*, 1901; Dobbs, A., *Essay upon the Trade and Improvement of Ireland*, 1729–31; Boulter, Archbishop, *Letters*, 1770.

filth and vermin", wrote Swift in 1727; "the younger labourers could not get bread and pine away for want of nourishment to a degree that if at any time they are accidentally hired to common labour they have not the strength to perform it."[1] In these terrible years "the poor were sunk to the lowest degree of misery and poverty".[2] Even worse were the years which followed the great frost at the end of 1739. "Want and misery", reported a contemporary, "are in every face; the rich unable to relieve the poor, the roads spread with dead and dying bodies, mankind the colour of the docks and nettles it feeds upon."[3] Migration from place to place in search of food and work was a result. After the middle of the century there was no general famine comparable with those of the earlier half, but local shortages were chronic, and made their contribution to the army of strolling beggars who, as Lecky suggests, began their wandering under pressure of want and acquired a liking for a vagrant life. Arthur Dobbs, writing in 1731, estimated their number at over 34,000.[4]

In spiritual as well as in material matters the bulk of the Irish peasantry, as members of the Roman communion, suffered from disabilities which, at most, affected but a small minority of the Highland people. It was the considered policy of the Government to rid the country of Popish priests and illegal schoolmasters to whom, not without reason, it ascribed the creation of a public opinion inimical to the Protestant ascendancy. The penal laws which prohibited the holding of civil and military offices under the Crown, the exercise of the parliamentary and municipal franchise, membership of parliament, of the universities, gilds and corporations, were outside the interests of the peasantry;[5] but the Act of 1697, which prohibited a succession of Popish clergy, thereby threatening the existence of the Roman priesthood in Ireland, touched them closely and directly.[6] The thousand priests who in 1704 took the oath of allegiance to the Crown were registered and

---

[1] Swift, T., *Collected Works*, 1752, vol. IV, p. 232.
[2] Sheridan, T., *op. cit.* p. 3.
[3] *The Groans of Ireland*, 1741.
[4] Dobbs, A., *op. cit.* vol. II, Part II, pp. 45–8.
[5] 2 Anne, c. 6 [Irish Statutes]; 3 Will. and Mary, c. 2 [English Statutes]; 10 Will. III, c. 13; 7 Geo. I, cc. 5 and 6; 2 Anne, c. 6; 7 Will. III, c. 4; 2 Anne, c. 3 [Irish Statutes].
[6] Irish Statutes, 9 Will. III, c. 1.

permitted to remain in their parishes, but no bishop was allowed to remain in the country in order to ordain new priests, and as none were permitted to enter the country from abroad, it was anticipated that when the generation which had taken the oath in 1704 died out there would be none to replace them. By 1710 a sensible decrease of Popish priests was reported, and the extinction of "the whole succession" within a few years was confidently promised.[1] Instruction by Popish schoolmasters was forbidden by the Act of 1709, and rewards were offered by the Government for the discovery and apprehension of every unregistered priest and illegal schoolmaster.[2]

That the memory of two bloody rebellions in the seventeenth century, and the threat of foreign invasion in the first half of the eighteenth century, made the penal restraint of Catholic activities necessary for the preservation of the Protestant Succession in England and the Protestant Ascendancy in Ireland explains the severity of these enactments. Regarded as political measures they are easier to justify than the penal laws imposed by a Catholic majority on a Protestant minority, as in France, or by a Protestant majority on a Catholic minority, as in England. In a country where Catholics were to Protestants as 2 : 1 the power of Rome to unloose a subject from his allegiance to his temporal ruler created very real and acute alarm, and provides a better justification than can normally be made for intolerance.[3] On the other hand the attempt of a minority to proscribe the religion of a people deserves the greater condemnation. Laws forbidding a succession of Roman clergy and restricting Roman Catholics from "teaching school" were enactments designed to exterminate the priests and schoolmasters, and to deprive the mass of the people of instruction in their religious beliefs. "If we should measure our temper by our laws", admitted William King, Archbishop of Dublin, "I think we are little short of the Inquisition."[4]

[1] See Memorial presented to the Duke of Ormonde in 1710 printed in Mant, R., *History of the Church of Ireland*, 1840, vol. II, pp. 220–27.

[2] Irish Statutes, 8 Anne, c. 3, reinforcing 7 Will. c. 4.

[3] Petty, Sir W., *op. cit.*, returned the proportion of Roman Catholics to Protestants in 1672 at 8 : 3. In 1731 the proportions were returned at 2 : 1. In 1805 at more than 8 : 3. See Newenham, T., *A Statement of Historical Inquiry into the Progress and Magnitude of the Population of Ireland*, 1807.

[4] Letter of Archbishop King to Bishop Burnet [n.d.], quoted in King, C. S., *A Great Archbishop of Dublin*, 1906, p. 90.

A study of Popish education in the first half of the century shows, however, that law and temper were not always identical. Sometimes both the will and the power were lacking to put the law into execution; sometimes a breach of the law was winked at by officials of Church and State; sometimes Protestants, disliking it, deliberately broke it. The Protestant squires of the new land system, from whose ranks the country magistrates were drawn, were not normally on terms of violent antagonism with their Catholic neighbours, nor were they always eager to play the informer. It is not impossible to find Roman bishops working and living unmolested in Ireland in the first half of the century, nor can the steadily growing number of unregistered priests and illegal schoolmasters, confounding the promise of their early disappearance, be explained except in terms of Protestant indifference. It is significant that the persons whose conduct the legislature most deplored were Protestant schoolmasters, who, in order to attract pupils to their schools, employed, in direct contravention of the law, Roman Catholic ushers and assistants to serve under them.[1] Time and place played their part in the alleviation of anti-Catholic legislation in Ireland, as in England and Scotland, and, after 1748, the laws were repealed one by one. But it is nevertheless true that the penal laws, described by Edmund Burke in a memorable passage as "a machine of wise and elaborate contrivance for the oppression, impoverishment and degradation of a people", pressed heavily upon the priests, and only less heavily on the schoolmasters.[2] The law was not the less severe because its execution was incalculable. Priests and schoolmasters were not seldom hunted like beasts; they were at the mercy of spies and informers, and a price was put upon their heads. Their courage and devotion in setting the law and its penalties at defiance brought them into close touch with the peasantry, and strengthened the ties of gratitude and affection which gave both priest and schoolmaster an impregnable position as leaders and champions of the people in later years. While the Government offered £10 a head for the discovery of every Popish priest and teacher, the people gave them food and shelter, and paid the dues that they could afford.[3] With the connivance of the peasantry these

---

[1] Irish Statutes, 7 Will. III, c. 4; 8 Anne, c. 3.
[2] Burke, E., *Letter to Sir Hercules Langrishe*, 1792.
[3] Irish Statutes, 8 Anne, c. 3; see also *Charge to the Grand Jury at Bandon Bridge*, *Co. Cork, Jan. 13, 1740*, by Sir Richard Cox of Dunmanway, 3rd ed., 1741.

men carried their particular brand of religious and political instruction to pupils awaiting them in the alleys of the towns or, as Arthur Young saw them in the second half of the century, in the ditches and hedges of the country-side.[1]

II

THE EARLY CHARITY SCHOOLS

The Irish charity school movement was directly related to the penal laws in restraint of Popish education. Conscious of the loss which the native Irish suffered from the prohibition of Popish schoolmasters and unregistered priests, without whose guidance, as Protestant reformers admitted, "the children were abandoned to the grossest ignorance of Christian and moral duties", and aware of the success of the charity school movement in England in tackling the twin devils of pauperism and infidelity, Irish Protestants found in the charity schools a means by which "the whole nation might become Protestant and English and all such rebellions as have heretofore arisen from the difference between us in Religion, Language and Interest may for the future be prevented".[2]

Ireland has with justice been called in modern times "the laboratory of English education".[3] Two centuries before the charity school movement began the Tudor sovereigns had initiated an educational policy which offers one of the earliest illustrations of State legislation directing under legal penalties the teaching of youth.[4] As early as 1537 the maintenance of parish schools, where "the rude and ignorant people of a certain wild kind and manner of living may learn the English tongue, language, order and habit", had, in Ireland, been placed by the Education Act of Henry VIII upon the shoulders of the clergy within the Pale, who, for default, were liable to fines of 6s. 8d. and 20s. respectively for the first and second offences, and to deprivation of their benefices for a third offence.[5] Elizabeth's supplementary Act of 1570 ordered ecclesiastical persons of each diocese in

[1] Young, A., op. cit. Part II, p. 202.
[2] Methods of Erecting, Supporting and Governing Charity Schools. An Account of the Charity Schools in Ireland and Some Observations thereon, 1718, 1721.
[3] See Balfour, G., Educational Systems of Great Britain and Ireland, 1903, pp. 78, 82.
[4] See de Montmorency, J. G., State Intervention in English Education, 1902, p. 125.
[5] Irish Statutes, 28 Hen. VIII, c. 15.

the kingdom to erect and maintain schools in which, under English schoolmasters appointed by the Deputy, "the loathsome and horrible errors" might, "by good discipline", be avoided.[1] These two acts presupposed the existence of a body of parish clergy, numerous enough to teach the children of the parish, or sufficiently well-to-do to contribute towards the expenses of a parish schoolmaster. But the condition of the parish clergy of the State Church in Ireland in Tudor and Stuart times precluded the possibility of success. Usurpations of temporalities were not unknown before the Reformation, but in Tudor times lay and ecclesiastical impropriators succeeded in despoiling the Church and left it without the means to support an adequate and qualified body of clergy. "The benefices themselves are so mean", wrote Edmund Spenser in 1569, "that they will not yield any competent maintenance for any minister to live upon, scarcely to buy him a gown",[2] and the correspondence of Wentworth and Archbishop Laud shows that the intervening century had witnessed little improvement.[3]

The parish schools, which by the Act of 1537 were to be financed by a tax upon the beneficed clergy aided by school fees, could not flourish in conditions such as these. The parishioners, wretchedly poor and mainly Roman in sympathy, afforded the ministers little financial support, and it is doubtful whether Henry's Act, which was not generally enforced as late as 1835, had any effect in the seventeenth and eighteenth centuries. In 1695 it was again re-enacted, "so that no pretence may be made or used that there are not sufficient number of schools in this realm",[4] but the small band of 600 poor clergy, serving parishes whose numbers were returned at 2300 in 1740, ignored the re-enactment as their predecessors had ignored the original Act.[5] It was left to a handful of Protestant enthusiasts to undertake, on a voluntary basis, the business of education in which the State had failed.

The aim of the early Irish charity schools movement was to provide schools in which children of both Catholics and Protestants might be

[1] Irish Statutes, 11 Eliz. c. 1.
[2] Spenser, Edmund, *View of the State of Ireland, 1596*, ed. by H. Morley, 1890, p. 127.
[3] Strafforde, *Letters and Despatches*, 1737, vol. I, p. 187.
[4] Irish Statutes, 7 Will. III, c. 4.
[5] *Sermon preached by the Bishop of Dromore in Christ Church Dublin*, Oct. 23, 1733. Archbishop Boulter in his *Letters*, vol. I, p. 179, gives the number of incumbents as "about 800".

decently clothed and usefully educated in the English language, the three R's and the Principles of the Christian Religion as professed by the Anglican Church. Some of the schools were for Protestants only; in others preference was given to children whose parents were members of the Established Church and "next to them the children of Papists and Dissenters"; in others, established primarily for Roman Catholic pupils, it was emphatically and clearly laid down that "mild and gentle methods were to be employed that Popish children taken care of along with our own may be won by our affectionate endeavours".[1] Set up in imitation of the English schools, with whose founders philanthropists in Cork and Dublin had carried on a long and enthusiastic correspondence, the Irish schools provided similar religious and moral training, and a similar curriculum. Instruction in reading the Bible and the catechism in English absorbed most of the school day. It is curious, in the light of recent history, that the language question, which from the middle of the century in the Highlands, and throughout the century in Wales, was a question of burning importance in the history of the schools, received little attention from Protestant or Catholic in eighteenth-century Ireland. The proposals of John Richardson, one of the few organised attempts before the nineteenth century to mobilise public opinion in England and Ireland upon the need of conducting the services of the Anglican Church in Irish, and of providing the adult natives who could not read English with Bibles, catechisms, prayer books and pious works in Erse, did not extend to the education of their children. They were to be taught in the charity schools set up for them to read the *English* Bible.[2] Protestant opposition, which wrecked Richardson's scheme of adult instruction, alleged not only that it would reverse the policy of the Government since the time of Henry VIII, and would thereby threaten the English interest in Ireland, but, also, that it was unnecessary, since the Irish language "as to the reading of it" was a "dead letter to the Natives", who for "trading and dealing with

[1] *An Account of the Charity Schools that have been erected and are now erecting in Ireland*, 1719.
[2] Richardson, Rev. J., rector of Belturbet, diocese of Kilmore, *A Proposal for the Conversion of the Popish Natives of Ireland to the Protestant Religion by Printing the Bible, Liturgy, an Exposition of the Church Catechism and other useful treatises in Irish...as also by Erecting Charity Schools for the Education of the Irish Children gratis in the English Tongue and Protestant Religion*, 1712. See also Mant, R., *op. cit.* vol. II, pp. 217–30, and King, C. S. *op. cit.* pp. 292–5.

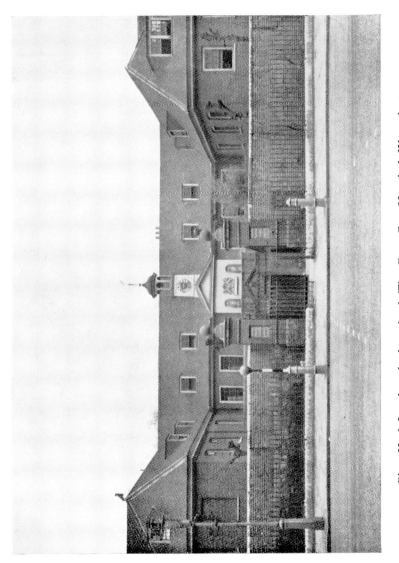

Plate II. A London charity school. The Grey Coat Hospital, Westminster

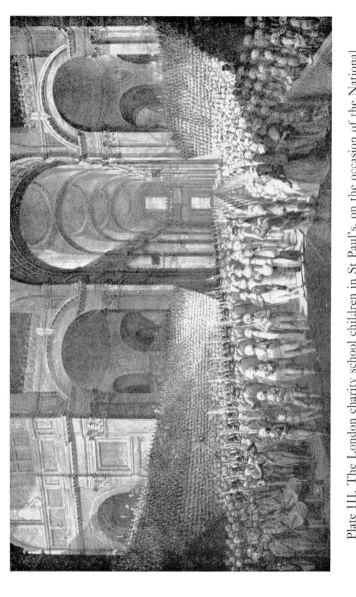

Plate III. The London charity school children in St Paul's, on the occasion of the National Thanksgiving for the recovery of George III, 1787

Plate IV. A country charity school, at Bottisham, Cambs.

Plate V. Wall tablet, showing figure of a charity school girl, in All Saints' Church, Northampton

Plate VI. Figures of charity school boy and girl at the Bishopsgate Ward charity school, London

Plate VII. Interior of Gravel Lane Dissenters' charity school

Plate VIII. An Irish charity school. Doorway and figures
of the Green Coat Hospital, Cork

their English landlords" were "all desirous to read, write and speak the English tongue".[1] Whether this was so or not there was no organised effort in Ireland during the eighteenth century to introduce the native tongue into the Protestant schools, nor was there any attempt to exclude English from the Popish schools. While Irish was their medium of instruction, the English language formed part of their normal curriculum.[2] Its value as a political instrument was too well recognised by Popish schoolmasters to allow it to be neglected. Anglican parson and Roman priest in Ireland were alike champions of the English tongue.[3]

In finance and management the Irish charity schools followed the methods adopted in England. Subscription schools were managed by committees of subscribers, whose contributions were augmented by collections taken at the church door on Sundays, by fines for debauchery and breaches of the penal laws, and by donations from cathedral chapters and city corporations. Dublin, whose filthy slums and alleys harboured children no less poor and ignorant than those of London, led the way in 1704, and by 1717 fifteen charity schools had been set up in the city parishes. Endowed schools were, as in England, controlled by their patrons. A few of the more go-ahead of the Protestant gentry, who found themselves, after the resettlement of the land, owners or tenants of undeveloped estates, on which "useful hands" were lamentably lacking, saw in schools which would "breed up the children of their poorer sub-tenants to trades and callings" a method of coping with their new properties. The Earl of Abercorn at Strabane, Sir Dermot O'Brien at Newmarket, Lord Percival and the gentry in County Cork, put the children to school, paid their apprentice fees, and, when they were out of their time, leased to them small parcels of land in the desolate and uncultivated parts of their estates, which they reported "thereby abounded in improvements". Elsewhere, as at Kilmacowen, Co. Sligo and at Tertarghan, Co. Armagh, the Anglican clergy financed the schools or collected money for them. Those "round about Sligo", eight in number, were established by the benevolent and energetic cleric Edward Nicholson of Cumin, who stirred up both

---

[1] *Sermon preached by the Bishop of Dromore*, Oct. 23, 1733; Rawlinson MSS. Letter of Edward Nicholson to the S.P.C.K. on Richardson's scheme [n.d.].

[2] See *Report made by His Grace the Lord Primate from the House of Lords Committee appointed to enquire into the Present State of Popery in this Kingdom* [etc.], 1731. [3] For Archbishop King's views see King, C. S., *op. cit.* pp. 293–5.

gentlefolk and townsfolk to finance them. Hollymount School, Co. Mayo, was erected by Edward Synge, Archbishop of Tuam, who settled a fund payable out of his estate for its maintenance.[1]

Further support, in these early years, came from the trustees of the Linen Board, established by Act of Parliament in 1710, to encourage the manufacture of linen, hitherto localised mainly in Ulster, in the southern provinces.[2] The establishment of spinning schools formed part of the Board's programme. The charity schools already in existence offered an opportunity for co-operation of which the Linen Board and the patrons and managers of the schools were not slow to take advantage. Spinning was introduced into the curriculum of the schools at Armagh, Killogh and elsewhere, to the mutual satisfaction of the Board and the school managers.[3] Private persons were not averse from following the lead given by the Board. The gentry, faithfully portrayed by Miss Edgeworth at the end of the century, were alive to the advantage of a curriculum which would appease their charitable impulses and provide them with household linen at small expense. Children on the Castle Rackrent estate, who were taught "to read and write gratis", were "kept well to spinning by my lady in return".[4] From 1720 to 1730, a period of great activity on the part of the Linen Board in setting up spinning schools, many of the charity schools added spinning to their curriculum.[5]

Conspicuous among the early charity schools for the munificence of its supporters and its care of the children was the Green Coat Hospital in the parish of St Mary Shandon in Cork city, whose flourishing provision trade made it one of the few prosperous urban centres in Ireland. There, in 1715, religion, learning and labour were combined to the admiration of all concerned. The romantic history of the school was known throughout Ireland. Its story, told in the tract *Pietas Corcagiensis*, a replica of Francke's tract *Pietas Halliensis*, was in essentials the same as that of Francke's Poor School at Halle. Believing that what "the excellent Augustus Francke" had done at Halle for the children of the poor could be achieved in Cork, the enthusiastic and

[1] *Methods of Erecting, Supporting and Governing Charity Schools [etc.]*, 1721.
[2] See Gill, C., History of the Linen Industry in Ireland, 1925.
[3] *An Account of the Charity Schools [etc.]*, 1718.
[4] Edgeworth, M., *Castle Rackrent*, 1799; 1895 ed. p. 5.
[5] *Accounts of the Charity Schools*, 1720–30.

efficient vicar of the parish, Henry Maule, later Bishop of Meath and Dromore, and the recognised leader of the charity school movement in Ireland, gathered gifts and subscriptions for a parish charity school. To the building of a large and commodious school-house he contributed the site and building materials; timber was given by a benefactor who "desired to have his name concealed"; tiles for the flooring, woollen cloth for the whole of the first year's clothing for the children, and books for the school library, were contributed by the townsfolk. And "because many might not wish their left hand to know what their right hand doeth" the effigies of a charity boy and girl, in their proper habits, holding boxes for alms, were set up, in the English fashion, outside the school-house, the one bearing the inscription "Naked and ye cloathed me", the other, "Inasmuch as ye have done it to the least of these ye have done it unto Me". A steady flow of money gifts from unknown and unexpected sources filled up the constantly depleted exchequer in so miraculous a manner that it was clear to the promoters that God's blessing rested on their work. A hundred children, fifty of whom were clothed each year, were taught the principles of the Christian religion and the three R's, and were given instruction in manual work. In co-operation with the trustees of the linen manufacture looms were set up under a master weaver for the boys, and the girls were employed under a mistress in spinning flax and hemp. In this pattern school care was taken "to study the genius of the children and to fit them, as best suited them, for the sea, husbandry, trades, or services".[1]

Dr Maule's work was not confined to the Green Coat Hospital. In conjunction with Edward Synge, Archbishop of Tuam, and Brigadier-General Stearne, corresponding member in Ireland of the London S.P.C.K., he formed, in 1717, a voluntary society in Dublin for Promoting Christian Knowledge for "the more general establishment of charity schools".[2] The Society advertised the schools in its annual reports, drawn up on the English model, and encouraged clergy and laymen to support them. Before the end of 1717 a hundred schools, with some 2000 pupils, were returned by the Society; two years later the schools numbered 130; in 1725 the number had increased to 163, and their pupils, who did not increase at the same rate, to about 3000.

[1] *Pietas Corcagiensis, or a View of the Green Coat Hospital and Other Charitable Foundations in the Parish of St Mary Shandon, Corke [etc.]*, 1721.
[2] S.P.C.K. Abs. of Correspondence, Letter from Henry Maule, Oct. 8, 1717.

Then came a halt. The advance ceased. In the five years 1725 to 1730 only nine new schools were set up, and the number of children remained almost stationary. Voluntary effort appeared to be exhausted.

Two stubborn facts were responsible for the failure of the early charity schools in Ireland. Lack of adequate support, in the first place, made progress impossible. The enthusiasm aroused in England and the quiet persistence of the Society in Scotland were alike absent in Ireland. The large, prosperous middle class, who in England financed and managed the schools, had no counterpart in Ireland. Indeed, during the greater part of the eighteenth century, Ireland lacked a middle class. "The only division which a traveller can make", said Arthur Young, describing Irish society as late as 1762, "would be into persons of considerable property and mob; the intermediate divisions of the scale, so numerous and respectable in England, would hardly attract the least notice in Ireland."[1]

The commercial restrictions, which England in its own interest imposed upon Ireland in the eighteenth century, were, in the main, responsible for the absence of a middle class. Unlike the agrarian policy and the penal laws, they fell with impartial severity upon Protestant and Catholic. The prevailing mercantilist policy of economic nationalism thrust Ireland into the position of a colony, whose function it was to supply the mother country with the raw materials it required, and to refrain from competing in trade and manufacture. The destruction of the once flourishing woollen manufacture confined the large majority of the population to the land, on which, by the land system, they were prevented from finding a means of decent livelihood. The towns were, for the most part, merely centres of distribution. The only industries which were permitted to flourish in Ireland were the trade in provisions and the linen manufacture. Dublin, living on the remnants of the woollen manufacture, Cork, enjoying a prosperous trade in provisions, and Belfast, which, later in the century, became the centre of the linen industry, were among the few exceptions to the general stagnation of urban life.[2] Charity school children who could read and write and cast accounts were not wanted in this small and backward industrial world. There was little work for them to do, even in the relatively important

[1] Young, A., op. cit. Part II, p. 201.
[2] Ferrar, J., The Prosperity of Dublin displayed in the State of the Charity Schools in Dublin, 1796.

corporate towns. In the market towns, when the novelty of the schools and their pupils had worn off, subscriptions quickly ceased and the schools disappeared.

Nor was there the same steady support of the schools from the parish clergy which marked the movement in England, Wales and the Highlands. For this, poverty was again the main cause. The letters of Archbishop King and Primate Boulter testify, as did those of Laud and Strafford a century earlier, to the scarcity and poverty of the parish clergy. "There are in the diocese of Ferns", wrote Archbishop King in 1712, "one hundred and thirty-one parishes, of these seventy-one are impropriate in lay hands, twenty-eight are appropriated to the bishop, dignitaries and prebendaries of the cathedral, and thirty-two in the hands of the clergy that serve the cures, and generally these are the worst, for the monks seldom troubled themselves but with the best. There is neither bishop, dean, nor archdeacon residing in it. There are only thirteen beneficed clergymen in it, and nine curates, and these very poorly provided, about £30 per annum to a curate, and very few of the beneficed clergy have £100 per annum, I cannot reckon five."[1] Plurality of livings, which in Ireland, as in England, was applied as a palliative for the poverty of the cures, nullified the State's educational policy. One man could not adequately perform his ecclesiastical duties in parishes eight, ten, twelve, or fourteen miles long, nor did the smaller parishes when united always provide the minimum required for a curate's pay. "The bishops", wrote the Archbishop of Dublin and the Bishop of Derry in a memorial to George I, "are frequently obliged to give three or four, or even in some places, ten parishes, that lie contiguous, to produce a maintenance of £50 a year only."[2] Laws were not lacking which permitted the exchange of glebes, united and divided parishes, recovered tithes, and other ecclesiastical dues, and increased the curate's pay, but reform was slow in making itself felt.[3] Betwixt the law and its execution, not seldom was a great gulf fixed.

[1] King, Archbishop, Transcribed Correspondence, Trinity College, Dublin. June 7, 1712. See also Archbishop Boulter's *Letters*, vol. I, *passim*.

[2] State Papers, Ireland (P.R.O. Belfast), Bundle 388. Memorial of William King, Archbishop of Dublin, and St George Ashe, Bishop of Derry, to George I submitting proposals as to Crown Rents affecting the Clergy [n.d].

[3] Irish Statutes, 2 Anne, c. 10, 8 and 9 Anne, c. 12, 1 Geo. II, c. 19, 1 Geo. II, c. 12, 6 Geo. I, c. 13.

Generalisation is dangerous in Irish history and is particularly so in the history of the Anglican Church in Ireland, for conditions and personnel were not everywhere alike. Parishes varied in size from the small compact parishes of the Pale to the vast moorland and forest parishes of Ulster. Emoluments were not uniform, nor was non-residence a uniform custom, as the returns to the visitation articles of the Bishops of Ossory and Raphoe in 1731–2 and 1733 bear witness.[1] While Strafford's condemnation of the Irish clergy in the seventeenth century as an "unlearned" body of men[2] holds true of their fellows in the eighteenth century, they were not all, in the opinion of at least one able and informed observer, lacking in "commendable and considerable general knowledge".[3] It was not impossible to find men of high character and devotion to duty resident in their cures.[4] Nevertheless, the bulk of available evidence paints a grey picture of a Church whose poverty was a by-word and whose officers were ill-equipped for their difficult and many-sided task. Catechising was neglected, and with a few conspicuous exceptions little effort was made by the parish clergy to set up schools for the children of the poor.

Consistent support from the higher clergy, which marked the initiation of the movement in the Highlands and England, was also lacking. William King, the greatest of Dublin's Anglican Archbishops in the eighteenth century, was lukewarm in his approval. Representative of the Irish, as opposed to the English, or "foreign", interest in Ireland, he stood unswervingly for the predominance of the Anglican Church in a country where Papists were in a majority and Protestant Dissenters not a negligible factor. While the maintenance of the Protestant Succession, in King's opinion, demanded restraints upon the political liberty of those who by their religion could not in conscience support it, he lacked belief in religious intolerance as a method of conversion. In a series of letters to Archbishop Wake and to members of the London and Dublin Societies for Promoting Christian Knowledge he expressed his distrust of education organised to this end.[5] The

---

[1] *History of the Church of Ireland*, ed. W. A. Phillips, 1933, vol. III, chap. v.

[2] Strafforde, *op. cit.* vol. I, p. 187.

[3] Rundle, Thomas, Bishop of Derry, see *History of the Church of Ireland*, ed. W. A. Phillips, 1933, vol. III, p. 216.

[4] See Burdy, S., *Life of the Rev. Philip Skelton*, 1816.

[5] Wake MSS. Arch. W. Epist. 12. Ireland, Sept. 2, Nov. 21, 1717; Archbishop King, Transcribed Correspondence, *loc. cit.* Mar. 18, Dec. 20, 1719.

drastic and startling proposal of the Lower House of Convocation in 1710, that the attendance of Popish children should be made compulsory at Protestant charity schools, was not acceptable to him.[1] He deplored a project for "uniting and breeding any bodies of men under colour of religion in any way". His distrust found expression in a general criticism of the attempt to educate the Irish natives. It was in his opinion unnecessary if the clergy did but their duty in teaching the children the catechism; it was unfair "to give poor children a taste of something above the vulgar without providing suitable employment for them when they grew up"; it was unwise, since "to ease poor people of their children would merely give the landlords an excuse for screwing more rent from them"; it was impolitic, since already in England the charity schools had got into the hands of persons "disaffected to the Revolution and the Government". Despair of improvement in Irish conditions informs his correspondence with Archbishop Wake and the members of the London and Dublin Societies. It provides a significant contrast to the enthusiastic support of the schools by high-placed ecclesiastics in England. "Once the schools have legal and settled endowments," said the Archbishop prophetically, "they will be managed as other charities that are on that foot."[2]

[1] "Resolved that it will be necessary that beside the Schools already provided by Law, such other School or Schools as the Bishop and Minister shall judge convenient, be appointed in every Parochial Cure or Union of this Kingdom, where the Children of such Natives may be taught *gratis* to speak and read the *English* Language, and be instructed in the Principles of the Christian Religion...and to the End that the charitable Design of such Schools may not be defeated by the Obstinacy of Popish Recusants, and that in Time the Irish Language may be utterly abolished: Resolved, that all Popish Natives of this Kingdom, who are not possessed of some Real or Personal Estate to the value of £50, or who do not hold, by Lease, Lands to the value of £10 *per annum*, be obliged, during Four Months of every Year, to send their Children, after they have attained the age of Seven Years until they arrive at the age of Twelve Years, to such publick Schools, to be taught and instructed as aforesaid under a Penalty of   per Month, to be levied by a Warrant from a Justice of Peace, and paid to the Minister and Church Wardens of the respective Parishes to be disposed of by them, as they shall think fit, for the better Encouragement of the said Schools." Sessio 242. Die Jovis, viz. 25to die Mensis 8bris 1711. Quoted in Corcoran, T., *Some Lists of Catholic Lay Teachers and their Illegal Schools in the Later Penal Times*, 1932, pp. 16, 17. See also Mant, R., *op. cit.* vol. II, pp. 226–30; Richardson, J., *op. cit.*

[2] Archbishop King, Transcribed Correspondence, *loc. cit.* Mar. 18, 1719. See also Dec. 20, 1719 and Wake MSS. *loc. cit.*

A second difficulty, more stubborn than that presented by Protestant apathy, was the failure of the penal laws to restrain the activities of the Popish priests and schoolmasters. Far from discouraging them the restrictions had stimulated rather than diminished their zeal. Unknown numbers of unregistered regulars and seculars assisted the parish priests, and went into hiding when warning was given that magistrates and soldiers were approaching. Their numbers were estimated by Archbishop Boulter in 1727 at over 3000.[1] An unnumbered body of Popish schoolmasters were, at the same time, slowly drawing away the Popish, and in some places the Protestant children also, from the charity schools. The growing anxiety of Church and State was expressed in the demand for a House of Lords' committee to inquire into the state of popery in the Kingdom. The returns, published in 1731, showed that the disproportion between Popish and Protestant schools was so great as to give "just and reasonable apprehensions". A rough estimate placed the number of illegal schools as high as 549, and the report made clear that many schools and schoolmasters had escaped identification. From Clonfert the Lord Bishop reported that there was commonly a Popish school in every parish. Tuam's provincial report stated that there was a school in almost every two or three villages, so much so that "a Protestant schoolmaster, when to be had, can scarcely get bread". From Cork the mayor replied that he had failed to find out the number of Popish schoolmasters, there were so many of them. In Dublin there were no less than forty-five illegal schools. Success so alarming was in marked contrast to "the slow advance of Protestantism".[2] A new effort was required if "the Protestant religion was to be established universally in the Kingdom".[3] This time the children were the victims, and the method adopted, in Lecky's opinion, excited "an intensity of bitterness hardly equalled by any portion of the penal code".[4]

[1] Boulter, Archbishop, *Letters*, vol. I, Feb. 13, 1727.
[2] *Report made by His Grace the Lord Primate from the House of Lords' Committee*, loc. cit.
[3] Boulter, Archbishop, *Letters*, vol. II, Feb. 19, 1736.
[4] Lecky, W. H., *History of Ireland in the Eighteenth Century*, 1892 ed. vol. I, p. 234.

III

THE INCORPORATED SOCIETY

The Edinburgh Society provided the model for the new attempt. Local initiative and local control on the English plan had failed. A national organisation incorporated by the Crown and able to draw upon sources which would not be subjected to the caprice and indifference of local patrons and subscribers formed the basis of the scheme proposed in 1733. Twice before the idea had been mooted and turned down. A memorial presented to the Viceroy Ormonde in 1712 had asked that a society should be founded by royal charter for the establishment of charity schools in every parish in Ireland as the most effectual method of promoting the conversion of the Popish natives to the Protestant Religion.[1] It was ignored by the Government. A similar fate met the proposal submitted by Dr Maule to the Lord-Lieutenant in 1716.[2] It was not until Bishop Hugh Boulter of Bristol was translated to Armagh in 1724, as resident manager of the English interest in Ireland, that the new plan began to take shape and that Archbishop King's measured opposition was met and overcome.[3]

The new Primate, perturbed by the alarming growth of Popery revealed by the report of the House of Lords' committee, welcomed the reappearance of Dr Maule's scheme with enthusiasm. His support ensured at last the success of the scheme. It assured the co-operation of the leading Protestant notables in Ireland and a favourable reception by Walpole and the Government in England. A petition faithfully expressing the policy of the promoters was presented to the Crown in 1730.[4] It stated

That in many parts of the Kingdom there are great Tracts of Mountainy and Coarse Lands of Ten, Twenty or Thirty Miles in Length and of a considerable Breadth, almost universally Inhabited by Papists; and that in most Parts of the same and more especially in the Provinces of Leinster, Munster, and Connaught the Papists far exceed the Protestants of all Sorts in Number.

[1] See King, C. S. *op. cit.* pp. 296–8.
[2] S.P.C.K. Abs. of Correspondence, Letter from H. Maule, Cork, July 5, 1717, enclosing proposal addressed to his Excellency the Duke of Bolton.
[3] See Dunlop, R., *Ireland from the Earliest Times to the Present Day*, 1921, p. 135.
[4] State Papers, Irel. 396; Brit. Departmental Correspondence, 2970, Ireland.

That the Generality of the Popish Natives appear to have very little Sense or Knowledge of Religion, but what they implicitly take from their Clergy, to whose Guidance in such Matters they seem wholly to give themselves up, and thereby are kept, not only in Gross Ignorance, but in great Disaffection to your Sacred Majesty and Government, scarce any of them having appeared to be willing to Abjure the Pretender to Your Majesty's Throne; so that if some Effectual Method be not made use of to Instruct these great Numbers of People in the Principles of True Religion and Loyalty, there seems to be little Prospect but that Superstition, Idolatry, and Disaffection will, from Generation to Generation, be propagated among them.

Among the Ways proper to be taken for converting and civilizing these poor deluded People, and bringing them (through the Blessing of God) in time, to be Good Christians and Faithful Subjects, one of the most necessary, and without which all others are like to prove ineffectual, has always been thought to be that a Sufficient Number of English Protestant Schools be Erected and Established, wherein the Children of the Irish Natives might be instructed in the English Tongue, and the Fundamental Principles of true Religion, to both of which they are generally great Strangers.

In pursuance thereof the Parish Ministry throughout the Kingdom have generally endeavoured, and, often with some Expense to themselves, to provide Masters for such Schools, within their respective Parishes, as the Law requires them to do; but the Richer Papists commonly refuse to send their Children to such Schools and the Poorer, which are the greater Number, not being able to pay the accustomed Salary as the law directs for their Children's Schooling, such School masters, where they have been placed, have seldom been able to Subsist, and in most Places Sufficient Masters are discouraged from undertaking Such an Employment; nor is it, as we conceive, to be expected that the Residence of the Protestant Clergy upon their respective Benefices will ever be a Sufficient Remedy for this growing evil, if some Effectual Encouragement be not given to such *English Protestant Schools.*

To the Intent thereof that the Youth of this Kingdom may generally be brought up in the Principles of True Religion and Loyalty in all Succeeding Generations, We, Your Majesty's most Dutiful and Loyal Subjects, most humbly beseech Your Majesty, that out of Your Great Goodness You would be pleased to Grant Your Royal Charter for Incorporating such Persons as Your Majesty shall think fit, and Enabling them to Accept of Gifts, Benefactions and Lands to such a value as Your Majesty shall think to be proper; that the same may be Employ'd under such Rules and Directions as Your

Majesty shall approve of for the Supporting and Maintaining such Schools as may be erected in the most necessary Places where the Children of the Poor may be taught *gratis*.

And we are the more Encourag'd to make this humble Application, from the good Success which the same Method has already had, and (through God's Blessing) we hope will further have among Your Majesty's Subjects of North Britain, and also in some measure by what We have seen already done in this Kingdom, in some few Places where such Schools have been Erected and Maintained at the private Expense of charitable Persons.[1]

The petition was signed by the Lord Primate, the Lord Chancellor, the Archbishops of Dublin, Cashel and Tuam, six earls, five viscounts, twelve bishops, six barons, and by over a hundred gentlemen and beneficed clergy. In 1733, convinced by the Lord-Lieutenant that the trustees of the proposed society would be drawn from men of the first rank in the kingdom, Letters Patent were granted by the Crown for the establishment of a "Society Corporate and Body Politic" by name of the Incorporated Society in Dublin for promoting English Protestant Schools in Ireland, "for the advancement of true religion and the increase of the Protestant interest in that Kingdom"; and with the Lord-Lieutenant as president and the Lord Primate as treasurer, and an influential body of notables forming an executive committee, the Incorporated Society was launched with pomp and circumstance in the council chamber of Dublin Castle.

Extraordinary enthusiasm greeted the new and powerful Society. Statesmen appealed for "this most prudent as well as most compassionate charity",[2] and leading ecclesiastics throughout the century preached sermons on its behalf to crowded congregations of *le beau monde* in Christ Church, extolling "the settled habit of industry and piety", deploring the "notorious disaffection to our Happy Constitution in Church and State", and appealing for funds "to rescue the souls of thousands of Popish children from the dangers

[1] *A Humble Proposal for Obtaining His Majesty's Royal Charter to Incorporate a Society for Promoting Christian Knowledge among the Poor Natives of the Kingdom of Ireland*, 1730.

[2] The Lord-Lieutenant, the Earl of Chesterfield. Quoted in the *Proceedings of the Incorporated Society*, henceforth referred to as *Proceedings*, for 1744. These *Proceedings*, published in Dublin, are printed as appendices to the sermons preached before the Society.

of superstition and idolatry and their bodies from the miseries of idleness and begging". It was not unusual, said Wakefield, for young women of fashion to make their *début* into Dublin society on these occasions. Ladies distinguished by rank or personal attractions were chosen to collect the contributions from the congregation and "all who had the slightest pretensions to fashion" crowded to the services.[1]

The powers granted by the Crown placed the Society on a satisfactory financial basis. In a country in which money was never plentiful it was but natural that the commonest gift should be that of land. Before the end of the century valuable estates had been vested in the Society for general or specific purpose by the landed gentry, enterprising manufacturers, city corporations and, as permitted by the act of 1722, the clergy of the Established Church.[2] Funds were raised by subscriptions and donations in Ireland, and by a Corresponding Society set up in London at Archbishop Boulter's suggestion, to collect and remit contributions to Dublin from those absentee landlords who were "English by blood and Anglican by profession", and sums, considerably in excess of those raised in Ireland, were received annually from the London branch. In 1738, as the funds collected were still inadequate for the elaborate scheme planned by the Society, the Primate petitioned the Crown for a grant, and annually until 1794 the Crown contributed £1000 to the work of the Society. Its response paved the way for securing "the settled fund" which was the goal of the Society's efforts. "If we are once able", wrote the untiring Archbishop in 1736, "to set on foot about 20 working schools in the several distant parts of the Kingdom and put them into a right method we shall meet with support and encouragement from the Legislature."[3] To this end the early work of the Society was directed.

Beginning in 1734, its first school was set up at Castledermot on lands given by the Earl of Kildare. Built to house as well as to instruct the twenty children of its establishment, it served as a model school to the rest. Minola, Co. Mayo, was the scene of the Society's second

---

[1] Wakefield, E., *op. cit.* "The collection is generally made before the sermon," reported Wakefield, "but when a charity sermon is preached the collection is not made until the feelings of the congregation have been aroused by the pathos and eloquence of the minister." Vol. II, pp. 788–9.

[2] Irish Statutes, 8 Geo. I, c. 12.

[3] Boulter, Archbishop, *Letters*, vol. II, Feb. 19, 1736.

venture, in 1735. John and William Brown, who had planted a linen manufacture on their estate, offered ten acres of land in perpetuity. In the same year a good slated house was set up at Shannon Grove, Co. Limerick, on lands given by the landlord, William Bury. Ballynahinch School, Co. Down, was endowed with two acres of land belonging to the see of Dromore, and the school at Castle Caulfield, Co. Tyrone, with an acre of glebe land granted by the incumbent of the parish. During the next few years the schools multiplied rapidly. To this period belonged those at Creggane, Co. Armagh, Ballycastle, Co. Antrim, Templestown, Co. Wicklow, Killogh, Co. Down, Kilfinane, Co. Limerick, and Ballinrobe, Co. Mayo. The decade 1740–50 represented the period of the Society's greatest activity, twenty schools being erected.[1]

To their upkeep the local gentry and clergy contributed, with gifts of land, money, or gifts in kind. In the forties and fifties, when "improving" methods of agriculture and industry made some headway among a small group of Irish landlords, the Society co-operated with them by setting up schools on their estates. In the famous experiment of Sir Richard Cox at Dunmanway, which Robert Stephenson in his *Journal* declared to be "the best plan of any outside of Ulster",[2] the charter school, built by Sir Richard for forty children, played its part in transforming the face of the country-side and the character of the inhabitants. Fields of great extent were divided into small enclosures for flax raising, and prizes were offered for the best crop, and for spinning and weaving the flax. Begging was severely punished, holidays curtailed, the morals of old and young carefully inspected, and one and all were compelled to labour. As a result the language, dress and behaviour of the common people were pleasingly altered. Smoky, sooty cabins were henceforth despised and "neatness crept into the houses". At Innishannon Cox's friend and neighbour, Sir Thomas Adderley, engaged in reforms of a similar character. To the Society he leased lands and defrayed part of the expense of erecting a school-house for forty children.[3] By 1754 thirty-eight schools had been set up, and

[1] See Appendix III, 2.
[2] Stephenson, R., *Journal of a Tour of Inspection in the Southern Provinces*, 1755, p. 185.
[3] Letter of Sir Richard Cox to Thomas Prior, Esq., Dublin, 1749; *Proceedings*, 1752, 1753.

their value was recognised by Crown, Church and gentry. It remained only for the Legislature to express its approval in a concrete fashion. Before the Dublin Parliament adjourned in 1747 it made the first parliamentary grant to elementary education in the history of the United Kingdom.

Grants from Parliament marked a new stage in the life of the Society. From 1733 it had lived on the limited support of its friends at home and abroad. From 1747 it was backed by the unlimited resources of the Legislature, from which it drew supplies with increasing assurance. Parliamentary grants, which in the ten years 1751–61 averaged £3500 per annum, reached a total of over £11,000 in the decade 1794 to 1804. In the ninety-one years of its life, from its inception in 1733 to the investigation of its financial position in 1824, over a million pounds had been poured into its coffers by the State and over half a million pounds had been received in addition from private sources. Its income at the beginning of the nineteenth century fell short by a few pounds of £10,000.[1]

IV

THE CHARTER SCHOOLS

The large income from private and public sources received by the Incorporated Society differed as much from the limited means of the Edinburgh Society, or from the paltry sums at the disposal of charity school supporters in Wales, as did their plans and methods of instruction. For the Irish Society, established when disillusionment with day-school education and enthusiasm for a labour curriculum was at its height in England and Scotland, determined to meet the joint problems of pauperism and proselytism by setting up schools which were both

[1] Parliamentary grants from 1751–1808 were as follows:

First ten years average	£3,500	p.a.
Second	„	5,800 „
Third	„	6,100 „
Fourth	„	9,000 „
Fifth	„	11,800 „
Last seven years nearly		20,000 „

See *First Report of the Commission of Irish Education Inquiry*, 1825, Appendix 172. See also abstract of the accounts of the Incorporated Society, 1754–5, published in the *Proceedings* of 1755.

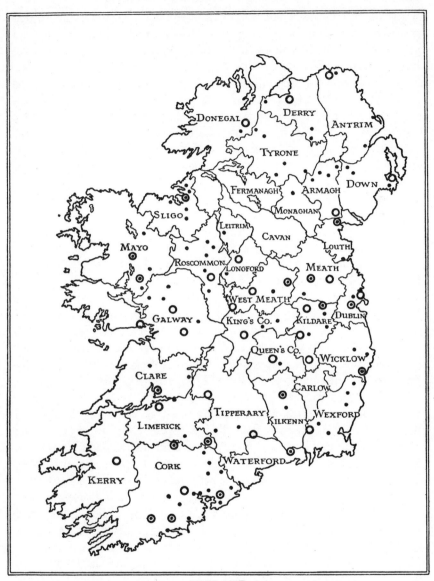

IRELAND

Map showing the distribution of the Schools of the S.P.C.K. •,
and of the Incorporated Society ○.

working and boarding schools. Endowed with considerable landed property for this purpose, it expended its funds on erecting substantial school buildings in which a score, or two score children, the master, his wife and family could be housed, and devised a curriculum which allowed the hours of school instruction to be devoted, in the main, to agricultural and industrial labour. In the early years, before the resources of Parliament were tapped, the existence of the schools was bound up with their success as self-supporting institutions. It was estimated that a school-house for twenty to thirty children cost £300; furnishing and materials £35; clothing and maintenance, salary and repairs at least £100 a year. These were items, the Society assured its supporters, which would become lighter as the children grew up and their labour became more valuable. It was assumed throughout that the schools would pay their way, and to this end the efforts of the children were directed. Three parts in four of their time was to be employed in labour. The work of the boys was to feed, that of the girls to clothe, the little colonies.

Report after report published in the *Proceedings* of the Society during the first half of the century told of the prodigious amount of manual work done by the children, whose ages ranged from four to fourteen years. A vision of the Irish country-side as a nursery for fruit and forest trees, gripped the Charter Society as it had already gripped its contemporary, the Royal Dublin Society, founded in 1731. The schoolmasters were instructed to use part of the land belonging to the schools as nurseries, where the boys were to be taught to raise and manage the trees. Reports from Ballynahinch school in 1734 showed that the dream had become a reality. 200 crab stocks, 200 cherry trees, 200 plum stocks, 100 pear stocks, 600 sets of osiers, 60 elm trees, 30 sycamore trees, 30 barberry trees, quantities of gooseberry and currant slips; ash, haw, birch, walnut, chestnut and horse-chestnut seedlings, and in the ditches 1800 white thorn, 2000 crab guides and 1800 ash had been planted and enclosed. The digging, fencing, trenching and hedging for the plantation was done by the boys. The committee of Minola school reported that five acres of school land had been fallowed by the children for flax, potatoes and oats. At Stradbally the boys, without any outside help, dug, planted and weeded the kitchen gardens, levelled and cleaned five acres of land, sowed them with flax seed, and cut and stored forty cartloads of hay. Even greater results were achieved by the boys at New Ross, who worked like Trojans at their labours, foddering cattle, gathering dung, digging land for flax, wheat, cabbage, peas, potatoes, parsnips, beans; ditching, levelling and clamping turf; rippling, watering and swinging flax; carding wool and knitting stockings. Threshing alone was beyond their strength.

The girls of the schools were equally busy. To them fell the work of cleaning, cooking and laundry, and of spinning the flax and wool, out of which the children's garments were fashioned. At New Ross, where the boys' heroic efforts had to be emulated, the girls, in addition to domestic work, spun, in one year, much fine linen yarn, and 73 lb. of coarse yarn; carded and spun 8 stones of wool, and shackled 14 stones of flax. At Shannon Grove the girls, for the year, spun enough linen yarn to serve all the children, and, in addition, manufactured 67 yards of cambric, which so pleased the local manufacturer that he bought each of the girls a new hat to wear at church on Sundays. At Minola they turned out 83 yards of drugget made of linen and woollen yarn for the dresses, 88 yards of woollen cloth for the boys' suits, and 60 yards of linen for shifts and shirts, in all 231 yards of material. Some of the schools became in part self-supporting, others entirely so, to the satisfaction of the Society, who saw as a result of their little labour colonies not only the wilderness blossoming as the rose, but a new generation of trained and industrious workers in the place of their slothful and unreliable parents. But the efforts of the children, directed by ignorant and unscrupulous masters, made the economic success of the schools a temporary one only. The silence of the reports after 1750, on the output of the children's work, is significant. Perhaps this date marks the beginning of the end, as described by John Howard in 1782.[1]

More important in estimating the work of the Incorporated Society, than the training it afforded the children in industry, is its religious policy. By the charter of 1733 it was empowered to erect schools in the most remote and Popish parts of the country "to convert the poor deluded natives to be good Christians and faithful subjects, by instruction in the English tongue and the Fundamental Principles of True Religion". As in the English parish charity schools the Anglican catechism formed the backbone of instruction, but whereas the English and Highland schools were designed to strengthen Protestant children in the tenets of their faith, or to carry the Gospel to barbarians, "on

[1] See *Proceedings* from 1750 to the end of the century.

17

whom the light of the Gospel had not yet shined", the Irish charter schools were "Protestant manufactories". "What our Charter Schools are labouring after", said Archbishop Boulter, "is the most rational push that has ever been made for establishing the Protestant religion more universally in this Kingdom."[1] To this end the schools were deliberately set up in the most remote and Popish parts of the country, and instructions were issued to the local committees of the schools to admit only those who were "the children of popish parents". In 1776 the Society put on record its resolution to restrict the schools "to the children of papists, or at least where one of the parents are, or have been, papists, or in case the parents are dead, or they being deserted, are in the utmost danger of being bred up papists".[2] In the early years of the nineteenth century these instructions were withdrawn, on the ground that they were not warranted by the Charter. But the evil had been done. The schools by these practices had become associated in the minds of the Irish peasantry with proselytism to the Anglican faith, an association only too well supported by the Protestant catechism written especially for the children, which Wakefield still found in use in the schools as late as 1812.

"Q. Is the Church of Rome a sound and uncorrupt Church?
A. No, it is extremely corrupt in Doctrine, Worship and Practice.
Q. What do you think of the frequent crossings on which the Papists lay so much stress?
A. They are vain and superstitious. The worship of the crucifix or figure of Christ upon the Cross is idolatrous and the adoring and praying to the Cross itself is of all the corruptions of the Popish worship the most gross and intolerable."[3]

In the early years of the Society, when the schools drew their pupils from the peasantry in the neighbourhood, they received a by no means unfriendly welcome from the native Irish, to whom a persistent tradition ascribes a passion for learning. There is enough evidence to show that

[1] Boulter, Archbishop, *Letters*, vol. II, Feb. 19, 1736.
[2] *Proceedings*, 1752. For the Resolution of the Society see the *First Report of the Commissioners of Education in Ireland*, 1809–12, vol. v, Appendix.
[3] Wakefield, E., *op. cit.* p. 411. The reference is to *A Protestant Catechism shewing the Principal Errors of the Church of Rome, in Four Parts. Published by order of the Incorporated Society for Promoting English Protestant Schools in Ireland.* Dublin, 1767.

the provision of free board and schooling for their children was pleasing to parents too poor to afford the modest fees of the hedge-school-masters. Reports of parents on their knees, imploring members of the Society to accept their children, of others turning away in despair because there was not enough room to receive them, and of eager application for the next vacancy which should occur, were common in the early years of the schools' existence.[1] It is not difficult to find explanations for native support. Poverty was the prime factor, and the terrible famines of the thirties and forties, which pass almost unnoticed in history, aggravated the general wretchedness. At such times starving parents were glad enough to find food and shelter for their children.[2] Schools where, in return for a signed contract promising not to demand the children during years of schooling and apprenticeship, food, clothing, instruction and binding out fees could be obtained proved too great a temptation to many Roman Catholic parents. Bribes of 2s. wherewith to pay the hearth tax provided a further incentive to send their children to the schools, and a bonus of £5 was offered by the Society to every pupil educated in the schools who should marry a Protestant.[3] That the children would become converts to Protestantism was, however, unlikely, while priestly and parental influence could operate to neutralise the Protestant atmosphere and Anglican teaching of the schools. Neither parent nor priest believed that Protestant propaganda would win child converts from Rome.

Parental support was, however, of short duration. As early as 1735 the Society placed on record its intention, when a sufficient number of schools had been established, of transplanting the children from schools in the neighbourhood of their homes to schools distant from them, so that the influence of priests and parents might be eliminated.[4] Poverty

---

[1] "The poor inhabitants are so well satisfied of the benefit their children receive that great application is made for others as vacancies occur", Report of Roundwood School. "The lower sort of people in this country are extremely Popish yet shew a great satisfaction in having their children admitted", Report of Killmalloch School. "The prejudice of the Popish parents is wearing off though the Priests are as busy as ever", Report of Creggane School. *Proceedings*, 1737-8.

[2] "Their poverty being so pressing that they think they cannot part with their children on better terms than to have them lodged, dieted, cloathed, educated and, at a proper age, put in a way to earn their own livelihood." *Proceedings*, 1735.

[3] Introduction to the *Proceedings*, 1748; Resolution of the Society, March 28, 1748.   [4] *Proceedings*, 1749.

again made the children the easy victims of this ruthless policy, which became practicable in 1741, when two successive years of famine had followed the great frost of 1739. When the children were admitted they were transplanted to distant schools, and to facilitate the removals the Society secured house-room in Dublin workhouse, in which the children were kept until they were carted across the country "to such remote schools as shall demand them".[1]

When this policy became general the Roman Church, which had hitherto contented itself with a close watch upon the schools, bestirred itself. The priests, alarmed, refused communion and absolution to parents who permitted their children to attend the schools, and as a result the number of pupils began steadily to decline. "Few Catholics pass by these schools without looking on them with a jealous eye and vent their feelings in curses and execrations", wrote Wakefield in 1812, "the words constantly in their mouths are—'Have not they, the Protestants, robbed the necessitous poor of their children to bring them up in their own religion'".[2] Only in times of stress would parents part with their children. When times improved they encouraged them to run away from the schools, or organised rescue parties, which lay in wait at the cross roads for the carts conveying the children to distant parts.[3]

New methods were therefore evolved to fill the schools. Attempts to cope with the ever-increasing number of beggars in Ireland had hitherto met with little success. In 1750 the Incorporated Society had been authorised to remove beggar children between the ages of five and fourteen years, whom nobody claimed, and one of whose parents was a Roman Catholic, to the nearest charter school.[4] In order to make the act effective the Society obtained from Parliament in 1758 an extraordinary grant of £5000 towards setting up in each of the four Provinces a nursery school, "a kind of storehouse", where the unwanted babies could be lodged until they were old enough to be transplanted to the depleted schools, and from this date, to the end of the century, the majority of the unhappy inmates of the schools were "pauper brats", with neither parent nor priest to defend them. "I am

---

[1] A Brief Review of the Rise and Progress of the Incorporated Society, 1743.

[2] Wakefield, E., op. cit. pp. 410–14.

[3] See Sermon preached before the Incorporated Society by the Bishop of Killala and Achonry, March 28, 1761.

[4] Irish Statutes, 23 Geo. II, c. 11.

assured", reported Campbell in 1775, "that a Papist would suffer any loss except that of his child rather than send it to one of these schools. Such is the bigotry of these deluded people that nothing but absolute want could prevail on them to suffer their children to receive an education which they conceive endangers their salvation."[1]

The difficulty of filling the schools in the second half of the century was increased by the slowly improving condition of the peasantry. While poverty and squalor remained the characteristic features of Irish peasant life, there was a conspicuous difference between the misery of the early years and the indigence of the later years of the century. Famine was no longer chronic or acute, as it had been in the thirties and forties. Regular and plentiful supplies of potatoes and milk, the common food of the Irish peasantry in the eighteenth century, provided a diet removed from the margin of subsistence. Arthur Young's comparison of the English labourer and the Irish cottier in the seventies redounds to the advantage of the Irish peasant, who at least "had a belly full". "Mark the Irishman's potato bowl placed on the floor, the whole family on their hams around it, devouring a quantity almost incredible, the beggar seating himself to it with a hearty welcome, the pig taking his share as readily as the wife, the cocks, hens, turkeys, geese, the cur, the cat, and perhaps the cow—and all partaking of the same dish. No man can often have been a witness of it without being convinced of the plenty, and, I will add, the cheerfulness that attends it." Had the charter boarding schools refrained from proselytism it is improbable that the peasantry would have supported them. While there was enough to eat at home, the children, who were not considered in Ireland, as Young remarked, a burden by their parents, would have remained at home.[2]

Until the last quarter of the century the lonely mountain places and the high stone walls of the buildings hid the charter schools from the world outside. Occasionally in the first half of the century inspectors sent out by the Society, and travellers in the neighbourhood of the schools, visited them and reported favourably upon them. Such scraps of information as are available suggest that the schools were, on the whole, well conducted. Smith and Harris, writing in 1744 their respective accounts of the charter schools at Waterford and Down,

[1] Campbell, T., *Philosophical Survey of the South of Ireland*, 1775, Letter I.
[2] Young, A., *op. cit.* Part II, pp. 186, 200.

gave details of the work done by the children, and concluded with a eulogy of "this happy institution", and of "the public spirited gentlemen who had encouraged it".[1] Bishop Pococke's diary of his tour through Ireland in 1752 affords similar testimony in respect of the twenty-four schools which he visited.[2] But, after the middle of the century, few persons troubled to enter them, or if they did so they lacked the interest and public spirit to publish their findings. The charity school sermons and reports, which were the only source of public information, did not, as John Howard's evidence showed, describe the schools as they were, but as the preachers imagined them to be.[3] But the public was not easy in its mind. Wesley, travelling in Ireland in 1782, heard disquieting rumours,[4] and John Howard, inspecting the Irish prisons from 1779 to 1782, was moved to turn aside and inspect the schools.

Howard's work in the cause of prison reform has been recognised by reformers throughout Europe, but it is not always remembered how widespread were his activities, nor along how many now almost forgotten by-ways they led him. "He trod an open and unfrequented path to immortality", says the legend at the foot of his statue in St Paul's Cathedral, and in one of the most unfrequented of these paths he found the lonely and neglected Irish charter schools and prepared the way for a belated reform of their worst abuses.

In the years 1782, 1784, 1787 and 1788 he visited the schools, gathering evidence which later he placed before the commission appointed to enquire into their abuses. Travelling in the remote parts of Ireland, "which are indeed more barbarous than the wilds of Russia",

[1] Smith, C., *History of Waterford*, 1845, pp. 78–80; Harris, W., *The Ancient and Present State of the County of Down*, 1744, p. 77.

[2] The School at Innishannon was "finely built", Clonmell's was "a sumptuous school"; Stradbally had "a very handsome school". Pococke, R., *Tour in Ireland*, 1752.

[3] *Journals of the House of Commons*, Ireland, April 14, 1788, vol. XII, appendix, p. DCCCXVI. On his first visit Howard carried with him the *sermon preached on behalf of the schools by the Bishop of Raphoe in* 1781. "Let the benevolent Patriot and Christian hear", said the preacher, "that in these schools above two thousand two hundred children, who otherwise must have become the Pests of Society and augmented the List of Souls doomed to destruction, are annually maintained." The actual number of children in the schools, reported Howard, was 700; less than a third of the number stated.

[4] Wesley, J., *Collected Works*, vol. IV, pp. 307–8.

was exhausting work, but more exhausting to patience and temper were the "sinister interests" which impeded his inspection. "One school has sheltered itself under the wing of a bishop, another under that of a lord, and for party purposes all the barriers of honour and honesty have been broken down."[1] Vested interests in the schools were strong, but Howard, with the support of Orde, the Secretary of State, the new Lord-Lieutenant, the Earl of Westmoreland, and Hely Hutchinson, Provost of Trinity College, was stronger still. To Howard and Sir Jeremiah Fitzpatrick, H.M. Inspector of Prisons, whose evidence before the Commission surpasses that of Howard in its detailed information, were given the right of entry, and to these two men the schools reluctantly gave up their secrets.

To travel in imagination with Howard or Fitzpatrick is to gain an intimate knowledge of the charter schools. The 700 victims of a powerful and merciless charity, sickly, dirty, underfed and uneducated, were brought by them before a public which had forgotten their existence. Outwardly the schools gave little warning of their internal condition. The strong buildings and high stone walls gave them a prison-like appearance, "well adapted to their purpose", as the Society stated in earlier years. Inside filth reigned undisturbed; the walls and floor reeking with dirt and swarming with vermin, and the infirmaries, used as pigsties or fuel-houses, loudly proclaiming that they had not been cleaned for months, prepared the visitor for the close and offensive bedrooms, for the disgusting beds and the filthy, torn and rotten sheets. In these beds of tickings stuffed with straw three or more children were commonly huddled, gaining from close bodily contact at night the warmth denied them in their working day.

With some few exceptions the same tale was repeated of all the schools with sickening detail; scarcity of water, no privies, scanty and unchanged linen, and clothing so ragged that in many of the schools the children were almost naked. Even worse was the condition of the puny, ill-fed, bodies so badly covered. Disease arising from the insanitation and neglect was rife; limbs were deformed by long hours of work at the large spinning-wheels, bodies were wasted by the perpetual use of saliva to moisten the flax in spinning. Skin diseases on the hands, the itch and scald head were common. The almost universal neglect of

[1] Howard, J., Letter to Dr Price, March 24, 1788, quoted in Baldwin Brown's *Memoirs of the Public and Private life of John Howard [etc.]*, 1818.

bodily cleanliness, the long working hours, the insufficient warmth and the absence of fresh air and exercise go far to explain the sickly appearance of the children, but perhaps the chief contributory cause was their unsuitable and inadequate food. Howard and Fitzpatrick call witnesses from school after school to testify to their chronic ill-treatment.[1]

The material condition of the schools so greatly occupied the attention of the visitors that they barely touched upon the *raison d'être* of the schools' existence. Thrice only in his "particular account" did John Howard mention the religious side of school life; once to comment on the assiduous and unusual attentions of the worthy clergyman, Mr Foster, at Stradbally school, a second time when explaining that the improvement of the boys at Ballinrobe was due to the attention paid to them by the clergyman, and the third when stating that at Castlemartyr there was not a Testament in the house.[2] Fitzpatrick mentions only that the Roscommon girls were kept to their

[1] See *Journals of the House of Commons*, Ireland, *loc. cit.*: evidence of John Howard and Sir Jeremiah Fitzpatrick.

Castlecaulfield. Several of the children had sore heads; the girls were eating hot potatoes.

Clontarf. Linen scanty, cutaneous eruptions on the hands.

Castlebar. Children almost naked, sheeting much wanted; no pump. Almost all had the itch and sore head. Puny sickly objects.

Connaught Nursery. The children from 2–4 years in a very sickly condition with itch, scald head, sore eyes.

Castledermot. The house out of repair. No diet table, nor had the mistress ever heard of any.

Clonmel. The children half starved.

Castle Island. The children scantily fed.

Dundalk. The children seemed by their countenances to be scantily fed.

Dunmanway. The master excused himself from going with me into the bed rooms by saying that he was afraid of catching a disorder. The bolsters matted with dirt. The children sickly. 12 beds for 39 boys and girls.

Frankfort. House very offensive. Fowls, ducks and pigs in the kitchen. The children sickly.

Farra. The children very dirty, water too distant, clothes in rags.

Galway. No towels. The house in good repair, but wants whitewashing.

Innishannon. The house out of repair; the children suffered from the itch and other cutaneous disorders.

Loughrea. 16 beds for 40 children. Dirty sickly objects.

Leinster Nursery. The children very dirty. Their heads not kept properly.

Trim. The bread very bad; the children badly clothed.

[2] Howard, J., *Account of the Principal Lazarettos in Europe*, 1789. Section VII.

catechism and lessons from 6 to 9 a.m., those at Loughrea school from 5 to 7 p.m., and that the children at Newmarket seldom went to church because of the distance. In the absence of contrary evidence it may be assumed that the children commonly attended church on Sundays, and it is probable that the catechist examined them in church after the morning service. Whether they received any religious teaching other than this is open to question. It is difficult to believe that the clergy can have visited the schools for this or any other purpose, and it is improbable that the masters and mistresses who neglected instruction in secular subjects for which they were responsible would have troubled themselves, except in rare cases, to give religious teaching. The picture which Fitzpatrick draws of hungry children in the early morning, or tired children at the end of the day, sitting down to learn their catechism by heart for the coming Sunday defines the religious instruction which they received.

Even greater was the neglect of the secular subjects of the curriculum. The reports of the visitors tell of schools in which no education was attempted. "What are they taught?" asked John Wesley after his visit in 1785 to Ballinrobe school. "As far as I could learn just nothing."[1] Once or twice Howard discovered a school where attention given to learning permitted a word of negative praise, but, in general, his and Fitzpatrick's reports agree with Wesley's. Children in their early and later teens, who had been years in the school, could scarcely write their names; others read very badly; some could not spell. The absence of books, pens, ink and paper, and the inadequate schoolroom accommodation, shows conclusively that this side of the Society's work was not considered important. Education, to quote Fitzpatrick, was "criminally neglected". In the schools where ushers were employed learning was sometimes entrusted to them; in the others little pretence at schooling existed. On the industrial side only of the charter school work was the Society's aim to any degree realised, and this in such a manner that the spirit was destroyed in adherence to the letter. The children were indeed employed in manual work; spinning indoors, or agricultural work outside, occupied the greater portion of their day. To their incessant toil Fitzpatrick attributed their sickly appearance and their many physical deformities. The time-table at Loughrea school, where the girls were employed in spinning, knitting and reeling, shows that they

[1] Wesley, J., *Collected Works*, vol. IV, pp. 307–8.

rose at 6 a.m.; cleaned themselves and the school until 9 o'clock; breakfasted and worked at their handicrafts until noon. From 12 to 2 p.m. they attended school; they returned to their labour from 3 to 5 p.m.; and from 5 to 7 p.m. were kept at their catechism, etc.; in all, a working day of twelve hours. At Roscommon, a school reserved exclusively by its founder, Lord Ranelagh, for the children of Protestants, the conditions were equally bad. No advantage accrued to the children of the poor from the faith of their parents. Protestant and Catholic were subjected impartially, by the Society's instructions, to the same *régime* of labour and religious instruction.[1] It is probable that these two schools, whose time-tables alone are given, were worse than the average,[2] but evidence drawn from other schools in Fitzpatrick's and Howard's reports show that the industrial conditions were uniformly bad. The indoor workers suffered most; confined to the close atmosphere of the unwarmed workrooms during the day and breathing the unhealthy exhalations of the filthy beds and bed-clothes at night the children lacked, as Fitzpatrick remarked, "the athleticity so strongly marked in the children of the poor in this Kingdom".[3] The agricultural workers, whom Bishop Maule had seen in his imagination, under the care of proper directors, transforming the desolate and uncultivated land into little farm colonies, well-hedged and manured, planted with trees, corn, flax-seed and potatoes, and with grazing land sufficient for three or four cows, spent their days as unskilled labourers. The vocational side of their work was completely neglected. Cheaper than beasts of burden, they carried water and carted manure or dug and picked potatoes, not as part of their training for agricultural life when they left the school, but as the casual labourer works from day to day.

---

[1] This was also the case in the school for boys on the Ranelagh foundation at Athlone. "I found", wrote Howard, "the boys dirty and ragged and employed in carrying heavy loads of dung to a lighter. The children in general did not appear cheerful." Howard, J., *op. cit.* See also *Journals of the House of Commons, loc. cit.*

[2] See *Journals of the House of Commons,* Ireland, *loc. cit.*

Clonmel. Proper attention is now paid to reading.

Killoteran. Their reading is not neglected.

Castleisland. Formerly their learning neglected but now they have a careful visitor.

[3] *Idem. Schedule annexed to the Report of the Committee on the State of the Protestant Charter Schools,* April 14, 1788.

In no single department of the schools had the Society's aim been realised; religious, scholastic, industrial, all had failed, and the ungrateful task of apportioning the blame must be considered. It may be urged on behalf of the Incorporated Society that its aims and methods were those of its age and that society as a whole rather than the Society in particular was responsible for the charter schools. But even if this be admitted the responsibility of the Society for the shameful condition of the schools is deplorably heavy. A glance at the names of the Dublin committee of fifteen which formed the central executive of the Society in part explains its failure. Many were those of men of position or of high professional standing, peers busy with their estates or parliamentary duties, ecclesiastics occupied with affairs of Church and State, judges concerned with matters far removed from schools and children, to whom the work of the Society ranked not as a primary, but as a secondary duty; and, as the work of the Society increased, the control of the schools devolved more and more upon the paid officials, the secretary and his clerks. Few if any of the members were men of practical experience in school affairs. Good solid stone houses were erected and paid for. Their value was self-evident, their cost could be estimated by the most amateur of committees, but the upkeep of the schools, the cost of adequate maintenance and the essentials of a sound education could, on the other hand, be judged only by men and women possessing a knowledge of boarding-school conditions. This knowledge the central committee never possessed; and as the years went by to ignorance was added indifference. One of the causes of the unsatisfactory condition of the schools as alleged by the Commission of 1809–12 was the difficulty of procuring a constant and regular attendance of the committee of fifteen in Dublin.

Heavy as the indictment of the Dublin committee must be, censure for the schools' maladministration must in part be borne by the local committees. The schools were too scattered, too remote, to make the constant control of the Dublin committee feasible. Hence at one of its earliest meetings, the Society resolved that wherever a charity school should be set up it would request the minister of the parish or his curate to act as catechist to the school, and the resident gentry to form themselves into a local committee to inspect the schools and to report to the standing committee in Dublin.[1] A system of dual control was thus set up, which depended for its success not only upon the efficiency of the central and local committees, but also upon the unity between the two bodies. On these two conditions rested the administrative success of the Society, and a cursory investigation shows that the majority of the local committees were as deficient in a sense of responsibility as was the central authority. In the early half of the century much local interest was evoked. School sites were offered by local clergy and gentry for the erection of schools in their neighbourhood and buildings like the Waterford girls' school, one of the prettiest and most commodious buildings of its kind in the kingdom, were erected at the expense of the local families. The lists of subscribers and benefactors attached to the reports of the local committees illustrate the local interest.[2] But when

[1] See the *Report of the Commissioners of Education in Ireland*, 1809–12, vol. v, p. 18: "Each school is under the immediate direction of a local committee, consisting of the principal resident Protestant Gentleman and Ladies of the neighbourhood and of a catechist, who is always the Curate of the Parish in which the School is situated. It is the duty of the catechist to superintend the Education of the Children generally, and more especially their religious instruction and to communicate monthly his observations on the state of the School and the conduct of the Masters, and, in concert with the local committee, to exercise general control, examine, and settle Accounts and report every quarter to the Committee of Fifteen in Dublin."

[2] See *Proceedings*, 1758, for the Report of Stradbally School, Queen's Co. "This school in which there are forty children owes its rise to Pole Cosby Esq. who expended £300 in the Building, gave an Acre of Land in Perpetuity and leased thirty acres at £11 per annum for which the Master pays £15. The annual subscribers to the school:

Pole Cosby Esq.	£10.	0.	0
Rt Hon. Earl of Upper Ossory	5.	13.	9
Hon. Mrs Bridges	11.	7.	6
Col. Nathaniel Mitchell	1.	10.	0
John Pigott Esq.	1.	10.	0
Matthew Cassan Esq.	2.	5.	6
Miss Sarah Cosby	2.	5.	6
William Pole Esq.	3.	8.	3
Hon. General Humphrey Bland	3.	8.	3
Rev. Frederick Trench	1.	10.	0
Rt Hon. Lady Sarah Pole	2.	5.	6
Warner Westenra Esq.	2.	5.	6
Rev. Mr Hatfield, Vicar of Stradbally	1.	10.	0
Walter Weldon Esq.	2.	5.	6
Total	51.	15.	3 "

the novelty of the movement had worn off, and a new generation arose, to whom the enthusiasm and interest of the founders made little appeal, neglect steadily encroached upon attention. The schools were too well provided with funds to be dependent upon the interest and subscriptions of "well disposed Christians". The system of dual control which, in theory, appeals by its freedom and elasticity, failed because the local authorities did not honour their obligations. Beyond an annual subscription, or the renewal of a lease, the local gentry and clergy took little personal interest in the schools and signed reports testifying to conditions which they had not troubled to examine.[1]

The inefficiency of both local and central bodies explains in part the general mismanagement, but equally important as an explanation was the lack of co-operation between them. It was no man's business to inspect the schools. The local committees drew up their own reports and the discrepancy between them and the conditions as disclosed by John Howard and Sir Jeremiah Fitzpatrick blatantly proclaims the freedom of the schools from inspection and control. In its early years the Society sent its secretary or appointed inspectors to visit the schools then established, and their report satisfied it of the excellence of the existing arrangements.[2] In 1788 Mr Gibbon, the secretary, admitted to the committee of inquiry that it was fifteen years since he had visited any of the schools except the Strand school, Dublin. Instead of establishing an effective control of the local committees the Society left the management of the schools and the care of the children in the hands of masters and mistresses, who either deliberately neglected their duties or were incapable of meeting the difficulties of their many-sided task.

Lack of competent teachers handicapped all educational schemes in England during the eighteenth century. "The starving wretches" of Mandeville's bitter gibe, the "brutal and incompassionate masters" whom Dr Watts deplored, "the refuse of other callings" condemned in later years by Macaulay, are to be met with in all types of eighteenth-century schools. But in Ireland the lack of competent and responsible teachers was even greater, for in a country where the majority of the population, and almost all the poorer classes, were Roman Catholics, the area from which Protestant masters and mistresses could be drawn was a small one. Further, the master of a charter school was expected

[1] *Journals of the House of Commons*, Ireland, *loc. cit.* See also Howard, J., *op. cit.* p. 105.
[2] See *Proceedings*, 1745.

to combine in himself the offices of teacher, parent, workhouse master and medical officer. Educational history abounds in fantastic pictures of the ideal teacher, but even Rousseau's "veritable phoenix" is an insignificant figure compared with the ideal required by the Incorporated Society. There does not, however, at any time, seem to have been a lack of candidates; on the contrary, canvassing for posts was common, and the interest of the leading members of the Society was eagerly sought.[1] The cause of this keen competition is easily explained. The ideal masters could not be obtained and the Society was obliged to fall back on men and women who, in Mandeville's words, "think themselves qualified". These persons, attracted by a free house and wages, and by the possibility of making money out of the industrial and agricultural side of the work, presented themselves in large numbers to the Society, which approached mechanically the distasteful task of selecting the best of the bad. "It would excite indignation and disgust", wrote William Disney, a member of the Dublin committee of the Society, in 1806, "to see the description of men and women to whom the education of children in these schools has been sometimes, almost necessarily, committed; men of vulgar habits, coarse manners, often ignorant in the extreme of everything but the common rudiments of reading, writing and arithmetic, exhibiting nothing in conduct or example that could raise the minds of the children above the level of that semi-barbarism which has been the character of the lower class of people in this country."[2]

The organisation of the schools played into the hands of unscrupulous men and women. Financially the schools were dependent on the central committee of control and the accounts were ordered to be examined annually by the local committees, but, since the Society contracted with the masters for feeding and clothing the children, and since the local committees consistently neglected their duty of supervision, opportunities for peculation were rife, and the wretched children were starved and ill-clothed. Howard's and Fitzpatrick's reports illustrate the criminal neglect of the most obvious duties of cleanliness and

---

[1] "There was a regular canvass on every vacancy and scarce any one conceived the idea of offering themselves that did not think himself previously sure of what is called the Interest of some of the leading members of the Society." Disney, W., *Observations on the Present State of the Charter Schools in Ireland and the Means of Improving them*, 1808.

[2] Disney, W., *op. cit.*

decency. They show that the schooling given was a farce, and that the moral and religious influences designed to raise the children from irreligion and immorality were conspicuously absent. But worse than the negative treatment was the positive cruelty which the more brutal masters inflicted on the children. Fitzpatrick tells in detail the incident which induced him to persevere in his inspection of the schools.

> Kilkenny School. 12th February 1785.

The House is situated a mile from the City. There were 32 children there, all of them very small and almost all looked miserable, and their wretched appearance was enhanced by their being barelegged and ragged. Though boys they were employed in carding and spinning and sat on stools and stone seats in a cold workshop. On the morning of the day of my visit it snowed heavily, yet the room in which they were at work was without a fire, although it was ready for lighting. I asked why it was not lighted. A person who superintended the labour of the children demanded (with an angered tone of voice) why they had not lighted it before? Two of them with a look of terror arose and instantly obeyed. After having examined the situation of the House where I found the beds abominably filthy, education most culpably neglected and many of the children afflicted with the itch and the scald I rode off, but suspecting from what I had seen that the children would not long enjoy the benefit of the fire I returned on foot through the fields and found that they had already extinguished it by pouring water on it. The barbarity of this treatment of the wretched objects of public benevolence was one of my first and principal inducements to persevere in the Inspection of the Charter Schools.[1]

Some measure of the vitality of vested interests in Ireland may be obtained from a study of Howard's and Fitzpatrick's reports. They sketch the master who disclaimed any obligation to instruct the children or to take them to church, and his fellow who considered himself capable of adding medical supervision to his other duties, with the result that eleven coffins for his baby victims figured in his quarterly account. They show the mistress of the filthy Castlebar school, who when reproved insolently retorted that she had powerful friends at court, and the usher of Loughrea who stood rod in hand to keep forty dirty, sickly objects, shivering with cold, at their knitting and spinning.

[1] *Journals of the House of Commons*, Ireland, *loc. cit.* vol. XII: Schedule annexed to the *Report on the State of the Protestant Charter Schools*, April 14, 1788.

They tell of the comfortable apartments of the masters and mistresses, and of the difference between their own children and the wretched paupers, and they give in outline a picture which Messrs Thackeray and Lee, sent by the Society to inspect the schools in 1817–18, and the witnesses before the Commission of 1824–5 fill in with hideous detail.[1]

It is easy to fulminate against men and women of this type. They took advantage of opportunities which offered to win a home and livelihood. The responsibility for their selection rests directly upon the Incorporated Society and indirectly upon society as a whole, which permitted such men and women to be engaged in educational work. The salaries paid illustrate the opinion in which the age held their work. £12 a year was the average; the ushers' wages ranged between £5 and £7. In addition bounties for satisfactory service were made and the masters and mistresses were at liberty to sell the children's labour. A skilful farmer-master, if the lands around the school were fertile, could raise the greater portion of the food required for the children, and could sell the occasional surplus in the neighbourhood; an experienced spinner or knitter could not only clothe the children in the school but could also supply the local market, and in this manner the small salaries were augmented.

Food and clothing poor and inadequate, dirt and disease unchecked, left the children at the mercy of the cold and damp. Fires, which the masters and mistresses and their children and hired labourers enjoyed, were not lit for the paupers in the workrooms. At the beck and call of master and mistress and usher for thirteen long hours every day, no time could be found for fresh air and invigorating exercises. Frightened, hungry, dirty and cold, utterly helpless and unprotected, they dragged out a miserable existence from day to day. Escape was possible only by "elopement" or by apprenticeship. Children ran away when they could, and it was considered a high recommendation of Killoteran school that not one child had deserted for several years.

By the Society's regulations the children were to be bound out as apprentices at the age of fourteen years. But here again the indifference of the Society to its regulations and the self-interest of the masters blocked the way. In the early years of the Society's history the children were regularly apprenticed as they reached the school leaving age, but before Howard's visit the numbers had steadily diminished. Instead of

[1] *First Report of the Commissioners of Education in Ireland*, 1825, Appendices 55–74.

well-trained boys and girls fitted for agricultural and domestic work, would-be employers found sickly children incapable of sustained labour, so filthy in body and undeveloped in mind that respectable homes would not receive them. Fitzpatrick stated plainly that the masters and mistresses worked for this result. The apprenticeship system meant a loss of the pupils just when they were becoming useful, hence the masters found it to their advantage to keep them dirty and ignorant so that no person would wish to take them apprentice, and in his report appear the wretched figures of lads in their later teens who had spent their lives in the schools and for whom the way of escape was barred.

Such was the picture drawn by John Howard and Jeremiah Fitzpatrick and presented to the Irish House of Commons in 1788. The shameful story aroused comment in England and in Scotland, but it is significant of the sinister interests which John Howard deplored that in Ireland public opinion and the Legislature were unaffected by it. "In this country", wrote Howard to Samuel Whitbread, "every public institution is a private emolument; all are corrupt or totally ineffective, from the highest to the lowest."[1] "The strong remonstrance" which was organised against his report was more powerful than the efforts of the greatest philanthropist of the age, backed by the sympathy of the Executive. Howard's and Fitzpatrick's evidence, which fills several pages in the Journals of the Irish House of Commons, was as effectively ignored as if the pages had been torn out of the volume. "I can find no trace", wrote Robert Steven in his *Demand for an Inquiry into the Abuses of the Chartered Schools in Ireland* in 1818, "of any steps having been taken by the Irish Parliament in consequence of the report", and the disclosures of the Commissioners of Education in 1825 confirm his indignant protest.[2]

---

[1] Field, J., *Life of John Howard*, 1855, p. 249, July 6, 1787.

[2] Two Commissions of the Board of Education, Ireland, reported upon the schools of the Incorporated Society in the first quarter of the nineteenth century. The Commission of 1809–12, whose reports were based on the evidence of visitors appointed by the Society to inspect the schools, was, on the whole, favourable. Richard Lowell Edgeworth congratulated the Society, of which he was a member, upon the reforms introduced into the schools since the visits of John Howard and Sir Jeremiah Fitzpatrick. "The education of the children is efficacious, practical, free from bigotry, and in every respect such as to put it beyond the reach of private defamation and public censure." The report of the Commission of 1825 was, on the

18

The schools set up under the auspices of the Irish S.P.C.K. and the Incorporated Society are not commensurate with the charity school movement in Ireland. Sixty-four non-classical schools endowed in the eighteenth century were returned by the Commissioners of Education in 1791. Some among them had their origin in the early efforts of the S.P.C.K.; others, endowed at later dates, were established independently of the Society. To arrive at an approximate estimate of the full extent of the efforts to provide elementary education for the poor in Ireland the number of parish schools assisted by the charity of the Protestant gentry and clergy should be added. Their numbers are unknown, but as the returns collected from the parishes at the end of the century showed that in at least half the benefices of the country no schools were maintained, their numbers were not great.[1] Again it is not possible to estimate the number of children whose fees in hedge, or cabin, schools were paid by subscriptions or by endowments for schooling, but when allowance is made for their existence it appears incontestible that the provision of instruction on a Protestant basis by the State, voluntary associations and individual beneficence, was lamentably in-adequate. Their failure was reflected in the formation of a new society —The Association for Discountenancing Vice and Promoting the Knowledge of the Christian Religion—as the century was drawing to a close.[2] The new society, whose scholastic history lies outside the eighteenth century, took its colour from the current dread of "French democracy and infidelity". It was an Anglican society, acting in close relationship with the Established Church. Concerned in its early years primarily with the provision of Bibles, Testaments and prayer books and with the encouragement of catechetical instruction by the clergy, it turned its attention to the setting up of day schools for the children of

whole, unfavourable. It condemned many of the schools, and attributed the favourable findings of its predecessor to collusion between the teachers and the members of the local committees when the schools were inspected. The evidence of witnesses before the Commission of 1825 revealed conditions in some of the schools comparable to the worst of those described by Howard and Fitzpatrick. As a result of these disclosures the parliamentary grant was gradually reduced and withdrawn in 1832. During the last hundred years the work of the Society devoted to the instruction of Protestant children has given it an honourable place in Irish education.

[1] *Report of the Commissioners of Irish Education Inquiry*, 1791. Printed in the *Endowed Schools (Ireland) Commission Reports*, 1856, vol. II, pp. 341 *et seq.*

the poor of all denominations. The schools were Anglican schools, the masters and mistresses were members of the Anglican communion and the Anglican catechism held its place as the backbone of instruction. Like the charter schools, they were supported by voluntary subscriptions and by parliamentary grants, which from 1800 to 1827, when the grants were withdrawn, exceeded a total of £100,000. The measured success of the new society in the first quarter of the nineteenth century in providing instruction for children whose parents would permit them to attend, flings into even greater relief the failure of State and voluntary efforts in the eighteenth century.[1]

V

THE HEDGE SCHOOLS

While the failure of the charity school movement in Ireland must in the main be attributed to the gross mismanagement of the Incorporated Society, the presence of a successful rival in the field of elementary education contributed to it in no small degree. In the Highlands the schools set up by the S.P.C.K. were the chief, and, in many parts, the only means of instruction for the poor. This was not so in Ireland. The effect of the penal laws in a country predominantly Catholic was to drive beneath the surface the determined and unremitting efforts of the Roman Church to control the education of its children. Its success in providing instruction for the superior orders, in the face of legal prohibitions, was considerable; more remarkable still was the network of schools for the children of the poor which it encouraged. Too loosely organised to be termed a system, but so numerous at the beginning of the nineteenth century as to make State action obligatory, if the Government were to exercise some form of control over popular education, the hedge schools provided, throughout the eighteenth century, and in particular after the repeal of the penal laws in 1782, a means of

[1] See *Reports of the Committee of Education appointed by the Association for Discountenancing Vice and Promoting Religion and Virtue in the Dioceses of Clogher and Kilmore, Armagh and Dromore*, 1800. See also *First Report of the Commissioners of Education in Ireland*, 1825, pp. 30–36; Appendix 173, pp. 339–406. The Association was founded in 1792 and incorporated in 1800.

education for the mass of the Irish people on a Roman Catholic basis.[1]

The origin of the schools is obscure. All that can safely be asserted is that in Cromwellian Ireland, and again in the eighteenth century, Roman Catholic priests and schoolmasters ignored the loosely administered laws, and, to avoid detection by Government officials or chance travellers, kept school out of doors, where

> Still crouching 'neath the sheltering hedge,
> Or stretch'd on mountain fern,
> The teacher and his pupils met
> Feloniously to learn.[2]

So successful were the Popish schools at the end of the seventeenth century that they threatened the schools endowed by the Cromwellian soldier, Erasmus Smith, at Drogheda and Galway with a total loss of their pupils, and by their presence elsewhere undermined the health of Protestant schools "as succors do starve the tree".[3] The alarm occasioned by the steady increase in the number of illegal schools was not allayed by the House of Lords inquiry in 1730. The number of schools then returned was clearly an under-statement, for the teachers did not advertise their presence. On the contrary, elaborate devices were used to prevent discovery, and, as the people could seldom be prevailed upon to give information concerning priests or schoolmasters, full and complete returns of their numbers and activities could not be assured. The life of the hedge schools depended upon their obscurity.

Their history in the eighteenth century, built up out of scraps of contemporary information, unveils an aspect of "Hidden Ireland" usually ignored by historians. The schools were peasant schools. While the fees of the very poor who attended them were sometimes defrayed by the charity of Roman priests, or country gentry, or Anglican clergy, the schools were normally financed by parents, who either paid the schoolmaster trifling fees of a few shillings per quarter for each of the subjects taught by him, or recompensed him in kind. Sometimes they

[1] For a recent study of the hedge schools see Dowling, P. J., *The Hedge Schools of Ireland*, 1935.
[2] O'Hagan, *The New Spirit of the Nation*, 1894, p. 16.
[3] Minute Book of the Governors of the Schools of Erasmus Smith, 1680; letter of Erasmus Smith, June 6, 1682, quoted in Corcoran, T., *State Policy in Irish Education*, 1916.

supplied him with a barn or outhouse for his work, and housed him with their families, or hastily erected a cabin for him in the ditch by the wayside, which provided, without expenditure of time or energy, two ready-made walls, and required only a back of clay and wattle, and a roof of green twigs "interlaced with strips of bog", to be complete. The common choice of the roadside explains Arthur Young's comment that in Ireland many a ditch was "full of scholars".[1]

The pupils attending the schools were peasant children, of all ages and stages, without distinction of sex or religion. Their curriculum extended from the spelling of English words, at one end of the scale, through reading, writing and arithmetic, to Hebrew, Latin, Greek and Mathematics at the other.[2] In some parts instruction was bilingual. Both English and Irish were spoken; in others good Latin scholars were to be found who did not understand the English tongue. The diocesan register of Cashel and Emly, from 1740 to 1759, establishes a close connection between the hedge schools and the Roman Church. It reveals the presence of Roman bishops in a country where they were forbidden by law to remain, working in close connection with Popish schoolmasters on whose heads a price was set.[3] Records from other parts of the country for the first three-quarters of the century appear to be non-existent, but the register makes incontestably clear that in Cashel and Emly and, it may be assumed, elsewhere, Roman bishops exercised supervision over the schools. There is evidence that in some of them the children were taught the Roman catechism, and that they were examined in "Christian Doctrine"[4] by the Roman clergy.

[1] Young, A., *op. cit.* Part II, p. 202.

[2] "It is well known", wrote Dr Charles Smith in *The Ancient and Present State of the County of Kerry*, 1756, "that classical learning extends itself even to a fault among the lower and poorer kind in this country many of whom, to the taking them off more useful works have a greater knowledge in this way than some of the better sort in other places", p. 418.

[3] See Corcoran, T., *Some Lists of Catholic Lay Teachers and their Illegal Schools in the Later Penal Times*, Dublin, 1932, *passim.*

[4] See Brennan, M., *The Schools of Leighlin and Kildare from 1755 to 1835*, published in 1935, which is an important contribution to the history of the Irish hedge schools. Using the parochial returns to a questionnaire addressed by the Commissioners of the Irish Education Inquiry, in 1825, to the clergy of the Established Church, the Presbyterian ministers and the Roman Catholic priests, the Commissioners drew up their Second Report (the Blue Book Summary) in 1826. The returns from which the summary was made were not published and it may be

The success of the peasant schools depended almost entirely upon the personality and efficiency of the schoolmaster. Himself a peasant, receiving his education at a hedge school, he was, as a rule, drawn from the ranks of the "poor scholars", the promising pupils who were ambitious to become priests and schoolmasters. The course of training demanded from candidate-teachers affords a measure by which the importance of pedagogy in Irish peasant life may be judged. A "Munster Diploma" was the immediate aim of the lads who set out from their homes to seek learning in the southern province, which, throughout the eighteenth century, was famed for its schools. "They traverse", said Croker, writing in 1824, "the southern parts of the Island, visit every village, sojourn in every school, examine every local curiosity, and return to their birthplaces after, perhaps a year's absence, without having for that space of time expended, or even possessed a single half-crown. So warm is the hospitality of the peasantry and so high their respect for learning."[1]

Sometimes on his return, sometimes before he set out, the candidate-teacher, ambitious to become pedagogue of the village school, would challenge his master in an open contest of scholarship and mental agility, before the parish priest and a crowded audience of villagers. If unsuccessful the young man stayed on awhile and tried another throw with his elder, or with the master of a neighbouring village school. A series of such contests was considered an essential part of every school-master's training.

Criticism severe, and in part deserved, has been passed upon the attainments and the character of the Irish hedge schoolmasters. In the writings of the novelists, Carleton, Banim, Lover and Lady Morgan, they appear often as drunken, cruel, ignorant brutes, bullying and ill-treating their pupils. Their morals were questionable, their conceit overwhelming, their ignorance hidden by a veil of pretended erudition, while their disloyalty to the Government was notorious. On the other hand there is not lacking evidence which demands considerable modi-

assumed were destroyed. For the dioceses of Kildare and Leighlin the returns of the Roman priests were made in duplicate and over three-quarters of them have been preserved in the Diocesan Archives. Published as an Appendix to Dr Brennan's work they provide new and valuable information about the hedge schools in the early nineteenth century.

[1] Croker, T. C., *Researches in the South of Ireland*, 1824, pp. 326–7.

fication of this unflattering picture.[1] There were sober, decent, lovable and even erudite scholars among them. Some, like their Highland fellows, were poet-teachers, "sweet singers", such as Brian Merriman in Co. Clare, or Dennis Macnamara in Co. Waterford, or Owen Roe O'Sullivan in Knockmagee, whose fame spread throughout Ireland. It appears incontestable that the hedge schools, like all other schools for the poor in the eighteenth century, drew upon men unfitted by character and attainments to be teachers; but it is equally clear that, pretentious as many of the hedge schoolmasters appear, there was among them an enthusiasm for learning and an interest in teaching which was not conspicuous among the charity school teachers. Public opinion demanded, and not seldom secured, the services in the hedge schools of men unlike the dull grey mediocrities who staffed the majority of the elementary schools. The hedge schoolmaster not infrequently aroused and maintained among his pupils an interest in learning and a fervour for politics which left its mark on the Irish peasantry.

To the attraction of "disloyal principles industriously insinuated",[2] and a smattering of Greek and Latin tags, the Protestant teachers of the charter schools could present no rival. Labour and the catechism were not enlivening or absorbing subjects of instruction, nor were the textbooks of Bible and catechism comparable with the Latin classics, or the coarse but enthralling chapbooks which the children brought with them for the reading lessons in the hedge schools.[3] The education of

[1] See Dowling, P. J., *op. cit. passim*; Brennan, M., *op. cit. passim*, "These are the schools", wrote Master Fitzgibbon, in *Ireland in 1868*, "described in Oliver Goldsmith's *The Deserted Village*, 'kept by masters severe and stern to view'."

[2] Carleton, W., *Traits and Stories of the Irish Peasantry*, 4th ed. 1836, vol. II, p. 398.

[3] Controversy has raged around the text-books used to teach children to read English in the hedge schools. Witnesses before the Commissioners of 1825 reported adversely upon their "immoral character", and upon the countenance given to them by the priests. The presence of such books was as vigorously denied. The available evidence suggests that the critics of the schools did not always distinguish between books which were offensive to morality and those which were offensive to religion and politics: the supporters of the schools, on the other hand, in denying the existence of immoral literature, forget that the reading books used not only in the Irish hedge schools but in the common schools in England and Wales were not as a rule provided by the schoolmasters, but by the pupils, who brought to school such books as their parents possessed. They varied from an innocuous nursery tale such as the *Seven Champions of Christendom* to the *History of Freny the Robber* and

young peasants "with a Cicero or Virgil under their arms",[1] or with chapbooks proscribed by the London S.P.C.K. for the English schools at the beginning of the century in their pockets, might be deplored by statesmen and educationalists, but they did not fail to attract to the schools, in ever-increasing numbers, children whose parents could ill afford to pay for their instruction.

The more enlivening curriculum of the hedge schools, and the less rigid methods of instruction used by men who were trained to quickness and repartee, and who prided themselves on their eccentricities, were not without their effect on their pupils. John Howard, comparing the children of the hedge schools with those of the neighbouring charter schools, remarked upon their "clean and wholesome, appearance", and found them "much forwarder than those of the same age in the charter schools".[2]

By the beginning of the nineteenth century the hedge schools had become the common schools of the Irish people. The withdrawal of penal legislation between 1782 and 1829 coincided with the period of rapid increase in the population and, as a result, of the rapid increase in the number of hedge schools, and of the children attending them.[3] "The strong passion for education", which "mark(s) the lower classes of our people", wrote John Leslie Foster to the Secretary of the Board of Education in 1811, "assures us that if we do not assist them instructed nevertheless they will be."[4] Recognition of this fact was responsible for

the *Irish Rogues and Rapparees,* a "eulogium", in Carleton's opinion, "of murder, robbery and theft". These "cottage classics" were read by the peasantry, and were used as reading-books in the schools. They form an interesting commentary on the reading of the people in the eighteenth century. A list of the books found by the Commissioners in use in the different types of Irish schools is printed in Appendix 221 of the *First Report of the Commissioners of Education in Ireland,* 1825, p. 553. A selected list is given in Dr Dowling's *Hedge Schools of Ireland,* Appendix.

[1] Sir Robert Peel, Speech in the House of Commons, Hansard, *Parliamentary Debates,* 2nd Series, vol. xv, March 20, 1826.

[2] Howard, J., *op. cit.* p. 119. See also the evidence of the Rev. Wm. Lee in the *First Report of the Commissioners of Education in Ireland,* 1825, Appendix 55, p. 125.

[3] See *Reports of the Commissioners of Education, Ireland,* 1809–12, vol. v, p. 342: "The Charter School at Newport (Co. Tipperary) built to hold forty children contained only 12 children in 1824, but in a cabin school within a short distance were found 96 children, 38 of whom were Protestants whose parents preferred paying for their instruction there rather than accept the free education supplied by

the establishment in Ireland of the first State department for education in the British Isles.

the Charter school. There was another Pay School at a distance of two miles held in a stable which a young man had taken for the Summer season. This was so crowded with children that the youngest were placed in a manger, there being no room for them on the floor."

The Seal of the Society for Promoting English Protestant
Working Schools in Ireland

CHAPTER VIII

WALES

CHARITY AND PIETY

"The Practice of Piety consists in knowing God and glorifying Him aright." Lewis Bayly, Bishop of Bangor, *The Practice of Piety*, 1613.

I

THE BACKGROUND

The charity school movement in Wales presents a curious contrast to the parallel movements in England, Scotland and Ireland. It was not primarily concerned with attempts to condition the children of the poor for their work in life, nor to instruct them in the blessings of an alien civilisation, nor to rescue them from the toils of Rome. It was concerned chiefly, and almost exclusively, with the desire to save the souls of the Welsh people.

For this distinctive aim the political, social and religious conditions in Wales, at the end of the seventeenth and throughout the eighteenth century, were, in the main, responsible. They may be described, in contrast to the conditions prevailing in the three neighbouring countries, in a series of negations. Jacobitism as a political force counted for little in eighteenth-century Wales. This is not to say that the Welsh squirearchy did not support it, or the Welsh clergy and peasants sympathise with it, for there is evidence of their warm sentimental attachment to the Stuart cause. In North Wales Sir Watkin Williams Wynn, prominent in the secret society of the Circle of the White Rose, and in South Wales the Pembrokeshire squire, Sir John Philipps, a leading member of the Society of Sea Sergeants, a similar Jacobite association, were ardent adherents of the absent Stuarts. But, tested by the events of 1715, 1717 and 1745, Welsh Jacobitism appeared a thing of straw. Rioting in Wrexham in 1715, and the failure of the Earl of Mar to land a force at Milford Haven in 1717, were the most outstanding incidents in the Old Pretender's attempts to win a crown. Nor was Welsh support of the Young Pretender, in the Forty-Five, of greater moment. The example of men like David Morgan, who devoted themselves to his cause, won few followers.[1] Support from Wales, upon which Prince Charles Edward had confidently counted, was not forthcoming, and evidence of any considerable ferment on the part of the people is lacking. Yet none had shown a greater devotion to the King in the civil wars than the landowners, clergy and peasantry of the Cymry. Possibly the steady succession of Hanoverian bishops, in the Welsh sees, was responsible for the lack of support for the Stuarts; more probably the work of religious reformers in the later seventeenth and early eighteenth centuries had diverted popular interest from politics to religion, just as, later on, the Methodist movement, strongly and officially anti-Jacobite, effectively side-tracked Jacobitism in Wales. Be this as it may, there was no need in Wales, as there was in England, Scotland and Ireland, to make a special effort to train the children in loyalty to the House of Hanover. The dominant political issue of the first half of the eighteenth century left the Welsh people curiously unmoved.[2]

Further, the politico-ecclesiastical changes of the sixteenth century did not create, in Wales, the bitter religious antagonisms which were factors of considerable importance in Highland history, and which have dominated Irish history ever since. Little groups of Roman Catholics were to be found here and there, and fear of their activities was not lacking, but the Welsh people, who, as a whole, had accepted the Protestant reformation with indifference, were equally unaffected by the Catholic counter-reformation efforts. Roman influence, so effective in producing opponents of the Hanoverian Church and Crown elsewhere, played a part of minor importance in Wales. Little garrisons of infant Protestants were not needed to stem the tide of Rome's advance.[3]

Nor did social conditions lend themselves in Wales, as they did in England, to the middle-class social policy of conditioning the poor. For in Wales, during the greater part of the eighteenth century, the middle classes were negligible. The towns, with few exceptions, lacked

[1] See Llewellin, W., "David Morgan, the Welsh Jacobite" in *The Cambrian Journal*, Series II, vol. IV, 1864; separately issued, Tenby, 1862.

[2] See Vaughan, H. M., "Welsh Jacobitism" in *Transactions of the Honourable Society of Cymmrodorion*, 1920–1.

[3] See Hughes, Stephen, Letter prefixed to the 1672 ed. of *Gwaith Mr Rees Prichard*; Owen, Huw, Introduction to *Translation of the Imitation of Christ*, 1684; Jones, Griffith, Letter to a Friend, in *Welch Piety*, Nov. 22, 1746.

seldom grudge many times, for several hours, to gather in their damp and cold Churches to await the coming of their Minister."

Nor were they entirely dependent for their religious pabulum upon church and clergy. "There are many of the common people", he continued, "who gladly make the best use of what little knowledge they have gained, and take the pains, privately and by Reading and Discoursing, to instruct one another in their Houses." Among them it "was not uncommon to see servants and shepherds, as they have an opportunity, strive to do these good offices to one another".[1] John Wesley's oft-quoted remark, that the Welsh were as ignorant of the Bible as the Cherokee Indians, is remembered, when his statement that in the parts of Wales traversed by him the inhabitants were "indeed ripe for the Gospel" is forgotten. Whitefield, in his *Journal*, made similar testimony. The acid comment of William Morris, of Holyhead, upon Charles Wesley's preaching does not lack significance. "Either he was demented or we were. He was like a man preaching the Gospel to a group of pagans without faith and without knowledge."[2]

Such reports demand consideration in any attempt to estimate the religious life of the Welsh people in the eighteenth century. It is probable that the common tendency of puritan reformers, of all denominations, to estimate religion in terms of ability to read the Bible, is the explanation of their agreed opinion upon the ignorance of the people. Protestantism, as Professor Halévy has said, is a "book religion".[3] Even more so was puritanism. Little allowance was made by its adherents for oral tradition and instruction, still less for music as the handmaid of religion among a people passionately devoted to it. Yet the *Halsingod* and *Carolau*, in which the doctrinal and historical parts of Scripture, or the lives and acts of "Saints of extraordinary Piety and Virtue", were set to music, were a never ceasing delight to them. The young people "got the Hymns by heart" and sang them "with emulation, excelling each other".

> A verse may find him who a sermon flies,
> And turn delight into a sacrifice

[1] Saunders, E., *A View of the State of Religion in the Diocese of St David's about the beginning of the Eighteenth Century*, 1721, *passim*.
[2] Wesley, J., *Journals*, ed. by N. Curnock, Oct. 20, 1739, vol. II, p. 296. Whitefield, G., *Journal*, 1756, pp.145–6; *Letters of the Morris Brothers*, vol. I, p. 150.
[3] Halévy, E., *History of the English People in 1815*, 1924, p. 457.

said George Herbert; but for this "most laudable practice of the primitive church", eighteenth-century religious reformers cared little.[1] Reading, and the repetition of the catechism, was their test of piety. A people who could not read the Holy Writ were ignorant and neglected. This must be remembered. Nevertheless, when allowance is made for the peculiar emphasis of puritan tenets, there remains a picture of a people to whom religion was not, in the early years of the century, the matter of absorbing concern which it later became. Leisure which remained, when the exacting business of rearing a family and earning one's bread was accomplished, was spent in games and dance and song, and in the ever popular interludes or rustic dramas, in which gentry and peasantry collaborated. The increasing output of chapbooks, ballads and anthologies of popular poetry, which appeared, side by side with religious works, in the middle and second half of the century, is proof that secular writers were not without readers.[2] The sermons and letters of religious reformers, denouncing the professional harpers and fiddlers who ministered to the demand for dance and song, present, all unwittingly, a picture of a gay and virile people, to whom music, poetry and drama were the source of lively intellectual amusement. "In the Summer months", testified an unsympathetic observer, writing of mid-century Wales, "men and maids met every Saturday night from the surrounding country-side," and "diverted themselves by singing to the harp until the dawn of the Sabbath." Throughout the day they danced and sang and played tennis against the Town Hall. "In every corner of the Town", deplored the writer, "some sport or other went on until the light of the Sabbath day had faded away."[3]

Whether such light-hearted enjoyment of secular pleasures be regarded as an infallible sign of irreligion or not, there is no question but that it was so regarded by religious reformers of all denominations in Wales in the eighteenth century, nor did they fail to lay the responsibility for the apathy they deplored at the door of the Anglican Church.

[1] Saunders, E., op. cit.

[2] See Jones, D., Life and Times of Griffith Jones of Llanddowror, 1902, pp. 185 et seq. and Pryce, A. I., The Diocese of Bangor during Three Centuries, Cardiff, 1929, p. lix.

[3] Trysorfa Ysprydol, 1799, An Account by the Rev. John Evans of the State of Wales in 1742, pp. 30–31; see also Letters of the Morris Brothers, passim; and MS. diary of Mr William Bulkeley of Brynddhu, Anglesey, 1734–43, 1747–60, quoted by Pryce, A. I., op. cit. p. lx.

19

The indifference of the Church to its duty was a commonplace of puritan opinion under the Commonwealth and Protectorate, which could find no good thing in Anglicanism. It was repeated, with vehemence, in the later years of the seventeenth century, when Nonconformists charged the Anglican bishops and clergy with negligence, ignorance and indifference.[1] At the beginning of the eighteenth century Anglican reformers took up the theme. Letters and reports of clergy and laymen to the S.P.C.K. repeat the Nonconformist criticism.[2] Later, Griffith Jones, most loyal of Anglicans, condemned, in vigorous language, the indifference of the bishops and clergy to the work of reformation.[3] A survey of Methodist opinion also makes clear that the lack of fervour of the Anglican clergy rather than doctrinal differences was the root cause of Methodist efforts for reform. Yet, here again, as in the attempt to estimate the truth of conflicting opinion on the religious life of the people, some modification of the accepted view is required. As an organisation whose *raison d'être* was the spiritual instruction of the people, the Church in Wales, during the eighteenth century, lacked spiritual force and administrative vigour. Disorganised more thoroughly than the Church elsewhere during the Interregnum, devitalised by the expulsion from its ranks of not a few men of scrupulous conscience, diverted from concentration upon the substantial things of religion by the arid deistic controversy, the Church in Wales needed, to a peculiar degree, the leadership of men of piety and intellect, prepared to spend their energies in the religious and administrative reform of their sees. Such, with rare exceptions, it was denied. Throughout the century it suffered from an alien and non-resident episcopate. Remote and unpopular, its four sees were regarded in contemporary opinion as stepping-stones to, or as "insurance for some other bishopric".[4] Among the Welsh bishops of the eighteenth century were men of high character and intellectual power, but their terms of office were, as a rule, too short, their periods of non-residence too long, and their ignorance of Wales and the vernacular language too great to allow

[1] Hughes, Stephen, Letter prefixed to the 1672 ed. of *Gwaith Mr Rees Prichard*.
[2] See S.P.C.K. Abs. of Correspondence, Mar. 4, 1699–1700, Mar. 4, 1700–1.
[3] See *Welch Piety*, Letters of Griffith Jones, Mar. 30, 1738; Aug. 16 and Oct. 11, 1739; Sept. 16, 1740; Oct. 27, 1742. See also Letters to Madam Bevan, Jan. 2, 1735; Jan. 8, 1737, quoted by Jones, Rev. D., *op. cit.* pp. 87, 88.
[4] Saunders, E., *op. cit.*

them to cope with the needs of the Church or the people.[1] Little was done by the Welsh bishops to tackle "the scandal of lay impropriations", whereby the stipends of the majority of the clergy were reduced to "shameful poverty",[2] nor, with two or three exceptions, did they encourage the efforts of clergy or laymen in the work of education.[3] The absence of leadership profoundly affected the history of the Church in Wales, for it left the parish priests, whose intellectual qualifications were seldom remarkable, and whose character was not always above reproach, without guidance and discipline during a period when they were in urgent need of them.

Nowhere was this more obvious than in the great diocese of St David's, the scene of strenuous reforming efforts on the part of Nonconformists, Anglicans and Methodists. Second only to Lincoln in size, covering more than half the territory of the Principality, yet containing within its vast area but 308 parishes, its administration demanded the continuous and unremitting care of men of organising ability. Ill-paid and remote, it was the least popular of the unpopular Welsh dioceses. Twelve of its seventeen bishops, appointed in the eighteenth century, vacated the see by translation to other bishoprics, after short tenures of office. Lack of easy communication and imperfect administrative machinery still further handicapped its effective organisation. Archidiaconal duties were not performed by its archdeacons in the eighteenth century, nor were the rural deans in evidence until the last decade. There was, as the historian of St David's diocese has said, "no intermediate link between the bishop and the parochial clergy", and no machinery of guidance or control.[4] Left to themselves in their vast cures, few in number, and, in general, receiving stipends lower

[1] "It is an astonishing fact", wrote the Rev. D. Ambrose Jones in his *History of the Church in Wales*, 1926, "that no bishop in Wales from 1714 to 1870, as far as can be ascertained, knew enough Welsh to ordain and confirm in the language of the people. Worse than that, they deliberately neglected those that did minister to the people in their native tongue" (p. 208).

[2] Saunders, E., *op. cit.*; see also Ecton, J., *Liber Valorum et Decimarum*, 1711, *passim.*

[3] Welsh bishops were to be found among the members of the S.P.C.K., but except for men such as Bishop Bull of St David's, Bishop Humphreys of Bangor, Bishop Beveridge of St Asaph and Bishop Fleetwood of Llandaff, in the early years of the eighteenth century they did not actively co-operate in its work.

[4] Bevan, Archdeacon W. L., *Diocesan Histories: St David's*, 1888, p. 203.

than the none too high level of remuneration in other dioceses in England and Wales, their poverty and indifferent intellectual equipment contributed to the popular contempt of the clergy. They were not seldom obliged, because of the dilapidated state of the "mean cottages used as parsonage houses", to reside outside the parish, and the poverty of the "single churches" forced them, for their subsistence, "to undertake the care of many". Plurality of livings, the recognised palliative in the eighteenth century for clerical poverty, diminished still further the priest's opportunities of ministering to his people. Not infrequently parishes were handed over by absentee clerics to the care of curates, who served three or four churches for £10 or £12 a year, "as many miles distant from one another". Hurrying, "like hasty itinerants", from place to place, they preached ill-prepared sermons, or no sermons at all, and scampered through the services, leaving their flocks "to go astray, or to take up with this, or that, or any, or with no religion". Neither the means nor the leisure was theirs to care for the poor, "to inform the ignorant and resolve the doubtful", or "to be conformable to the canons in their dress and habits".[1] Lack of access to their parish priests, and the want of plain, practical and zealous preaching in a language and dialect the people were able to understand, was Griffith Jones's explanation of the failure of the Church to satisfy the needs of the people.

The men upon whom rested their care and instruction refuse, however, in Wales, as elsewhere, to conform to the cut and dried standards which historians have imposed upon the clergy of the Established Church in the eighteenth century. It cannot be denied that the majority were unequal to their many-sided task. Some, like their bishops, were non-resident, others were aliens, unable because of their ignorance of the language to communicate with their parishioners in church or home; others, presented to their livings by lay impropriators, desirous of extending their patronage to an old servant, or a "petty A-B-C-Darian schoolmaster," lacked the intellectual and religious qualifications required for work of prime importance. But it is not difficult to find among the Welsh clergy men of piety and character and education, whose devotion to their work was above reproach. Nor can the remarkable output of books written by them be ignored. Their contributions to Welsh literature are sufficient to rescue them, as a body,

[1] Saunders, E., *op cit. passim.*

from the charge of indifference to learning.[1] And if there are not enough men whose devotion to their calling can be established, and not enough books to attest the intellectual vigour of more than a small minority of Welsh clergy, their interest in the most practical form of eighteenth-century piety demands some modification of the criticism showered upon them. The charity school movement in Wales owed its success, in the main, to the clergy of the Established Church. Their interest in the education of the poor allows a new and more favourable estimate to be made of them and their work. At the same time it fixes upon them part of the responsibility for the spectacular change in the habits and interests of the bulk of the Welsh people, to whom, before the end of the century, religion had become the supreme concern. Strict Sunday observance, Bible reading, prayer meetings, catechetical exercises and hymn singing had replaced, in great part, the older customary habits and interests of the people. This religious absorption is generally ascribed to the influence of the Methodist revival. The history of the charity school movement in Wales divides the responsibility between Nonconformists, Anglicans and Methodists, who for a hundred years directed the social, religious and intellectual interests of their compatriots to the practice of piety.

II

THE WELSH TRUST

It was not an accident that Wales was the scene of the most successful and sustained movement for the education of the poor in the eighteenth century, for the ground had been prepared in the preceding century by State and voluntary efforts to an extent unknown elsewhere in the British Isles.[2] As the laboratory of puritan social and religious experiment, the country had suffered with peculiar violence from the religious

[1] See Jones, Rev. D. Ambrose, *op. cit.* chap. VIII, *passim*, and Pryce, A. I., *op. cit.* Introduction.

[2] For religious affairs in Wales during the Commonwealth, Protectorate and Restoration periods see the erudite and exhaustive studies by Dr Thomas Richards of Bangor: *The Puritan Movement in Wales, 1639–53*, 1920; *Religious Developments in Wales, 1654–62*, 1923; *Wales under the Penal Code, 1662–87*, 1925; *The Religious Census of 1676, An Enquiry into its Historical Value in Reference to Wales*, 1927, *Wales under the Indulgence, 1672–5*, 1928, *Piwritaniaeth a Pholitics, 1689–1719*, 1927. No student of Welsh history can afford to neglect the vast accumulation of information in these volumes.

strife of the seventeenth century. For seventeen years government by committees, composed almost exclusively of Englishmen, imposed the religious and political ideals of triumphant puritanism upon the country. Acting first through the Committee for Plundered Ministers, and later through the Commission set up for the Better Propagation of the Gospel in Wales, and later still through successive Committees of Triers, the governments of the Commonwealth and the Protectorate disestablished and partially disendowed the Anglican Church, established tests for the trial and removal of clerics guilty of moral misdemeanours, and expelled nearly three hundred clergy from their livings. On the constructive side, numbers of the Welsh cures were filled by the Committees with "godly and painful men of approved conversation", and to meet the dearth of ministers an itinerant preaching ministry was established. More remarkable than these changes in Church government and personnel was the educational policy of the Government. During the period of the Propagation Act (1649–53) it made the first State grant to education in the history of the British Isles, created a new type of puritan "preaching schoolmaster" of approved piety and learning, and set up over sixty free schools in which instruction irrespective of class, and in some cases of sex, was given.

From so comprehensive a scheme much was legitimately expected. But puritan hopes were not realised. In the first place Wales did not take kindly to puritanism. It was an English importation, imposed too hurriedly and too forcibly upon an unready people. "Over much zeal", admitted the puritan divine, Dr John Owen, in a sermon before Parliament in 1656, had "hurried the people with violence beyond their principles, and even beyond the truth....Overdriving the cattle and the young ones has almost destroyed the whole flock."[1] Further, differences of opinion upon government divided moderates and extremists, and among puritan preachers were men who were neither indifferent to the things of this world nor lacked craft in obtaining them. Above all, the supply of preachers who were to carry the Gospel to the remote hills and valleys remained, even at the height of puritan power, an acute problem. "If some course be not taken", wrote Major-General Berry to Thurloe, from South Wales in 1656, "these people will, some of them, become heathens."[2]

[1] Owen, Dr John, *Works*, ed. Russell, 1826, vol. VIII, p. 452.
[2] Thurloe, J., *op. cit.* Papers IV, 565, Feb. 28, 1655–6.

The puritan edifice crumbled at the Restoration. The schools set up under the Propagation Act were not permitted to stand, and, deprived of State support, disappeared. Glamorgan, reported Bishop Lloyd of Llandaff in 1662, "was utterly destitute of schools".[1] A policy of persecution, as discreditable as that for which puritan excesses had been responsible, accompanied the new *régime*. One hundred and eighteen ministers in Wales suffered the loss of their livings, before the passing of, and under the Act of Uniformity,[2] and schools kept without a licence from the bishop or ordinary were prohibited. The Conventicles Act of 1664 laid an interdict upon meetings of more than four persons outside the family in whose house they were held, and set up a savage tariff of penalties for meetings in excess of that number. The Five Mile Act, the following year, deprived men and women, who refused to declare that they would not at any time "endeavour any alteration either in Church or State", from "teaching school".[3] Lack of uniform administration modified these harsh enactments. Ambiguities in the law provided loopholes of escape for Nonconformists, and the impossibility of executing the code without a standing army made its administration an exhausting problem. Royal tactics at the centre of Government and the puritan sympathies of local justices gave, from time to time, and from place to place throughout England and Wales, relief from its harsh enactments. It was, however, severe enough, as a recent writer has said, to save puritanism, for it purged Nonconformity of "the dangerous company of opportunists and self-seekers", who had threatened to undermine its spiritual health in the days of its power, leaving only "an irreducible minimum of tender consciences".[4]

This was conspicuously so in Wales. There, militant puritanism had won few converts, but, during the troublous times of the penal laws, the Nonconformists, who numbered but a fraction of the population, played a part in Welsh history out of all proportion to their numbers.[5] Their ministers cared for their small and scattered flocks in the "gathered churches", and founded new churches, meeting their

---

[1] Antony à Wood, *Athenae Oxonienses*, ed. P. Bliss, vol. IV, p. 835.
[2] Richards, T., *Religious Developments in Wales, 1654–62*, p. 391.
[3] 14 Car. II, c. 4; 17 Car. II, c. 2.
[4] Richards, T., *Wales under the Penal Code*, p. xi.
[5] See Richards, T., *Religious Developments in Wales, 1654–62*, and Clark, G. N., *The Later Stuarts, 1660–1714*, Statistical Note on Religion, p. 26.

courageous congregations, when persecution was acute, in the sheltering woods and caverns which a mountainous country provided for them. Nor did they confine their activities to the adult members of their congregations. "Despight law and coercion" they set up schools.[1] Some measure of their success may be derived from a comparison of the number of legal and illegal schools returned by the Bishops of Bangor and St David's to their Metropolitan, Sheldon, at the end of the first twelve years of Charles II's reign. While Bishop Lloyd of Bangor could find but five legal schools in his diocese, and Bishop Lucy but ten licensed schoolmasters in the huge diocese of St David's, the number of Dissenting schoolmasters was returned in a provisional list at sixteen.[2] Brecon, Carmarthen, Haverfordwest, Swansea, Cardigan and "several other places", complained Lucy to Sheldon, harboured unlicensed schoolmasters.[3] Figures such as these establish the indifference of the Restoration Church to the instruction of the people. Persecution of Dissenting schoolmasters, rather than the provision of parish schools for the children, was its negative policy. Had it not been for the voluntary efforts of a group of Welsh divines, Anglicans and Dissenters, whose concern for the spiritual welfare of their compatriots was greater than their interest in religious differences, it is improbable that Wales would have been the scene of the first concerted movement to instruct the children of the poor.

The initiative appears to have come from Stephen Hughes, ejected in 1662 from his living of Mydrim, Carmarthenshire. "He was", said Calamy, "a plain methodical, affectionate preacher who insisted much upon the substantial things of religion."[4] A moderate and tolerant Nonconformist, he continued to preach after his ejection, not only to fellow Nonconformists, but, with the connivance of the clergy and the support of the gentry of the county, in the parish churches.[5] Alive to the importance of the written word, in a county with a sparse and scattered population, and at a time when the Roman Church was busying itself to provide doctrinal literature in Welsh, he called on

[1] Tanner MSS. vol. CXLVI, No. 138: Letter of William Lucy, Bishop of St David's, to Archbishop Sheldon, Feb. 20, 1672.
[2] Richards, T., *Wales under the Penal Code*, chap. 14.
[3] Tanner MSS. *loc. cit.*
[4] Palmer, S., *Nonconformist's Memorial*, 1777, vol. II, p. 621.
[5] Tanner MSS. *loc. cit.*

parents and masters to teach their children and servants to read the Bible, opened school himself and was excommunicated for the offence, and turned his main energies to the production of religious literature for the Welsh people, among whom Bibles were so scarce that "workmen, servants, and especially poor shepherds, cannot reach them".[1] His literary fame was well established in his lifetime. New editions of the poems of the "old vicar" of Llandovery, Rees Prichard, translations of the Assembly's catechism, the psalms in prose and metre, the New Testament and Bunyan's *Pilgrim's Progress*, published in 1688, are but a selection of the works for which he was responsible, either singly or in collaboration with the distinguished Welsh writers he gathered around him. Samuel Jones, founder of the first Nonconforming Academy in Wales, Charles Edwards, the gifted Oxford scholar and author of *Y Ffydd Ddi-ffuant* (The History of the Faith), Richard Jones, the future translator of Baxter's *Call to the Unconverted*, and James Owen, author of the widely read *Trugaredd a Barn* (Mercy and Judgment), were, like himself, Nonconformists. Among his Anglican friends and helpers were William Lloyd, vicar of St Petrox, Hugh Edwards, vicar of Llangadock, and the eminent Dr William Thomas, Precentor of St David's from 1660 to 1665, who succeeded Lucy and Stillingfleet as Bishop of St David's and Worcester respectively. With their assistance he produced the New Testament in Welsh in 1672. To-day the importance of his work is recognised by students of Welsh literature and history. By the conjoint efforts of Stephen Hughes and his friends the language was preserved and the means of religious instruction provided for the people.[2]

In England, simultaneously, a movement complementary to the movement in Wales was on foot. By the Act of Uniformity the pious and philanthropic Thomas Gouge, who in character and religious devotion bore a marked resemblance to Stephen Hughes, was ejected from his living of St Sepulchre's, Southwark. His wide circle of friends, including Tillotson, Dean of St Paul's, Richard Baxter, the famous

---

[1] Hughes, Stephen, Preface to Letter prefixed to the 1672 ed. of *Gwaith Mr Rees Prichard*.

[2] For an excellent modern account of Stephen Hughes and his work especially on the literary side see Williams, G. J., *Stephen Hughes a'i Gyfnod*, in *Y Cofiadur* (Transactions of the Welsh Congregational Historical Society, No. 4), March, 1926.

Nonconformist divine, and the Socinian, Thomas Firmin, London's leading philanthropist, is witness to his broad and tolerant spirit. Wales, remote and backward, made, to him, an imperative demand for help. Under his leadership Welshmen and Englishmen, Anglicans and Dissenters, joined forces. Possibly in London he had come into personal contact with the Welsh *literati*, when they superintended the passage of their translations through the press, and had learned from them of the neglected state of the country. His interest in the Principality was "set all on fire" after reading in 1671 the life of Joseph Alleine, the Nonconformist minister of Taunton, whose passionate desire it had been to evangelise Wales.[1] A scholar and a man of independent means, Gouge devoted the remaining years of his life to his "living of Wales". His first visit, presumably in 1671–2, was confined to "the skirts of Wales, bordering on England", where many could speak English. There he rode from place to place, like a Commonwealth itinerant, preaching in villages, where the people were without instruction, and paying small sums to men and women to teach the children. His early sojourns in Wales made indisputably clear to him that the immediate need of the Welsh people was a supply of Bibles in their own language. He returned to London and set up a Trust to provide the funds.[2]

The Welsh Trust was the remarkable result of his efforts. Its neglect by historians is curious, since it provides a rare concrete illustration of the ideals of seventeenth-century "men of latitude". In it Tillotson, Stillingfleet and Benjamin Whichcote, the giants of "accommodation", Henry Bridgeman, Bishop of Sodor and Man, and Symon Patrick and Simon Ford, later, respectively, Bishops of Ely and Gloucester, were the leading representatives of the Established Church. Richard Baxter, William Bates, Matthew Pool, and Cromwell's "most excellent Mr Thomas Firmin", contributed the Nonconforming element.[3] The second decade of Charles II's reign provided them with a favourable opportunity for latitudinarian effort. It is true that the Conventicles Act of 1670 was more severe in its restrictions than the earlier Act of 1664, but the penalties attached to it, to secure its execution, reveal the difficulty of persuading magistrates and officials to administer it. The

[1] Clark, S., *op. cit.* pp. 141–2.
[2] Tillotson, J., Archbishop of Canterbury, *Works*, 1707; *Sermon preached at the Funeral Service of Mr Thomas Gouge, with a short account of his life*, 1681.
[3] See the *Reports of the Welsh Trust*, 1675 and 1678.

Lord Mayor of London "laid the laws asleep", and there was not wanting evidence from other parts of the country of officials who, instead of executing the law, "winked at Conventicles".[1] The violent unpopularity from which Nonconformists had suffered after 1660 was considerably modified by 1670. Roman Catholicism, rather than Dissent, held the chief place in public dislike, and suspicion of the King's policy was gradually replacing the earlier fear of Nonconformist plots and revolts. The Declaration of Indulgence of 1672 allowed the growing sympathy with the Nonconformists to express itself openly, for the King, "by virtue of his supreme power in ecclesiastical matters", suspended "all manner of penal laws in matters ecclesiastical against whatsoever nonconformists or recusants", and, to afford them protection, licences were granted by the King, at pleasure, to places and persons, without which Nonconformists were not permitted to meet, or their preacher-teachers to officiate. The withdrawal of the Declaration by the King, under pressure from Parliament in 1673, and, later, of the licences which he had issued, did not, however, obliterate the effects of the Declaration. Its results were permanent. The respite which it had offered to Nonconformists allowed them to consolidate their position. By it Dissent "had been given a start, which even the persecution in 1682 could not reduce".[2]

The initiation of the Welsh Trust coincided with the publication of the King's Declaration of Indulgence. Leading men of different denominations, who had for years been working for accommodation, formed its central committee. Public support rallied to the lead of these men of latitude. The City of London, generous and tolerant, "encouraged by the most bountiful example of the Lord Mayor and Court of Aldermen",[3] responded liberally to the appeal for funds. Subscriptions were received from some of "the quality in and about London", and from the bishops and clergy. Persons of all ranks and conditions made their contributions. The response from Wales was equally satisfactory. An influential group of landowners, deputy lieutenants, justices of the peace, and members of parliament, several of whom had played parts of local importance under the Governments of the Commonwealth and Protectorate, subscribed to the Trust, and testified "by their

[1] *Cal. State Papers, Dom.* 1671, p. 47.
[2] Bate, Frank, *The Declaration of Indulgence*, 1908, p. 143.
[3] Tillotson, J., *Sermon, op. cit.*

personal knowledge or certain information" that its work was carried on "with all impartiality and fidelity". Edward Harley, Edward Mansell, Thomas Moston, Trevor Williams, John Trevor, John Awbrey, Henry Owen, John Wyndham, Evan Seys and Erasmus Philipps, names to conjure with in Wales, were members of the local organisation of a society which had its headquarters in London.

The work of the new Society fell into two main divisions. For the adult poor it supplied devotional books in their own language. Acting first as a distributing centre it collected, after strenuous efforts (for Bibles were so scarce in Wales that "they were not to be had for money"), 32 Welsh Bibles, 479 New Testaments and 500 copies of *The Whole Duty of Man* in Welsh, and distributed them in Wales. Then, in co-operation with Stephen Hughes and his friends, the Trust, inspired by Thomas Gouge, helped to finance the publication of works written or translated by them for their compatriots. The remarkable output of new books, new editions of Welsh classics and translations of English religious writings, was crowned, in 1677–8, by the appearance of a new impression of the Welsh Bible, bound up with the singing psalms, and sold in Wales at the printer's price of 4s. 2d. a copy. The distribution of these books was, in itself, a problem. Yet under Gouge's able administration over a hundred towns and villages were selected as centres, from which Bibles and books of devotion were given away without charge to the poor who could read Welsh, but could not afford to buy them.

Schools for the children accompanied the provision of books for the adult poor, but the medium of instruction differed. In the schools the children were taught to read, not in Welsh but in English, whereby, in the opinion of the Trust, they might be enabled to read "our English Bible, and be more serviceable to their country and to live more comfortably in the world". The boys, in addition, were given instruction in writing and casting accounts. By midsummer 1675 the clergy and churchwardens, who acted as managers, returned over eighty schools to the Trust. The number of their pupils ranged from sixty at Haverfordwest, to ten at St Hilary, Glamorgan. In all, over 2000 boys and girls were put to school, some at the personal charge of Thomas Gouge, others at that of the Trust's funds, and others at the expense of the most considerable Welsh towns, which were "excited to bring up at their own charge, the like number of children in the like manner".[1] Arch-

[1] See the *Reports of the Welsh Trust, op. cit.* and Appendix IV, 6.

bishop Tillotson, who speaks with authority as a manager of the Trust, stated in 1681 that between 1600 and 2000 children received instruction under Gouge's inspection and care in every year of the Trust's existence.[1] It is not, however, possible to estimate, with any degree of accuracy, the total number who passed through the schools, for the length of the school course is not known, nor can it be ascertained with certainty when the Trust began, or when it came to an end. It is improbable that it was founded before 1672, or carried on its educational work after 1681.

A concatenation of causes was responsible for the shc.. life of the schools of the Welsh Trust. The vitality of the Society depended upon the co-operation of Welshmen and Englishmen, and upon the maintenance of a spirit of religious toleration. Neither of these conditions was easy to secure. The English curriculum of the schools was unacceptable to the leader of the Welsh literary and religious revival, Stephen Hughes. It is possible that the scarcity of Welsh books, when Gouge began his work, was, in part, responsible for the emphasis laid upon the value of English in the school curriculum, but it is clear from the report of 1675 that the Trust was determined that children in its schools should be taught the English tongue. Neither English ecclesiastics, nor Welsh squires, who, as a body, were English in their sympathies, would finance instruction for children in the Welsh language. Adults, who were too old to learn English, were, for the salvation of their souls, provided with Welsh books, but the younger generation could best be secured for the glory of God and the service of man by an English education. Such a policy was in direct opposition to that of Stephen Hughes, who, as early as 1672, had protested vehemently against English instruction for Welsh children.[2] No open breach appears to have occurred between the Welsh and English supporters as a result of the Welshman's protest. Welsh books continued to appear as late as 1682 under the joint editing of Hughes and Gouge, but there was a noticeable lack of co-operation between the Welsh *literati* and the English members of the Trust in its scholastic work.

More destructive of the work of the Trust than the question of language was the adverse criticism of its religious opponents. To an

---

[1] Tillotson, J., *op. cit.*

[2] Hughes, Stephen, Letter prefixed to the 1672 ed. of *Gwaith Mr Rees Prichard*.

age in which the idea of liberty of conscience was not only unfamiliar but even repellent, the tolerant attitude of seventeenth-century latitudinarians was anathema. A society which included Churchmen and Dissenters, and which entrusted the supervision of its work and funds to a Nonconforming clergyman, did not receive uniform support. The persecution of the Anglican clergy and the proscription of the liturgy of the Church were too recent to be forgotten. Dread of a revival of puritan power remained acute. Fear and dislike dominated the mind of those clerics who shared the intolerant spirit and narrow ecclesiastical policy of their Metropolitan, Sheldon. From North and South Wales came vehement protests to the Archbishop. Bishop William Lucy of St David's, by implication, and Bishop Humphrey Lloyd of Bangor, explicitly condemned the activities of Gouge and his schools. In spite of law and coercion unlicensed schoolmasters and schoolmistresses, supported by patrons and "great purses", kept school in the diocese of St David's, and appeared entirely indifferent to episcopal censure. To Lucy's colleague, Bishop Lloyd of Bangor, it was intolerable that Gouge, a Dissenter from the Church of England, should collect funds for a new edition of the Welsh Bible, unauthorised by the bishops, and should be allowed "to drop 30s." on "little schole masters and schole mistresses", selected by him, to teach the children to read. In his letter to Sheldon, Lloyd described Gouge as an "itinerant emissarie of the leading sectaries", and roundly charged him with drawing "the credulous common people into a dissaffection to the government and liturgy of the Church", and with "insinceritie, not to say false dealing", in engaging the Bishop's name to the list of supporters for the new Welsh Bible. It is probable that Gouge, who "paid a greater veneration to divine truths and ordinances, than to such usages as are merely human", employed "women and excommunicate persons", who were equally deleterious in episcopal estimation,[1] but it is inconceivable that Gouge, the loved and trusted agent of Tillotson and his friends, who were as one man in agreeing that none was "more worthy to be a pattern for men of all Persuasions whatsoever",[2] should have been guilty of false dealing, or that his work was directed against the Church

---

[1] Tanner MSS. vol. CXLVI, No. 138; vol. XL, p. 18, Letters from William Lucy, Bishop of St David's and Humphrey Lloyd, Bishop of Bangor, to Archbishop Sheldon, Feb. 20, 1672; Aug. 10, 1676.

[2] Tillotson, J., op. cit.

of England. On the contrary he was, as Calamy asserted, "so far from the narrowness of spirit and bigotry that he procured the Church catechism, the Common Prayer, the Welsh Bible, the Whole Duty of Man, and the Practice of Piety, and other practical books containing such things only as good Christians are generally agreed in".[1] The Trust in raising funds for a new edition of the Bible was doing what the Welsh bishops should have done. Lloyd's embittered recognition of this explains his animus towards Gouge and his work.

While the nobility and gentry and local magistrates encouraged the work of the schools, nothing was left to the bishops but censure. Patrons and impropriators on the spot could insist upon the willing or unwilling co-operation of the parish clergy, whether the bishops, non-resident, and without adequate administrative control, approved or not. In 1670 the important case of the schoolmaster William Bates, decided in the King's Bench, strengthened still further the hands of patrons, and deprived the episcopate of an effective weapon against Dissenting schoolmasters. For the law laid down that a bishop's licence was not required by teachers who held office by presentation of the founder.[2] School patrons were thus at liberty to appoint teachers without episcopal permission, and it is clear that in Wales some among them, latitudinarian or indifferent, were not unwilling to extend their patronage to "excommunicates" from the Church of England. The weapon of episcopal censure was, nevertheless, not without effect upon timid clerics and laymen, and when it could count upon the support of the civil authorities, as it could in different localities and at different times in the fluid political conditions of the reign, it was a force to be reckoned with. The reduction in the number of schools returned in the report of 1677–8 may not be unrelated to Bishop Lloyd's vigorous opposition to Gouge and his work.

It is, however, in the political situation of the later years of Charles II's reign, rather than in the curriculum and government of the schools, that the explanation of their decline is to be found. Their continued existence depended upon factors which the Trust could not control. While the Crown was "the Patron of Nonconformist Liberties", as, in spite of changing tactics, it remained for the first twenty years of the reign, moderate Churchmen were able to co-operate with

[1] Calamy, E., *Historical Account of my own Life*, 1829, vol. I, p. 147.
[2] Ventris, B., *Reports*, Part I, p. 41.

Dissenters in a semi-social, semi-religious enterprise, aware that while high Anglicans might disapprove, the civic magistrates in London and the country-side took their lead from the King, doing as Richard Baxter remarked, "for the most part what they perceived to be his will".[1] But when the King in 1681, by his dramatic dissolution of the Oxford Parliament, successfully parried the prolonged attack of the Whigs, his patronage of Dissent came to an abrupt end. To win allies for himself, in the last round of the struggle with Shaftesbury's disorganised forces, he threw the Dissenters to the wolves, securing thereby the support of the Anglican clergy, who turned "the force of their zeal almost wholly against the Dissenters".[2] A subservient judicial bench assisted in the policy of repression, and country justices, to whose growing tolerance Nonconformists had become accustomed, were permitted to treat the Dissenters with a severity reminiscent of the early days of the reign. The slowly cooling embers of religious persecution were again fanned into a flame.

It was not possible for an undenominational society to ride the whirlwind. Gouge's death in 1681 removed the only member of the Trust whose devoted efforts on its behalf were "unaffected by the strange occurrences of this troublesome and busy age".[3] Richard Baxter was thrown into prison; the election of John du Bois, a lay member of the Trust, as sheriff of the City of London, was disallowed, and even Stillingfleet, erstwhile champion of religious liberty, condemned the Dissenters as schismatics, and advised them not to complain of persecution.[4] Tillotson, whose faith in the work of the Trust did not waver, stated in his funeral sermon on Gouge that it was under deliberation to find a successor who would carry on the good work. In the absence of evidence supporting the continued existence of the schools, it is generally assumed that they disappeared. That none of them survived in Wales is however unlikely. Many of them, as the reports show, were financed independently of the Trust. It is not without significance that no less than thirty of the schools returned by the S.P.C.K. in the early years of the eighteenth century were to be found

[1] *Reliquiae Baxterianae*, Book III, p. 87, ed. M. Sylvester, 1696.
[2] Burnet, Gilbert, *History of His Own Times*, Book III, p. 330, ed. 1838.
[3] Tillotson, J., *op. cit.*
[4] Neal, D., *History of the Puritans*, 1732–3. Abridged edition, ed. E. Parsons, 1811, vol. II, p. 583; Sylvester, M., *Reliquiae Baxterianae*, Book II, p. 883.

in towns and villages where schools had been set up by Thomas Gouge.[1]

The Welsh Trust forms a link between the abortive State experiments of the seventeenth century and the voluntary organisations for popular education of the eighteenth century. It establishes continuity of idea, and a remarkable continuity of personnel. The men who were responsible, as State Commissioners under the Commonwealth, for the administration of the Propagation Act of 1650 supported voluntary efforts when State control came to an end. Sir John Trevor and Sir Erasmus Philipps, two of the Commissioners appointed to apply the State scheme, were members of the local committees of the Welsh Trust. Symon Patrick, Bishop of Ely, Edward Fowler, Bishop of Gloucester, and John Meriton, a London member of the Trust, were among the earliest members of the S.P.C.K. Sir John Philipps, a leading member of the Society, played the same part in establishing schools in the Principality, in the eighteenth century, that his father, Erasmus Philipps, had done under the Propagation Act and the Welsh Trust, in the seventeenth century. The close connection between the Trust and the Society is attested by John Strype, who, describing the annual gathering of the London charity schools in 1720, stated explicitly that "this favour of the Londoners towards poor children began divers years ago in North and South Wales"; and when "it lessened in Wales, it began nearer home".[2] The Welsh Trust may therefore be considered the parent of the voluntary societies for the education of the poor in the eighteenth century. By their piety and enthusiasm Thomas Gouge and his Welsh and English colleagues aroused their generation to a consciousness of its responsibility to children and adults, to whom the Bible was a closed book.

III

THE SOCIETY FOR PROMOTING CHRISTIAN KNOWLEDGE

It was in a country prepared by the labours of the Welsh Trust that the Society for Promoting Christian Knowledge began its work in the early years of the eighteenth century. The ignorance of the people was

[1] See Appendix IV, 1, 2.
[2] Strype, D., 1720 ed. of Stow's *Survey of London*, Book V, p. 43.

20

still a matter of perturbation to men of piety. The Society was warned not to expect response to its attempts to provide the peasantry with instruction. "Ignorance and unconcernedness are the reigning diseases", wrote the dean of Bangor, when he reported to the Society his attempts to establish schools in the diocese. A South Wales report lamented "the spirit of atheism and indifference which has run through whole families for some generations, so that the peasantry frequent neither church nor assembly", and it was "the miserable blindness" of his own people which was the reason given by the vicar of Llanddowror, Griffith Jones, for refusing the invitation of the S.P.C.K. to take up work in the foreign mission field.[1]

When the Society got into touch with its clergy correspondents in Wales, in 1699–1700, the movement to establish schools for the poor made good progress. Many of the Welsh squires and their ladies threw their influence and money into the scheme. John Vaughan of Derllys, whose work in supplying the Welsh people with devotional literature in the early years of the eighteenth century was complementary to his work in education, called together the freeholders of his lordship and with their help set up a school for the children; the lord of the manor of Marros, Carmarthenshire, paid the schoolmaster and provided him with a house; the gentlewomen of Brecon gathered subscriptions for a girls' school; Edward Vaughan's lady endowed the schools at Llanfihangel and Llanfyllin with £1200; Sir Humphrey Mackworth, one of the original five members of the S.P.C.K., incited industry to follow the lead of the land, and persuaded the company of the Mines Adventurers, of which he was deputy-governor, to support schools at Neath, in Glamorganshire, and at the Esgair Hir mines, Cardiganshire, for the children of the miners and workmen belonging to the company.[2]

But the enthusiasm which welcomed the work of the Society in Wales was due in the main to the guidance and energy of the South Wales squire, Sir John Philipps of Picton Castle, Pembrokeshire. Like Robert Nelson, he was a combination of puritan and Jacobite High Churchman, regulating his life according to the dictates of godly dis-

---

[1] S.P.C.K. Abs. of Correspondence, Dec. 16, 1699; June 12, 1701; June 11, Sept. 3, 1713.

[2] S.P.C.K. Minutes, July 26, 1705; Catalogue of Add. MSS. National Library of Wales, Williams MS. 202; S.P.C.K. Abs. of Correspondence, May 20, 1722; *Accounts of the Charity Schools*, 1712 and 1717.

cipline and Christian charity. The religious and philanthropic associations of the age, the societies for the reformation of manners and the religious societies, found in him an enthusiastic and generous benefactor. He was a member of the religious society in Fetter Lane, and was on terms of personal friendship with John Wesley, John Clayton, and John Gambold, members of the Oxford Holy Club. It was his generous financial assistance which enabled George Whitefield to remain at Oxford to superintend the affairs of the Methodists in 1736. The S.P.C.K. found in him one of its earliest and most munificent patrons. He was the first person whom the founders of the Society invited to join them, and at his death, in 1737, they lamented him as the "Ornament", and, "in great measure, the support of the Society".[1]

His interest in education owed much to heredity and environment. His father, Sir Erasmus Philipps, had been one of the Commissioners under the Propagation Act during the Commonwealth, and a leading member of the Welsh Trust. Four of the Gouge schools were set up within a stone's throw of Picton Castle, another was at Haverfordwest, another in Pembroke Town. Sir John Philipps spent his youth surrounded by schools which his father had helped to finance, and, as his work in the S.P.C.K. attests, he shared his father's interest in education.

The number of schools in Wales for which he was wholly responsible cannot be ascertained, for many of the reports returned to the Society "concealed his name", but the records of the S.P.C.K. tell of over a dozen schools set up and maintained by him.[2] An even greater tribute to his generous and high-minded enthusiasm is found in the exertions made by laymen and clerics under his leadership. All sorts and conditions of persons offered gifts and service, but generous as was the response of the laity to the Society's appeal, perhaps the most interesting point which emerges from a study of its work in Wales was the interest and support which it evoked from the clergy. For a short period in the history of the Church in Wales the four Welsh Bishops supported a movement for the education of the people. Dr Beaw of

[1] For a detailed account of Sir John Philipps and the work of the S.P.C.K. in Wales see the late Rev. Thomas Shankland's article in the *Transactions of the Honourable Society of Cymmrodorion*, 1904–5.
[2] In Pembrokeshire at Marloes, Walton East, Walton West, Puncheston, Boulston, Rudbaxton, Llanychaer, Maenclochog, Penally, Templeton, Bigely, and Hascard. In Carmarthenshire at Laugharne, St Clears, and Llanddowror.

Llandaff "by his great age, and long distance from Wales", and Dr Watson of St David's, by ridiculing the meetings of the clergy, "hindered the good work" in its initiatory stages, but in the early years of the eighteenth century Bishops Humphreys and Evans of Bangor, Bishop Beveridge of St Asaph, Bishop Bull of St David's and Bishop Tylor of Llandaff gave their support, and by so doing contributed in no small degree to the success of the Society's work in Wales. Under the auspices of the Welsh Bishops and of the Bishops of Worcester and Hereford, new editions of the Welsh Bible were published in 1717 and 1727. Clergy societies were set up immediately in the counties of Denbigh, Flint and Montgomery, and a society "was begun" in Pembrokeshire. Among the higher clergy Dean Jones of Bangor, second only to Sir John Philipps in his consistent efforts for education, and Edmund Meyricke, Canon and Treasurer of St David's Cathedral, gave unfailing support during their lifetime, and left generous endowments after their death. On the parish clergy, however, in Wales, even more than in England, rested the responsibility of encouraging the peasantry to send their children to be instructed and of supervising the work of the schools. At a time when the moral and intellectual apathy and indifference of the clergy as a body brought them into contempt, the records of the S.P.C.K. show that there were among them not a few men who bestirred themselves to support the charity schools, and to arouse the interest of their parishioners in them, undeterred by the ever-present difficulty of keeping afloat an enterprise erected upon the shifting sands of subscriptions and Sabbath Day collections. Letters in the possession of the Society bear witness to their interest and care. Out of slender stipends they may be found paying for the hire of a schoolroom, buying books for the children, or providing "the schoolmaster's diet". Some of them taught and examined the pupils in the schools, and "exhorted the masters to proficiency", and, with admirable courage, they carried on their work when schools were demolished through "the covetousness of persons who withdrew their subscriptions", or when the squire's heirs were "not pleased to continue his encouragement".

The tasks of supervising the schools and correcting the capricious habits of subscribers were of less moment than that presented by the indifference of the people to education. It was difficult to persuade parents to send their children to school, or to allow them to remain there for any length of time. Poverty kept the children away, for their labour was needed in the fields, or on the hill-sides. "It is impossible in these parts", wrote Dean Jones from Bangor in 1716, "to fix the poor children constantly and regularly at school, because they must go, ever and anon, to beg for victuals, there being no poor rates settled in these parts. It is the constant method to relieve the poor at their doors, and the houses of the several parishes being so scattered about at considerable distances from each other, increases the difficulty the poor children labour under; in harvest the poor parents take them out of school, and declare they had rather they should not be taught at all than debarred of the use and service of them." From Pembroke, richly endowed with charity schools, came similar reports. "The masters cannot prevail upon the parents of poor children to keep them constantly at school." Help for the parents had to be provided, if the children were to be educated, and it became increasingly common in Wales, as in England, to provide clothing and even maintenance for the children while they were at school. Grants of twenty shillings a year were given to parents whose children attended Sir John Philipps's school at Rudbaxton, and similar sums were promised to the pupils attending his school at Haverfordwest. In other places the poorest children were given clothing, on condition that their parents did not remove them for twelve months.[1] The heavy expense involved in clothing and maintenance grants led to a slowing down of the charity school movement in Wales, when it became evident that education was a luxury which the very poor could not afford, unless it were combined with material assistance. Yet there remain records of ninety-five schools set up under the auspices of the Society between 1699 and 1737.[2]

The provision of charity schools for the poor in Wales is not exhausted by the enumeration of those recorded by the S.P.C.K. Twentynine schools, other than those returned by it, were set up and endowed between 1699 and 1737.[3] Nor did schools cease to be established after this date. The returns of the Charity Commissioners report the existence of thirty-four schools established or re-endowed between 1737 and the

---

[1] S.P.C.K. Abs. of Correspondence, March 4, 1699–1700; April 29, Aug. 1, Dec. 7, 1700; Aug. 10, 1701; June 20, 1716; Dec. 16, 1699; June 5, 1700; Nov. 28, Dec. 19, 1710; Dec. 13, 1712; April 26, Dec. 16, 1715; Feb. 13, 1715–16; May 2, 1716; Dec. 16, 1699; June 20, 1716; July 14, 1716.

[2] See Map and Appendix IV, 2.   [3] See Appendix IV, 5.

end of the century, and it may safely be assumed that in Wales, as in England and Ireland, subscription schools, born to-day to die from lack of support to-morrow, were neither reported by the S.P.C.K. nor found a place in Lord Brougham's returns. Further, the schools set up by Nonconformist denominations were ignored by the Society. In North Wales the trustees of the estate of Dr Daniel Williams, Dissenting minister of Wrexham, founded charity schools under his will in the counties of Denbigh, Caernarvon, Montgomery and Merioneth.[1] In Carmarthen town the Dissenting minister taught twelve poor children,[2] and it is inconceivable that other schools, whose records have disappeared, were not set up by Nonconformist churches.

A comparison of the efforts of the S.P.C.K. in Wales and elsewhere reveals two significant differences. Welsh reformers did not share the enthusiasm of their fellows in England, Scotland and Ireland for the "mixt curriculum" of labour and learning. There was little need in Wales to inure children to labour, or to provide technical training for them, when work was awaiting them in the fields, on the sea, or in domestic service. Occasionally a successful English experiment, such as that at Artleborough, excited interest and emulation, but the weight of Sir John Philipps's influence, during his lifetime, was exerted against any attempt to divert the children from agriculture to the "mechanics trades". A four-year course in the literary subjects and in singing, denounced in England because of its alleged disruptive social and political influence, remained the ideal of the Society's schools in the Principality.[3]

More significant was the difference of opinion upon the place of the vernacular language in the curriculum. Supporters of the Welsh

---

[1] See the *Reports of the Royal Commission to Inquire Concerning Charities*, 1819–37, under the counties of Denbigh, Flint, Caernarvon, Montgomery and Merioneth. By his will, dated June 26, 1711, Dr Daniel Williams made provision for the founding of eight schools in "Denbigh, Flint, Caernarvon, Montgomery, Beaumaris, *or* else Conway, Merioneth *or* Holt and Chelmsford". One in Wrexham was already established. The teachers were to be selected by his trustees and paid £8 each per annum. Instruction was to be given in the Assembly's catechism. Opposition to the schools from the clergy and leading inhabitants prevented their establishment at Flint, Beaumaris and Conway. The trustees finally set up the schools at Denbigh, Caernarvon, Montgomery, Llanuwchllyn, Newmarket and Pwllheli.

[2] S.P.C.K. Abs. of Correspondence, July 2, 1717.

[3] S.P.C.K. Abs. of Correspondence, Dec. 13, 1712; July 31, 1727.

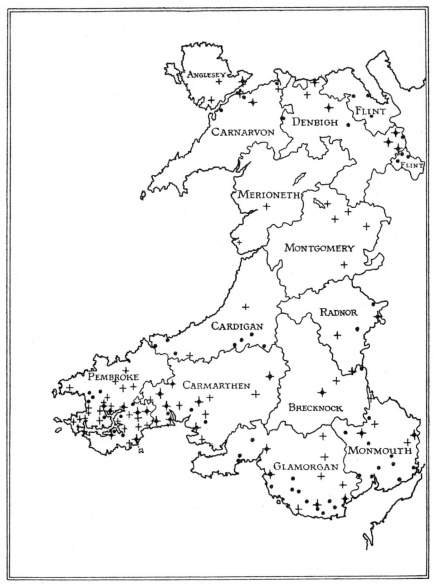

WALES

Map showing the distribution of the Schools of the Welsh Trust, 1674–5, ●
and of the S.P.C.K., 1699–1737 ✝

charity schools who urged that the children should be taught English only, were not lacking, but there is evidence that some at least of the Welsh clergy who managed the schools were alive to the folly of teaching Welsh children to read the Bible in a foreign tongue. The clergy societies of Flint, Denbigh and Montgomery decided as early as 1700 to set up Welsh schools, "that being the language which the parents best understand". The schools established by Dean Jones of Bangor were, as his will explicitly stated, "for the instructing of poor children for ever to read Welsh so perfectly as that each of them might be able to read the Bible and Common Prayer Book in Welsh well, and be also taught the catechism of the Church of England in Welsh".[1] Indeed, it seems probable that the majority of the schools in North Wales were vernacular schools. The absence of evidence of a like nature from South Wales suggests that the South was less successful in establishing Welsh as the language of the schools, and perhaps explains the neglect of education which Griffith Jones deplored when he began his work. But whether English or Welsh predominated in the schools, the demand for books in the native language grew steadily. Letter after letter was received by the Society asking for Welsh Bibles and prayer books, and for "good books" translated into Welsh, and the Society responded by one of the most remarkable efforts in its history. Acting first as a clearing house, distributing all the Welsh books it could find, and, when these were exhausted, as the publisher of new editions, it supplied its Welsh *clientèle* with translations of English devotional works, and encouraged its Welsh correspondents to supply it with manuscripts in the vernacular for publication. In 1717, 10,000 copies of a new impression of the 1630 edition of the Welsh Bible were issued. It was followed in 1727-8 by another impression. Prayer books, psalters, catechisms, manuals, family prayers and pastoral letters poured out from the Society's presses. When the peasantry were too poor to pay for Bibles, they found their way, as gifts from Sir John Philipps, into farm-house and cottage, in the most remote corners of the country-side. Before the middle of the eighteenth century the ground was well prepared for a religious and national revival.

[1] S.P.C.K. Abs. of Correspondence, April 15, 29, June 5, 1700. See Appendix IV, 6.

IV

THE CIRCULATING WELSH
CHARITY SCHOOLS

When Sir John Philipps died in 1737 his mantle fell upon the shoulders of Griffith Jones, the most distinguished figure in the history of education in Wales. The scraps of material which the labours of his countrymen have unearthed relating to his birth, childhood, education and personal life have allowed of more than one interpretation of his character and personality. Of his work among the peasantry there is, on the other hand, ample evidence, and there is no great difference in the estimate of its value.[1]

From 1713, as clergy correspondent for Pembrokeshire to the S.P.C.K., and, later, as the brother-in-law and colleague of Sir John Philipps, under whose patronage he became rector of Llanddowror, this earnest and conscientious parish priest lived in a circle of men and women whose interests centred upon the religious instruction of the poor. Through Sir John Philipps and the S.P.C.K. his work links up with that of Stephen Hughes and Thomas Gouge, and stretches out, after his death, through Madam Bevan and Williams Pantycelyn to Thomas Charles of Bala.

The quality of leadership which distinguished Gouge and Sir John Philipps was in a marked degree a characteristic of Griffith Jones. It does not detract from the worth of his contemporaries Moses Williams, vicar of Llanwenog, Thomas Ellis, vicar of Holyhead, John Thorold, the London banker, John Vaughan and Madam Bevan, whose work in the Welsh charity school movement is sometimes ignored, to recognise that his was the inspiration and the direction of the movement. He possessed, to a marked degree, confidence in himself and a strong sense of vocation. His conviction that he was "wonderfully called to be a shepherd of men" explains much of his influence over the young men

---

[1] The main contemporary sources for the life and work of Griffith Jones are the reports of the Welch Circulating Charity Schools, called *Welch Piety*, including letters and addresses, written by Griffith Jones and, after his death, by Madam Bevan. The known reports cover the period 1737–77, the year usually running from Michaelmas to Michaelmas. W. Rowland's *Camb. Bibl.*, 1869, records reports for 1777–8 and 1778–9. See p. 587, No. 10 and p. 593, No. 4.

who took service under his leadership, and upon the parish clergy whose co-operation was essential to the success of his work.

Before Sir John Philipps's death modifications of the existing scheme of charity school instruction had been considered by the two reformers, and the new plan of circulating Welsh catechetical schools for adults and children was worked out in seclusion, until it was ready to be made known to the public. The existing charity schools were too few in number to serve more than a fraction of the sparse peasant population in the Welsh hills and valleys. The attendance of children at the schools was unsatisfactory; few of the poor could afford to keep their children from three to four years at their books, and instruction, when it was given through the medium of the English tongue, did not enable even those who stayed the requisite course to do more than "learn very imperfectly to read the easy parts of the Bible without knowing the Welsh of it".[1] To meet the need of a national system of religious instruction Griffith Jones adopted the plan of itinerant Welsh schools.

It is probable that the memory of the itinerant preachers of the Commonwealth still persisted in Wales; it is possible that Griffith Jones may have heard in Scotland of the success of the ambulatory schools in the Highlands;[2] it is clear, from the correspondence of Sir Humphrey Mackworth with the S.P.C.K., that he had recognised the advantages of itinerant schoolmasters as early as 1719.[3] But to whatever source the idea of the circulating schools, or, as they should more correctly be termed, "school-sessions", owed its origin, its adoption and its organisation was Griffith Jones's work. The schoolmasters were trained and

---

[1] *Welch Piety*, Letter to a Friend, Oct. 11, 1739.

[2] See the *Journal of the Calvinistic Methodist Historical Society*, vol. VII, March 1922, for "The diary of a journey made by Griffith Jones with Sir John Philipps to the North of England and across the Scottish Border". One of the earliest ambulatory schools set up under the auspices of the S.P.C.K. in Scotland was in the neighbourhood of Dumfries.

[3] S.P.C.K. Abs. of Correspondence, Letter from Mr O'Connor at Neath, Glamorganshire, Sept. 17, 1719. "That he is desired by Sir Humphrey Mackworth to acquaint the Society that there has been several overtures for a school-master at Neath, but that they seem not altogether qualify'd, especially to sett up the first School. He therefore submits to the Society's consideration whether it may not be proper to pitch upon one of the best school-masters in London to begin the setting up of schools in Wales, who may be a sort of Itinerant Master, when he has sett up one School and brought up an Usher, then to sett up another. N.B. Referred to the Committee."

sent out to their different stations, usually in the winter months when farm work was slack; they reported to him the progress they had made, and were paid by him. "'Tis commonly", he wrote in 1738, "but three or four Months that these Schools are continued in the same Place; poor People cannot stay longer at one time from their Labour; and sometimes they have the Schools again for so many months afterwards in the following Year, to perfect what was deficient before: this being thought the best Way, as also a sufficient Length of Time for willing Learners to accomplish their Desires. And then the Schools are re-moved to other and distant Neighbourhoods, where they are most desired and like to meet with the best Success. And whereas the Benefit of Hired Servants, Day-labourers and married Men and Women, as well as the younger Sort is intended by them, 'tis found necessary to give them the Offer of these Schools at such Times or Seasons of the Year as they can best spare from the greatest stress of their several Employments; which in almost all Places here is between September and May. The Inconveniency of the Days being then shorter than in Summer is no Disadvantage to the Design; for they commonly used to be together for four or five Hours in the Night; and several Labourers, whom the pressing Necessities of their poor Families will not admit to attend the Schools by Day, do in some Places constantly resort to them by Night; as a considerable Number of very poor (and lately very profane) People did in our *Welsh* City of *St. Davids*'; and Instances of this we have also in other Schools. Besides, Servants can more easily find Labourers to serve cheaper in their room while they are at School in the Winter than they could do at any other Season: And when there is Encouragement or Opportunity for it there are some few Schools continued for Part of the Summer."[1]

For the success of such a scheme the willing co-operation of the parish clergy was the first essential. Their permission was desirable before a school was set up in their parishes. Few of them could have been blind to the implication of Griffith Jones's request to be allowed

[1] *Welch Piety*, 1740, Letter to a Friend, March 30, 1738. An interesting local study of the circulating schools in the adjoining parishes of Conwil-Elvet and Abernant, Carmarthenshire, shows that the school sessions were held regularly in these parishes for periods usually of three months' duration from 1738 to 1757. The nineteen places in which the schools were held were, with few exceptions, farm houses and the number of children in attendance varied from 8 to 79. See the *Transactions of the Carmarthenshire Antiquarian Society*, 1909–11, pp. 5–6.

to send a schoolmaster to teach the children the Church catechism. In the early years of his work such requests were met frequently by blank refusal, or grudging assent, but, before his death in 1761, the opposition had in great measure been overcome. Writing in *Welch Piety* in 1745–6 he says: "I am glad to inform you that I am spared the trouble of answering such objections as are wont to be started by unthinking or uninformed people against all religious undertakings at the first appearance of them. I think these schools have now got above and quite vanquished all this."[1]

The change of attitude was due, in the first place, to the noticeable alteration in the habits and behaviour of the peasantry among whom the teachers had set to work. They carried out the founder's instructions to teach the children to read and sing psalms, to pray to God in school and with their families at home, and to frequent public worship on the Sabbath. Twice every day the master catechised the children and inculcated the principles and duties of religion, admonishing them against the reigning vices of the times. In the annual reports of the schools published in *Welch Piety*, extracts from hundreds of letters, received by Griffith Jones from lay and clerical correspondents, are extant.[2] They tell of the "visible change for the better in the lives of the people", and in the behaviour of the children who "now prefer praying to playing". "I may boldly say", wrote the curate of Llandyssul, "that the Welsh Charity School did more good in our parish than all our preaching for many years, for the people bring their children to Church to be catechised, every Sunday evening, twenty or thirty at a time." "These schools", reported the incumbent of Llanengan, "have greatly revived the spirit of Christianity in the hearts of people, as is visible from their eagerness, poor as they are, to procure Welsh Bibles and other good books, a passion so dead, indeed, a few years ago that one might fancy himself transported to another climate." "The Welsh Schools", wrote the curate of Gelligaer, "have been the means, under God, to reform the profanation of the Sabbath Day, which the

[1] *Welch Piety*, 1745–6, Letter to a Clergyman, Nov. 22, 1746.

[2] "I have now before me about two hundred certificates or letters received this year about them [the schools] from clergymen to others, all but few personally unknown to me, several of which I beg leave to annex to this Account. Were I to trouble you with all such testimonies as have been sent me about them from all parts where the schools have been from the beginning the number would amount to near two thousand." *Welch Piety*, 1751–2, Letter to a Friend, Oct. 25, 1752.

generality of the common people formerly spent in tippling, gaming etc, notwithstanding all the good laws in force against it. Many of them, at present, are as fervent for the sanctification of it as before they were in profaning it; for as then they assembled for their plays and diversions without much interruption, neighbours associate now on the Lord's Day evening to read their Bibles, or other good books, and to repeat what they remember of the instruction given them from the pulpit in the morning, singing Psalms and praying with their families, which, before they were taught to read, they neither did nor could do. They gratefully own the light and reformation they are now blessed with to be owing (next under God) to the charitable supporters of these Schools, which they acknowledge to be the most beneficent charity that ever could be offered towards promoting religion among the poor and ignorant."[1]

A second factor in the change of attitude towards the schools was Griffith Jones's power of appreciating the difficulties under which the parish clergy of the Welsh Church laboured in the eighteenth century. To clerics unfitted for the ministry or those who, like their diocesans, were non-resident, or unable to speak the Welsh language, he was unsparing of criticism, but his indignation did not extend to "the lowest class of clergy resident in their parishes, upon whom the work of the ministry—almost all of it—in this country, devolves". It was his sympathy with "the curates and meanly beneficed ministers", serving, as Erasmus Saunders had stated a quarter of a century before, three or four churches set far apart for £10 a year, which helped to change the attitude of hostility and suspicion to one of co-operation and good-will. His understanding of their difficulties was matched by his tact in dealing with them. No school was to be set up except at the invitation of the clergy of the parish. "These schools", he assured them, "never intrude or force themselves, but are given where desired." The choice and appointment of the teachers was commonly submitted to the parish ministers, and the care and conduct of the schools and schoolmasters, he promised, should always be their affair.[2]

The collection of funds for the circulating schools appears to have occasioned their founder comparatively little anxiety. Unlike the

[1] *Welch Piety*, 1746–7, Letters of July 16, 1741; May 25, 1747; June 10, 1755; see also *Letters of the Morris Brothers*, April 27, 1752; Dec. 13, 1759.

[2] *Welch Piety*, 1740–41, Letters to a Friend, Aug. 16, 1739; Sept. 16, 1741.

charity school enthusiasts in England, Scotland and Ireland, Griffith
Jones did not establish a Society to organise the work. The circulating
schools were carried on "as part of the laudable but more extensive
labours of the S.P.C.K.", of which he was a corresponding member for
forty-eight years. When his health appeared likely to fail the idea of a
society was mooted, but did not mature. His attitude towards the
mundane problem of funds for the schools was that of Hermann Francke
of Halle, or the founders of the Green Coat Hospital at Cork. God's
blessing rested on the work; He would provide the means. With
"singular pleasure" Griffith Jones explained to his contemporaries that
the funds of the "national organisation", which he had established,
began "with no other Fund, to defray the Expense of it, than what
could be spared from other Occasions out of a small Offertory by a
poor Country Congregation at the Blessed Sacrament; which being laid
out first to erect one, and then a little time afterwards two, *Welch
Schools*, answered so well that this gave Encouragement to attempt to
setting up a few more; and Divine Providence was not wanting to
bring in Benefactions to support them".[1] From this small beginning,
presumably in or about 1730, the numbers steadily increased, until, in
1738, when the first report of the schools was published, they numbered
thirty-seven. When he died, in 1761, *Welch Piety* recorded 3498 schools,
which had been set up in less than half a century. This astonishing
number of schools was financed by collections from "people in inferior
circumstances", and from "poor country congregations". Occasionally
contributions were made by the gentry, "some of whom were well
satisfied that they could not see how to lay out their money to a better
purpose", and by "unasked and unexpected supplies", collected by
the English benefactors, but, from the early years of the movement,
"the generous and compassionate assistance" of Bridget Bevan, the
heiress of John Vaughan of Derllys, and wife of Arthur Bevan, who
represented Carmarthen in Parliament for fourteen years, relieved
Griffith Jones of the financial anxieties inseparably connected with
eighteenth-century voluntary efforts.[2] The laying out of the funds at

---

[1] *Welch Piety*, Letter of Oct. 11, 1739; Letters to a Friend, March 30, 1738;
Sept. 15, 1740; S.P.C.K. Abs. of Correspondence, Sept. 22, 1731.

[2] A list of benefactors and supporters was appended to the *Annual Reports of
Welch Piety*. Among them the names of Sir John Thorold, the London banker,
Sir Francis Gosling, Alderman of London, and Slingsby Bethell are conspicuous.

his disposal to the best advantage was, however, no easy task. His ambition to send his schoolmasters through the length and breadth of Wales involved the strictest economy. Only on "books and the essential business of teaching" was money to be spent, and not much on them. None was wasted on "pompous preparations", or "costly buildings", on office expenses, or a salaried inspectorate. The funds received for the support of the schools were laid out directly upon "the main and chief design of it, avoiding as much as may be all cost about lesser convenience and such circumstantial expenses incident to some other works of charity". That extreme parsimony was employed the figures returned in the report of 1741 bear witness. 12,754 pupils had received instruction in the four years, 1737–41, at a total cost of £850.[1] But saving in money meant, as it invariably does, spendthrift expenditure of time and energy. Clergy and churchwardens had to be approached for permission to hold the school in church or chapel, letters were written begging them to condescend to inspect the schools and to sign certificates testifying to the work and behaviour of the masters, farmers were asked if they would lend kitchen or barn for a night school, rules were drawn up for the conduct of the schools,[2] teachers were instructed to keep a strict account of the names, ages, condition in the world and progress in learning of all the scholars, of the books they used, and the number of months, weeks and days they were at school, and every schoolmaster, at the end of three months, was required to send or to bring his reports to be inspected by Griffith Jones at Llanddowror. There, possibly at the cottage in the village which still bears the name of *Yr Hen Goleg* (the Old College), he gave a short intensive training course of a few weeks' duration on catechetical instruction. In 1738 some fifty

The lists are significant, as the Rev. D. Ambrose Jones remarks, on account of their omissions. "Not a single bishop, dean, or archdeacon are among them, and no landowning magistrate with the exception of Sir John Philipps from the whole of Wales." See *History of the Church in Wales*, p. 199.

[1] *Welch Piety*, Letters to a Friend, March 10, 1738; Aug. 16, Oct. 11, 1739. Occasionally a clergyman was paid a small fee for inspecting the schools. See Letter to a Friend, Aug. 16, 1739, "A judicious person was employed as an Inspector". See also the *Letters of the Morris Brothers*, vol. 1, p. 150, and *An Address to the Charitable and Well Disposed*, 1741, p. 7.

[2] See *Welch Piety*, Feb. 8, 1744–5, for the Rules of the Welsh Schools. A revised translation of the rules is given in Professor Cavenagh's *Life and Work of Griffith Jones, of Llanddowror*, 1930, pp. 47–52.

teachers had completed their training, and were sent out to the far corners of the country-side.

The aim of the schools, their founder did not tire of repeating, was the promotion of piety. This was the exclusive object of the "pious nurseries". They were to restore catechetical instruction to the position it had occupied "in the primitive church and among the Mohamedans, Jews and Jesuits". In his opinion, as in that of his English and Irish contemporaries, the neglect of catechising was the root of the irreligion and ignorance which they deplored. Neither church service nor sermon could stem the torrent. Catechising alone could help "the gross and dull understandings of the common people", and catechising, so far, had failed because the minister "be he never so willing and desirous, cannot perform this Duty without the People come to be catechised, and the People, be they never so desirous to comply, cannot learn to say the Catechism without they are taught it". The business of the schools was to teach the children the catechism. In those set up in his lifetime this principle was consistently adhered to. They did not, as did the English and Highland schools, teach writing and arithmetic; nor, like the Irish schools, did they give manual instruction. They were simply catechetical schools. "It is but a cheap education, we desire for them", their founder declared, "only the moral and religious branch of it."[1]

The orders given to the teachers emphasised this end. "Neither the Poor, nor any others are at all to be taught Writing and Cyphering in these Schools, that the Masters may exert *all* their Endeavours and lay out *all* their Time and *all* their Pains to instruct (the children) in the catechism." The one indispensable duty of the teachers, he taught at Llanddowror, was to instil instruction to this end. They were "not to elate the Minds of the children, but to make them, by the Grace of God, good Men in this World and happy in the next", and, lest they should, with the enthusiasm of the teacher, forget to restrict their instruction, he reminded them that the schools were not designed "to make them *Gentlemen*, but *Christians* and *Heirs* of Eternal Life". They were "the poor men's guide to Heaven".[2]

The normal difficulties of raising funds, securing local support, selecting and supervising teachers, which were inseparable from the

[1] *Welch Piety*, Letters of Aug. 16, 1739; Dec. 24, 1744.
[2] *Welch Piety*, 1749–50, July 24, 1741; Nov. 17, 1750.

efforts of educational reformers in all four countries of the British Isles, were increased in Wales by the coincidence of the Methodist movement with that of the circulating schools. Fourteen years before Wesley took orders, and twenty-five years before Whitefield became a priest, Griffith Jones faced in Wales the problems which they later faced in England, and met them in a manner which anticipated theirs. He was possessed, as they were, with the passion for saving souls, and consecrated his life to this end. Pastor, teacher and doctor in his own parish, he found it too small for his missionary spirit and powers of organisation, and travelled, as did his two great contemporaries, outside its confines to the villages around, preaching with passionate conviction the doctrine of faith and repentance, and in his early years, when the churches could not hold those who came to hear him, he taught in the fields and churchyards. Such was the conduct of the Methodists. His friendship with Whitefield and the Countess of Huntingdon in England, and with the leaders of the Methodist movement in Wales, establishes also his sympathy with Methodist ideas. Howell Harris, Daniel Rowland and Howell Davies, the remarkable trio of Methodist leaders in Wales, looked to Llanddowror as their spiritual home, and to the schools as agents of regeneration.[1] Wielding as he did exceptional influence in the religious life of mid-century Wales, it is impossible to dissociate Griffith Jones from the Methodist movement. St David's diocese, the chief scene of his labours, was the cradle of Methodism in Wales. Among his teachers were missionaries of Methodism; his practice of itinerant preaching, his championship of psalmody, conference and brotherly exhortation, opened the door to irregularities which the Church condemned.

On the other hand it should be remembered that, during Griffith Jones's lifetime, the Methodist movement was a movement within the

---

[1] Lack of space precludes more than a brief and inadequate selection from the vast bibliography devoted to the life and work of Howell Harris and his confrères, some acquaintance with which is indispensable to an understanding and an interpretation of modern Wales. See the following: *The Trevecka Letters, or the Unpublished Correspondence of Howell Harris and his contemporaries*, by the late M. H. Jones, ed. R. T. Jenkins, Caernarvon, 1932; *Brief Account of the Life of Howell Harris*, 1791; Bulmer, J., *Memoir of Howell Harris, with an Account of Calvinistic Methodists in Wales*, Haverfordwest, 1824; Morgan, E., *Life and Times of Howell Harris*, 1882; "Howell Harris, Citizen and Patriot", by M. H. Jones, in the *Transactions of the Cymmrodorion Society*, 1908–9.

Church of England, and that loyalty to the Church was his guiding principle. Because the indifference of the higher clergy filled him with indignation, and the timidity of the lower with an itch for reform, it was difficult for his critics to realise that salvation, not schism, was the outstanding passion of this faithful, but despairing, son of the Church. It was left for a later age to attribute to his influence the fact that, while the Methodist movement began in Wales four years earlier than it did in England, the final separation of the Methodists from the Anglican communion took place over a quarter of a century earlier in England than it did in Wales. Whether Griffith Jones's loyalty to the Anglican Church, a loyalty which he shared with the leaders of Methodism in Wales, would have stood the test of time remains an open question. Before his death in 1761 his opponents had denounced him as a Methodist and his schools as agents of Methodism.[1] Had he lived he would have found the loyalty of a devoted and conscientious Anglican even more severely tested by the apathy of the Church in the second half of the century than in its earlier years.

Adverse criticism was not confined to the founder of the schools. His teachers were the object of outspoken and bitter attack from clergy and gentry. Sometimes they were "barbarously abused".[2] In Wales, as elsewhere, the existence of charity school teachers was a reproach to the clergy, whose privilege it was by the 78th Canon of 1604 to undertake, if they so desired, the office of schoolmaster. That the circulating school teachers were drawn in the main from the ranks of the peasantry, without intellectual qualifications of any kind, and in receipt of wages lower than those of day labourers, added to the reproach.[3] Their success was attributed to an abuse of their position as teachers. Among them were men who did not limit themselves to teaching the Bible and catechism. Some of them indulged in exhortation, others were not sparing in their criticism of the Established Church and its clergy. "Your Welch Charity Schools in their Great Progress", wrote the Chancellor of Bangor and eleven Caernarvonshire clergymen in 1743,

[1] See Evans, Rev. J., *Some Account of the Welsh Charity Schools and of the Rise and Progress of Methodism in Wales Through the Means of them, under the sole Management and Direction of Griffith Jones, Clerk, Rector of Llanddowror in Carmarthenshire* [etc.], 1752.

[2] See *Welch Piety*, Letter to a Friend, Oct. 27, 1742. See also Rees, T., *History of Protestant Nonconformity in Wales*, 1861, p. 399.

[3] According to the Rev. J. Evans, *op. cit.*, they received £3–£4 a year.

"have unhappily reached this Corner of *Carnarvonshire*. We say unhappily, as their Effects here are apparently so, in disturbing the Consciences of poor weak People almost to Distraction thro' the Ignorance, to say no worse, of your *School Masters*, wresting the Scriptures to the Confusion of their Hearers and perhaps their own. This Assertion will be made clear from the following Facts. These *South Wales, Enthusiastick Itinerants* pretend to be Church of England *People*, and come to Church; but at *Nights* they creep into such Houses as they are able to work themselves a way to, and there *delude* Ignorant Men and lead Captive Silly Women and Children by *despising* the *Clergy* and accusing them of *not preaching the Truth of the Gospel*, assuring their Hearers that We are all *Dumb Dogs, Blind Guides, False Prophets, Hirelings*; that we *lye* in our Pulpits. But that *they* and *none others* are the *Elect, the Chosen of God, the Predestinated, the Regenerated*—that they *cannot Sin* in their *Regenerate State*; that *They only* are the *true Ministers of Christ*. They promise Heaven to their Followers: and, as if the Keys of Heaven were intrusted to them alone, they *Damn* all others in order to terrify the *Illiterate* into their *Faction*—They assure them that their *Fathers* and *Grandfathers* are in Hell: and that they see visible *Marks of Damnation* in the *Faces* of such as *will not* become *Methodists*—And to alienate the Affections of Weak People, yet further from the *Established Church*, they maintain that our most excellent *Liturgy* is a dead *Letter*; a *Heap of Popish Rubbish composed by Devils*."[1]

The men and women whom Griffith Jones gathered around him were chosen not for their scholastic qualifications, but for their religious devotion. Sometimes the curate or the parish clerk officiated; occasionally a converted harper or fiddler, convinced of the error of his ways, joined the ranks of the teachers; more often farm-servants of both sexes, though the women were few in number, or labourers, who had received instruction in the schools, became teachers of others.[2] Their lack of intellectual qualifications did not perturb him. But it is evident from his letters that the excesses of some of them were an embarrassment to Griffith Jones, and impeded his design of establishing a parochial system of schools under the aegis of the bishops, and with the co-operation of the whole body of clergy. The rules drawn up by

---

[1] Quoted in Evans, Rev. J., *op. cit.* p. 86.
[2] See Williams of Pantycelyn, *A Serious Address presented to the Consideration of All Well-disposed Christians* [etc.], 1790.

him for the schools show that members of the Anglican Communion, "not contending about questions of religion", were required, but, as they were not always easy to find, Griffith Jones drew some of his teachers from the ranks of Nonconformity.[1] The available evidence shows that all such teachers were induced to communicate in the parish church,[2] but their appointment supported the criticism of Griffith Jones's opponents that the schools aimed at making Dissenters.[3] Other teachers became infected with the spirit of enthusiasm, and brought the schools into disrepute. Masters who favoured Methodism were not, he asserted, of his appointment. "I have sought very carefully", he wrote in 1741, "that this design should be carried on in everything as orderly and consistently with the Church of England as was possible."[4] Letters from clergy correspondents and churchwardens show that by no means all of the parish ministers subscribed to the opinion of the Chancellor of Bangor and his confrères. Many were at pains to testify that the teachers had behaved "according to the prescribed rules"; that they had "not taken upon themselves to be exhorters"; that they were "sober and careful men".[5] But, whether

[1] See article by the late Rev. M. H. Jones in the *Transactions of the Carmarthenshire Antiquarian Society*, vol. xv, part 37, col. 832, referring to Baptists and Congregationalists as teachers in the schools.

[2] I am indebted to Mr R. T. Jenkins for this information.

[3] See Evans, Rev. J., *op. cit.* pp. 115–6.

[4] *Welch Piety*, Letter to a Friend, Sept. 16, 1741.

[5] See extracts from a letter from the inhabitants of Llanvihangel-Rhos-y-Corn, Carmarthenshire, to Griffith Jones, July 7, 1741: "We whose names are hereunto subscribed, being the inhabitants of the Parish of Llanvihangel-Rhos-y-Corn, and other adjacent neighbours, do hereby humbly acknowledge ourselves very much indebted and obliged to our benefactors for the much esteemed favour and loving kindness of bestowing on us...a Welsh Charity School, to teach our poor children and other ignorant people to read the Word of God in their native language...For which your Great Charity and Mercy towards us we return our most humble and hearty thanks, and pray God to bless and reward you...and we beg leave to certify that the Master has been very painful and diligent in teaching his scholars not only to read, but likewise to instruct them in the Church catechism...And whereas we are informed that his diligence has been represented by some (who are not for these things) as if he had taken more upon him than became a School-Master, we think it our Duty to certify that there was no cause or foundation for it, but what we shall freely testify, viz. that the Master, when invited to lodge over night with some or other of his scholars in their houses, did use to examine them in the Church Catechism by the help of his Book, in the long winter nights, and sometimes read a Chapter or part of a Chapter, in the Bible, bidding them to mind and take notice of

they be classed as Methodist or as Evangelical Churchmen, they penetrated into the farthest corners of the country-side, and left behind
them, where they rested, children and adults who found in the Bible
the spiritual and emotional experience they desired; and, as they
travelled, they blazed a trail for Howell Harris and the leaders of the
Methodist revival.

Two characteristics distinguish the circulating charity school movement in Wales from the charity day-school movements elsewhere. The
first was the large scale on which it was planned and carried out.
Beginning in 1730–1, with two schools in the neighbourhood of
Llanddowror, it spread rapidly over the South Wales counties in the
years 1738–9, and, moving north, reached Denbigh in 1739–40, Anglesey in 1746, and Flint in 1751. In 1737, thirty-seven schools had been
opened; when Griffith Jones died in 1761 there were 210 schools in
existence, and no less that 3495 were set up between 1737 and 1761.[1]

The number of pupils was proportionately large. The 2400 scholars
returned in 1737 had increased by 1761 to over 8000; the total number
of registered pupils at the schools, during the twenty-four years 1737–61,
was returned at 158,237. To this large number of day scholars, mainly
children, must be added the unregistered adult scholars of the night
schools, whose presence was a characteristic of the circulating school
movement. In some of the day schools as many as two-thirds of the
scholars were adults, "many above *Fifty*, and *some* above *Sixty*, and
even *Seventy* years of age", who learned to read sitting side by side
with their children and grandchildren.[2] In the night school, half
prayer-meeting, half catechetical class, special provision was made for
adult scholars, whose work in the day time prevented their attendance

the plainest and most observable things, and the practical Duties contained therein;
concluding with a singing of a Psalm and Prayer, and that only in a Private House
at the request of the House-holder, and his Family... Which all here about, as well
as we, know to be very necessary for us of this neighbourhood; our lately deceased
Vicar, (we are sorry to say it), taking little care of us, having neither Sermon nor
Service for several Sundays together in Winter time; he living remotely from us,
and having three Churches to serve, besides a fourth he employed a Curate in. And
therefore the Master of the Welsh Charity School has been very useful and much
desired to instruct us, and many others of our mean rank and capacity, about our
misery as fallen by sin, and concerning our recovery by redeeming Grace through
Jesus Christ..." *Welch Piety*, 1740–1.

[1] See Appendix IV, 3.   [2] *Welch Piety*, Letter to a Friend, Aug. 16, 1739.

at the day schools. Their numbers were estimated by Griffith Jones at about twice, or thrice, as many as the pupils of the day schools, making the immense total of some 300,000 to 400,000 people instructed by his teachers in his lifetime. The possibility of incorrect returns, as Griffith Jones admitted,[1] cannot be eliminated, but even if the figures show exaggeration it is more than clear, from the reports which came in from all parts of the country, that the schools received popular support from young and old. To adult education the Welsh circulating schools made a permanent contribution. Theirs was the pioneer movement in the four countries of the British Isles.

It must, however, be remembered that this large-scale movement was established at the cost of a rigidly restricted curriculum. Compared with the charity day-school movement elsewhere, or with the schools of the Welsh Trust and the S.P.C.K. in Wales, it was a retrograde movement in the history of elementary education. It is probable that no great proportion of the children attending the charity schools in any of the four countries advanced beyond the reading class, but the majority of the schools offered writing and arithmetic to pupils who could take advantage of more advanced instruction. The circulating schools confined their instruction to reading. It may also be questioned whether the impermanent character of the schools, designed to meet the combined difficulties of inadequate finance and a scattered population, was not, in the long run, an additional handicap to educational progress, since it discouraged the growth of local responsibility, upon which the earlier movements had laid stress, and upon which the modern educational system is based. The Welsh circulating schools made a breach in the slowly growing tradition of the three R's, and of local control.[2]

Of peculiar interest and importance to Wales, in the second place, was the founder's insistence that the instruction of the people should be carried on through the medium of the Welsh tongue. It was due to Griffith Jones that the Welsh language was firmly entrenched in the schools. Like those of the Welsh Trust and the S.P.C.K., his schools were financed in great part by English subscribers, some of whom disapproved of the use of Welsh. In a series of forceful letters he cut the

---

[1] *Welch Piety*, 1740–1, Letter of Sept. 15, 1740.

[2] See the late Rev. Thomas Shankland's article in *Seren Gomer*, 1903, for criticism of the schools on these lines.

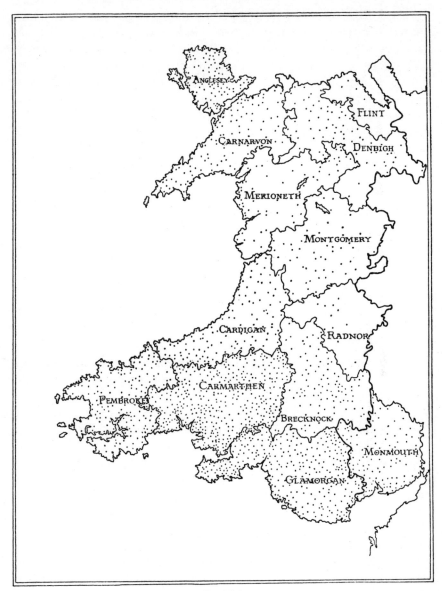

WALES

Map showing the distribution of the Welsh Circulating Charity Schools.

ground from under their objections. English schools in English-speaking districts were opened by him in Pembrokeshire, and bilingual masters were employed in schools on the border, but English charity schools in Wales were, he declared, as absurd as French charity schools would be in England. To insist upon the English language was to show more concern for its propagation than for the salvation of the Welsh people. In the race with Satan the English tongue was a stumbling-block. Speed was the essential. Before English could replace Welsh, "what myriads of poor ignorant souls must launch forth into the dreadful abyss of eternity and perish for want of knowledge". He claimed that children and adults who could read English but imperfectly after three or four years' instruction, could read Welsh well in three or four months' time. The ease with which Welsh (a phonetic language) could be learned marked it out, in his opinion, as a super-excellent means of serving "the Glory of God, the Interest of Religion, and the Salvation of the poor Welsh People".[1]

To supply Welsh books for school use, and, later, to meet the demands of the reading public, which the schools had created, was in itself an immense task; one which, but for the co-operation of the S.P.C.K., would have proved impossible. As early as 1713 Griffith Jones, unable to buy the Bibles he required for his parishioners, wrote begging the Society to publish a new impression of the Bible. In 1714 the Welsh bishops bestirred themselves to raise subscriptions for a new edition of the Bible, and in 1718 and again in 1727 impressions of the Welsh Bible were published by the Society. The steady increase of schools and scholars synchronised with a steady demand for Bibles. In 1743 the earlier editions were exhausted and in 1748 a new impression of 15,000 copies, bound up, as were the earlier editions, with the common prayer and the psalms in metre, was published, but "such was the Zeal and Thirst of Good Christians throughout Wales for having the Holy Scriptures in that language, wherein alone they could possibly read them; that this Impression, large as it was, fell exceedingly short of the Universal Demand that was made for it".[2] In 1752 another edition of 15,000 copies came from the press. Sixteen years later this edition, too, was exhausted, and 20,000 copies of a new edition were published by the Society in 1768. From its presses poured out psalters, bound up

[1] *Welch Piety*, 1740–1, Letter to a Friend, Oct. 11, 1739.
[2] *Account of the Charity Schools*, 1776.

with the Welsh alphabet, common prayer books, church catechisms and devotional works such as *The Book of Homilies* and *The Whole Duty of Man*. Especial provision was necessary for the beginners in the day and night schools and, since suitable books were not forthcoming, Griffith Jones wrote tracts for their use, such as *Concerning the Nature and Necessity of Sound Christian Knowledge, The Scriptural Explication of the Baptismal Vow, The Duty of Householders and of Family Worship*, and the *Exposition of the Church catechism, relating to the Christian Covenant, the Christian Creed, the Christian Duty, the Christian Prayers and the Christian sacraments*. As the books and tracts filled the dual rôle of reading primers and religious manuals, the common Welsh practice of adding the alphabet and a list of words of one syllable as a preface was followed. Bibles and tracts were given away free of charge to poor persons "of proper age and an earnest disposition", who could produce certificates from their parish minister testifying that they could read.

When Griffith Jones died in 1761 he left his personal property and the schools' funds in trust to his friend and helper, Madam Bevan of Laugharne, who had lived and moved among charity school enthusiasts. After his death she carried on the duty of supervision and control, not without discouragement.[1] Under her care the schools continued to increase. In 1763 their number touched the high-water mark of 279; in 1773 the number of scholars reached a total of 13,205. Little is known of the schools under her guidance. One of the few contemporary notices of them after Griffith Jones's death is to be found in a report drawn up by the Russian commissioner authorised by Catherine the Great in 1764 to investigate and report upon English education. "On y enseigne aux Personnes de tout Âge et des deux Séxes, à lire leur Langue natale, la Brétonne; et on les instruit dans les Principes et les Devoirs de la Réligion, en se servant pour cet effet, du Catechisme de l'Église, et de l'Explication que Mr. Jones en a donnée outre les Prières, pour le Matin & pour le Soir & pour les Répas, etc. Cela se fait chaque jour; Même plusieurs qui n'ont pas le tems de venir a l'École pendant le Jour, y viennent pendant la Nuit. Ces Écoles se tiennent durant l'Espace de 4 ou 5, et quelquefois de 6 Mois, ou plus longtems, suivant les Bésoins de ceux qui souhaitent d'apprendre, & dans les Saisons de l'année, où les Pauvres, étant moins occupés, peuvent plus commodé-

[1] See Jenkins, R. T., *Griffith Jones of Llanddowror*, Cardiff, 1930, p. 51.

ment les fréquenter. Ce sont les Ecclésiastiques des Endroits où se
trouvent les Écoles, qui en ont l'Inspection, & qui, de tems en tems,
examinent, tant en public à l'Église, qu'en particulier à l'École, ou chés
eux. Ils en font leur Rapport à quelque Personne considérable, qui
contribue à cette Charité, qui est établie dans la Principauté de Galles.
L'annee passée c'étoit une Dame, à qui les Ecclésiastiques envoyoient
ces Attestats; et vrai-semblablement c'est encore elle cette année."[1]
With Madam Bevan's death in 1779 came a sudden collapse of the
system so laboriously established. Her will, leaving a sum of about
£10,000 to trustees to continue the work, was questioned by her next
of kin and the whole fund was invested in the Court of Chancery,
where it remained for thirty-one years. Deprived at one blow of their
director and their funds, the scholars dispersed and the schools disappeared.

V

THE SUNDAY SCHOOLS

The final decision of the Court of Chancery was not made known until
1809. Pending the decision of the Court, attempts were not lacking to
carry on the work which Griffith Jones and Bridget Bevan had established. In the South, Williams of Pantycelyn, "the sweet singer of
Wales", who as curate at Llanwrtyd had welcomed itinerant schoolmasters in Griffith Jones's day, appealed in 1790 for help to found
new schools for a generation deprived of instruction. His death, five
months after his appeal, paralysed efforts in the South. In North Wales
Edward Williams, Congregational minister at Oswestry, met with some
success by converting Sunday schools, which he had set up in the
borderland towns and villages, into day circulating schools in which,
in 1793, 300 children were taught to read and say the catechism. But it
was the vigour and personality of Thomas Charles of Bala which again
set on foot Welsh circulating schools in the Principality.[2]

[1] The MS. copy of this report formed part of the Philipps' Collection of MSS. It
has been in my possession since 1923. See also Richardson, C. M., *History of
the Institution called Welch Piety but now known as Mrs Bevan's Schools*, 1870;
Burgess, Bishop, *Tracts*, 1815, p. 148; *Life and Times of Selina Countess of Huntingdon*, vol. I, p. 454.
[2] See Williams of Pantycelyn, *op. cit.*; Gilbert, J., *Memoirs of the Rev. Edward
Williams*, 1825; *The Evangelical Magazine*, 1798, pp. 231–2; Jenkins, D. E., *op. cit.*

Once more Carmarthenshire, which had already provided two out of three leaders in the Welsh charity school movement, supplied the new movement in the North with its leader. Thomas Charles, in his boyhood a pupil at Llanddowror school, was one of the growing band of loyal Churchmen, for whom the Church had no use in the eighteenth century. Ordained in 1778, he had by 1784, because of his enthusiasm, been "turned out of three churches in this country without prospect of another".[1] After a long period of doubt and indecision, he accepted the invitation of the Calvinistic Methodists at Bala in 1784 to take up his ministry among them. During his lifetime the Methodists, hitherto a group within the Anglican Church, separated from it, and became, in spite of the extreme reluctance of Charles, a new denomination in 1811. It was due, in the main, to his efforts that Methodism became the religion of so great a number of the Welsh people, and that the Sunday school movement became a national movement for education in Wales. His plan was a continuation of that of Griffith Jones: "To teach the children to read their *native* language correctly and to instruct them in the principles of Christianity and *nothing more*, as the Salvation of their Souls is the only point we have in view."[2] The itinerant method was employed; school in the day time for the children, and at night and on Sundays for adults. Funds were gathered in like manner by collections in the locality and by subscriptions and donations from England, and, to meet the shortage of suitable books, Charles composed catechisms and elementary readers. His "greatest care", like that of Griffith Jones, was the appointment of proper teachers and their supervision. The first group he instructed himself, and the work of the teachers was personally inspected before they moved on to new posts.

The actual numbers of the circulating schools set up by Charles in North Wales does not appear to be stated, but a rough estimate can be obtained from the number of his teachers and the length of their stay in a locality. In 1786 seven schoolmasters were in his employ; in 1789 fifteen; and in 1794 twenty. They stayed six or nine months in each place. Hence forty schools would be an outside estimate for the year 1794, nine years after Thomas Charles began his work. This slow development is in striking contrast to the rapid growth of the earlier

[1] Jenkins, D. E., *op. cit.* vol. I, p. 490, Letter of Thomas Charles, June 12, 1784.
[2] Jenkins, D. E., *op. cit.*, vol. II, p. 29, Letter of Thomas Charles [n.d., possibly 1789].

movement in the South, where in the nine years, 1737–46, 120 schools had been set up. The more backward condition of the North, the strong opposition of the country gentry to the Methodist preachers, and a lack of that support from the country clergy which had made Griffith Jones's work possible, explain, in part, the slower rate of development.[1] Difficulties such as these Thomas Charles was capable of overcoming, but the limited success of his circulating schools was due primarily to the new and rival attraction of the Sunday schools, to which, after considerable hesitation, he capitulated. To whom the honour of introducing Sunday schools into Wales belongs is still a matter of dispute in the Principality. The evidence available does not permit a ruling in favour of one or other of the claimants, nor does a decision appear to be of any real importance. Three distinguished Welshmen, Morgan John Rhys, Baptist minister in South Wales, Edward Williams, Congregational minister at Oswestry, and Thomas Charles of Bala, to all of whom the work of Raikes and the English Sunday School Society appears to have been known, set up Sunday schools in Wales.[2] While Rhys's influence was, in the main, confined to his writings, and the schools of Edward Williams operated in the neighbourhood of Oswestry and the border, Thomas Charles, less easily convinced than either of his contemporaries of the value of Sunday school instruction, organised them with so much success among the Welsh Methodists that other denominations followed suit. "As for your Sunday Schools in England", he wrote in 1785, "I have heard of them, but it would be impossible to set them up here in this wild country, where the inhabitants of every parish live so distant from each other."[3] Itinerant schools were, he considered, the only

[1] "There is", wrote Edward Williams in 1789, "a material difference between South and North Wales; the former has been for a considerable number of years more civilised and enlightened with religious knowledge so that between serious ministers and people in the establishment, commonly called Methodists (and they are not a few) and the Dissenters, who are very numerous, the means of religious knowledge among the poor and particularly catechising are little inferior to any parts of England. But this cannot be said of North Wales...The gentlemen of fortune are generally very much prejudiced against the strictness of religious profession....Where the gentlemen of influence are not friendly and where there are no masters of manufactories to exert any authority it is not easy to keep up the number." Gilbert, J., op. cit. Letter of Edward Williams, May 14, 1789, pp. 286–8.

[2] See Gilbert, J., op. cit.; Griffith, J. T., Morgan John Rhys, 1910; Evans, J. J., Morgan John Rhys a'i Amserau, 1935.

[3] Charles, Thomas, MS. Letter, July 6, 1785, in the National Library of Wales.

possible system for Wales. The astonishing success of the Sunday school movement in England could not, however, be ignored. It appealed to Charles, to whom, like Griffith Jones before him, speed was the essential in the salvation of souls. While he was still convinced of the superiority of itinerant day schools, the advantages of the Sunday schools pressed for recognition. His teachers were instructed to attend on one or two nights in the week and especially on Sunday evenings to instruct "servants and such persons as have not time at their disposal".[1] And, as these "supplementary Sunday schools prospered exceedingly", Charles, in 1798, asked for and received financial help from the English Sunday School Society, whose correspondent he became. Under his vigorous leadership night schools and Sunday schools were set up in all parts of the country.[2] The circulating schoolmasters were retained to carry the light to dark places, and to those parts of the country "where none were found willing or able to set up Sunday schools",[3] but as the unpaid Sunday school teachers (figures characteristic of the Welsh Sunday school movement throughout its history) gradually superseded the salaried schoolmasters, the new movement, free from the stranglehold of inadequate finance, took easy precedence of all other forms of educational activity in the Principality.

The Sunday school movement in Wales, as in England, was primarily a nineteenth-century movement. As such its history lies outside the scope of eighteenth-century experiments. Like the English movement it owed its appearance to the combined influence of economic change and the religious revivals of the late eighteenth century. Arriving later in Wales than in England, and operating in a more strictly delimited area, the industrial revolution did not affect Welsh life as profoundly as it affected English life in the last years of the eighteenth century; but indigence, always present in Wales, was intense and widespread in the last twenty years, when the rise in population, a trait of Welsh social life as of that of the neighbouring countries, and the steady increase in rents and prices, upset the delicate balance between poverty and

[1] Jenkins, D. E., *op. cit.* vol. II, p. 30, Letter of Thomas Charles, 1787.

[2] "In Carnarvonshire there are now thirty schools and 1,500 scholars. In Anglesea there are now twenty schools and 12,000 scholars, and new ones are rising up every week. In Denbighshire and Merioneth the same spirit prevails, though I have not been able as yet to ascertain the exact number." Jenkins, D. E., *op. cit.* vol. II, pp. 183–4, Letter of Thomas Charles, Dec. 8, 1798.

[3] Jenkins, D. E., *op. cit.* vol. III, Letter of Thomas Charles, Sept. 12, 1808.

pauperism. The Sunday school offered in Wales, as elsewhere, a cheap and rapid means of education to a people, who, under the influence of strong emotional forces, were eager for instruction, and had neither leisure nor means to afford a day-school education.

Comparison of the Welsh and English Sunday schools reveals several characteristic differences.[1] The practice of piety was the supreme aim of the schools organised by Charles and the Calvinistic Methodists. The "grand principle of subordination" which bulked so large in the English Sunday schools was not ignored; but the formation of manners took a back seat. Over and over again did Charles assert that the purpose of the schools was not to teach morals to children, but to bring about their eternal salvation; "the salvation of souls is the *only* point we have inview". In accordance with this aim the children learnt to read their native tongue. By teaching Welsh first, asserted Charles, with a vehemence reminiscent of Stephen Hughes and Griffith Jones, "we prove to them that we are principally concerned about their souls, and thereby naturally impress their minds with the vast importance of acquiring the knowledge of divine truth in which the Way of Salvation, our Duty to God and Man is revealed, whereas that most important point is totally out of sight by teaching them English, for the acquisition of English is connected only with their temporal concerns".[2]

The administration of the Welsh Sunday schools reinforces the contrast. The autocracy of the parson and lay helpers under the English system gave place, in Wales, to a democracy of the teachers. Their services were voluntary. Unlike the English teachers, who, until 1811, were the paid servants of parson and patron, they formed the government of each individual school. Representatives to the strongly centralised Methodist "associations", which exercised control over the schools and the superintendents of the single schools associations were elected by them, and when faults or misdemeanours were committed by a member of the teaching body, judgment was given by his peers.[3]

[1] See Griffith, D. M., *Nationality and the Sunday School Movement*, Bangor, 1925, for a comparative study of the Welsh and English Sunday schools.

[2] *First Annual Report of the Society for the support of Gaelic Schools*, 1812, p. 58, Letter of Thomas Charles to the Society, Jan. 4, 1811, pp. 58–60.

[3] Traethawd ar Angenrheidrwydd a buddioldeb Cyfarfodydd Athrawon ynghyd a'r Dull goreu idd eu cynnal. *Rules of the Denbigh, Flint and Cardiganshire Schools*, 1820.

A mixture of classes, not to be found in the English schools, was a third striking characteristic of the Welsh Sunday schools. They were not the preserve of the poor. They were open to all, gentle and simple, and if the poor predominated, comfortable tradesmen and artisans, well-to-do-farmers and professional men attended them, brought their children with them, and taught in the schools.

Lastly, the methods employed in the Welsh and English Sunday schools were dissimilar. The presence of adult scholars in the Welsh circulating and Sunday schools permitted a greater freedom of intercourse between teacher and pupil than was possible where children only were concerned. The small group for intensive study, the discussion class, and the training in self-expression had no counterpart in the early English Sunday schools.[1] When the Sunday schools became established institutions in Wales they worked as power stations creating fresh stores of religious enthusiasm, and transmitting it alike to town and countryside. In the early years of the movement the doctrinal strife of the later stages was conspicuously absent. The schools welcomed all, men and women, adults and children; no tests were demanded, no creeds imposed. Churches of all denominations in the Principality opened schools, which in more than one place formed the nucleus of a new church. Statistics convey little idea of the astonishing religious enthusiasm shown in the later years of the eighteenth and the early years of the nineteenth century. As the movement developed massed meetings of from fifteen to twenty schools were held. So great were the numbers that came together from the villages that often no chapel could contain them. The whole day was spent in religious exercises; parents and children left their homes in the early morning to travel across mountain and valley in time for 8 o'clock service. On these occasions stands were erected out of doors, on one of which the scholars took their places, on the other the teachers. Between them a congregation of the peasantry stood in profound attention, listening to the questions asked, and

---

[1] See Hanway, J., *op. cit.* p. 32: "In some [English Sunday schools] young women learn to read. As to young men, they do not appear to have any such ambition. If they have not been taught in their childhood they prefer ignorance." For a charming description of a Welsh Sunday school in the nineteenth century see Davies, J. H., *The Life and Opinions of Robert Roberts, a Wandering Scholar, as told by himself*, pp. 18–21, Cardiff, 1923.

applauding the answers given.[1] Many of the children, reported Charles, could repeat whole epistles by heart. They made response to almost any question asked them, "with great seriousness and accuracy, and loud enough for two or three thousand people to hear them".[2] An insistent demand for devotional works was met by a flood of religious and educational publications, which poured out from the presses in England and Wales. "A loud and general cry for Bibles" predominated.

[1] Charles, Thomas, Letters to a Young Lady, Oct. 1806 and 1808, in *The Evangelical Magazine*, 1806, and *The Christian Guardian*, 1809. A typical *Pwnc ysgol* (school theme) on the subject of *Envy*, sent by Charles to the schools to be prepared for his arrival and published, since, in the Sunday school periodical, *Cronicl Yr Ysgol Sabbothol*, illustrates the methods employed by him:

Q. What is Envy?

A (I). Envy is a feeling of sorrow to see another prospering; for example:

(1) In Riches. Psalm lxxiii, 2, 3; Gen. xxvi, 14.

(2) In respect and eminence. Daniel vi, 4.

(3) In doing good and uprightness. Eccles. iv, 4.

(4) In being loved. Gen. xxxvii, 4, 11; Acts vii, 9.

(5) In religion as regards talent, usefulness, approbation of man and recognition by God.

(II) Or to feel glad on perceiving another's troubles, or some misfortune befalling him. Prov. xvii, 5; xxi, 10 and xxiv, 17; Psalm xxx, xxxv, 15, 26 and xxxviii, 16.

Q. Does God in his word speak against envy?

A. Yes. Prov. xxiv, 1, 19; Gal. v, 26; Psalm xxxvii, 1; I Pet. ii, 1.

Q. What considerations show the heinousness of this sin?

A. 1. That envy arises from vanity, pride and ignorance. I Tim. vi, 4.

2. That it leads to strife, confusion, etc. James iii, 16.

3. It is a sign of men serving their lusts. Titus iii, 3.

4. It is a rottenness to the bones. Prov. xiv, 30.

5. It kills. Job v, 2.

6. A man under the domination of envy knows nothing of charity. I Cor. xiii, 14.

7. It is worse than wrath and anger. Prov. xxxvii, 4.

8. What one from envy wishes and intends for another is most likely to come upon himself. Ezek. xxxv, 11; Psalm vii, 15; Prov. xxvi, 27; Psalm lvii, 7; compare Esther v, 11–14 and vii, 9–10.

9. Miriam was struck with leprosy because of this sin. Num. xii, 1, 2, 9, 10.

10. It was for envying Moses and Aaron that Korah, Dathan and Abiram were swallowed alive into the earth. Psalm cvi, 16, 17; Num. xvi, 1, 3, 30.

11. It is a devilish sin. James iii, 14, 15.

12. It shuts out the kingdom of heaven. Gal. v, 21.

Quoted in Evans, D., *The Sunday Schools of Wales*, 1883, p. 189.

[2] Charles, Thomas, *ibid*.

No edition had been published since 1767. In the schools the children held before them tattered scraps, with neither beginnings nor endings. The S.P.C.K., whose co-operation had made the work of eighteenth-century Anglican reformers possible, did not show the same willingness to supply the Bibles required for the new movement. Hence the Bible Society, later known as the British and Foreign Bible Society, was founded, in 1804, to supply the need.[1] An English traveller who witnessed the arrival of the cart carrying the first load of New Testaments sent by the Society recorded his impressions. "The Welsh peasants went out in crowds to meet it and welcomed it as the Israelites did the ark of old; drew it into the town and eagerly bore off every copy as rapidly as they could be dispersed. The young people consumed the whole night reading it, and labourers carried it with them to the fields that they might enjoy it during the intervals of their labours."[2] The schools had created a reading public.

VI

THE NATIONAL REVIVAL

It would be difficult to exaggerate the importance and effect of the charity school movement upon the history and character of the Welsh people. The steady concentration upon piety as the aim and end of all instruction changed a gay and simple people, indifferent to religion and lacking in political consciousness, into a people whose dominant interests were religious and political. The Bible had become the Welshman's manual. Its language was his language, its teaching dominated his social and political life. In it, and in the hymns of Williams of Pantycelyn, the emotional and intellectual interests of the peasantry found satisfaction.

The political influence of the charity school movement was no less important. Modern Welsh nationalism is the child of the literary and linguistic renaissance of the eighteenth century, and in this, as in the religious revival, the charity school movement played a part of chief importance. Before the schools began their work Welsh, once "the language of princes and poets", was in danger of destruction. By the end

[1] See Appendix IV, 6. Bibliography of the Welsh Bible.
[2] *The Christian Observer*, July, 1810, quoted by the Rev. John Owen in *The History of the First Ten Years of the Bible Society*, 1816, vol. I, p. 263.

22

of the eighteenth century it was again the medium of poetry and prose, no longer princely, but bearing upon it the marks of its peasant origin and pious inspiration. When the promoters of the Welsh Trust set the charity school movement afoot in the last quarter of the seventeenth century, Welsh nationalism had been, for two hundred years, asleep. Welsh had been threatened more than once during the middle ages with extinction; the early Tudor period witnessed its destruction as the language of culture and office, and thereby reduced the danger of rebellion. No one holding office under the Crown was permitted to use it.[1] The Welsh gentry, acquiescing in the anglicisation of government and customs, became English in language and thought. Little by little English replaced Welsh as the language of culture, and the use of the vernacular became the mark of a lower social class. Indeed, the only Welsh spoken was the illiterate patois of the peasantry, no better than "the chatter of wild birds or the roaring of beasts", and in the market towns English was "as rife as Welsh".[2]

The first check to the flowing English tide was set by the Act of 1563, which commanded the bishops of the Church in Wales to provide a Welsh translation of the Bible and of the book of common prayer for every church throughout Wales, so that "the Welsh people might, by conferring both languages together, the sooner attain the English tongue".[3] In 1567 came Richard Davies's translation of the prayer book and William Salesbury's translation of the New Testament and in 1588 Bishop Morgan's Bible, which, revised and amended by Dr John Davies in 1620 and published in a cheap edition in 1630, is substantially the Welsh Bible of to-day.[4] Severely classical, the Bible of 1588 and 1620 checked the growth of dialectical differences and, by the adoption of the language of scholars and artists, established a literary standard of remarkable beauty and purity. Unwittingly, the Anglican Church had counteracted the policy of the English Crown. The Welsh Bible and prayer book kept alive the Welsh language, the foundation upon which Welsh nationalism is based.

The restoration of a national weapon did not, however, mean that

[1] 27 Henry VIII, c. 25.
[2] Salesbury, W., *Oll synnwyr pen Kembero*, f. A iii, 1546; Penry, J., *An humble Supplication in behalf of the Countrey of Wales*, 1587, p. 52.
[3] 4 Eliz. c. 28.
[4] See Edwards, O. M., *Wales*, 1902, p. 349.

Welshmen were ready to use it. Clergy and gentry continued to receive an English education, in anglicised grammar schools and English universities. They wrote letters and memoirs in English, and their contributions to scholarship were made in English or Latin. No longer were *y gwŷr mawr* "the patrons of sweet song and perfect tale".[1] Welsh literature, deprived of their support, declined. By the beginning of the seventeenth century few of the gentry employed bards or minstrels, and it is significant that there was no eisteddfod in North Wales between 1568 and 1798.

Nor was the puritan revolution, in its turn, of direct influence upon the intellectual revival in Wales. It was an English importation, which produced comparatively little effect upon the people. There was little enthusiasm for it. It was not until puritanism had ceased to be a militant force, and had become the expression of a devout and pious temper of mind, that its exponents, passionately determined to rescue the souls of the Welsh people, used the language as a means to that end.

Their policy was in marked contrast to that of contemporary reformers in Ireland and the Highlands, to whom English, alone, was the means of salvation and "civilitie". The difference cannot be explained simply in terms of the greater common sense of the Welsh reformers. From the beginnings of the movement in Wales they recognised, as their contemporaries in Ireland and the Highlands failed to do, that the vernacular was a short cut to the Scriptures; but there is, running through the demands of Stephen Hughes and Griffith Jones for Welsh Bibles and literature, an appreciation of their native language, and a faith in its intrinsic worth, which is not to be found among the reformers of Highland and Irish life. "If thirteen thousand conscientious Englishmen", wrote Stephen Hughes, with vehemence, "were to keep school, at the same time, in the thirteen counties of Wales, it would still be impossible for the commonality of one county to lose their native tongue", for it was "unbecoming for the people to lose their language".[2] More forceful, and more sustained, was Griffith Jones's championship. His letters reveal his love and admiration for his native tongue. It was

---

[1] See James, Ivor, *The Welsh Language in the Sixteenth and Seventeenth Century*. Reprinted 1887. See also the *Report of the Departmental Committee appointed by the President of the Board of Education to inquire into the position of the Welsh Language and to advise as to its promotion in the Educational System of Wales*, 1927.

[2] Hughes, Stephen, Letter prefixed to the 1672 ed. of *Gwaith Mr Rees Prichard*.

a language which was "the same for the higher and lower people", whereas other tongues were rather dialects; it was "old, unaltered, and unmixed", the same now as it was in the days of Taliesin, whereas Englishmen had need of interpreters to understand their language as it was talked but a few centuries ago; and it was a language of force and beauty, "full stately and masculine, and perhaps the chastest in Europe".[1]

The language policy of educational reformers in Wales was inseparably connected with their nationality. They were Welshmen, who, in Griffith Jones's words, "had not unlearned their Mother tongue". They possessed a knowledge of their country and its language, which was conspicuously lacking in the alien reformers of the two Gaelic-speaking countries. Although admittedly the preservation of the language was a secondary consideration to the practice of piety, their language policy was productive of unexpected and remarkable results, for despite the fact that they have been criticised not undeservedly, by contemporaries and posterity, for diverting the literary and traditional interests of Wales into religious channels, it remains true that by creating a nation of readers of classical Welsh they were primarily responsible for the literary renaissance of the eighteenth and nineteenth centuries.

One final point demands consideration. Laws of social subordination do not flourish in institutions devoted exclusively to the saving of souls. The supreme importance of the individual, not the reform of society, was the lesson taught in them. While Methodism, "the bitterest foe of freedom in England", maintained in the eighteenth and early nineteenth centuries its opposition to radical thought, it checked the political consciousness of the Welsh people, but when, in the second half of the nineteenth century, it adopted the radicalism of the older Nonconformist denominations, it released from its embargo on politics

---

[1] "She has not lost her *Charms*", wrote Griffith Jones of the Welsh language, "nor *Chasteness*; remains unalterably the same, is now perhaps the same She was *Four thousand Years ago;* still retains the Beauties of her Youth; grown *old in Years,* but not *decayed.* I pray that due Regard be had to her *great Age,* her intrinsick Usefulness, and that *her long-standing Repute* may not be stained by wrong Imputations: let it suffice that so great a Part of *her Dominions* have been usurped from Her; but let no *Violence* be offered to *her life.*" *Welch Piety,* Letter to a Friend, Oct. 11, 1739.

men and women, who were not only imbued with a strong sense of personal values, but who possessed, also, some experience in the working of democratic institutions, and had been trained in dialectic and self-expression. The schools made the Welsh people free of their national literature; they taught them the political importance of the individual. Modern Wales owes not a little to their influence.

CHAPTER IX

CHARITY OR THE STATE

"The private purse immediately and of itself closes when the public purse opens, and nothing can force open the former until the latter be securely shut."
State Education destructive of Voluntary Education, Letter of Edward Baines, Junior, to Lord John Russell, October 9, 1846.

I

THE TRIUMPH OF THE VOLUNTARY PRINCIPLE

The organisation of popular education by means of endowed and subscription day and Sunday schools satisfied all but the most progressive minds throughout the greater part of the eighteenth century. Judged by modern standards the provision of education was lamentably inadequate. Judged even from the standpoint of the early eighteenth century the charity school movement had fallen short of the standards then set up. The avowed aim of the Society for Promoting Christian Knowledge in 1699 had been to encourage a national provision of day schools offering instruction in religious knowledge and the three R's to the children of the labouring poor. This aim was in turn adopted by Scotland, Ireland and Wales. Nowhere was it realised. The withdrawal of the S.P.C.K. from its rôle as leader and protector, the distrust of a literary curriculum as a redemptive agency and the Jacobite taint which clung to some of the schools were responsible for the lack of enthusiasm in England after the end of the first quarter of the century. The Highland Society had placed self-imposed limitations upon its activities by its fixed policy of refusing to set up schools in parishes which had no legal school. An unhappy legal dispute, by depriving the Welsh circulating schools of their main source of income, suspended the movement in Wales, and in Ireland, where alone funds were plentiful and steady, the schools were tabooed by the peasantry. The Sunday school movement of the last quarter of the century was but a provisional means of providing the children of the poor with discipline and instruction. The decrease in child mortality and the increasing demand for child labour forced into prominence the question of State provision of education. Voluntary effort was clearly insufficient and unsuitable. It had become, as Malthus argued in 1798, "a great National disgrace" that the education of the lower classes should be left to "a few Sunday schools, supported by a subscription from individuals".[1] Yet in the first half of the nineteenth century the privately financed, semi-publicly administered provision of elementary instruction received a new lease of life which enabled it to rivet itself upon the country as the voluntary system of national education.

The triumph of the voluntary principle was not due to the indifference of the public in the early years of the nineteenth century, when once again, as at different times during the eighteenth century, enthusiasm for the education of the poor infected all classes in England. Opposition to their instruction was indeed still voluble. Davies Giddy's speech in opposition to Samuel Whitbread's education bill of 1807 was reminiscent of Mandeville's and "Cato's" diatribes eighty-three years earlier. "Howsoever specious in theory the project may be of giving education to the labouring classes of the poor it would in effect be prejudicial to their morals and happiness; it would teach them to despise their lot in life, instead of making them good servants in agriculture and other laborious employments to which their rank in society has destined them; instead of teaching them subordination it would render them factious and refractory, as was evident in the manufacturing counties; it would enable them to read seditious pamphlets, vicious books, and publications against Christianity; it would render them insolent to their superiors, and in a few years the result would be that the legislature would find it necessary to direct the strong arm of power towards them, and to furnish the executive magistrate with much more vigorous laws than were now in force." More remarkable as an illustration of the opinion of a section of the public upon the education of the people was the speech of William Cobbett in the grant-in-aid debate of 1833. The great "Tribune of the People" opposed the vote on the ground that education was not improving the condition of the country. In the country districts, he declared, the father was a better man than his son. Education did nothing but increase the number of schoolmasters

[1] Malthus, T. R., *Essay on the Principle of Population* [etc.], 3rd ed. 1806, vol. II, p. 418.

and schoolmistresses, that new race of idlers. To tax the people for the increase of education was nothing but an attempt to force education. He would oppose "this French, this doctrinaire plan".[1]

While the opinions of Giddy and Cobbett serve as a reminder that the public was not uniformly converted to a belief in popular education, the demands for the instruction of the people, which thrust themselves into prominence in the years just before and after the Great War, differed not only in volume but in character from similar eighteenth-century demands. Philanthropists and men of piety, anti-Romanists and social disciplinarians were still in evidence, but behind them, infusing the agitation with a new character, stood the philosophic liberals and a steadily growing phalanx of working-class men and women, whom French radical thought had inspired with enthusiasm for education as a means of political enlightenment and social betterment. Public interest showed itself in a growing appetite for educational literature. The indefatigable Edgeworths, who popularised a pedagogy derived from Locke and Rousseau, were widely read. Pestalozzi's work at Stanz and Verdun aroused interest in his writings, translations of which appeared in England during the twenties. Of more direct bearing upon the education of the poor were the accounts of Fellenberg's heroic efforts among the peasant children in Berne, made known to the public, in England, by Lord Brougham's report to the Select Committee on Education in 1818. Twenty editions of Brougham's famous pamphlet on *The Education of the People* appeared in 1825. Robert Owen's remarkable essays on *The Formation of the Human Character*, and David Stow's account of his infant schools, found readers both eager and critical.[2] From 1798 to 1808 Sir Thomas Bernard and his friends, in the *Reports of the Society for the Betterment of the Poor*, informed an interested public of the efforts made by the charitable to set up new schools and reform old ones. It was the consciousness of public support which inspired the "education-mad" group of liberals in Parliament to demand from a Government, already tackling the problems of factory labour, pauperism, and negro slavery, consideration for a social problem of equal importance.

[1] Hansard, *Parliamentary Debates*, 1st Series, vol. ix, cols. 798–806, July 13, 1807; 3rd Series, vol. xx, cols. 734–5, Aug. 17, 1833.

[2] See Owen, R., *A New View of Society*, 1813–16; Stow, D., *The Training System*, 1836.

But the growing interest in the education of the poor which characterised the early years of the nineteenth century was not accompanied by enthusiasm for State intervention. Except in Ireland, "the experimental laboratory in the problem of state control", State interference was successfully repelled by voluntaryism. There the Commission appointed by the Lord Lieutenant in 1788 was revived, after the Union of 1801, by the new Parliament, and sat from 1806 to 1812. It reported in favour of State assistance provided that "no attempt was made to influence or disturb the peculiar religious tenets of any sect or description of Christians".[1] The Kildare Place Society, founded in 1811 by men of all religious denominations to promote schools in which the Bible should be read without note or comment, fulfilled the Government's requirements, and was authorised in 1814 to disburse a parliamentary grant of £6890 to schools and societies which accepted the principle of religious neutrality. Unhappily, by supporting the schools of two Protestant denominational societies, antipathetic to Roman Catholicism, the Society betrayed its own principles, and lost the opportunity of establishing itself as a national organisation for popular instruction. Its failure forced the Government to take action. Following the recommendation of the Select Committee of the House of Commons, the Board of Commissioners of National Education in Ireland was set up in 1831, and annual parliamentary grants were paid to this new agency of public education. It was the Government's intention to use the new scheme, if successful, as a working model for the control of elementary education in England and Wales.[2]

In England and Wales a long and stubborn struggle was fought between the supporters and opponents of State intervention, resulting, in 1833, in a compromise which testified to the strength of the voluntary principle. Influenced by the Scottish parish system, English educational reformers in the nineteenth century first proposed to throw the cost of the schools they demanded upon the rates. Whitbread's poor law reform bill of 1807, which among other reforms proposed the establishment of parish schools, supported by a parish rate, in parishes where there were parents who could not afford to educate their children, was thrown

[1] *Reports of the Commissioners of the Board of Education, Ireland,* 1809–12, Fourteenth Report.

[2] Sadler, M. E., *Outlines of Educational Courses in Manchester University,* 1911, p. 6.

out. The bill, which made the provision of parish schools compulsory, placed their supervision under the control of the parish clergy and officers, but left the operation of the law in the hands of magistrates, who were given the power to purchase land, or to rent holdings to be used as school-houses. It was attacked on all sides. In committee it suffered the removal of financial compulsion; in the House of Lords it was defeated without a division. According to the Archbishop of Canterbury it violated the first principle of education in this country, namely that schools should be under the control and auspices of the Establishment.

Lord Brougham's parish school bill of 1820, by which buildings for the new schools were to be financed from the Consolidated Fund and the teachers paid from the local rates, met with a like fate. Avoiding Whitbread's mistake he fell foul of the Nonconformists. His measure, introduced with a warm eulogy of the clergy of the Established Church, gave legal recognition "to the persons whom Providence had appointed to assist in this great work of educating the poor". To the parish clergy he entrusted the drawing up of the curriculum, the arrangement of school fees, and the examination of the children. They were given "not a nominal but a real and effectual veto" in the appointment of teachers, who were to be regular communicants of the Anglican Church. Finally, to bishops, archdeacons, deans and chancellors were given the right of visitation and power to dismiss the schoolmasters. This time Protestant Dissenters and Roman Catholics offered vigorous opposition, and the bill was withdrawn.

Comparison of Roebuck's measure of 1833, the third attempt of the reformers to induce the Government to take action, with those of Whitbread and Brougham shows a marked advance in educational thought. The difficulties of clerical control and parish rating were met, first, by the democratic proposal that the people, operating in each district through committees elected annually by heads of families or by contributors to the schools, should be the guardians of the children's education, and, secondly, by the creation of a ministry of public instruction, presided over by a cabinet minister, whose function it would be to apportion the grants for each district. Radical as were these suggestions, Roebuck's proposal that education should be compulsory was not less so: every child between the ages of six and twelve in Great Britain and Ireland was, by law, to attend school. The fate of the bill could have been foreseen. State compulsion was profoundly distasteful to all shades of political opinion in the House, and Roebuck withdrew his motion.[1]

Lack of support for popular education based on parish rating or Government grants had already turned the attention of the "education mad" set in Parliament to the existing funds for the education of the poor. Investigation of the old endowments, earmarked for education, was the first step. Until all the returns made under the Act of 1786[2] were received by Parliament in 1788 no composite record of the innumerable and varied charitable benefactions of dead and gone philanthropists existed.[3] Out of the 13,000 parishes and townships in England and Wales from which returns had then been required only fourteen omitted to make a reply, but the information given did little more than record the existence of charities, their aggregate income, estimated at £528,710, and their common maladministration. Almost complete public ignorance of the number and value of these charitable donations prevailed, until 1816, when Lord Brougham's Committee of Inquiry into the Education of the Lower Orders printed the returns. The Committee, which included Samuel Romilly, William Wilberforce and Francis Burdett, with Brougham as chairman, published its reports between 1816 and 1818. In spite of their unreliability on matters of fact, and their error in interpreting the phrase *pauperes et indigentes*, describing the beneficence of educational endowments, as though it were used in the sense conveyed by the English term "the indigent poor", the reports were of unique value in presenting the first composite picture of the existing means of education for the poor.[4] The returns showed that there were over 478,000 children attending the 14,300 unendowed schools and 165,432 children attending the 4100 endowed schools. Using the Breslau Tables, based on the calculation that children of school age, i.e. those between the ages of seven and thirteen years, constituted one-ninth of the population, Brougham made effective play, when introducing his education bill of 1820, with

---

[1] Hansard, *Parliamentary Debates*, 3rd Series, vol. xx, cols. 139–74, July 30, 1833.   [2] 26 Geo. III, c. 58.

[3] *Abstract of Returns of Charitable Donations*, 1786–8. Printed 1816.

[4] See *Letter to Samuel Romilly, Esq., M.P., F.R.S., from Henry Brougham, M.P., F.R.S., upon the Abuse of Charities*, August 20, 1818, and Fearon, J. P., *The Endowed Charities*, 1855.

a comparison of the figures supplied by Switzerland and Holland, where the proportions were respectively one in eight and one in ten, with those of England, where "the average means of education" was one in sixteen; of Wales one in twenty, and of Scotland one in nine to one in ten. Of equal interest was the information respecting the unequal distribution of the schools. Out of 13,000 parishes in England 3500 "had not the vestige of a school, endowed, unendowed or dame". Of the remainder, 3000 had endowed schools, the rest, some 5500, relied entirely upon unendowed schools, "fleeting and casual". In Westmorland, conspicuous as the best educated county, the proportion of children attending school was as high as one in seven; in the six Midland counties, Buckinghamshire, Bedfordshire, Cambridgeshire, Northamptonshire, Hertfordshire and Huntingdonshire, where lace-making, "the great enemy both to children and to morals", was the ordinary occupation, the average was one in twenty-four.[1]

The abuse of charitable endowments, brought to the notice of the committee during its investigations, led to Brougham's bill of 1818, which demanded the establishment of a Royal Commission to make a thorough inquiry concerning charities in England and Wales. Pressure from the trustees of vested interests at once made itself felt. By a majority of one vote only the bill passed its second reading, emerging eventually in an emasculated form which confined its terms of reference to charities "unambiguously intended for the very poor and destitute".[2] The reports of the Commission, published at intervals from 1819 to 1837, informed the public that there was a sum of half a million pounds applicable to the education of the poorer classes, and that serious abuses had diverted considerable sums from the educational purposes intended by their pious founders. But not until 1835 was a permanent Board of Commissioners for the supervision of charities recommended; not until 1853 was the Board set up.

[1] See *Reports of the Committee to Inquire into the Education of the Lower Orders*, 12 Parts, 1816–18; and Hansard, *Parliamentary Debates*, vol. II, cols. 49–89, for speech of Mr Henry Brougham in the House of Commons, June 28, 1820.

[2] Adamson, J. W., *A Short History of Education*, 1919, p. 262. The Commissioners were authorised "to investigate the Amount, Nature and Application of all Estates and Funds of what Nature or Kind so ever and the Produce thereof, destined or intended to be applied either to the purposes in the said recited Act mentioned, *or* to the support of any Charity or Charitable Donation or Donations for the benefit of Poor Persons in England and Wales" (59 Geo. III, c. 81).

Unable because of religious jealousies to compel the application of
the rates to education, and because of the jealousy of vested interests to
control endowments for the education of the poor, educational reformers fell back upon the demand for financial assistance from the
State. Late in the session of 1833, in a thin house, after a heated debate,
the Commons, by a majority of 50 to 26, voted in supply the sum of
£20,000 a year in aid of private subscriptions for the creation of school
houses for the education of the poorer classes in Great Britain. No
machinery was set up. Subject only to the condition that half the cost
of the new buildings should be met by voluntary contributions, the
Treasury, relying on the recommendations of two voluntary societies—
the National and the British and Foreign—for the education of the
poor, made grants-in-aid for new school buildings.

The first parliamentary grant to English education, under the
modern educational system, has acquired an importance as a landmark
which is undeserved. The sum earmarked for elementary education was
small, too small, as Joseph Hume pertinently remarked, to constitute a
national system. "It committed the Government to no policy, and did
not increase their responsibilities."[1] It was, indeed, merely a recognition by the State of the voluntary system of education.

Three factors were in the main responsible for the continuity of the
voluntary method, not least of which was the success of Andrew Bell
and Joseph Lancaster in establishing the "mutual system of education"
and the controversy which ensued between the two men and their
supporters.[2] The method which they developed was an old one, used,
as the need arose, in eighteenth-century week-day and Sunday charity
schools. Its elaboration into a system coincided with the new wave of
enthusiasm for popular instruction. The education of the poor became
again, as it had been a hundred years before, the interest of the moment
to the fashionable and learned world. Like other successful plans of the
schoolroom it owed its appearance in its new form to accident. The

[1] Hansard, *Parliamentary Debates*, 3rd Series, vol. xx, cols. 732–7, August 17,
1833.
[2] For Lancaster and his work, see Salmon, D., *Joseph Lancaster*, 1904; Articles
in *The Educational Record*, 1905–29; *The Practical Parts of Lancaster's Improvements and Bell's Experiments*, Cambridge, 1932. J. M. D. Meiklejohn's *An Old
Educational Reformer, Dr Andrew Bell*, 1881, remains the best account of Bell and
his work.

teachers employed in an orphan charity school at Madras in India refused to obey the instructions of the superintendent, the Reverend Andrew Bell. The elder boys were called upon to take their place in the school, and carried out their duties so efficiently that the superintendent in 1797 set pen to paper, and in his pamphlet on *An Experiment in Education made at the Male Asylum at Madras* told the public of the success of the mutual system of education.

A year later the Quaker, Joseph Lancaster, master of a school, half pay, half charity, for the children of the poor in Southwark, developed the idea. The plan, which a later age does not hesitate to condemn as cheap and mechanical, appealed to Lancaster because of the difficulty in finding suitable teachers for the children of the poor, and in paying them when found. Dame schools for children under seven years of age abounded, according to him, in every poor neighbourhood of London. Pay schools run by masters for elder children were also plentiful. But the weekly pence demanded for their tuition restricted instruction to the children of the more respectable poor. The unsavoury character of many of the teachers in these schools, their general lack of intellectual qualifications, and the crowded and insanitary schoolrooms, in which they taught their pupils, made even the few pence demanded an excessive charge. Small as were the fees, the very poor could not afford them, and Lancaster, whose school began as a pay school, touched by the desire of poor parents that their children should be instructed, collected subscriptions to defray the expense of their schooling. His benevolence, his enthusiasm, his remarkable powers as organiser and teacher, and the rewards and punishments which he devised, attracted vast numbers of children. They came for education "like flocks of sheep" but, at the lowest estimate, the cost of each child's instruction worked out at a guinea a year, and, as the subscriptions were limited, the number of charity children whom he could admit were few. The "Mutual or Monitorial System" solved his problem for him. It made a "cheap education possible". "It came to be demonstrated that seven children could be educated for a guinea instead of one."[1] Success bred success. Subscriptions poured in, the pay element was eliminated, and a charity school financed on the same lines as the old charity schools was established.

[1] Lancaster, J., *Improvements in Education as it respects the Industrious Classes of the Community* [etc.], 1803 ed., pp. 2–3.

The new plan of education, which aroused the enthusiastic support of the king, the royal family, the nobility and gentry, the intelligentsia and the middle classes, depended for its success upon the pupils. It was a mode, as Dr Bell explained, of "conducting education through the agency of the scholars themselves".[1] The pupils became the instruments of their own discipline and instruction. In Lancaster's enormous school of 1000 children in the Borough Road the whole system of tuition was almost entirely conducted by the boys. "The Master", said Lancaster, "should be a silent by-stander and inspector. What a master says should be done; but if he teaches on this system he will find authority is not personal—that when the pupils, as well as the schoolmaster understand how to act and lean on this system, the system, not the master's vague discretionary uncertain judgment, will be in practice. A command will be obeyed by any boy because it is a command, and the whole school will obey the common, known commands of the school, from being merely known as such, let who will give them. In a common school the authority of the master is personal, and the rod is his sceptre. His absence is the immediate signal for confusion and riot; and in his absence his assistants will rarely be minded. But in a school properly regulated and conducted on my plan, when the master leaves school, the business will go on as well in his absence as in his presence, because the authority is not personal. This mode of ensuring obedience is a novelty in the history of education."[2]

The amount of red tape required in a school is in inverse proportion to the moral and intellectual powers of the teachers. Instruction and discipline which depended upon ignorant and unformed children demanded, for its success, mechanical and rigid regimentation. Schools conducted on Bell's Madras plan appear to have been rather more flexible than the Lancasterian schools. In both the essential was a large single room, with desks around the walls for the writing lessons, and a floor space chalked out into squares, in which the children stood in classes for their lessons. In the Borough Road school eight to ten children formed a class in charge of a monitor. Under the Madras plan the assistant teachers, whose age ranged from eleven to fourteen years, aided by the tutors, whose age might be anything between seven and

[1] Bell, A., *Report of the Madras Asylum*, Part I, p. 24.
[2] Lancaster, J., *The British System of Education* [etc.], 1810, p. 45.

eleven years, attempted to teach and discipline from twenty-four to thirty-six children.[1]

The methods employed by Bell and Lancaster show little advance on those of the eighteenth-century charity schoolmaster, except for the prompt hearing of short and easy lessons.[2] The meaning of the book read, or of the passage written, was no concern of the youthful teacher; the development of number concept in the arithmetic lessons was outside the scope of his imagination; but memory, "the pack-horse of Parnassus", was driven hard. Question and answer, formal and memorised, was the nearest approach which the teacher made to the business of imparting and co-ordinating knowledge. Nevertheless, the schools of Bell and Lancaster made an important contribution to the education of the poor, for they re-established the principle of full-time attendance for their pupils at a time when the success of the Sunday school threatened to break the older tradition of day-school instruction, and when the cheap and unskilled services of the monitors offered a temporary solution to the ever-present difficulty of financing and staffing day schools for the poor.

The moral training of the children found the two men in agreement. "To train children in the practice of such moral habits as are conducive to their future welfare as virtuous men and useful members of society"[3] was Lancaster's avowed aim. Bell was concerned to make "good scholars, good men, good subjects and good Christians".[4] To this common end they taught responsibility by emphasising the mutual obligation of teachers and pupils; they provided mental and physical

---

[1] Sir Thomas Bernard discovered other advantages in the monitorial system. "Such assistants may be had without expense and at the moment they are wanted. They may be dismissed without any pension from the funds and without any call for that pity which in some cases induce the Governors of schools to vitiate the whole system rather than discard or supersede unworthy or incapable ushers." *Report of the Society for Bettering the Condition of the Poor*, 1801.

[2] No lesson with the younger children, Bell insisted, should take more than a quarter of an hour, or with older children more than half-an-hour. This practice was in marked contrast to that used in other schools "where children learn one lesson a day" and waited "the convenience of the master" to hear it. *An Experiment in Education made at the Male Asylum at Madras*, 1797, Part II, chap. I, Introduction.

[3] Lancaster, J. J., *Improvements [etc.]*, p. 25.

[4] Bell, A., *op. cit.* Preface to 2nd ed. 1805.

discipline by the unremitting drill in the three R's, and, by inciting rivalry and emulation, they encouraged the active participation of the children in the work of the school. These are the factors which help to explain the warm contemporary approval of the monitorial system, and its influence on educational practice in the British Isles during the greater part of the nineteenth century. The mechanical character of its instruction did not offend the age of machinery. Indeed, the similarity of the new schools to the new factories was a matter of commendation rather than of condemnation. "The principle in schools and manufactories is the same", wrote Sir Thomas Bernard, with warm approval. "The grand principle of Dr Bell's System is the division of labour applied to intellectual purposes."[1] The increased speed, skill and dexterity of workers under the factory system was confidently expected from children under the monitorial system. State intervention became unnecessary when voluntary effort could devise machinery for mass education without its aid.

Before enthusiasm for the new method began to wane bitter and prolonged religious controversy diverted attention from the obvious defects of the monitorial system to the differing religious convictions of its founders. Lancaster, a Quaker, demanded that education should be unsectarian in character. He appealed to "the friends of youth among every denomination of Christians" to put aside the religious differences, which had deprived many thousands of children of the benefits of instruction, and to "exalt the standard of education". "The grand basis of Christianity" was, in his opinion, broad enough for the whole of mankind to stand on. Upon it the "National Concern of Education", free from the peculiar tenets of any sect, should be founded.[2] On these lines he proposed the establishment of a new voluntary society for the reform and encouragement of existing schools and the creation of new schools.

His proposal acted as a trumpet call to the redoubtable Anglican and anti-Jacobin, Mrs Sarah Trimmer. Lancaster's methods won her modi-fied approval; Lancaster's plea for public education on a non-sectarian basis was, in her opinion, a threat, not only to Anglicanism, but to Christianity. Her kindly, but obtuse, mind saw the twin devils of deism

[1] Bernard, Sir T., *Of the Education of the Poor*, 1809, pp. 35–6. Bell and Lancaster use the same analogy and show the same appreciation.
[2] Lancaster, J., *op. cit.* 1805 ed. p. 184.

and infidelity, rampant in France, in the most unlikely places. "Of all the plans that have appeared in this kingdom likely to supplant the Church", Lancaster's scheme appeared to her to be the most formidable, and an education founded "on general Christian principles, ill-grounded and mischievous".

Not only was the plan of "this Goliath of schismatics" a danger to Christianity, it was also, in her view, unnecessary. A national system of grammar and charity schools was already in existence. The catechism and book of common prayer were, by law, the prescribed subjects of study, and bishops and clergy were the authorised guardians of education. If Lancaster won his way, and his army of influential supporters made him appear a formidable figure, undenominationalism would supplant Anglicanism in all schools of public elementary instruction, and the authority of the Church would be undermined. She called on Anglicans to save the Church, which was once again in danger.[1] Bell, who after the publication of his pamphlet had played no active part in the new scheme of education, was dragged by Mrs Trimmer from his retirement. The creator of the monitorial system was prevailed upon to establish it against Lancaster, who treated the system as his own, and to press for its adoption by all Anglican schools throughout the country.[2]

Mrs Trimmer's intervention changed an educational into a politico-religious question. Tories and Churchmen took up their stand behind Bell; Whigs and Dissenters supported Lancaster. A storm in press and pulpit, reminiscent in its violence of the outburst caused by Mandeville and "Cato" in 1723, raged for years. *The Edinburgh, The Quarterly* and *British Reviews, The Anti-Jacobin, The Orthodox Churchman, The British Critic, The Morning Post, The Pamphleteer*, provided platforms for the rival schools. Wilberforce, Romilly, Brougham, Robert Owen, Bentham, James Mill, Wordsworth, Southey, Samuel Rogers, Whitbread, Thomas Bernard, and, most trenchant of publicists, Sydney Smith wrote on one side or the other, and anonymous pamphleteers added fuel to the fire.

[1] Trimmer, Sarah, *A Comparative View of the New Plan of Education promulgated by Mr Joseph Lancaster in his Tracts Concerning the Instruction of the Children of the Labouring Part of the Community; and of the System of Christian Instruction founded by our Pious Forefathers for the Instruction of Young Members of the Established Church in the Principles of the Reformed Religion*, 1805, *passim*.

[2] For an account of the controversy see Salmon, D., *The Educational Record*, vol. XVIII, Nos. 43–5; vol. XIX, No. 47.

In 1810 the Royal British or Lancasterian Association, informally in existence since 1808, was founded. Money poured in from all sides, and ninety-five new schools were established on an undenominational basis within two years. In 1811 a concerted movement to divert the new enthusiasm for education into Anglican channels was set on foot. Dr Marsh, Lady Margaret professor of Divinity at Cambridge, on whose shoulders Mrs Trimmer's mantle had fallen after her death in 1810, summoned the Church, in a sermon delivered at the anniversary meeting of the London charity schools, to take action. The national religion, he asserted, was the foundation of national education, but the national religion of the people was not the religion of the Bible alone, as Lancaster taught, but of the Bible in conjunction with the liturgy of the Anglican Church.[1] To maintain this "essential association" in popular education the National Society for the Education of the Poor was formed, under the auspices of the S.P.C.K. In its offices the new Society was established. To it the old Society handed over its century-old interest in the education of the poor. The appeal for funds brought in over £20,000 in gifts and £1500 in promises of annual subscriptions. New schools were set up, and old charity schools such as those in Whitechapel and Marylebone and at Kendal changed their name, and became National schools. 230 schools and 40,484 pupils were returned by the National Society in 1813.

The remarkable response of Anglicans and Nonconformists seated the voluntary system firmly in the saddle. It met the dual demands for popular instruction and for religious liberty by leaving the control of education in the hands of two societies, which were agreed in refusing to contemplate education for the people which did not provide religious instruction. The rivalry between them did not allow either party to relax its efforts. Both National and British schools grew apace, and State control of a national service receded still further into the background.

Distrust of State control was a second factor which contributed to the longevity of the voluntary principle. The recognition which continental nations had given before the end of the eighteenth century to education as a public service under State direction was delayed in England by the resolute opposition of liberal opinion. Montesquieu's essay on *L'Esprit des Lois*, published in 1748, may be considered as a convenient point of

[1] Marsh, H., *Sermon preached in St Paul's Cathedral, June 13, 1811, on The National Religion the Foundation of National Education.*

divergence between English and European schools of thought on the rôle which should be played by the State in the provision of education for its citizens. His thesis that the laws of education ought to be in relation to the principles of Government won general recognition in his own country. La Châlotais carried it to its logical conclusion in claiming for the nation an education dependent upon the State alone, "because education belongs essentially to the State".[1] The conception of education as a public service became a commonplace of French political thought after 1789, when public instruction, "universal, compulsory, gratuitous and secular"[2], expressed the attitude of Revolutionary France to its citizens.

In Austria, in Prussia and Bavaria, and other of the German States, the same tendency towards the steady extension of State controlled and secularised education manifested itself.[3] In England, on the contrary, the idea hung fire. Thomas Sheridan's prolix essay on *British Education*, published in 1756, developed Montesquieu's thesis. Dr John Brown, nine years later, demanded a prescribed code of education, in conformity with the doctrines of the Established Church, to which all members of the community should legally submit themselves. Mary Wollstonecraft, at the end of the century, acknowledging her debt to Talleyrand's "very sensible pamphlet on public education", demanded the establishment of schools for public instruction supported by the State.[4] But the bulk of advanced opinion in England was opposed to the control of education by the State.

The men who were responsible, during these years, for the moulding of liberal opinion, were in no degree indifferent to the need of instruction for the labouring classes. Those who, like Joseph Priestley, Richard Price and William Godwin, held the doctrine of the progressive perfectibility of man, looked to education as the chief instrument of human advance. Adam Smith demanded the education of the common people as a safeguard against the delusions of enthusiasm and supersti-

---

[1] Montesquieu, *L'Esprit des Lois* [etc.], 1748, Book IV; La Châlotais, *Essai d'Education Nationale, ou Plan d'Etudes pour la Jeunesse*, 1763, p. 31.

[2] Adamson, J. W., *English Education, 1789–1902*, 1930, p. 7.

[3] See Paulsen, F., *German Education Past and Present*, 1908, *passim*.

[4] See Sheridan, T., *British Education, or the Source of the Disorders of Great Britain*, 1756; Brown, J., *Thoughts on Civil Liberty, on Licentiousness and Faction*, 1765; Talleyrand-Périgord, *Rapport sur l'Instruction Publique* [etc.], 1791; Wollstonecraft, M., *A Vindication of the Rights of Women*, 1792.

tion, and as a corrective to the temper of mind and body produced by the division of labour in civilised and commercial societies. In *The Rights of Man* Thomas Paine urged the grant of family subsidies from the State for the education of the children of the poor, declaring that under a well-regulated Government none should remain uninstructed. But liberal opinion fought shy of State interference. Education, flexible, experimental and diversified, giving "free scope to everything which may bid fair for introducing more variety among us",[1] was, in the opinion of Priestley, incompatible with a fixed and uniform system. Adam Smith's argument in favour of public assistance for elementary education was coupled with criticism of endowments for education and, inferentially, of State aid. Paine's scheme of State-aided instruction left the provision of schools in private hands, and their choice to the parents. Godwin's rigid individualism permitted no truck with the State. In his *Enquiry Concerning Political Justice* the distrust of the State reached its apotheosis. A system of national education under its superintendence would establish a permanence of opinion inimical to progress and individual initiative, and would provide the State with an alliance of "a much more formidable nature than the old and much contested alliance of church and state".[2]

When the French wars were over the influential body of philosophic radicals associated with Bentham and the elder Mill played a leading part in creating a public opinion favourable to the provision of education for the people, but whereas they were as one man in demanding opportunities for public instruction, they showed little disposition to take popular education out of the hands of its voluntary administrators. With one or two exceptions, State supervision operating through existing machinery, and State contributions disbursed by voluntary organisation, defined the limit of their concessions. Their compromise helped to establish the principle of "voluntaryism" firmly in the saddle at a moment when, as the advance guard of political and social reform, they might have been expected to see in State control of education an essential public service.

[1] Priestley, J., *Remarks on a Code of Education proposed by Dr Brown in a late Treatise entitled Thoughts on Civil Liberty*, 1765, p. 149.

[2] Godwin, W., An *Enquiry Concerning Political Justice and its influence on Morals and Happiness*, 2 vols. 1793, vol. II, p. 144. See also Smith, Adam, *An Inquiry into the Nature and Causes of the Wealth of Nations*, 1776, and Paine, T., *The Rights of Man*, 1791–2, Part II, Chap. V.

Speeches delivered inside and outside Parliament and articles in the reviews and the daily press show that the opposition to State intervention drew part of its strength from the belief, firmly held by Anglicans and Liberals, that State control of education would be inimical to religious freedom and individual liberty, but the third and a far more potent cause of opposition was to be found in the widespread and deep-seated conception of popular education as a philanthropic enterprise. No period before the eighteenth century had witnessed the creation of so many societies for associated effort on behalf of the ignorant and helpless, or the same devoted personal service of so many pious men and women. Robert Nelson, Henry Hoare, Thomas Bray, Lady Elizabeth Hastings, John Phillipps, Henry Maule, Edward Nicholson, Edward Synge, John Wesley, John Howard, Elizabeth Fry, William Wilberforce, John Clarkson, Captain Coram, Hannah and Martha More, Griffith Jones, Bridget Bevan, Thomas Charles, Jonas Hanway, Henry Thornton, Sarah Trimmer, William Allen are typical in their different philanthropic interests of an immensely wide section of their countrymen, who by their individual and collective efforts had built up voluntary organisations for social service. Their like was not to be found elsewhere. They were a product of eighteenth-century England.[1] They were proud of their benevolence and none could deny that they had done well by their countrymen. The provision of schools for the children of the poor held first place among their charitable activities. They had kept the movement for education alive for over a hundred years, and, but recently, had revived it with such extraordinary success that Brougham, champion in his early years of State intervention, withdrew his support of Roebuck's bill, on the ground that the voluntary system was both adequate and successful. The roots of voluntary charity were too deep and too strong to allow the half-hearted efforts

[1] See Ruggles, T. (ed.), *Histoire des Pauvres par l'Amiral du Quesnay*, prefaced by an advertisement by the editor [n.d.]; Paterson, J., *Pietas Londonensis*, 1714; Highmore, A., *Pietas Londonensis*, 1814; Portus, G. V., *Caritas Anglicana*, 1912; Gray, Kirkman, *History of English Philanthropy*, 1905. See also Wilberforce's remark upon the part played by women in philanthropic work at the end of the eighteenth century. "There is no class of persons whose condition has been more improved within my recollection than that of unmarried women. Formerly there seemed nothing useful in which they could be naturally busy, but now they may always find an object in attending the poor." *Life of William Wilberforce*, 1839, by R. and S. Wilberforce, vol. I, p. 238.

of early nineteenth-century reformers to change the established order. Its supporters could not brook the idea of State interference. Philanthropy to them was incompatible with bureaucracy. The one would destroy the other. The private purse, they held, would close when the public purse opened, and men and women would be deprived of the spiritual reward which accompanied the care of the ignorant and helpless. By their determination to regard education as a voluntary service, bestowed by patronage upon the poor, they renounced the one method by which permanent reform could have been secured.

II

EPILOGUE

The charity school movement has received little recognition from historians of eighteenth-century history. The stalwarts of the antislavery movement, and of prison and factory reform, have won their measure of commendation from contemporaries and from posterity. The men and women who struggled valiantly for the education of the poor against the indifference and obscurantism of their day have not, with the exception of Robert Raikes, received even a modicum of praise. Instead they have been subjected to a steady stream of adverse criticism, because their aims were propagandist and their methods objectionable. It is not possible to deny the truth of such judgments. It may be questioned whether, with rare exceptions, the company of pious and philanthropic men and women who financed and managed the charity school movement had any conception of education except as a redemptive agency. They did not envisage it as a basis of common citizenship, nor as a means of developing the personality and intellectual powers of the children. They were concerned with the propagation of moral discipline, or English "civilitie", or the Protestant faith, or the salvation of souls for the glory of God. Schools for the poor were regarded by them as a shield and defence against the specific religious, political and social perils of the age. Their supporters were responsible for the conception of elementary education as an act of grace, and as a system complete in itself, from both of which ideas it has with difficulty freed itself. The schools were inadequate in number, their management was not lacking in corruption, nor their discipline in brutality. The instruction given in them was limited and mechanical; the spirit which informed it was that of class discipline enforced by religious sanctions. Such a conception of education is so distasteful to modern minds that the value of the work is forgotten or ignored. Yet it is clear, from a study of the movement, that the schools provided tens of thousands of children in the eighteenth century with their only means of instruction. Except in Ireland the State played no part; the schools owed nothing to it. The crusade of science on behalf of education was yet to come. Religion alone laid the foundation of public elementary education.

It has been customary to compare, to their detriment, the educational ideals of the eighteenth century with those of the sixteenth century, as expressed in the schools established in the two periods. The characteristic contributions of the one are condemned as class and propagandist institutions; those of the other are commended as institutions engaged in the liberal study of the classics and open to all. But it is possible to exaggerate the differences. The grammar schools of medieval and modern times were not the free institutions which history has made them out to be. They did not provide free instruction for the poor. At best they left the door open to the intellectual aristocrats among the lower orders, who could afford entrance fees and had received sufficient preparatory instruction, to enter upon a classical education. That door was not closed by the advent of the charity school. It is as absurd as it is unfair to suggest that a system of schools, in which the elements were taught in an avowedly superior manner to that of the pay schools of dame and parish clerk, prevented its pupils from pushing open the door of the grammar schools.

It is, again, often forgotten that dogmatic religious instruction played no small part in the grammar school curriculum. Grammar school masters were frequently clerics; the bishop's licence was required before they could teach, and religious instruction, in Bible and catechism, and attendance at church on Sundays and holy days bulked large in the life of the grammar school as it did in that of the charity school. The religious emphasis in charity school instruction was not peculiar, but was in keeping with established grammar school practice. Education, without religious instruction, was an idea foreign to sixteenth-century grammar school and eighteenth-century charity school alike. The restricted character of charity school instruction cannot be denied, yet narrow as it was, it was too wide for public taste. The curriculum was, in the main, confined to reading and repetition. But as the common text-book of the schools was the Bible, the liberal value of charity school education is consistently underrated. It would be difficult to find a text-book which clothed instruction in so perfect a literary form, or to find teaching more conducive to intelligent criticism of social conditions than the gospel of the poor. A sense of the beauty of words, an appreciation of poetry, and a burning fire of indignation for social ills, are not uncommon possessions of Bible students. Nineteenth-century writers who express astonishment when they find that few among the working classes could not read, and historians who are surprised by the rapid reception of radical thought in the early nineteenth century, show themselves ignorant of New Testament ethics and unaware of the innumerable charities bestowed for the express purpose of teaching the poor to read.

The value of the charity school movement is not confined to these points. It was responsible for experiments in school method and management, with which it has rarely been credited. It provided semi-public instruction for girls, whose education was ignored, in fact if not in law, by the grammar schools, sometimes by the establishment of schools specifically for their instruction, sometimes by co-educational methods. While girls are seldom mentioned in grammar school statutes, and the term "children", found in them, was commonly translated by the word "boys", innumerable eighteenth-century wills and deeds of gift left funds specifically for the education of boys *and* girls, and the term "children" was uniformly translated to cover both sexes. The lead given by the charity school movement was but slowly followed in secondary and higher education. "A girl", said Sir Joshua Fitch, as late as 1873, "is not expected to serve God in Church and State, and is not invited to the university, or the grammar school, but she may, if poor, be wanted to contribute to the comfort of her betters as an apprentice or servant, and the charity schools are therefore open to her."[1] It was these same charity schools whose endowments have since helped to provide secondary education for girls.

Another experiment followed close upon the heels of the provision of elementary schools for girls. While the three R's were regarded by the majority of the schools' supporters as suitable mental pabulum for

---

[1] *The Westminster Review*, April, 1873.

boys, there was general unanimity that reading, sewing, knitting, and, when possible, housework, was the correct curriculum to fit girls for their life of toil, either as servants in the homes of others, or as wives in homes of their own. Some of the schools attempted to provide boys with similar work. Such instruction was vocational in character, and deserves consideration as an attempt to establish a relationship between life in school and the world outside, which modern education has failed to accomplish. Unhappily lack of funds and criticism of the schools as literary institutions, unfitting their pupils for their future work as hewers of wood and drawers of water, side-tracked this experiment in vocational instruction. Labour, which turned the schools into little factories and the children into wage earners, met the "popular clamours" against the education of poor children, and thrust the vocational element out of mind.

Of more lasting importance were the new methods of organisation, which the charity school movement inaugurated. To philanthropy in general it contributed, in a highly developed form, the idea of association as the machinery for philanthropic effort. Voluntary societies for all sorts and conditions of social work followed in the wake of the London S.P.C.K., and its sister societies. A central body working in conjunction with local committees, advising and encouraging them in co-ordinated effort, became the common organisation of associated philanthropy and an invaluable training ground for democratic government.

The modern State system of elementary education owes the movement an even more specific debt. It supplied an interim organisation for semi-popular education until the State was ready to take up its duty, and it was responsible, in no small degree, for the peculiar structure of the modern educational system. It had shown that central control and local initiative were not incompatible, and could with advantage be developed in company.

One debt remains, the importance of which it is not possible to estimate. A warm tribute to the heroic efforts of church schools, chapel schools, night schools, and ragged schools, in transforming the manners and morals of the working classes in London during the last three-quarters of the nineteenth century, has been paid by two distinguished English historians.[1] The eighteenth-century charity schools, in their

[1] Webb, S. and B., *London Education*, 1904.

different forms, were too thinly distributed, and the quality of their instruction was too uneven to produce a spectacular change of a like nature in the country at large. But it may be claimed for them that they provided the means whereby no inconsiderable number of the lower orders were enabled to modify their ignorance and their helplessness.

Appendices

APPENDIX I: *ENGLAND*

1. *Endowed Non-Classical Schools*

Table showing the number and distribution of *English* schools endowed or re-endowed before and during the eighteenth century, as returned by the Commissioners of Inquiry into Charities, 1818–1843.

County	Before 1698	1698–1710	1710–1720	1720–1730	1730–1740	1740–1750	1750–1760	1760–1770	1770–1780	1780–1790	1790–1800	Not dated	Total
Beds	7	1	0	4	0	0	0	0	0	0	0	1	13
Berks	10	6	3	1	1	0	1	1	0	2	3	2	30
Bucks	3	3	5	2	1	0	0	2	0	1	2	0	19
Cambs	8	3	3	9	5	1	0	1	0	0	0	5	35
Co. of Chester	15	2	3	4	1	0	4	1	2	9	0	17	58
Cornwall	3	3	2	0	0	1	2	1	1	1	1	2	17
Cumberland	4	0	3	5	1	1	5	2	2	1	4	7	35
Derby	14	4	10	13	3	8	1	3	2	1	3	11	73
Devon	16	4	7	2	6	3	2	3	0	2	3	1	49
Dorset	6	2	2	1	4	2	2	1	1	1	2	4	28
Durham	1	1	4	5	2	4	0	6	2	2	3	4	34
Essex	15	3	5	6	3	0	3	4	3	1	0	2	45
Glos	12	7	5	5	5	1	2	3	5	1	0	2	48
Hereford	12	2	2	3	0	0	1	2	1	3	5	5	36
Hertford	9	2	1	5	0	0	0	2	1	0	0	2	22
Hunts	3	3	4	3	0	1	0	1	0	0	0	1	16
Kent	23	5	9	6	2	2	1	2	2	4	3	3	62
Lancaster	22	7	11	11	10	7	10	7	5	4	7	24	125
Leicester	10	1	2	3	3	1	1	9	0	0	1	3	34
Lincoln	29	12	22	11	2	2	1	3	0	2	1	10	95
Middlesex	13	16	5	1	2	0	1	3	1	4	1	8	55
City of London	26	14	10	1	2	0	0	0	0	0	0	6	59
City of Westminster	3	7	0	1	0	0	0	0	0	0	0	0	11
Monmouth	4	0	1	1	2	0	0	0	0	0	0	0	8
Norfolk	11	3	4	7	2	0	0	1	1	0	1	5	35
Northampton	21	6	11	2	3	0	2	5	2	1	1	7	61
Nottingham	3	7	2	6	6	2	0	0	0	3	1	7	37
Northumberland	2	5	5	1	1	0	0	1	2	0	3	4	24
Oxford	9	4	5	4	3	1	1	0	1	2	0	7	37
Rutland	5	0	0	2	0	0	0	0	0	0	0	2	9
Shropshire	13	3	6	5	3	1	1	1	2	3	1	10	49
Somerset	12	2	9	7	2	0	7	3	0	1	2	4	49
Southampton	8	2	4	6	3	2	2	2	1	4	1	1	36
Stafford	15	5	1	10	4	3	3	5	1	5	4	10	66
Suffolk	11	4	3	4	2	1	1	0	0	0	0	6	32
Surrey	9	3	10	1	1	2	0	0	1	2	1	0	30
Sussex	5	3	3	4	3	1	2	1	1	1	1	0	25
Warwick	15	8	9	5	5	0	1	3	3	2	0	9	60
Wilts	8	3	6	7	2	2	2	1	5	2	3	5	46
Worcester	10	8	10	4	3	2	1	1	2	1	2	8	52
Westmorland	7	0	0	1	1	0	0	2	3	0	1	2	17
Yorkshire	28	19	28	18	16	9	7	10	2	6	12	38	193
Totals	460	193	235	197	115	60	67	93	55	72	73	245	1865

2. Charities not attached to Endowed Non-Classical Schools

Table showing the number and distribution of charities for elementary education before and during the eighteenth century, as returned by the Commissioners of Inquiry into Charities, 1818–1843.

County	Before 1698	1698–1710	1710–1720	1720–1730	1730–1740	1740–1750	1750–1760	1760–1770	1770–1780	1780–1790	1790–1800	Not dated	Total
Beds	6	3	3	3	2	1	0	1	1	1	0	7	28
Berks	7	2	3	5	0	0	5	1	2	1	6	11	43
Bucks	7	0	6	6	4	0	1	2	1	1	3	5	36
Cambs	6	1	0	3	0	1	0	1	0	0	0	5	17
Co. of Chester	3	0	1	4	0	2	2	1	0	0	4	1	18
Cornwall	7	1	4	0	1	2	2	1	2	3	0	2	25
Cumberland	0	0	1	2	2	1	1	5	5	7	3	5	32
Derby	9	1	3	3	3	6	0	0	1	2	3	4	35
Devon	27	6	11	14	19	5	1	5	5	3	4	33	133
Dorset	4	1	0	1	0	0	1	1	1	0	1	5	15
Durham	2	2	1	2	0	1	0	0	0	3	0	1	12
Essex	7	3	1	3	8	1	4	2	7	2	4	12	54
Glos	12	3	10	15	6	7	3	4	0	5	2	18	85
Hereford	2	2	4	3	1	1	0	1	1	1	0	3	19
Hertford	7	0	1	3	4	1	1	0	0	2	2	5	26
Hunts	1	3	2	0	0	0	0	2	1	1	0	4	14
Kent	6	3	9	9	5	1	6	4	5	3	4	6	61
Lancaster	10	1	6	2	3	3	3	2	0	1	2	15	48
Leicester	5	4	7	6	5	1	2	4	3	3	5	20	65
Lincoln	9	2	5	5	5	0	2	0	0	2	0	11	41
City of London	5	0	2	2	1	0	0	0	1	0	0	2	13
Middlesex	7	2	2	2	0	0	1	3	2	2	6	6	33
Monmouth	1	0	0	2	0	0	0	0	0	0	0	1	4
Norfolk	17	0	5	9	2	0	0	1	4	2	5	7	52
Northampton	10	5	2	1	2	2	3	1	1	3	1	18	49
Northumberland	0	0	1	3	2	1	1	0	0	0	2	4	14
Nottingham	7	0	3	4	1	6	0	1	3	3	1	15	44
Oxford	7	4	7	9	0	1	0	1	0	5	0	6	40
Rutland	1	0	0	0	0	0	0	1	0	0	1	4	7
Shropshire	2	3	1	8	4	1	0	1	0	1	0	13	34
Somerset	6	4	5	7	6	3	3	4	3	5	5	17	68
Southampton	9	3	2	7	2	1	4	2	6	3	1	5	45
Isle of Wight	3	0	0	2	0	0	0	0	0	0	0	0	5
Stafford	12	1	5	5	2	0	2	1	1	2	6	15	52
Suffolk	12	9	9	10	3	2	1	2	1	1	2	25	77
Bor. of Southwark	1	0	1	0	0	0	0	0	0	0	0	0	2
Surrey	7	3	4	8	1	1	3	2	3	2	0	1	35
Sussex	3	3	5	5	4	0	1	4	2	0	1	5	33
Warwick	7	2	5	1	2	2	0	4	4	3	2	2	34
Westmorland	1	0	1	1	2	0	1	1	1	0	2	3	13
Wilts	5	6	1	5	4	1	2	2	1	4	1	8	40
Worcester	3	1	2	4	1	0	2	0	0	2	2	6	23
City of York	3	2	1	3	0	0	0	0	1	0	0	2	12
Yorkshire:													
E. Riding	5	8	5	6	1	1	0	3	2	4	4	11	50
N. Riding	8	6	3	5	1	0	5	7	3	4	1	20	63
W. Riding	12	0	10	10	4	5	4	7	1	6	10	33	102
Totals	291	100	160	208	113	61	67	85	75	93	96	402	1751

3. *A list of the Non-Classical Schools in England, endowed or re-endowed during the eighteenth century*

as returned in the *Digest of Schools and Charities for Education*, 1842

S. Signifies schools which were originally Subscription schools, or, at the time of the Inquiry, were financed in part by subscription.

D. Signifies schools connected with the Dissenting Interest.

H. Signifies Hospitals or Boarding schools, in which all, or part, of the pupils were maintained.

Co. of Bedford

Bedford Town
Biggleswade
Cranfield
Dean
Dunstable S.
Renhold

Co. of Berkshire

Abingdon
Abingdon
Appleton
Binfield
Blewbury
Buckland
Chaddleworth
Chieveley
Hurst
Kingston-Bagpuze
Lambourne
Newbury
Pangbourn
Reading S.H.
Reading S.H.
Reading
Shinfield
Sonning
Sparsholt D.
Thatcham
Wargrave
New Windsor S.
New Windsor S.
Old Windsor
Winkfield
Wokingham
Wokingham

Co. of Bucks

Buckingham
Burnham
Chalfont St Giles S.
Denham
Eton
Farnham Royal S.
Hanslope
Iver S.
Great Linford
Moulsoe
Newport Pagnell
Ravenstone
Soulbury
Stoke Hammond
Stoke Poges
Swanbourne
Wavendon
Winslow

Co. of Cambridge

Babraham S.
Borough Green
Bottisham
Cambridge S.
Chippenham
Cottenham
Coveney
Doddington
Doddington
Ely
Graveley
Haddenham
Histon
Kingston
Orwell

Co. of Cambridge

Over
Swaffham Bulbeck
Swaffham Prior
Waterbeach
Whittlesea
Whittlesford
Willingham
Wisbech St Mary
Wisbech St Peter S.

Co. Palatine of Chester

Alderley S.
Barthomley
Barthomley
Bowdon
Bowdon
Great Budworth
Little Budworth
Bunbury
Cheadle
Cheadle S.
Christleton
Davenham
Farndon
Frodsham
Gawsworth S.
Nether Knutsford
Lymm
Malpas S.
Mottram in Longden-
    Dale D.
Nantwich
Prestbury
Prestbury

2 k

354

354 APPENDIX I

Co. Palatine of Chester

Prestbury
Prestbury S.
Rosthern S.
Sandbach
Sandbach
Stockport
Tattenhall
Thornton-on-the-Moors
Wybunbury
Wybunbury

Co. of Cornwall

Anthony St Jacob
Cambourne
Landrake
Linkinhorne
East Looe
Madron
Menheniot
Morval
St Dominick
St Erth
St German S.
St Stephen-by-Launceston

Co. of Cumberland

Addingham
Aikton S.
Ainstable
Alston with Garrigill
Bridekirk S.
Brigham
Bromfield
Carlisle S.
Carlisle
Carlisle
Carlisle
Croglin S.
Dacre
Dearham
Distington S.
Edenhall
Gilcrux
Greystock
Greystock
Hayton
Hutton-in-the-Forest

Co. of Cumberland

Ireby
Lazonby
St Bees
St Bees
Skelton
Wetheral
Wetheral

Co. of Derby

Alfreton
Ashborne
Bakewell
Bakewell
Bakewell
Bakewell
Brighton
Bonsall
Breadsall
Church Broughton
Carsington
Castleton
Castleton
Chaddesden
Chapel-en-le-frith S.
Chesterfield
Chesterfield
Clown
Denby
Dronfield
Dronfield
Dronfield
Duffield
Duffield D.
Eckington
Eckington
Eckington
Eyam
Glossop
Glossop S.
Glossop
Hartington
Hathersage
Hathersage S.
Hathersage
Hault Hucknall
Hope
Hope

Co. of Derby

Killamarsh
Kniveton
Langley
Melbourne S.
Mickleover
Morley
Mugginton
Quarndon
Radbourn S.
Spondon
Staveley
Sutton-on-the-Hill
Ticknall S.
Walton-upon-Trent
North Wingfield
Youlegreave
Youlegreave

Co. of Devon

Ashburton
Axminster S.
Barnstaple S.
Bishopsteignton S.
Bovey Tracey
Branton S.
Brixham
Broadhembury
Buckland Monachorum
Clist St George
Comb Martin
Crediton S.
Crediton
Exeter S.
Exeter S.D.
Malborough
Modbury S.
South Molton S.
Moreton Hampstead
Plymouth S.
Plymouth H.
Plymouth S.
Plymstock
St Budeaux S.
Silverton
Tamerton Foliott
North Tawton S.
Thorverton S.

Co. of Devon

Tiverton S.
Great Torrington S.
Totnes S.
Walkhampton
Whitstone
Widworthy
Witheridge
Wolborough D.

Co. of Dorset

Abbotsbury
Bere Regis
Blandford
Bradford Abbas
Bradford Abbas, with
 Clifton Maybank
Bridport
Corfe Mullen
Dorchester S.
Evershot
Frampton
Iwerne Courtney
Melbury Osmond
Piddle Trenthyde
Poole
Shaftesbury
Sherborne
Sherborne
Spettisbury
Stower Provost S.
Sturminster
Sydling St Nicholas
Toller Porcorum

Co. of Durham

St Andrew, Auckland D.
St Helen, Auckland S.
Bishop Middleham S.
Chester-le-Street
Darlington S.
Easington D.
Easington
Gainford
Hart
Haughton-le-Skerne S.
Haughton-le-Skerne S.
Houghton-le-Spring S.

Co. of Durham

Houghton-le-Spring
Hurworth S.
Jarrow
Lanchester S.
Middleton St George
Middleton in Teesdale
Middleton in Teesdale
Middleton in Teesdale
Norham
Staindrop
Staindrop
Great Stainton
Stanhope
Stanhope
Stanhope
Stockton S.
Stranton
Sunderland D.
Sunderland
Whickham S.
Winston
Witton Gilbert

Co. of Essex

Great Baddow
Little Baddow
Great Bardfield
Little Bardfield
Boreham
Bradwell-juxta-Mare
Chelmsford S.
Colchester S.
Great Easton
Great Easton
West Ham
Harwich
Havering-atte-Bower
Maldon
Netteswell
Orsett
Prittlewell
Purleigh
Rettendon
Romford
Roothing Margaret
Roydon
Saffron Walden S.

Co. of Essex

Springfield D.
Stanford-le-Hope
Stapleford Abbots
Wethersfield
Wethersfield
Writtle

Co. of Gloucester

City of Gloucester
Ampney Crucis
Arlingham
Great Badminton
Berkley
Bisley
Bourton-on-the-Hill S.
Bourton-on-the-Water
Buckland
Cam
Cheltenham S.
Chipping Campden S.
Chipping Campden
Churchdown
Cirencester S.
Dirham
Dursley D.
Dymock S.
Eastington S.
Fairford
Henbury
Horsley
Kempsford S.
Marshfield
Minchinhampton
Minchinhampton D.
Minchinhampton
Minsterworth
Mitchel-Dean S.
North Nibley
Painswick S.
Pebworth
Pucklechurch
Randwick S.
Stapleton
Stonehouse S.
Tetbury
Tewkesbury S.
Thornbury

356 APPENDIX I

Co. of Gloucester

Weston-upon-Avon
Wotton-under-Edge S.

Co. of Hereford

Bishop's Froome
Brampton Brian
Bredwardine
Breinton
Burghill
Dilwyn S.
Dore or Abbey Dore
Fownhope S.
Huntington
Kentchurch
King's Caple S.
Kinnersley S.
Ledbury
Leinthall Starks
Letton
Michael-Church-Eskley
Norton Canon
Pembridge
Ross S.
Upper Sapey
Stanton-upon-Wye
Stretton Grandsom S.
Upton Bishop
Weobley

Co. of Hertford

Aspeden
Barnet, Chipping S.
Berkhamstead S.
Much Hadham
Hertford S.
Hitchin S.D.
Hitchin S.
Pelham
Rickmersworth S.
Standon
Tewin
Watford
Welwyn S.

Co. of Huntingdon

Bluntisham, with Earith S.
Buckden

Co. of Huntingdon

Elton S.
Fenstanton
Holme
Huntingdon S.
Pidley S.
Ramsey
St Neots S.
Somersham
Great Staughton
Woodstone
Yaxley

Co. of Kent

Canterbury H.
Ash-by-Sandwich
Ash-by-Wrotham S.
Aylesford
Birchington
Charing
Charlton
Chilham
Chislehurst
Chislehurst
Cray, St Mary
Dartford S.
Deptford, St Paul S.
Dover, St Mary S.
Elham
Feversham
Gravesend
Greenwich
Greenwich H.
Greenwich S.H.
High Halden
Hardres-cum-Stelling
Harrietsham
Hawkhurst
Hothfield
Maidstone
Maidstone S.
Marden
Milton-next-Sittingbourne
Rochester
Rochester S.
Rochester
Rochester
Rolvenden

Co. of Kent

Sandwich S.
Smarden
Strood
Tonbridge S.
Tonbridge (South-
borough)
East Wickham S.
Woolwich
Wye
Yalding

**Co. Palatine of
Lancaster**

Aldingham
Ashton-under-Lyne
Ashton-under-Lyne
Blackburn S.
Blackburn
Blackburn
Bolton le Moors
Bolton le Moors S.
Bolton le Moors
Bolton le Moors
Bolton le Moors
Bolton le Moors
Bolton le Moors H.
Bolton le Moors S.
Bolton le Sands
Bury
Bury
Bury
Bury
Childwall
Childwall
Chipping
Cockerham
Croston
Dean
Dean
Eccles
Eccles S.
Eccles
Garstang
Garstang
Garstang
Garstang
Halshall

Co. Palatine of
Lancaster

Halton-with-Aughton
Hawkshead S.H.
Hawkshead
Hoole
Huyton
Kirkham
Kirkham
Kirkham H.
Kirkham
Kirkham
Lancaster
Lancaster
Lancaster
Lancaster
Lancaster
Lancaster
Leigh
Leyland
Leyland
Leyland
Leyland
Leyland
Leyland
Liverpool
Lytham
Manchester
Manchester S.
Manchester S.
Manchester S.
Manchester S.
Manchester S.
Melling
Middleton
Oldham S.
Ormskirk S.
Ormskirk
Ormskirk
Ormskirk
Penworthan
Penworthan
Poulton
Poulton
Prescot S.
Preston
Prestwich
Prestwich
Rochdale D.
Rochdale

Co. Palatine of
Lancaster

Rochdale
Rochdale
Rochdale
Rochdale
Rochdale S.
St Michael-upon-Wyre
Sephton
Standish
Ulverston
Ulverston
Ulverston S.
Urswick
Walton
Walton
Warrington H.
Whalley
Whalley
Whalley
Whalley
Whittington
Wigan
Wigan
Wigan S.
Winwick
Winwick
Winwick

Co. of Leicester

Ashby-de-la-Zouch S.
Ashby-de-la-Zouch
Barrow-upon-Soar
Barwell
Bottesford
Breedon S.
Long Clawson
Claybrook S.
Coleorton
Diseworth S.
Easton Magna
Enderby
Hinckley
Kimcote
Kirkby Mallory
Langton S.
Leicester
Lutterworth S.

Co. of Leicester

Medbourne
Newbold Verdun
Thornton
Thurcaston

Co. of Lincoln

Lincoln H.
Lincoln
Aisterby S.
Alford
Bardney
Barkstone S.
Barton
Benington
Boston
Boston S.
Burton Coggles S.
Great Carlton
Cowbit
Cranwell
Crowle
Digby
Eagle
Epworth S.
Fleet
Folkingham
Freiston
Frodingham
Hagworthingham S.
Haxey
Hemingby
Holbeach
Horncastle
Kirkby-on-Bain
East Kirkby
Laceby
Lavington
Maltby-le-Marsh
Marston
Morton-cum-Hanthorpe
Morton
Newton
Owston
Great Ponton
Quadring
Middle-Rasen
Ropsley

CO. OF LINCOLN

Ruskington
Saleby
Scawby
Sedgbrook
Sibsey
Sleaford
Spalding S.
Spilsby S.
Stamford S.
Surfleet
Sutton St Mary S.
Swineshead
Syston
Timberland
Tydd St Mary
Ulceby
Waddingham
Washingborough-cum-
Heighington
Welby
Whaplode
Wigtoft
Wooton
Wroot

CITY OF LONDON

All Hallows, Bread Street
S.
All Hallows, London Wall
S.
Christ Church, Newgate
Street S.
St Alphage S.
St Andrew, Holborn S.H.
St Anne, Blackfriars
St Anne and St Agnes,
Aldersgate S.H.
St Bartholomew the Great
S.
St Bartholomew the Great
S.D.
St Botolph, Aldersgate S.
St Botolph, Aldgate S.
St Botolph, Aldgate
St Botolph, Aldgate S.H.
St Botolph, Billingsgate S.
St Botolph, Bishopsgate S.

CITY OF LONDON

St Botolph, Bishopsgate S.
St Bride, Dorset Street
St Bride S.
St Dunstan-in-the-East S.
St Dunstan-in-the-West S.
St Ethelburga, Bishopsgate
S.
St Giles, Cripplegate S.
St Giles, Cripplegate S.
St James, Garlick Hithe S.
St Mary Magdalen, Old
Fish Street
St Michael, Crooked Lane
S.
St Nicholas Cole Abbey S.
St Peter, Cornhill S.
St Sepulchre Within, New-
gate
St Sepulchre Within, New-
gate S.
St Sepulchre Within, New-
gate S.H.
St Stephen, Coleman Street
S.

CITY OF WESTMINSTER

St Ann, Soho
St Clement Danes S.H.
St George, Hanover Square
St James
St James S.H.
St James
St Margaret S.
St Margaret S.H.
St Martin-in-the-Fields
S.H.
St Mary-le-Strand S.
St Paul, Covent Garden
S.H.

CO. OF MIDDLESEX

All Saints, Poplar and
Blackwall S.
Chiswick S.H.
Christ Church, Spitalfields
S.
Clerkenwell S.

CO. OF MIDDLESEX

Clerkenwell S.
Ealing S.
Ealing S.
Fulham S.
Fulham S.
Great Greenford
Hackney S.
Hackney S.
Hanwell S.
Hayes D.
Hornsey S.
Isleworth S.
Islington S.
Littleton S.
Stoke Newington S.
Norton Folgate S.
St Anne, Limehouse S.
St Katherine near the Tower
S.
St Dunstan, Stepney S.
St Dunstan, Stepney S.
St Dunstan, Stepney S.
St Dunstan, Stepney S.
St Dunstan, Stepney H.
St George-in-the-East S.H.
St George the Martyr S.
St Giles and St George,
Bloomsbury S.
St John, Wapping S.
St Leonard, Shoreditch S.
St Leonard, Shoreditch S.
St Luke, City Road S.D.H.
St Luke in Golden Lane S.
St Mary, Stratford, Bow
St Mary, Whitechapel S.
St Matthew, Bethnal Green
St Matthew, Bethnal Green
S.
St Paul, Shadwell S.
St Paul, Shadwell S.D.
St Paul, Shadwell S.
St Sepulchre S.
St Sepulchre S.
Sunbury
Tottenham S.
Tottenham S.
Twickenham S.

Co. of Norfolk

Norwich D.
Norwich S.D.
Bawdeswell
Blofield
Bressingham
Coltishall
Colton S.
Happisburgh S.
Hevingham
Mileham
Northwold
Ormesby, St Margaret S.
Redenhall-with-Harleston
Ringland
Shipdham
Swaffham S.
Terrington, St Clement S.
Thorpe-next-Norwich
Walpole, St Andrew and
  St Peter
West Walton
Great Yarmouth D.

Co. of Northampton

Arthingworth
Cold Ashby
Long Buckby S.
Chelveston-cum-Caldecott
Cottingham
Culworth S.
Daventry S.
Dodford
Finedon H.
Glinton and Peakirk
Green's Norton S.
Harpole
Irthlingborough S.
Kettering S.
Kingscliffe
Lamport-with-Faxton
Lowick
Mears Ashby S.
Northampton S.
Northampton
Northampton
Oundle
Oundle

Co. of Northampton

Paulerspury
Peterborough
Preston Capes S.
Staverton
Sulgrave S.
Thornhaugh
Warmington S.
Watford
Weedon Beck
Welford
Wellingborough S.
Weston Favell
Whilton
Whittlebury S.
Yelvertoft S.

Co. of Northumberland

Newcastle-on-Tyne S.
Newcastle-on-Tyne S.
Newcastle-on-Tyne S.
Newcastle-on-Tyne S.
Newcastle-on-Tyne S.
Bellingham
Bothal
Corbridge
Embleton
Haltwhistle
Howick
Lesbury
Newburn
Ponteland
Rothbury
St Johnlee
Shilbottle S.
Shotley
Slaley
Stannington
Berwick-upon-Tweed S.

Co. of Nottingham

Nottingham S.
Balderton
Beckingham
Bunny-with-Bradmore
Calverton
Clayworth
North Collingham D.

Co. of Nottingham

Edingley
Edwinstowe
Farnsfield
Flintham
Greasley
Harworth
East Leke
Mansfield S.
Mansfield
East Markham
Misson
North Muskham
Normanton-on-Trent
Norwell
Oxton S.
West Retford
South Scarle
Sutton-on-Lound
Weston
Wilford
Winckbourn
Woodborough

Co. of Oxford

Albury
Asthall
March Baldon
Banbury S.
Bicester S.
Bladon
Ensham
Goring
Great Haseley
Henley-on-Thames
Islip
North Leigh
Oxford S.
Oxford
Sarsden
Standlake
Stanton St John
South Stoke
Swinbrook
Great Tew
Thame
Witney
Wootton

CO. OF RUTLAND

Belton
Glayston
Lyddington

CO. OF SALOP

Baschurch
Bishop's Castle S.
Cardington
Cheswardine
Church Stretton S.
Claverley
Cleobury Mortimer
Cleobury Mortimer
Clunbury S.
Ellesmere
Hopesay
Llanyblodwell
Middle
Great Ness
Prees S.
Preston-upon-the-Wild-
  Moors H.
St Martin
Selattyn
Shiffnall
Shrewsbury
Shrewsbury S.
Shrewsbury
Stanton
Stoke St Milborough S.
Tong
Upton Magna
Much Wenlock
Wentnor
Westbury
Whitchurch D.
Whittington

CO. OF SOMERSET A

City of Bristol

Queen Elizabeth's Hospital
  H.
Colston's Hospital H.
Colston's School
Charity School for Girls
  S.

CO. OF SOMERSET A

City of Bristol

Dissenters' School D.
Wesleyan Methodists D.
St Leonard
St Mary Redcliff
St Michael
St Michael and St Augus-
  tine S.
St Nicholas S.

CO. OF SOMERSET B

Babington
Banwell S.
Bridgewater
Queen Charlton S.
Cheddon Fitzpaine S.
Chewstoke S.
Chewton Mendip
Chewton Mendip
Crewkerne
Crowcombe
Cutcombe
Dulverton
Frome S.
Frome H.
Higham
Kilmersdon S.
Lovington
Milverton
Midsomer Norton
North Petherton
Norton St Philip
South Petherton S.
Shepton Beauchamp
Timberscombe
Trull
Wellow
Wells S.
Winscombe S.

CO. OF SOUTHAMPTON

Andover
Andover
Brockenhurst S.
Broughton
Burghclere S
Dummer

CO. OF SOUTHAMPTON

Knight's Enham S.
Fareham
Froxfield
Headley
Hinton Ampner
Lyndhurst
Odiham
Petersfield H.
Preston Candover
Romsey
Rotherwick S.
Sherfield-upon-Loddon
Southampton
Stratfieldsaye
East Tisted
East Titherley
Twyford
Winchester

ISLE OF WIGHT

Chayle
Freshwater
Gatcombe
New Church
Newport S.H.
Niton

CO. OF STAFFORD

Aldridge
Alstonefield S.
Alstonefield
Audley
Betley
Biddulph S.
Blithfield
Bobbington
King's Bromley
Burslem S.
Burton-upon-Trent
Cannock
Castle Church
Cheddleton
Clent
Colton S.
Dilhorne
Envil H.
Grindon

Co. of Stafford

Hanbury
Hanbury S.
Harborne S.
Harborne
Ipstones S.
Kingsley
Leek
Lichfield
Lichfield
Newcastle-under-Lyme
Norton-under-Cannock
Pattingham
Penkridge S.
Penn
Rowley Regis
Rowley Regis S.
Rugeley
Sedgeley D.
Stoke-upon-Trent
Stoke-upon-Trent
Stoke-upon-Trent
Stone S.
Stone
Tamworth
Tipton S.
Tutbury
Waterfall S.D.
Whillington
Wolverhampton
Yoxall

Co. of Suffolk

Ampton
Benhall S.
Blundeston
Bramfield
Coddenham
Hacheston
Hadleigh
Halesworth
Hintlesham
Holton St Mary S.
Horningsheath
Hoxne
Hundon
Laxfield
Newmarket

Co. of Suffolk

Rougham
Sibton
Stradbrooke
Sudbury
Whepstead

Co. of Surrey

Battersea S.
Bermondsey S.
Bermondsey
Camberwell
Chertsey
Chipstead
Christchurch S.
Croydon
Egham
Esher
Godstone
Guildford S.
Lambeth
Lambeth S.
Lambeth S.
Leatherhead
Morden
Mortlake S.
Putney H.
Reigate
Richmond S.
Rotherhithe S.
Streatham
Wandsworth S.
Weybridge

Borough of Southwark

St Thomas S.D.
St Thomas S.

Co. of Sussex

Battle
Boxgrove
Brighthelmstone
Brighthelmstone S.
Brightling
Burwash S.
Chichester
Chichester S.
Chichester S.

Co. of Sussex

Guestling
Hartfield
Horsted Keynes
Mayfield S.
Newick
Northam
Petworth
Rotherfield
Rye
Sedlescomb
Storrington
Uckfield
Walberton

Co. of Warwick

Coventry D.
Coventry D.
Coventry
Coventry S.H.
Anstey
Foleshill
Allesley
Arley
Aston
Bedworth
Berkswell
Bilton S.
Birmingham H.S.
Budbrooke
Coleshill S.
Dunchurch
Farnborough
Fillongley
Fillongley
Frankton
Hampton-in-Arden
Hampton-in-Arden
Harbury
Hatton
Hillmorton
Kenilworth
Leek Wootton
Mancetter
Prior's Marston
Middleton
Middleton S.
Nuneaton

Co. of Warwick

Rugby
Shustock
Solihull
Southam
Stoneleigh
Stratford-upon-Avon
Studley
Bishop's Tachbrook
Warwick
Wellsbourn S.
Wishaw S.
Wootton Wawen

Co. of Westmoreland

Appleby
Barton
Barton
Kendal S.
Kendal
Kirkby Lonsdale S.
Kirkby Lonsdale S.
Kirkby Lonsdale S.
Kirkby Stephen S.
Kirkby Stephen
Kirkby Shore

Co. of Wiltshire

Amesbury
Avebury
Great Bedwin
Berwick Bassett
Bishopstone
Box S.
Bradford
Bradford
Bulford
Great Cheverell
Chilton Foliat
Chippenham
Cliffe Pypard
Devizes S.
Donhead St Andrew
Fisherton Anger
Fittleton
Fonthill Bishop
Highworth S.
Broad Hinton S.

Co. of Wiltshire

Little Hinton
Kingswood
Kington St Michael
Lyneham
Malmesbury
Pitton and Farley
Poulshot S.
Purton
Rodborne Cheney
Salisbury
Steeple Ashton
Swindon S.
Trowbridge
Upton Lovell
Whiteparish
Whiteparish
Wilton
Wishford
Wroughton S•

Co. of Worcester

Worcester
Abberley
Astley Abbots
Bellbroughton S.
Birts Morton
Blockley
Bredon D.
Chaseley
Cropthorne
Droitwich
Dudley S.
Dudley S.
Dudley S.D.
Evesham Borough
Grimley
Hanbury S.
Kempsey
Kidderminster S.
Kidderminster S.D.
Kidderminster
Kidderminster S.D.
Northfield
Ombersley S.
Rushock
St John-in-Bedwardine
Salwarpe

Co. of Worcester

Great Shelsley
Shipston-on-Stour
Stone
Strensham
Suckley
Old Swinford
Old Swinford S.
Old Swinford
Tredington
Upton-upon-Severn
Upton Warren
Warley Wigorn
Yardley

Co. of York

City of York

City of York
City of York

East Riding

Beverley S.H.
Bilton
Brandsburton
Catton
South Cave S.
Cottingham
Eastrington
Gate Fulford
Hemingborough
Hessle
Kingston-upon-Hull
Kingston-upon-Hull S.
Nether Poppleton
Riccall
Skipwith
Sproatley
Thorganby
Thorparch
Walkington
Market Weighton
Wheldrake

North Riding

Appleton-le-Street
Aysgarth
Aysgarth
Ayton

Co. of York

North Riding

Patrick Brompton
Easby H.
Glaisdale
Guisbrough S.
Hutton Bushel
Ingleby Greenhow
Levisham
Masham
Melsonby
Middleton
Normanby
Rudby
Skelton
Slingsby
Strensall
Westerdale

West Riding

Aberford
Ackworth
Aldmondbury
Armthorpe
Aston-cum-Aughton
Bardsey
Batley S.
Bentham
Bingley S.
Birstall
Birstall
Bolton-by-Bolland
Brayton
Carlton
Cawood H.
Clapham
Clapham
Clapham
Clapham
Collingham
Darton
Dewsbury S.
Dewsbury S.
Dewsbury S.

Co. of York

West Riding

Doncaster S.D.
Ecclesfield
Ecclesfield
Ecclesfield
Ecclesfield
Ecclesfield
Fewstone
Monk Fryston
Garforth
Giggleswick
Halifax
Halifax
Halifax
Halifax D.
Halifax
Hampsthwaite
Handsworth
Harewood
Hatfield
Huddersfield
Huddersfield
Keighley
Kirkburton
Kirkburton
Kirkby Malzeard
Kirkby Malzeard
Kirkby Overblow
Kirk Deighton
Knaresborough
Knaresborough
Leathley
Ledsham
Ledsham
Leeds S.H.
Leeds
Maltby
Church Marton
Mirfield
Mitton D.
Newton Ryme
Nun Monkton
Penistone

Co. of York

West Riding

Pontefract
Ripley
Ripley
Ripon
Ripon
Ripon
Ripon
Ripon
Rotherham S.
Rotherham
Royston
Royston
Sandal
Sedbergh
Selby
Selby S.
Sheffield
Sheffield
Sheffield
Sheffield
Sheffield
Sherburn
Silkstone
Silkstone
Skipton
Slaidburn
Snaith
Thorne
Thorner
Thornhill
Thornton-in-Lonsdale
Thrybergh
Wakefield
Wath-upon-Dearne
Wath-upon-Dearne
Wath-upon-Dearne
Whiston
Whitgift
Whitgift
Whitkirk
Wistow
Sherburn D.

4. *A list of the Charity Schools in England*
as returned in the *Account of Charity Schools* for 1724

The figures before and after the place-names show respectively the number of schools and the number of scholars. The geographical position of the places, and the spelling of the place-names given in the Report, have been retained.

BEDFORDSHIRE

Ampthill (26)
Arlesey (6)
Battlesden
St Paul's Bedford (40)
(2) Biggleswade (16)
Caddington (10)
Chalgrave Hochliff
Clifton
Cranfield (20)
Dean (20)
Dunstable
Flitton cum Silfo (23)
Hawnes (30)
Henlow (10)
Leighton Beaudefert (10)
(2) Malden
Metchburn (12)
Mepperfall (8)
Milbrooke
Milton Earneys
Norhill (20)
Sandy (20)
Southill (12)
Stretley (18)
Studham
Sutton (6)
Thurleigh (6)
Tuddington (7)
Wilden (5)
(2) Woburn (45)
Yelden

BERKSHIRE

(2) Abingdon (26)
Bingfield (6)
Blewbury (50)
Boreton (7)

BERKSHIRE

(4) Bray (61)
Buckland
Chadleworth
Childrey
Cholfey
Cleworth (16)
Colshill (12)
Commer and Wootton (27)
Compton
Cranburn (15)
Farringdon (30)
Hinton Parva
Hurst (14)
Longcott (24)
Maidenhead (19)
Newbury (40)
Pangbourne (12)
Peasmore
(2) Reading (48)
Shinfield (12)
Shotsbrook (6)
Shrevenham (30)
Sparholt (13)
Speen (30)
Sunninghill (13)
Sunning (12)
Sutton Courtney (12)
Thackham (26)
Uffington and Woolston (12)
Wallingford (12)
Wantage
Warfield (12)
Wargrave (47)
Watchfield (12)
Welford (30)
West Ifley (10)

BERKSHIRE

White Waltham (20)
(2) Windsor, New (70)
(5) Windsor, Old (36)
(2) Wingfield (40)

BUCKINGHAMSHIRE

Aston Clinton
Aston Sandford
(2) Aylesbury (120)
Beaconsfield (5)
Blechley (20)
Bow Brickhill
Great Brickhill (23)
Brill (23)
Chalfont St Peter (40)
Chesham (40)
Colnbrook (10)
Coblington
Denham (30)
(2) Gerard's Cross (35)
Grendon Underwood
Hambleden (40)
Great Hampden (6)
Hardwick (10)
Iver (24)
Ivingo (10)
Great Kimble (6)
St Leonard's (6)
Great Linford (20)
Great Marlow (30)
Medmenham (6)
Moulso
Newport Pagnel (40)
Quainton (20)
Stoke Goldington (6)
Stoke Hamond (20)
Stony Stratford (8)
Swanbourn (8)

BUCKINGHAMSHIRE

Waddesden
Wavendon (20)
Wendover
Westbury
Weston Turvil (12)
Wing (20)
Wingrave (8)
Wormenhall

CAMBRIDGESHIRE

Barrington
Brinkley
Borough Green
Burwell (40)
(12?) Cambridge (300)
Chippenham (8)
Croxton (15)
Elme and Elmesly
(2) Ely (60)
Fen Ditton
Fordham (30)
Fulbourn
Gamlingay (20)
Haddenham
Histon
Linton (20)
Little Gransden (10)
Horseheath
Kennet (6)
Soham (100)
(2) Wisbeach (140)

CHESHIRE

(2) Chester (66)
Darnhall
Holm's Chapel (10)
Little Budworth
(2) Namptwich (70)
Northwich (10)
(2) Stockport (14)
Whitegate
(2) Wybunbury (10)

CORNWALL

(2) St Colomb (20)
Grampond
(2) Lanceston (16)

CORNWALL

Liskard
Looe
Morvel
Penzance
Polperra
Saltash

CUMBERLAND

Carlisle (20)
Croglin
Kirk Andrews upon
    Eske (60)
Longtown (60)
(2) Penrith (50)

DERBYSHIRE

Barlborough (4)
Darly (20)
Derby in Parish of St
    Alkmund (20)
St Werburgh (20)
Etwal (6)
Hiedge
Kirk Ireton (16)
Matlock (8)
Melbourn (18)
Risley (25)
Smalley (16)
(2) Spondon (60)
Sutton on the Hill
Swarkston (14)
Ticknel (30)
Whilwell (38)
Winster (30)

DEVONSHIRE

(2) Barnstaple (80)
Brixham
(3) Buckland Monachorum
    (18)
South Buddocks (20)
Chudleigh
Crediton (40)
Clyst-Heydon (18)
Dodbrook
Exminster (12)
(4) Exon (200)

DEVONSHIRE

Gittisham (20)
Heanton (14)
Honiton (30)
Paignton
(5) Plimouth (128)
Plimouth (30)
(2) Plymstock (29)
Rockbeare (9)
Sidbury (12)
South Moulton (30)
Stoke Gabriel (16)
(2) Tiverton (110)
Topsham (40)
Torrington (32)
Trusham (6)
Walkhampton (20)

DORSET

Beaminster (20)
Beere Regis
Catsloke (12)
Corsmullen
Dorchester (6)
Litchet (9)
Maiden Newton (10)
Pool (20)
Sherbourne (10)
Spetsbury
Charlton
Stalbridge
Yetminster (20)

DURHAM

City of Durham
Darlington (23)
Gateshead
Houghton le Spring
    (20)
Swalwell (30)
Whickham (60)
Winlaton (40)
Winlaton Mill (30)

ESSEX

Bradfield (20)
Brentwood (6)
(2) Chelmsford (61)

ESSEX

Chigwell (10)
(2) Chipin-Ongarp (38)
(3) Colchester (150)
Dedham (40)
Frierling (10)
Great Birch
Great Oakley
Halstead (30)
Heydon
Ingatiston (10)
Langford (7)
Low Leyton and Walt-
  sham (17)
Malden (6)
(2) Rumford (70)
Saffron Walden (32)
South Okenden (14)
Stansted Mount (10)
Fichet
Tilbury Fort (8)
(2) Withersfield (40)
Wivenhoe (15)
Woodham Water
Writtle (10)

GLOUCESTERSHIRE

Almondsbury
Ampney Crucis (30)
Badminton
Berkley (20)
(9) Bisly (136)
Bourton on the Waters
Breem (23)
Cam (20)
(2) Campden (54)
Cheltenham (25)
(2) Cirencester (100)
Cleve (40)
Deerhurst
Doynton
Dumbleton
Gloucester City (70)
Huntley
Kempley (12)
Laberton (20)
Leonard Stanley
Marshfield (24)

GLOUCESTERSHIRE

Michell Dean (25)
Mincing Hampton (9)
Naunton (11)
Newent (20)
(2) Oxenhall (20)
Painswick (11)
Prestbury
Puckle-Church
Randwick (8)
Rodborough (20)
Sandhurst (20)
Stanton
Staverton (26)
Starton
Stonehouse (12)
Stroud (60)
In the Neighbourhood
  of Stroud (34)
Tainton (14)
Tewksbury (30)
(2) Westerleigh (20)
Weston Birt (10)
Wick
Woodchester
Wotton under Edge
  (60)

HAMPSHIRE

(2) Alton (60)
Amport (30)
(2) Andover (44)
(3) Basingstoke (56)
Bishop's Waltham (12)
Broughton
Chilbolton (24)
Chiddensden
Corhampton (8)
Drummer

Isle of Wight

Caresbrook (12)
Freshwater (14)
Gatcomb
Godshill
Shorewell (7)
Milbrook (6)
Odiam (30)

HAMPSHIRE

Overwallop
Rumsey (20)
(3) Selbourn (46)
Sherbourne
West Sherbourne (24)
Silchester (5)
Soberton and Meon (24)
Southampton (40)
South Stonham (26)
Southwick (24)
Tichfield (12)
(3) Winchester (105)
Wounston (12)

HEREFORDSHIRE

Aymstry
Brampt Bryan (50)
Dower
Hampton Court (12)
(2) Hereford (100)
Hentland
Kingsland (15)
(2) Kington (26)
Laisters
Ledbury (24)
Leominster
Linton (8)
Little Laintol
Long Laintol
Lucton (100)
Much Marcle (20)
Pyon Regis (17)
Richard Castle (18)
(2) Ross Castle (50)
Titley (12)
(2) Weobly (43)
(2) Weston under Penyard
  (20)
Withington (20)
Yarpol (12)

HERTFORDSHIRE

St Albans (40)
Albury (12)
Aldenham (60)
Aspenden (12)
Ashwel (24)

HERTFORDSHIRE

Aston (6)
Barkway (40)
Berkhamstead
Braughin (12)
Buntingford (28)
Cheshunt (30)
Datchworth (6)
(2) Hatfield (40)
(4) Hertford (95)
Hitchin (30)
Kimpton
North Mims (26)
Ofley (20)
(2) Rickmersworth (30)
Sabridgeworth (36)
Shephall (20)
Stevenage (25)
Tewing (4)
(2) Therfield (30)
Tring (20)
Ware (10)
Watford (40)
Wotton (20)
Welwin (4)
Westmill (4)

HUNTINGDONSHIRE

Abbot Ripton
Bluntsham cum Erith (20)
Buckden (34)
Catworth (6)
Croxton (20)
Farcet (20)
Fenny Stanton cum Hilton (6)
Folkesworth (4)
Glatton (12)
Godmanster (30)
Graffarn
Great Gidding (4)
Hamarton (10)
Holme in Glatton (12)
Holywell (15)
Huntingdon (12)
St Neots (25)
Pidley

HUNTINGDONSHIRE

Ramsey
Somersham (30)
Stilton (14)
Great Stoughton (15)
Thurning (6)
Warefly (6)

KENT

Adisham
Ash (20)
Ashford (20)
Ailesford (20)
Barham (16)
Brastead (28)
(3) Canterbury (124)
Chelsford
Chevening (30)
Cowdham (12)
Deal (27)
Doddington
(3) Dover (160)
(2) Ethham (30)
Feversham (20)
Folkestone (20)
Grain
Gravesend (24)
Hemingford Grey (5)
Hyth (33)
Keiston (4)
Lidd (40)
Loose (26)
(4) Maidstone (100)
(3) St Mary Cray (36)
Newnham
(2) Sandwich (50)
Sevenoaks (15)
Shoreham (25)
Sittingbourne (8)
Staple
Stroude (25)
Sundrich (26)

Isle of Thanet

Birchington (12)
St John Baptist (20)
(2) Minster (28)
St Nicholas (8)
St Peter (20)

KENT

Throwleigh and Sheldwich (16)
Tunbridge Wells (70)
Wickhambreux (10)
Wingham (20)
Witresham
Wye (30)

LANCASHIRE

Aughton in Halton
Great Bolton (30)
(2) Castleton (12)
Fulwood
Liverpool (50)
Littleborough in Rochdale (10)
(2) Manchester (80)
Newton (10)
Overkellet in Bolton Parish
(2) Preston (50)
Ratcliffe Bridge (12)
Rossendale (10)
Stalmyn
Todmordin (6)
Whalley
Warrington (24)

LEICESTERSHIRE

Appleby (100)
Ashby de la Zouche (24)
Little Ashby
Barrow (6)
Barkly (10)
Blaby
Bringhurst
Church Langton (12)
Cole Orton
Cotesbach
Congeston (12)
Croxton Kyrier (6)
Diseworth (6)
Freaby (16)
Garthorpe (10)
Great Gaston in the Parish of Bringhurst (6)

LEICESTERSHIRE

Hallaton (26)
Hinkley Stoke
Goldington
Husbands Bosworth
  (30)
Ibstock
North Kilworth (6)
South Kilworth
(2) St Margaret's Leicester
  (50)
Lockington (20)
Loddington (15)
Loughborough (20)
Rothely (12)
Sileby (14)
Stony Stanton (14)
Swineford
Thruffington (15)
Thurcaston (12)
Waltham on the Wolds
Wimondham (37)
Withcock

LINCOLNSHIRE

Asserby (50)
Barnoldby (7)
Barrowby (12)
Barlinges
Barnach (16)
Bennington (12)
Billingborough (16)
Billingshay
Bilsby (10)
Binbrook St Gabriel
(3) Boston (125)
Brent Broughton
Bucknal (12)
Burgh
Burton Coggles (14)
Great Carleton (25)
Carleton Mereland (3)
Church Hickam (16)
Croft (30)
Crowle (20)
Denton (30)
Digby (3)
Dowsby

LINCOLNSHIRE

Edenham (25)
Epworth (6)
Eresby (40)
Foldingworth
Fillingham (20)
Folkingham (14)
Glentworth
Gosberton (10)
Grantham
Gretford cum Wils-
  thorpe
Haconby
Great Hale
Hannestone
Hanworth
Harmston
Hatcliffe
Hatton
Holton cum Beckering
  (10)
(2) Horbling (20)
Ingham (10)
Kelsey St Mary (10)
Kilby (4)
(3) Lincoln (120)
Louth (40)
Ludborough (12)
Maltby
Marsh Chappel (4)
Marston (15)
Netlam (12)
Nocton
North Coates
North Somercoates
Owersby (12)
Rathby (20)
Rippingale (24)
Ruskinton (20)
Scawby (20)
Sedgebrook (15)
Sifton (6)
Shellingthorp (25)
Spalding (24)
(2) Spilsby (40)
Stallinburgh (4)
Stamford (42)
Stickney (30)

LINCOLNSHIRE

Stow (20)
Surfleet (20)
Thorpe
Trusthope
Utterby (3)
Waddingham (16)
Waddington (20)
Washingburgh (10)
Wibberton (20)
Wilsford (4)
Witham-on-the-Hill
Wooton
Wrangle
Wrawby
Wroot (20)

MIDDLESEX

(2) Bedfont (18)
Brentford (30)
Chiswick (30)
Craneford (20)
(2) Ealing (20)
Finchley (15)
(2) Fulham (36)
(2) Hammersmith (39)
Harefield (20)
Harlington (30)
(2) Hendon (30)
Highgate (24)
Houndsloe (12)
Shepperton
Stanes (25)
(2) Stanwell (45)
Teddington (26)
(2) Thistleworth (80)
Tottenham (22)
Twickenham (50)
Whitchurch (30)

NORFOLK

Attleborough
Bremerton (30)
Brigham
Castlerising (12)
Denton (50)
Diss (20)
Easterling

NORFOLK

Eaton-by-Norwich
  (32)
Hetherset
(8) Norwich (240)
(4) Norwich (160)
Northwold
(2) Shottesham (55)
Stoe Beedle and Cason
Terrington-in-Marsh-
  land (20)
Thorp (10)
Weeting
Wyndham (30)
(2) Yarmouth (80)

NORTHAMPTONSHIRE

Achurch
Addington
Aino
Alwinkle (9)
Artleborough, alias
  Irthillingborough(60)
Ashton near Oundle
  (30)
Barnwell (15)
Brigstock (30)
Great Brington (30)
Castle Ashby (12)
Creke
Dainton (50)
Daventree (8)
Disworth (20)
Findon (20)
Geddington (20)
Greens Norton (20)
Harringworth
Helmdon (10)
Hemington and Lud-
  dington (10)
Luffwick
Little Houghton
(2) Kettering (34)
Northampton (40)
Norton (14)
(2) Oundle (42)
Peterborough (10)
Pilton (5)

NORTHAMPTONSHIRE

Polebrook (4)
Preston (20)
Rance
Rockingham (12)
Scaldwell
Syresham (6)
Soulgrave
Stow
Walgrave (20)
Weekly and Warkton
  (10)
Wellingbro (26)
Weston Favil
Whiston (12)
Whitfield (8)
Woodford (6)
Yelverton (16)

NORTHUMBERLAND

Benwell (70)
Berwick (60)
Embleton
(6) Newcastle-on-Tyne
  (220)
Rothbury

NOTTINGHAMSHIRE

Annesley (14)
Best-Thorp
Bingham (30)
East Bridgford (10)
East Markham (20)
Finningly
Gonalston
Harworth
Harringworth
Hartshorn
Mansfield (36)
Newark (36)
North Collingham
(3) Nottingham (78)
Westhallom

OXFORDSHIRE

Bampton-in-the-Bush
  (20)
(2) Banbury (50)

OXFORDSHIRE

Blocksom
Bisceter (30)
Brize Norton (20)
Cuddesden (12)
Deddington (32)
Great Hasely (14)
Henly-upon-Thames
  (20)
Islip (21)
Kirtlington (30)
Middleton Stony (4)
Mixbury
(4) Oxford (160)
Shiplake (5)
(2) Whitchurch (20)
Witney (10)

RUTLANDSHIRE

Empingham
Exton
Greetham (20)
Langham
Oakham (24)
Thistleton

SHROPSHIRE

Bishops Castle (14)
Cherbury (6)
Farlow (8)
Ledbury North
(2) Ludlow (80)
(2) Mainston (20)
Newport
Norton (6)
Oswestry (40)
Shifnal (6)
(4) Shrewsbury (120)
In the Suburbs of
  Shrewsbury (30)
Sylvington
Wem (40)

SOMERSETSHIRE

(2) Bath (100)
Bath Easton (10)
(4) Bristol (390)
Brushford

SOMERSETSHIRE

Chewstoke (20)
Crookhom
Cutcombe
Exford
Farmborough (15)
Froom
Kainsham (20)
Keinton
Kilmersdon (40)
Luxborough
Mells (20)
Midsummer Norton (42)
Newton St Loe
North Peterton (20)
Porlock (15)
Stanton-drew (15)
Spaxton (15)
Trent (20)
Wellow
(2) Wells (40)
Wrington
Yeovil (30)

STAFFORDSHIRE

Bilston (10)
Brewood
Cheadle
(2) Eccleshall (40)
Grindon
(2) Lichfield (48)
Rowley Regis (20)
Stoke-upon-Trent (40)
Stone (40)
(3) Wolverhampton (120)

SUFFOLK

Beures St Maries (30)
Boxford (20)
Great Bradley (24)
(3) Bury St Edmunds (90)
Balham (20)
Dunwich
Eye (30)
Freckenham (10)
Gazeley
(2) Glemsford (40)

SUFFOLK

Halesworth (20)
Hartest and Somerton West (40)
Haverhill (7)
Horringer
(3) Ipswich (110)
Lidgate
Martlesham (6)
Market Weston
Nacton (6)
(2) New-Market (40)
(2) Neyland (60)
Owsden (15)
Parham-Hacheston (12)
Rusham
Stowmarket (20)
Stradbrook (20)
Sylham (10)
Tuddenham (6)
Wickambrook (30)
Wingfield (34)
Witnesham (10)

SURREY

(2) Beddington (30)
Great Buckham (8)
Cobham
Croydon (20)
East Horley (50)
Egham (50)
Epsom (40)
Ewhurst
Farnham
Godalming (50)
Guildford (50)
Horne
Kingston (30)
Leatherhead (21)
Mortlake (34)
(2) Richmond (100)
Rygate
Stretham (12)
Sutton (10)
(2) Walton (40)
Wandsworth (40)
(2) Wimbledon (50)
Wonersh (10)

SUSSEX

Battel (40)
(2) Brighthelmeston (70)
Bucksted (10)
(2) Chichester (60)
Ditchling (20)
(2) Hastings (200)
Horsham
Horstead Keynes (20)
Lewes (28)
Plumpton
Ringmer (18)
Rye (30)
Seaworth (12)
Streat
Waldron
Westmeston-cum-Chiltington
West Terring (12)

WARWICKSHIRE

Alcester
Atherstone (20)
Atterbury
Ausley
Badgely
Bagington
Baxterly (16)
(2) Bedworth (60)
Berkenwell (50)
Birmingham (60)
Castlebromwich
Chaldecot
(2) Colesholl (21)
Coventry (12)
Dunchurch (12)
Dunchurch
Hampton-in-Arden
Kingsbury (10)
Lea Marston (10)
Mancester
Middleton (10)
Polesworth (20)
(2) Rugby (30)
Sheldon (50)
Solihull
Southam (20)
Temple (20)

WARWICKSHIRE
Tisoe
Walter Orton (10)
(3) Warwick (104)
Wasperton

WESTMORLAND
Kendall (26)

WILTSHIRE
Ambresbury (30)
Bishopston (4)
Box (30)
Bradford (60)
Broadhinton (18)
Calne (40)
Calston (16)
Chippenham (24)
Cholderton
Clevepepper
Deverelhongbridge (30)
(2) Devizes (86)
Hacklestone
Hannington
Highworth (50)
Hullavington (20)
Little Hinton (4)
Littletondrue (7)
Market Lavington (36)
Marlborough (44)
Nettleton (24)
Potterne (50)
Ramsbury
(3) Salisbury (120)
Salthrop
Seend (24)
Southmarston
Westkinton (10)

WILTSHIRE
Wooton Basset
Wroughton (30)

WORCESTERSHIRE
Alvechurch (20)
Bingworth (30)
Bortsmorton
(2) Blockly (60)
Broadway
Bromsgrove (12)
(2) Dudley (70)
Elmbridge (30)
Evesham
Feckenham (12)
Fladbury (20)
Hadzor (30)
Hartlebury (38)
(3) Kidderminster (60)
Leigh
Madresfield
Mitton
Northfield (20)
Ombersley
Riple (20)
Salwarpe (10)
Spetchly
Stourbridge (60)
(3) Old Swinford (66)
Upton-upon-Severn (16)
(2) Worcester (80)
Yardley (10)

YORKSHIRE
Addle (25)
Askew (8)
Bedel
Beverly (40)
Carleton (8)

YORKSHIRE
Cleasby
Copgrave (3)
Crostone (12)
(2) Doncaster (56)
Eland (20)
Greasbrook (15)
(2) Hawnby (8)
Hoton Roberts (22)
Great Houghton
Hoyland (24)
Hunsinger (12)
Hutton Wanesley, alias
    Long Marston (20)
Keighley (40)
Kingston-on-Hull (65)
Kirkdeighton
Kirkleatham in Cleave-
    land (50)
Kirkby Overblow
(2) Leeds (100)
Marston (20)
Nunmounton
Pontefract (36)
Reavey
Ripley
Rotherham (42)
Selby
(2) Sheffield (50)
Silsden
Skern
(2) Skipton (55)
Skipworth
Slaidburn
Spofforth (40)
Wakefield (63)
Wath (15)
Wentworth (50)
Wetherby (5)
(2) York (80)

5. *A list of the Subscription Charity Schools in and about London and Westminster,*

as returned in the *Account of Charity Schools* for 1799

The figures before and after the place-names show respectively the number of schools, normally one for boys and one for girls, and the number of scholars.

(2) Aldgate Ward Within (40)
(2) St Alphage (25)
(2) St Andrew, Holborn (151)
   In the Same Parish, Navigation School (40)
(2) St Anne, Aldersgate (103)
(2) Aldersgate Ward (60)
(2) St Anne, Blackfriars (103)
(2) St Anne, Soho (140)
(2) St Anne, Limehouse (50)
   St Anne, Limehouse (50)
(2) St Bartholomew the Great (60)
(20) Battersea, Surry (812)
   St Botolph, Aldersgate (40)
   Billingsgate Ward (40)
(2) St Botolph, Aldgate (101)
(2) St Botolph, Bishopsgate (60)
(2) St Brides Parish (70)
(2) Bridge, Candlewick and Dowgate Ward (100)
(2) British or Welsh School, Gray's Inn Lane (91)
(2) Broad Street Ward (80)
(2) Camberwell, Surrey (65)
(2) Castle Baynard Ward (58)
(2) Chelsea, Middlesex (55)
   In the Same Parish (33)
(2) Christ Church, Spitalfields (100)
(2) Christ Church in Surrey (80)
(2) St Clement Danes (100)
(2) In the Same Parish of St C. (30)
(2) Colman Street Ward (65)
(2) Cordwainers and Bread Street Ward (80)
(2) Cornhill and Lime Street Ward (80)
(2) Cripplegate Ward, Without in Redcross Street (202)
(2) Cripplegate Ward Within (75)
   In the same Parish (70)
(2) Deptford in Kent (70)

(2) St Dunstan-in-the-West (90)
   St Edmund the King
(2) St Ethelburga (56)
(2) Farringdon Ward Within (100)
(2) French Charity Schools, Spitalfields (31)
(2) Finsbury Charity School (45)
(2) St George, Middlesex or Rayne's Hospital (140)
(2) St George the Martyr (100)
(2) St George, Southwark (65)
   St George Wheeler's Chapel in Spitalfields (36)
(2) St Giles-in-the-Fields, and St George, Bloomsbury (181)
   Greenwich, Kent (40)
   In the Same Parish (20)
   In the Same Parish (50)
(2) Hammersmith, Middlesex (40)
   Highgate, Middlesex (20)
(2) St James, Clerkenwell (100)
(2) In the Same Parish (30)
(2) Peter Joys' School (61)
(2) St James, Westminster (130)
(2) In the Same Parish in King Street (156)
   In the Same Parish of St James, Westminster (70)
(2) St John at Hackney (60)
(2) St John Wapping (90)
   St John South (36)
(2) St James, Clerkenwell (100)
(2) Isleworth, Middlesex (60)
(2) St Katharine near the Tower (50)
(2) Kensington, Middlesex (50)
   Lambeth in Surrey (50)
   Langbourn Ward (60)
(2) St Leonard, Shoreditch (110)
(2) St Luke, Middlesex (150)
   In the Same Parish (20)
(2) St Margaret, Westminster (86)

(2) In the Same Parish (86)
(2) St Martin-in-the-Fields (120)
(2) St Mary, Islington (60)
(2) St Mary Magdalene, Bermondsey (80)
(2) St Mary Overee, alias St Saviour, Southwark (110)
(2) St Mary, Rotherhithe (55)
(2) In the Same Parish (36)
(2) In the Same Parish (40)
(2) St Mary-le-bone (94)
(2) St Mary-le-bone School of Industry (56)
St Mary le Strand (20)
(2) St Mary, Whitechapel (100)
(2) St Matthew, Bethnal Green (60)
(2) Mile End, Old Town (50)
In the Same Parish (100)
(2) Mortlake in Surrey
(2) Newington Butts, Surrey (50)
Norton Folgate School (36)

St Olave, Southwark (40)
(2) St Paul, Covent Garden (40)
(2) St Paul, Shadwell (80)
St Pancras (40)
(2) Pentonville (24)
(2) Queen-Hithe Ward (48)
(2) Radcliffe Hamlet, Stepney (50)
Richmond in Surrey (130)
St Sepulchre, London (51)
In the Same Parish (51)
In the Same Parish (21)
In the Same Parish (30)
(2) Saint Stephen, Walbrook (80)
St Thomas, Southwark (30)
(2) Tower Ward (120)
Vintry Ward (50)
Wandsworth, Surrey (25)
(2) Westminster (37)
French Charity School

6. *Books recommended for Teachers and Children,*

compiled from Reports of the S.P.C.K. and the Accounts of Schools

Abridgement of the History of the Bible. 1*d.*
Anatomy of Orthography, or a Practical Introduction to the Art of Spelling and Reading English.
Apocrypha. 4*d.*
Art of Spelling and Reading, in two Parts. The first, containing a variety of Lessons, Prayers, Psalms, Hymns, Proverbs and other things proper and useful for Children; the second, an Introduction to the English Tongue, etc.
Ayres. Youths Introduction to Trade.
Beveridge, Bishop. Church Catechism Explained. 1*s.* 6*d.*
Brewster, S. The Christian Scholar. 1704.
Christian Education of Children. 1*s.*
Christian Monitor, The.
Church Catechism broke into Short Questions. 1½*d.*
Common Prayer and Singing Psalms. 4½*d.*
Dialogue between a Protestant Minister and a Romish Priest, wherein it is shewn that the Church of Rome is not the only true Church, and that the Church of England is a sound part of the Catholic Church. 2½*d.*
Disney. First and Second Essay Concerning the Execution of the Laws against Immorality and Profaneness. 5*s.*
Dixon, H. The Parents' and School-Masters' Spiritual Assistant for grounding the Charity Children.
The English Instructor, or the Art of Spelling improved.

Ellesby. A Caution against ill-company; the Dignity and Duty of a Christian and the Great Duty of Submission to the Will of God.

Exemplary Life of James Bonnell. 3s.

Francke, A. H. A Short and Simple Instruction how Children are to be guided to a True Piety and Christian Wisdom, formerly drawn up for Christian Tutors, and now by desire printed. 1702; trans. 1707.

Green, T. The Principles of Religion for Charity Children. 1750.
  Catechetical Instruction by way of Question and Answer. 1751.
  Pastoral Advice to Young Persons. 1759.

Hanway, J. A Comprehensive Sentimental Book for Scholars learning in Sunday Schools, containing the Alphabet, Numbers, Spelling, Moral and Religious Letters, Stories and Prayers suited to the growing powers of Children for the advancement in Happiness of the Rising Generation. 1786.

Hatton. Arithmetic. 4s.

Johnson. Arithmetic.

Ken, Bishop. Exposition of the Church Catechism. 1s. 6d.

Kennett, White. The Christian Scholar, or Rules and Directions for Children and Youths sent to English Schools, more especially designed for the Poor Boys Taught and Cloathed by Charity in the Parish of St Botolph's, Aldgate. 1710.
  The Excellent Daughter.

Lessons for Children, Historical and Practical, drawn up for the Use of a Charity School in the Country. 4th ed. 1725.

Lewis. Exposition of the Church Catechism.

Lincoln, Bishop of. Exposition of the Church Catechism. 2s.

Lucas. The Influence of Conversation.

Monro, G. Just measures for the Pious Instruction of Youth. 2 vols. 9s.

Nelson, R. The Whole Duty of a Christian, Designed for the Use of the Charity Schools in and about London. 1704.

Nowell, Dean. The Elements of Christian Piety, designed particularly for the Charity Children. 1715.

Osterwald, J. F. The Grounds and Principles of the Christian Religion, explained in a Catechetical Discourse for the Instruction of young people: Rendered into English by Humphrey Wanley.

Prayers for the Use of Charity Schools.

Present for Servants, A.

Protestant Catechism.

Raikes, R. The Sunday School Scholars Companion; consisting of Scripture Sentences disposed in such order as will quickly ground young learners in the Fundamental Doctrines of our most Holy Religion, and, at the same time, lead them Pleasantly on from Simple and Easy to Compound and Difficult Words. 1794.
  Catechism for the Use of Sunday Schools. 1810.

Sacrament of the Lord's Supper explained in Questions and Answers. 2½d.

Salisbury, Bishop of. Exposition of the Church Catechism.

Seasonable Caveat against Popery.

Short Computation of the principal errors of the Church of Rome. Popery tried and condemned by the Holy Scriptures.

Short Refutation of Popery.

Snell. New Copy Book. 5s.

Sunday Scholars' Companion. 1794.
Talbot, J. The Christian Schoolmaster. 2s.
Taylor, Bishop. Holy Living and Dying. 5s.
Tillotson, Archbishop. Concerning the Hazard of being saved in the Church of Rome.
Trimmer, Mrs Sarah. The Charity Spelling Book: The Teacher's Assistant, consisting of Lectures in the Catechetical form, being part of a plan of Appropriate Instruction for the Children of the Poor. 2nd ed. 1808.
  The Œconomy of Charity. 1786.
  An Abridgement of Scripture History. 1804.
  An Abridgement of the New Testament. 1809.
Turner. Spelling Book. 1s. 6d.
Vernon. Compleat Counting House. 9d.
Wake, Archbishop. Commentary on the Church Catechism.
Watts, Isaac. Divine Songs for Children.
Williams, Bishop. Brief Exposition of the Church Catechism.
Whole Duty of Man, The.
Woodward. Short Catechism, with an Explanation of divers hard words.

7. *An Account of the Rates of Cloathing Poor Children belonging to Charity Schools,*

taken from *An Account of Charity Schools in Great Britain and Ireland,* 1712

THE CHARGE OF CLOATHING A BOY

	£	s	d
A Yard and half-quarter of Grey Yorkshire Broad Cloth 6 quarters wide, makes a Coat	00	03	00
Making the Coat, with Pewter Buttons and all other Materials	00	01	00
A Wastcoat of the same Cloth lined	00	03	06
A pair of Breeches of Cloth or Leather lined	00	02	06
1 Knit Cap, with Tuft and String, of any Colour	00	00	10
1 Band	00	00	02
1 Shirt	00	01	06
1 Pair of Woollen Stockings	00	00	08
1 Pair of Shoes	00	01	10
1 Pair of Buckles	00	00	01
1 Pair of Knit or Wash-Leather Gloves	00	00	07
The Total	00	15	08

THE CHARGE OF CLOATHING A GIRL

	£	s	d
3 Yards and half of blue long Ells, about yard wide, at 16d. p. Yard, makes a Gown and Petticoat	00	04	08
Making thereof, Strings, Body-lining, and other Materials	00	01	00
A Coif and Band of Scotch-Cloth with a Border	00	00	09
Ditto of fine Ghenting	00	01	00
A Shift	00	01	06
A White, Blue, or Checquered Apron	00	01	00
A pair of Leather Bodice and Stomacher	00	02	06
1 Pair of Woollen Stockings	00	00	08
1 Pair of Shoes	00	01	08
A Pair of Pattens	00	00	08
1 Pair of Buckles	00	00	01
1 Pair of Knit or Wash-Leather Gloves	00	00	07
The Total	00	16	01

N.B. The different Stature of Children is allowed for here; and 50 Children between the Ages of 7 and 12 (one with another) may be cloathed at these Rates.

APPENDIX II: *SCOTLAND*

1. *A list of some of the Ambulatory Schools of the Scottish S.P.C.K.,*
compiled from the Reports and Minutes of the Society, 1711–1800

The figures in brackets show the number of scholars returned in the Report of 1774. The geographical position of the places, and the spelling of the place-names, given in the Reports, have been retained.

ABERDEENSHIRE

School Station

Aboyne
Allanquaich
Altanlargue
Ardlier
Auchairn
Auchernoch
Ballatrach
Ballochan
Ballochan (50)
Balmannock
Bellamore
Belno
Blairnamuck
Bridge of Gurnick
Broadley
Camafour

Castletown of Braemar
Coldrach (68)
Craigylea
Crathie
Dorrinsilly
Doubrich in Corgarph
Easter Balmoral (66)
Graystone
Inchmartin (72)
Invercauld
Inverchanlick
Inverey
Inver of Muck
Keanvoan
Kindyside
Kinnore

Little Kinord
Lynorn
Migvie
Mill of Cossack
Newbigging
Newbyth (62)
Ruthven
Ruthven (48)
Sockach (40)
Tilliecairn
Tullicairn
Tullich
Tordarroch
Torrancroy (68)
Wester Micras
Whitsheal

ARGYLLSHIRE

School Station

Ambrisbeg (75)
Appin (36)
Appin
Ardchattan
Ardchattan
Ardentrive (29)
Arisaig
Arross in Mull
Auchalader
Auchinbreck
Barbay
Barnaline (52)
Barr (40)

Barrichareil (62)
Bellsuil
Bowmore
Bowmore
Brodie
Cairndow (67)
Campbelton
Caollaig
Cappachine in Arisaig
Carniewhinny
Coll
Craiganich
Dalavech

Dergachy (55)
Doet
Dripp
Drumfern (21)
Duachai
Duntroon (30)
Fanmore
Ferlochan
Garvie
Gigha
Glenan
Glenary (41)
Glenco

APPENDIX II

ARGYLLSHIRE

School Station

Glenlaogh
Glenshiray (38)
Icolmkill, Isle of
Islay
Jura Island
Keanvy
Keill
Kenmore (32)
Kerrera Island
Kerry
Kerston
Kikrapol
Kilbranden
Kilbride
Kilbride (42)
Kildalton
Killearndale
Kilmachalmiag (48)
Kilmichael
Kilmorie
Kilmun

Kinlochspelvie
Kintrae
Knockcrom
Kyle
Lagavoilin
Laggavoulin
Lagg in Jura
Laroch
Laroch
Lesmore
Locharcaig
Lochgilphead
Luing Island
Mamore
Maryburgh
Muckairn (82)
Mull of Kintyre (43)
Mungostell
Neriby
New Pitsligo
Otterferry (59)

Port Appin (36)
Queenish
Savarie
Scalasaig (34)
Shalunt
Shirgrim
Skipness
South Hall
Strath
Strone
Strone
Strontian (20)
Taynraich
Tiree Island
Tobermory
Torloisk
Torloisk
Torosay
Toward
Ulva Island
Whitehouse (35)

BANFFSHIRE

School Station

Abercharder (32)
Auchinabridge
Ballintomb
Baudfoor (102)
Bolintruan
Broadley
Buckie
Clashtyrum (61)

Crofts of Minmore
Delavorar
Delnabo
Enzie
Glenrinnes
Grange
Inverlochie

Kinore of Abercharder
Knock (40)
Letterlaindach
Mulben
Portsoy (72)
Ruthven
Shorr of Buckie
Thornybank

CAITHNESS

School Station

Assery
Auchanarris (38)
Barrack
Bighouse (43)
Blackbridge
Brabster
Bualcrappie
Buckies
Bunahaven

Clardon
Clyth
Dunbeath
Emster
Harpsdale
Hevackcroy
Kirkton
Keiss (34)

Mey
Milnton
Milton of Dunbeath
Noss (39)
Quoysdale
Stroma Island
Thrumster
Ulbster (18)
Weatherclate

DUMBARTONSHIRE

School Station

Dumfin
Inversnaid (91)

Mill of Halden (83)
Muirland (86)

Salachy

DUMFRIESSHIRE

School Station

Halfmorton

Tynron

Whinnyhill (46)

EDINBURGH

School Station

Charity Workhouse (76)

Dalkeith

Orphan Hospital (60)

ELGINSHIRE

School Station

Archieston
Broom of Moy (27)
Coneycavil (26)
Cottertoun of Brodie
Craigroy
Culphairn (16)
Dallas Broughty
Daugh of the Knock

Dornaway
Dunduff
Earlsseat
Findhorn (41)
Goldford
Kellas
Kintisack

Mevistoun
Pluscarden
Pitnuisk
Presley
Speymouth
Tillidivie (21)
Westground of Brodie

FORFARSHIRE

School Station

Bridge of Tarf
Clantlaw
Dalforth

Drumfork (80)
Folda (63)

Glenisha
Glenprossan
Miltown (67)

INVERNESS-SHIRE

School Station

Aberachan
Aberchalder
Achadrome
Aird (15)
Alvey
Armadale
Aviemore (32)
Ballantruan (30)
Ballentomb
Badavochill (88)
Barra
Barra (37)
Bellnagordanach

Belloch
Belnain
Benbecula
Bohuntine
Boisdale
Borbh
Borlum
Bornick
Borve
Bourg
Bracadale
Bracadale
Braes of Abernethy

Braeroy
Braes of Lochaber
Brechlich
Bridge of Truin
Bunloit
Burn
Burnstod
Cabrichie
Canna
Clachanmore
Croachy
Crostcarnoch
Culclachie

INVERNESS-SHIRE

School Station

Culmulin
Dalroy
Daviot
Dell of Rothiermurcus (23)
Deshar
Deskie
Dochearn
Dochfour
Drumcudden
Drynachan
Dughgarrioch
Dunachton
Easter Bunloit
Egg
Erlesbeg
Eskadale
Fannellan
Farr
Farr in Croachie
Flemington
Fort Augustus (115)
Frobost
Gargoch
Gavlarig
Glasnacardock
Glenconvent
Glenessie
Glenfessie
Glengary
Glenlivet
Glenmorison (21)
Glenorquhart

Glenshee (73)
Glenshiero
Glentrum
Grantoun
Harris Island
Insbabry
Insh
Inverey
Invergeseran
Inveruglas
Kilbar
Killichuiman
Kilmartine
Kilmore (26)
Kilmuir
Kincardine (27)
Kingussie
Kinkell
Kirkhill
Kirkton
Kirkton of Glenelg
Knoidart
Knockandow (36)
Levisie
Leys (60)
Lyoll
Mickly
Milton of Urquhart (60)
Minginess
Muccoul
Moy
,Muck

Muckrach
Nevie
Newtoun of Leys
North Moror
Obriachan
Pable (12)
Perry
Pitgown
Portree
Raining's School (208)
Roadil (14)
Rum
Scarista
Shenvail (61)
Shirgrim
Shirramore
Skiradvie
Slait
St Kilda Island
Stonebridge
Strathglass
St Richard's
Tarransay
Teighinnataim
Tomintoul (98)
Tomnacharich
Tomnaclagan
Torbreck
Tullich
Tynahalnich
Uist
Urquhart

KINCARDINESHIRE

School Station

Glenfarquhar

LANARKSHIRE

School Station

Glasgow

NAIRN

School Station

Calder
Dalcroy
Nairn

ORKNEY AND SHETLAND

School Station

Brandequoy
Bremer (39)
Burra
Calfsound
Costay
Costay
Cross and Burness
Cunningburgh
Delton
Edday Island
Eithston
Fair Isle (24)
Faulda Island
Firth
Flota (31)
Foula Island (24)
Garmiston (31)
Gela
Gela in Fair Isle

Graemsay
Greny (31)
Harray (82)
Hoy (33)
Inatoun (25)
Ingsay (32)
Kirkwall
Konsger
Laxfobigging
Marwick (48)
Melsitter
Midby
Newhouse and Stronza
Norbie
Oback
Oback (45)
Orphir
Quendale

Ridewick
Sanday
Sandness
Sandwick
Scatness
Sorren
Stenness
Strand
Unst
Uphouse
Walls
Walls (35)
Weisdale
Weisdale
Westray
Whinyester
Whytness (29)
Yarpha (53)

PERTHSHIRE

School Station

Aberfoyle
Aldvad
Amulree
Anney
Ardeonaig (85)
Ardtallanaig (73)
Auchgoil
Auchtermuthill
Balquhidder
Berryhill
Bishop of Dunkeld (66)
Blairvoyaig (76)
Blairvuick
Bohally
Bridge of Kelty
Bridge of Turk
Camagouan
Carie
Cluniemore (47)
Craignafarrer
Craignafarrer
Cullintogle
Culmuline
Dalguise

Dalnamein
Dercullich
Drumcastle
Drumoor
Edradynate (37)
Fincastle
Finnart
Fordynate
Foss (47)
Gairntully
Gartmore
Glenalmond
Glenalmond (64)
Glenartney
Glendochart
Glenfernat
Glenlednoch
Glenquaich
Glenroar
Glenshee (73)
Innervan
Innervar
Innerwick of Glenlyon
Invercharnaig

Kilchonan
Kilchonanrannoch
Kindallachan (66)
Kinlochard
Lawers (86)
Lochearnhead
Loch-earn-side
Logiealmond (51)
Methven
Morenish
Nether Cloquhat
Orchilmore
Perth
Pitcastle
Pittagown
Roro
Shian
Straloch (40)
Strathfillan
Strathtummel (41)
Strathyre
Strelitz
Strowan
Trochry in Strathbrand

APPENDIX II

ROSS AND CROMARTY

School Station

Achillibuie
Achmore
Allangrange
Allanreich
Arnat (29)
Arrean
Auchnach
Auchtihairn
Balnakill
Balvraid
Barvas (43)
Belblair
Belmungy
Blairninich
Boath
Bolintruan
Bybell
Calrichie
Carloway
Craigholm (41)

Croftnacrich
Croftnacriech
Culbain
Culbockie (86)
Davidstoun
Drumcudden (85)
Drumcudden
Fairburn
Gairloch
Glasnacardoch
Glenurquhart
Goathill
Inverlael
Inver of Tain
Jollie
Kanrive (41)
Keos
Killearnan (69)
Kilmuir
Kilmuir Wester

Kinnahard
Kintail
Kirktoun of Lochbroom
Kishorn
Little Strath
Lochalsh
Lochcarron
Lochs (27)
Milton of Reidcastle
Milnton of Urquhart
Ness
Ratagan
Rianteer
Strathascaig
Strathchonan
Strathgarvie
Swainpost
Tollie
Tolly
Ullapool

ROXBURGH

School Station

Carlenridge

STIRLING

School Station

Calness
Dalmary (55)

Gartinstarry
Gurtfarren

Inversnaid
Salachy

SUTHERLAND

School Station

Aschylmore (54)
Ashilbeg
Auchness
Borible
Cain
Cambusnaden
Duibill
Eddiachilis
Evelack
Gruid
Homlean

Inverchasley (41)
Invershean
Kildonan
Kilfederbeg
Knockbreck
Lairg
Langdale (21)
Ledbeg
Lettermore
Little Crosty
Melness

Old Shores
Philine
Rivigil
Skibo
Skiness
Skirra
Strathmore
Strathbeg (56)
Stronza
Torrisdale

2. *The Scriptures in Scottish Gaelic*

Date	Edition	Promoters	No. of copies
1767	12mo. First edition of the New Testament	S.S.P.C.K.	10,000
1767	8vo. Edition of above, followed by amplified rules for reading the Gaelic language	S.S.P.C.K.	
1787	John Smith's Metrical Version of the Psalter		
1796	Revised edition of the New Testament of 1767	S.S.P.C.K.	21,500
1801	First edition of the Old Testament	S.S.P.C.K.	5,000
1807	Revised edition of the Old Testament of 1801	S.S.P.C.K.	
1807	First edition of the Bible	British and Foreign Bible Society	

Before 1767 copies of the Scriptures in Irish Gaelic were in circulation among the Gaelic-speaking inhabitants of Scotland, e.g. the New Testaments of 1681 and 1754; the Old Testament of 1685; the Bible of 1690; the Metrical Psalms of the Synod of Argyle, 1659; Kirke's Psalter, 1684; the Gaelic Psalter of the Synod of Argyle, 1694, and Macfarlane's revision of this in 1753.

3. *The Establishments of the S.P.C.K. in Scotland for the year 1st May* 1800 *to 1st May* 1801,

taken from the ABSTRACT of the Scheme of the Society, 1801

	Salaries
200 schools on the first patent,	£2459 0 0
19 superannuated teachers on ditto,	147 0 0
13 missionaries and catechists,	336 0 0
6 Gaelic bursaries	90 0 0
94 schools on the second patent,	459 0 0
1 superannuated teacher on ditto,	5 0 0
333	£3496 0 0

The Number of Scholars usually taught at the above Schools, at an average, on the First Patent, viz.-for the purposes of religion, and the first principles of literature, is computed to be   10,000
At the Schools for Industry, on the Second Patent   1,880

In all,   11,880

APPENDIX III: *IRELAND*

1. *A list of the Charity Schools in Ireland,*

extracted from the *Accounts of the Charity Schools* from 1716 to 1730

The figures before and after the place-names show respectively the number of schools, when more than one, and the number of scholars when stated.

Co. ANTRIM

(2) Belfast (100)
Ramone

Co. ARMAGH

(2) Armagh (40)
Ballintoy (20)
Benburb (6)
Portadown (12)
Laughall
Lurgan (16)
Tertaraghan
Eglish (12)

Co. CAVAN

Cavan (14)
Kilmore (10)

Co. CLARE

Correfin (20)
Killaloo (10)
Newmarket (24)
Kilfenora

Co. CORK

Bantry
Ballyclogh (12)
Burton (24)
Carrigalin
Castlelyons
Castlemartyr (20)
Charleville
Cloyne (20)
(5) Cork (188)
Corryglass (20)
Drishane

Co. CORK

Dunmanway
Farragh
Great Island (6)
Inishonane (9)
Killworth
Killshanich
Kinsale
Middleton (6)
Mitchellstown (10)
Mourn Abbey (12)
Ovens
Youghal (40)

Co. DONEGAL

Ramoghey (10)
Raphoe (27)

Co. DOWN

Dromore
Killogh (20)
Moyrah (24)

CITY OF DUBLIN

St Anne (42)
(2) St Andrew (46)
St Audeon (2)
St Bridget (4)
St James (21)
St John (20)
St Katherine (40)
(2) St Mary (60)
(2) St Michael (60)
(2) St Michan (60)
St Nicholas Within (20)
St Nicholas Without (20)

CITY OF DUBLIN

(4) St Patrick's Liberties (82)
St Paul (25)
St Peter (76)
St Warbourgh (14)

Co. DUBLIN

(2) Finglas (30)
Castlenoch
Clonmethan (4)

Co. GALWAY

Aghrim (16)
Dunmore (12)
Headford
Tuam (24)
Cloonburn (16)

Co. KILDARE

Castle Dermot (20)
Kildare
Kildrought (18)
Maynooth (8)
Naas

Co. KILKENNY

Kells
Kilkenny City (28)
Drumheen (15)

Co. KERRY

Ballihaigne
Dingle (15)
Killarney
Tralee (26)

KING'S COUNTY
Bor (6)
Geshell (20)
Killeigh (20)

Co. LEITRIM
Drumahare (24)
(2) Kilfinane

Co. LIMERICK
(4) Limerick City (115)
Kilmalloch

Co. LONDONDERRY
Lisson
(2) Londonderry (50)
Magherafelt (18)

Co. LONGFORD
Lanesborough (24)
Longford (22)

Co. LOUTH
Drennishin
Drogheda (24)
Dundalk (20)

Co. MAYO
Ballinrobe (24)
Castlebar (24)
Foxford
Hollymount (40)
Kilmain (24)
Killala (15)

Co. MEATH
Rathmoylan (24)
Trim

Co. MONAGHAN
Monaghan (10)

QUEEN'S COUNTY
Abbeyleix (40)
Stradbally (4)

Co. ROSCOMMON
(2) Abbey-Boyle (52)
Athleague (24)
Carrick
Castlereagh (26)
Easter-Snow (16)
Elphin (24)
French Park
Tessararah (12)

Co. SLIGO
(3) Castlebaldwyn (62)
Coloony (22)
Kilmacowen (18)
Primrose Grange (18)
Skreen (14)
(3) Sligo (50)

Co. TIPPERARY
Cashell
(2) Emly
Thurles

Co. TYRONE
Castle Caulfield (20)
Clogher (16)
Strabane (12)
Tullyhog
Newton Steward (14)

Co. WATERFORD
(2) Waterford (95)
Dungarven (20)
Lismore

Co. WESTMEATH
Castle Pollard (12)
Christ Church (24)
Lizard (14)
Slane

Co. WEXFORD
Leskinfair (24)
Camolin (20)
Cowsduff
Old Ross (24)
Taghmun (4)
Ross (20)

Co. WICKLOW
Delalassery
(2) Wicklow (19)
Baltinglass (6)
Donoghmore (12)
Dunlaven (12)

2. *A list of the Schools of the Incorporated Society, Dublin,*
as returned by the Commissioners of Irish Education Inquiry, 1791

Date of foundation	County	School	Establishment strength	No. of children in 1790
1734	Kildare	Castledermot	40	38
1735	Down	Ballynahinch		
	Mayo	Minola*		
	Limerick	Shannon Grove	100	63
1736	Tyrone	Castle Caulfield		
1737	Armagh	Creggane	40	40
	Antrim	Ballycastle	40	34
	Wicklow	Templestown		
1738	Down	Killough†		
	Limerick	Kilmallock†		
	Louth	Dundalk	40	36
	Queen's County	Stradbally	50	39
	Limerick	Kilfinane	20	14
	Mayo	Ballinrobe	40	30
1740	Galway	Newtown Eyre		
	Monaghan	Newtown Corry†		
	Donegal	Ray	30	32
1741	Wexford	New Ross	40	39
1743	Clare	Ballykett†		
1744	Dublin	Santry	40	36
	Waterford	Waterford	40	41
1745	Kilkenny	Kilkenny	60	34
	Meath	Ardbraccan	50	38
1748	Cork	Charleville	30	39
	Down	Strangford	50	39
	Kildare	Castle Carberry‡	50	46
	Tipperary	Clonmell	40	39
	Meath	Trim	40	38
	Wicklow	Arklow	40	41
	Limerick	Mountshannon		
1749	Cork	Kinsale†		
	Cork	Castle Martyr	40	33
	Dublin	Clontarf Strand	100	63
	Galway	Loughrea	50	39
	Kildare	Manooth	40	34

* Discontinued on a general plan of economy, 1764.
† Discontinued on a general plan of economy, 1773.
‡ Burnt down by the rebels in 1798.

Date of foundation	County	School	Estab-lishment strength	No. of children in 1790
1751	Tipperary	Cashell	40	30
	Cork	Dunmanway	40	40
	Tipperary	Newport	40	40
1752	Derry	Ballykelly	50	45
	Cork	Innishannon	50	47
1753	King's County	Frankfort	40	33
	Longford	Longford	60	43
1755	Galway	Galway	40	23
	Galway	Monivae		
	Sligoe	Sligoe	80	52
1758	Westmeath	Farra	40	31
	Armagh	Armagh*		
1760	Cork	Inniscarra	50	44
1763	Kerry	Castle Island	45	22
1768	Mayo	Castlebar	50	43
	Clare	Newmarket	40	37
			1775	1455
		Nurseries:		
	Galway	Monivae		
	Limerick	Shannon Grove		
	Kildare	Monasterevan		
	Dublin	Miltown, near Dublin		263
Schools on the Ranelagh Foundation for Protestants:				
		Athlone Roscommon		80
				1798

* Discontinued on a general plan of economy, 1773.

APPENDIX IV: *WALES*

1. *A list of the Schools of the Welsh Trust,*

as returned in the Report of the Society for 1674–1675

The figures after the place-names show the number of scholars.
The geographical position of the places, and the spelling of the place-names given in the Report, have been retained.

CARMARTHEN-SHIRE

Laughorne (40)
Penboyne (20)
Lanboydy (30)
St Cleeres (20)
Marrows (20)
Llanelthy (20)
Llandovery (20)
Kidwelly (40)
Llanactkany (12)
Llandiowrer (20)
Carmarthen Town (24)

PEMBROKESHIRE

Carew Town (20)
Lampeder Welfry (10)
Usmoston (20)
Pembroke Town (60)
Haverfordwest (60)
Nolton } (30)
Trefgarn }
Brawdy (10)
Frestrop (10)
Langham (10)
Martheltwy (20)
Slebbish (15)
Roch-Parish (20)
Cosheston (24)
Tenby (25)
Narbarth (12)

GLAMORGAN-SHIRE

Cardiff (50)
Margam (20)
Cunfigg (20)

St Nicolas (12)
Lancarvan (20)
Lantrithed } (20)
St Mary Hill }
Penmark (20)
St Hilary (10)
Wenvoe (14)
Cowbridge (40)
Swansey (20)
Neath (40)
Llandilotabont (20)
Bridg-End (20)
Bettws (15)

BRECKNOCHSHIRE

Brechnoch-Town (20)
Hay-Town

MONMOUTHSHIRE

Chepstow (20)
Llantrissent (20)
Newport (42)
Caerlion (40)
Langiby (20)
Machen (20)
Basslegg (20)
Usk (32)
Monmouth (50)
Abergavenny (40)
Pont le Pool (16)
Michelstone de Vedo (32)

CARDIGANSHIRE

Cardigan-Town (40)
Lambeder (24)
Myvod (32)
Welsh-pool (40)

Kinnerly (20)
Llanchfrochwell (12)
Oswestry (25)

RADNORSHIRE

New Radnor (20)
Knighton (40)
Prestain (40)

CAERNARVON-SHIRE

Carnarvon Town (20)
Conweigh (36)
Llandegay (12)
Llanllechid (12)

DENBIGHSHIRE

Ruthen (40)
Denbigh-Town (50)
Markeweell (16)
Wrexham (40)
Gresford (12)
Llanrwst (20)
Abergelly (40)
Holt (12)

FLINTSHIRE

Bangor (50)
Flint-Town (24)
Northop (20)
Caerwys (15)
Mould (30)
Ourton (50)
Worthenbury (20)

ANGLESEY

Bewmarris (48)

2. *The Schools of the S.P.C.K. in Wales*, 1699–1737,

extracted from the Minutes and Reports of the Society
The figures before the place-names show the number of schools
when more than one

ANGLESEY

Beaumaris
Llanfihangel
   [Ysgeifiog]
Llangeinwen

BRECKNOCKSHIRE

(3) Brecon
(4) Glasbury (partly in
   Radnorshire)
Llandilo

CARDIGANSHIRE

Esgair Hir Mines
Llandyssul

CARMARTHEN-
SHIRE

Abergwilly
(2) Carmarthen
Laugharne
Llanboidy
Llandovery
Llanddowror
Llangadock
Llangan
Llangunnog
Marros
Pembrey
Penboyr
St Clears

CAERNARVON-
SHIRE

Bangor
Gyffin
Llanllechid

DENBIGHSHIRE

Bettws, Abergele
Denbigh
Gresford
Marchwiail
Wrexham

GLAMORGAN-
SHIRE

Cardiff
Cowbridge
Laugharne
Llantwit-Major
(2) Llantrissant
Llanwonno
Margam
(3) Merthyr Tydvil
Neath

MERIONETHSHIRE

Dolgelley
Towyn

MONMOUTHSHIRE

Abergavenny
Llanthony
Llantilo Bertholeu
Michel Troy
(3) Monmouth

MONTGOMERY-
SHIRE

Kerry
Llanfihangel
(2) Llanfyllin
Llangunnog
Welshpool

PEMBROKESHIRE

Amroth
Bigely
Boulston
Dinas
Heraldston-west
Hascard
Haverford-west
Lambston
Lampeter Velfrey
Lawrenny
Llanychaer
Maenclochog
Marloes
Mounton
Narberth
(3) Pembroke
Penally
Prendergast
Puncheston
Rudbaxton
Slebech
St Bride
St Issel
Steinton
Templeton
Tenby
Usmaston
Walton East
Walton West

RADNORSHIRE

Glasbury (see Breck-
   nockshire)
Maesgwin
Presteign

3. A list of places where the Welch Circulating Charity Schools were set up, 1738–1761,

compiled from the Annual Reports of Welch Piety

The spelling of the place-names is not uniform in the Reports. This list adopts one of the several modes used in Welch Piety.

The geographical position of the places found in the Reports has been retained.

The figures after the place-names show the number of day scholars attending the schools in 1759–1760.

ANGLESEY

Aberffraw
Bodedern
Bôdwrog (40)
Bodlossion in Llangefni
Bryngwydrin in Llanidan parish (41)
Brynsiencyn in Llanidan
Caer-Eurych in Llángristiolos
Cefn-Esgob in Llanfihangel Tre'r Bardd
Ceirchiog (39)
Cerrig-Ceinwen
Clynog-Fawr in Llangeinwen
Efel-fach in Trewalchmai
Hên-Eglwys (37)
Holyhead near Holyhead Town
Llanallgo
Llanbabo
Llanbadrig (40)
Llan-Bedr-Gôch
Llanbeulan
Llanddaniel (35)
Llanddeusant
Llanddona (50)
Llanddyfynan (55)
Llandegfan
Llandrygarn
Llandyfrydog
Llan-Elian
Llanenghenell
Llan-Engrad
Llanfachraeth (42)
Llanfaelog (53)
Llanfaes (46)
Llanfaethlu
Llanfairmathaferneitha (36)
Llanfeirian
Llanfflewin
Llanfigel (33)
Llanfihangel Tre'r Bardd (22)

Llanfwrog (44)
Llangadwaladr
Llangaffo (28)
Llanfihangel-matha-farneitha (36)
Llanfair-pwll-y-gwyngill
Llanfair-ynghornwy
Llanfair-yn-neubwll (30)
Llangefni (47)
Llangeinwen (34)
Llangoed
Llangristiolis
Llangwillog
Llaniestyn (68)
Llanrhwydrus
Llanrhyddlad (40)
Llansadwrn
Llantrisant
Llan-enghenel
Llechcynfarwy (49)
Merddyn Cetyn in Llanrhyddlad
Newborough (35)
Olgra in Llanddyfnan
Penmôn
Penmynydd (46)
Penrhos
Pentre'r-lludw in Llangristiolis
Penrhoslligwy
Rhoscolyn (33)
Rhydpont in Rhosgelyn
Trefdraeth
Tregauan
Trewalchmai
Ysgubor-fawr in Llanfihangel-Manadd-fwyn

BRECKNOCKSHIRE

Abercar in Vaynor
Aber Car in Taf-fawr
Abergwersin

Arddlâs in Defynnog
yr Allt in Llanfigan
Abercludach in Llanfigan
Bwlch in Cathedin
Brynbach in Talgarth
Blaen y glais in Vaynor
Brelch in Cwmdu
Buyllt
Brecon Town
Buddwn in Llanhamlach (32)
Bodwicced in Penderyn
Bedw-in-Llan y wern
Battel
Blaen glyn tawe in Defynnock
Bryn Llws
Capel-y-ffin in Llanygon
Cwmcrwynon in Llangynider
Coed-y-cymmar in Vaynor
Capel Dyffryn Honddi
Carnant in Penderyn
Cantref
Crughowel
Crosgwyn in Llanddewi Cwm
Cwm-y-Rhos in St Michael Cwmdu
Cilgattws in Llanspyddyd
Cilian in Crig-Cadarn
Cwarter Garth in Ystradgynlas
Doley Gâr in Crughowel
Dyfynog (67)
Derwen y Groes in Llanfigan
Efordd Isa in Glasbury
Felindre in Llanfernach
Felin Issa in Llanfihangel-Nant-Brân
Felindre in St Davids
Gwern-y-badd in Bronllys
Gwenddwr
Groyne Fychan
Gelli, *alias* Hay
Glyn collwyn
Glyn in Devynock
Gallt y fan in Llywel
Gwern-y-frân in Devynock
Groes in Cilfannus Hamlet in Vaynor
Garn in Vaynor
Heol y knappie in Llangors
Illtyd Chapel in Defynog
Llywel Village
Llanfihangel Bryn Buan
Llanwrtyd

Llanfillo
Llanllowenvel near Garth
Llandilo'r Fan (46)
Llanthew
Llangynog
Llechwallten
Llanganten
Llanafan Fawr
Llangammarch
Llangadog Crig Howel
Llangors
Llanddewi Abergwersin
Llanwrthwl
Llechfaen in Llanhamlach (51)
Lloegr fychan in Llanfihangel-Nant-Brân
Llangynide
Llangwern
Llwyngweision in Llangammarch
Llanathow
St Michael cwmdu
Mynydd-Ylltyd on the borders of Llan-
    byddyd and Defynog
Merthyr Cynog
Maes-Mawr in Llanthety
Nayath in Ystrad Gynlais
Neuadd in Kerrig Kadan
New-Bridge in Llanafanfawr
Penisa'r Waun in Llanddew
Pont-âr-Dâf in Vaynor
Pentre in Llangors
Ponde in Llandevalley
Pant-y-Dery in Llanfeigan
Penderyn
Pompren Llwyd in Penderyn
Pant y ffordd in Dyfynog
Pont Sticcil in Vaynor
Penbryn y Groes in Dyfynog
Rheol-newydd in Llanfigan
Selydach in Llywel
Ty Rees y Gôf in Llangors
Tŷ-newydd in Llanddevalley
Ty-mawr-y-cwm in Cwmdu
Ty-fru in Llangynnider
Trevecka
Taf-fechan in Llanddeffy
Ty-Fri in Llanfigan
Talachddu
Ty yn y Rheol in Llandefelog
Trallong

Tal-y-llyn
Waun Lwyd in Llandilo'r Fan
Ystrad-wellte
Ysgubor-y-twyn in Talgarth
Ystrad Gynlais

CAERNARVONSHIRE

Aberdaron (33)
Abererch
Aber
Bwlch in Llaningen
Bidwesliog
Bettws-Garmon
Bedd-Celert (43)
Bryn-croes
Bettus-y-coed (37)
Bôdvean (32)
Bryn in Llangwnadl
Cappel-Curug
Caerhun
Clynnog
Carnguwch (45)
Crickeith
Cefn-buarthau in Llanaelhaiarn
Coetgae in Llan-armon
Croes-ynyd in Llanglynnyn (35)
Caer Helygen in Llanwnd (39)
Corsor in Llanvihangel y Pennant (43)
Dol-wyddelan (32)
Dolbenman (4)
Denio
Derwyn-ucha in Clynnog
Dwygofylchi
Edern
Hendre in Aberdaron
Holeburn in Nevyn
Keidio
Llangybi (28)
Llangian (20)
Llanryg
Llaniestyn (54)
Llanberis
Llanddeniolen
Llandegai
Llaneingan
Llanystindwy
Llanunda
Llanllyfni (37)
Llanvihangel-y-pennant (62)

Llanvalerhys
Llangwynhoydyl
Llanberr-Cennin
Llanhaiarn
Llanarmon (31)
Llanwnda
Llawnda
Llanllechid
Llanvihangel-Bachellaeth (9)
Llan-Beblig
Llannor (27)
Llanfaglen
Llandwrog (26)
Llidiardgwyn in Llanbeblig
Llanfair-fechan
Llanbedrog (18)
Llanwrog (26)
Llan-ael-haiarn
Llanrhychwyn
Llandidwen
Llanengan (32)
Llangwnadl (45)
Llandegwnning (39)
Llecheiddior in Llanvihangel y Pennant
   (62)
Mellteyrn (37)
Nefyn
Pentre-bach in Llanwnda
Penllech
Pentir
Pentir Chappel in Bangor Parish
Pistill
Pen-rhos Chapel
Penrhos
Penmachno
Penmorfa
Rhyw (37)
Rhywgofylchi
Rhos y lan in Llanistindwy (57)
Sgybor-bach in Clynnog
Trefrhyw
Tydweiliog
Tŷ newydd in Gyffin (35)
Tŷ yn y Nant in Llandwrog

CARDIGANSHIRE

Abereinon in Llandyssul
Aberporth
Aberporth

Argoed in Llanddewi-brefi
Aberystwyth
Adpar in Llandyfriog
Argoed fawr in Tregaron
Blaenporth
Brongwyn
Brynyrarian in Llandyssilio-Gogo
Bangor
Bettws Lickys Chapel by Llanddewibrefi
Blaensilltin in Brongwyn
Blaen Harthen in Trevdroir
Blaen Cil-llêch in Llandyfriog (64)
Blaenllan in Llangunllo (30)
Bryn yr Amber in Llanddewibrefi
Berllandwyll in Llanddewibrefi
Bach y Rhew in Llandyssul
Blaen y Plwy in Ystrad
Cappel St Silin
Cil-Llech in Llandyfriog (63)
Cwm in Verwick
Cardigan Town
Cwmdu in Bettus Joan
Canllyfae in Tremain
Cwm in Blaenporth
Coed y cwm in Llandigwydd
Cellan (48)
Cnwc y Neuadd in Llandysilio-Gogo
Chancery Lane in Llanychaiarn
Caron
Dan-yr-Allt in Penbryn
Dihewyd
Dyffryn Hâfnant in Penbryn (65)
Dol Ifor in Llanfair Orllwyn
Doithie Fach in Llanddewibrefi
Dan yr Allt in Llanfihangel Glyn
Duffryn in Llanbadarn Fawr
Ffynnon y Gareg in Llandygwydd
Felin Ganol in Troed-yr-Aur
Glan-ryyd in Troed yr Aur
Gilfachheda in Llanina
Glandwr in Llangoedmor
Gweyn dunni in Blaenporth
Gwesyn in Llandyssil (58)
Glanymor in Llansantffraid
Gwar-y-Cefel in Llandyssil
Gellifraith in Llandyssil
Glandwr in Llandyssilio Gogo
Hen Hafod in Llandyfriog
Henllan Dyfi

Henfenyw
Kilkennyn
Llwyn-Llwyd in Llangoedmor
Lampeter
Llandygwydd
Llechryd (65)
Llety'r Cymro in Llangranog
Lleiniau in Ystlym Gwili in Abergwili
Llanon in Llansantffraid
Llangoedmor
Llansantffraid Village
Llanfair-Orllwyn
Llangynllo (62)
Llandyfriog
Llanfair Treflygen
Llangeitho
Llanddewi Aberarth
Lledrod
Llanilar
Llanddiniol
Llanbadarn Trefeglwys
Llanarth
Llanina
Llethbrad
Llanwenog
Llanllwchaiarn
Llandissilio-Gogo
Llanrhystyd
Llanddewi-brefi
Lampiter Pont Stephen
Llanfair-Clydog
Llandysil
Llanbadarn Odwyn
Llanfihangel-Ystrad
Llanwynnen
Llanddowlas
Llanerch Euron
Llangranog
Llwyn-bedw-Bach in Llandyssil (10)
Lleiniau in Tremain (37)
Llwyn y Gronwen in Gwnws
Llwyn Piod in Llanbadarn Edwin
Lluast-y-Bwlch in Llandabarn Fawr
Llangynog
Login in Verwick (78)
Llanwrtyd
Llwyn-Dafydd in Llandysilio Gogo (112)
Nant-fawr in Mount
Neuadd lwyd in Henfenyw

Nantcwnlle (43)
Nant yr Henryd in Llanbadarn Fawr
Pen-y-Parcau in Llandysilio Gogo
Penylôn in Troed-yr-Aur
Penbryn
Penygraig in Gwnwys
Penbryn-arian in Llandisilio Gogo
Penwernfach in Llandygwydd (15)
Penwernfawr in Llandygwydd
Pentre Gwynedd in Llandygwydd
Penallt Gybbie in Llandygwydd
Penplas in Llandyssilio Gogo (63)
Pencarreg
Panty Mawr in Llangrannog
Penybont in Llandysilio Gogo
Penylan in Cilcennin
Pant Glâs in Llangranog
Pant y Gwayr in Llanllwchaiarn
Pant y Castell in Llandysilio Gogo
Rhiw-lûc in Llandissyl
Rhosdie
Rhyd-Cradog in Llandysul
Rhydowen village in Llandysul
Rhyw-Lâs in Llanychaiarn
Spytty-ystrâd Meyrick
Sylian
Trewimmod in Blaenporth
Ty'r Lan in Llandyfriog
Trerhedyn in Llandyfriog
Tremain
Tybach yn y Weyn in Llandysul
Troed yr Aur
Tregaron
Trewen in Brongwyn (86)
Tynewydd in Llangoedmor (73)
Tresilian
Ty-Gwyn in Llangoedmor (41)
Ty'n-yr-allt in Nantcwnlle (61)
Ty-yn-y-Pwll in Llanbadarn Fawr
Ty-ny-y-Graid in Llanbadarn Fawr
Verwick (73)
Vaynor Hamlet in Llanbadarn Fawr
Yspytty-Cefnyn in Llanbadarn Fawr
Ystrad

CARMARTHENSHIRE
Aberarad in Cenarth (38)
Abernant
Abergorlech
Abergwily

Abergolau in Brechfa
Aber-dau-ddwr in Llangan
Bwlch-Melin in Cenarth
Bola-haul in Llantharog
Blaen-nant-y-blaidd in Conwyl Elfedd
Bryn-llefrith in Pencareg
Blaen-y-coed in Conwyl Elfed
Bwlchgolau in Llanfihangel Abercowyn
Blaenau in Llandebie (52)
Beuly mawr in Llangan
Bronhydden in Penboyr
Bryn y maen in Llandilofawr (60)
Berth Lwyd in Llandilofawr
Bryn y Whîth in Conwyl Elfed
Blaen-y-Ffynonan in Ciffig
Bryn-bach in Llanpumsaint
Byr gwn in Llanegwad
Bettus fach
Blaen-Tymmhorau in Llanboidy
Blaen-y-gelli in Llanwinno
Bryn Magog in Cayo
Bol-haul in Llangwnnwr
Blaen-hiraeth in Llanfallteg (33)
Blaenywern in Llanfihangel Abercowyn (20)
Blaen-y-wayn olen in Trelech a'r Bettws (38)
Bron y gaer in Mydrim
Blaen y parsel in Abernant
Brechfa
Broadlay in St Ismaels
Blaen Eyrch in Llangan
Cappel-y-bettus Trelech
Cappel-Llanlluan (80)
Cappel dyddgen in Llangendeirn
Clun-uchel in Llanarthney
Cum-nant-y-gôf in Conwyl Elfed
St Clear's
Caer Coed in Llangathen
Cwrt-Henry in Llangathen
Cwm-y-Pandy in Trelech
Cyffig
Cilmaenllwyd Cenarth
Cilrhedyn
Cilycwm
Cydweli
Cilfod in Cenarth
Cappel y Drindod in Penboyr
Cwm-Cawdden in Moddfei
Clos-y-Graig in Llangeler (40)

Carmarthen Town (40)
Cryg-y-stydyr in Trelech
Cwm Sarah in Cenarth
Clun-du in Pencarreg
Cwrt Maenororion in Llangeler (25)
Castleheli in Ciffig
Colomendy in Abernant
Cwm-amman in Llandebie
Clyn-Glas in Llandebie
Castell-dwyfran Cappel
Cwmpedol in Llandilo-fawr (72)
Castell-du in Llanfihangel Ararth
Clos-y-Felin in Llanglwydwen
Clos-y-graig in Penboyr
Carnau in Cenarth
Croes yr Heul in Llanon
Castell Howel in Llandilofawr (73)
Cwmdowe in Pencarreg
Cwm coly in Kiffig
Cilarddu in Conwyl-elvet
Castell y Ferwd in Cilrhedyn (71)
Cappel Joan in Cilrhedyn
Crug y bar in Caio
Cilcarw in Llangyndeirn
Clyn-caled in Llangeler
Court in Llanegwad (50)
Cenarth (36)
Cynwyl Caio in Caio
Clawdd Côch
Cwrt y Cadno in Caio
Cwm Brwyn in Laugharne (45)
Cae'r Dole in Pemboir
Cwm-forgan in Cilrhedyn
Conwyl Elfet
Cothi-Bridge in Llanegwad
Cilgryman in Llanwinio
Cwm Gwyddyl in Llanwinio
Cwm-dwyfran in New Church
Caer Canvas in Llanelli
Craig yr Auryn in Llangan
Cwm in Llangan
Cwm deri Cyrn in Llannon
Coedu in Llannon
Cwm-amman in Llandilo
Cwmnant in Llanon
Cwmcennin in Llandilofawr
Clunwallis in Llanfihangel Rhos y Corm
Coedeiddig in Pencarreg (38)
Cwmgwenhendy in Llanfynydd (100)
Cwm-y-frân in Llanfynydd

Cwm-crwth in Llanfihangel Cilfargen
Coedgain in Llangynnwr
Coynant in Mydrym
Caerhoeliw in Llanegwad
Cae Howel in Llanfihangel Aberbythych (55)
Ca-llifer in Llanfihangel Aberbythych
Caio
Dan y Gribin in Penboyr
Dan y Graig in Conwyl Elfet
Dol-fan in Liangan
Dyrslwyn in Llangathen
Dan-yr-allt in Llanfihangel Ararth
Dan-y-Coed in Llangeler
Dan-y-Graig in Llandyfeilog
Dan y Gaer in Llangyning
Dyffryn Tywy
Drasgell in Llanfihangel Abercowyn (33)
Dol y Saefon in Conwyl Elfed (35)
Dalfa-ddu in Cilycwm
Dyffryn Broidir in Llanboidy
Eglwys Fair (Llantaf Church)
Eitheyn Duon in Llansawel
Eglwys fair Chapel
Evel vac in Llanfihangel Aberbythych
Ffôs lâs in Trelech ar Bettus
Ffynnon-freuddig in Llanfihangel Aber-buthych
Felindre in Trelech
Ffôs-y-Wion in Llanllawddog
Ffair-fach in Llandilo-fawr
Felin Gwm in Llanegwad (47)
Felingenaur Coed in Llanllawddog
Felindre sawddau in Llangadog
Felin Marlais in Llanfihangel
Fel in Issa in Llangan
Forest in Llandingad
Forest-fâch in Cilrhedyn
Ffinnant in Cenarth (62)
Felin fâch in Llanybyddar (52)
Ffynon Dudyr in Llangeler
Ffordd in Llanstephan
Fron Las in Trelecha'r Bettws
Ffos-ddu in Abernant
Felin-fâch in Llanarthney
Ffynon y Gôg in Llanfihangel Rhos y Corn
Ffynnon Newydd in Llangynnock
Gelli Dywyll in Cenarth
Gellifach in Llangynog

Glawsawdde in Llangadog
Gwaen-yr-Helfa in Llanpumsaint
Glasfryn in Llanfihangel Abercowyn
Gelli-gatti-fàch in Cenarth
Glyn-y-Geifr in Trelech
Glyn-y-Cefn in Llanfihangel Aberbythych (34)
Glyn in Henllan Amgoed (51)
Gelli'r-fawnen in Llandebie
Gwynvey Chapel in Llangadog
Garn in Llanddarog
Gorse by Mynydd bâch in Llandilo fawr
Glyn Claiar in Llansadwrn
Garth Tal-llychan
Gwaen Clunda in Llansadwn
Glyn rhyd y mor wynion in Llanegwad
Gwarnogau in Llanfihangel Rhos y Corn
Glan Gwily in New Church
Glaucwmbychan in Llanedi
Gwaun-y-fwyalchen in Brechfa
Gelli Wen in Trelech
Gellifach in Llandilo fawr
Gweyn-clyn-da in Llansadwrn
Godre'r-bryn in Abernant
Gwndwn bach in Llangyndeirn
Kilmaenllwyd
Kilcarw
Kilrhedyn
Kidweli
Kilcwm
Hafod-hir in Llanfihangel Abercowyn
Henllan-Amgoed (62)
Neuadd in Gwynfei Hamlet Heol-y-Llangadog
Hên Effel in Llangeler
St Ismaels
Llan y Bri in Llanstephan
Llangynog
Llwynhendy in Llanelly
Lower-Court fach in Llanfihangel Abercowyn
Llangan
Llanfihangel Abercowyn village
Llanddowror (18)
Llannewydd
Llanllwch
Llwyn-y-piod in Llanfihangel Abercowyn
Llangorse in Llanfihangel Abercowyn
Llangwnnor

Llannant in Llandyfeilog
Leger in Mydrim
Llanglydwen
Llansadwrn
Lleiniau in Cilrhedyn
Llainrhydwen in Cenarth
Llan in Llangan
Llwyn-yr-haf in Llandebie
Llanpumsaint
Llwyngoedisa in Llanon
Llandybie
Llandre in Llanllawddog
Llanelly
Llanvihangel Kilfargen
Llangeler (32)
Llanycrwys
Llanfynydd
Llanwinio (92)
Llangyndeirn
Llanddarog
Llanfihangel-Orarth
Llanfihangel-Aberbythych
Llanybyddar
Llangathen
Llangunnor
Llandingad
Llansawel
Llanegwad
Llangynin (14)
Llethergarw in Llanfihangel Aberbythych
Lletyr Hurdd in Llangynin
Llangynwr
Llenarth
Laugharne (60)
Llechglawdd in Llanboidy
Llanhafren in Mydrim
Llanycefn
Llanllian Chapel
Llandylas
Llangunheiddon in Llandyfeylog
Llangattock
Llangwendraeth in Llangendeirn
Llanddeusant
Llanfair ar-y-Bryn
Llanwrda
Llandeilo-Abercowyn
Llwyn-yr-Haf in Llandilo Fawr (61)
Llanedi
Llwyn Kelyn in Llanvallteg

Llanarthey
Llandyfeilog
Llangain
Llandisilio
Llandyfaen Chapel in Llandilo-Fawr
Llanfihangel Rhos-y-Corn
Llanon Village
Lletty mawr in Llanvihangel Aberbythych (42)
Maengwyn in Llangeler
Meddygan in Conwyl Elfed
Meddfyn Fŷch in Llandybie
Mydrym
Maen-ar-dilo in Llandilo Fawr
Moddfey
Merthur
Mynydd bach in Llandilo Fawr
Marros
Mynydd Ycha Llandyfeiliog
Machros in Abergwili
Morlech in Llanon
Merlyn's Gate in Abergwili Village
Melin Bibwr in Llangunnor
Nant-y-cernydd in Abernant
Nant-uwch-gwili in Llanllawddog
Nant-bai in Llanfair ar y Bryn
New Well in Llangynog
Newcastle Emlyn (53)
Nant-y-Blaidd in Conwil Elvet (11)
Nant-y-ffin in Llangendeirn
Nant y frân in Llanarthney
Nant y Garreg in Llangeler
New Church
Pen-y-Pontpren in Cilrhedyn
Pentre'r Garn in Llanddarog
Pen-yr-Allt in Cenarth
Pant-y-Groes in Llangan
Pass-By in Llangan
Pencader in Llanfihangel-Orarth
Pen-y-Caerau in Conwyl Elfet
Perth-y-Gwenyn in Trelech
Pen Pont ar Sawdde in Llangadog
Penlan in Llanddewsant
Parc-cethin in Llandilo-Abercowyn
Pwll-y-March in Trelech
Pen-y-Bont in Llanfihangel Orarth
Pistyll Gwynn in New Church
Pencarreg
Penton in Penboyr
Penhill in Moddfey

Priory Street in Carmarthen Town
Pen-y-bach in Llanddowror (49)
Pen-y-Bont in Trelech
Parc-Gwyn in Llangan
Penybank Llanllawddog
Penlanfawr in Penboyr
Plas-y-Parce in Penboyr (31)
Pantiouryn in Ystlym Gwili in Abergwili
Pant-yr-Hebog in Penboyr
Pwll-y-trap in St Clears
Penrhiw Goch in Llanboidy
Pen y ddwy ffordd in Llangadog
Pant yr Helyg in Llangathen
Penbrey
Pant-y-llyn near Llandybie
Penboyr
Pentre Tywyn in Llanfair-ar-y-Bryn
Pen y Rheol near Cothy Bridge
Penybank near Woodhouse
Pant-y-Gwyddyl in Llanwinio
Pant y Ddafaad in Llanwinio
Pen-y-vedw vach in Llanedi
Penygraig in Trelech
Pompren maur in Llanboidy
Penrhiw-onnen in Llanfair-ar-y-Bryn
Parc y deunaw in Llanarthney
Peny Banc in Llanarthney
Porth-y-Rhyd in Llanddarog
Pantycelyn in Llanfair ar y Bryn
Pant y Berllan in Llanfynydd
Penrhognwg in Llanfihangel Abercowyn
Pen-yr-heol in Llanegwad
Pant y Kelyn in Llanfair
Pen-y-bauli (8)
Penybeili in Conwyl Elfed
Plas-y-Gwer in Llanfihangel Abercowyn (54)
Penpompren in Llanegwad
Pen-allt-cillo in Cenarth
Plâs Bâch in Henllan Amgoed
Pont-y-Cleision in Llanvihangel Abercowyn (48)
Pont ar Gothy
Pen y Ffin in Llanfihangel Orarth
Pentre in Llanfihangel Abercowyn
Panty-y-ffynon in Llanddarog
Pant-y-Ffynon in Abergwili
Penderi March
Plâs Newydd in Llandyfeilog

Pen-yr-hoel in Llangendeirn
Pant y glâs in Llandingad
Pen y coed in Eglwys Fair
Pen yr hoel in Cappel Ifan
Penrhyw in Llangeler
Pantglâs in Llandilo fawr
Pencraig in Llanwinio
Pantglas in Llanarthney
Pont-y-Llan in Llanddarog
Pen-yr-allt in Llanboidy
Pen-yr-heol in Llanfair ar-y-Bryn
Rhyd y ddrysien in Llanwinio
Rhydfoyr in Penboyr
Rhiwau in Llanllawddog
Rhyd y ffwolbert near Castell Cerrig
　Cynnen
Rhosyn coch in Mydrim
Rhandir ganol in Llanvair Bryn
Rhiw-ddu in Llanfihangel Aberbythych
Rhos-y-Maen in Llandilofawr (64)
Rhydwynnog in Trelech
Rhywlas in Llandeilo fawr
Rhandir y Bruscod in Moddfey
Rhyd-y-Wrach in Henllan Amgoed
Rhydtal-Esgob in Llanvallteg
Rhyd-y-Bont in Llanybydder
Rhydwithan in Llangeler
Rhegwm in Eglwys Fair
Rhŷd-y-Saint in Llangadog
Rhŷd-y-dal in Llanddarog
Rhyd-goch in Llanarthney
Rhwng dau fyngdd in Llandilo fawr
Rhyd y cerfeaed in Llanginin
Seybor fach in Llandeveylog
Sidenyn in Abernant
Sarnau in Mydrim
Sticklau in Llangendeirn (19)
Sarngoch in Llanboidy
Taldu in Llanfihangel Abercowyn
Tynewydd in Henllan Amgoed
Tycenol in Abernant
Twyn-llanan in Llanddensant
Ty gwyn in Trelech
Taldy in Mydrim
Tybâch in Cilrhedyn
Trelech ar Bettus
Ty'r-felin in Llangeler
Tynewydd-cilai in Llanddarog
Troed-y-Rhiw in Cenarth

Ty-Hên in Trelech
Tyisa near Ffynon Felen (70)
Troed y Rhiw in Llanfihangel Ararth
Ty'r Bank in Llanedi
Tynewydd in Llanarthney
Troed yr Oyr in Tal-llychan
Troed y Rhiw in Llanfihangel Rhos y
　Corn
Tŷ-issa in Bettws
Tyucha'r Fforest in Llanedi
Tredai in Llangan
Ty'r Eithin in Llangeler
Ty-yn-y-Garn in Llanfihangel Aberby-
　thych
Trallwyn cau in Llanvair bryn
Tygwyn ar Daf
Ty-jets in Llangyndeirin
Tal-lluchan
Ty-dan-y-Graig in Cilcarw
Ty-newydd in Llanegwad (24)
Tre-newydd in Laugharne (36)
Trepiod in Llandyfeilog
Trecadwgan in Llanfihangel Abercowyn
Troed y Rhyw Cappel in Kilrhedyn
Ty-hen in Peuboyr
Talsarn in Llanelly
Trewynt in Trelech a'r Bettws
Trenewydd in Llanfihangel Abercowyn
Tandalardd in Llanllwni
Ty'r clai in Llanfynydd
Ty yn y Ffordd in Llanegwad
Tre-hîr in Llanboidy
Wern newydd in Ystlym Gwili
Wern-y-Brics in Llanfihangel Abercowyn
Weyn Fach in St Clears
Wern in Llanarthney (81)
Waun in Llandyrnog
Ystym gwili in Abergwili
Y Glog ddu in Llangynnog
Ysgol-fach in Llangathen
Ysgybor fâch in Llandilofawr
Ystrad ffin
Yscar goch in Llanfair-Bryn
Yscar Hoeliw in Llanegwad
Yscar Owen in Pencarreg
Ysgybor fach in Llandefeilog
Ysgwin in Llangathen
Ysgybor fawr in Eglwys Fair Llantaf
Ysgar fychan in New Church

DENBIGHSHIRE

Blaenau Llangerniw
Bettus-Abergeley
Banker in Llandyrnog Parish (45)
Cefn Llwyd in Llanufudd
Crinlle in Llansannan (34)
Denbeigh Town
near Denbeigh
Derwen
Eglwys-fach
Efenechtyd
Ffynhonnau in Llanufudd
Gyfylliog
Gwytherin
Glyn-glas in Llanddoget
Gwern y Llyfion in Llansannan
Glan-yr-afon near Llandyrnog
Hirwawn in Llanbedr-dyffryn-clwyd
Hen-y-bryn bach in Llanufudd
near Henllan Church
Llanddyrnog
Llanbedr (53)
Llangwyfan
Llanfwrog
Llanarmon-Dyffryn-Ceiriog
Llanrhaiadr in Mochnant
Llanfair-talhaiarn
Llangerniew (36)
Llan-Elidan
Llanrwst
Llansannan
Llanynys (32)
Llansaintfraid
Llandyrnog
Llanddoget
Llandegle
Llanfwrog, at Rich Parry's house in
Llansantffraid-Clan-Conway
Llanarmon in Yale Village
Llanfair-Dyffryn-Clwyd
Llansannan Village
Llanvair
Mochdre in Llandrillo in Rhos
Maes-llwrf in Llanfair Talhaiarn (41)
Nantglyn
Pentre-Llanbedr in Dyffryn-clwyd
Petrual in Llanfair-talhaiarn
Pandûbudr in Llangernew (28)
Plas issa in Llanbedr

Rhyd Loyw in Llansannan near Gyffy-
lliog
Rhydgaled in Henllan
Rhaiadr-arjan in Llansannan
Rhyd-yr-arian in Llansannan (38)
Rhŷd-loyw in Llansannan
Rhiw'r-fudde in Llanfair Talhaiarn
Ruthin in Llanfwrog Parish
Tŷ'n y Llidiard in Llanrdaiadr
Tyddyn-isaf in Llanrhaiadr
Ty'n y Rhôs in Llangernew
Tŷ'n y llidiad in Llangerniw
Tal-y-bryn in Llanufudd
Wain-breian in Llanrhaiadr
Waun-fôr in Llanufudd
Waun in Llandrynog
Waun in Llanbedr
Yspyttu Ivan

FLINTSHIRE

Cwm
Dysert Village
Gallt-Melyd
Melidan

GLAMORGANSHIRE

Aber-avan
Aberbargoed-Bridge
Aberdare (31)
Angel Town in Newcastle Bridgend
St Andrews
Abertridwr in Eglwys Llan
Abertwrch in Llanguick
Allt-wen in Cilbebyll
Aberlonga in Ystrad-Owen Parish
Alltgrig in Llanguick
Byeastown in Coyty
Brombil in Margam (38)
Bayden Hamlet in Llangynwyd
Bid-gelyn in Eglwys-Llan
Brychton in Wick
Baglan
Bedwellty in Cwm Syrewi
Bettus near Neath
Berthyn in Llanblethian (28)
Bwlch-dau-Fynydd in Michaelston
Bwrthing in Llanblethian (28)
Bryn-Cethin in St Bride's Minor (21)
Blaen-Hondda in Cadoxton

Britton Ferry
Bryn y Lloi in Bettws
Blaencrymlyn in Coychurch
Bettws Llangunwyd
Bolegoed in Llandilo Talybont (59)
Bryn in Michaelston
St Bride's Minor
Bryn-coch in St Bride's Minor
Bath-newydd in Llangyfelach
Bryncallo in Laleston
Bridgend
Cwm in Llanwonno
Cwmcylleu in Gellygâr
Cadoxton
Cross-wen in Radyr
Craig-tre-wyddfa in Llangyfelach
Cynffig Hall in Cynffig
Cefn-Donn in Llwyd-Coed, Aberdare
Cwmdâr in Aberdâr
Cwm rhyd y filast in Llangyvelach
Cnap-y-llwyd in Llangyfelach
Cwm-brombil in Margam (38)
Cefn Cribwr in Tythegston
Caerphilly Town
Colvinston (26)
Cae-helyg in St Brides Minor
Clyngwyn in Llanwonno
Castlychwr
Cors-Eynon in Llangyvelach
Clwyd-y-fedw in Gelligâr
Capel Newydd
Clynogwr
Cefneseison in Llanylltyd
Croynant Chapel in Cadoxton
Cygerwen in Llanguick
Cwm-maenllwyd in Cilbelyll
Cwm in Llansamlet
Croesfach in Panteg
Coity, alias Coychurch (44)
Cemickston in Llangennith
Cefn-machen in Llangwinor (42)
Crosswen in Eglwys Llan
Cwmllwydrew in Machyn
Clyn y Castell in Llantwit
Chapel Glyn Castell
Cefncribwr in Llandidwg
Cwm-dwr in Llangyfelach
Cefn-hengoed in Gelligar
Cappel-tal-y-garn in Llantrissant

Colwyn Village in Colwynston (26)
Cwm-mawr in Llwchur
Croes-y-Ceiliog in Llandefeylog
Dan-y-Graig in Llangyfelach
Dinas in Llantrisant
Denis Powis in St Andrew
Dyffryn Mill in Margam (42)
Drewen Deg in Christ Church
Dunsant in Llanrhidian
Dyffryn in Merthyr Tydfil
Dyffryn House in Aberdare
Eglwysilian
Eglwys Helen
Ffilocks in Llandaf
Forest Hamlet in Merthyr Tydvil
Fedw fach in Gelligar
St Fagan's Village
Felin fâch in St Brides Minor (40)
Flimston
Fernhill in Rosilly
Fonmon Village in Penmarc
Felyn-wen in Llangyfelach
Gellifeddgar in Upper Hamlet of Coy-
    church
Gelligâr Village
Gwar y canau in Hafod Hamlet in Margam
Gelli gron in Llanguick
Glyn Tâf in Eglwys Llan
Goston in Llangan
St Goris
Gellifelgaws in Cadoxton
Gylfach yr Haidd in Llanguick
Garth Gynyd in Gelligaer (21)
Gelli-fedi in Llanbedr-fynydd (33)
Gaelfael Penmain in Mynydd Islwyn
Gilfach in Llangynwyd (30)
Gelli wastod in Llangyvelach
Garnlwyd in Llangynwyd
Green-y-quills in St Bride's Minor
Gadlais in Aberdare
Gwn Dwr in Llangyfelach
Hirwain in Aberdâre
Heol-y-sheet in Pyle
Henffig near Margam
Hawdd-dre in Baglan
Hills in Portynon
Hills in Rylastown
Heol-Bryn-Cettyn in St Bride's Illan
St John

Kil-bebyll
Llangewydd in Laleston
Llandyfydog
Laleston
Llysfaen
Llwst-y-nant in Llanwonno
Llanharan (33)
Llangewydd in Laleston
Llanishan
Llwyd-goed Hamlet in Aberdâr (42)
Llantrisant
Llantwit Vardre
Llangan
Llanharry Village
Llanmaes
Llwyn Helyg in Laleston (29)
Llansamlet
Llanguick
Llangynwyd
Llandilo-Tal-y-bont (77)
Landow
Lysworney
Llan St Fred
Llangattwck
Llangrallog
Llannynno
Llanylltyd fair dref
Llangyfelach
Llanynewir Chapel in Llanrhidian
Llanddiddan near Cowbridge
Llanblethian (25)
Llanfabon
Lynon in Ilston
Llanrhidian
Llwyn Helygwr Talygarn Chapel in Llan-
    trisant (32)
Llwyn Owen in Baglan
Llantwyn in Hyttri
Llusendy in Coychurch
Llusendy in Bettus
Llanbedr near Llanharan
Llangynni
Lusendy in Llandyvodick
Llangenith
Llwyncellyn in Llanguick
Llan gafty Tal-llyn
Llandidwg
Maesteg in Llantwit-Vardre
Merthyr Mawr Village

Melin-pwill-y-glaw
Michaelston upon Avon
Maes-y-bryn in Llanedarn
Monachdy in Llanwonno
Melin y Cwm in Gelligâr
St Michael
Melyn Gwryson near Neath
Middle Stormy in Tythegston
Michaelston-le-pit
Merthyr Tydfil
Mynydd-Bach in Tythegston
Meline, Ystrad y Mynach
Megin-y-bwlch in Mynydd Islwyn
Mynydd-cadle in Llangyfelach
Margam
Molton in Llancarfan
Machyn or Machen
St Mary's Hill Common
Neath Abbey in Cadoxton
New-Castle Bridge-End
Newton
Nottage
St Nicholas
Neath
New Inn in Panteg
Newton in Oystermouth
Neuadd in Llanguhe
Old Castle Bridgend (21)
Olchfa in Swansea
Pwll Flawydd in Llanwonno
Peterston super Montem (33)
Pen-y-darren in Hengoed
Pont-yr-Ynn in Merthyr Tydfil
Penlline Village
Pandy House in Merthyr Tydfil
Penybont Newydd in Gelligar
Pantmawr in the hamlet of Hafod
Pen y pryst in Coychurch (20)
Pont-Eynon, in Llanwonno
Pont y ty Prîdd
Pen yr Aly in Coed Fraink Cadoxton
Pentyrch
Pool y pant
Penylan in Swansea
Pencoed in Coychurch (30)
Pen-yr-heol in Llandilo Talybont (52)
Pilton in Rosilly
Pen y fan near Newcastle
Pomprenllwyd in Penderin

Penheol fawr in Llanvabon
Penrhyw in Margam
Penybank in Llangatwg ar Caerleon
Person-dy in Llanharry
Pwll-y-bath in Pile
Pentre Estyll
Pentile in Baglan
Pentre trybaid in East Margam
Penhydd-Waelod in Margam
Penrice
Pesked Wyn in Llandilo Taly-Bont
Pant-y-môch in Margam
Pont Cadifor in Merthyr Tydfil
Roath
Ryddry
Rhyd-yr-Eithinen in Llantwit Vardre
Reeding in Cadoxton
Sheet Lane in Pyle
Siggai in Llantwit
Swansea Town
Silly Village
Ty-taldon in Merthyr Tydfil
Ty'r Bont in Merthyr Tydfil
Tyn-y-Garddau in Coychurch
Ty-dan-y-Graig in Rhyddry
Tybach Dany-graig in Llyswerry Llys-
    vane
Ty dan y lan in Llangyfelach
Tŷ-yn-y-cwm in Merthyr Tydfil
Tŷ-yn-y-cwm in East Margam
Treforyg in Llantrisant
Ty yn y cae in Whitechurch
Tre-r-rhingyll in Llanblethian
Tontraethwg in Llantrisant
Tal y garn in Llantrisant (32)
Ty Lloyd in Cadoxton
Ton y planwydd in Cadoxton
Treguff in Llancarvan
Tongwnlas in Whitechurch
Trane Hamlet in Llantrissant
Tonnau in Llanylltyd
Tranch in Trevethyn
Tonnau im Llantwit
Ty-yn-ffram, Margam
Tynewydd in Llangwm
Ty-ar-y-cefn in Laleston
Ty yn y Cae in Goitre
Ty'r Pwyf in Llangwinor (28)
Trallwm in Trissent Hamlet (28)

Tnys fach in Llanylltyd fawr
Ty yn Rheol in Llanelltyd
Tymaen in Laleston
Ty'r Rhôs in Gelligaer
Tres-oes in Llangan
Tŷ-ucha in Llangyfelach
Tŷ mawr in Panteg
Ty-issa in Michaelston in Avon
Tyn y Croft in Baglan
Tyn y Graig in Llansawel
Trisaint in East Margam
Tewgoed in Michaelston on Avon
Tŷ yn y Waen in Lantwit
Ty'r Cyrnel in Tythegston
Ty-picca in Colwinston
Ty-uwchlaw'r Eglwys in Michaelstone
Undy Village in Undy
Vedw in Peterston-super-Ely
Whitchurch
Wenallt in Llantwid
Wolves Newton
Wayn fawr in Bedwellty
Wain Cygurwen in Llanguicke
Walton in Lantwit Major
Windmill in Llanrhidian
Welch-moor in Llanrhidian
Ynys fach in Llantwid
Ystrad Gynlais
Ymlaen-y-Glais in Vaynor
Ynys y Bwl in Llanwonno
Ynys fach in Llanylltyd fawr
Ystrad Yfodwg
Ynys Bowys in Llangrannog
Ynys y Maerdre in Britonferry
Ystrad Owen
Ygadles-issa in Aberdare

MERIONETHSHIRE

Adwydda in Llanvihangel y Traethau
Bala
Barmouth in Llanaber
Bodgadvan in Kelynin
Brithdir in Dolgelly Parish (26)
Cae'r Crydd in Llanfawr
Corwen
Cefn-Coch in Llanvihangel Traethau
Cynwyd in Gwyddelwern (34)
Corwen Town
Dinas-y-mowddwy in Mallwyd (18)

Dolgelley Town
Ffestiniog
Garthgoch in Llanfawr
Garnedd near Rhiwedog in Llanfawr
Gwyddelwern (47)
Harlegh Town
Kregenan in Kelynin
Llanychllyn
Llanfawr
Llangower
Llanelltyd
Llanfrothen
Llanfachreth
Llandrillo (42)
Llanaber
Llanfair, near Harlech
Llanenddwn
Llan-Bedr (25)
Llantower
Llan y Mowddwy
Llan-enddwyn
Llandderfel
Llansant-ffraid-Glandyfrdwy
Llangar (41)
Llwyngweril in Celynnin (29)
Llanfihangel y Pennant
Maentwrog
Mallwyd
Maes y Groes in Llan y Mowddwy (34)
Maerdre in Llandrillo (43)
Nant y deiliau in Llanuwchllyn
Pennal (40)
Penrhyn-Doctor in Llanaber (28)
Penrhyn bach (29)
Perthsaethydd in Gwyddelwern
near Riwaedog in Llanfawr
Rhos-y-gwaliau in Llanfawr
near Ragat in Corwen
Rhiwlas in Llanfihangel y Pennant
Tal-y-llyn
Trawsfynydd (38)
Ty newydd in Dolgelley (34)
Ty Cerrig in Llangelynin

MONMOUTHSHIRE

Aberystryth
Aberbargoed Bridge in Bedwellty
Abergwiddon in Mynyddyslwyn
Bettws

Blaenafon in Llanfoist
St Brides
Bedwas
Brynhyddyn in Bedwellty (28)
Blaenafon in Llanwernath
Blaenau Gwent
Croesfach in Panteg
Castell-y-bwch in Henllys
Cosgarneinon in Bassaleg
Cwm in Graig Hamlet
Coed-bychain in Raglan
Cwmbran in Llanvrechva (14)
Caingoed in Llandenny
Carreg Bicca in Bedwellty
Coedcamawr near Aberṣychan (32)
Carleon
Cwm-nant-yr-odyn in Mynydd Islwyn
Coed-Gwnnwr in Llangefiw
Cleidda in Llanarth
Cefn ty'r Marchog in Bassaleg
Cefn Cribwr in Laleston
Dan yr Heol in Aberystruth
Derwen-deg in Christ-Church
Elusendy in St Mellans
Five-Lanes in Bassaleg
Glas-coed in Usk
Goitre (46)
Gwchelwg Common in Usk
Gavel-Land in Llanwenarth
Glan y Dwfr in Aberystruth
Glascoed in Llanbadoc (36)
Glascoed in Trefethyn
Gellygryg in Aberystryth (30)
Gwernesney
Gurhay in Mynydd Islwyn
Gafael Penmain in Mynydd Islwyn
Henllys
Heol y fforest in Bedwellty
Hatrel in Cwmyoy
Holy Bush in Sîr Newton
Kemmeys Commander
Kevenllwyn Common in Llanddewi vach
Llandowlas in Llangibby
Llanfachas
Llanelan
Llanfrechfa near Cwmbran
Llanbadock
Llanwenarth
Llantony

Llwetrog in Llanover
Llwyn Celyn in Llanfihangel Fedw
Llanfihangel
Llanfihangel Fynachlog
Llanhileth
Llanelli Common
Llanishen
Llanwyddyn
Llanidloes Town
Llanddewi Rhydderch
Llanover
Lusendy in Rhymney
Mynyddyslwyn (34)
Migin y Bwlch in Mynydd Islwyn
Monk's wood Chapel Hamlet
Machen
Magor in Magor
Mamhilad
Marshfield
Pont y Felin in Panteg
Penrhyw-gyngi in Bedwellty
Pont-gwaith-yr-harn
Pont-da-bean in Trevethin
Panty Fforest in Aberystryth (30)
Pentwyn mawr in Mynydd Islwyn
Pen-y-twyn in Malpas
Pengam Bridge in Aberystryth
Pen-y-rhiw in Rhysca
Pen-yr-heol in Pantêg
Persondy in Llanfrechfa
Pandy in Llanfrechfa
Panteg near New Inn
Pen Parc Newydd in Bassaleg
Pentre bach in Llanfihangel Llantarna
Penbank in Llangattwg
Rhyd-nant-Melyn in Bedwellty
Rhwŷthog in Cwm Joy
Rhymney
Sîr Newton
Sweet Well in Mynydd Islwyn
Twyn-yr hychod in Trefethyn (22)
Ty-yn-y-cae in Goytrey
Twyn Singreg in Llanfihangel-vedw
Tŷ ar y nant in Aberystryth
Tŷ yn y Lelyn in Rocheston in Bassaleg
Tŷ-Pant-Sychpant in Aberystryth
Ton Sawndwr in Llanfihangel Fynachlog
Tŷ Dan-y-Wal in Aberystryth (26)
Typoeth in Glasgoed Hamlet near Usk

Tŷ mawr in Pantegue
Twyn yr Hychod in Trevethin (22)
Trostra in Glasgoed Hamlet near Usk
Ty ar y mynydd in Cwm Joy
Tycoch in Bettws
Tranch in Trefethyn
Ty Pentwyn in Llangatwck Caerleon
Tŷ coch in Caerleon
Tŷ Llwyd near Ponty pool
Tynewydd in Llangan
Usk
Undy
Ysgybor Newydd in Raglan
Wolves Newton

MONTGOMERYSHIRE

Bwlch y Ca-haidd in Aberhafes
Bwlch-yr-Helygen in Tref Eglwys
Cappel banhadlog
Cwm Carnedd in Llanbryn mair
Cae-Gilbert in Llanbrynmair
Capel in Llanbrynmair
Cefn Llwyd in Llanfair Gaereinion
Cemmes (28)
Carno
Darowen
Esger-wgan in Carno
Hendre in Carno
Hen-dŷ'r-gô in Llanlligan
Henvas in Llangwrig
Kerry
Llanwyddelan
Llanddinam
Llan-bryn-Mair (33)
Llanvair Kereinio
Llanwyddyn
Llanidlos Town
Llidiard vawr in Llanlligan
Llangadfan
Llanwddin
Llangwrig
Llangynnog
Llanwryn
Llanlligan
Moughtrey
Pentyrch in Llanfair Careinion
Pont-dôl-goch in Llanwennog
Pen-y-Gochel in Llanfair Gaereinion
Pen-planwydd in Llangwrig

Pennant
Pen-Egos
Rhôs aflog in Llanvair Kareinion
Rhyd-y-cwmllwyd in Carno
Tref-Eglwys
Ty yn y Coed in Llanlliccan
Ty'n y Wain in Llanwyddelon
Ty yn y Wain in Aberhafes
Ty-yn-yr Helyg in Carno
Ty main in Llangwrig
Under-garn-fawr in Llangwm
Ystradynog in Llanidlos

PEMBROKESHIRE

Abergwayn
Amroth
Ambleston
Blaenhiraeth in Llanfallteg
Bridell
Blaengafren in Eglwys Wrw
Bramble-Bush in Lampeter x Velfrey
Blaenllechog in Maenchochog
Barn's Hill in Hay's Casstle
Brengast in Cilgerran
Brodey
Bletherstone
Bayvil
Cilgerran (91)
Cilgwyn Chapel in Nefern
Cilfachwrnell in Llanfihangel Penbedw
Cross Inn in Llantwyd
Castle Bigh
Clydey
Carfarchell in St Davids
Castell Newydd Bach
Cwm in Lampeter Velfrey
Castell Ely in Cyffig
Creffty-Cornel in Castell Haidd
Cilgwyn Cwarter in Nefern
Castell Haidd
Clyn-fyw in Manor-dwi
Cwm bach in Clydey
Dinas
St David's Town
St Dogmals (45)
St Donats
Eithyn Duon in Llandysilio
Eglwys Erow
Fynachlog-ddu

Ford Chapel in Hays Castle (17)
Fishgard
Felin y dyffryn-mawr in Whitechurch (22)
Fachelych in Whitechurch
Gwryd mawr in St David's
Gilfach in Mathry
Henllan Amgoed
Hendy in Letterston
Henry's Mote
Hiraeth in Llanvallteg (34)
Jeffreyston
Kilmanllwyd
Kilcam
Kilrredyn
Llanfair-Nant-gwyn (30)
Llangoed in Eglwys Wrw
Lampeter Velffrey
Llanfallteg
Llandysilio
Letterston (107)
Llanhowel
Llangafru
Llantwyd
Llanfihangel-Penbedw (51)
Llanychllwydog
Llanychaer (51)
Llandilo fach
Llanfyrnach (28)
Llanllawer (42)
Little Newcastle
Llysyrane
Llanunda
Llanrhidian
Llanglydwen
Llwyndyrus in Egrmond
Llangalman
Llandeilo
St Lawrence
Llanrhian
Lamphey
Llangan (42)
Llwyncrwm in Maenordivy (51)
Llanfair Nantygof
Llangwm
Llanfeygan in Bridell
Llandeloy
Llan y Cefn
Llantood
Llwydart in Llan y Keven

Monington
Maenordivi (38)
Moylgrove
Morfa-dû in Penrhydd
Monachlogddu
Maenclochog
Mathry
Morfil
Morfa in Castellan (23)
Moor in Llanfyrnach (19)
Monk Town
Meline in Lampeter Velfrey
St Michael's in Pembroke Town
Machelych in Eglwyswen
St Mary's in Pembroke Town
St Martin
St Nicholas
Nant-yr-helygen in Eglwys Wrw
Nant-yr-Angell in Llanvihangel Penbedw
Nant-y-Nydd in Clydey
Neddadd Wen in Letterston
Nanlydd in Llanvyrnach
Newport
Nant-y-Geifr-fach in Llanfyrnach
Nant y deilian in Llanwachllyn
Nant y Nywl in Clydey
Pen-y feidir in St David's
Pencnwc-bach in Meline
Pontgynon Mill in Meline
Plas-y-Berllan in Manordeifi
Penffordd in Meline
Pont-faen in Whitechurch (30)
Penallt y Felin in Manordivi
Pigws Park in Amblestone
Pen Rhydd
Pont Rhyd-seli in Manor-dwi
Penygraig in Manordivi
Pen-y-cnwck in Fishguard
Plwyf y Groes near St David's
Pentre ys yllt in Nefern
Pembroke Town
Puncheston
Punch-Castle Village
Penhescwarn in Llanwnda
Porskilly in Mathry
Pontpaldan in Nefern
Porth-hiddi in Llanrhian
Rhostwarch in Meline

Rhyd y gelan in Brawdy
Rhŷdlangwege in Ambroth
Richeston
Rhuddbach
Rhinaston
Rhosgerdd in St Dogmels
Roch
Rosemarket
Ramswood in Rudbackstown
Solfach
Stradland in Ambleston
Stepside in St Lawrence
Sheyvoch in St David's
Trevecca in St David's
Trefin
Teg y pistyll in Moylgrove
Tŷ yn y Gilfach in Llan y Keven
Trewyddyl
Trelettart
Trefwomon
Troed y Rhiw in Penrhydd (40)
Tannerdy in Cilgerran (40)
Tresysyllt in Llanrhian
Tresare in Mathry
Tretio in St David's
Trefair in Llanglydwen
Tregidreg in Mathry
Trurhos in Llandilofach
Treslanog-Fach in Mathry
Trefelin
Whitechurch Cemmaes
Woodstock in Ambleston

RADNORSHIRE

Boughroad
Bog in Abi-cwm-hîr in Llanbister
Cwmteiddwr
Crig cadarn
Dyserth
Dolfrwynog in Llananno
Grochren in Llanbadarn Fynydd
St Harmon's
Llansaint frêd
Llandrindod
Llandegle
Llanwrthwl
Nammel
Pains Castle

4. *The Circulating Welsh Charity Schools*, 1737–1777,

as returned by Judge Johnes in his *Causes which have produced Dissent from the Established Church in Wales*, 1870

Year	Schools	Scholars	Year	Schools	Scholars
1737	37	2400	1758	218	9,834
1738	71	3981	1759	206	8,539
1739	71	3989	1760	215	8,687
1740	150	8767	1761	210	8,023
1741	128	7995	1762	225	9,686
1742	89	5123	1763	279	11,770
1743	75	4881	1764	195	9,453
1744	74	4253	1765	189	9,029
1745	120	5843	1766	219	10,986
1746	116	5635	1767	190	8,422
1747	110	5633	1768	148	7,149
1748	136	6223	1769	173	8,637
1749	142	6543	1770	159	9,042
1750	130	6244	1771	181	9,844
1751	129	5669	1772	219	12,044
1752	130	5724	1773	242	13,205
1753	134	5118	1774	211	11,685
1754	149	6018	1775	148	9,002
1755	163	7015	1776	118	7,354
1756	172	7064	1777	144	9,576
1757	220	9037			

5. *A list of Non-Classical Schools in Wales endowed or re-endowed during the eighteenth century*

compiled from the *Digest of Schools and Charities for Education*, 1842,
and from the Reports of the Schools Inquiry Commission, 1870

S. Signifies schools which were originally Subscription Schools, or, at the time of the Inquiry, were financed in part by subscription.
D. Signifies Dissenters' Schools.
H. Signifies Hospitals or Boarding Schools, in which all, or part, of the pupils were maintained.

Co. OF ANGLESEY

Aberffraw S.
Llan Badrig
Llan Fihangel Ysceifog
Pentraeth

Co. OF BRECON

Builth
Llanbeder-cum-Partrishow
Llanigon
Llanwrtid

Co. OF CARDIGAN

Llanbadarnfawr S.
Llandewibrevy
Llanilar

Co. OF CAERMARTHEN

Abergwilly
Caermarthen
Caermarthen
Cynwyll S.
Llandilo Fawr
Llanfynydd
Llangendeirn
Llangunnog S.
Llansadwrn
Trelech-ar-Bettws

Co. OF CAERNARVON

Aber
Bodfean
Bryn Croes
Cricaeth S.
Gyffin
Llan Lechid

Llan Ystyn Dwy S.
Pen Machno

Co. OF DENBIGH

Bettws In Rhos S.
Bryn Eglwys S.
Denbigh D.
Eglwysfach S.
Gresford
Holt
Llanarmon-in-Yale
Llanfair Dyffryn Clwyd S.
Llanfair Talhaiarn S.
Llanferras
Llangollen
Llanrhaiadr S.
Llanrhaiadr-yn-Mochnant
Ruabon S.
Wrexham
Wrexham
Wrexham D.

Co. OF FLINT

Bangor Iscoed
Mold
Mold
Newmarket or Trelofonyd D.
Tryddyn
Whitford

Co. OF GLAMORGAN

Cardiff
Eglwysilan
Gelligaer
Neath

Co. OF MERIONETH

Llan Uwch-y-Llwyn D.
Tywin

Co. OF MONTGOMERY

Castle Caercinion
Churchstoke
Kerry H.
Llanbrynmair
Llanbrynmair D.
Llanerfyl S.
Llanfihangel
Llanfyllin
Llangynog
Montgomery S.
Myfod
Newtown

Co. OF MONMOUTH

Bedwas
Caerleon
Llanvihangel Istern Lewern
Matherne
Penalt

Co. OF PEMBROKE

Amroth
Pwllcrochan S.
St Issel

Co. OF RADNOR

Beguildy
Llandegley
Pilleth and Whitton
New Radnor
Rhayader

6. The Welsh Bible. Bibliography

compiled from *The Bible in Wales* by John Ballinger and from the *Historical Catalogue of the Printed Editions of Holy Scripture in the Library of the British and Foreign Bible Society*, by T. H. Darlow and H. F. Moule, vol. II.

Date	Edition	Promoters	Name	No. of copies
1588	Folio. For use in Churches. The first complete Bible in Welsh	Wm Morgan, later Bishop of St Asaph, editor and translator	—	800–1000?
1620	Folio. For use in Churches. Revision of edition of 1588	Richard Parry, Bishop of St Asaph, assisted by Dr John Davies of Mallwyd	—	800–1000?
1630	8vo. First People's edition. Reprint of edition of 1620	Patrons: Sir Thos Middleton and Rowland Heylin	Beibl Midltwn	about 1500
1654	8vo. People's edition. Reprint of editions of 1620 and 1630	Patron: Oliver Cromwell, according to tradition	Beibl Cromwel	6000
1677–8	8vo. People's edition	Edited by Stephen Hughes. Assisted by Thos Gouge, who collected subscriptions for it	—	8000
1689–90	8vo. People's edition. Reprint of edition of 1677–8	Edited by Stephen Hughes & David Jones. Patron: Lord Wharton	—	10,000
1690	Folio. For use in Churches	William Lloyd, successively Bishop of St Asaph and Worcester	Beibl yr Esgob Llwyd	10,000
1717–18	8vo. People's edition	Edited by Moses Williams. First Welsh edition. Published by S.P.C.K.	Beibl Moses Williams	10,000
1727	8vo. Reprint of edition of 1717–18	Corrected by Moses Williams. Published by S.P.C.K.	—	Not known

Date	Edition	Promoters	Name	No. of copies
1746	8vo. People's edition	Edited by Richard Morris. Published by S.P.C.K.	Beibl Risiart Morys	15,000
1752	8vo. People's edition. Reprint of edition of 1746	Published by S.P.C.K.	—	15,000
1769	8vo.	Edited by John Evans. Published by S.P.C.K.	—	20,000
1770	8vo. Issued in 1s. parts from 1767 to 1770. Complete edition, 1770	Edited by Peter Williams. First Bible printed in Wales, at Carmarthen	Beibl Peter Williams	8600
1779–81	8vo. Reprint of the edition of 1770. Issued in 1s. parts	—	—	6400
1780–81	8vo. People's edition. Reissue of edition of 1779–81	—	—	—
1789	Folio. For use in Churches	Edited by H. Parry. Published by the S.P.C.K.	Beibl Parri, Llanasa	1000?
1790	8vo. People's edition	Edited and published by Peter Williams and David Jones	Beibl John Cann	4000
1796	8vo. People's edition	Comments by William Romaine	—	4000
1797	8vo. People's edition. A reprint of the edition of 1770	Edited by Peter Williams	—	4000

SELECT BIBLIOGRAPHY

A. SOURCES[1]

I. MSS

ABERYSTWYTH. National Library.	The Ottley Papers. (Papers of Adam Ottley, D.D., Bishop of St Davids, 1712–23 and of Adam Ottley, Registrar of St Davids, 1713–52.) The Plasgwyn Papers. (Letters relating to the S.P.C.K., 1699–1712.) The Williams MSS. (Letters written between 1745 and 1783 by correspondents in England and Wales to the secretaries and officials of the S.P.C.K.) The Charity of John Vaughn of Derllys. The Bodewyrd MSS. (Papers relating to the charity school at Ross, 1712 and 1745, and at Hereford, 1723 and 1745.)
BELFAST. Public Record Office.	State Papers relating to Ireland, 1715–1800.
DUBLIN. Public Record Office.	State Papers relating to Ireland, 1700–1800.
Trinity College	Archbishop King's Transcribed Correspondence.
DURHAM. Auckland Castle	Returns to Episcopal Visitation Articles, 1792.
EDINBURGH. H.M. Register House.	S.P.C.K. records: Minutes of (a) General, (b) Committee Meetings, 1737–1800; (c) Reports of Schools; (d) Misc. Papers. Forfeited Estates papers: General Management, II, Schemes of Improvement, I.
National Library.	Wodrow Correspondence. Letters from Henry Newman, Secretary of the S.P.C.K.
University Library.	Laing MSS. Div. II, Folios 177 and 626. Report upon the suitable sites for establishing linen manufacturing colonies in the Highlands and of the established colony at Lochcarron 1755. Scheme of Lord Gardenstone for improving the village of Lawrence Kirk, 1789.
Library of the Church of Scotland.	Records of the General Assembly of the Church of Scotland. Letters, memorials, petitions, schemes relating to the Society in Scotland for Propagating Knowledge, to 1732. Acts of the Church of Scotland. Walker MSS. 1755. Kirkwood MSS. Collection. Letters to Sir Francis Grant, Lord Cullen, George Meldrum and to the members of the London S.P.C.K., 1707–8.

[1] Only those sources and secondary authorities relating to education have been included in the bibliography. Contemporary and modern works on the religious, social and economic history of the period have been omitted.

ELY. Diocesan Registry	Returns to a *Questionnaire* of the Bishop of Ely on the state of the schools in the diocese, 1786, 1801, 1884.
HARTLEBURY CASTLE.	Misc. Papers.
LINCOLN. Diocesan Registry.	Misc. Papers.
LLANDAFF. Diocesan Registry.	Returns to Episcopal Visitation Articles, 1771.
LONDON. British Museum.	The Place Collections. Add. MSS. 27823. Stowe MSS. (Letters relating to the S.P.C.K.)
Guildhall.	Journals of the Common Council, July 23, 1783, Feb. 22, 1785, March 4, 1785.
Guildhall Library.	Minute and Account Books of Aldgate Ward Charity School, 1716–91. Minute and Account Book and Register of Peter Joy's school in St Anne's, Blackfriars, 1706. Misc. Papers.
House of Lords Library.	MS. Petition of Trustees of Charity Schools in London and Westminster, June 5, 1716.
Lambeth Palace Library.	Cod. Miscellaneous, 952.
Public Record Office.	State Papers Domestic to 1783. State Papers Scotland. Series 2. Report of George Walker to the General Assembly of the Church of Scotland, 1755.
Sion College Library.	Misc. Papers.
S.P.C.K. House	S.P.C.K. records: (*a*) Minutes, (*b*) Letters, (*c*) Abstracts of Correspondence, (*d*) Reports of Schools, (*e*) Misc. Papers, 1698–1800. Wanley MS.
NORWICH. Diocesan Registry.	Returns to Episcopal Visitation Articles, 1784.
OXFORD. Bodleian Library.	Tanner MSS. Nos. XL, 18 and CXLVI, 133. Letters of Humphrey Lloyd, Bishop of Bangor and Wm. Lucy, Bishop of St Davids to Archbishop Sheldon. Rawlinson MSS. (Papers of Henry Newman, Secretary to the S.P.C.K.) Order Papers. A Plan of Education for Ireland [1787].
Christ Church Library.	Wake MSS. Misc. Papers.
ST DAVID'S. The Palace, Abergwili.	Returns to Episcopal Visitation Articles, 1705–10, 1755, 1804. Misc. Papers.
SCHOOLS at Bath, Blewbury, Greenwich, Hendon, New Brentford, Rotherhithe, St James's, Westminster, St Martin's-in-the-Fields, St Margaret's, Wesminster, West Ham.	School Papers, Minute Books, Registers, etc.
WORCESTER. Diocesan Registry.	Misc. Papers.

II. PRINTED SOURCES
(a) OFFICIAL DOCUMENTS

Statutes at Large.

Irish Statutes.

Acts of the Parliament of Scotland.

Acts of Parliament under the Commonwealth (ed. H. Scobell).

Acts of the Privy Council of Scotland.

Acts of the Assembly of the Church of Scotland.

Abstract of Returns of Charitable Donations for the Benefit of Poor Persons, made by the Ministers and Churchwardens of the Several Parishes and Townships of England and Wales, 1786–88. Printed 1816.

Reports: Commissioners of Irish Education Inquiry. 1788–91.

Commissioners of the Board of Education, Ireland. 1809–12.

Select Committee on the State of the Children Employed in Manufactories. 1816.

Select Committee on the Education of the Lower Orders. 12 parts, 1816–18.

Commission to Inquire Concerning Charities. 32 Reports, 1819–37. Digest of Schools and Charities for Education. 1843.

Commissioners on Education in Ireland. 1825.

The Select Committee on Education in England and Wales. 1835.

The Select Committee on the State of Education in Scotland. 1838.

Commissioners of Inquiry into the State of Education in Wales. 1847.

Commission of Endowed Schools, Ireland. Commissions, 1854–8.

Commissioners on the State of Popular Education in England. 6 vols. 1861.

The Schools Inquiry Commission. 21 vols. 1866.

Commissioners to inquire into the State of the Schools in Scotland. 10 parts. 1865–7.

The Departmental Commission to inquire into the position of the Welsh Language, and to advise as to its promotion in the Educational System of Wales. 1927.

Parliamentary History, ed. by W. Cobbett, to 1803; Parliamentary Debates, ed. by Hansard, from 1803.

Journals of the House of Commons, England.

Journals of the House of Commons, Ireland.

Calendar of Home Office Papers, State Papers Domestic. 4 vols. 1760–73.

Thurloe, J. Collection of State Papers, ed. by T. Birch. 1742.

Educational Census 1851, compiled by Horace Mann.

State Trials, Collection of, ed. by T. B. Howell. 1816–26.

(b) REPORTS AND ACCOUNTS OF SOCIETIES

Account of the Rise and Progress of the Religious Societies in the City of London. 1697.

Account of the Several Societies of Religion. 1700.

Reports of the Societies for the Reformation of Manners in London and Westminster and other parts of the Kingdom. 1699–1738.

Accounts of Charity Schools in Great Britain and Ireland, being the Annual Reports of the Society for Promoting Christian Knowledge on the State of the Charity Schools. 1704–1800.

Account of the Society of the Patrons of the Anniversary of Charity Schools. 1803.

Circular Letters of the Society for Promoting Christian Knowledge to its Correspondents. 1699–1725.

Annual Reports of the Society in Scotland for Propagating Christian Knowledge. Edinburgh. 1709–1800.

Annual Reports of the Society in Ireland for Promoting Christian Knowledge. 1716, 1717, 1718, 1719, 1721, 1725, 1730, Dublin.

Proceedings of the Incorporated Society, Dublin. 1737–99, Dublin.

Reports of the Society in London Corresponding with the Scottish S.P.C.K. 1776, 1791, 1792, 1793, 1794, 1800.

Reports of the Society in London Corresponding with the Incorporated Society, Ireland. 1744, 1745, 1747, 1749, 1751, 1753, 1755, 1759, 1761.

Welch Piety: Reports of the Circulating Welch Charity Schools. 1737–67, 1768–9, 1770–77.

Reports of the Society for Promoting Religious Knowledge among the Poor. 1750, 1762, 1766, 1800.

Reports of the Society for Discountenancing Vice and Promoting Religion and Virtue. 1800–2, Dublin.

Reports of the Gaelic Society. 1811–19, Edinburgh.

Reports of the Society for Bettering the Condition and Improving the Comforts of the Poor. 1797–1808. Digest of same, 1801.

Reports of the Sunday School Society. 1787, 1788, 1789, 1797, 1799.

Circular Letters of the Sunday School Society. 1784–5.

Report of the Sunday School Union. 1803.

Reports of the National Society for Promoting the Education of the Poor in the Principles of the Established Church, 1812–30.

Reports of the British and Foreign Schools Society. 1815–30.

Report of the Finance Committee of the British and Foreign Schools Society. 1810.

Report of the Philanthropic Society. 1788.

Reports of the Central Society of Education. 1837–8–9.

Accounts of the Proceedings of the Charitable Society. 1719–35.

(c) SERMONS

SERMONS PREACHED:

At the Anniversary Services of the Charity Schools in and about London and Westminster. London, 1704–1800.

At the Anniversary Services of the Society for Propagating Christian Knowledge in Scotland, in the High Church of Edinburgh. Edinburgh, 1710–1800.

Before the Incorporated Society in Ireland, at Christ Church, Dublin, and at other Dublin Churches. Dublin, 1731–1800.

Before the Society in London Corresponding with the S.P.C.K. in Scotland. 1776, 1791, 1792, 1793, 1794, 1800.

Before the Society in London Corresponding with the Incorporated Society in Dublin. 1739, 1740, 1741, 1742, 1743, 1744, 1745, 1747, 1749, 1751, 1752, 1755, 1757, 1759, 1767, 1773.

At Anniversary Services on behalf of the Dissenters' Charity Schools in Gravel Lane, Southwark, 1719, 1723, 1724, 1728, 1729, 1733, 1735, 1744, 1751, 1763, 1792; Bartholomew Close, London, 1770; Horsely Down, Southwark, 1779, 1781, 1796.

(d) REPORTS AND ACCOUNTS OF SCHOOLS

Artleborough [Irthlingborough].	The Working Charity School. In An Account of Workhouses in Great Britain in the year 1732.
Bamborough Castle.	The School of Industry. In the Appendix to The Œconomy of Charity, by Sarah Trimmer.
Barrington School, The.	An Account of, by Sir Thomas Bernard. 1815.
Bartholomew Close, London.	An account of the Dissenters' Charity School. 1779, 1781, 1796.
Bath.	Plan of a Sunday School and School of Industry established in the City of Bath. [n.d.]
Boldre.	The Working Charity School. In the First Report of the Society for Bettering the Conditions of the Poor. 1798 (henceforth referred to as S.B.C.P.).
Borough Road, London.	An Account of Mr Joseph Lancaster's School, by John Walker. 1804.
Brentford, Old.	An Account of the Sunday Schools and Schools of Industry. In the Appendix to The Œconomy of Charity, by Sarah Trimmer.
Broughton Blean.	The Sunday School. In the Appendix to Sunday Schools Recommended, by G. Horne, D.D.
Bristol.	The Dissenters' Charity School. Bristol, 1785.
	Proposals for Supporting by an Annual Contribution a Charity School for the Education and Clothing of Poor Girls of the Parish of Temple in the City of Bristol, together with Rules and Orders of the Said School. 1779.
Bristol, Baldwin Street.	The State of the Ladies' Charity School. Bristol, 1756.
Cambridge.	Short Account of the Rise, Progress and Present State of the Charity School. Cambridge, 1763.
Canterbury.	The Sunday Schools in the Parishes of St Alphage and St Mary, Northgate. In the Appendix to Sunday Schools Recommended, op. cit.
Chelsea.	Memorial of the Charity School at Chelsea. [n.d. 1718?]
Chester.	Plan of the Education for Poor Children, by Dr Haygarth. 1797.
Cork.	Pietas Corcagiensis, or a View of the Green Coat Hospital and Other Charitable Foundations in the Parish of St Mary Shandon, Corke [etc.]. Cork, 1726.
Deptford.	Account of the Charity School. [n.d.]
Dublin.	The Prosperity of Dublin Displayed in the State of the Charity Schools. Dublin, 1796.
Edgeware Road.	The School of Industry. In Reflections upon the Education of Children in Charity Schools, by Sarah Trimmer. 1792.
Ely.	Steps to Establish Sunday Schools. 1780.
Exeter.	Account of the Charity School. Exeter, 1741.

Finchem.	The Working Charity School for Poor Children. In the First Report of the S.B.C.P.
Findon.	The Working Charity School. In An Account of Workhouses, 1732.
Gloucester.	The Rules for Sunday Schools, drawn up by Thomas Stocks and Robert Raikes. 1783.
Gravel Lane, Southwark.	Report on the State of the Dissenters' Charity School, from 1719 to 1800.
Gray's Inn Road, London.	A Brief Account of the Rise, Progress and Present State of the Most Honourable and Loyal Society of Ancient Britons for Supporting the Charity School erected at the North End of Gray's Inn Road, London. 1839.
Greenwich.	The Girls' Charity School. In An Account of Workhouses. 1732.
Harwood, Wales.	Report of the Sunday Schools at. 1789.
Hatton Garden, London.	The Mathematical Charity School, Account of. 1749.
Hawkestone, Salop.	Account of a School, by Sir Thomas Bernard, 1804.
Hendon.	Rules of the Government of the Charity Schools at Hendon. 1802.
Highgate.	The Ladies' Charity School House Roll of Highgate [etc.]. [n.d.]
Horsely Down, Southwark.	A Brief Account of the Dissenters' Charity School. 1779, 1781, 1796.
Kendall.	An Account of the School of Industry. 1811.
Lambeth.	The Working Charity Schools at. In An Account of Workhouses. 1732.
	An Account of the Charity Schools. 1794.
Leeds.	The Ladies' Charity Schools. In the Eighteenth Report of the S.B.C.P. 1801–2.
	The Sunday School at Kirkstall. In the Eighteenth Report of the S.B.C.P.
Lewisham.	The School of Industry, Account of. In the First Report of the S.B.C.P. 1798.
Liverpool.	Report of the Blue Coat Hospital. 1801–3.
	An Historical Introduction to the Prayers Psalms and Hymns used by the children in the Blue Coat Hospital. 1814.
Mendips.	An Account of the Mendips Schools. In the Eleventh Report of the S.B.C.P.
Newcastle-on-Tyne.	History of the Charity School in Hanover Square. 1796.
Norwich.	Proposals to Erect Charity Schools in the City of Norwich. 1707.
Oxford.	An Account of the Charity School. 1715.
Rotherhithe.	St Mary's Parish, An Account of the Amicable Society's School. 1739.
St Anne, Aldersgate, London.	The Rules and Orders of the Charity School. 1808.
St Bride, Fleet Street, London.	A Brief State of the Charity School. 1795.
St Catherine Cree Church, London.	An Account of the Charity School. 1718.

St Ethelburgha's Society.	An Account of the Charity School supported by. 1802.
St James, Westminster.	An Account of the Girls' Charity School. 1732.
St Luke, Middlesex.	An Account of the Working School. 1755.
St Margaret, Westminster.	The Grey Coat Hospital. In An Account of Workhouses. 1732.
St Marylebone Charity School, London.	An Account of the Establishment, Rise and Present State of. 1798.
St Sepulchre, London.	The Plan of the Ladies' Charity School. 1805.
Scilly Isles.	An Account of the Charity Schools. 1796.
Stroud.	Rules for the Management of the Sunday School. 1784.
Weston, Somerset.	A School for Poor Children. In the Eighteenth Report of the S.B.C.P. 1801–2.
Wisbech.	An Account of the Charity School. 1814.
Worcester.	An Appeal for the Charity School. 1781.
York.	An Account of Two Charity Schools, by Catherine Cappe. 1800.

(e) NEWSPAPERS, MAGAZINES, REVIEWS

Annual Register, The. From 1758.
Anti-Jacobin, The. 1807, 1809, 1811.
Applebee's Weekly. 1723.
Arminian Magazine, The. 1785.
Baptist Monthly Magazine, The. 1785.
British Apollo, The. 1708.
British Gazetteer, The. 1716, 1723, 1751.
British Journal, The. 1723.
Christian Guardian, The. 1809.
Christian Monthly, The. 1745.
Daily Advertiser, The. 1722, 1743, 1752.
Daily Courant, The. 1724.
Edinburgh Review, The. 1802, 1806, 1807, 1810, 1811, 1813.
European Magazine, The. 1798.
Evangelical Magazine, The. 1798, 1806, 1815.
Evening Post, The. 1723.
Flying Post, The. 1716.
Gentleman's Magazine, or The Monthly Intelligencer. 1731, 1737, 1742, 1758, 1767, 1784, 1788, 1790, 1791, 1793.
Gloucester Journal, The. 1783, 1784, 1787.
Guardian of Education, The. 1802–6.
Guardian, The. 1713.
Intelligencer, The. 1730.
London Journal, The. 1723.
London Advertiser, The. 1751.
Morning Advertiser, The. 1742, 1750.
Morning Penny Post, The. 1751.
Morning Post, The. 1811.
Newsletter, The. 1716.

Pamphleteer, The. 1811, 1812, 1813.
Post Boy, The. 1718, 1719, 1722, 1723.
Philanthropist, The. 1812.
Quarterly Review, The. 1811, 1812.
Read's Weekly Journal. 1751.
Saturday Post, The, or the Weekly Journal. 1716, 1719, 1720, 1721, 1723.
Spectator, The. 1712.
St James's Evening Post, The. 1716.
Tatler, The. 1709.
Universal Magazine, The. 1784.
Weekly Medley, The. 1718, 1719.
Wrongs of Children, The. 1819.

(f) LETTERS AND DIARIES

Boulter, Hugh. Letters written by His Excellency Lord Primate of All Ireland (etc.) to Several Ministers of State in England and Some Others, containing an Account of the Most Interesting Transactions which passed in Ireland from 1724 to 1738. 2 vols. Oxford, 1769–70.
Brougham, Henry. Letter to Sir Samuel Rommilly on the Abuse of Charities. 1818.
[Burt, E.] Letters from a Gentleman in the North of Scotland to a Friend in London. London, 1754.
"Cato." Collection of Letters published in The British Journal. London, 1723.
Charles, Thomas. Letters of, ed. by the Rev. E. Morgan. 1832.
Francke, A. H. Letter to the S.P.C.K. enclosing a Report of the Schools and work at Halle. 1710.
Grant, Mrs Anne, of Laggan. Letters from the Mountains, 1773–1803. 3 vols. 1806.
Hanway, J. Letters on the Importance of the Rising Generation, and To the Guardians of the Infant Poor. 1767.
Howard, John. Letters of, ed. by J. Field. 1855.
Hughes, Stephen. Letter prefaced to the 1672 ed. of Gwaith Mr Rees Prichard.
Jones, Griffith. Letters in Welch Piety. Letters to Madam Bevan, ed. by the Rev. E. Morgan, 1832; and in the Transactions of the Carmarthenshire Antiquarian Society, ed. by M. H. Jones. Nos. 38 and 39. 1921.
King, Wm, Archbishop of Dublin. Correspondence of, ed. by S. C. King. In A Great Archbishop of Dublin. 1906.
Lancaster, J. Letter to John Foster, Esq., Chancellor of the Exchequer for Ireland, on the best means of Educating and Employing the Poor in that Country. 1805.
Le Blanc, D. B. Lettres d'un Français. 1745.
Letters of a Clergyman to his Friend in the Country, being a short Account of the Charity Schools. 1725.
Letters to the Patrons and Trustees of Charity Schools. 1788.
More, Hannah. Memoirs of the Life and Correspondence of, ed. by W. Roberts. 1835. Letters of, ed. by Brimley Johnson. 1925.
More, Martha. The Mendip Annals, the Journals of Martha More, ed., with additional matter, by Arthur Roberts. 1859.
Morris Brothers, The. The Letters of, ed. by J. H. Davies. 1906.

Nisser, F. C. Rector of the Swedish Church, London, Letters on the Patriotism, Charity and Philanthropy in Great Britain. 1797.

O'Sullivan, H. Hedge School Master at Callin, Diary of. Part I, ed., with Introduction, Translation and Notes, by M. McGrath. Irish Texts Society, 1936.

Pococke, Bishop. Tour in Ireland, 1752, ed. by G. T. Stokes. Dublin, 1891.

The Trevecha Letters, or the Unpublished Correspondence of Howell Harris and his Contemporaries, by the late M. H. Jones, ed. by R. T. Jenkins. 1932.

Thoresby, Ralph. Diary and Correspondence of, 1677–1724, ed. by J. Hunter. 4 vols. London, 1832.

Trimmer, Mrs Sarah. Some Account of the Life and Writings of, with Original Letters [etc.]. 2nd ed. 1816.

Wesley, J. Letters of, 1721–9, ed. by J. Telford. 1931.

Wesley, John. Journals of, ed. by N. Curnoch. 8 vols. 1909–16.

Whitefield, George. Journal of, with Appendices, ed. by W. Wale. 1905.

Wodrow, R. Correspondence, ed. by T. M. McCrie. 3 vols. 1843.

Woodforde, Rev. James. Diary of a Country Parson, 1758–81. 4 vols. ed. by J. Beresford, 1926–9.

(g) OTHER CONTEMPORARY WORKS

I. ENGLAND.

Anon. Considerations of the Fatal Effects to a Trading Nation of the Excess of Public Charity. 1763.

Anon. Defence of the Private Academies and Schools of the Protestant Dissenters. 1714.

Anthems and Psalms as performed in St Paul's Cathedral on the day of the Anniversary Meeting of the Charity Children in and about the Cities of London and Westminster. 1800.

Baptist Annual Register. 4 vols. 1790–1802, ed. J. Rippon.

Barnard, T. An Historical Character relating to the Holy and Exemplary Life of the Right Honourable Lady Elizabeth Hastings. 1742.

Bell, Andrew. An Experiment in Education made at the Male Asylum at Madras, suggesting a System by which a School or Family may teach itself under the Superintendence of the Master or Parent. 1797.

Bernard, Sir T. Account of the Foundling Hospital. 1799.
  Of the Education of the Poor. 1809.
  The New School: An Attempt to illustrate its principles, details and advantages. 1809.
  The Barrington School. 1812.

Bowles, N. L. Education of the Lower Classes. 1808.
  Thoughts on the Education of the Poor. 1820.

Boyer, W. Schools for Spinning. 1795.

Brewster, S. The Christian Scholar. 1704.

Bridges, W. Methods and Management of Free Schools. 1699.

Brokesby, F. Of Education. 1701.

Brougham, H. Observations on the Education of the People. 1825.

Brown, J. Baldwin. Public and Private Life of John Howard. 1823.

Bruce, Mr. The Advantage of changing the Bell and Lancaster Schools from Charity to cheap Pay-School. 1819.

Burnet, Gilbert. History of His Own Time. 6 vols. Oxford, 1833.
  Supplement to Burnet's History of His Own Time, by H. C. Foxcroft. Oxford, 1902.

J. B., Under Master of the Charity School in St Alban's, Holborn. Charity in Perfection this Side Heaven. A Poem. 1716.

Chamberlayne, E. Notitiae Angliae, or the Present State of England. 1700–2–4–7, Continued by his son, J. Chamberlayne as Magnae Britanniae Notitiae.

Clarke, S. The Lives of Sundry Eminent Persons in the Later Age. 2 Parts. 1683.

Colquhoun, P. A New and Appropriate System of Education for the Labouring People. 1806.

Complaints of the Poor. 1792.

Cooper, S. Definitions and Axioms relating to Charity, Charitable Institutions, and the Poor Laws. 1760.

Cowper, Wm. Tirocinium, or Review of Schools. 1784.

Crutwell, C. Life of Bishop Thomas Wilson. 2 vols. Bath, 1781.

Davies, David. The Case of the Labourers in Husbandry. 1795.

Defoe, D. Giving Alms No Charity. 1704.

    Charity Still a Virtue, or an Impartial Account of the Trial and Conviction of the Rev. W. Hendley for Preaching a Charity Sermon at Chislehurst. 1719.

    Everybody's Business is Nobody's Business. 1725.

    Of Royal Education. 1728.

Dixon, H. The Parents' and School-Masters' Spiritual Assistant for grounding the Charity Children. 1732.

Doddridge, P. Collected Works, ed. by E. Williams and E. Parsons. 10 vols. 1802–10.

Dyer, G. The Theory and Practice of Benevolence. 1818.

Eachard, J. The Grounds and Occasions of the Contempt of the Clergy inquired into. 1698.

Eden, Sir F. State of the Poor. 3 vols. 1797.

Edgeworth, M. Practical Education. 3 vols. 1801.

Educational Record, The, with the Proceedings of the British and Foreign School Society, vols. XV–XXII. 1899–1929.

The Expediency and Means of elevating the Profession of the Educator in Society. 1839.

Firmin, T. Some Proposals for the Imployment of the Poor and the Prevention of Idleness. 1681.

Firmin, Thomas. Life of. 1698.

Fox, J. Comparative View of the Plans of Education as detailed in the Publications of Dr Bell and Mr Lancaster. 1811.

    A Vindication of Mr Lancaster's System. 1811.

Francke, A. H. Pietas Halliensis, or a Public Demonstration of the Footsteps of a Divine Being yet in the World, or an Historical Narrative of the Orphan House and Other Charitable Institutions at Claucha, near Halle in Saxony. 1707.

    A Short and Simple Instruction how Children are to be guided to a True Piety and Christian Wisdom, formerly drawn up for Christian Tutors, and now by desire printed. Trans. 1707.

Gaskell, P. The Manufacturing Population of England; its Moral, Social and Physical Conditions and the Changes which have arisen from the use of Steam Machinery; with an Examination of Infant Labour. 1833.

Gibson, Edmund. The Peculiar Excellency and Reward of Supporting Schools of Charity. A Sermon preached on May 24, 1716.

    The Charge of Edmund, Lord Bishop of London, to the Clergy of his Diocese in his Visitation begun in the Cathedral Church of St Paul, May 28, 1730.

Gibson, Edmund. Directions given by, to the Masters and Mistresses of the Charity Schools within the Bills of Mortality and Diocese of London, Nov. 14, 1724.

Gisborne, T. An Inquiry into the Duties of Men in the Higher Ranks and Middle Classes of Society in Great Britain. 1797.

Gloucestershire Tracts, No. 13. [n.d.]

Gouge, T. The Surest and Safest Way of Thriving. 1694.

Hanway, Jonas. A Letter from a Member of the Marine Society, Shewing the Generosity and Utility of their Design. 1757.

An Account of the Marine Society. 6th ed. 1759.

A Candid Historical Account of the Hospital...for Exposed and Deserted Young Children. 1759.

An Earnest Appeal for Mercy to the Children of the Poor. 1766.

The Importance of the Rising Generation of the Labouring Part of our Fellow Subjects. 1768.

A Sentimental History of Chimney Sweepers in London and Westminster, with a Letter to a London Clergyman on Sunday Schools, calculated for the preservation of the children of the poor. 1785.

A Comprehensive View of Sunday Schools for the Use of the more Indigent Inhabitants of Cities, Towns and Villages, through England and Wales. 1786.

A Comprehensive Sentimental Book for Scholars learning in Sunday Schools. 1786.

Hendley, W. A Defence of Charity Schools. 1724.

Henry, Matthew. Sermon Concerning the Catechism of Youth. 1713.

Herring, Archbishop. Visitation Returns, 1743. 5 vols. Ed. Ollard, S. L. and Walker, P. C. Yorkshire Archaeological Society. 1928–31.

Huntingdon, Life and Times of Selina, Countess of. By a Member of the Houses of Shirley and Hastings. 2 vols. 1844.

Hymn Sheets prepared for the Anniversary Services of the Charity Schools in the parishes of St Mary, Rotherhithe, 1768, 1776, 1794; All Hallows, London Wall, 1752; Christ Church, Spital Square, 1755.

Hymn Sheets prepared for the Anniversary Services of the Charity Schools in and about London and Westminster. 1709, 1711.

Ivimey, J. History of the English Baptists. 4 vols. 1824–30.

Memoirs of William Fox. 1831.

Kennett, White. The Christian Scholar, or Rules and Directions for Children and Youths sent to English Schools, more especially designed for the Poor Boys Taught and Cloathed by Charity in the Parish of St Botolph's, Aldgate. 1710.

Kidder, R. Charity Directed, or the Way to Give Alms. 1676.

Knox, V. Remarks on the Tendency of a...Bill now pending...to degrade Grammar Schools. 1820.

Ladies' Memorial Praying for a Charter for the Foundling Hospital (1737).

Lancaster, J. Improvements in Education as it respects the Industrious Classes of the Community [etc.]. 1803.

Outline of a Plan for educating Ten Thousand Poor Children. 1806.

An Account of the Progress of Mr Lancaster's Plan. 1809.

A Remarkable Establishment at Paris. 1809.

Instructions for forming...a Society for the Education of the Poorer Classes. 1810.

The British System of Education. 1810.

Schools for all. 1812.

Leach, A. F. Educational Charters and Documents. 1911.

Lee, Francis. History of Montanism. 1709.
  Memoirs of the Life of J. Kettlewell, compiled from the Collections of G. Hickes and R. Nelson. 1718.
Lloyd, W. F. Life of Robert Raikes. 1826.
Maidwell, L. The Necessity and Excellence of Education. 1705.
Maitland, W. History and Survey of London. 2 vols. 1772.
Malthus, T. R. Essay on the Principle of Population as it affects the future Improvement of Society. 1798.
Mandeville, B. The Fable of the Bees on Private Vices Public Benefits. Ed. K. F. B. Kaye. 2 vols. Oxford. 1924.
Marsh, H. Vindication of Dr Bell's System of Tuition. 1811.
  The National Religion the Foundation of National Education. A Sermon preached in St Paul's Cathedral, June 13, 1811.
Massie, J. A Plan for the Establishment of Charity Schools. 1758.
Matthews, H. Reasons for Promoting the Interests of Charity Schools. [n.d.]
  Memorial presented to the S.P.C.K. for setting up Charity Schools Universally in All Parishes of England and Wales. 1710.
Mill, James and John, on Education, ed. F. A. Cavenagh. Cambridge, 1931.
Milner, I. Strictures on Some of the Publications of the Rev. Herbert Marsh, intended as a reply to his objections to the British and Foreign Bible Society. 1813.
Monro, G. Just measures for the Pious Instruction of Youth. 2 vols. 1701.
More, Hannah. Collected Works. 12 vols. 1854.
  Cheap Repository Tracts. 1795–8.
Navy, The. An Infallible Project for the more effectual and easy manning of. 1745.
Neal, Daniel. The History of the Puritans or Protestant Non-Conformists from the Reformation to...the Act of Toleration. 2 vols. 2nd ed. 1754.
Nelson, R. The Life of Bishop Bull of St David's. 1713.
  The Whole Duty of a Christian, Designed for the Use of the Charity Schools in and about London. 1704.
  Ways and Methods of Doing Good. 1715.
  Festivals and Fasts. 1739.
Orders read and given to the Parents on the Admission of their Children into the Charity Schools. 1708.
Orphanotrophy, A Memorial Concerning, or the Hospital for the Reception of Poor Cast-off Children or Foundlings, in order to the Saving of the Lives of many poor Innocents yearly, and to the rendering of all useful to the Public, instead of hurtful Members thereof; as those who survive by being brought to begging generally prove. By a Rector of one of the Parish Churches without the City Walls. 1728.
Owen, J. History of the Origin and First Ten Years of the British and Foreign Bible Society. 2 vols. 1816.
Owen, Robert. New View of Society, or Essays on the Principles of the Formation of Human Character and the Application of the Principles to Practice. 1813.
Parr, Samuel. A Discourse on the Plans Pursued in Charity Schools. [n.d.]
Parson, W. and White, W. History, Directory and Gazetteer of the Counties of Durham and Northumberland. 2 vols. Leeds, 1827–8.
Patrick, Symon, Bishop of Ely. Autobiography. Oxford, 1839.
Patrons of Charity Schools, List of. 1784.
Peterson, J. Pietas Londoniensis. 1714.

Pitt, W. M. Plan for the Extension and Regulation of Sunday Schools. 1785.

Place, Francis. Improvement of the Working People. 1834.

Porteus, Beilby, Bishop of Chester. Letter to the Clergy of the Diocese of Chester. 1785.

Potter, R. Observations on the Poor Laws. 1775.

Proposals for Establishing a Charitable Fund in the City of London [etc.]. 1706.

Pugh, J. Life of Jonas Hanway. 1787.

Raikes, R. The Sunday School Scholars Companion. 1794.

Secker, Thomas. The Works of, with Life by Beilby Porteus. 6 vols. 1811.

Service Papers at the Anniversary Meetings of the Charity Schools in St Dunstan's in the West. 1791–1843.

Shenstone, W. The Schoolmistress. 1740.

Smith, Adam. An Inquiry into the Nature and Causes of the Wealth of Nations with... Supplemental Dissertations, by J. R. McCulloch, Esq. New ed. 1872.

Southey, R. Life of John Wesley. 1820.

The New System of Education, reprinted from an article in the Quarterly Review. 1812.

Southey, R. and C. C. Life of the Rev. Andrew Bell. 3 vols. 1844.

Speculum Dioeceseos Lincolniensis sub episcopis Gul: Wake et Edm: Gibson, ed. by R. E. G. Cole.

Stow's Survey of London...brought down from 1633...to the Present Time. Ed. J. Strype. 1720.

Talbot, J. The Christian Schoolmaster, or the Duty of those who are Employed in the Public Instruction of Children, especially in Charity Schools. 1707.

Taylor, T. Memoirs of John Howard. 1836.

Temple, W. Essay on Trade and Commerce. 1770.

Trimmer, Mrs Sarah. The Œconomy of Charity. 1787. 2 vols. 1801.

Reflections upon the Education of Children in Charity Schools, with an Outline of a Plan of Appropriate Instruction for the Children of the Poor [etc.]. 1792.

A Comparative View of the New Plan of Education promulgated by Mr Joseph Lancaster in his Tracts Concerning the Instruction of the Children of the Labouring Part of the Community, and of the System of Christian Education founded by our Pious Forefathers for the Initiation of Young members of the Established Church in the Principles of the Reformed Religion. 1792.

Trimmer, Mrs Sarah. The Guardian of Education. 1802–6.

The Charity Spelling Book: The Teacher's Assistant, consisting of Lectures in the Catechetical form, being part of a plan of Appropriate Instruction for the Children of the Poor. 2nd ed. 1808.

Ventris, P. V. Reports of Select Cases. 2 vols. 1696.

Watts, Isaac. Essay on Charity and Charity Schools. 1724.

Treatise on the Education of Children and Youths. 1725.

Divine Songs attempted in Easy Language for Children. 21st ed. 1752.

Wesley, John. Works of. 14 vols. 1840–2.

Conference Minutes, 1794–8. 1862.

Whiston, W. Memorial for the Setting up of Charity Schools. 1710.

Sermon preached at Trinity Church in Cambridge, January 25, 1704/5, at which Time and Place the Teachers of the Charity Schools lately erected in Cambridge appeared with the Poor Children under their Care, in Number about Three Hundred. 1705.

Whiston, W. Memoirs, Written by Himself. 1753.

Whole Duty of Man, The. 1650.

Wilberforce, R. and S. Life of William Wilberforce. 2nd ed. 1839.

Wilberforce, W. A Practical View of the Prevailing Religious Systems of Professed Christians in the Higher and Middle Classes of the Country contrasted with real Christianity. 1797.

Young, A. The Farmer's Tour through the East of England. 4 vols. 1771.

II. SCOTLAND.

Anderson, J. The State of Society and Knowledge in the Highlands of Scotland. 1827.

B. de —, Mons. Reflections on the Causes and Probable Consequences of the Late Revolution in France, with a view to the Ecclesiastical and Civil Condition of Scotland. Trans. Edinburgh, 1799.

Carlisle, N. Topographical Dictionary of Scotland. 1813.

Gillies, J. Historical Collections relating to Remarkable Periods of the Success of the Gospel. Glasgow, 1754.

The Highlands of Scotland in 1750 from the MSS. 104, in the King's Library, the British Museum. 1898. Ed. Andrew Lang.

Hunter, H. A Brief History of the Society in Scotland. 1795.

Lockcarron and Glenmoriston Experiments, The. In The Scots Magazine, vols. xv and xvi. 1753–4.

MacFarlane, J. The History of the Society in Scotland. 1783.

Moral Statistics of the Highlands and Islands, compiled from returns received by the Inverness Society for the Education of the Poor in the Highlands, to which is prefixed a Report on the Past and Present State of Education in these Districts. Aberdeen, 1826.

Shaw, Lachlan. History of Moray. 1778.

Sinclair, Sir J. Statistical Account of Scotland. 21 vols. 1790–99. Edinburgh, 1799. Analysis of Statistical Account. 1825.

Stewart, D. Sketches of the Manners and Character of the Highlands of Scotland. 1825.

Wodrow, R. Life of James Wodrow. 1828. Analecta. 4 vols. Publication of the Maitland Club. 1842–3.

III. IRELAND.

Anderson, C. Memorial on behalf of the Native Irish with a View to their improvement in Moral and Religious Knowledge through the medium of their own Language. 1815.

Berkeley, G. Works and Life of, ed. by A. C. Frazer. 4 vols. Oxford, 1901.

Birch, T. Life of the Hon. Robert Boyle. 1744.

Bradshaw Collection of Irish Books in the University Library of Cambridge.

Caldwell, Sir J. Penal Laws relating to Ireland. 1764.

Campbell, T. Philosophical Survey of Ireland. 1776.

Carleton, W. Traits and Stories of the Irish Peasantry. 2 vols. 4th ed. 1836.

Carr, Sir J. The Stranger in Ireland. 1806.

Croker, T. D. Researches in the South of Ireland. 1824.

Disney, W. Observations on the Present State of the Charter Schools in Ireland and the Means of Improving them. Dublin, 1808.

Edgeworth, M. Castle Rackrent. 1895.

Edgeworth, R. L. Memoirs of. Begun by himself and concluded by his Daughter Maria Edgeworth. 2 vols. 1820.

Halliday Collection of Pamphlets. Royal Irish Academy, Dublin.

Harris, W. The Ancient and Present State of the County of Down. 1744.

Hood, T. The Irish School-Master. Collected Poems. 1876.

Howard, J. An Account of the Principal Lazarettos in Europe. 1789.
State of the Prisons in England and Wales. 4th ed. 1792.

Latocnaye, de. Promenade d'un Français dans l'Irlande. Dublin, 1797.

Mason, W. S. A Statistical Account or Parochial Survey of Ireland drawn up from the Communications of the Clergy. 3 vols. Dublin, 1814–19.

Newenham, T. A Statement of an Historical Inquiry into the Progress and Magnitude of Ireland. 1771.

O'Brien, W. S. Education in Ireland. 1839.

Richardson, J. A Short History of the Attempts that have been made to convert the Popish Natives of Ireland to the Established Religion. 1712. A Proposal for the Conversion of the Popish Natives of Ireland to the Established Religion. 1712.

Smith, C. The Antient and Present State of the County of Waterford. Dublin, 1745.
The Antient and Present State of the County of Kerry. Dublin, 1756.

Steven, R. An Inquiry into the Abuses of the Chartered Schools in Ireland. 1817.
The Education of the Lower Classes in Ireland. 1815.

Swift, J. Collected Works. 10 vols. 1752.

Synge, E. Brief Account of the Laws now in force in the Kingdom of Ireland for Encouraging the Residence of the Parochial Clergy and Erecting English Schools. Dublin, 1723.

Thoughts and Suggestions on the Education of the Peasantry in Ireland. 1820.

Twiss, R. A Tour in Ireland. 1755.

Wakefield, E. An Account of Ireland. 2 vols. 1812.

Warburton, J., Whitelaw, J. and Walsh, R. History of the City of Dublin from the Earliest Accounts to the Present Times, containing its Annals, Antiquities, Ecclesiastical History and Charters, etc. 2 vols. 1818.

Ware, Sir J. Antiquities and History of Ireland. Dublin, 1705.

Young, Arthur. A Tour in Ireland with General Observations on the Present State of that Kingdom made in the Years 1776, 1777, 1778 and brought down to the end of 1779. Selected and edited by C. E. Maxwell. Cambridge, 1925.

IV. WALES.

Alleine, Joseph. The Life and Death of Mr. 1762.

Birch, T. Life of J. Tillotson. 1752.

Burgess, Bishop. Tracts on the Origin and Independence of the Ancient British Church. 2nd ed. 1815.

Calamy, Edmund. An Historical Account of my Own Life, 1671–1731, ed. by J. T. Rutt. 2 vols. 1829.

Calamy Revised, being a revision of E. Calamy's Account of the ministers and others ejected and silenced, 1660–2, by A. G. Matthews. Oxford. 1934.

Edwards, Charles. Fatherly Instructions. 1686.

Evans, John. Some Account of the Welsh Charity Schools, and the Rise and Progress of Methodism in Wales through the Means of them, under the sole management of Griffith Jones, Clerk, Rector of Llanddowror in Carmarthenshire [etc.] 1762.

Gilbert, J. Memoir of the Life and Writings of the late Rev. Edward Williams. 1825.
Harries, E. Sketch of the Life of the Rev. Griffith Jones. [n.d.]
Harris, Howell. Brief Account of the Life of. 1791.
Jones, Robert. Drych Yr Amseroedd, 1820, ed. by Owen Edwards. 1899.
Life and Character of the Reverend and Pious Griffith Jones, late Rector of Llanddowror
    in Carmarthenshire; the First Projector and Conductor of the Welch Circulating
    Schools throughout the Principality of Wales. 1762.
Malkin, B. H. The Scenery, Antiquities and Biography of South Wales. 2nd ed. 1807.
Middleton, E. Biographia Evangelica. 1786.
Morgan, E. Life and Times of Howell Harris, 1852.
    The Life and Labours of the Rev. T. Charles. 1828.
    Brief account of Daniel Rowland. [n.d.]
Palmer, S. The Non-conformists Memorial [etc.]. 2nd ed. 1777.
Saunders, Erasmus. A View of the State of Religion in the Diocese of St David's about
    the beginning of the Eighteenth Century. 1721.
Tillotson, John. The Works of, with the Life of the Author, by Thomas Birch, M.A.
    10 vols. 1820.
Williams, Daniel. A True Copy of the Will of. 1717.
Williams, William, of Pantycelyn. A Serious Address presented to the Consideration of
    all Charitable and Well-disposed Christians for Contributing Some Part of their
    monied properties to raise a small fund to carry on Welsh Charity Schools upon a
    Similar Plan with that established by the late Reverend Mr Griffith Jones, and
    continued by Mr Bevan. Caefyrodin, 1790.
Wynne, W. (ed.). Caradoc of Llancarvan, History of Wales. 1697.

B. LATER WORKS

(i) GENERAL AND FOREIGN

Adamson, J. W. Pioneers of Modern Education, 1600–1700. Cambridge, 1905.
    A Short History of Education. Cambridge, 1905.
Balfour, Sir G. The Educational Systems of Great Britain and Ireland, 2nd ed. 1903.
Darlow, T. H. and Moule, H. E. Historical Catalogue of the Printed Editions of Holy
    Scripture in the Library of the British and Foreign Bible Society. In Four Parts.
    1903–11.
Encyclopédie Methodique. Paris, 1873.
Fosseyeux, M. Les Écoles de Charité à Paris sous l'ancien régime et dans la première
    partie du XIXe siècle. Paris, 1912.
Francke, A. H. Schriften über Erziehung und Unterricht, ed. by Karl Richter. Berlin, 1872.
Guibert, J. Histoire de St Jean-Baptiste de la Salle. Paris, 1901.
Hippean, C. L'Instruction Publique en France pendant la Revolution. Paris, 1881.
Kramer, G. A. H. Francke, Pädagogische Schriften. 1885.
Levis, M. de. L'Angleterre au commencement du dix-neuvième siècle. 1814.
Paulsen, F. German Education Past and Present. 1908.
Histoire des Pauvres, par l'Amiral du Quesnay [prefaced by an advertisement by the
    Editor, T. Ruggles]. [n.d.]
Rigeaud, G. Saint Jean-Baptiste de la Salle. 1925.

Weber, M. The Protestant Ethic and the Spirit of Capitalism, trans. by T. Parsons, with a foreword by R. H. Tawney. 1930.

Young, T. P. Histoire d'Enseignement Primaire et Secondaire en Suisse plus spécialement de 1560–1872. 1907.

(ii) ENGLAND

Abbey, C. D. The English Church and its Bishops, 1700–1800. 2 vols. 1887.

Abbey, C. D. and Overton, J. H. The English Church in the Eighteenth Century. 2 vols. 1878.

Adamson, J. W. An Outline of English Education, 1760–1902, reprinted from the Cambridge History of English Literature, vol. xiv. 1928.

English Education, 1789–1902. Cambridge, 1930.

Allen, William. Life of, with Selections from his Correspondence. 3 vols. 1846.

Allen, W. O. B. and McClure, E. Two Hundred Years, 1698–1898. The History of the Society for Promoting Christian Knowledge. 1898.

Baptist Historical Society's Transactions, The, vol. iv. 1914–15.

Birchenough, C. History of Elementary Education in England and Wales from 1800 to the Present Day. 1920.

Body, A. H. John Wesley and Education, 1936.

Bourne, M. A. The Trust Estate of Benjamin Herold. In The Educational Record, June 1902.

Canton, W. History of the British and Foreign Bible Society, vol. i. 1904.

Carlisle, N. Endowed Grammar Schools in England and Wales. 2 vols. 1818.

An Historical Account of the Origin of the Commission appointed to enquire concerning Charities in England and Wales. 1828.

Carpenter, L. Matthew Henry. 1824.

Carter, E. H. The Norwich Subscription Books, 1637–1800. 1937.

Congregational Historical Society Transactions, The. 1904–27.

Darton, F. Harvey. Children's Books. In the Cambridge History of English Literature, vol. xii, ed. by A. W. Ward and A. R. Waller. Cambridge.

De Montmorency, J. G. State Intervention in English Education. 1900.

Dobbs, A. E. Education and Social Movements, 1700–1850. 1919.

Doran, J. London in Jacobite Times. 2 vols. 1877.

Educational Record of the British and Foreign School Society, The. 1902–19.

Fearon, J. P. The Endowed Charities. 1855.

Fitch, Sir J. G. Charity Schools and the Endowed Schools Commission. 1873.

Furniss, E. S. The Position of the Labourer in a System of Nationalism [etc.]. Boston and New York, 1920.

Gamble, H. R. An Eighteenth Century Visitation. In The Church Times, November 4, 1921.

Gardiner, D. English Girlhood at School. Oxford, 1929.

Garrard, T. Edward Colston the Philanthropist. His Life, Times [etc.]. 1852.

George, D. London Life in the Eighteenth Century. 1925.

Gilbert, Wm. Contrasts. 1873.

The Girlhood of Maria Josepha Holroyd, ed. J. H. Adeane. 1896.

Gordon, A. Addresses, Biographical and Historical. 1922.

Gray, Kirkman. History of English Philanthropy. 1905.

Gregory, A. Robert Raikes. A History of the Origin of Sunday Schools. 1880.

Hadden, R. H. An East End Chronicle. [n.d.]

Halévy, E. History of the English People in 1815. 1924.

Hawkes, J. The Rise and Progress of Wesleyan Sunday Schools. 1885.

Hazlitt, W. C. Schools, School-books, and School Masters. 1888.

Hyett, F. Glimpses of the History of Painswick. 1928.

Jayne, R. E. Jonas Hanway. 1929.

Kay, J. Education of the Poor in England and Europe. 1846.

Khan, S. A. Ideals and Realities. Madras, 1921.

Leach, A. F. Articles on Schools in the Encyclopaedia Britannica, 11th ed., vol. xxiv.
  Articles on Schools and Education in the Victoria History of the Counties of England;
      Beds, Berks, Bucks, Derby, Durham, Essex, Glos, Hants, Herts, Lancs, Lincoln,
      Notts, Somerset, Suffolk, Surrey, Sussex, Warwick, Yorks.
  Articles in The Dictionary of English Church History. 1919.

Lecky, W. E. H. History of England in the Eighteenth Century. 7 vols. 1892.

Le Keux, J. Memorials of Cambridge. 1842.

Loch, C. S. Charity and Social Life. 1910.

London, 1844, ed. by Charles Knight.

Low, S. The Charities of London. 1850.

McClure, E. A Chapter in English Church History. 1911.

McLachlan, H. English Education under the Test Acts, being the History of Non-
  Conformist Academies, 1662–1820. Manchester, 1931.

Meiklejohn, J. M. D. An Old Educational Reformer, Dr Andrew Bell. 1881.

Mill, James and John, on Education, ed. F. A. Cavenagh. Cambridge, 1931.

Murray, T. B. An Account of the Efforts of the S.P.C.K. on behalf of National Education. 1848.

Nichols, R. H. and Wray, F. A. A History of the Foundling Hospital. Oxford, 1935.

Nightingale, B. History of Lancashire Non-Conformity. 3 vols. 1890–93.

North, E. M. Early Methodist Philanthropy. 1914.

Ollard, S. L. History of the Church of England. 1914.

Overton, J. H. The Evangelical Revival in the Eighteenth Century. 1900.
  The Church in England. 2 vols. 1897.

Overton, J. H. and Relton, F. The English Church. 1714–1800.

Palliser, B. History of Lace Making. 1865.

Portus, G. V. Caritas Anglicana or an Historical Inquiry into those Religious and
  Philanthropic Societies that flourished in England, between the years 1678 and
  1740.

Salmon, D. Joseph Lancaster. 1904.
  The Education of the Poor in the Eighteenth Century. In The Educational Record,
      October 1909.
  Articles on Bell and Lancaster in The Educational Record, 1902–7.

Schools. Histories of:
  Bishopsgate Schools, 1702–1889, by J. Avery. 1923.
  Bishopsgate Ward Charity School. In the Central Foundation School Bicentenary
      Magazine. 1926.
  Bridge, Candlewick and Dowgate Wards Charity Schools. Account of. 1852.
  Cheltenham. Bicentenary History of the Parish Charity School. 1902.
  Greenwich. History and Position of the Blue Coat Girls School, by G. B. Airy. 1867.

Schools. Histories of (*cont.*):

Greenwich. History of the Roan School, by J. W. Kirby. 1929.

Ratcliffe. History of Hamlet of Ratcliffe Charity School, by J. V. Pixell. 1910.

Rotherhithe. A Statement of the Charity Schools belonging to the Parish of St Mary, Rotherhithe. 1878.

St Alphage Society, City of London. Some Account of. 1849.

St Botolph, Aldgate Charity School. Account of. 1852.

St George the Martyr Charity School, by E. C. Bedford.

St Giles', Cripplegate, Charity School. Account of. 1851.

St Margaret's Westminster. An Old Westminster Endowment, being a History of the Grey Coat Hospital [etc.], by E. S. Day. 1902.

St Martin's-in-the-Fields Charity School, by J. McMaster. 1916.

St Martin's-in-the-Fields High School for Girls, by Dora H. Thomas. 1929.

Shakespeare's Walk, Protestant Dissenters School, by M. A. Bourne. In The Educational Record, February 1902.

Soho. The Story of a Charity School [etc.], 1699–1899, by J. H. Cardwell. 1899.

Stockport. History of the Stockport Sunday School, and its branch schools, by W. I. Wilde. 1891.

Wandsworth. All Saints Charity School, by W. J. Moore. 1910.

Secretan, C. F. Memoirs of the Life and Times of the Pious Robert Nelson. 1860.

Sessions, W. York and its Associations with the Early History of the Sunday School Movement. 1882.

Smith, F. The Life and Work of Kay-Shuttleworth, 1923.

A History of English Elementary Education, 1760–1902. 1931.

Stamp, W. W. The Orphan House of Wesley. 1863.

Stanford, C. Joseph Alleine, His Companions and Times. 1861.

Stoughton, J. History of Religion in England. 8 vols. 1901.

Sunday Schools. The Origin of. 1841.

Sykes, Norman. Edmund Gibson, Bishop of London, 1669–1748. Oxford, 1926.

Thompson, Henry. Life of Hannah More. 1838.

Townsend, W. J., Workman, H. B. and Eayers, G. A new History of Methodism. 1909.

Tudor, O. D. The Law of Charities and Mortmain, ed. Briscoe, Hunt and Burdell. 4th ed. 1906.

Tuer, A. W. Children's Books. 1899.

The Horn Book. 2 vols. 1896.

Turberville, A. S. (ed.). Johnson's England. 2 vols. Oxford, 1933.

Twining, T. A Country Clergyman of the Eighteenth Century. 1882.

Tyerman, L. Life of George Whitefield. 2 vols. 1876.

Urwick, W. Nonconformity in Worcestershire. 1897.

Nonconformity in Hertfordshire. 1884.

Victoria County Histories.

Watson, W. H. History of the Sunday School Union. 1853.

Webb, S. and B. London Education. 1904.

Whitley, W. T. The Contribution of Nonconformity to Education until the Victorian Era. In The Educational Record, June 1915.

Wilson, Mrs R. F. The Christian Brothers. Their Origin and Work. 1883.

(iii) SCOTLAND

Bellesheim, A. History of the Catholic Church of Scotland. 4 vols. Trans. Hunter Blair, 1883.

Blundell, Dom Odo. Ancient Catholic Houses of Scotland. 1907.

The Catholic Highlands of Scotland. 1909.

Dean, I. F. M. Scottish Spinning Schools. 1930.

Kerr, J. Scottish Education. Cambridge. 1910.

Leith, W. Forbes. Memoirs of Scottish Catholics during the Sixteenth and Seventeenth Centuries. 2 vols. 1909.

McCulloch, John. The Highlands and Western Isles of Scotland, their history [etc.]. 4 vols. 1834.

Mackay, J. Education in the Highlands in the Olden Times. Inverness, 1921.

The Church in the Highlands. 1914.

Urquhart and Glenmoriston in the '45. Inverness. 1893.

MacKenzie, A. History of the Highland Clearances. 1914.

Maclean, D. Typographia Scoto-Gadelica [etc.]. 1915.

The Counter Reformation in Scotland, 1500–1930. 1931.

Maclean, Magnus. Historical Development of the Different Systems of Education in the Highlands. In the Old Highlands, Gaelic Society of Glasgow, vol. I. 1895.

Mason, J. History of Scottish Experiments in Rural Education. 1935.

Wright, H. History of the Old Parish Schools of Scotland. 1898.

Warden, A. J. The Linen Trade. 1864.

(iv) IRELAND

Brennan, M. The Schools of Leighlin and Kildare, 1775–1835. Dublin, 1935.

Church of Ireland, History of. 3 vols., 1933–4, ed. by W. A. Philipps.

Corcoran, T. State Policy in Irish Education. Dublin, 1916.

Some Lists of Catholic Lay Teachers and their Illegal Schools in the Later Penal Times. Dublin, 1932.

Education Systems in Ireland from the Close of the Middle Ages. Dublin, 1928.

Corkery, D. The Hidden Ireland. Dublin, 1925.

Dowling, P. J. The Hedge Schools of Ireland. 1935.

The Irish Charter Schools. In The Dublin Review, January 1932.

Dunlop, R. Ireland from the Earliest Times to the Present Day. 1921.

Godkin, J. Education in Ireland. 1862.

Ireland and her Staple Manufactures, being a sketch of the History and Progress of the Linen and Cotton Trades...connected with the Northern Province. Belfast, 1870.

Lecky, W. E. H. History of Ireland in the Eighteenth Century. 5 vols. 1892.

Le Fanu, W. R. Seventy Years of Irish Life. 2nd ed. 1893.

Mant, R. History of the Church of Ireland. 2 vols. 1840.

O'Hagan. The New Spirit of the Nation. 1894.

Walsh, J. E. Sketches of Ireland Sixty Years Ago. Dublin, 1847.

(v) WALES

Ballinger, J. The Bible in Wales. 1906.
Bibliography of the History of Wales, ed. by R. T. Jenkins, and W. Rees. Cardiff, 1931.
  History of Carmarthenshire, ed. for the London Carmarthenshire Society, by Sir J. E. Lloyd, vol. I. Cardiff, 1935. (Vol. II in the press.)
Cavenagh, F. A. Griffith Jones. 1930.
Davies, E. J. Hanes Griffith Jones. 1930.
Davies, J. H. Diary of the Rev. Griffith Jones. In Cylchgrawn, Cymdeithas Hanes y Methodistiaid Calfinaidd, vol. VII, No. 1.
  West Wales Historical Records, vol. II. 1913.
Edwards, A. G. Landmarks in the History of the Church in Wales. 1912.
Evans, D. The Sunday Schools of Wales. 1883.
Evans, J. J. Morgan John Rhys a'i Amserau. Cardiff, 1935.
Griffith, D. M. Nationality in the Sunday School Movement. Bangor, 1925.
Griffith, E. The Presbyterian Church of Wales. Calvinistic Methodist Historical Handbook, 1735 to 1905.
Griffith, J. T. Morgan John Rees. 2nd ed. Carmarthen, 1910.
Jenkins, D. E. The Life of the Reverend Thomas Charles of Bala. 3 vols. Denbigh, 1908.
Jenkins, R. T. Gruffydd Jones, Llanddowror, 1683–1761. Cardiff, 1931.
  Hanes Cymru yn y Ddeunawfed Ganrif. Cardiff, 1931.
  A Conspectus of Griffith Jones Schools in North Wales, 1738–61. In The Bulletin of the Board of Celtic Studies, vol. V, Part 4, May 1931.
  One of Griffith Jones' School-masters. In The Bulletin of the Board of Celtic Studies, vol. VII. 1935.
Jeremy, W. D. The Presbyterian Fund and Dr Williams' Trust. 1885.
Johnes, A. J. Causes which have produced Dissent from the Established Church in Wales. 1870.
Jones, David. Life and Times of Griffith Jones of Llanddowror. Bangor, 1902.
Jones, D. Ambrose. Griffith Jones, Llanddowror. Wrexham, 1923.
  History of the Church in Wales. Carmarthen, 1926.
Jones, E. J. Gruffydd Jones, Llanddowror. In Yr Athro, vol. III. 1930.
Jones, M. H. Hanes Tarddiad a thwf yr y sgol sul Gymreig in Cyfarwyddwr, vol. I. 1922.
  Griffith Jones, Llanddowror. In The Welsh Outlook, September 1927.
Jones, Rhys, of Kilsby. The Educational State of Wales. 1851.
Knight, L. S. Welsh Independent Grammar Schools to 1600. 1926.
  Welsh Schools trom A.D. 1000 to A.D. 1600. In Archaeologia Cambrensis, Sixth Series, vol. XIX, Parts I and II. 1919.
Lewis, S. Williams Pantycelyn. 1927, 2nd ed. 1883.
Morrice, J. C. Wales in the Seventeenth Century. Bangor, 1818.
Owen, J. D. Morgan John Rhys. In Cylchgrawn. Cymd. Eithas Hanes y Methodistiaid Calfinaidd. March, 1922.
Phillips, Sir T. Wales: the Language, Social Conditions, Moral Character and Religious Opinions of the People considered in relation to Education, with some account of the Provision made for Education in other Parts of the Kingdom. 1849.

Rees, Thomas. History of Protestant Nonconformity in Wales. 1861, 2nd ed. 1883.

Richards, T. The Puritan Movement in Wales, 1639–53. 1920.

    Religious Developments in Wales, 1654–62. 1923.

    Wales Under the Penal Code, 1662–87. 1925.

    The Religious Census of Wales. 1676. In The Transactions of the Hon. Soc. of Cymmrodorion. 1927.

    Wales Under the Indulgence. 1672–5. 1928.

    Piwritaniaeth a Pholitics. 1689–1719. 1927.

Richardson, C. M. History of the Institution once called Welch Piety, but now known as Mr Bevan's Charity. 1890.

Salmon, D. The Welsh Circulating Schools. In The Educational Record. 1900.

    A Brief History of Education in Pembrokeshire. In The Educational Record. 1926.

Shankland, T. Sir John Philipps and the Society for Promoting Christian Knowledge and the Charity School Movement in Wales. In The Transactions of the Hon. Soc. of Cymmrodorion. 1904–5.

    Stephen Hughes. In Y Berniad, vol. II. 1912.

    Diwygwyr Cymru. In Seren Gomer. 1900–4.

    Dechreuad yr Ysgolion Sabbothol yng Nghymru. In Cymru, vol. XXII. 1902.

Vaughan, H. M. Welsh Jacobitism. In The Transactions of the Hon. Soc. of Cymmrodorion. 1920–21.

Williams, G. J. Stephen Hughes a'i Gyfnod. In y Cofiadur, March 1926.

Williams, I. Thomas George, Pioneer of Popular Education. In The Welsh Outlook, vol. XVII, Part 2, February 1930.

UNPUBLISHED THESES

Larcombe, H. J. The Development of Subscription Charity Schools in England and Wales from the close of the Seventeenth to the close of the Eighteenth Century, with Special reference to London and District. Theses deposited in the University of London Library, 1928.

Owen, T. J. The Educational and Literary Work of Griffith Jones of Llanddowror. Thesis deposited in Bangor University Library, 1928.

Williams, Ffowe. The Educational Aims of Pioneers in Elementary Welsh Education. 1730–1870. Thesis deposited in Bangor University Library, 1929.

INDEX

Abercorn, Earl of, and charity school at Strabane, 225

Aberlour, opposition of priests to charity school at, 193

Abertarf, opposition of clansmen to charity school at, 176, 192–3, 205

Acts of the General Assembly of the Church of Scotland:
Act 5, Sess. 5 (1707), 177

Acts of Parliament:
27 Hen. VIII, c. 26 (1535), Concerning the Laws to be used in Wales, 322
8 Eliz. c. 28 (1562), For Translating the Bible into Welsh, 322
43 Eliz. c. 2 (1601), Poor Law Act, 48, 87
43 Eliz. c. 4 (1601), Charitable Uses Act, 55
Acts of the Commonwealth (1649), For the Propagation and Preaching of the Gospel in Wales, 16–17
14 Car. II, c. 4 (1662), Act of Uniformity, 279
16 Car. II, c. 4 (1664), Conventicles Act, 279
17 Car. II, c. 2 (1665), Five Mile Act, 279
22 Car. II, c. 1 (1670), Conventicles Act, 282
3 Will. and Mary, c. 2 (1691), For Abrogating the Oaths of Supremacy, etc., 219
4 and 5 Anne, c. 14 (1705), For the Better Collecting of Charity Money, 122
10 Anne, c. 6 (1711), Occasional Conformity Act, 112
13 Anne, c. 7 (1714), Schism Act, 112
1 Geo. I, c. 54 (1714), For Securing the Peace of the Highlands, 179
4 Geo. I, c. 8 (1718), Forfeited Estates Act, 179
6 Geo. I, c. 11 (1719), Forfeited Estates Act, 179
9 Geo. I, c. 7 (1723), For Relief of the Poor, 88
13 Geo. I, c. 30 (1727), For Encouraging and Promoting Fisheries and Manufactures, 200
20 Geo. II, c. 43 (1747), For Abolition of Heritable Jurisdictions, 180

20 Geo. II, c. 50 (1747), For Abolition of Tenure of Ward Holding, 180
20 Geo. II, c. 51 (1747), For Abolition of Highland Dress, 180
25 Geo. II, c. 41 (1752), For Annexing of Forfeited Estates, 180, 202, 208
24 Geo. III, c. 57 (1784), "The Healing Act", 208
26 Geo. III, c. 58 (1786), For Return of all Charitable Donations, 331
59 Geo. III, c. 81 (1819), Concerning Charities for the Education of the Poor, 332

Acts of Parliament (Ireland):
28 Hen. VIII, c. 15 (1537), For the English Order, Habit and Language, 222
12 Eliz., c. 1 (1570), For the Erection of Free Schools, 223
7 Will. III, c. 4 (1695), To restrain Foreign Education, 223
9 Will. III, c. 1 (1697), For sending Popish Ecclesiastics out of the Kingdom, 219
10 Will. III, c. 13 (1698), To prevent Papists being Solicitors, 219
2 Anne, c. 3 (1703), To prevent Popish Priests from coming into the Kingdom, 219
2 Anne, c. 6 (1703), To prevent Growth of Popery, 217
2 Anne, c. 10 (1703), For Exchange of Glebes, 229
8 Anne, c. 3 (1709), To prevent the Further Growth of Popery, 217
8 and 9 Anne, c. 12 (1708–10), For uniting Parishes, 229
6 Geo. I, c. 13 (1719), For better Maintenance of Curates, 229
8 Geo. I, c. 12 (1721), For enabling the Clergy to reside, 236
1 Geo. II, c. 12 (1727), For recovery of Tithes, 229
1 Geo. II, c. 19 (1727), For division of Parishes 229
23 Geo. II, c. 11 (1750), For better regulation of Charity Schools, 244

Acts of the Parliament of Scotland:
1633, c.5, V, 21–2; 1646, c. 45, VI, 216; 1696, c. 26, X, 63–4, 166
1700, c. 3, X, 215–9, 175

Date Due

Demco 293-5